REMEMBERED
LAUGHTER

COLE LESLEY

REMEMBERED LAUGHTER

The Life of Noel Coward

Alfred A. Knopf   New York   1976

THIS IS A BORZOI BOOK
PUBLISHED BY ALFRED A. KNOPF, INC.

Copyright © 1976 by Cole Lesley
All rights reserved under International and Pan-American Copyright Conventions.
Published in the United States by Alfred A. Knopf, Inc., New York,
and simultaneously in Canada by Random House of Canada Limited, Toronto.
Distributed by Random House, Inc., New York.
Originally published in Great Britain as *The Life of Noel Coward*
by Jonathan Cape Ltd, London.

Since this page cannot legibly accommodate all acknowledgments,
they appear on pages xv–xvi.

ISBN: 0-394-49816-X
Library of Congress Catalog Card Number: 76–13701

Manufactured in the United States of America
First American Edition

For Graham Payn
without whose help this book
might have been written
but would not
have been the same.
With Love.

When I have fears, as Keats had fears,
Of the moment I'll cease to be
I console myself with vanished years
Remembered laughter, remembered tears,
And the peace of the changing sea...

—From 'Noel's Last Poem'

'Really, my life has been one long extravaganza...'

—Noel Coward, on re-reading
his journals

CONTENTS

ILLUSTRATIONS

(Photographs, unless otherwise indicated, are from the Noel Coward collection.)

following page 72

Playing the piano at Goldenhurst *(Newnes and Pearsons)*

Rehearsing with Mary Martin in Blue Harbour, 1956 *(Life)*

Firefly Hill *(Amador Packer)*

With Marlene Dietrich and Douglas Fairbanks, Jr, 1954 *(Radio Times)*

With Merle Oberon and Judy Garland, Hollywood, 1956 *(C.B.S.)*

Las Vegas, 1955 *(U.P.I.)*

following page 392

In Stanley Donen's *Surprise Package*, 1959 *(Keystone)*

On location for *Our Man in Havana*, 1959 *(Popperfoto)*

With Vivien Leigh, Kay Kendall and Lauren Bacall,
    1959 *(Associated Newspapers)*

With Sean Connery in Jamaica for *Doctor No*, 1963

With Sophia Loren in Montreux for *Lady L*, 1964 *(Camera Press)*

Sunday morning in Trafalgar Square, 1964 *(Lord Snowdon)*

Coward by Beaton *(Cecil Beaton)*

With Kay Thompson at Les Avants

With Peter O'Toole

The Wink *(Arnold Weissburger)*

With Richard Rodgers, 1967 *(U.P.I.)*

With Dame Edith Evans at a rehearsal of *Hay Fever*, 1964 *(Angus McBean)*

Firing the noonday gun, Hong Kong, 1968

With the Queen Mother, July 1968 *(Swaebe)*

With Charles and Oona Chaplin *(Camera Press)*

Noel Coward and friends *(Horst Tappe)*

In the drawing room at Les Avants in the early 'sixties

Lornie at Les Avants, January 1960

With Gladys Calthrop and Joyce Carey at Noel's investiture as Knight
    Bachelor, 1970 *(Cole Lesley)*

With Lady Diana Cooper, January 1972

ACKNOWLEDGMENTS

For encouragement, help, advice and permissions to use material immediately and generously given, I am deeply grateful to:

The Lady Diana Cooper	Mrs Gladys Calthrop
Sir John Betjeman	Miss Joyce Carey
Sir Bernard and Lady Miles	Mrs Joan Hirst
Miss Lillian Gish	Mr Irving Paul Lazar
Mrs Anne Morrow Lindbergh	Mr Tom Maschler
Miss Lilli Palmer	Mr David Machin
Miss Stella Gibbons	Mr Robert Gottlieb
Miss Monica Stirling	Mr Geoffrey Johnson
Miss Adrianne Allen	Mr Sheridan Morley
Mrs Nesta Obermer O.B.E.	Mr Raymond Mander
Dame Rebecca West	Mr Joe Mitchenson
Sir Terence Rattigan	Mrs Patricia Etherington
Mr Beverley Nichols	Professor Dan H. Laurence
Mr Cleveland Amory	Mr Beverley Griffin
June (Mrs Edward Hillman Jr)	Madame Ginette Spanier
The Hon. Lady Maclean	Mr John Merivale
Miss Elizabeth Salter	Mr Norman Newell
The Lord Boothby	Mr Jeremy Wilson

Permission to reproduce copyright material has been kindly granted as follows:

For the George Bernard Shaw letters, from the collection of the Humanities Research Center of the University of Texas, by the Society of Authors on behalf of the Bernard Shaw estate. The note to Mr Vedrenne on p. 57 is © 1976 the Trustees of the British Museum, the National Gallery of Ireland and the Royal Academy of Dramatic Art;

For the T. E. Lawrence letters, by the Trustees of the T. E. Lawrence Letters Trust;

For the Dame Edith Sitwell letters, by Mr Francis Sitwell;

For the Maurice Baring letter, by the Hon. Lady Maclean;

For the Patrick Campbell article, by the author and the *Sunday Times*;

For the Patrick Garland article, by the author and *Vogue*.

FOREWORD

ONE winter Monday morning in 1947, Noel Coward and I set out from 'White Cliffs', his country house at St Margaret's Bay in Kent, to drive to London, Noel at the wheel. The day was particularly beautiful; snow had fallen heavily, the sky was cerulean and the entire hoar-frosted landscape sparkled in very bright sunshine. From every branch hung Christmas-tree-like little icicles. We were happy, I remember, laughing and talking, until we got nearly to the top of steep Wrotham Hill—that beauty-spot dreaded by drivers—when we were silenced. The car started to skid slowly backwards on the icy road, then gained momentum until it became out of control, Noel having to let it have its way while it waltzed and reversed during its descent. His sang-froid throughout these frightening minutes was remarkable, even to putting a reassuring hand on my knee and saying, 'Don't worry. It'll be all right.' No other car had appeared from either direction, thank God, and we at last came to rest on level road at the base of the hill. Shaken, we lit cigarettes and agreed that it had been a Near Thing, and how in the midst of life we are—though happily unaware—often near death. 'Think what a fuss there'd have been,' he said, 'if we'd been killed. Can you imagine the headlines? NOEL COWARD DEAD IN CRASH; in papers all over the world, I suppose.' At the next attempt he made the top of the hill in one and then, for the remainder of the journey to London, we talked about Death, our own deaths in particular. The eternal verities lasted us till about Sidcup, after which we played a game of guessing who might write the official biography of Noel Coward. To tease him I said that Hannen Swaffer—well-known journalist on the London *Daily Express* and Noel's *bête noire* at that time —might write one about him anyway, and should have anticipated his reply: 'Over my dead body.'

Many famous names were mentioned—'I should like Rebecca best of all'—then as though to end the matter, and to my astonishment, he said, 'I'll tell you who could do it. You. I'm sure you could do it and I should like you to do it. And I want you to tell the truth.' (In those days nobody Told All as they do today, when one so often wishes they wouldn't.) 'Anyway, this is all hypothetical.' Then followed the refrain which constantly recurred throughout his life: 'I shall outlive you all. You'll leave me one by one and I shall be left all alone, very very old and crotchety like Willie Maugham. I don't know what I shall do without you, but don't worry. I shall manage somehow. I always have.' The subject of my writing the book was never again mentioned between us, although there is one very slight hint in a letter to me from Jamaica in 1950, included in this book, in which he wrote, '... if ever this witty letter is published in your memoirs.'

Now, twenty-eight years later, through force of circumstances, I, who have never before written a book, find myself doing what he asked me to do so long ago. I have had to rely for certain aspects of his childhood and youth—though not many, for new material has come to light — on the first volume of his autobiography, *Present Indicative*. His second volume, *Future Indefinite*, deals with the Second World War years in much detail; use of this I have on the whole been able to avoid and to write from my own memories and experience, for I had entered his service in 1935, at the age of just twenty-seven. By the time the war started in 1939 I had become companion rather than servant, and later his secretary and friend until he died.

The new material covering the first twenty years of his life I found in 'Mum's Suitcase'. Ever since Mrs Coward's death in 1954, the big suitcase had been with us, though I cannot remember Noel ever going through it thoroughly, there being far too much of Auntie Vida's (his mother's sister's) correspondence with Lord Lyon King of Arms regarding their Veitch ancestry, which bored him. I can—just—remember persuading him, because of his habit of never properly dating his letters, to try to 'place' all those found in the suitcase which he had written to his mother, and this he neatly did. At least he got as far as eight envelopes, seven of which he marked in his own writing with the years, or with 'Charley's Aunt Tour', or 'Davos–Berlin–The Young Idea', or 'New York–White Sulphur Springs–Honolulu', until he tired of the task and thrust most of the others into the eighth, frustratingly described as 'Odd Letters'. The top one of the loose elastic-banded remainder begins, 'Orient Express, Saturday. Darlingest, here I am joggling along through Serbia ...' But when?

Postmarks would have dated them for us but Mrs Coward did not save all the envelopes, nor did she name all the people in her albums of yellowing snapshots. These two omissions aside, Mrs Coward scrupulously saved every relevant scrap of information from Noel's

birth until his early manhood, as though she foresaw he was to become
—as Alexander Woollcott later named him—Destiny's Tot.

Before going further I must point out that if any of the facts given
in this book are at variance with those in Noel's autobiographies, it is
because of the later knowledge obtained from Mum's Suitcase. Noel did
not have this advantage; did not know that his early letters and press-
cuttings still existed, and Mrs Coward seems not to have pointed out
the discrepancies, most probably having forgotten them herself after
so many years. For example, Noel wrote that he got his first part in
The Goldfish through his mother having answered an advertisement in
the *Daily Mirror*. This was naturally repeated in other books, and by
Noel himself in countless interviews; eventually, during his seventieth
birthday celebrations, the *Daily Mirror*'s files were searched for the
famous advertisement that 'changed his life'. In vain; there had in fact
been no such advertisement.

For the hitherto unpublished material from 1940 to the end, I have
had the enormous benefit of access to Noel's diaries and journals,
which he began to keep from that year onwards. But here again
variations will occur, to any future reader of the diaries especially. Two
glaring examples are our differing accounts of his performance of
Present Laughter in Antwerp and of his arrival at Blue Harbour, his
newly built house in Jamaica. I was present at the former, Graham
Payn at the latter, and we can vouch for the accuracy of my recounting;
in fact both events ranked high among Noel's oft-told tales, his telling
much more hilarious, vivid and true than his diary entries, in which
they are dismissed in a few words. One can only suppose that he was
too tired to write more at the end of such exhaustingly long days, or
perhaps wished to gloss over, rid himself of the day's disappointments.

For the veracity of all the stories I relate I cannot accept responsibility; stories are well known to improve with retelling, but I can and
do swear to the accuracy of my reporting of them as they were told to
me, and of course I vouch for my accounts of conversations and events
at which I was present.

The greater number of Noel's friends were and are famous—many
of them world famous—and name-dropping is therefore unavoidable.
Name-Dropping was in fact going to be the title of one of the last books
he ever planned, half in fun, after a memorable evening spent in the
company of Swifty and Mary Lazar. The evening consisted of a never-
ending stream of stories from his vast store of reminiscence, most of
which are incorporated in this book.

My interpolations in quotations from Noel's writings and letters are contained within square brackets, which will I hope make for smoother reading and will avoid the bane of footnotes, which Noel would have hated. He could never bring himself to glance at one, he said, after John Barrymore expressed the opinion that having to look at a footnote was like having to go down to answer the front door just as you were coming.

When J. B. Priestley tackled Noel in 1964 with, 'What is all this nonsense about you being called the Master?', Noel replied, 'It started as a joke and became true.' It seems that it did, in the 'twenties, start as a joke in his immediate circle, probably a self-defensive one made to forestall any accusations of their being yes-men, which they were not. Like most of the people who worked for him both in and out of the theatre I called him Master, as finally did the newspapers and many of the public. But the name perforce recurs so often in this book that it became tedious to look at, and I have also forgone the use of his beloved diaeresis over the 'e' in his name, having no wish to dizzy the eye of the reader.

REMEMBERED LAUGHTER

I

'DESTINY'S TOT'

THE first example extant of Noel Coward prose, later to become famous for this very quality of concision, was written at the age of seven from Charlestown, Cornwall. You will note that at that early age he had already become an entertainer of resource:

> Darling Mother I hope you are well. Girlie has taught me to row with two oars and I row her along. I had some little boys over yesterday afternoon to tea and I dressed up in a short dress and danced to them and sung to them and we all went round the lake and on it. xxxx ooo oxo I am writing this in the kitchen with love from Noel Coward give this to Maggie and Winnie.

There are many more x's representing kisses, o's representing hugs and oxo's scattered around and between the last few lines. Maggie and Winnie must have been the maids at the Coward Family's home at that time, and one gathers that some of the x's and o's are for them. I found this letter in Mum's Suitcase. With the letter are some drawings and caricatures in pencil embellished by watercolours, all signed 'Noel Coward' and mostly dated 1912; one of a fat-faced ballerina in a red tutu firmly entitled 'Anna Pavlova', and two of Nell Gwynn, one with her oranges and basket and the other after she had come up in the world, *décolletée* with a necklace and earrings. Noel's lifelong infatuation for King Charles II, Minette and all those close to the King must already have begun.

In his Address at the Service of Thanksgiving for Noel Coward, at St Martin-in-the-Fields on May 24th, 1973, Sir John Betjeman described St Alban's Church, Teddington-on-Thames, as 'a fine, soaring Gothic Revival building ... it looks like a bit of Westminster Abbey that has been left behind further upstream.' In St Alban's, on October 8th, 1890, Arthur Sabin Coward, 34, Bachelor, by profession a clerk, son of James Coward, Professor of Music, married Violet Agnes Veitch, 27, Spinster, daughter of Henry Gordon Veitch, Captain, Royal Navy. The bride-groom's entire family were very musical indeed; he and his brothers Randolph, Walter, Percy and Gordon and his sisters Hilda (known as the Twickenham Nightingale), Myrrha, Ida and Nellie all sang in the choir of St Alban's, and his brother Jim played the organ. The bride also lived in Teddington with her mother, her sister Vida and an unspecified relation called Borby, who was understandably rather eccentric as she had fallen out of a porthole on to her head at the age of two. She, the bride, was also musical and belonged to the choir. Here she met her Arthur, who courted her with ardent looks during the services, furthered by meetings at the many social activities connected with the church. Evidently an eager theatre-goer, she saved all the programmes of her youth, some of them with notes against the actors' names such as v.g. or n.v.g.; poor Weedon Grossmith gets 'Can't dance a bit, or act much either.' Judging by the programmes she must have seen every single production Henry Irving ever put on at the Lyceum, some of them several times over. Ellen Terry she adored, she could do no wrong, she was perfection. She must have admired Irving, or she would not have gone many times to see him, even without Ellen Terry, or somehow get herself into his Memorial Service in Westminster Abbey. But I can remember Noel persuading her to admit that he must have been an old ham, and encouraging her to do her imitation of him, which consisted of pulling a face and emitting jeering sounds of 'Myurr-myurr-myurr-myurr-*myurr*.'

There is no mention of a honeymoon. Arthur took Violet to live at 'Helmsdale' in Waldegrave Road, Teddington, a small and cosy house which remained their home for the next ten and a half years. One year after the marriage a son, Russell Arthur Blackmore, was born to them, his godfather being R. D. Blackmore, the famous author of *Lorna Doone*, who lived at Teddington and most probably, like Violet and Arthur, attended St Alban's. Mr Blackmore wrote:

> My dear Mrs Coward. What a peaceful and delightful baby! I shall be proud to have such a little godson; who deserves, and (I trust) will have a very happy life. With kindest wishes, I am truly yours, R. D. Blackmore.

His mother doted on Russell; everybody seems to have agreed with

her that he was a little angel, and indeed he does look rather angelic in
the misty photograph of him, colour-tinted on white glass. Mrs Coward
had not been vaccinated herself, did not believe in vaccination and
refused to have any of her three sons vaccinated (though in Noel's case
this was rectified by the Army in World War One). This omission may
or may not have had anything to do with the fact that Russell died of
meningitis six years later, greatly mourned by his mother.

Eighteen months after Russell's death, and only fifteen days away
from the birth of the twentieth century, on December 16th, 1899, a
second son was born and christened Noel Peirce. He was named Noel,
of course, because his birthday was only nine days before Christmas;
it was always a sore point with him that throughout his childhood one
present had to make do for the two that other children received.
Another sore point was Peirce. His godmother was Jessie Peirce, alias
'Flower'(presumably a nickname). Throughout his life Noel complained
that he had been saddled with a name he actively disliked, from
godparents he had never seen since and who had not even given him a
christening present. Why could he not have had as illustrious a godfather as his brother? His lucky star seems to have shone on him and
protected him from as early as the font, for Mr Blackmore refused:

> My dear Mrs Coward, I have been thinking long & sadly over your
> kind and flattering wish; & the more I am convinced that I must
> not do as I should like. It must be more than mere mishaps, or
> casual fortune that attends my dear Godchildren. Four out of five
> have been taken already—one more since your dear little Russell
> was called away—& I think it is a warning to me that precious
> young lives must not be subject to the risk I seem to cause them.

In March 1930, inspired presumably by preparations for the 'Famous
Children' exhibition, Mrs Coward was moved to write the following
account:

> We had a very festive christening and our small house was crowded
> with guests—our Vicar [The Reverend F. L. Boyd, who preached
> vitriolic sermons, his eyes flashing fire, his fingers pointing
> accusingly at old ladies in the congregation] called it The Coward
> Crush. We had a huge christening cake and a most lovely tree of
> white lilac on the buffet table [afterwards planted in the cemetery].
> Singing and music. Mrs Walt[er] Coward quartette, etc. Nurse,
> very grand, brought Noel down and handed him round, in a

lovely Madeira worked robe—he had five given him. It was all great fun and he was such a jolly, healthy baby and everything went off beautifully. Thick snow and none of the guests could leave till quite late. He was very big for his age always, and very forward and amusing. When we took a much larger house in Teddington 18 months later, I had a lovely nursery for him at the top of the house. Knocked two rooms into one so there was plenty of room to run about and I am sadly afraid he was very much spoilt—my mother and sister adored him and I had my work cut out to keep him in order. He was a most attractive child, never a bit shy.

Mum's Suitcase is rich with such treasure-trove. Among my favourites is a slim blue cloth-bound book with 'Baby's Record' gilt-printed on the cover. Inside the cover, 'With The Compliments of Mellin's Food For Babies As Used By THE ROYAL MOTHER [Queen Mary-to-be] Of The FUTURE KING OF ENGLAND [Edward VIII].' With the ominous exception of the blank against 'vaccination', she has straightforwardly filled in the questions asked ('baby's eyes, blue', 'hair, Golden Brown'); knowing Mrs Coward, I feel sure it was with naughty pleasure typical of her that against 'baby's food' she wrote the names of Mellin's two great rivals, Allen & Hanbury's and Benger's. Noel too would have enjoyed the joke. In August 1901 he 'cut his *last* tooth, thank goodness! He says "I'll kill ye!"'

He had already made his first journey by train, to Fleet in Hampshire, during which he had stayed wide awake, staring at everything all the time, which made his mother fear he was a bad traveller. Could this have been the first manifestation of his enduring passion for trains and for travelling in them? More than sixty years later, in the library at Les Avants, he had so many paintings of trains (plus a needlepoint cushion of one worked by Joan Sutherland for his birthday) that the butler announced after dinner that coffee was served in the Buffet de la Gare.

When Noel was still two the doctor pronounced that his brain was much in advance of his body and advised that he should be kept very quiet, that all his curls should be cut off and that he was to go to no parties. When Mrs Coward later disobeyed the third edict and took him to one she wrote proudly that Noel was the star. They were shown into a room filled with people; Noel made a most dignified entrance and climbed up into an armchair, on which he sat down comfortably, tightly clasping his tin soldier. By the time he was three

he always wanted to come down on his mother's At Home days, all
dressed up and ready, but she never rang for him unless he was asked
for. If she did not ring there was, she said, all hell to pay in the nursery.
If she did, he came down with perfect composure, danced to her piano
accompaniment, and a general fuss was made, always hugely successful.
He went to his first theatre when he was just four, the pantomime of
Aladdin at Kingston Theatre, during which he sat quite quietly all the
time—watching, watching.

Except for those odd fifteen days each year, Noel's age marched in
step with the twentieth century; thus he was five when in 1905 the
family moved to a villa at Sutton in Surrey, and soon after the move his
brother Eric was born. (In the years to come the spelling was changed
to Erik.) Noel thought him on first sight to be singularly unattractive
and—though everybody else seemed to be delighted—could not
imagine what all the fuss was about. Noel always maintained that he
had never cared very much for his father or his brother, although,
judging from the letters exchanged during childhood separations such
as holidays, the Cowards seem to have been a devoted and affectionate
family. Noel's favourite holidays were spent with Aunt Laura, favourite
out of his many aunts, at Charlestown, near St Austell in Cornwall.

She was of a full-blown prettiness, vain and addicted to wearing
tea-gowns. The garden was beautiful and there was a large lake with an
island in the middle and a blue punt in which to get to it. In later years
he used to think that his memory made him imagine the lake larger than
it had actually been, but when *Sail Away* was being tried out in Bristol
in 1962, we motored there and Noel was happy to find everything
exactly as he remembered and had so often described it. During one of
those halcyon summer holidays he wrote:

Dear Darling old Mother, Thank you very much for your letter I
could not send a card and this was scacely odd because there
were no cards to send I have been out in the yaught this after noon
it was very very rough and I was fearfly sea sick and uncle Harry
took me ashore and I was going to wait on the beach for 2 hours
but a very nice lady asked me to go to tea with her I went and had
a huge tea this is the menu 3 seed buns 2 peacises of cake 2 peacises
of Bread and jam 3 Biscuits 2 cups of tea when I thanked her she
began to Preach and said we were all put into the world to do kind
things (amen) I am afraid she did not impress me much but I
wished her somewhere I shant go in that yaught again for months
and months and months Auntie Laura sent my washing to the

village I hope you are not miserable it makes me miserable to think
you are I have got to go to bed now so good bye from your ever
loving sun Noel. Squillions of kisses to all love to Eric [There follow
37 x's.] the name of the lady that gave me tea is Mrs Penrose Walter
The dogs are so nice down here Nan and Marcus, Marcus sits on a
chair and smokes a pipe he looks so funny and if you drop anything anywhere Nan goes and fetches it. I had 3 little boys to tea
yesterday each about the size of a flea *I* had to amuse them and
didnt enjoy it much Elephant sends her love. [Was Elephant
Aunt Laura?—I suspect she was.]

In her six-page recollection of Noel's childhood, Mrs Coward wrote,
'There is so much I could tell, of his dear ways and loving affection
when he was a boy, no mother ever had such a son and I always feel
that I am really and truly more proud of his love for me than of his
great success.' What she does not mention is his extreme naughtiness,
which he freely admitted and loved to recall, sometimes referring to
himself as mischievious (as he liked to pronounce it), and sometimes
saying, 'I must have been an absolute little devil.' From his peram-
bulator days he was given to terrible fits of screaming until he got his
own way; he manufactured one such fit outside a shop, so long and
spectacular that in the end his mother was forced to slap him, causing
a passer-by to stop and ask her indignantly how she could be so cruel
to the poor little mite. In spite of his precociousness he had still not, by
the age of six, learnt to tie the bow of his bootlaces; when he was sent
to a nearby day-school, where they would not do this for him, Mrs
Coward was forced to take him away because of the scenes he made.
At his next school, irritated—he says—by Miss Willington over a little
question of English grammar, he announced he was not going to stand
it any longer and marched out. When Miss Willington tried to prevent
him, he bit her arm quite badly; in Noel's version he said he bit it to
the bone, and never regretted this action for an instant.

In the later years of his childhood, after the family had moved to
Battersea, ringing doorbells with playmates from neighbouring flats
and then running away was a commonplace, as was harassment of the
keepers in Battersea Park. Mrs Coward's temper could flare up every bit
as quickly as her son's; Noel came home crying one evening, complaining that a girl called Doris had hit him with her tennis-racket, whereupon she dragged Noel with her to confront Doris in her flat. She
found Doris having her tea in the kitchen, produced a racket from
behind her back and hit Doris over the head with it. '*That* will teach

you to hit children smaller than yourself,' she said. The supreme example of Noel's naughtiness, almost amounting to wickedness, also took place in Battersea when, so Mrs Coward told me, he poured a kettle of boiling water down the speaking-tube into the hall-porter's ear.

Noel not only stole quite a lot of books from the Army and Navy Stores, he first of all stole a suitcase to put them in and then walked out undetected. His theft of a coral necklace from a friend of his mother's was committed for the same reason—his craving for books and not having enough money with which to buy them. His budget was already severely strained; each week he simply had to buy—what boy did not—the *Magnet* and the *Gem* in order to follow the manly adventures of the eternally adolescent Tom Merry and Harry Wharton, and *Chums* and the *Boy's Own Paper* were equally necessary. He had also fallen in love, quite literally for the rest of his life, with the books of E. Nesbit—probably best known today for the film of her enchanting book, *The Railway Children*. After trying to manage by buying for one penny back-numbers of the *Strand Magazine* in which her books were serialised, he found there were numbers missing from *The Magic City*, so he pawned the necklace for five shillings, bought the complete book for four-and-six, paid a penny for the bus-fare home and was still fivepence to the good.

Noel seems to have been accident-prone in childhood; a merciful Providence always dramatically providing aid where none could be expected. He was paddling on a very lonely beach and trod on a broken bottle, severing an artery; the water around him turned scarlet, and so did the towel his mother applied. There was only one far-off figure on the beach, to whom his mother yelled frantically for help; he turned out to be a labourer who with startling good luck had just completed a course of lessons in first aid. He skilfully applied a tourniquet, made from a big pebble and a torn-off strip of the towel. Then he pushed Noel, with his leg up on the handlebars, all the way home on his bicycle, and the doctor who arrived after a long wait—there was no telephone— thought Noel might easily have bled to death had it not been for the timely tourniquet. As it was, he was laid up for weeks. Again, he was walking in a lane near Sutton with the nurse and Eric in the pram when he was knocked down against a fence by a boy learning to ride on a wobbling bicycle, one of the wheels hitting his head. He was concussed. Not a soul to be seen until two men at last materialised; one of them a policeman, the other a doctor.

Despite these Providential interventions in his boyhood, Noel took

little interest in such matters: whenever he had to fill in a form which
required to know his religion, Noel would say, 'I suppose I'd better
put good old C. of E.' Apart from the drama of his being, at the age
of two, so carried away by the music that he got out of the pew, and
danced in the aisle and then had to be taken from the church because of
his ungovernable rage at being thwarted, he never spoke much about
the religious aspect of his childhood. But it must always have been there,
for his mother went regularly to church on Sundays until old age
prevented her, and she and his father must have induced him to join the
choir in his boyhood. He often told of his disappointment at the lack of
applause after he had triumphantly concluded the treble solo of the
anthems and, as he still remembered and could sing these in his old age,
one may presume (although he only admitted to singing occasional
solos) that he consistently sang in the choir for some years. Religious
feeling is still evident at the age of twelve, when he drew and coloured
with crayons TO DEAR MOTHER in mauve and then, surrounded by
flowers and garlands,

> Easter brings greetings
> Easter brings love
> Easter brings Happiness
> From far above

He was confirmed, to please his mother, on March 7th, 1915 (not
in June, as Noel states in *Present Indicative*), by the Bishop of Kingston
at Holy Trinity, Clapham. After his first preparation his instructor tried
to make a pass at him. He had by this time been on the stage for over
four years and was not innocent, having as early as 1910 had his knee
pinched in a railway-carriage by a clergyman who gave him sixpence,
and having later been told the facts of life by Philip Tonge, while they
were appearing together in *Where the Rainbow Ends*. He always recalled
the incident with indignation; I suppose to a boy of fifteen who had
tried hard to get himself into a suitable frame of mind for the occasion
the shock was genuine. At any rate, he rounded on his instructor and
ticked him off firmly, and the remaining preparations were given him
by the vicar, Mr Tower. And that, he would lead one to believe, was
the end of regular church-going; it is therefore surprising to find him
writing more than a year later, during the tour of *Charley's Aunt*, 'No,
I didn't go to the Cathedral on Sunday, we went to All Saints.'

Before we leave childhood, here is the only remaining letter, of that
period, from his brother:

Dear Noel. Tink swallowed a bone today and she was sick three times and brought it up the first time. she was a good dog yesterday she went to her box three times running. Did you like the Forth Bridge? Good bye for now. From Eric.

Although Noel got only one make-do-for-both gift at Christmas, his lack of a present on December 16th must have been more than made up for by his birthday treat. From the age of five his mother always took him to a theatre, and from about seven onwards this became an even more exciting outing, starting in the morning for the West End and then waiting in the queue for the matinée of a musical comedy. Noel never forgot the rapture of attaining the front row in the pit. He was allowed to choose the menu for the meal at home after their return, but it never varied—roast chicken with 'simply masses' of bread sauce generously flavoured with onion and a coffee *mousse* with cream, the latter in later years changed to a more sophisticated chocolate sauce. So, by the time he was 'rushing headlong towards puberty', Noel had seen *A Waltz Dream*, *The Chocolate Soldier*, Lily Elsie in *The Merry Widow*, and Gertie Millar, by whom he was enslaved, in anything— but especially in *The Quaker Girl*. He had developed the extraordinary gift of being able, as soon as he got in the door, to rush to the piano and play by ear most of the score complete with verses and the correct harmonies. With the aid of a booklet of the lyrics which you could in those days buy for sixpence he was able to play and sing them, words and all, straight away. He never forgot those much-loved scores, and forever after would gladly play and sing them for us at the drop of a hat. We have seen that he was capable of entertaining anybody who would watch or listen to him from the age of three. Then came his appearances with Uncle George's Concert Party during holidays at Bognor; he invariably won a prize in the Competition for the Kiddies, and perhaps his professed disillusionment with life began when he discovered that only the top layer of the large box was chocolates, the rest being filled with shavings.

Noel had made his first public appearance at the age of seven at a concert at Miss Willington's school, bringing the house down by singing 'Coo' from *The Country Girl* and accompanying himself on the piano. The only amateur concert programme in Mum's Suitcase is of a Grand Variety Entertainment in connection with St Alban's Fête and Bazaar. The Coward family were prominent throughout the pro-gramme; Master Noel Coward was the third item with 'Song and Dance', the first was enigmatically announced as 'Bigotphone Quartette' and the second was a plantation song, 'De Ole Banjo', by his uncle and aunt Mr and Mrs Alcock. His father, with his sweet tenor voice, appeared twice, and an orchestra of fourteen played Haydn's *Toy Symphony* with Noel's cousin Doris Alcock on the bells. Master Noel Coward reappeared with another 'Song and Dance' in the second half, already in the best solo spot 'one before the end'.

Noel's education, one way and another, was sporadic, but from time to time his parents would have stirrings of conscience and yet another attempt would be made to send him unwillingly to school. One such was made through his Uncle Walter, whom Noel described as an eminent member of the Chapel Royal Choir, and it was decided that he should attend the Chapel Royal School at Clapham. This he did more or less regularly, though for how long is not known. The Headmaster was Mr Claude Selfe, a kind and sometimes jocular man with calves so tremendous that they looked as though they would burst through his trouser-legs. Noel got on quite well with his seven or eight fellow scholars, but hated the superior twelve who had already graduated to the choir, and with reason—they bullied him, forcing ink pellets down his collar and sometimes holding him head-down in the lavatory pan. When the time came for his vocal examination by Dr Alcock, the organist, for entry into the choir, Noel failed. He put this down to having sung Gounod's 'There is a Green Hill Far Away' with too much dramatic abandon. His mother, simmering with rage, remonstrated with Dr Alcock that Noel's voice had once moved the Queen of Portugal to tears, and then decided it was all for the best and that the whole lot of them, including Uncle Walter, looked common. Noel felt lighter-hearted, having escaped a sentence of several years of singing sacred music to no applause, and who knows but that once more his lucky star had shone on him, leaving him free to accept his first professional engagement, only a year or so away.

Mrs Coward made a lightning decision to let the flat in Battersea for six months. Off they all went, Mother and Father, Noel and Eric, to stay with Grannie and Aunts Vida and Borby at The Myrtles, Beach Road, Southsea, where the boys were perfectly happy while their parents searched for a suitable cottage in the country. Bay Tree Cottage, near Meon, where they settled, was a minute thatched dwelling with a lavatory at the bottom of the garden, and it was there that Noel first learned to love the country, with its delights of haymaking, nutting and blackberrying. He recalled the eagerness with which he sped across the fields on the days when the *Gem* and the *Magnet* came out and how loiteringly he returned, deep in the magazine from the moment he left

the shop, often having to stand stock still, carried away by the breathtaking adventures of Harry Wharton and Tom Merry.

The six months sped by, and then they all went back to Southsea for
a further six weeks, which included Christmas. All this time Noel had
run carefree, without thought of school, and his parents' sudden
determination to send him back alone to London and to Mr Selfe came
as a shock. January fogs, thick and dark yellow, shrouded London and
invaded the tall house in St George's Square in which he stayed with
Aunt Amy and Uncle Ran, and also the classroom, gaslit all day long,
in which Mr Selfe for the first and last time caned him. One thinks of
Noel as so self-assured throughout his childhood that one has to
remember he was for the first time separated from his family, a frightened, homesick little boy of ten when he wrote this letter:

> Dear darling old Mother, I am still very unhappy and I shant get
> over it till I see you again. I would rather see you than Alladin but
> I suppose I cant. I saw the portsmouth train going off the other day
> and I longed to get in it. I wish you would let me come back to you
> please do, for I do want to so I could never be happy without you
> I cry every night and day and are so miserable do let me come
> back. I am quite alright now but I wish you were here. The dinners
> are alright, at school there are six new boys. I have to get up very
> early in the morning. Auntie Amy and Uncle Ran send there love
> to you they were taken in by Miss Smith of southsea oh Mother do
> send me some money to come down to you please do I am not very
> happy here without you. send my love to all and heaps of kisses
> for Nora good bye now darling old Mother from your loveing son
> Noel. please do do do do send back for me.

He was not sent for; instead the family came back to him and the
Battersea flat within a week.

The spring and summer of 1910 passed fairly uneventfully. Noel's
dancing, though graceful, was technically uncertain, and perhaps it
was because at one concert he had, after a series of turns, ended up
with a mortified back to the audience that his mother sent him to Miss
Janet Thomas's Dancing Academy in Hanover Square. Thus the monotony of school was broken for two afternoons a week, Noel making
the journeys across London to Hanover Square and back by himself
and learning for the first time the joy of independence. He easily
extended this joy because of the irregularity of his school attendance,
giving more dancing lessons as an excuse for frequently playing truant.

Although the truancies were spent harmlessly enough watching the
trains at Clapham Junction or Waterloo, they made him feel enjoyably
wicked, and to add to his wickedness he took to talking to strangers,
lying about his home life, his brutal father, gin-soaked mother and his
starving brothers and sisters, some of them dying from lingering
diseases. As he always used a false name and address it mattered not
at all when one old lady reported the matter to the police.

We come, in the autumn of that year, to Noel's first professional
engagement. In the *Daily Mirror* of September 7th, 1910, there is a
half-column interview with Miss Lila Field which I give in part; the
sentences in italics were scored by Mrs Coward. After some grandiose
dreams of a London Theatre for Children which never came true, Miss
Field continued:

SEARCH FOR CHILD ACTORS

'For many months past now I have been busy collecting my cast; as I want thirty or so bright children between the ages of ten and fourteen, this has been far from an easy task. *To get suitable boys has been especially difficult. I have got sufficient girls at last, but am still badly in need of five or six boys. The Goldfish* ... will be the first play given ... I start rehearsing almost at once.' Miss Field has obtained most influential support for the Children's Theatre. Princess Dolgorouki, Princess Hatzfeldt, the Duchess of Norfolk, the Duchess of Marlborough and the Marquis de Soveral are among those who are supporting and taking a most active personal interest in it.

The most active interest of these dazzling names must have been an
exaggeration, for they were never mentioned again, but one can be
sure they added excitement—for she dearly loved a title—to Mrs
Coward's state of mind when she decided that September morning to
write to Miss Field care of the *Daily Mirror*.

Miss Field's postcard is dated September 11th, only four days later:

Many thanks for your letter, I shall be pleased to see your little son on Tuesday next at *10.45* at my studio, 24 King Street, Baker Street, W. Yrs. v. truly, Lila Field.

Noel wore his brand-new Norfolk suit with an Eton collar for the
audition, his mother grand in grey satin. He sang his tried-and-true
standby, 'Liza Ann' from *The Orchid*, and as there was no piano Mrs
Coward la-la-la'd the accompaniment for his dance which followed.

When Miss Field accepted him and said that the fee would be a guinea and a half a week, Mrs Coward flushed red and said she was sorry, she couldn't afford it. No no, no, said Miss Field, that was what Noel would *receive*, and the two of them triumphantly floated down the stairs and into nearby Selfridge's for festive ice-cream sodas.

The handbill for *The Goldfish* describes it as 'A Fairy Play In Three Acts with a STAR CAST OF WONDER CHILDREN'. In their review of the play on January 28th, 1911 – it opened at the Little Theatre the afternoon before – the *Mirror* quite rightly took credit for the fact that all the boys and some of the girls had been obtained through their help; they had received over two hundred applications the day following Miss Field's interview and from these had themselves made the selection to send on to her. (Luck again: what if they had not selected Mrs Coward's letter?) So their review is understandably favourable, including, 'Great success is scored by Master Noel Coward as Prince Mussel'. The *Daily Graphic* went further and said that he not only acted well but sang with remarkable feeling for one so young. In all reviews Noel got good mention; when the play moved to the Court the *Evening Times* said he should be heard of again, as he had a sympathetic voice and a quiet manner, although they started their review with, 'Performances by children are usually boring and last night's ... was no exception.'

Thirty-seven years later Lila Field and her sister Bertha came backstage to see Noel after a matinée of *Present Laughter*,' ... and in a moment the past and the present became one. Neither Lila or Bertha had had the grace to change at all, looking exactly the same, with the same charming voices talking nineteen to the dozen and shouting each other down.' They still believed in *The Goldfish*, and hoped to have it published for Christmas 1947. They had updated it, which meant cutting the first two words Noel Coward spoke in a theatre, later to become so famous in another context: 'Hello Dolly.' Gone too with the modernization was his second line: 'Crumbs, how exciting!' There were references to Fred Astaire and gangsters, characters called Wise Crack and Rib Tickler and I am afraid some of the music was still, as it had been in the original production, attributed to Ayre O'Naut. Not surprisingly, the revised version was never published, in spite of the fact that it was dedicated to Noel 'with Affection and Deep Admiration', and that Noel agreed to write a foreword, which I quote in part:

During the weeks immediately before production the excitement rose to fever pitch – anxious mothers, clutching their offspring's shoes, shawls and Dorothy bags, lined the rehearsal room walls whispering and swaying slightly as the winds of rumour eddied round them — 'Miss Field says Doreen's solo is to be cut,' 'Miss Field says this,' 'Miss Field says that' ... Life and Death and the stars in their courses depended upon what Miss Field said ... Occasionally there was an outburst of hysteria, faces were slapped, tears were shed; mothers bowed icily to each other and sat tight-lipped watching with disdain the cavortings of their rivals' progeny who, serenely unaware of these primeval undertones, were enjoying themselves tip-top. Finally the great day dawned. The curtain rose at 2.30 disclosing a pretty garden scene, 'Hollyhock Villa', Little Sunny Cove, crowded with bright and eager children hell-bent on future stardom all under fourteen with the exception of one who we suspected then, and I still suspect, was nineteen if she was a day. The opening chorus was led by a radiant, fair little girl and a plumpish, very assured little boy in a white knicker-bocker suit. The girl was described in the programme as Little June Tripp [later to become famous as June, the musical-comedy star] and the boy as Master Noel Coward and they sang with extreme abandon:

'School, School — Good-bye to school
Now we are always playing ...'

In addition to June and Noel, two others of those children hell-bent for stardom achieved that end; Alfred Willmore became Micheál MacLiammóir, and Ninette Devalois (as her name is spelt in my first Diaghileff programme of *Aurora's Wedding* in 1928) became — well, Dame Ninette de Valois. Collectively, Miss Field's children were considered clever, Mrs Coward said, and in demand, and she seemed not in the least surprised that Sir Charles Hawtrey should send for her son that autumn. (Noel said he was sent for by Bellow and Stock, the agents, to go to E. M. Tarver, Mr Hawtrey's stage-manager.) The excitement began again, and they went next day to the Prince of Wales's Theatre where a dress rehearsal of *The Great Name* was already in progress. After leaving his mother in the stalls for some time, Noel returned from back-stage with the glad tidings that he had got the part of the pageboy as he had such a beautiful speaking voice. This last may have been the reason she over-rehearsed Noel that night and caused him to say his lines next day with such throbbing intensity that Hawtrey said wearily, 'Tarver, never let me see that boy again.' He did relent, however, after Tarver hurriedly rehearsed Noel to gabble the lines in Cockney.

Noel hero-worshipped Hawtrey from then on, remembering always his kindness, his patience, how strongly he smelt of eau de Cologne, and how much he learned from his hero. He was in several Hawtrey productions before he was twenty; hardly ever leaving the side of the stage when Hawtrey was on, absorbing and retaining all he could of the great light comedian's technique, of how he got his effects. Hawtrey gave him lessons in the difficult art of laughing naturally on the stage and forbade him ever to keep his hands in his trouser pockets except on the rare occasions when a part demanded it. Noel's wonderfully free and effective use of his arms and hands can never be forgotten by those who saw him perform, especially in his cabaret appearances, and this he attributed entirely to Hawtrey's early training. His comedy timing, too, he said he 'caught' from listening to, and acting with, Hawtrey. He also learned resource; Noel never forgot watching Hawtrey with fascination in one play, alone on the stage for twenty-five minutes yet keeping the audience entertained. He emulated his master in this in the last act of *Present Laughter*, though for not quite as long, having the audience in fits simply by settling down comfortably and then spotting yet another ashtray he had to get up and walk over to, and then empty. But this was not all he learned in those formative years; the craft of playwriting was unconsciously, or perhaps intuitively being acquired by practical knowledge of it: 'The second act takes a terrible dip half-way through,' which had to be put right, or 'She's got to have a funnier exit line,' or 'The first act curtain isn't nearly strong enough.' It was wonderful training for the future playwright, strengthened by Noel's ever-quick acquisition of knowledge, never missing a trick.

The Great Name closed after two months, but by then Noel was already rehearsing for Hawtrey's production of *Where the Rainbow Ends*. Though only eleven he already loved to hear an audience laughing and applauding, 'loved the smell of "Size" drying on canvas scenery, the pungency of hot "Gelatines" in the limelights and footlights and the unforgettable, indescribable dressing-room smell of greasepaint, face powder, new clothes and cold cream.' He admitted that he must have driven Hawtrey mad, never leaving his side, pestering him with questions and distracting him so much that once he made him miss an entrance— an unforgivable sin, but Noel was soon forgiven. Hawtrey for his part must have liked the entertaining boy who tried to make him laugh, and often succeeded. 'The Aunt' in *The Rainbow* had to smack Noel's face, to which he objected; when Hawtrey asked him why, saying, 'It doesn't really hurt, does it?', Noel said, 'It isn't so much the smack, it's the anticipation.' His first-night message read, 'Best of luck and I hope a good hard smack. Charles Hawtrey.'

Noel was never a pupil of Italia Conti's, though her school did provide most of the children for *The Rainbow*, including two more future stars and lifelong friends, Hermione Gingold and, in the next year's production, Brian Aherne, who at that time thought Noel an unpleasant youth with large ears and too much assurance. Esmé Wynne played Rosamund and became Noel's close friend for the next ten years. Noel refers to Miss Conti as the ballet mistress, but she must have been more than that, probably co-directing with Hawtrey. By the time she gave this interview in the 'thirties it really had become 'my' production; she had bought or taken over the rights:

When I founded my school for stage children in 1911, I like to think I established a family which has done me more credit than I ever deserved. Some of those boys and girls who were with me in the early days are now famous men and women. Without asking their permission I am going to claim the prerogative of a parent and visualize them as children again. There was a little boy who played with great success in my production of *Where the Rainbow Ends*. From the first I realised that he was no ordinary child, possessing as he did strong affections and dislikes, and being of a rather emotional and rebellious temperament. I think he broke every rule I made. In my mind's eye I see him very distinctly in Manchester when we were on tour. The other children are having the time of their lives but he is telling me in sobbing tones how terribly homesick he feels. This same child had a wonderful ear for music, a charming voice and a facility for writing plays which the other children acted. Well, I am sure everyone has now guessed ...

... and she presumably went on to mention her other famous children, Gertrude Lawrence, Brian Aherne and Hermione Gingold, but Mrs Coward got out her scissors and cut them off.

Noel's education became more convulsive than ever during the spring of 1912; he was allowed, now that he and his mother considered him a professional actor, to take two days off each week to make the rounds of the agencies, searching for another job. At last he found one and appeared in June in Miss Ruby Ginner's ballet *An Autumn Idyll*, 'to music by F. Chopin'. Miss Ginner had not choreographed but had 'invented and arranged' the ballet, and herself was the *Première Danseuse* as the Autumn Leaf, a role for which Noel considered her much too large and well-developed to be blown about so easily by the Wind (Mr Alan Trotter). Twenty-six girls, one of whom was Saza Putt-farcken, were Leaves, also blown about by Mr Trotter, and it was presumably he too who caused the eight little Mists to swirl. There were four female Toadstools and a male one, the latter danced by Master Eric Coward; his one and only appearance on the stage. In larger print, Master Noel Coward is billed as the Mushroom with Miss Joan Carrol as the Toadstool. The Mushroom made an exuberant entrance, high-kicking until at last he spotted the Toadstool in pink, became enamoured of her, and they executed a tender *pas de deux* to tepid applause.

In October, Hawtrey again engaged Noel to appear with him, this time in a sketch called *A Little Fowl Play*, the most important number in the variety bill at the Coliseum. The engagement provided Noel with four heaven-sent weeks; he always got to the theatre early, stood at the side and watched the other turns, from performing seals to stars such as George Robey, Nellie Wallace, and Beattie and Babs, learning much from the solo performers—you had to 'get' your audience quickly, and from then on you had to hold them: 'There was an excitement about the Music Halls from the noisy, brassy overture onwards. I found it thrilling to watch the numbers of the turns change on the illuminated plaques at either side of the proscenium arch, each one filling me with fresh anticipation.'

One of his favourites was Phil Ray, the stand-up comedian, because he loved any playing about with words and Phil Ray's patter consisted mainly of abbreviations: 'I always abbreve, it's a hab.' Then there was Maidie Scott. Long before Sophie Tucker gave the very young Mary Martin such good advice over 'My Heart Belongs to Daddy', 'When you have a blue line to sing always look upwards,' the charming Maidie Scott, Noel said, was singing with gentle innocence some pretty hot stuff in 'If the Wind Had Only Blown the Other Way', and would give an imitation of her to prove it.

In between performances Noel always stayed in the Coliseum so that he could sing and dance on that vast stage to the empty and even vaster auditorium, all alone except for the cleaning-women, who paid no heed to him. He explored each cranny and nook backstage, and once in the property room opened the lid of a basket and released a number of snakes, who were there imprisoned when they were not being charmed thrice daily. There were shrieks from Madame Alicia Adelaide Need-ham's Ladies Choir when they arrived for the next performance to find all the snakes coiled round their radiator, to which they had writhed for warmth. Noel never said a word to anyone, of course.

His lucky star shone on him from the start; I have mentioned the Merciful Providence that guarded him from accident, and there does seem to have been a destiny that ruled his end, all along the way. While he was playing in *Where the Rainbow Ends* for a second time, this winter of 1912, the husband of a friend of Mrs Coward, an electrical engineer, was robbed of a valuable roll of copper wire. Her friend had already gone twice without success to the Coliseum, where Anna Eva Fay the thought-reader was topping the bill, to ask Miss Fay its whereabouts. The friend persuaded Mrs Coward to go with her for a third try; Miss Fay had created a sensation in America and the place was packed, but they succeeded in getting seats in the crowded balcony. A man came round with slips of paper on which people who wished could write their questions, and the friend induced Mrs Coward, rather against her will, to write one.

Now Mrs Coward had for some time been troubled in her mind, and what is more pestered by her multitudinous relations-in-law, as to the wisdom or not of keeping Noel on the stage at the expense of his education, and in such a precarious profession. So she wrote in pencil on a slip which was later handed back to her, and which is in front of me as I write: 'Do you advise me to keep my son Noel Coward on the stage? Violet Coward.'

There was a hush when Miss Fay at last appeared and spoke a few words; she sat down, an assistant put a sheet over her and she held her arms out wide, ghost-like. After answering one or two questions she shouted, 'Mrs Coward, Mrs Coward! You ask me about your son—keep him where he is! Keep him where he is! He has great talent and will have a wonderful career!' After a few more questions, Miss Fay was near collapse and had to be helped off the stage. The Coliseum holds 2,500 people, and Mrs Coward might well write, 'My feelings were beyond words, I was flabbergasted. How could she know, and *why* should she answer me amongst so many people?' Her friend's wire was never found, and when Mrs Coward triumphantly told all the relations about her wonderful experience, they listened to her with scepticism and pitying smiles. This made her determination to keep Noel on the stage all the more inflexible.

She wrote, on a modest note of self-justification, that 'Noel did get some schooling in during 1912', and that his spare time was spent constantly in the company of Esmé Wynne, both of them perpetually writing stories, poems and plays. They acted the plays, the two best parts reserved for themselves, Eric being forced to fill a gap if there was one, 'which he was not overjoyed at'. Mrs Coward did not quite like Noel going to Liverpool and Manchester for three weeks without her in March 1913 to play in Basil Dean's production of Hauptmann's *Hannele*; but he was thrilled at having obtained the double part of schoolboy and angel, and was so very anxious to go that she allowed it. While in Manchester he and the other children were forced by magistrate's order to attend a local school, which so enraged him — no one ever being able to force Noel to do anything — that he refused to answer the pince-nez'd master's questions or learn any lessons and threatened to walk out if he were caned or in any way punished. For the remaining days he took books with him which he read unmolested at the back of the classroom. That is the last we hear of Noel's education.

He was seen off at Euston by his mother, who was assured by Miss Conti — in charge of the ten or so boys and girls in *Hannele* — that he would be well looked-after. On the train the theatrically historic first meeting took place between Gertrude Lawrence and Noel Coward. Gertie was fifteen, already *mondaine* in a black satin coat and cap; she shamelessly powdered her nose in public and told Noel some enjoyably risqué stories, and from then on Noel loved her and she loved him. A friend of ours says that Noel told her that during this engagement Gertie took him to the bedroom and demonstrated, more practically than Philip Tonge had verbally done the year before, the facts of life.

Hannele was Noel's first encounter with Basil Dean as a director. Mr Dean, a young man of twenty-five, was already a bully. Noel, thirteen, even then knew how to deal with him. He advanced downstage and calmly but firmly proclaimed his ultimatum: 'Mr Dean, if you ever speak to me like that again, I shall go straight home to my mother.' Basil Dean, most likely an unconscious bully, reacted as browbeaters always do when they are stood up to; he never tried to intimidate Noel again. He directed five of Noel's plays in the 'twenties, and directed him in *The Constant Nymph*, which was justly famous for its perfectly assembled minute details of direction. Noel's stories of him were monotonously alike — of how he and Edna Best, the stars, had to threaten to walk out for the rest of the day unless he stopped terrorising the small-part actors; and how Jane Cowl, in *Easy Virtue*, when Dean had reduced yet another elderly actor to a gibbering mass, near to tears, came down to the footlights and said cooingly in her 'beautiful' voice, 'Mr Dean, you do want this gentleman to give a good performance on opening night?' 'Yes, of course I do.' 'Then LAY OFF him!'

'Why on earth did you put up with him?' we would ask Noel. 'He sounds a terrible man.' 'He was a fine director, he just didn't realise that actors have one skin less than other people.' (He should have, one thought.) 'Besides'—and this would end the matter—'I was really rather fond of him.'

After *Hannele*, Noel's next assignment was in June 1913 in a sketch called *War in the Air* on the variety bill at the Palladium. The author, Frank Dupree, wrote prophetically of what was to come true a few years later, describing it as the Hovering Peril. Noel, with a toy aeroplane, played a little boy who combined precocious aeronautical knowledge with piety, ending the prologue on his knees praying, 'Please God make me a great big aviator one day.' His prayer was answered with startling rapidity, seconds later at the beginning of the next scene. Noel had become not only a grown-up aviator, but his accent had changed to refined Cockney and his looks had altered completely, even to the colour of his eyes. The adult aviator stepped into a large mock-up aeroplane and flew off on a wire round the Dress Circle, or rather halfway round where (to Noel's delight) it stuck and the whole thrilling effect had to be abandoned.

Meanwhile during this happy summer (though Noel felt it may not have been so happy for his mother) the Coward family moved to the upper maisonette of a house on the south side, Clapham Common. The rooms were larger than those of the Battersea flat, commanding at the front a view of the Common, prettier than it sounds and in those days even more rural, and at the back of a large private garden. Finances were at a low ebb, a servant of any kind being out of the question, and Mrs Coward pretended—for Noel's sake especially—that all the house-work she had to do, the laundering, cooking and scrubbing, was fun. Noel and Eric, now aged eight, helped with the washing up. Mr Coward was by this time travelling for Payne's pianos, but his travelling had become more and more spasmodic, much of his time being unprofitably spent sailing a model yacht on a pond nearby on the Common; Eric, more docile than Noel, squatted obligingly opposite and prodded the toy with a stick to start its return voyage to his father.

Noel had a matchbox of a room under the roof, but it was his very own. In this room, as well as on his journeys by Underground to the West End in search of work and back, he read every book he could. Though faithful always to E. Nesbit, he had by now graduated to the spy thrillers of E. Phillips Oppenheim and William Le Queux, *Doctor Nikola* by Guy Boothby and the historical novels of Stanley Weyman. He started to build his library with the charming little scarlet-and-gold

uniform series published by Nelson & Sons; the novels of Mrs
Humphrey Ward, Miss Braddon's *Lady Audley's Secret* and the romances
of Anthony Hope and C. N. and A. M. Williamson. Now began his
lifelong addiction to any book, novel or biography, dealing with the
French Revolution, Marie Antoinette endlessly fascinating him.
Baroness Orczy's *The Scarlet Pimpernel* was a great favourite, and later,
when it was dramatised for Fred Terry and Julia Neilson, he saw it
many times and loved to quote from it: 'Hoity-toity, Citizen Alice,
what in the world are ye doing in Calaiss?' Then there was the actress
who was allowed to play in it on tour but not to come into the West
End because of the uncertainty of her French accent: 'Ze men zey are
terreeble, and ze women zey are even more terreeble zan ze men'—now
in refined English—'Marguerite St Just in particular.'

Noel wrote that they all went down that summer of 1913 to stay
with Auntie Vida at Lee-on-Solent, but at some time during that
month he must have been separated from his mother, for he wrote
from there:

Dear and most august Parent, This *is* a letter although *you* may not
think so. [He has drawn four long lines across the page.] these
lines are to show how much I adore you. I am still as beautiful as
rotten Mangold-Wurzel. I met the Douglas woman to-day and
told her what fun I had when I was at my Zenith! (I hope that
isent a rude word!!!) Farewell Beloved. Your Sweet Son Noel.

'Farewell Beloved' is most probably a joking quote from Tosti's
'Good-Bye', the song forced through more throats than any other at
that time, in every drawing-room and front parlour throughout the
land. With both his parents so musical, many of Noel's childhood
evenings were spent listening, whenever they had company, to drawing-room ballads. His mother would carefully remove her rings and
place them at the end of the keyboard before bravely embarking on the
introductory chords and then accompanying his father's 'light tenor
voice of great sweetness' in the 'Indian Love Lyrics', Paul Rubens's
'I Love the Moon', 'Comin' through the Rye', 'Sweet Lass of Richmond
Hill' and many more; Noel knew and remembered them all and
remembered too the tremendous responsibility of being asked to 'turn
over' for the pianist, as well as a joke that went with it; 'I *am* so sorry,
I didn't realise it was a flymark. I thought it was a dotted crotchet.'

Charles Hawtrey provided another example of his kindness towards
the end of this holiday. He offered Noel a part in *Never Say Die* but the

letter was laggingly forwarded, and although he and Mrs Coward at once scurried up to London they were too late; Reggie Sheffield had already been engaged. Noel's disappointment was so plain to see that Hawtrey sympathetically gave him the understudy. This was better than nothing, and Noel was happy to be in the company because, apart from Hawtrey, he had a special admiration for the beautiful leading lady, Winifred Emery. What is more, he was bringing home—where it was very badly needed—two pounds ten a week.

Only four months later, Noel's cherished dream of appearing in *Peter Pan*, then a youthful annual of only ten Christmases, was to be realised. The Duke of York's Theatre was packed with children when Noel went for his audition, all of them accompanied as he was by their mothers and, like him, all burning with the same ambition—to get into *Peter Pan*. When Noel's turn came they both went up on to the stage but Mrs Coward 'kept well in the background as I always did, such good policy ...' Dion Boucicault, who was taking the audition, called out, 'Only one verse,' but when Noel and the accompanist stopped he again called out, 'Go on. Go on!' and Noel did go on, to the end of the song. Mr Boucicault asked Mrs Coward what part Noel wanted; she rather daringly asked for Slightly and even more boldly asked for four pounds a week. He told them to go away and come back in an hour, which time they spent feverishly walking about. Mrs Coward wrote (after he had granted both her requests) that he was a nice kind man, with the most charming manners. About a week later there arrived a letter, the most exciting letter Noel had until then ever received in his life. The paper is headed CHARLES FROHMAN, LONDON AND NEW YORK:

Dear Master Coward, on behalf of Mr Frohman, I engage you to play the part of 'Slightly' in 'Peter Pan' on or about December 23rd, at a salary of £4 a week. Kindly write and confirm this and oblige. Yours truly, W. Lestocq, General Manager.

The *Observer* thought Noel excellent in the part and another critic wrote, 'The immortal Slightly, as acted by Master Noel Coward, is quite a young boy [the older A. W. Baskcomb had previously played him] and his grave pretence at wisdom is all the funnier.' Micheál MacLiammóir, who played John, did not agree; he remembered Noel's performance as too intelligent, probably thinking it should have been as bumbling as Baskcomb's had been. Mrs Coward admitted that her opinion was probably prejudiced, but thought it much more suitably played by a boy than a grown man, and stated flatly that Noel made a hit. The last night became a gala; it was the adored Pauline Chase's last performance as 'Peter' in the West End, after playing him for eight seasons running; there were crowds waiting outside, some of whom called, 'Good old Slightly!' when Noel came out, and nearly shook his hand off. He and his mother drove home luxuriously in a taxi, 'loaded with boxes of chocolates and flowers'. (One would not wish to detract from Mrs Coward's exciting account, but according to Noel all the children were given the same, though on that night he did get more than most, perhaps from the numerous relations.)

After very little sleep, they had to hurry the next morning to catch the nine o'clock train for Glasgow, the start of a four-week tour. Mrs Coward was also in charge of a boy called Donald Buckley who shared their digs; the tour was a new experience for her and she described it as a charming one, except when she discovered lice in Donald Buckley's hair during the week in Newcastle.

Noel was wretchedly disappointed the following year when A. W. Baskcomb was again given Slightly, until a telegram arrived asking Noel to take over immediately, since Baskcomb was ill. To Noel's elation was added the fact that he would actually be appearing on the same stage as the great Madge Titheradge, who was that year playing Peter. And on his very first matinée he ran into her on the stairs; she shook his hand warmly, said, 'My name's Madge, what's yours?' and his bliss was complete. Miss Titheradge was a dramatic actress of enormous power, and in the scene when Tinker Bell will die unless we all applaud and help to save her, she asked, '*Do* you believe in fairies?' and commanded, '*Say quick* that you believe!' so ferociously that little children whimpered and clung to their mothers instead of clapping their hands, and Miss Titheradge never played Peter Pan again.

Graham Payn, who was to become very close to Noel and me during the last thirty years of Noel's life, also played in *Peter Pan*, with Jean Forbes-Robertson as Peter; and as I had seen and read the play many times (the three of us agreeing that Jean Forbes-Robertson was the best Peter ever), we could and did quote from the play with ease and enjoyment. 'A little less noise there', 'And now to rescue Wendy!', 'Straight on till morning', were in everyday use, as were 'That is the fear that haunts me', and 'Oh the cleverness of me!' Much of it could be shortened and used as a code: 'That's Nana's bark when she smells danger', for instance. A *sotto voce* 'Nana's bark' from Noel at, say, a business meeting, would be enough to warn Graham and me to beware.

2

THE YEARS
OF PROMISE

AFTER the tour of *Peter Pan* in early 1914, Noel was out of work for almost the rest of the year. He wrote in *Present Indicative* that these periods in his memory were difficult to recapture, oddly jumbled and nebulous without the chain of the theatre to hold them together. It is true that there are discrepancies, even with the theatre; he wrote that by the time he met Madge Titheradge he had already seen her in *Tiger Cub* [*sic*] at the Garrick, when as a matter of boring accuracy *Tiger's Cub* was not produced at the Garrick or anywhere else until January 29th, 1916. Also at variance are the accounts of the strange cough which Noel developed and which proved to be caused by a tubercular gland in his chest. Noel stated that it was in 1915 that Doctor Etlinger, an old friend of the family, examined him; in his mother's version it was early in 1914 that she 'was very glad when Noel ran across a friend, a Doctor Etlanger, who had a sanatorium down in Gloucestershire'. Noel said he spent a little time at the Pinewood Sanatorium at Wokingham. At any rate, it is from Cranham, near Stroud in Gloucestershire that Noel wrote, his letter as usual undated:

Darling Mummy, it *is* simply perfect down here its a dear little cottage on the side of a very steep hill, woods at the back and woods at the side and a lovely valley in front with a lake, a cow, a horse, two puppies and a good many snakes! To day I have seen an Adder, a Grass Snake, and a blind-worm they abound, Mrs E[tlinger] is so nice so is the Doctor. There is a lovely pony I ride I am going shopping on him this afternoon. There is a forest opposite us. Out of my bedroom window I can see and hear a Waterfall, The Regent's Canal begins in this garden I had a grass Snake round my neck to-day!!! (me don't think!) Do send old clothes quickly. I have bare legs, arms, and head, and I paddle in the lake. Do send my bathing dress. I dident feel a bit homesick last night. love to everything, everybody, anyhow, anywhere Your ever loving son Noel P.S. I was up to my calfs in mud at 7 oc this morning.

Also from the same address:

Darling Mummy, I *am* having a fine time I have had some real adventures Yesterday (The pony is a dear and he gallops a lot and I can ride very well) I dressed up as an Arab and two very jolly Girls friends of the Doctor dressed up as Arabs too I rode on the pony he was all dressed up in beads and hangings and we three went through the village throwing flowers at everyone and telling their fortunes It *was* fun. This morning The Doctor and I built a log hut in the woods and The girls and I started at a quater to nine at night (I am writing this at 10-15) with larntens and this is a list of what we brought, — 1 Billy Can, ½lb of Potatoes, 2 Eggs (one of which talked and broke), ½ loaf of Bread, 1 bit of Cheese (that got up and flew away) 2 larntens, 1½ Candles, 2 Matchboxes, 4 Apples, Coca and sugar and water, 1 Kettle.

The good Doctor Etlinger's advice, that Noel should be allowed to run wild in clean country air, proved to be sound and the mysterious cough disappeared quickly. While on this holiday-cum-convalescence he first learned to play croquet, a game to which he became devoted and eventually extremely skilful—much sought-after as a partner and absolutely dreaded as an opponent. The Doctor further advised Mrs Coward to send Noel to the sea for the rest of that summer and autumn.

In the spring of this same year, 1914, Noel wrote that he had met— without explaining how or where—an artist named Philip Streatfield, who had a studio in Chelsea. Philip Streatfield was then about thirty to Noel's fourteen; Noel of course was older than his years, considerably more sophisticated than an average schoolboy of the same age would have been, and one supposes that Philip found in him a highly enter- taining and amusing companion. Noel for his part loved going to tea at the studio; the theatre must have been a bond between them, for Philip was at that time painting a portrait of Phyllis Monkman in the pink velvet dress she wore in her 'Pom Pom' dance in the revue at the Alhambra. He was also painting a nude of a girl called Doris, who would casually break her pose in order to make the tea; Noel felt this was only to be expected in such a Bohemian atmosphere and would talk about it off-handedly to the family when he got back to Clapham. Mrs Coward does not mention this friendship in her notes of Noel's youth, but she carefully kept the pencil portrait Philip drew of him.

We shall never know exactly what the relationship was between them, but Mrs Coward must have approved of it, for when Philip decided in May to go on a motor tour of the West Country in search of a cottage from which to paint landscapes, she gave her permission for Noel to go with him. Noel found the trip doubly exciting because he had never been in a fast car in his life, let alone for two whole weeks. After this fortnight on the road he dropped him off at Aunt Laura's house in Charlestown. He was delighted to be back in the house with the lovely garden and the lake and found the spell of its beauty to be as potent as ever. Now occurred the memorable incident of Noel being encouraged by his cousins, Walter and Connie Bulteel, to dress up as a girl. There were in those days no Freudian implications; it was just a jolly good jape. He would soon be wearing Esmé Wynne's clothes and she his, even in the street when they felt like it. The idea had been that Noel should deceive the other guests that evening for as long as he could; Noel was tall and with whatever make-up there was in those days he appeared older and succeeded so well that one young man became besotted and over-ardent during a walk in the garden. Noel quickly brought him indoors, but continued the masquerade until all the guests had gone. When the eager young man appeared early next morning Walter and Connie lied that their friend had already left, but comforted him by promising to forward a letter to her. They all laughed their heads off when they opened the letter, Walter and Connie told me that Noel had been wonderful in carrying the joke right through to the end, and it was no surprise to them that he later became such a brilliant actor:

My Dear Little Flapper, You can imagine my feelings when I arrived at the Bulteel's this morning, to find you had flown. I was fearfully sick as I was looking forward to spending an exceedingly pleasant morning with you on the lake and was beastly disappointed. I do call it real hard lines and I am still feeling beastly depressed. I have got a little remembrance of you which I am loth to part with—your cigarette holder. Am I to send it on to you? If so ... I will grudgingly do so. Will you let me write to you occasionally, and if so, will you answer my letters? Should I be presuming too much if I asked for your photo? I hope that you are not going to ignore me and forget me altogether. With best love, yours ever, A.S.

In the years when I knew him, Noel disliked the idea of men dressed as women and thought it extremely unfunny. On the stage was a different matter, if it was well done. He and Sir Gerald du Maurier, of all unlikely people, played two coy débutantes in one of the *Grand Giggle* plays at a Theatrical Garden Party in the late 'twenties; and he went many times to see Danny La Rue at his club or in the theatre — the point being not that Danny made him roll about with laughter because he was in drag, but that, in or out of drag, Danny is such a fine comedian.

Philip Streatfield had found a house during their two-week tour and a little while later asked Noel to stay with him. Noel wrote from there, for the first time using morsels of French, the diaeresis over the 'e' and the firm downward stroke of the 'l' in his signature, and with two Phil Ray abbreves at the end of the letter:

Polperro, Cornusarl sur le Corn: Dear Darling old Mummysnooks, I *am* enjoying myself so much it really is perfectly Heavenly here. Donald Bain has got the most ripping pair of field-glasses that ever happened in this wide universe and the next! We are right opposite the 'Eddistone Lighthouse' and it looks so tall and white standing straight up in the sun. We havent had such very lovely weather its generally been a leetle beet to cold a wind to be really nice but we bathe from a sandy cove about a mile along the cliffs and then lie in the sun and dry. I am now the coulour of a boiled lobster with which these shores abound (not to say sharks! O-o-ee-r-r Auntie!) This house is perfectly ripping so beautifully furnished and its about 300 feet above the sea and I climb right down every morning to catch fish for my aquarium which is a clear pool in the rocks Philip has bought me a net with which to catch le denizens de la deep (Bow-wow!) ... I received le sweater et le lettre all right and it fits me Tres Chic!!! (More bow-wows!) I havent been very homesick but I have been a little (bless you) I shall have to stopppp now as I am going to wallow in Bacon and eggs so good-bye and love to Daddy and Eric and Florrie and Tinker and any old thing you like to mench! Hope you are well as leaves me at pres. Your evereverevereverever loving Noel P.S. I will write every Saturday.

The peace of the holiday was shattered when they read in the papers on August 4th that war had been declared on Germany. Philip took Noel to Looe railway station, where Hugh Walpole materialised; he kindly took charge of Noel during the journey to London, and, even more kindly, gave him the handsome present of half-a-crown at parting. The remainder of 1914 was for Noel uneventful, some of the autumn spent pleasantly enough with the aunts at Lee, the rest not so pleasantly in London searching for work. His birthday and Christmas passed with Noel unemployed until, as we have seen, he was sent for to replace Baskcomb in *Peter Pan* in January but, says Mrs Coward, 'the war had started and nobody felt gay anymore'.

Noel, however, seems cheerful enough. The following letter is difficult to place exactly, but appears to have been written just before he went into *Peter Pan*. The revival of *The Little Minister* had been running at the Duke of York's since September, presumably by Christmas only in the evenings, while *Peter* played matinées, so Noel was able to obtain free seats for both from Mr Matthews, the front-of-house manager. The letter also proves that he had achieved enough independence from his parents to stay with Philip Streatfield as often as he pleased. Many years later Marie Lohr gave him a reproduction of Shannon's famous portrait of herself, slim, young and beautiful, as Lady Babbie in the play:

> 53, Glebe Place, Chelsea, Friday: Ducky old Diddleums, Philip is now a soldier! (cheers) and I am going to stay to-night with him too as I shant see much of him when he is drilling all day. I took him to the 'Little Minister' last night and Mr Matthews promised to let me have two more seats when I wanted them. I couldnt say anything about Peter Pan because he was surrounded by people but I will when I go with you. The play is ripping the most beautiful scenery you ever saw and Marie Lohr is sweet but its all in very broad Scotch so unless we get stalls you wont hear a word. I am going to see Captain Charlton this morning and Captain Somer is going to take Philip and Captain C. and yours truly to a box at a Music Hall to-night. No evening dress required. Good bye now, Ever your own, Dinkybobs.

By June 1915, Philip was training with the Sherwood Foresters in Essex. While he was there Noel received a letter from Mrs Astley Cooper inviting him, at Philip's suggestion, to stay with her at Hambleton Hall, her house in Rutland. Philip thought that Mrs Cooper would like the fifteen-year-old boy, that Noel would benefit from the country air and from the astringent wisdom of Mrs Cooper's friendship. He did more for Noel than he knew. This was Noel's first taste of 'county' and of staying in a well-run country house. There was a fire in his bedroom, shining brass cans of hot water, and his dinner clothes were laid out for him each evening. There can be no doubt that Noel learned much social nerve and poise from his visits to Mrs Cooper; henceforth he would feel perfectly at home either staying with, or writing about, the upper classes.

Mrs Cooper turned out to be the most jolly and stimulating company. She hadn't asked Venus to take her votive glass, since she was not what she was, but had herself hung scarves over all the mirrors because she could no longer find any charm in her own appearance. Noel always described her as a perfect old duck, with the endearing habit of lying flat on a chintz-covered mattress in front of the fire in the drawing-room, shooting off witticisms in a petulant wail while from time to time breaking wind fore and aft without self-consciousness.

Hambleton is in the middle of the Cottesmore country; Noel drove himself to meets in the dogcart and followed the hunt until the pony rebelled and would gallop no farther. Surely he could not have written his second comedy, *The Young Idea*, in 1921 had not these visits made him familiar with the hunting set and their jargon. Further, he owed to Mrs Cooper his lifelong friendship and collaboration with Gladys Calthrop, whom he met while staying with her in Alassio, also in 1921. Noel wrote, 'Philip died the following year without ever realising to the full the kindness he had done me.'

He had yet one more reason to be grateful to Mrs Cooper. On a later visit to Hambleton, while still in his teens, he made a joyful discovery. There, on a round table in the hall, lay a copy of *Beasts and Superbeasts* by Saki (H. H. Munro), which he took up to his bedroom. He was unable even to think of going to sleep until he had finished it. He had been captivated from the first paragraph by the verbal adroitness of Saki's dialogue and the brilliance of his wit. He crystallised in Noel's mind, by the effortless evocation in his novels of the atmosphere and social charm of Edwardian country-house parties, how such events could and should be written about. Mrs Cooper, articulate and with just the right amount of eccentricity, Noel now saw as a character straight out of Saki, and she would of course be the hostess whose witticisms would explode like fire-crackers. 'There was apple-blossom everywhere'; 'Only on the apple trees, surely,' is dialogue exactly to

Noel's taste and, as he admitted, influenced his own youthful efforts in the delicate, precise art of high-comedy writing.

He read all the other Saki books as soon as he was able, including the two successful essays in the macabre, 'The Easter Egg' and the even more sinister 'Shredni Vashtar', which he recalled (and would often re-read) with an authentic shudder. So Saki, very early on, joined E. Nesbit as the first true loves in his growing passion for reading, and his love for them both remained unabated.

At last, just before Christmas 1915, Noel found work; he was re-engaged for *Where the Rainbow Ends*, but this time, since he had grown too big for the Pageboy, he played the Slacker, a short but showy part which he enjoyed to the limit. The Slacker is half-man, half-dragon (complete with tail), and Noel smothered his cheeks with yellow make-up, emaciated them with blue and, his eyelids glittering with green sequins, played the part full-out. He made his exit laughing long and hysterically and never failed to get a round of applause.

Again in the cast with Noel was Esmé Wynne, and when the run ended the two of them got jobs in the spring tour of *Charley's Aunt*, Esmé as Amy and Noel as Charley, a part he regarded as one of the most unrewarding ever written. Charley has to 'feed' everybody else; they get all the laughs while Charley gets none, and Noel was far from pleased. His and Esmé's friendship developed; in his weekly letters home her name crops up continually. Noel's other close friend at this time was John Ekins; handsome, one year older than Noel and even more stagestruck, already with two good West End parts to his credit. The three were inseparable, John rushing from London to see the others whenever he could.

Noel and Esmé read quantities of poetry, the more romantic and passionate the better, and both attempted to write it. Noel's very first efforts inclined much more towards the funny; in Introductions both to his *Collected Lyrics* and to his book of verse *Not Yet the Dodo* he refers to this early 'Vegetable Verse' and quotes two examples:

> In A Voice Of Soft Staccato
> We Will Speak Of The Tomato

> The Sinful AspaRAGus
> To Iniquity Will Drag Us

He was relieved to say that the rest had disappeared completely. But his shade is benevolent, and I am sure he would have allowed these further quotations had he known that his mother had so carefully kept them with his letter from Blackpool ('I have written two more nonsense rythmes which I enclose':)

> I had a little Onion
> Its smell was rather strong
> But it couldn't help its odour
> 'Twas its nature that was wrong
> It was Coarse and Avaricious
> Peculiarly Pernicious
> And Disgustingly Suspicious —
> *Pas Bon.*

The second may be a take-off of Esmé's love-poems, though I am only guessing:

> 'Love Ditty to a Turnip'

> Oh Turnip Turn
> Those lovely eyes once more
> To me
> And let true love be ours
> Eternally
> Others I have loved before
> But none
> As much as thou, Thou art
> My Moon my Sun
> My Star of Stars from out
> The Heavens above
> Come Turnip Mine
> And let us yield ... to Love!

At last the tour of *Charley's Aunt* came to an end. After the long separation from their parents, Noel and Esmé were delighted to be home; she lived not too far away at Stockwell and John Ekins with his uncle at Lewisham. Mrs Coward wrote that the three of them were quite inseparable, always together in their spare time, and thought they had a very happy time of it. Which they did, though sometimes Esmé and Noel quarrelled so violently that they drew up Rules of Palship which forbade arguments over certain subjects, especially religion; this may have given Noel the idea of the word 'sollocks', which puts an immediate stop to Amanda and Elyot's squabbles in *Private Lives*.

Noel's romantic friendship with John continued all through 1916. They adored one another's company, excitedly going to every play or musical they could, and Noel often walked on in the crowd scenes when in September John got a part in *The Best of Luck* at Drury Lane. To add to the glamour, Madge Titheradge was the star; and again some of the lines became part of Noel's language. 'May God forgive you, Blanche Westermere, for I never shall!' he would exclaim years afterwards, to other people's bewilderment. He and John indulged in silk socks, blue and pink and mauve, with, to Noel's later shame, handkerchiefs to match, though at the time they fancied themselves in their carefully pressed navy-blue suits. They were equally happy staying with John's parents at the Rectory at Rame, near Plymouth, where John's father was the incumbent. Much of their time was spent in deck chairs in the garden, which overlooked the sea, gloating over the pictures in back numbers of *Play Pictorial*. They naturally went to matinées at the Theatre Royal in Plymouth, always followed by tea in the Palm Court of the Royal Hotel.

Noel recalled their friendship as one of unalloyed happiness — they seem never to have quarrelled — and with a certain amount of emotion because of its ending. In the following year, 1917, when John was training as an Air Force cadet at Farnborough, Noel received a letter from him arranging for them to go to a matinée at the Criterion Theatre. But by the same post there was another letter, from John's mother, to say that he had died suddenly of spinal meningitis. Noel felt brave when he made the decision to go to the matinée alone and couldn't understand why he foolishly started to cry during the second interval. This was his first brush with death, the first time he had had to apply the dreadful words 'never again' to all the memories of someone he had loved.

Some long while before this, Arthur Scott-Craven had written to Robert Courtneidge, saying, 'I particularly wish to bring young Noel Coward to your direct and personal attention. He is the possessor of the most exquisite boy's voice I ever heard.' (He dreamed of dramatising Lewis Carroll's *Sylvie and Bruno*, with Noel as Bruno.) Now, in the summer of 1916, Courtneidge engaged Noel to play in a musical, *The Light Blues*, in which his daughter Cicely was to appear with Jack Hulbert, her husband of a few weeks. Noel had only a small part, but he also understudied Jack; he prayed that Jack would fall ill so that he could show the West End how brilliantly he could sing, dance and act in a grown-up part. Cis recalls that Noel seemed to know every-thing and infuriated her because he was always right. He also in-furiated her father; at one rehearsal he became so angry with Noel that he shouted at him, threw his hat on the ground and stamped on it in his rage. Noel remained maddeningly cool and smiled a superior smile. 'Why are you laughing, boy?' roared Mr Courtneidge. 'Because it's your hat you're jumping on, not mine,' replied Noel.

Noel did not take the West End by storm, and neither did the play, which petered out after a run of two weeks. Three months later, Noel found himself back once more in a children's play at Christmas time, called *The Happy Family*, though no longer playing a boy's part. He had matured into a young spriggins of a Sandhurst cadet, wearing a red-and-white striped blazer and a pillbox hat with, for the first time, a number all to himself. This was 'Sentry Go', which he sang and danced with such dash and verve that one critic—alas of a weekly with a limited circulation—said that he combined the grace and movement of a Russian dancer with the looks and manner of an English school-boy. Together with him in *The Happy Family* were Mimi Crawford and Fabia Drake. Fabia christened Noel 'Cowardy Custard' and called him 'Custard' for the rest of his life. Mimi Crawford became Countess of Suffolk, and the last time she and Noel met was on the staircase at Wartski, the jeweller's in Regent Street; they hugged so all-embrac-ingly that they lost their balance, fell over, and rolled down the last four steps in a bundle. They remained reminiscing, sitting on the bottom step, and I on the top one heard them singing the opening number from *The Happy Family*:

> Isn't it awfully jolly
> Doing a little revue?
> Never could be a more happy idea
> It's nobby and nutty and new.

This same year, 1916, Noel wrote and composed the lyrics and music of his first completely integrated song, 'Forbidden Fruit'. In the first three lines he makes clear that he is already aware of the hopelessness inherent in most human endeavour:

> Ordinary man
> Invariably sighs
> Vainly for what cannot be ...

'Things go from bad to worse in the refrain which, although it begins fairly skittishly with the objective statement "Every peach, Out of reach, Is attractive", ends on a note of bitter disillusion':

> For the brute
> Loves the fruit
> That's forbidden
> And I'll bet you half a crown
> He'll appreciate the flavour of it much much more
> If he has to climb a bit to shake it down.

The song, though a remarkable achievement for a sixteen-year-old, as is its worldly cynicism, is only very nearly good enough, and had to wait thirty-seven years for publication in *The Noel Coward Song-Book*, and then only for its exceptional curiosity value. But it did usefully come into its own fifty-two years after its composition in the film *Star*, in which Daniel Massey portrayed—not imitated—his godfather, and sang and played it at an audition for André Charlot.

From now on ideas for songs, either the words or the music or both, crowded in his brain. In August of the next year, 1917, he wrote from the Gaiety Theatre, Manchester, where he was appearing in *Wild Heather*:

My Darling, at the moment I am nearly mad with excitement, it is awful not having you here to tell about it all! My Dear I am collaborating with Max Darewski in a new song, I wrote the lyric yesterday after breakfast, I hummed it to him in the Midland lounge at 12 oc, we at once rushed up to his private room and he put harmonies to it, there were some other people there, when they had sung it over once or twice, Max leapt off the piano stool and danced for joy and said it was going to take London by storm! We are putting the verse to music this morning it is to be published next week and probably sung by Lee White or Phyllis Dare! I am arranging business part of it to day. I shall probably make a lot of money out of it, it is called When you come home on leave, written and composed by Noel Coward and Max Darewski. You see he is one of the most influential men in town, he owns three theatres, at last I am beginning to make my way, really Manchester has been astonishingly lucky for me. Good bye now my Snig, I am too mad to write about anything else. Your Baby, Snag (*Dramatist and Composer*)

That nothing came of all this over-excitement is sad to relate; on the other hand Darewski continued to encourage Noel with kind enthusiasm. In the following May, when Noel bought a fat hard-covered notebook in which to scribble lyrics, Darewski wrote inside the cover his telephone number and a surprising address, 'c/o Marquis [*sic*] of Winchester, St Mary's, Andover'. His kindness extended to inducing his brother Herman to give Noel a contract for lyrics, £50 for the first year, £75 for the second, and although Noel dutifully reported to his office every week or so with the bursting notebook in hand, he never even clapped eyes on Herman Darewski, let alone had a lyric accepted. Noel went with anxiety on the last day of the third and final year, but need not have worried; Mr Darewski's secretary gave him a cup of tea in the outer office and handed him a cheque for £100 with a charming smile. Noel was not in the least surprised when the firm went bankrupt shortly afterwards. As a matter of interest, this is the very first of the lyrics which Mr Darewski did not accept, entitled 'Anna the Auctioneer':

Verse: Annabel Devigne
       Had a flat at Golder's Green
       And her ways were really most endearing
       She desired to learn a bit
       And she thought she'd make a hit
       If she did a little auctioneering
       On a box she'd take her stand
       With a hammer in her hand
       And a firm resolve to keep from skidding
       But don't think that she fell,
       She went most awfully well
       With the men who came to do her bidding.

Refrain: Anna was an Auctioneer
       Tho' what she sold is not quite clear
       And as a business woman she
       May never quite have shone
       She discovered young men's choice was
       To hear how nice her voice was—
       Going, Going, *Gone!*

Another telephone number inside the cover is that of Miss Doris Joel. Miss Joel's keenness as a composer of songs at that time almost matched

Noel's; at all events they worked very hard together, and eventually succeeded in getting their 'The Baseball Rag' published by Ascherberg, Hopwood and Crew. The cover is very gay indeed, with red and blue baseballs flying in all directions on a white background; this was the first time Noel had the thrill of seeing his name on a sheet-music cover, and in quite large letters too: 'Words by Noel Coward, Music by Doris Doris'—as she preferred to be known professionally. Noel admitted afterwards that the song was not as All-American as they thought it was at the time:

> I've got a ripping new sensation
> There's just no need for hesitation
> Baseball's the game that
> Makes the world go round
> It gets your heart a-palpitating
> You can't sit still
> You'll go mad, you'll go bad
> Because you'll never be contented
> Until ...
>
> You, do, that, Raggy Rag
> It's just a baseball tune
> And it gets you syncopated mad
> Like any old coon
> You simply glide along dear
> You never want to lag
> It's a joy, it's a dream
> It's a yell, it's a scream
> Oh, that Baseball Rag.

The notebook provides a lot of material that is unexpected from such a youthful lyricist:

> Give me a girl with a dull brown eye
> And I know just where I am
> I don't care a damn
> For the grey eyes and the green eyes
> And the just what might-have-been eyes
> People may rave over Kirchner Girls
> But I can pass them by
> It's the shyness that entrances

And the slightly frowning glances
Of the Girl with the Dull Brown Eye.

The three weeks spent in Manchester with *Wild Heather* were for Noel packed with far-reaching incident. He appeared only in the first two acts, which left him free to hurry to the Palace and catch Ivy St Helier and Clara Evelyn, singing and playing at two grand pianos back to back. He made himself known and they invited him to tea in their suite at the Midland Hotel, where he immediately played and sang them some of his songs. He always remembered the wise advice that Ivy gave him that afternoon. The value of 'authority' at the piano, for one thing; she taught him several commanding, striking chords which could be used as introduction to almost any song, and would straight away claim the audience's attention. He profited greatly from Ivy's counsel and from then on always used her method of 'attack' when starting to play the piano.

Then, stepping off a tram one day outside the Midland, Noel ran into Robert Andrews and Ivor Novello. Bobby had been a friend since their contemporary days as boy actors, and at that time also an envied and hated rival because Bobby, with his strong advantage in good looks and slight advantage in age, was always given the plum parts. But that was long ago, and Bobby now introduced him to Ivor, already the great and romantically handsome Matinée Idol he was to remain. Noel was shocked: the idol was yellow-faced, unshaven and wearing an old overcoat and a deplorable brown hat, having just finished a morning rehearsal. But that evening Noel, free at the end of his second act, flew to the Prince's to see the last act of Ivor's musical *Arlette*. He afterwards watched the transformation as Ivor prepared to go to a company supper-party and envied everything about him; his looks, personality, assured position, his suite at the Midland and above all the supper party at which he felt sure Ivor would be laughing gaily as he sipped champagne, surrounded by adorers. Noel begrudged him none of this, even though he envied him; but it was a sharp reminder of how far he himself, at seventeen years of age, still had to go before he could achieve such glamorous eminence. That evening in Manchester was the beginning of what Noel called their hilarious friendship, an account of which will have to wait until Noel did scale the same heights.

There was one more excitement during the three weeks in Manchester:

Darling, I felt I must write and tell you my news, I was sent for to see Gilbert Miller at the Midland. My Dear he had come down *specially* to see me in Wild Heather and he said I was *really splendid* and that I hadn't half enough to do! Also that it would be all right about the extra week now that he had seen me play, he felt absolutely certain that I should make my name in The Saving Grace. He says it is a terrific part and I have to play with Marie Lohr! isn't it gorgeous. He is going back to Hawtrey today to say that he had perfect confidence in me and that I am thoroughly natural and unaffected etc: Oh I am a star! Your ownest, Noel.

Gilbert Miller, then young, was as famous an American impresario as his father Henry Miller had been before him, and Noel was surprised and flattered when he was asked to supper at the Midland after the play. Like Charles Hawtrey, Mr Miller seems to have had a strong belief in Noel's future, and extended the same benign guidance to him over many years. By the end of the following year, Noel had dashed off three plays; two bad ones (unnamed) and one slightly better, *The Rat Trap*, which he asked Mr Miller to read. He had, as we have seen, picked up many of the less important, albeit very useful, tricks of the playwriting trade and could write dialogue by the yard. Miller told him that the plays were not good enough, that their construction was lousy, and then gave Noel a lecture which he never forgot. The construction of a play, Miller's father had told him, was as important as the foundation of a house, and must be strong and solid enough to support the entire structure. Dialogue, however brilliant, should at most be thought of as embellishment of the firm foundation. From then on, Noel regarded his great gift for dialogue as 'my dangerous facility, which I must beware of Gilbert Miller warned me about it years ago.'

The Saving Grace was the big chance Noel had been longing for; a grown-up part at last, the juvenile lead in a witty comedy, playing in the West End. After all the years of gazing at photographs in *Play Pictorial* of famous actors and actresses, there he was himself, playing opposite Emily Brooke (not Marie Lohr after all) and in the distinguished company of Charles Hawtrey, Ellis Jeffreys and Mary Jerrold. Mary Jerrold was a most charming actress and famous in the profession for being one of the worst gigglers on-stage, Fay Compton being the other. Miss Jerrold and Noel were supposed to sit quietly together on a sofa while Hawtrey was playing an important scene with Ellis Jeffreys, but one night she suddenly jumped up on to the sofa, gathered her skirt up round her and let out a stifled scream. Hawtrey was furious. It was useless for Noel to explain that he had only murmured 'Nice' when he noticed Miss Jerrold's new shoes, and that she thought he had said 'Mice'; he should not have been talking at all, and they were both in disgrace.

After five years of genteel but increasing poverty in Clapham, Mrs Coward rebelled. Like her son she never put up with anything for long; she took action. Aunt Ida (Noel's father's sister and not to be confused with Aunt Vida) had been successfully running a guesthouse in Ebury Street for some years. When the tenants of a house opposite, No. 111, decided to sell the remainder of their lease, and all the furniture plus the goodwill, Mrs Coward bravely signed the rather frightening legal documents and they all, including Auntie Vida, moved in. Eric continued his education at Manor House School, and Mr Coward was probably happier sailing his model yacht on the Serpentine than on the pond on Clapham Common. Noel had a tiny attic to himself and was definitely happier for being within walking distance of the West End. The house was tall, and although there were two maids to begin with, Mrs Coward took on a dreadful load of drudgery with the lease; Mr Coward helped by carrying trays and turned out, because of his jocularity, to be immensely popular with the Paying Guests. Noel later insisted on calling these the Lodgers and made his mother do the same, whereas there was in fact a wide and socially significant gulf between the two: the Paying Guests, like true-blue Englishmen in the jungle, changed every night into evening dress for dinner. Miss Daubeny, niece of Lord Brassey, lent tone by occupying a third-floor room for several years. Mr and Mrs Farina on the ground floor frequently asked Noel to dine with them, and though he felt guilty at the thought of his mother having spent hours over a hot stove preparing the delicious food, he was only too pleased to be told that Mrs Farina liked being read aloud to. He read her everything he had ever written and she was only very occasionally critical.

George Moore, famous for his books *Esther Waters* and *The Brook Kerith*, lived nearby at 121, and their cats fell in love. They caterwauled and carried on such a passionate affair that Mr Moore stopped Noel in the street and in the end asked him to tea on the strength of it. Noel went several times, and though I longed to hear every detail, Noel would only say he was a nice enough old boy, always very kind, but that teatime was quite long enough to spend with him; the cats were really their only bond.

Across the street—though this was some years later, in the 'twenties —lived a strange family, Lady Dean Paul and her son and daughter.

The son, Napper Dean Paul, writes of his mother as having three personalities; Irène Wieniamska, Irène Poldowska and Irene Dean Paul. As Poldowska, she and her close friend Cecile Sartoris gave recitals of Verlaine, set to music by herself, in the homes of the wealthy; in spite of her fun and high spirits she was a tragic figure, a musician of integrity, and though poor thought nothing of tearing up a cheque and throwing the pieces in the face of the hostess if she felt like it. She and Cecile were immensely kind to Noel when all three were poor together in New York in 1925. Brenda Dean Paul, the daughter, is described by her brother as 'what happens when Genius mates with Scottish Lowland Gentry'. She became notorious; always in and out of the courts on drugs charges, rather beautiful until her looks disintegrated into emaciation. She eventually died of excessive drug-taking. She wrote:

Back in London [has] made me think of other happy moments that have occurred in my life. First among them is my recollection of Noel Coward. My mother and I had rooms opposite Noel's house in Ebury Street. We were great friends. Neither of us had much money. Both suffered from the affliction of shilling-in-the-slot gas meters. Quite often the gas would go out, in his house or our own, without a shilling available for the meter. Noel, on such an occasion, would cross the street in his dressing-gown to borrow a shilling, and when we were deprived of gas we would cross in more conventional attire to him.

Mrs Coward has left a note of those days:

Noel loved to look after me when he was a boy, he was so capable that I depended on him perhaps more than I should, when he was so young. He always knew the right thing to do, his opinion was really law to me, for he was always right. When I was at my wits' end and quite desperate at Ebury Street several times for money, he would talk and reassure me, and go off and get money somewhere and bring relief and joy to me. Oh dear those were happy days when the boys were young and I had them all to myself. Fortunately mothers don't realise that those times will come to an end and that when the children grow up they must live their own lives, and the mother who was simply everything to them in their young days must stand aside and try to make another life of her own without them.

Before *The Saving Grace*, in the summer of 1917, Noel made his first film appearance, impressively enough in *Hearts of the World*, directed by D. W. Griffith. His part, however, was far from impressive; in fact only a few days as an extra, pushing a wheelbarrow in a French village street which was filmed on location at Broadway in Worcestershire. Although he was only too glad to earn the money, he hated having to get up at five in the morning and walking about with his face made up bright yellow. But from this experience two typical examples emerge of Noel going 'straight to the top' and succeeding, aided no doubt by his already strong and winning personality. He persuaded the great Mr Griffith that it would be more sensible for him to push his wheel-barrow towards, instead of away from, the camera (which today allows us the pleasure of being able to see him in the famous 'still' with Lillian Gish). In addition he, the seventeen-year-old extra, made instant friends with the two stars of the film, Lillian and Dorothy Gish, and with Mrs Gish their mother; all three inviting him each day to their carriage to share the lunch Mrs Gish had provided. Noel's gift for making friends in all the productions with which he was connected has already been made evident, and this was no exception; his friend-ship with Lillian in particular remained undiminished.

The First World War had so far made little personal impact on Noel; he had been much too occupied trying to get ahead in his chosen profession, and in any case for the first three and a half years he had been too young to enlist. But in January 1918 he had to appear before an Army Medical Board which, after examination, pronounced him unfit for active service because of the slight tubercular tendency of some years before, and told him to hold himself in readiness for some kind of service in due course. Sure enough, after *The Saving Grace* had closed and Noel was already rehearsing a rattling good part for fifteen pounds a week in a play by a lady named Hazel May, an un-pleasant grey card dropped through the letter box at 111 Ebury Street, commanding him to another medical at Camberwell Baths. From here, with fifty others, he was marched to Waterloo, entrained to Hounslow and put into uniform.

Noel's career in the British Army was without glory and its brief nine months seemed to him an eternity, one long exercise in futility. He got himself transferred to the Artists' Rifles and did his square-bashing at Gidea Park in Essex. He did at first try to conform but only succeeded in regarding the whole dreary interlude as an infuriating interruption to his career, an obstacle delaying him from achieving his avowed intention of becoming famous as quickly as possible and rich enough to keep his mother and himself in comfort. The Army, at any rate in the ranks, was then no place for individuality; he hated the almost anonymous homogeneity of it; he must get out of it by some means or other and as quickly as possible. He had been graded B2 physically and ill-health seemed to be the obvious way to achieve his end. A certain amount of scrimshanking went on and he afterwards admitted that some of his spells of illness were self-induced. Others were psychosomatic, of emotional origin, and therefore very real, such as the unexplainable headaches, so violent that he became incapable of standing upright. His mother's account of his service is more to the point: 'He could not stand the drilling and kept on getting ill and really spent more of his time in hospital than he did in training ... I am afraid he was more trouble than he was worth in the Army and did not help the War along very much.' He was at last given his discharge, a pension of seven-and-six a week for six months, a suit, an overcoat and a medal, and felt no shadow of embarrassment at his unheroic showing as a soldier. There was no room in his heart, he says, for anything but thankfulness that he was free again to shape his life as he wanted.

While in hospital during his last months in the Army, Noel gave full rein to a passion for the novels of both G. B. Stern and Sheila Kaye-Smith, to such an extent that he felt compelled to write to them and express his admiration. Both ladies answered and such an animated correspondence ensued that by the time they met they found they had already become old friends. Miss Kaye-Smith's novels are set on the Kent–Sussex border and evoke, especially when dealing with Romney Marsh, a strongly insular atmosphere out of that flat bit of country, which she makes even more strange and slightly 'foreign' than it actually is. She and her novels contributed greatly to Noel's later love for the Marsh, for Dymchurch and Dungeness, for the peace of the little village of St Mary-in-the-Marsh in which he wrote his early plays, and eventually, when he had enough money, for Goldenhurst Farm, on the rising land just above the Marsh, which remained his country house for thirty years.

'Peter' Stern's novels were readable but he very soon began to complain to her face of their tendency to verbosity and, when she came to write her entertaining though rambling volumes of reminiscences, that she made more and longer digressions from the subject at hand than any writer he ever read, not excepting Proust. He lent Peter Stern's novels and showed her letters to the only friend he seems to have made in the Army, a young New Zealander named Geoffrey Holdsworth, who immediately wrote to her and a few months later married her. (She mentions casually in a letter she wrote in 1931 or 1932, 'Got my Decree Nisi last month. Be careful whom you introduce me to another time.')

Before the marriage Noel went to join Peter for two weeks' holiday at St Merryn in Cornwall, where she was staying with Mrs Dawson-Scott and her family, none of whom he had met. According to Noel Mrs Dawson-Scott wore long loose gowns and no shoes or stockings and wrote intense novels seething with primitive love and childbirth, earth, sea-wrack and hot, sweet breasts; and so for once one of his jokey telegrams — 'Arriving Padstow 5.30. Tall and divinely handsome in grey' — failed to raise a laugh. His reception was frigid, his suggestion that they call him Noel met with, 'I think we'd rather wait a little, Mr Coward', and he only stuck out the fortnight because he had paid for his keep in advance and because of his rapidly ripening friendship with Peter Stern. She and Noel got away by themselves as much as they could and she allowed him to talk as much as he liked about his ambitions as a playwright, novelist, lyric-writer and composer without ever suggesting that he might be taking too much upon himself. For this he was grateful: even then he was beginning to suffer from the Jack Of All Trades label. His and Peter's accounts of the rigours of the holiday were hilarious and may have improved and become funnier with the years. Peter was startled when in the 'thirties a friend reported that he had sat next to Mrs Dawson-Scott at dinner and she poured out the whole indignant history of their stay at St Merryn in 1918 from *her* point of view. He had been absolutely riveted because, he said, it didn't tally with her and Noel's version at all.

In any event Mrs Dawson-Scott can have borne Noel no grudge, for after their return to London she asked him to dine with her in Hampstead and to meetings of the Tomorrow Club of which she was a founder member and which later developed into the P.E.N. Club. And so it was through her that Noel found himself, by the time he was twenty, in the remarkable position of knowing, or having met, that abundant pride of literary lions of the day: John Galsworthy, Rebecca West, May Sinclair, Charles Scott-Moncrieff, Somerset Maugham, Hugh Walpole, H. G. Wells, Compton Mackenzie, E. F. Benson, Rose Macaulay and Arnold Bennett.

Not knowing the form, Noel arrived at his first meeting with the Tomorrow Club in evening dress, to find everybody in day clothes. He paused only a moment in the doorway as the eminent heads turned towards him. 'Now I don't want *anybody* to feel embarrassed,' he said.

The morning and afternoon of November 11th, 1918, Noel spent with the mafficking crowds in the streets of the West End, celebrating the Armistice. By the evening he was with two wealthy and attractive Chileans, Tony and Juanita Ganderillas, in their red Rolls-Royce, so entirely surrounded by the same screaming crowds that it took them two hours to get through Trafalgar Square to the Savoy. Once there, they celebrated more grandly with champagne in the crowded gala atmosphere where Alice Delysia, glittering in pink, time and again was made to stand on her table to sing, thrillingly and movingly, the *Marseillaise*.

Apart from his dreary nine months in the Army, Noel had not been noticeably affected by the war; although he later realized to the full its tragic significance, at the time he thought of it only as an oppressive background to four years of his youth. Now the oppression was lifted, that was all. Yet within a few years from that carefree Armistice night he had somehow become, in the press and in the public mind, the prototype of the disillusioned, cynical young post-war generation. How this came about remained to Noel forever a mystery, but whether that particular generation was in fact so blighted was to him no puzzle. It was not, though a handful of poets and intellectuals were articulate enough to voice the disillusionment of the minority. The majority, with at the helm the Bright Young Things and the Prince of Wales (even the Sitwells enjoyed themselves), was out to have a good time as the younger generation has always done and always will and, Noel included, succeeded in having one. Noel's inherent pessimism ('What is there to strive for, Live or keep alive for?') was not to rear its head till ten years later, by which time it had indeed become representative of his age group in the 'thirties, with the splendid idea of a War to End War already a mockery and the threat of a Second World War more apparent every year.

After his Army discharge Noel found no work in the West End until, in December 1918, he at last obtained a negligible part in *Scandal* at the Strand, with Kyrle Bellew and Arthur Bourchier as the stars. They took a liking to him as Hawtrey had done and put up with a great deal from him because he made them laugh. His two cronies in the cast were Norah Swinburne and Mary Robson. Mary, a few years older than Noel, had a strongly warm and lovable personality; or rather has, for she is alive and well and living in Maine. She influenced his taste in music for the better, giving him leather-bound volumes of songs from French operas such as *Mireille* and from French *opérettes*, plus a few saucier songs such as ' 'Ello Tu-tu, 'Ow are you?' She was also the first to inflame him with an ambition to go to America, to New York in particular, where she had appeared several times and which she described in such dazzling terms that in his dreams he could see the name Noel Coward in huge letters picked out and flashing in electric lights on Broadway.

Noel behaved very badly indeed to the old ladies in the cast, making fun of them in front of Mary and Norah, to whom were added Esmé and her friend Aishie Pharall when he had them to tea on matinée days. Millie Hylton spoke with a slight cackle, so he made clucking-hen noises whenever he was within her hearing, even when she was on stage. Gladys Ffolliot always brought her dog Daphne to the theatre and was furious when she overheard Noel say that Daphne stank like a drain. From then on he would hurry past Miss Ffolliot with his head averted and his fingers elaborately held to his nostrils or, if her dressing-room door was open, stagger and pretend to faint to the ground outside it from what he described as the overwhelming stench, after which he and the four girls flew to his or Mary's room, shrieking with laughter. In the end Arthur Bourchier had to give him a talking-to, warning him in future always to behave well to the older actresses in a company because, once aroused, their enmity could become implacable. He thought Noel an excellent young actor and would be sorry to lose him and advised him to send in his notice to the management before they fired him. Noel went home and enjoyed composing a dignified letter of resignation, which the management accepted with relieved alacrity; when he got to the theatre next night he was given his pay-packet and half an hour in which to clear out of his dressing-room. For the first and last time in his life Noel was given the sack.

He celebrated Peace Day in 1919 as glamorously as he had the Armistice, by being invited by Fay Compton to her box at the Victory Ball, held at the Albert Hall. Among the other occupants of Fay's box were Beatrice Lillie and the pretty young actress Billie Carleton—then appearing in *The Luck of the Navy*—and her man-about-town companion. The revellers revelled until the early hours, and who went home with whom and how he got home himself, Noel could never exactly remember. Beatrice Lillie has always had, among her many talents, a special one for achieving intoxicated high spirits on a sip or two of lager. She has in consequence never suffered from a hangover, and was as gay as a cricket when she went next day to the Savoy desk and asked for Miss Carleton's suite. Upon being told by the desk clerk that Miss Carleton had been found dead, Beattie, still in gala mood, cried, 'Lead me to the body!' and made her way to the lift. It was only too true; Billie Carleton had died from an overdose of cocaine.

Noel often talked to Graham and me about this incident. He evidently knew Billie Carleton and her companion, who supplied the cocaine, quite well. Drug-taking seems in those days to have been prevalent and rather taken for granted among the people he knew. His name eventually became associated with the use of drugs, especially after *The Vortex*, in which, five years later, he played the drug-taking son. Graham and I never asked him whether he had himself taken drugs at that time because he made it so apparent that he had not. Broad-minded as he was, he had a surprisingly puritanical side to his nature, as well as an absolute horror of losing control of his senses from too much alcohol, let alone drugs. (He drank as much as the next man and from time to time thoroughly enjoyed a binge, but never became insensibly drunk or had to be helped to bed, except on a few occasions when helpless from too much laughter.) He remained an innocent all his life as far as drugs were concerned, re-telling with the utmost drama of the only occasion, in New York in the 'thirties, on which he had given marijuana a trial. He took the joint back to his apartment, went to bed and then puffed away in expectation of hitherto unknown rapturous transports; instead he was so violently sick that he telephoned for his doctor to come round at once. He felt sure he would be unconscious before the doctor arrived and dragged himself on all fours to the front door, between which and the jamb he put a cushion to make sure it would remain open, and then crawled back to bed. The doctor came quickly, made him a pot of boiling black coffee, sat on the edge of the bed and to Noel's surprise smoked the remaining three-quarters of the joint because he thought it would be a pity to waste it.

Forty-three years later in a speech at a literary luncheon Noel, speaking of his writing, said he had been so overpoweringly witty at the age of eighteen that he shuddered to think of it. He also described the two novels he had already written at that age. The first of these was *Cats and Dogs*, which dealt with the adventures of a brother and sister, filched unscrupulously from Shaw's *You Never Can Tell*. These two bright young things prattled away with unparalleled vivacity for nearly eighty thousand words until the story mercifully and untidily came to an end.

'The second novel was in a more fanciful vein and was entitled *Cherry Pan*. Cherry Pan, I regret to tell you, was the daughter of the Great God Pan and was garrulous and tiresome to the point of nausea. Having materialised suddenly on a summer evening in Sussex, she proceeded with excruciating pagan archness to wreak havoc in a country parsonage before returning winsomely to her woodland glades and elfin grots. I remember being bitterly offended by a friend [could it have been Esmé?] who suggested that the title should be changed to *Bedpan*.'

For three weeks in Birmingham in August 1919 Noel played Ralph the Apprentice in Beaumont and Fletcher's *The Knight of the Burning Pestle*, which came to London for a longer run the following year. For ever after he considered Elizabethan comedy extremely unfunny, and never cared much for Restoration comedy either. But for some reason he did consider the two names Beaumont and Fletcher in conjunction were funny and used them surprisingly in his jokes, as when Dame Edith Evans repeatedly inserted the word 'very' into a line in *Hay Fever*. Eventually Noel said, 'No, no, Edith. The line is, "You can see as far as Marlow on a clear day."' He then added, 'On a *very* clear day you can see Marlow *and* Beaumont and Fletcher.'

Noel was not very good in *The Knight of the Burning Pestle*. Nigel Playfair directed and did nothing to stop him posturing and mouthing his part in a Mayfair accent. When Noel left the London production Nigel Playfair himself took over, gabbled the part in Cockney and got all the laughs; Noel never quite forgave him. Betty Chester, almost as young as Noel, played the Citizen's Wife, a bawdy matron of middle age; although she was comical, her casting didn't help much either. She and Noel had been friends for some time; she seems to have been able to entertain rather rowdily at her parents' house in Chester Square as often as she liked. Sadly, Noel's friendship with her was of short duration. When the Ebury Street rent became badly overdue and Noel asked her to lend him £40, which he could repay within a fortnight, she refused on the unlikely grounds that she had only just been robbed of that very amount, hoping to add verisimilitude by saying she had reported the robbery to the police. Typically, Noel went straight to the local police station to check, was told—as he expected—that she had done no such thing, and that was the end of their friendship.

It was at Betty's house that Noel got to know two important friends-to-be—Meggie Albanesi and Lorn Macnaughtan. Meggie and Noel became deeply attached; she was one of two understanding companions—Gertie was the other—whom he could take dancing at Murray's or Rector's. When relying on his own funds, she or Gertie would suddenly feel faint when the waiter came to take the order and declare themselves unable to face a morsel, whereupon Noel ordered one dish which they both polished off when the waiter wasn't looking, as well as as many bread rolls as there were on the table. Gertie, two years older, was already much in demand as a partner for many of the smartest and most dashing young guardees in town. She once refused an invitation from Noel and Roy Royston (who had been in the company of *Hannele* with Noel and Gertie back in 1913) to go dancing at Ciro's, but when they arrived on their own, there she was, revolving in the arms of one of these god-like young men and, with her capacity for playing to the hilt whatever role fell to her, as haughty as he. She cut Noel and Roy, which was not to be borne: Roy quickly found a partner, edged close to Gertie on the dance-floor, and then said, clearly and insinuatingly, 'Who gave Alf Zeitlin crabs?' Collapse of Gertie from her social pedestal, in fits of laughter.

Noel's other tie with Meggie Albanesi was their mutual friendship with Lorn, who at that time did secretarial work for Meggie's mother, E. Maria Albanesi, a prolific writer of popular novels. Later she worked in the same capacity for Meggie, after the latter had become a famous young actress. During these years Lornie married Rupert Loraine, had a son, Peter, and a daughter, named Meggie after her godmother. The baby Meggie was also Noel's godchild, the first of his family of sixteen godchildren.

Since Ellen Terry, no actress seems to have inspired the admiration and love from her friends, the members of her profession and the public as did Meggie Albanesi. She succeeded in every part she undertook, from her dramatic intensity in the last act of Clemence Dane's *A Bill of Divorcement* to the light comedy of *The Lilies of the Field*, and all who saw her predicted a future for her as one of the great actresses of this century. In rehearsal for a new play, she hoped that the peace, quiet and fresh air of a long weekend at Birchington-on-Sea would do her good; she had hidden from her mother and from even so intimate a friend as Lornie how ill, and in what pain, she actually was. She collapsed, alone, over her table in the dining-car of the train; Lornie hurried next day to her side and, with Madame Albanesi, was with her when she died. Her death at the age of twenty-four produced in all who knew her, and those who only knew her name, a shocking sense of irreplaceable loss. Noel wrote to Madame Albanesi:

It is utterly impossible to write what one really feels. Meggie will always be a very dear and sweet memory to me, and I shall always mourn her. I fully understand how utterly meaningless life must seem to you now that she has gone. If anyone in the world deserves eternal happiness it is Meggie, and perhaps because she was such a darling to us here we may be given the chance of meeting her again.

For Noel at that age even to hint at the possibility of an afterlife is unexpected. This may be a remnant of the religious background of his upbringing; more likely it was a lifeline he threw to Madame Albanesi, deep in her grief.

Lornie and Noel enjoyed an easy intimacy from their first meetings at Betty Chester's house onwards, and very soon reached a point at which they could not imagine a time when they had not been friends. After Meggie Albanesi's death, it was an easy transition for Lornie to go instead to Noel to help with his letters. Lornie was tallish and fair — pale of hair, eyes and skin, her accent well-bred though frequently giving way to the most common boisterous and infectious laugh that I for one have ever heard. Just to hear Lornie laugh in the next room, without hearing what had been said, made one laugh oneself. She paid little attention to her appearance which was in general rather colourless in those days (later Noel made her wear brighter colours and use a brighter lipstick) so that, despite her strong personality, she could disappear into the woodwork when she wanted to. This gift she deliberately cultivated for use at large parties, which she disliked and, if there was music to be listened to in silence, actively hated, and would be happily at home in bed an hour or two before she was missed.

Highly unlikely as it seemed to Noel when they first met, Lornie was herself on the stage and, even more incredible, singing and dancing in the chorus of *Irene* at the Empire. Her father, Malcolm Macnaughtan, belonged to the same club as Sir Seymour Hicks and was a crony of his, so when he confided to Sir Seymour that he 'didn't know what to do with his gal', the latter offered to try to find something for her and off she went in the tour of *Bluebell in Fairyland*. Lornie admitted that she could not have been very good on the stage; but by the time I got to know her she would when asked oblige us with a bit of buck-and-wing for our delight, or make us laugh singing snappy American songs such as 'Get Out and Get Under', but in a special bleating, refined South Kensington accent.

It was obvious that Lornie had adored the atmosphere of the chorus dressing-room and made many friends; her stories about the girls verged on the Rabelaisian. Most of the girls in *Irene* seem to have been, let us say, experienced, except for the youngest, over whom they worried when a beau appeared at the stage door to take her out to supper. Sure enough, the next night she admitted that she had let the beau have his way with her. She started to cry and through her sobs asked their old dresser if it was true that she would get her virginity back if she didn't do it again for seven years. 'I don't know about seven years, dear,' came the comforting reply, 'you can get it back in five minutes with a penn'orth of alum.'

Then once, when a slip in the programme of the revue at the Palace announced that the star was indisposed (actually she was in Hammersmith having an abortion), Lornie popped in to ask the other female star how she was getting on. 'All right,' the other star said, 'but oh, what a silly girl—fancy letting him put it *there*! In the mouth or up the arse yes, but fancy letting him put it *there*.'

As Noel says, all this accounted for the strange flashes of chorus-girl jargon which sprang from Lorn's lips bawdily at the most unexpected moments, and which, so surprisingly combined with her ladylike distinction, was what had attracted him to her in the first place. From then on he relied on her advice, and he could and did confide every secret of his life to her without even having to think about the possibility of betrayal. Her loyalty to him was entire and her devotion complete. The bond that bound them closest was laughter; pomposity was derided—their jokes often disgracefully irreverent—and above and beyond their ability to laugh at the world around them, they laughed at themselves.

3

THE SHINING
FUTURE

BACK in 1919, while in Birmingham with *The Knight of the Burning Pestle*, Noel received a cable from Gilbert Miller with the glorious news that Al Woods would pay five hundred dollars for a year's option on Noel's play *The Last Trick*. This was hotly followed by another, to say that the open-handed Mr Woods wished to buy the play outright for a further fifteen hundred. True, this was because he thought the play should be entirely re-written by a more experienced playwright, but no matter, Noel had never had such a windfall in his life. He bought several new suits, including a tail-suit for the evening, paid the overdue rent on Ebury Street and bought a second-hand piano from Harrods, his first, which not only added splendour to his room but enabled him to compose in privacy, instead of on his parents' old upright in the general sitting-room. On this piano he would compose the songs to become famous later on in the 'twenties and which are still famous, including 'Parisian Pierrot', 'Poor Little Rich Girl', and 'Dance Little Lady'.

Noel took to lunching almost daily at the Ivy in West Street, opposite the Ambassadors and St Martin's Theatres. The owner, Abel Giandolini, had been generous in allowing credit to Noel when it was unlikely that the bills would be paid; now Noel could begin to repay his kindness and his faith that Noel would one day make his mark. His fondness for Noel continued up until his retirement in 1953 when, to commemorate the event, he sent Noel a liberal cheque for the Actors' Orphanage. Mario Gallati, the head waiter, was a friend through all the years at the Ivy and also when he opened his own restaurant, the Caprice in Arlington Street, in 1947.

The Ivy started out as a small café with linoleum on the floor, paper napkins and two waitresses, but by the time it became Noel's home from home Abel and Mario had carpeted the floor and engaged a first-class chef. Throughout the 'twenties, apart from Gertie, Beattie, Tallulah, Delysia, Ivor and Noel, the illustrious of the film world, society, politics and the arts thronged to the Ivy. Winston Churchill, Pavlova, Jacob Epstein, Mistinguette, all three Barrymores, the Dolly Sisters, the Aga Khan; and as early as the linoleum days, Duff Cooper brought Lady Diana especially for the spaghetti. But primarily the Ivy was 'theatre', to an extent that it became, so to speak, a club, with Dame Marie Tempest and Dame Lilian Braithwaite as reigning, and almost resident, presidents. In 1929, when adjoining property and the big room above were acquired, Abel and Mario announced that the Ivy would be closed for months during the rebuilding. The habitués were aghast, so the little room remained open all through the very cold winter, and packed, with walls being pulled down round the customers. Waiters walked, Blondin-like, on a plank across a big hole in the floor, carrying loaded trays. The customers sometimes ate wearing fur coats and scarves, and one rainy day Marie Tempest dexterously held up her umbrella and finished her steak at the same time.

After asking, 'I wonder if I shall *ever* be a success?' (Noel had had a long spell out of work in 1919), only two months or so later he was thrilled to be able to tell Mario that, for the first time, a play of his was to be produced in the West End with himself playing a leading part. Mario joined him at his table to drink a toast to the play's success, and to Noel's pride and pleasure offered to hang a.playbill of *I'll Leave It to You* in the entrance hall of the Ivy. The play was tried out in Manchester for three weeks, where it was received with much enthusiasm by both public and critics. It is interesting, however, to note that Noel's very first critic of eminence, Neville Cardus in the *Manchester Guardian*, complained that its theme was restricted to that of the idle bourgeoisie; a grumble that would echo in Noel's ears for many years to come.

Amid all the success and excitement—Noel had to lead Kate Cutler forward every night in response to the cheers and then make a speech to more cheers—he naturally expected great things from Mrs Gilbert Miller and Mrs Charles Hawtrey when they came up from London to report back to their famous husbands. Instead, theirs were the only dissentient voices, not that they said much; they exuded sympathy not congratulations, kissed Noel, sadly shook their heads, and left to catch the train back to London with their heads still wobbling. They were right. Noel's fierce determination that his play should not peter out after three weeks in Manchester resulted in its finally being presented in London under Lady Wyndham's management. Despite a roaringly successful first night and good notices the piece, within five weeks, had come dimly to an end; Lady Wyndham having for economy's sake removed half the stage-lighting.

To offset the disappointment, *I'll Leave It to You* brought great encouragement to Noel as a novice dramatist. Almost all the critics agreed that a new playwright had been born and that he showed astonishing promise for one so young (he had not yet come of age and his father signed the contract for him). He was described in the papers as an infant prodigy, an amazing youth, and gave sparkling interviews as often as he was asked, exhilarated by all the publicity. One day he would write that once a playwright has been discovered, once his feet are on the ladder, he will be reproached, execrated and patronised until old age enshrines him as a Master. The public may flock to his plays and they may run triumphantly in all the capitals of the world but he will never again, poor beast, be allowed to recapture the thrill of that first glorious morning after that first glorious night when he opened the papers and saw, shimmering before him on the theatre page, the magic words 'Playwright of Promise'.

For the first time he found fans waiting for him outside the stage door, as he had done in earlier years for Pavlova, Gertie Millar or Lily Elsie. From then on, unless he were hopelessly late or for some other valid reason, he never refused to give his autograph. 'When I was young I wanted more than anything to be a star; when I became one I realised it brought certain obligations. As long as there are people who wait for my autograph, I shall give it. And if the day ever comes when no one waits, I shall miss it dreadfully.' The unthinking behaviour of fellow-stars who brushed their fans aside upset him. 'You mark my words, the day will come ... ' And it did for some of them; not for Noel.

He moved from his little attic at 111 Ebury Street to a room of more splendid proportions on the floor below, where his grand piano could be seen to greater advantage and where he could entertain his friends to tea. Esmé was married by now and would bring her husband, Lyndon Wynne-Tyson; 'Peter' Stern, Sheila Kaye-Smith, Betty Chester (before the rupture) and Lorn were habitual guests, occasionally joined by Mrs Cooper, and then one day by Stewart Forster, a lieutenant in the Coldstream Guards. Stewart, of whom we shall hear a little more later, invited Noel to dine with him the next week, when he would be on guard at St James's Palace. The dinner gave Noel his first glimpse at close quarters of military ceremonial splendour and a taste for it which he was never to lose. He and Stewart became friends, and they planned a week's holiday in Paris, a plan which could not materialise until the following January, in 1920. They stayed at the Ritz until next morning, when they became aware of the cost and hurriedly left for something smaller in the rue Caumartin. In the evenings they went to the Moulin Rouge and the Folies-Bergère and did all the things young men usually do in the evenings in Paris. During the day they saw the more orthodox sights, Versailles above all attracting Noel like a lodestone. They came home feeling distinctly more worldly, having picked up several French phrases, some of which were extremely impolite. Neither of them had ever been out of England before, and Noel had been immediately and forever trapped by the glamour of 'abroad'.

One month later Mrs Cooper asked him to go to stay with her in Italy, at Alassio. Travelling by train always excited him, or rather he brought an excitement to it, so that the undertaking became an adventure, more than just a journey. This was the longest train ride he had so far experienced; more than that, it was his initiation into the pleasures of the *wagon-lit*. On this first trip, though, he was too anxious not to miss a moment to be able to sleep for long; he watched the sunrise as he was whirled through Switzerland and down on to the plains of Lombardy. Alassio, too, was an eye-opener, with pastel-coloured houses, their walls blanketed with wistaria and vividly coloured bougainvillea, and, to crown it all, the agreeable shock of discovering that hot sunshine was possible in February. Henceforth he would never willingly submit to the rigours of winter, in England or anywhere else.

The London revival of *The Knight of the Burning Pestle* in the autumn of 1920 was received with lukewarm enthusiasm; it was only memorable for Noel because Mrs Patrick Campbell came one night to see it. Everybody behind the scenes was agog with excitement and gave of their best for the great lady, only to discover at the end of the evening she had been fast asleep in her box from the beginning. Noel was outraged and sent her a knuckle-rapping message. Mrs Campbell admired his pluck and was back in the box the very next evening; smiling, she evilly applauded his every entrance and exit, and every speech he made, to the enjoyment of the rest of the cast but to his own deep embarrassment. They were often to spar in the future: on this occasion Noel conceded that she had won the first round, 'the wicked old woman'.

Noel had a few weeks in which to kick his heels before his next engagement, *Polly with a Past*, in February, and decided to go again to Italy. After two lonely days in Rapallo, unable to talk to anybody for lack of Italian, he was only too thankful to exchange his independence for the cosy pleasure of Mrs Cooper's company at the Grand Hotel, Alassio. A few days later he sang at a concert at the English Club, assured and superior in manner—after all he was a professional—in spite of the jangling, out-of-tune piano on which he accompanied himself. This combination convulsed a striking-looking, smartly dressed young woman in the front row. He shot her several looks intended to kill, which only sent her off into further spasms. By the time he tackled her after the concert she had regained control and was evasive as to what exactly had made her laugh, but in the end admitted that she thought he had *looked* so funny. Her name was Gladys Calthrop. Like Mrs Cooper, Gladys was 'county', though the Arts had beckoned her early; at the age of twelve she started to write a novel with an opening sentence of much promise. ' "Fool, thrice fool!" he cried, as he paced the floor.'

For the remainder of his stay in Alassio, Gladys and Noel were seldom apart, walking in the olive groves, sitting on the beach or on terraces looking out to sea, and endlessly talking. Although it was of another calibre, Gladys possessed wit as quick as Noel's own, and each sharpened their wit on the other's. Then as now, she indiscriminately peppered her talk with the word 'thing' to funny effect: 'What exactly is the matter with Aunt Cordelia?' 'She had a little sort of stroky thing, you know.' Life and Death were discussed in depth, as were Religion and above all Art, Gladys having, Noel said, a slight tendency towards highbrow Bohemianism. As with all those who at this time became his friends, Gladys seems never to have questioned Noel's belief in his shining future, the future in which she was to play so large a part; instead she encouraged and helped to plan it with him. She never followed fashion, but created her own chic look; her necklaces, bracelets, clips and brooches verge on the barbaric but they are always a visual pleasure and, whether they have or not, appear to have come straight from the rue de la Paix. Noel wrote of her as being less attractive then than she is now, but in the portraits of her painted soon after by Oliver Messel and Sir William Rothenstein she looks serenely beautiful, her head held high, her clear grey eyes in striking contrast to her dark hair.

Before leaving Alassio they went to a *festa* at the Combattente Club which, though far from reaching the frenzy of a saturnalia, had about it enough paper streamers, sweet champagne and cheap Latin glamour for them to enjoy themselves and to give Noel the idea for a play called *Sirocco*, for which Gladys would do the designs.

Polly with a Past opened in March 1921; Edna Best was the leading lady and with her schoolgirl prettiness could not match the verve and sparkle Ina Claire had brought to the same part in New York. Up against players of the standard of Claude Rains, Aubrey Smith and Edith Evans, Noel found himself again the 'feed', as he had been in *Charley's Aunt*; by the end he was over-acting badly in an attempt to make any impression at all. Most nights Noel walked home from the St James's Theatre to Ebury Street with Edith Evans, who lived nearby. Edith had played five Shakespearean roles, toured with Ellen Terry and scored success in *My Lady's Dress* and *Milestones* (with Lynn Fontanne also in the cast); she could therefore already talk to Noel with the voice of experience. Chiefly, though, they talked eagerly of what was yet to come, their future stardom and how to achieve it. These walks home were what remained uppermost among Noel's memories of *Polly with a Past*, as they remained uppermost among Edith's.

Jeffery Holmesdale, now Earl Amherst, first appeared in Noel's life at this time. Of medium height, fair, with twinkling blue eyes, he was a captain in the Coldstream Guards with a brave war record which Noel thought incongruous, so young did he look. His manner was affable but with a certain amount of reserve, so although they dined together from time to time, even Noel, with his gift for an easy and quick transition from acquaintance to friendship, took ages to get to know him well. Once established, their friendship was to be put to the severest of tests, that of travelling together, sometimes in conditions of trying discomfort. At least two of their journeys lasted months, and Jeffery's gaiety never failed.

Noel's boredom with the routine of playing the same part night after night became evident during the comparatively long run of *Polly with a Past*. To offset this he had by now established the habit of working every day at some form of creative writing or composing, and he was bursting with ideas.

From among the miscellaneous outpourings of those months, one play emerged — *The Young Idea*. The brother and sister of *Cats and Dogs* had now become twins, which made the resemblance to Shaw's *You Never Can Tell* closer than ever, and Noel mentioned his slight guilt when he offered the play to the Vedrenne management. Vedrenne sent the play to Shaw, who not only had no objections, he never even hinted at plagiarism; instead he returned the script with constructive suggestions for re-writing the last act, and helpful injunctions written in his own hand in the margins, such as, 'Oh no you don't, young author!' He later wrote Noel a kind letter. Lornie believed the precious script and letter to have been stolen in the early 'thirties, though Noel says he was idiotic enough to lose it, but she remembered at any rate the letter being in her files. The script seems not to have survived but the letter, dated June 27th, 1921, is now safe in the University of Texas, having first re-appeared in Messrs Myers & Co's Spring Catalogue of Autograph Letters in 1954:

Dear Mr Coward,

I gather from Mr Vedrenne that he turned the play down because he had some misgivings about trying to repeat the old success of the twins in You Never Can Tell, and was not quite sure that you had pulled off the final scene which I suggested. But when once a manager has entertained a play at all, his reasons for discarding it are pretty sure to be business and circumstantial ones. When you put impudent people on the stage they are very amusing when the actor or actress has sufficient charm to make the audience forgive the impudence: in my youth Charles Mathews lived on impudent parts; and every comedy had a stage cynic in it. Hawtrey has kept up the tradition to some extent; but impudence has been long out of fashion; your twins will take some casting to make them pardonable. I daresay Vedrenne did not know where to lay his hands on the right pair.

I have no doubt that you will succeed if you persevere, and take care never to fall into a breach of essential good manners, and, above all, never to see or read my plays. Unless you can get clean away from me you will begin as a back number, and be hopelessly out of it when you are forty.

Faithfully,

G. BERNARD SHAW

Noel was, it goes without saying, overcome with gratitude, and wrote in his autobiography, ' … there was more than brilliance in the trouble that that great man had taken in going minutely over the work of a comparatively unknown young writer.' He never actually regretted having written this, but would often go as far as saying he wished to God he hadn't; it cost him dear. When his autobiography was published a steady stream of unsolicited play-scripts began to arrive and never abated; the accompanying letters, though varied in tone, almost always mentioned G.B.S., ranging from supplications for Noel to 'be as kind to me as Mr Shaw was to you' to the peremptory 'I am young and poor and struggling, now it is your turn to help me as Bernard Shaw helped you.' But history did not repeat itself; Noel never had the luck or the pleasure of being sent a script of promise equivalent to the one he sent to Shaw.

Noel sailed for New York in May 1921. He had never forgotten Mary Robson's exciting descriptions of that city, and now three motives combined at once to determine him to try his luck on Broadway. His new-born travel urge, for one; then at a party in Ivor's flat he had met and been magnetized by Jeanne Eagels and her vivid talk of American theatre and acting, which made him long to see these wonders for himself. The decisive factor, however, was Jeffery Amherst, who told Noel he was sailing in the *Aquitania* and suggested that Noel come too. Once Noel had obtained promise of his release from *Polly with a Past* there was nothing to stop him, save lack of money for the fare. This he scraped together within the necessary time, by borrowing and also by selling two of his songs to Lord Lathom, who had no use whatever for them, not at the time that is; a little later they would lead to bigger and better things. Noel already realized the value of at any rate appearing to live first-class, and rather than creep into New York with a return ticket on a freight boat he courageously bought a one-way passage on the *Aquitania*, which left him only seventeen pounds on which to live. Atlantic crossings were not to be undertaken lightly fifty years ago; fond farewells had to be said all round, for there were then no quick communications with loved ones left at home except cables, which Noel could not afford. Mrs Coward, ever fearful for his safety, prayed daily that her son be kept from peril; her apprehensions continued for years to come, by which time he had learned to rag her about them:

This is just a short line to reassure your yearning mother heart. I am well considering I had three operations for appendicitis yesterday—was run over by a bus on Tuesday—smitten down by peritonitis on Sunday and am going into consumption tomorrow. But you mustn't worry because apart from these things I'm *all right*. There are certain to be Icebergs, Hurricanes, Typhoons and Torpedos but Douglas Fairbanks I am sure will save me if you write him a nice letter. By the way there is a dreadfully dangerous lift in this apartment, several people are killed daily just getting in and out—and as the drains are notoriously bad Diphtheria and Typhoid are inevitable! But *Don't Worry*.

After the ship left Cherbourg, Noel admitted to 'fears twittering in his stomach like birds in a paper bag'; had he been too rash to bank on the benevolent Al Woods buying another manuscript? Or David Belasco and Charles Dillingham, to whom he had letters of introduction, condescending to see him? Yes, he had—but it was now too late to regret his recklessness. The weather was clement and the sea calm, and the only thing to do was to enjoy Jeff's company and to lean on him for help with the mysteries of life on board a liner and, when the time came, of American Immigration and Customs.

Jeff had four friends to meet him when the ship docked, two of whom, Lord Alington and Teddie Gerard, Noel already knew. Teddie Gerard was the American revue star, a great favourite in London and famous for wearing one of the first backless evening-gowns, which, when she turned round, caused the audience to gasp and the young gentlemen of the chorus to burst into song: 'Glad to See You're Back, Dear Lady'. Cecile Sartoris and Gabrielle Enthoven were the other two, and Noel could not know at this point that he would be living with them for the greater part of the coming months. Needless to say he made his way to Broadway that first evening, intent on seeing a play on his own and then joining the others for supper at Teddie Gerard's house in Washington Square. He chose *Nice People* by Rachel Crothers; Francine Larrimore was the star, with two greater stars-to-be supporting her—Katharine Cornell and Tallulah Bankhead. He was bowled over by the speed at which this otherwise gentle comedy was played. For the first twenty minutes all the cast seemed to be talking at once, until he realised he was hearing everything of importance that he was intended to hear; anything superfluous was intentionally thrown away, and nobody dreamed of waiting for laughs, the sin that Noel had been guilty of so recently in *Polly with a Past*.

Jeanne Eagels had been right; the tempo of the acting was more alive and exciting than in London. Noel learnt the lesson immediately and applied it when he returned to London—throw the laughs away in the first act and bring them in in the third—and used it ever after, to great success. True, it did cause many old ladies to complain that they hadn't heard a word, and when he told Yvonne Arnaud—another brilliant technician and also with perfect diction—that a fan had written, 'All I could hear was mumble, mumble, mumble,' she opened wide her eyes, her mouth and her handbag and produced from the latter a letter using exactly the same words, and from the same tormentor.

Through the cigarette smoke at Teddie Gerard's party that night, Noel spotted the aforementioned Irene Dean Paul; she had, like Noel, come to New York determined to make some money, and with Cecile Sartoris was earning a precarious living with their recitals of Verlaine's poems set to music. She was to prove herself a friend in need, and with Cecile and Gabrielle helped Noel through the almost penniless months ahead. Nobody had warned him that this was just about the worst time of year he could have chosen to come to New York; with, in those days, no air-conditioning, most theatres closed during the heat of summer. Although he managed to deliver in person his letters of introduction, all the recipients were on the point of going on vacation and said with unanimous finality that there would be nothing doing until the fall, whereupon Noel moved up to an even tinier room in the very eaves of the Brevoort Hotel. Jeffery had left to represent his family at ceremonies at Amherst College, Massachusetts, the first Baron Amherst having been Commander-in-Chief of George III's Army in North America, and had then returned to London.

Noel was now alone in the big city; he had as yet no close friends, and money was running out. In the nick of time Frank Crowninshield bought three sketches from Noel's collection of satires, *A Withered Nosegay*, for *Vanity Fair*, a magazine still unmatched in its own field for all-round excellence. Noel respected and admired Mr Crowninshield, and liked him, for he was an exceedingly kind man and a witty one; he remained a bachelor because he thought that married men made poor husbands. Frederic Bradlee, Crowninshield's nephew, later wrote that his uncle '… could never have envisioned what a Roman Candle he was helping to set off when he published those pieces by a totally unknown English boy in 1921.' Bradlee met Noel backstage in Boston in 1936 when he and Gertie were playing *Tonight at Eight-Thirty*, 'a memorable oasis in the bleak desert of a New England adolescence'. He remembers Noel's staccato accents rapping out, 'Your Uncle Frank paid me the first dollar I ever earned in America. As I was almost starving at the time, I was positively enchanted to get it.'

One by one, Noel made new friends. Irene Dean Paul became his companion in misfortune and always welcomed him to her flat on West 70th Street; when he could no longer afford even his attic in the Brevoort, Cecile and Gabrielle offered him a room in their studio on the understanding that he would pay them rent when and if he sold a play. All three women were fast friends, with temperaments so violently artistic that quarrels and furious rages were as frequent as high spirits. One of them, I forget which, came home one evening to find all her belongings in the street and had to stay there with them until after nightfall, when Gabrielle the peacemaker restored reason. Between the three of them life must have been anything but dull, but Noel contented himself with saying that he was grateful for their company. He stuck gallantly through the din to his habit of writing every day, and with memories of the Gala in Alassio still fresh in his mind worked at *Sirocco*, finished it quickly and had, to use his own words, no cause to regret it until several years later.

Like everybody else, Cecile and Gabrielle escaped from New York in August, leaving Noel to rattle about by himself in their studio. Now followed what must have been the loneliest and most poverty-stricken month of Noel's life. He took to sitting on the benches of Battery Park during the day; though hobos asked him if he couldn't spare a dime and the sight of ships sailing for England caused him painful nostalgia, this at least brought him the refreshment of cooling breezes from the sea. The heat and humidity of the dog-days made the nights almost unbearable, and on one occasion brought a swarm of bedbugs from their lair behind a tapestry of the Virgin Mary to crawl over himself and his bed. The neighbourhood cop befriended him and lent him a revolver, because in his opinion the district was dangerous for anyone living alone and unarmed. What little appetite Noel had was luckily reduced to almost nothing by the heat, and he lived sparingly on a diet of bacon-rashers charitably supplied on credit by the grocer on the corner. The frying of bacon was then Noel's sole culinary accomplishment, amounting to burnt sacrificial proportions, to the extent that he had to remove all his clothes because of the clouds of hot smoke in the kitchen. Noel's nakedness seen through the window was what had attracted the cop's attention in the first place, but his initial moral indignation was soon allayed by the offer of a glass of red wine, and dispersed altogether by the time he insisted that Noel should borrow his gun.

With the end of summer, friends began to trickle back from the country and the sea, Laurette Taylor and her family among the first. She was pre-eminently famous on both sides of the Atlantic for her portrayal of *Peg O' My Heart*. With her playwright husband Hartley Manners, she kept open house on Sunday evenings at their residence on Riverside Drive, large, austere and somewhat Gothic outside, splendid with brocades and Italian antiques within. Although her parties bristled with celebrities, Noel seems quickly to have become one of her favourite guests. The members of the family, sometimes one by one, would return in the late afternoons to find Noel already there at the piano, playing or probably trying to compose. Each would stop on their way upstairs and ask him if he wouldn't like to stay to dinner, and to each, while still playing, he would smile and say, 'Thank you, darling, I'd love to,' no doubt with the utmost sincerity, after his month on fried bacon. The most renowned feature of Miss Taylor's parties was the Adverb Game, which brought with it both terror and glee to her guests; glee to the assured professionals, only too eager to show how 'swooningly' they could drink a glass of water, and absolute terror to the young or tremulous when asked to do the same thing 'vivaciously' in front of every star in New York City.

Laurette Taylor, her luminous and larger than life-size personality, her family, her house, her parties and the word-games, together made a rich subject, ripe for any playwright's plucking; the wonder is that no one, her husband included, had done so until Noel thought of *Hay Fever*. Though they sparked him off and he used them and the material they unintentionally provided, the end-result is not and was never intended to be an accurate picture of themselves and their way of life. That Miss Taylor was hurt when she heard of *Hay Fever* makes for sad reading; when she saw the unsuccessful New York production with Laura Hope Crews acting 'her' part execrably she may have had more reason to say that she found it hard to forgive. The fact remains that Noel had written about them all and the fun they gave him as he always remembered them: with affection.

Laurette Taylor had seen Lynn Fontanne in *Milestones* in London, and ever since she met her at a tea-party at Lady Townsend's—admission five pounds, for war charities—had remembered the gawky young actress. In the end she sent for her to come to New York and play with her in *The Harp of Life*. (Lynn is always described in the memoirs of those days as gangly, gawky, scrawny or scraggly, but with stardom she assumed a lasting mantle of beauty which Miss Taylor put down to her having put on twenty pounds in weight, while a few diehards maintained they had recognised her beauty all along.) She played in four more productions with Miss Taylor, who paid her the best tribute an actor can pay: 'While acting with her I forgot we were actresses.' Lynn's stardom was just around the corner when she walked into one of the Sunday night parties with Alfred Lunt.

To put it delicately, Lynn and Alfred had been walking out for some time; Lynn and Noel had known one another off and on during the war years in London and the trinity seem to have come together and stayed together in as pre-ordained a manner as the heavenly one. Alfred, tall and exceedingly handsome, had from an early age obtained leading-man roles opposite star actresses with comparative ease because of his looks and charm. Margaret Anglin, the first, was twenty years older than he, and Laura Hope Crews, the second, was older still, more than old enough to be his mother. By the time he played with Lily Langtry she was sixty-three and could have been his grandmother; this was in a music-hall sketch called *Ashes* involving some compromising letters, which led one critic to inquire whether she had written him the letters in his cradle. All this had of course been excellent experience, which, with his immense talent, had made him a star in the title-role of Booth Tarkington's *Clarence*, two years before he met Noel. He and Lynn lived at Doctor Rounds', a theatrical boarding-house, 'untidily comfortable', on West 70th Street, and Noel only too thankfully went there to supper as often as they asked him. He read them his by now dog-eared manuscripts and they, more perspicacious than the New York managers, detected his playwriting skill at once. More than that, they believed without question in his own assurance of his brilliant future as an actor and it was after one of these suppers that the three of them dreamed up their future design for living. More substantial than a dream, it was to them a plan, to be carried out practically and simply. Whether Lynn could charm away Alfred's mother's dislike of her or not, she and Alfred would marry; they would all three of them become stars of international renown and then, having climbed these heights, they would scale a further pinnacle and appear together in a play which Noel of course would write, and in which they would enjoy a triple triumph. The final segment of their plan fell into place at the Hanna Theatre in Cleveland, Ohio, on January 2nd, 1933, twelve years later.

They had an agonising wait of several weeks until Lynn fulfilled her own contribution to the plan—her first starring part in the New York production of *Dulcy*. She was as sick as any mother-to-be, and Alfred and Noel as anxious as expectant fathers, until she sailed on in the first act in absolute control and made it apparent that her stardom was as certain as Alfred's had been in *Clarence*.

Mother had brought home the bacon, but Noel's financial plight was by now more grievous than ever and it took days for him to screw up enough courage to ask Lynn to lend him twenty dollars. His torture had been unnecessary; Lynn gave him twenty dollars out of her bag and went on with what she wanted to say, none too pleased at being interrupted. The very next morning the editor of *Metropolitan* asked him to lunch and offered him five hundred dollars if he would turn *I'll Leave It to You* into a short story; within three days he had repaid

Lynn, paid the obliging grocer for all those packets of bacon and sent forty pounds home to his mother.

He moved back into the Brevoort, and by now 'everybody'—the social set and the theatre managers—had moved back into the city. The latter were friendly, and though they steadfastly refused to produce his own two plays, over lunches they would discuss his making the adaptations of plays they had bought in Europe and, much to his liking, sent him complimentary seats for their first nights. He even extracted two out of the omnipotent David Belasco for the opening of Frances Starr in *The Easiest Way*. For two reasons this opening remained clear in his memory. One was Miss Starr's curtain speech. Life had dealt her blow after blow until she could stand no more, whereupon she proclaimed to her maid her intention of going to the bad, in (approximately) these shocking words: 'Doll me up, Annie! Dress up my body and paint up my face—I am going to Rector's to make a hit, and to hell with the rest!' Whenever in the future Noel had to face a dinner of prodigious boredom, he would remain supine on his bed until the very last moment, dramatically declaim this speech, and then drag himself reluctantly to dress.

The other reason was that, after the curtain fell on Frances Starr's sensational proclamation, Noel said within Alexander Woollcott's hearing that he had found one of the performances very 'vexing'. For Mr Woollcott, an eminent critic with the appearance of a disgruntled owl, 'vexing' was a word unexpected enough to appeal to him. The evening air was rent with laughter and Noel had found a place in his crusty heart for ever. His heart could be, perhaps essentially it was, as soft and sweet as a marshmallow, but he preferred it to be thought of as hard and crusty, and always expressed his undying affection for Noel in terms of terrible abuse, especially when squabbling over their interminable games of chance.

As for the New York social set, Lester Donahue was a pianist of distinction and it seems to have been mainly through him that Noel, often without a nickel in his pocket, was asked for weekends at the Easthampton houses of the rich. Lester, who was comparatively well-off, moved in to the Brevoort and became Noel's constant companion; moreover, he could afford the luxury of a piano in his hotel room, which he encouraged Noel to use. Hoytie Wiborg, who was fervidly interested in the arts, invited Noel to Easthampton, and her friend, Gladys Barber, took a great shine to him and presented him with a twenty-dollar gold piece as a mascot, though he knew perfectly well that it was given because he was broke.

More and more he longed to return to England and home, but as he frequently could not even afford a ticket on the subway, enough money for a passage across the Atlantic was an impossibility. In the end, when all was at its darkest and most hopeless, it was Gladys Barber who came to Noel's rescue. Through her husband, who was a shipping magnate, she procured for him a free cabin in the S.S. *Cedric*, sailing on October 31st, 1921. There was a little flurry of money-making before he left and he did in fact return with seven pounds more than he had arrived with. But the high hopes he had started out with had come to nothing. He could not know that he would never be as poor again; and on the immediate credit side there was a large amount for which to be thankful. He had seen, experienced and learned a great deal that was new to him, and had made many friends. He had grown to know and love New York City; actually, from the hotel suites, penthouses and limousines of the future he would never again know it so well, though his love for it would increase with fame and success.

4

<u>LONDON CALLING!</u>

THE *Cedric* was old and slow but comfortable, and after three days spent in his cabin pea-green with seasickness Noel emerged and began to enjoy the crossing. Among the few people on board was Doctor Marie Stopes, then a household name in England for her passionate pioneering of (to the public at large) a mysterious and vaguely dirty-sounding process which she called Birth Control. Noel, ever attracted to celebrities as they seem to have been attracted by him, made himself known and to his surprise found her a vivid conversationalist, deeply interested in the theatre. She had gone so far as to write several plays, the scripts of which she sent him on arrival in England and which he thought unproducible. When he went to stay with her she read one aloud to him, which quickly sent him into a deep sleep. As the reading took place rather late after dinner, she understood and forgave him and read it aloud all over again next morning. This unlikely friendship continued sporadically until after his success with *Cavalcade*, when she wrote, '*Do* be an angel and lend me three thousand pounds,' which terminated it.

The first inkling his family had of Noel's arrival was the telegram he sent from Lime Street Station after the ship docked in a storm of snow and sleet at Liverpool. This caused fever-pitch excitement at Ebury Street, and his homecoming a few hours later was hysterical, the new housemaid hopping from one foot to the other at her first sight of him.

Back in England, apart from the creature comforts of home, Noel's prospects appeared no less bleak than they had from his bench in Battery Park. Nobody wanted either him or his plays, Ebury Street was making only just enough money to keep the brokers' men at bay, and the strain of running it was beginning to tell on his mother, her fighting spirit for once near breaking-point. He had been paid a hundred pounds for making an adaptation of *Pour Avoir Adrienne*, which was stretched to last as long as possible; then he again had to swallow his pride, and this time asked Ned Lathom for a loan. He refused; he thought that a loan might spoil their friendship. Instead he gave Noel two hundred·pounds outright as a present. When trying to write about this spontaneous generosity, even at a distance of years later, Noel found it difficult to express his gratitude; his over-effusive words turned cold when put on paper.

After all the pressing debts were paid, neither Noel nor Ned Lathom could guess the blessings the remaining fifty pounds were to bring, some immediate, some long-range. The more distant benefits would become apparent within a year, resulting from his friendship with Ned Lathom, while an instantaneous one arose from his firmly making his mother go to the country for a rest, and to bring the roses back to her cheeks. This is the first instance—there were to be many more in the future—of Noel bossing other people about against their wishes but for their own good. Despite strong protestations, his idea was that his father could run the boarding house by himself, which he did with great success, dashing up and down the stairs with breakfast trays, smiling and popular with one and all, from the window-cleaner to the lodgers themselves, and especially with May the housemaid, to whom he allowed the unheard-of laxity of seldom wearing her cap and singing at the top of her voice all day long.

By great good fortune, Athene Seyler lent Noel her house at Dymchurch in Kent for a fortnight, during which time he and Gladys Calthrop scoured the countryside on bicycles looking for somewhere suitable for Mrs Coward and to which he could come at weekends to write. He called the cottage they eventually found in the pretty village of St Mary-in-the-Marsh 'small and tender', nestling up against the Star Inn, with four rooms and a privy in the garden. (For me the Star Inn itself from my boyhood possessed a romantic charm until I went back once too often, to find it 'improved' with formica and chromium.) Across the village street from the Star is the church, in the churchyard of which that summer Noel wrote *The Queen Was in the Parlour*.

Out of his walks and bicycle rides in early spring with Gladys, and then with his mother through that summer, arose Noel's long love-affair with Romney Marsh, a silvery green flatland laced with lazy canals, huge skies, clouds ever-changing and spectacular sunsets often as red as a blood orange. ('Too red. Very affected,' Noel would say.) The benefit furthest away, yet stemming from Ned Lathom's present kindness, was that Noel would one day buy the farmhouse, woods and verdant fields from Aldington Knoll, his favourite cycling objective, down to as far as the Military Canal, this vista stretching before him as he sat and rested.

While at St Mary's, Noel discovered that his idol, E. Nesbit, lived nearby at Jesson, and went at once to call. She lived in two huts joined together, with her husband T. T. Tucker, known as the Skipper. One hut was called 'The Longboat', the other, because it was squat and fat, 'The Jollyboat'; the kitchen was 'The Galley', and the bedrooms 'cabins'—all was nautical. Everything was shining and shipshape, Noel said, yet there was something in her character which made him think of her as one of the most truly bohemian persons he ever met. Although she was now an old lady within sight of the end of her life and with a severe code of behaviour, Noel found to his joy that there was no generation gap between them; she read his plays and listened to his 'modern' views with equanimity, encouraged him and advised him as though to a writer of equal status. They at once took to one another and Noel visited her often, but she by no means took to everybody; when his mother accompanied him on one occasion she met with a cool reception and from then on referred to Miss Nesbit as stuck-up.

There were plans that summer for a tour of *The Young Idea* in the autumn, which involved Noel's staying at Ebury Street. As had happened in America, his comparative poverty notwithstanding, Noel was by now always in demand in the houses of the rich and famous. Conversationally he was an enormous asset, the unexpected word quickly delivered; if the party wasn't going with a swing, he was only too willing to oblige with songs at the piano. There were weekends at stately homes and country houses, complete with tea on the lawn, cawing of rooks in immemorial elms, and the whack of cricket or tennis balls in the near distance. During one such weekend, while staying with Lady Colefax near Oxford, Elsa Maxwell blew into Noel's life with hurricane velocity. An immediate rapport was struck and by the following Tuesday Elsa and Dorothy (Dickie) Fellows-Gordon had invited Noel to spend two weeks in Venice with them. He described the invitation as being put with diffidence—though it is difficult to imagine either of those ladies ever being diffident—because their invitation included a ticket from Victoria Station via Paris to Venice and back to Victoria. Noel had no such scruples, accepted enthusiastically, and after two glamorous weeks (Elsa wasn't yet crowned, though this holiday marked the beginning of her long reign over the Lido) came home reflecting that the life of a kept boy, without the bother of amorous responsibilities, could be a very happy one.

The Young Idea opened in September at Bristol with Herbert Marshall in the cast, and Noel, at his own insistence and to everybody else's opposition, playing the lead. Bart Marshall, contrary to the starchy Englishman image he was later to project in the movies, turned out to be rather larky. He had lost a leg in the war, and the metal replacement, though he used it with apparent ease, often gave trouble technically. Noel was appointed mechanic, a cause of hilarity between them, Marshall having to drop his trousers while Noel with a spanner tightened a loose screw, or loosened it if—'you stupid sod'— Noel had screwed the knee unbendably tight. Their humour seems to have been centred exclusively below the waist; Marshall would gaze spellbound at Noel's flies until he had reduced him to the appalling certainty that he had come onstage with them undone. When they tired of this, Noel appeared with two or three buttons open, which sight he managed to make visible only to Marshall, whose turn it then was to be fascinated by what Noel might reveal to the audience.

By the time the tour finished it was discovered that no suitable West End theatre would be available for the play until the following February. With the money he had saved and more than three months with nothing to do, Noel wired to Ned Lathom, who was at Davos taking a long 'cure' for his tuberculosis, suggesting that he go out to join him for Christmas. The reply was flatteringly enthusiastic and Noel excitedly bought thick sweaters and socks and set off, first-class on the Channel boat and second-class on the trains, most likely the last time he ever intentionally travelled anything but first-class. He cannot however, as he states, have arrived 'next day, my eyes dazzled by leagues of white snow in strong sunlight', for he wrote from the Hotel de Londres in Paris:

Darling, I arrived *perfectly* safely this morning and have been received with open arms by everybody—divine lunch at the Ritz, now I'm off to dance at Claridges and then dining with Edward [Molyneux]. Elsa is giving a lunch party for me tomorrow to meet François de Croisset, Robert de Flers and [Henri] Bernstein, three of *the* best dramatists. They want me to play in this new comedy here in February—*such* a good gesture to refuse it for my *own* play—altogether I'm a *riot*! Rout out *Sirocco* and *Nadya* [*The Queen Was in the Parlour*] from those suitcases in my room and register them to Davos ... Paris is marvellous; wonderful plays and everything thrilling! I'll write the moment I get to Davos. All love, Snoop.

Again the start of a lifelong friendship; that with Edward Molyneux. As with the Lunts, he and Edward made a dream-pact; Edward, young, good-looking, ambitious, just starting his career, was determined to become one of the world's top dress-designers. Like Charles Worth, who had dressed the Empress Eugénie, Edward was English, but he too would storm the Paris fortress of fashion, and conquer. They planned that when he and Noel were both internationally famous— though in fact their improbable dream came true before that—no one but he was to make the gloriously beautiful clothes for Noel's leading ladies, who were of course going to be unimaginably glamorous. This was the decision they made in 1922 and that is in fact what happened. Except for the musicals and period-pieces, and even after Edward retired and the house of Molyneux was embodied in his cousin John Tullis, one read in the programme that the leading lady's clothes were 'by Molyneux', right up until Noel's last appearance in *Suite in Three Keys* in 1966. Not all the glamorous leading ladies were quite as sylph-like as they had envisaged in 1922, but their friendship survived several stars' tears and tantrums.

Ned Lathom had yet one more blessing to bestow: Noel arrived to find him looking better though still coughing badly, his suite in the Grand Hotel, Davos-Platz 'amazingly luxurious' and he as incurably stage-struck as ever. Noel, almost exploding with new songs and ideas for sketches and yet more songs, played and sang and expounded his ideas until Ned Lathom decided there was nearly enough for a revue and that he must send for André Charlot, whose last show, *A to Z*, he had financed.

> Darling, I've just played all the music to Charlot and he's delighted —he sat without a smile and then took me aside and said they were *all* good—so that's that. I now quite definitely enter the ranks of British Composers! ... it will be very thrilling to hear all my songs done by a good orchestra won't it? I am very excited as the music *is* good.

While Charlot was there Noel began his discipline of rising early, working hard and undisturbed during the long morning, playing and reading what he had achieved to the others in the afternoons and then enjoying what remained of the day as he pleased. The revue, later to be named *London Calling*, began to take shape, his only worry being that he might be stuck with a long run in *I'll Leave It to You*, for which he was under promise to Robert Courtneidge:

Charlot had a long talk with me to-day—if by any chance I find the whole undertaking too much, I am to do as much as I can— He is terribly keen on my playing lead, if Courtneidge will release me— he intends to boom me tremendously, of course it will probably mean £30 a week to *start* with! I must have a serious talk with Courtneidge ... I have a feeling everything will come out all right in the end but I am extremely what's known as 'put about' ... It really seems as tho' the chance that all the fortune tellers have fore-told is coming at last—the Revue is almost certain to run a year, It's going to be colossal, the whole production will cost about seven thousand to put on! And when you think that the bright particular star will be *me*, it's a bit breathless! ... it will be gorgeous to do, specially with people like Maisie [Gay] and Gertie, I have written Maisie a divine burlesque song, she is to wear a fair wig and very 'bitty' clothes and look *quite* 55, she does a parasol dance after the song with the male chorus, falling over once or twice on her fanny—it's one of the *wittiest* burlesques I've ever done ... I'm writing her a male impersonator burlesque, 'I'm Bertie from The Bath Club, but I've *never* learnt to swim'. Gertie will sing 'Prenez Garde, Lisette' (new and excellent), 'Tamarisk Town'—'Carrie Was a Careful Girl' with full chorus in lovely Victorian dresses—I am to give myself a new song to open with, then 'The Russian Blues', my *clothes* (*all* paid for by the management) will be marvel-lous. Isn't it all thrilling darling? I'm sunburnt and marvellously well—I'm afraid getting fat! Constant food and *such* food!

Two of Noel's enduring characteristics emerge from this letter. Every-thing he wrote, when fresh from his pen, was 'new and excellent' and was going to be marvellous and thrilling. Apart from being a most engaging trait, this was one of his greatest strengths; perhaps his greatest. Never mind what disaster had befallen a little while before, he was already eagerly looking ahead to the next project, which was always going to be 'one of the best things I've ever done'. The other trait was physical; a tendency to put on weight. His figure is remem-bered as being elegant and slim as a reed, which indeed it was, but from his schoolboy chubbiness onwards he had to guard against this tendency. In after years he worked out a diet of no more, often con-siderably less, than eleven hundred calories a day, by which he could drop fourteen pounds in a fortnight before appearing in a film or a play, and would say, '*Isn't* it curious about me; do you know as long ago as 1923 I had to go on a diet before I could appear in *London Calling*.'

Darling Lamb, here is another disappointment for you. I shall
have to return here for Christmas after Berlin. Edward Molyneux
is going to Cannes until the 24th when he comes here — it is frightfully important for me to see him as he is dressing the *entire* show
and Charlot wants me to produce [i.e. direct] and generally supervise. It will only mean a difference of four days before I come home
as I shall leave here on Boxing Day ... I do hope you won't feel
miserable at Xmas without me — *please* write and say you won't be
disappointed, it really is only a matter of sentiment and you really
will be sensible about it, I *know* you will. We will have a Christmas
day all on our own in the middle of the week — I shall bring home
some rich presents from Berlin.

With Edward not arriving until Christmas Eve and Ned Lathom
planning a star-studded Christmas house-party, one uncharitably
wonders whether much serious work would be got through in the few
days he had begged off from his mother; whether the pull of a first
visit to Berlin and all the famous people who were coming for Christmas was not too strong for Noel. Berlin, though Germany was in the
depths of a depression and the Mark at the height — if that is the word
— of inflation, was hectically gay; besides, with the Mark still plum-
meting, Noel was given *carte blanche* to buy the presents for the Christmas tree, a task which he enjoyed to the utmost and at which he
excelled. He never forgot the huge amounts of paper money one got in
exchange for a few pounds sterling; with typical exaggeration saying
that he had had to carry a bulging attaché case just to go out for the
evening and sometimes going still further and recalling that he'd 'had
to lug a suitcase'.

Berlin-Wilmersdorf, Sunday morning [December 10th]. My Lamb,
Two nice letters were waiting ... your last just came in with my
early tea (11.30!). I'm *so* relieved you're not upset over Xmas, I
knew you'd be sensible and sweet as usual. Last night we went out
and danced at various places. You'd never imagine Berlin was a
ruined country, it's gayer than anywhere, even Paris, and the
money! It's now 32,000 marks to the pound — one gets a delicious
dinner at any of the best restaurants for about 2/6 My lunch on the
train yesterday came to *exactly* fourpence halfpenny and I had *six*
courses all delicious *and* a bottle of red wine! One can drive all over
Berlin in a taxi for about a shilling — Tonight I'm going to this new
operette *Madame Pompadour* to see the greatest living German

Noel at age two

Noel in Cornwall,
1907

Philip Streatfield's drawing of Noel, 1914

In Charles Hawtrey's
Company, 1912

In *The Knight of the
Burning Pestle*, 1917

Noel's brother Erik vacationing
on the Norfolk Broads in 1924

With Esmé Wynne and John Ekins, 1915

Noel's father, Arthur, in 1932

Noel's mother, Violet, in 1915

Idol with idol:
a publicity shot of Noel
in the early 'twenties

Another publicity shot

With Gertrude Lawrence   >
in 'You Were Meant for Me',
choreographed by Fred Astaire;
from *London Calling!*, 1923

With Gladys Calthrop, 1924

Noel's farewell
to Marie Tempest and the cast
of *Hay Fever* before his
departure for America, 1925

Chicago, 1926: on tour with *The Vortex*

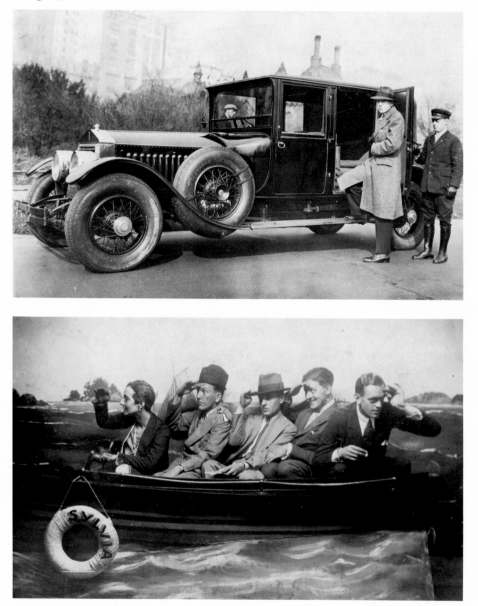

Coney Island, 1925: Gladys Calthrop, Noel, Robert Andrews,
Henry Kendall and Alan Hollis

On the set of *Private Lives* with Fredric March, Gertrude Lawrence
and Douglas Fairbanks, Jr, Phoenix Theatre, 1930

With Alexander Woollcott, New York, 'thirties

Discussing *Point Valaine* with Jack Wilson (*standing left*),
Osgood Perkins and Alfred Lunt and Lynn Fontanne, 1935

Oliver Messel's portrait
of Gladys Calthrop

With Madge Titheradge

<

Another publicity shot

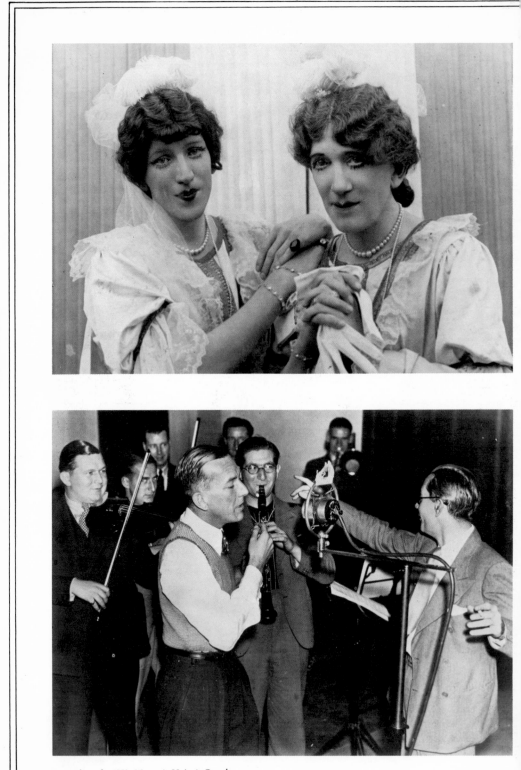

Recording for 'His Master's Voice', October 1934

<

With Sir Gerald du Maurier
at a Theatrical Garden Party
in the late 'twenties

Conversation Piece with Yvonne Printemps, His Majesty's Theatre, February 1934

November 1933: Noel is godfather to Daniel Massey,
with Raymond Massey (*left*), Adrianne Allen and Geoffrey Massey (*right*)

Trying to extricate
the Duke and Duchess
of Kent from the crowd
at a charity
Theatrical Garden Party
he hosted in Queen
Mary's Garden,
Regents Park, 1937

musical comedy artiste Fritzi Massary ... We have naturally booked most expensive seats in the front row — 2/– each! My pocket book is bulging, I've never felt so rich. You say you *expect* Ned is putting up money for the Revue — Certainly he is, *it's his solely and entirely*, Charlot is on a salary as Director! He is the usual taciturn manager — he's been charming to me and asked if I'd agree to let Clifton Webb play in it *with* me (Clifton's salary is £80) I said of course providing that I was indisputably in the superior position! Aren't I a *dear*!

Monday night: Just a line before I go to sleep — *Madame Pompadour* had *divine* music, I bought the score for 1/6. Today I got a huge bottle of hairwash for threepence — I've just come in from the Opera — your beloved *Tosca* — I've never heard it so well done — it was *enchanting* Good night my lamb! Snoop.

Tuesday and Wednesday: Darling, I've been shopping all day, things for Ned's Davos Christmas Tree — The shops are lovely — I'm looking out for a nice winter coat for you ... it's a lovely city, enormous squares and buildings and general grandeur. I've just re-met the boy from whom I wrote the hero in *Sirocco*. I haven't seen him since Alassio two years ago. My French has suddenly become *really* fluent in a miraculous manner so I could talk to him comfortably. German is a terribly funny language to listen to — I get weak at moments and laugh in people's faces! Goot Nacht mein Frau. Snoop Hohenzollern.

In ones and twos the celebrated guests began to arrive at Davos for Christmas. They must be listed because — yet again and without exception — they became and remained faithful friends of Noel's. There was the legendary Maxine Elliott, a favourite friend of Edward VII and Winston Churchill, with a theatre in New York named after her, and, though never a great actress, of a startling large-eyed beauty. Gladys Cooper, with Lady Diana Cooper one of the two most beautiful women in England, was at the height of her loveliness. She and Noel got off to a bad start. With a superiority which infuriated Noel — her voice could cut like ice when she wanted — she advised him to collaborate, to which he replied that as Shaw, Barrie and Maugham didn't, he didn't see why he should. One can hear Gladys saying, 'Well *really*! I've *never* heard such conceit, I might just as well compare myself with Bernhardt.' Noel quickly told her that that comparison would be *too* fantastic and the other luncheon guests nervously started to talk all at once about the weather.

The friendship between Gladys and Edward Molyneux started during this Christmas, and their association in the theatre lasted through the 'twenties and into the 'thirties when she starred in her own productions at the Playhouse. Edward designed her dresses for these, the most memorable one being the sheath glittering with beads she wore as Paula Tanqueray. Gladys never gave a hoot for her priceless complexion, exposing it to sun and wind and cold weather alike, although she did embark with a friend, Mrs 'Teddie' Thompson, on a business venture called 'Gladys Cooper's Beauty Preparations', which Noel regarded as hilarious after she told him the face cream had a base of gin and lemon juice. The venture had some acrimonious interludes towards the end when Gladys had tired of it and refused to travel to Leeds or Hull to promote the creams, to Teddie's fury.

Elsa Maxwell, Dickie Fellows-Gordon and Clifton Webb were also of the company, Elsa of course organizing all the parties. They went in for what they called 'tailing', the lot of them each on a small sled, hanging on to one another and trailing through the town in a long string with Elsa leading in a large horse-drawn sleigh, waving and 'screaming like a banshee', stopping the inhabitants dead in their tracks with amazement.

> Darling, we had a divine Christmas and I've had some lovely presents ... on Sunday we all went up to the Schatzalp, a restaurant on top of a mountain, then came down on luges. It's the most heavenly sensation in the world, two and a quarter miles zig-zag-ging through the trees like one long helter-skelter. It's perfectly safe because when you're going too fast you use your feet as brakes, and when you do fall off (which is *very* often) you only roll in the snow. The moment you reach the bottom you hitch on to a horse sleigh and gallop through the town to the Mountain Railway again. Then once more down ... Yesterday I went driving with a German Baroness right up the mountain opposite where we warmed our-selves with the most delicious hot chocolate. There were deep gorges with rushing torrents at the bottom and huge icicles hang-ing and desolate woods of fir trees – all snow almost up to your waist if you get off the road! I've just come in from skating at which I'm becoming quite roguish, doing figure eights *mostly* on my fanny but there, Vive Le Sport! Maurice [dancing partner of the lovely Leonora Hughes who was also at Davos] is very amusing and anyhow the best dancer in the world—the hotel is full of Spaniards who teach me marvellous Spanish rhythms on the

piano and shriek and gesticulate wildly. Goodbye now my Sniglet
I am getting too fat, Ned and I have bread-sauce with everything.
Snoop.

Noel got on the whole even more glowing notices for *The Young Idea*
when it opened in February 1923 than he had for *I'll Leave It to You*.
As a brilliant young playwright of great promise, that is, not as an
actor; James Agate, for instance, suggested that he was not primarily a
player. He seems already to have begun to attract his own fashionable
public, with its 'simply divine's and its 'too marvellous, darling's,
St John Ervine complaining in his *Observer* notice that he had unfortunately been wedged among a group of them.

But the play only ran eight weeks: 'London is outraged at the play
coming off, everyone is talking about it and it's doing me a *lot* of good.'
Years later he wrote, 'I learnt [from this] that good press notices are
not enough. If I had really cared about good notices I should have shot
myself in the early 'twenties.' His own favourite line from the play was,
'I lent that woman the top of my thermos flask and she never returned
it. She's shallow, that's what she is, shallow.'

With the play closed, Noel went off to join Gladys Calthrop at Cap
Ferrat, where the ever-hospitable Mrs Cooper had rented a villa. To
their dismay they found there a Dominican prior, to whom Mrs Cooper
seemed to be attached. Noel was in a holiday humour and tried hard to
make a go of it, but in spite of his efforts to charm and to make him
laugh, the prior remained sour in his dislike, which even Mrs Cooper's
jollity could not overcome. This went on until an afternoon when
Gladys and Noel returned unexpectedly and caught the prior in
Gladys's bedroom having himself a lovely time wearing nothing except
a minimum of her underclothing. They admitted defeat and left that
evening in torrents of rain for Italy, wandering about for two weeks
sightseeing, Gladys says, on very little money indeed. With Noel on
a recalcitrant mule and Gladys on a tiny donkey they rode to the top
of Vesuvius; by the time they got to Pompeii the gates were shut and
the guardian gone, so they simply climbed in and had the entire place
to themselves, unforgettably beautiful and pleasantly creepy in the
twilight.

Next day, broke, they were forced to ask an unwilling British Consul
for enough money to get them home to England. After a long bombard-
ment of Coward charm the Consul succumbed and agreed to accept a
cheque and left them while he went to get the money. 'Who shall I
make it payable to?' Noel called. 'Summers Cox.' 'And some hasn't,'

Gladys added. They took the money and fled, their violent *fous rires* not spent until after they had collapsed into their seats in the train.

London Calling! opened at the Duke of York's Theatre on September 4th, 1923, to reviews in general complimentary to the show as a whole, but uncomplimentary to Noel's own performance. Gertie's biggest success was with 'Parisian Pierrot', the idea for which had come from an elongated Pierrot doll fastened to and hanging limply from a curtain in a cabaret show which Noel had seen in Berlin the previous winter. The picture of it remained impressed on his mind and he often dreamed about it until he exorcised it by writing the song. Judging from the royalty returns, 'Parisian Pierrot' stays today as immovably as ever in Noel's own Top Ten. Gertie's all-round brilliance in *London Calling!* led to Charlot's taking her to Broadway in his *London Revue of 1924*, in which she achieved immediate and lasting stardom. Noel missed her dreadfully when she left for New York, although she was replaced more than capably by Joyce Barbour. Gertie had worn an elegant wisp of flame-coloured chiffon designed by Molyneux for their sentimental song-and-dance, 'You Were Meant for Me'; when poor Joyce suddenly appeared for the same number clad in dark tomato, Noel said, 'My God, you look like a redbrick villa,' and she melted into his arms in gales of giggles from which they never recovered. Literally never, until Noel left the show; every night as soon as they heard their introductory music they started to shake, and in the end it became a small nightmare.

London Calling! marked the beginning of Elsie April's long association with Noel as his musical amanuensis, and Danny O'Neil's as stage manager. Later they were joined by Cissie Sewell as ballet mistress, and the three of them were, through many musicals, a delight to Noel, a sort of permanent comedy act. When George Balanchine, who had choreographed several ballets for Cochran revues, came to Les Avants in 1968, he and Noel, to everyone's surprise and to the disappointment of some, talked exclusively about Elsie, Cissie and Danny; how funny they had been and how superlatively good at their jobs. With their down-to-earth humour, they were at their best at auditions, which can otherwise be a boring form of torture. Elsie, if some wretched girl had too shrill a soprano, would hiss, 'She's been at the birdseed, dear,' while Cissie, of an over-bright dancer, would say, 'She's a nice little arteeste, but she won't do onsomble.' As for Danny, Noel had a regrettable tendency to pick at his nose when deep in thought; whenever Danny caught him with an index finger exploring a nostril he would call out gaily, 'Wave when you get to the bridge!'

This is perhaps the moment to state once and for all that there is no truth in the rumour, still fairly widespread, that Elsie April wrote some of Noel's music. Nor do I believe that she ever said she did, because she was the first to admit that she couldn't. Noel called her mastery of musical technique miraculous; she possessed every possible musical talent except that of composition. A sixteen-bar 'link' was at one point needed in *Bitter Sweet* and Noel said to her, 'Go on, you can do that for me, surely.' She tried, but it was no use; she couldn't. Noel owed much to Elsie and to his orchestrators, the most brilliant of the latter being the young Pete Matz at Las Vegas, but every melody he wrote was his own, except, as Elsie was the first to point out, for an inadvertent little chunk of Richard Wagner in *Bitter Sweet*.

London Calling! must not pass without mention of the Sitwells' feud with Noel. The fabled feud lasted forty years, though why it began and what it was about Noel could never really understand or explain. Osbert Sitwell had stopped at Noel's table after luncheon at the Ivy and said that his sister Edith was giving a recital of poems from *Façade* to music by William Walton at the Aeolian Hall (always known by Noel as the A.E.I.O. Ulian Hall), from which Noel might possibly pick up some ideas. Noel went and did pick up an idea, though the resulting skit bore little resemblance to the Sitwells beyond the fact that it consisted of two brothers and a sister. The stage directions do say that Hernia Whittlebot's face should be white and weary with a long chin and nose, but Maisie Gay was plump and her pop-eyed face as round as a full moon. It is true the sketch made fun of what was then 'modern' poetry, but in fact Noel gave the Swiss Family Whittlebot the poem 'Beloved It is Dawn, I rise', which he had published in his collection of satires *A Withered Nosegay*, and which had therefore been around for a year for anyone to read, including the Sitwells. Hernia Whittlebot goes on to say: 'Life is essentially a curve and Art is an oblong within that curve. My brothers and I have been brought up on Rhythm as other children are brought up on Glaxo.

> Drains and Sewers support the quest
> Of eternal indulgence.
> Thank God for the Coldstream Guards.
>
> Guts and Dahlias and billiard balls
> Swirling along with spurious velocity
> Ending what and where and when
> In the hearts of little birds
> But never Tom Tits.'

The Sitwells, instead of laughing at such light-hearted nonsense, took it to heart and cut Noel dead from then on. Perhaps everybody concerned was too young and too earnest; the strange thing is that from then on Noel too took a self-instituted campaign of mockery of modern poetry earnestly and seriously. Arguments pro and con, verging on solemn quarrels, took place over the years between him and some of his friends, his opinion being that modern poetry wasn't poetry at all, it was too easy and that almost anybody could write it. To prove his point, one evening after dinner he read to two pro-Edith friends selections from her poems indiscriminately mingled with some from his own *Spangled Unicorn* and defied them to guess which was which. He did not cheat, he gave to everything he read equal importance. To his glee they could not differentiate between the two.

By July 1924 Noel had three completed plays up his sleeve: *The Vortex*, *Fallen Angels*, with which Gladys Cooper and Madge Titheradge dickered, and *Hay Fever*, which he envisaged for Marie Tempest. All three unprofitably went the rounds of the West End managements, but undeterred he joined his mother at the rather dreary cottage he had taken at Dockenfield in Surrey and wrote a fourth, called *Easy Virtue*. Once again, with funds perilously low, he received and accepted an invitation to stay with a wealthy friend, this time with Ruby Melville at Deauville for the rest of the summer. Here Sir James Dunn, an abundantly rich industrialist who had previously ignored him, quite suddenly—probably prodded by Ruby Melville—pronounced that Noel was a genius and that he would finance him. He offered one hundred pounds a month—a fortune to Noel—in return for twenty per cent of his earnings over the next five years. Noel was understandably tempted, as he was often to be throughout his career, to 'sell his soul', but on each occasion was saved by a friend's advice. This time it was Gladys (Calthrop) who, on his return to England, drenched the idea with such ice-cold contempt that he never signed the agreement, and—the pattern was always to be repeated—within a year his affairs took a sensational turn for the better.

Elsie Scott, whom Noel met during this holiday at Deauville, was a type of woman who held an eternal fascination for him. Her white Rolls-Royce was driven by a tall and handsome chauffeur, liveried from the cap on his head to his boots and leggings in gleaming white leather. She herself was coolly elegant, seemingly—perhaps indeed she was—well-bred, her manners impeccable and her conduct at any rate in public above reproach. Noel was to know many such women, Julie Thompson especially well, all of them kept by rich, titled and sometimes royal protectors, and though everybody knew who was whose *chère amie*, by general consent this was never mentioned. Their names and photographs seldom if ever appeared in the papers or in the smart magazines; in the period about which I am writing, that is. The word *déclassée* was still in use, as was *demi-mondaine*, and it was to this latter class that these lovely ladies belonged. They knew their place; they could be seen in public at the theatre and in restaurants and night clubs, though not with their protectors, but in spite of their popularity in their own circles they knew they would never be accepted by the hard upper crust of society or presented at Court, and they did not expect to be. Where, Noel always longed to know, had they been schooled in their exacting profession? How had they learned never to put a foot wrong, let alone never to go too far? One thing they had without exception learnt, Noel noticed, was never to make an enemy of another woman; they were all as nice to the ladies as to the gentlemen. Their mentors, he decided, had probably been their lovers; Gertie, though not of this class (actresses were different), had been taught everything by Philip Astley, who guided her taste in clothes and everything else, and she, monkey-quick, picked up every trick of social jargon and behaviour until the girl from Brixton emerged during their long relationship as a perfectly polished product of Mayfair. As the years went by the rigid rules were gradually relaxed, though never by the Old Guard.

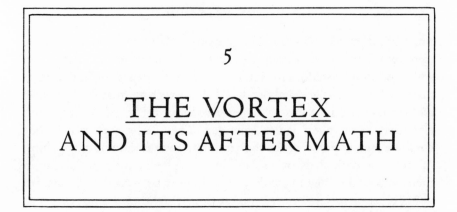

5

THE VORTEX
AND ITS AFTERMATH

THE events leading up to the theatrically famous first night of *The Vortex* at the Everyman Theatre at Hampstead in November 1924 were several and diverse. The idea for the play was planted in Noel's imagination by an incident he never forgot. He had maintained his friendship with the young Coldstream Guards officer Stewart Forster, and eventually stood godfather to Stewart's daughter Sarah; meanwhile he had become increasingly fond of Stewart's beautiful mother. In his autobiography Noel, at one point, is troubled that he may have left out several people who had been of considerable importance to him, Grace Forster among them: 'She should have made her entrance a long way back, swishing across shady lawns and night clubs, wrapped in gallant vanity and smelling slyly of amber.' Stewart one night asked Noel to join his party for supper and dancing at the Grafton Galleries; there, on entering, he noticed Grace across the room on a banquette with one of her young admirers. As soon as the party was seated one of the girls blurted out, 'Will you *look* at that old hag over there with the young man in tow; she's old enough to be his mother.' Noel sprang to his feet, walked across to Grace, kissed her, sat down beside her smiling and talking, with his arm deliberately and affectionately across her shoulders. Stewart paid no attention to any of this, but Noel could not get out of his mind the painful stab he must have received from the girl's remark, and thus was the mother-young son-young lover triangle conceived for the play. There the resemblance ended; he only needed another conflict between the mother and the son to provide an even stronger basis, and this came easily to him from his unlikely pre-occupation, already noted, with the subject of drug addiction.

Michael Arlen and Noel, who were both to become pre-eminent symbols of the 'twenties, were by this time friends of three years' standing. Mr Arlen had already achieved glittering success with *The*

Green Hat, one of the most sophisticated (in the Mayfair sense of the word) best-sellers there have been. Noel's success was yet to come, and he admitted to envy of Mr Arlen's and of the outward signs of it, such as his pearl and platinum watch-chain. However, when alone together, they discarded all worldly-mindedness and shared a warm and affectionate relationship which, to judge from their correspondence, continued for many years. So when Noel, over dinner with him at the Embassy Club, poured out his troubles about getting backing for *The Vortex*, Mr Arlen quickly wrote him a cheque for two hundred pounds with no stipulations, as though it were the most natural thing in the world. He was equally generous with his praise to Noel after the first night: 'Oh, how proud I should be if I had written it!'

But before that happy night Noel and Gladys were as one in taking arms against the sea of troubles that almost engulfed them: Kate Cutler's folly, for one thing, in walking out of the leading role of the mother one week before production because, she wrongly thought, Noel had built up his own part at the expense of hers. Noel spent such a sleepless night trying to think of a suitable replacement that he in the end worked from the other extreme; Lilian Braithwaite heading his list of unlikely type actresses to play the flamboyantly neurotic Florence Lancaster. Miss Braithwaite, tall, dark and an actress of great distinction, was about to start rehearsals for yet another cup-and-saucer comedy at an extremely good salary compared to the regulation five pounds a week offered by the Everyman. However, she agreed to see Noel that very morning, and, after he had read her the play, said with meaning that she had not yet signed a contract. Noel liked to think that the faraway look he detected meant that she could already see herself in the highly effective part, wearing outrageous clothes and a red wig, and he was quite right — she could.

Another trouble they had to face was the bloody-mindedness of Norman Macdermott, the manager of the Everyman, his furious rage that the important Lilian Braithwaite decision had had to be made without consulting him, and his insistence that the programme should mention that he had designed part of the scenery. The whole conception of the sets and clothes was Gladys's except for the fireplace, and this he tore out on the day of the opening, leaving a gaping hole to be patched over before the curtain rose. She had in any case had an agitating morning out in the street painting scenery, with the flats propped up against the pavement wall of the tiny theatre; Noel meanwhile having an equally turbulent morning in the Lord Chamberlain's office in St James's Palace, only persuading Lord Cromer in the nick of time to grant a licence for his 'unpleasant' play. The dress rehearsal the night before had been for Noel and Lilian a disaster, leaving them filled with nothing but gloomy foreboding. Joyce Carey, Lilian Braithwaite's young daughter, had been in front, however, and had been moved and electrified by their performances and by the play itself, then with excitement had rushed backstage only to find them utterly dejected. I suppose she had seldom argued with her famous mother, who was knowledgeable and experienced in theatrical matters, but she made a brave leap, prophesied out-and-out success and the next night was proved triumphantly right.

The first night of *The Vortex* is theatrical history; never to be forgotten by those present, actors and audience alike. *Le beau monde*, from Lady Louis Mountbatten to the omnipresent Eddie Marsh, turned out in force and in full fig, braving the icy weather, the hazards of the journey to darkest Hampstead and the discomforts of the tiny, hard-seated theatre. White ties and jewels abounded and the coconut matting went unnoticed, for it could not be seen, so great was the crush. The audience was agreeably shocked by the first-act comedy dialogue and then genuinely startled by the abrupt switch to near-tragedy in the third, and by the highly charged emotional tension of the acting. Lilian's sensational breakaway from drawing-room comedy added greatly to the general excitement; Noel cut his hand when he swept all the bottles off Florence's dressing-table in the last act and it obligingly went on bleeding, the handkerchief that bound it becoming redder and redder during the countless curtain calls.

The novelist Stella Gibbons has written:

I was present at the very first performance of *The Vortex* in a little kind of converted drill-hall in Hampstead and remember how shocked I was at the drug-addict boy (he would have been called a Drug Fiend in those days by ordinary people) and ever since I have had so much enduring pleasure and laughter from his songs and jokes. He seems to me to incarnate the *myth* of the 'twenties (gaiety, courage, pain concealed, amusing malice) and that photograph ... with prised fingertips held to hide the mouth, with the eyes delightfully smiling, is an incarnation in another form, even to the extreme elegance of the clothes.

Noel Coward had arrived, and was here to stay. Everything about himself that he had unswervingly believed would come true came true in a single night, two weeks before his twenty-fifth birthday. From the beginning he had seen his star in the east, and now that bright particular star was risen. Whether it was a meteor, soon to burn itself out, he sometimes had reason in the coming years to wonder. But for the moment with stardom, deservingly earned, came all the trappings he loved and had so eagerly wanted; the dressing-room jam-packed with admiring friends, the praise, and the crowd waiting for him outside the stage door. This last I believe meant more to him than almost anything, at first because he had so recently been one of that crowd himself, waiting for someone else, and then increasingly as the years went by seeing it as a tangible proof of the public's love. Young as he was, he had now proved himself to be a playwright, actor and director of good quality, and had already a year before in *London Calling* sung and danced, composed many of the songs and written their lyrics and the sketches leading into them. What young man had ever before — or has since — attempted and succeeded in so many branches of theatrical endeavour? No wonder he became society's hero and so quickly accepted as the darling of the 'twenties: Miss Gibbons is right, he *was* the 'twenties embodied, writing and speaking for his generation with wit, penetration and a brave use of sentiment of which he was never afraid, even in that supposedly cynical era. What is more, in the midst of all the adulation, he kept his head when all about him were doing their best to turn it; revelling in hard work and the self-imposed discipline of writing, and, when not working, observing and putting his observations to good use. John Osborne once described him as 'His own invention, his contribution to the twentieth century ... To be your own enduring invention seems to me to be heroic and essential. Even if you can begin to make it. It seems increasingly impossible.'

Comparisons have often been drawn between Noel's *The Vortex* in 1924 and John Osborne's *Look Back in Anger* thirty years later. They were both pioneer plays, both milestones in the history of English drama; both young dramatists spoke with startling effect for their contemporary generations and both of them influenced and indeed actually changed the style of dramatic writing with such certainty that there was no going back; both authors used a stomach-pump of realism on audiences grown complacent on what they had hitherto been fed. *Look Back in Anger* was quickly labelled 'Kitchen Sink', just as an outraged Sir Gerald du Maurier had used the word 'filth' and called *The Vortex* 'Dustbin Drama'. Noel vigorously defended in print the new reality he had injected: the years would pass until in 1961 he wrote and published in the *Sunday Times* three articles which by and large revealed his general attitude to be that of Sir Gerald so long before. To be fair to Noel, however, he did at this time express an admiring appreciation of some of the new young playwrights, Peter Shaffer and Harold Pinter, his favourite, in particular. And he knew with certainty during the first half hour of *Relatively Speaking* that at last, after a long barren patch, we had again a comedic writer of brilliance—his comedy solidly based on truth—in the person of Alan Ayckbourn, and he was pleased beyond measure.

No less than eight managements made bids for *The Vortex* and only two weeks after the Hampstead first night it opened at the Royalty Theatre in the West End. Lilian and Noel settled in for a long run which had from the beginning a gratifying glow of success about it. With the accompanying prosperity, Noel recklessly indulged in several suits, many silk shirts and pyjamas and a new car. Ebury Street also blossomed; the plumbing now gushed piping hot water and Noel's rooms were done over, his bedroom particularly striking with walls of scarlet further embellished with murals in Bakst-like colours by Gladys. Lorn was raised to the rank of Permanent Secretary for Noel's Affairs; she came into this riot of colour every morning and sat on the end of the bed armed with a shoebox called Shortly into which they piled all pending letters. They learned from experience that if Shortly was left undisturbed for a month or longer most of the letters had answered themselves and consequently always employed this efficient and time-saving method.

Noel's three nearest friends at this point were Lorn, Gladys and Jeffery, and to this trio was added a fourth, Joyce Carey, the daughter of Lilian Braithwaite and Gerald Lawrence, the matinée idol. Noel soon fell under the spell of her looks, charm and keen intelligence, to which is surprisingly added (when she occasionally chooses) a wicked and bawdy sense of humour, all the more effective expressed as it is in a well-bred way in her well-bred voice. She uses four-letter words very sparingly indeed and with great skill; devastatingly unexpected by the person to whom she is talking. Noel never forgot the comfort she had brought to him and to her mother on the wretched night of the dress rehearsal at the Everyman, but what really endeared Joyce to him in the first place was her reply when he asked her how her father had come to marry her mother. 'I've always wondered myself,' she said rather dreamily, 'how that stallion stampeded his way into the vicarage garden.'

One May evening in 1925, towards the end of the London run of *The Vortex*, Noel and Lilian were attracted by the rapt attention being paid to them and their performances by a handsome young man in the front row of the stalls. Audiences had become duller after such a very long run and they were so grateful to him for his obvious absorption that they played 'to' him and gave him a special bow when they took their final curtain. This was Noel's first sight of John Chapman Wilson. 'Jack' appeared backstage two nights later, and as he turned out to be an American, nearing the end of his first holiday in London, he and Noel promised to meet in New York as soon as *The Vortex* opened there. No warning bell had sounded to alert Noel that Jack was soon to become an intimate friend and would exert a potent influence on his private life and career during the years ahead.

Apart from the febrile intensity with which he threw himself into the part of Nicky eight times a week, Noel's industry during the run of *The Vortex* now seems scarcely credible. First came the revue *On with the Dance*, the first production of his nine-year association with C. B. Cochran, for which he wrote the book, lyrics and most of the music and of course sat in on the auditions and rehearsals in London. Came a Sunday when he travelled to Manchester with the company for the opening on Tuesday, casually leaving Nicky to be played for two nights by the understudy, unprofessional behaviour for which he later chided himself; later still, when the understudy, John Gielgud, had become famous, he decided that the public hadn't been cheated at all. Alice Delysia made an enormous success in *On with the Dance* singing 'Poor Little Rich Girl' to Hermione Baddeley, and Douglas Byng and Ernest Thesiger were hilarious as elderly ladies undressing and getting into a strange bed together in a boarding-house. Then there was a *Fête Galante* at a Church garden-party at Runcorn:

> We're six dirty little choirboys,
> With really frightful minds,
> We scream and shout and run about
> And pinch our friends' behinds.
> Nobody could admire boys
> With dirty hands and knees,
> But the countryside rejoices
> At our sweet soprano voices,
> So we do what we damn well please.

The revue abounded in astonishingly varied dancing; from Leonide Massine, superb in two ballets, to Florence Desmond's 'Danse Eccentrique', and to Terry Kendall, Kay Kendall's father, dancing as Valentin the Boneless Wonder.

The critic of the *Morning Post* wrote:

The speed ... of the performance is feverish, burlesquing the speed
of our modern life. At times the players seem mad, intoxicated
with the desire to force their bodies to do something faster,
faster. As befits Mr Coward's genius, many of the incidents are as
Nature seen through a glass crookedly ... The arid, futile people
that Mr Coward puts into his plays dash about the stage, worked
into a frenzy by the syncopated music.

Apart from one or two squabbles with Cochran, and the dress rehearsal
lasting twenty-seven hours, the whole successful enterprise passed off
without memorable incident for Noel except that Delysia lost her
temper when he thought he might also let Gertie use 'Poor Little Rich
Girl' in New York and said, 'Noel is a sheet and a bougairr.'

Before *On with the Dance* had come to London, Noel was already hard
at work on the production of *Fallen Angels*, one of the four plays he
had been forced to keep up his sleeve through lack of interest and
which were now suddenly in demand. Margaret Bannerman was to
have played Julia to Edna Best's Jane but after three weeks of rehearsal
collapsed with what Noel calls a brainstorm; the ebullient, beautiful
and sexy Tallulah Bankhead came bounding in to the rescue. Within
two days she was word perfect and four days after that gave a magnetic
and assured first-night performance. She was at the height of her outrageous popularity, idolised by socialites and the gallery alike. Everything she said and did was news; she was still smarting from Somerset
Maugham's resolute refusal to let her play Sadie Thompson (he was
wrong to give it instead to the nondescript Olga Lindo) so that when
she went and gazed longingly out of the window and said '*Rain!*'—not
in Noel's script—with intense meaning, she got a big laugh and
applause from all over the house, save from Noel. Her large following
coupled with the reviewers' shocked notices—'disgusting', 'degrad-
ing', 'vile', 'obscene' and so on—ensured that both the box-office's
telephone and its cash-register tinkled merrily for months.

Arising from this production there sprang up a most unlikely but
nonetheless very real friendship between Tallulah and Lornie. Gin was
one bond between them, with bawdy conversation accompanied by
raucous laughter far into the night another. Lornie was the recipient of
Tallulah's most intimate confidences and at this time she had much to
confide. Tallulah laughed most things off but, Lornie said, she took the
rumour that she was a lesbian very seriously and assured Lornie on her

word of honour that she *always* thought about a man when playing with herself and could thus prove conclusively—to the newspapers if necessary—that she wasn't.

The subsequent history of *Fallen Angels* has been chequered indeed, though pretty consistently successful. Its first major revival came in 1949, produced at the Ambassadors by Lance Hamilton, Charles Russell and Peter Daubeny Productions. Hermione Gingold and Hermione Baddeley used the play as a showcase for their differing though equally comic personalities and the public loved them. But this was the first time a play of Noel's had not been acted straight and regarded as sacrosanct, and he was therefore understandably upset when he saw the result. Noel went off in a huff on one of his far-flung holidays, leaving Lornie with the coffers very low and consequently only too grateful for the regular weekly royalties. Noel was eventually able to see the affair in proportion, but it took a very long time. He and I once thought we would pay our respects at Shakespeare's tomb after a matinée at Stratford-on-Avon; we happened upon the vicar, who took us close, inside the chancel rail, and while we were standing in silence and not without awe at that sacred spot, he suddenly said, 'We had a rare treat last autumn at the Memorial Theatre.' (A noble Hamlet? A glorious Cleopatra? we wondered.) 'The two Hermiones in *Fallen Angels*!' 'I do think it's a shame,' Noel complained as we left, 'I can't get away from that bloody production, not even at Shakespeare's tomb.'

Yet he condoned what to my mind was a much more exaggerated low-comedy performance by Nancy Walker in the same play a year later on Broadway, and gradually accepted the fact that the play had become a vehicle for the two leading ladies to do more or less as they liked with, as long as he didn't see or know what they were up to. We thought it better not to inquire; just to be grateful for its continued popularity in repertory and summer stock. Jane and Julia should be played by young women, but the stars became more and more mature until a few years ago Hermione Gingold asked Noel if she could take *Fallen Angels* to theatre-starved South Africa. He agreed, but when we got home said, 'I'm very very fond of Ging, so I couldn't say no, but I really can't have any more old ladies, drunk all through the second act and hanging about for a young French lover. From now on we really must make sixty the limit.'

For Noel, who had the two plays and the revue running simultaneously in the West End, there was never an idle moment. Marie Tempest, First Lady of the English Theatre and certainly its most scintillating comedienne, made up her mind after twelve months' indecision and declared herself willing, nay eager, to appear in *Hay Fever*. This may have been because everything Noel touched at this time turned to gold, or because she had had several failures in a row, or both. Noel, least timorous of men, was apprehensive when the great star (and a very determined lady) insisted that he direct her, but need not have been. From the first she took his direction like a lamb, calling from the stage, 'Young man, come up here and show me how to do it!' which convinced him once and for all that a director should himself have at least some working knowledge and experience of acting. Marie Tempest's husband, Willie Graham-Browne, who invariably acted with her, was notoriously slovenly about learning his lines, which after three weeks was slowly driving Noel mad, as indeed it was Miss Tempest: 'That's right, Noel, give him hell. Perhaps you can knock some sense into him; I can't!' She and the play enjoyed tremendous success for more than a year, though some of the critics began to bewail Noel's lack of advancement as a serious playwright and started what was to become a continual chorus of 'thin', 'tenuous', 'trivial', 'flippant' and 'brittle' until, about a quarter of a century later, this was at last changed to 'not vintage Coward' which is what *Hay Fever* had presumably been in the first place. As with all his comedies, some of the lines remained in Noel's personal repertory; he would fling himself on to chair or sofa and exclaim from the depths of extreme despondency (perhaps his typewriter ribbon had buckled), 'Life has dealt me another blow, but I don't mind.' I knew my duty and would murmur absent-mindedly, 'What did you say?' 'I *said*'—a dagger-like look at me, filled with hatred—'that Life had dealt me another blow, and that I didn't MIND'. This was especially enjoyable if done, as it usually was, in front of uncomprehending visitors.

Lilian and Noel took New York by storm when they opened in *The Vortex* at the Henry Miller Theatre in September 1925. They had played a dreary week in sweltering Washington by way of try-out, to sparse, lethargic audiences; the first night there only engraved on their memories by a stagehand, who, after Lilian had wrenched Nicky's box of drugs from Noel and thrown it dramatically out of the window, caught it and flung it straight back at her. What is more she caught it even more adroitly than he had, with one hand, to Noel's astonishment. 'That's what comes of having cricketers for brothers,' she explained afterwards.

They returned dejectedly to New York, steeled to face undoubted failure, and were therefore totally unprepared for what awaited them;

tumultuous welcomes on their entrances, completely absorbed attention throughout from a spellbound audience, and at the end a terrific, vociferous standing ovation. The whole cast had played as though inspired and Noel felt to his satisfaction that he had given the best performance of his life: 'I was hugged and kissed and crowned with glory, and that night is set apart in my memory, supreme and unspoilt, gratefully and forever.'

The press next day was as enthusiastic and as profitable for the box office as it had been only the day before for Michael Arlen's *The Green Hat*, starring Katharine Cornell as the romantically doomed Iris March. The smell of success was in the air for Michael Arlen and for Noel, relished by both, though the smarties made up their minds that they were rivals, and must be bitterly jealous of each other. To scotch this they could be seen dining, just the two of them, at least once a week in the most prominently fashionable restaurants in New York until rumour swung the other way and had it that they were having an affair, which of course added more to their enjoyment than ever.

Sure enough, Jack Wilson kept the promise made in London and asked Noel to lunch during the first week of rehearsals of *The Vortex* in New York. Noel dictated a letter of acceptance and then on the day appointed waited for ages; no Jack turned up and in the end he had to eat a drugstore lunch alone and in a filthy temper. It was later revealed that his secretary had never posted the letter, so when Jack appeared at the stage door after the first matinée (Noel had meanwhile become the most sought-after young man in New York) he professed to be in a rage and attacked Noel for not answering his invitation. After a heated exchange in the alley, Noel asked Jack to dine at his studio-apartment, where Gladys and Mrs Coward helped to smooth his ruffled feathers. There was an instant reconciliation, and a few months later Jack gave up stockbroking for ever in order to act as Noel's personal manager. In addition to his film-star looks, Jack had an immense amount of charm, and with his sharp wit he could be so funny that one forgave, or didn't even notice, the mocking irony with which his wit was edged.

Mrs Coward had come over with Noel and Gladys in the *Majestic* in August, leaving Daddy, Erik and Auntie Vida to bicker in, and run, Ebury Street. From the moment she first stepped on to American soil, she unflinchingly faced the strange mysteries of her new life, engaged maids, ran the apartment and quickly learnt enough American to do the daily marketing efficiently and economically. In fact she loved it all; her son's exciting success, his first Rolls-Royce, so many thrilling famous people in and out of the apartment at all hours and the constant theatrical and social activity. No sooner had *The Vortex* opened than Noel, as he had done in London, plunged other irons in the theatrical fire; *Hay Fever* was cast, or, more accurately, miscast, rehearsed, and Mrs Coward sat with her son and Gladys in a box on the Sunday-night opening and watched the play going inexorably down the drain. *Easy Virtue* was the next venture, the first ever of Noel's plays to be produced in New York before it was in London. A comedy built on foundations of Pinero-like drama, Jane Cowl—a blazing star if ever there was one—played it full out as the latter, particularly at the second-act curtain. She should have got a big laugh as she hurled a replica of the Venus de Milo (though not so large) to the ground and smashed it, but she declaimed, 'I've always hated that damn thing!' with such intensity and force that she thrilled audiences to the marrow, to Noel's chagrin. So, although George Jean Nathan rudely referred in print to *Easy Virtue* as an ancient whangdoodle, Miss Cowl triumphantly played to virtual capacity right through the winter.

At about this time Gladys went off to act as art director for Eva le Gallienne's newly founded Civic Repertory Theatre. This worthy enterprise was at once renamed the Civic Raspberry Company by Noel, and its high-mindedness automatically became a target for his disrespect. The Gospel According to Stanislavsky ordained that they went away for a month in the country during which to 'live' and grow into their parts for a play by Chekhov; Noel's levity can be imagined when they sat in a bed of poison-ivy and had to come trooping home again and go to hospital for treatment. Then there was a performance of *John Gabriel Borkman* at which Noel was present, and while Miss le Gallienne was emoting in the snow a metal coat-hanger fell out of the snow-bag and hit her on the head.

By the time *The Vortex* went on the road after the run in New York, Mrs Coward stepping westward with the company, Noel had wearied of playing his demanding role and made the firm decision never again to commit himself for so long a run. Three months in London and three in New York would be ideal, he thought: this was less high-handed than it sounded to managements and fellow actors because it would leave him freer for his writing, to which he attached more importance. And in the future he did find himself in the fortunate position of being able to carry out this agreeable plan.

But everybody in the company, above all Noel, avidly anticipated six glorious weeks in Chicago, the highlight of their tour. He had met Mary Garden, Queen of Chicago Opera, a year or so before in the South of France and their love at first sight was mutual. In the back of the car late that night Miss Garden began to nod and finally dropped off; her sister whispered to Noel, 'Thank God she's asleep and we can have a little peace,' whereupon, without opening her eyes, she bawled '*Depuis le Jour*' right through at the top of her lungs. And so on arrival, they found Chicago plastered with what Noel called Mary's frigid little message: 'My divine breezy city! You have with you four words that spell Genius—Noel Coward, The Vortex!'

The theatre was packed on opening night but for some reason—a mystery never solved—the smart audience sat morose and mute all through the comedy of the first half and then exploded with hysterical laughter at every tragic line in the second. Their six weeks were hurriedly reduced to an ignominious two, and years later Clifton Webb was alarmed to find on his dressing-room wall at the Selwyn Theatre an indelible epitaph: NOEL COWARD DIED HERE. Socially however Noel had a fine old time; Diana Cooper and Iris Tree were there with *The Miracle* and staying in the same apartment house, the Lake Shore Drive. It was now that his loving friendship with Diana burgeoned. Diana had brought her mother, as Noel had brought his, and the two unshrinking violets, Violet Duchess of Rutland and Violet Agnes Coward, quickly became buddies, shopped together at the Piggly Wiggly market and thought America wonderful—bacon was to be bought ready sliced and packeted, imagine!—and ran merrily up and down stairs between kitchenettes with food to feed their chicks. Diana, Iris and Noel shared a wealthy Stage-Door Johnny who twice lured them to his hideously gracious home, where a table laden for Lucullus rose magically from depths beneath the floor, and where he lingered insinuatingly in his bedroom, many-mirrored and sporting an emperor-sized love-nest. But which of them was he after? Probably a romp with all three, they decided, once they were safely home.

Jack, having flung his stockbroker's bonnet over the windmill, sailed for England in the *Olympic* in the spring of 1926 with Noel, Mrs Coward and the Rolls-Royce, while Gladys stayed on in America with the Civic Raspberry Company, to Noel's annoyance. He worried on the voyage, wondering how much Lornie would welcome or resent the introduction of Jack, the hard-headed American, into their slap-dash business lives. Lornie for her part was worried too; so far she had had the office to herself and did not look forward to his advent or like his being so swiftly given power of attorney, which at that time she did not possess. But she too soon fell for his fascination and more than anything for his rapid stream of wisecracks, a form of humour new to her as it was to most people, talkies not yet having arrived. Jack was at first known as Penny Eyes—his were dark brown—then as the Baybay (pronounced Biby, perhaps a mixture of his American enjoyment of Cockney and his being slightly the youngest of the group). None of us can remember why he was also nicknamed Dab. As he is almost always referred to by one or other of these names they must be given here or much of what follows will be incomprehensible. Jack called Noel Poppa or Pop.

Such an attractive young man had an immediate social success in London. Before long Lornie, who often left verses for Noel to come home to and find on his pillow, left this (Betty Shale was Maisie Gay's understudy, a good low comedienne in her own right and a bosom chum of Lornie's):

> Just because your friend from Yale
> Climbs to heights you cannot scale
> Don't forget your secretary
> Made her curtsey to Queen Mary.

> Yes, although I fail to please
> Sutherlands and Angleseys
> And the Pembrokes find me stale
> *I* am friends with Betty Shale.

The loving friendship between Noel, Jack, Gladys and Lorn never quite recovered from a financial rift years later, and it is astonishing to find, right from the start and all through the early years, Jack's extravagance always mentioned and his trustworthiness, financial and otherwise, always in question, albeit jokingly:

> It's quite a big expense to us
> Transporting Little Dab
> He never travels in a bus
> And seldom in a cab.

A cable to Jack at sea, from Noel:

> Baybay's gone, the mousies play
> Fifteen cheques went out today
> Richmond Park is grey with sorrow
> Thirty cheques go out tomorrow.

Jack's reply:

> Baybay's got Attorney's Power
> Growing richer every hour
> In a boatload full of smarties
> Baybay's giving lots of parties.

Again from Noel:

> Darling Baybay, darling Jack
> Just a kleptomaniac
> Pinching gifts from Poppa's house
> Like a predatory louse
>
> Taking slyly without stint
> Here a photo, there a print
> Still, although you snatch and grab
> Poppa loves his darling Dab.

Jack's reply from New York:

> Why is Pop in such a pox
> I only took a priceless box
> Shut down that reproachful lay
> And write a nice successful play
> The biggest hit on this here street
> Is Noel Coward's Bitter Sweet.

Rebecca West has written of Noel, 'He was a very dignified man ... There was impeccable dignity in his sexual life, which was reticent but untainted by pretence,' and this is true. He was homosexual. There is nothing sensational to report. He enjoyed sex as much as the next man and made no secret of it, but a list of people he went to bed with would, by and large, prove uninteresting, and in any case his own good taste and behaviour over this matter must be respected. But what is interesting is his behaviour during the four or five times in his life when he fell really in love. When not in love, he could write, 'How idiotic people are when they are in love. What an age-old devastating disease.' But when he himself caught this disease there arose a resentment in him, at himself, against the unexplainable fact that he had fallen physically in love. He hated this loss of control over himself just as deeply as he loathed the loss of control brought about by drunkenness, or by drug-addiction in others. He wrote:

> I am no good at love.
> I batter it out of shape,
> Suspicion tears at my sleepless mind
> And, gibbering like an ape,
> I lie alone in the endless dark
> Knowing there's no escape.
>
> I am no good at love.
> When my easy heart I yield,
> Wild words come tumbling from my mouth
> Which should have stayed concealed
> And my jealousy turns a bed of bliss
> Into a battlefield.
>
> I am no good at love.
> I betray it with little sins,
> For I feel the misery of the end
> In the moment that it begins,
> And the bitterness of the last good-bye
> Is the bitterness that wins.

These words were written from the heart and they give an exact description of himself when in this hapless condition. What were the 'little sins'? Elsewhere he wrote, 'Cruelty, possessiveness and petty jealousy are traits you develop when in love,' and again he must be writing about himself, and if he were, he wrote truly. Physical cruelty he couldn't abide and never practised it: the cruelty was verbal; wild words did come tumbling from his mouth. His wit, though sharp, was —I think one may safely say—never cruel: try as one may, out of all the devastating remarks he made to or about other people, it is difficult to find one that can be defined as cruel. But when he was passionately in love he was not himself, and with his command of language he could plunge many a barb into the loved one's heart. As for his possessiveness, it became total at these times; utterly untypical of him when he was not obsessed. He was the least jealous of men; never envious of his fellow actors and writers or indeed of anybody, he showered praise on those who were worthy of it, praise unjaundiced by jealousy. Yet, in love, he was guilty of this vice, his jealousy of the loved one did turn the bed of bliss into a battlefield. Ever entirely honest with himself, he admitted to the guilt of these three sins and his candour only worsened his self-torture: 'Why, why, why do I do it?' The only answer there was — 'Because I cannot help it' — got to the heart of the trouble but increased his dislike of himself when in this state. He, Noel, of all people, was hopelessly out of control, yet retained enough detachment to regard himself with an examiner's eye, and what he saw he despised. Of course there were also the many moments of bliss to be enjoyed, but never quite enough, except in one rare instance, to compensate for all the self-indictment.

He fell in love for the last time at the age of fifty-eight, with someone half his age, an eventuality he had for a long time dreaded. But it happened. He wrote:

My private emotions are going through the usual familiar hoops, hoops that I fondly imagined I had discarded years ago. I am sure it is good for the soul and the spirit to fall down into the dust again but it is now and it always has been painful for me. I scale heights and tumble down lachrymose ravines. I lie awake jeering at myself and, worst of all, pitying myself. All the gallant lyrics of all the songs I have ever written rise up and mock me. To me, passionate love has always been like a tight shoe rubbing blisters on my Achilles heel. (Oi, Oi, that's enough of that.) I resent it and love it and wallow ... and I wish to God I could handle it but I never have and I know I never will.

During the months that this affair lasted, apart from the object of his affections, he had myself to whom he could open his heart; this he did endlessly, which helped, although it could not cure. The pattern as above was repeated and the same small sins committed. Oh, those mornings after a sleepless night when the loved one hadn't kept a promised tryst, or the telephone hadn't rung as had been pledged. Why, Noel wanted to know, should these idiotically small things cause an actual physical pain, an ache which he literally could feel and from which he had suffered throughout his insomniac night? Over this subject Noel's sense of humour deserted him and he lost what had always been one of his greatest strengths — his ability to laugh at himself. 'Why do you think I suffer like this over anything so trivial?' he asked one morning. 'Because,' I said with truth, 'you're like Mrs Gummidge. You feel things more than other people.' At the thought of being compared with Mrs Gummidge, Noel fell back in a torrent of laughter and could not stop; he hadn't laughed like that for weeks, and from then on Mrs Gummidge greatly helped him: 'Now I'm being Mrs Gummidge again. I must stop it.' Six months of this dragged by until at last his good old 'geographical distance' came to his aid and from the safe vantage point of Jamaica Noel could write:

Now all is peace and sunshine and I am trying, not as yet very successfully, to adjust myself to a slower tempo. I have slept and slept and dreamed too much. I can remember—I can remember— the months of November and December and the ecstasy and the nightmare. I know I couldn't bear to live it all over again but I wouldn't be without it. Of course I regret much of my own foolishness because I should have been old enough to know better, but if I had been old enough to know better none of it would have happened and if none of it had happened I should not now be happier and more contented and a good deal duller and dryer. My only valid excuse is that, at moments, the pain was unendurable and when the heart is in pain it is liable to strike out.

We sometimes lived those months over again in reminiscence, Noel praying such an experience would never occur again, and it did not. Then we would talk about the importance of loving as opposed to being in love, and Noel would quote from that fount of wisdom, old Madame Hubrecht, the mother of his Dutch friend Daan: 'It's your capacity for loving, not whom you love, that matters.'

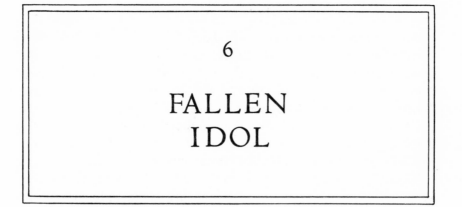

6

FALLEN
IDOL

THE year 1926 passed happily for Noel. Life took on new lustre viewed through Rolls-Royce windows, and he revelled in the assurance derived from his now solidly established international stardom. He delightedly gave his views on any question his countless interviewers cared to ask, his opinions on Flappers and Marriage evidently being the two most eagerly anticipated by readers. In June, Jane Cowl opened in *Easy Virtue* in London, smashing the Venus de Milo to even greater effect than she had in New York. This production remained memorable to Noel for the appearance in his life of the youthful Adrianne Allen. She played Nina Vansittart, one of the characters 'littered about the hall' in the third act, 'attired in a strikingly original rose-taffeta frock, with a ribbon of the same shade encircling her hair the wrong way—giving more the impression of a telephone apparatus', and, to use Adrianne's own words, 'swinging her Dorothy Bag and squealing at the gentlemen'.

Basil Dean, who directed the play in New York and in London, and to whom Noel had stood up so bravely as a boy, had now re-entered Noel's life for the next few years and five more productions as a director. Their association is puzzling to understand, for he was anything but pleasant to work with and Noel hated his ill-treatment of small-part actors. But there was a strange rapport between them; Noel had got his measure early on and had great fun watching the different methods the big stars employed to get their way with him—Edna Best with placidity, Madge Titheradge with a sort of determined indifference, and Jane Cowl fighting him all along the line. Ivor Novello laughed openly in his face; after the climax of one of his long and furious rages, Ivor asked demurely, 'Basil, is 'oo twoss wiv us?' Dean was soon to direct three of Noel's direst failures, but at the time of which I am writing Noel had faith in him as a director and jointly they must have had optimistic hopes for the future, for later this year Noel is writing on grand, pale grey paper headed in crimson BASIL DEAN INC, 'English Plays In America', with an office at 1674 Broadway. Meanwhile in London they got through the production of *The Queen Was in the Parlour*, Noel's only expedition into Ruritania, prompted by his boyhood admiration both for Anthony Hope's romantic *The Prisoner of Zenda* and for his dear Madge Titheradge, who starred in it and brought the rather cardboard drama splendidly to life.

When Noel tired of being cabin'd and confined in the villa at Dockenfield his thoughts turned, as did his mother's, to somewhere near the sea and that part of Kent where they had been so happy a few years earlier. Long searching and much advertising in the *Kentish Times* drew blanks until out of the blue came a letter from Mr Body, who had been their neighbour at St Mary's-in-the-Marsh, wanting to let Goldenhurst Farm at Aldington.

I, born west of the Medway and therefore a Kentish Man, knew every mile of the Marsh as minutely as Noel and loved it as devotedly, so that when I went to work for him and found to my delight that much of my time was to be spent at Goldenhurst Farm, it proved a bond between us—an unexpected bond, as strong as it was tranquil, far removed from the exciting, often agitating theatrical hullabaloo of London. The Marsh's most magical moments are at dusk, when mists rise and hang above it, when natives fastened their windows in the old days, fearful of the ague. Conveniently, this time would more or less coincide with the first drink of the evening, or in high summer after dinner when we would have another drink, romanticise and repeat old tales of the encroaching sea beneath which the bells of buried churches can still be heard, and of the smugglers for which the Marsh was famous. Once we got on to this subject—which made a welcome change from harrowing stories of leading ladies' outrageous behaviour over their wigs or dresses—and the last glimmer of light had gone, Noel loved to talk about the smugglers and recite:

> Five and twenty ponies
> Trotting through the dark
> Brandy for the Parson
> 'Baccy for the Clerk
> Laces for a lady, letters for a spy
> Watch the wall my darling
> While the Gentlemen ride by!

In spite of its grand-sounding name, Goldenhurst Farm itself turned out to be almost as poky as Dockenfield, though it did also have a barn and a lopsided new wing with a tin roof painted pink. They liked the tranquil atmosphere, though, and thought it would do for the time being. I can only write of it as I knew it ten years later and for the twenty years after that. By this time Noel had bought and transformed it, together with the surrounding 139 acres; the land Noel had so little dreamed would one day be his when he had gazed out across it from Aldington Knoll, across to the miles of low-lying Marsh beyond, some of it below sea level so that the distant sea looked high up in the sky. Lights on the French coast twinkled on clear nights like stars in a straight line, and far off to the right Dungeness lighthouse flashed its beams. The greater part of the property was leased out as working farm- and pasture-land except for a pretty bluebell wood, where poachers poached happily away for rabbits, undisturbed except for Old John the gardener's occasional angry shouts and stick-brandishing. The drive ran from the house through the wood to the main entrance, and was the ritual walk for Noel and his guests on Sunday afternoons. Young poplar trees were planted on each side of it, and it was quickly christened Twig Avenue by Lornie. Two ducks on the pond across the drive from the front door soon multiplied and for some long-forgotten reason were collectively known as Louisa ('Louisa are quacking like mad'). The pond came perilously near the edge of the drive and we once watched with fascination a car slide slowly backwards into it, till Jeanne de Casalis cried dramatically, 'My God, it's *my* car!' and we all sprang into action. Noel's Auntie Ida unknowingly dropped her imitation fox fur into the pond when getting out of the car, so she and Mrs Coward retraced their drive over the Marsh until nightfall to look for it and then called the police to send out a search-party. It surfaced next morning, covered with green slime; Old John shouted, 'There's a bloody great rabbit dead in the pond,' and fetched a long rake to pull it to shore. The parlourmaid went to Auntie Ida, still in bed, and said, 'What would you say if I told you they'd found your pussy?' Auntie Ida, after a sleepless night, said, 'Oh Ellen, please don't joke about it; it's far too serious.' Ellen then produced the dreadful object from behind her, washed it, and it spent the day with its jaws clenched on a piece of string from which it hung suspended over the radiator, Auntie Ida gently brushing the fur up the wrong way to restore it to its former dubious lustre.

There was a fig-tree, by no means barren, close to the front door; a croquet lawn—scene of many vicious battles—with bulging herbaceous borders nearby and to one side a mulberry tree which brought forth large and luscious fruit to stain our mouths dark purple. In my memory eternal summer gilds it yet and covers the house with roses and heady-scented honeysuckle, though Noel always put these sun-flooded recollections into perspective by pointing out that we never poked our noses outside the door when it was pouring with rain. Old farmhouses in books should always be rambling: Goldenhurst wasn't until Noel made it ramble by joining the farmhouse proper to the barn by a long passage. Off the passage he built a brand-new guest room, instantly haunted. The quite large barn he made his own, with a blue and white library at ground level and above this his bedroom, beamed with aged oak, and a bath- and dressing-room. Between the end of the passage and his barn he built a drawing-room always called the Big—though it might just as well have been known as the Huge—Room. The new rambling part was made to look as old as the farmhouse by the use of weathered brick and tiles, and all was made lovely inside by Gladys, Jack and David Herbert who successfully combed the Marsh, Folkestone, Deal and Hythe for antiques. They also went to a sale at Herstmonceaux Castle and returning with, among other finds, two large and triumphant trophies: a seven-foot-long Grinling Gibbons carving of a beribboned garland with a lascivious cherub's head in the centre, and an enormous pair of wings of gilded Cornish tin sprouting from an hourglass. Syrie Maugham did her costly best to supply what else was needed in the way of furnishings, especially in the Big Room, where the wings rightly had place of honour over the fireplace, in front of which stood one of the longest sofas ever seen, designed by Syrie. Two grand pianos stood back to back, on which before my time Noel had played jazzy double piano with Kreisler, and during my time with Richard Rodgers, Richard Addinsell, Ivy St Helier, Hugh Martin, Joseph Cotten's wife Lenore and anyone else who could come up to his mettle. Double piano improvisation was his favourite diversion, and when he had a musician of Kay Thompson's calibre, with a quick-witted brilliance to equal his own, one of his greatest joys. Kay was his partner *par excellence* at this game of skill, sitting at the piano with angular abandon, her legs at right angles to an ordinary mortal's position, one ankle crossed on the other knee, and carelessly—it seemed—leading or following Noel into double firework variations on an improvised theme. The whole of the big room had a feeling of Syrie's influence—greatly *à la mode* at the time—with the walls white rough-cast and the materials of pale beige and gentle faded greens.

Noel's own taste in decoration, when allowed to blossom later on, by which time he was 'sick to death of beige', turned out to be for bright colours unexpectedly and intrepidly put together to good effect. But to the end, for his own rooms, he remained faithful to walls of white.

Basil Dean had an overwhelming success with his production of Margaret Kennedy's *The Constant Nymph* in September. The starry cast included Cathleen Nesbitt, Elissa Landi and Mary Clare, with Edna Best touchingly constant as Tessa and Noel tweedy and pipe-smoking as the rather fierce Lewis Dodd. The part was long and taxing and he hadn't wanted to play it in the first place: it is not surprising that his nerves, already taut and then overstretched by his frenetic activities of the past two years, finally snapped and after only three weeks he played one whole performance in unexplainable tears. He was given strychnine injections and put to bed for a week. He then, against doctor's orders, insisted on sailing for New York to start rehearsals of *This Was a Man*, a comedy which Noel had written in Palermo earlier that summer, and which has never been produced, so far as is known, in England.

During his absence on the voyage, his first serious play, *The Rat Trap*, in fact his first play written at the age of eighteen, was given its one and only production at the Everyman, and should never have been taken out of the drawer in which it had languished for eight years, most people thinking of it as a retrogressive step in his career as a playwright. He called the last act an inconclusive shambles, based on the inaccurate assumption that the warring egos of the man and wife will simmer down into domestic bliss merely because the wife is about to have a baby. *The Rat Trap* is one of the two plays of his own writing that he never saw performed, and from what he heard from eyewitnesses he hadn't missed much.

Noel's stay in New York and the general climate of it is best portrayed by himself in these extracts from some of his long weekly letters to his mother:

October 28th, 1926: Darling, Everything is going very well here, I've got Francine Larrimore, A. E. Matthews and Nigel Bruce for *This Was a Man* which is rehearsing now. I went to Eva [le Gallienne]'s first night and it was more frightful than anything in the world, she was terrible, the production awful, and the play lousy! Two of Gladys's sets were very good ... Jack sends dearest love and is looking after me beautifully. Jack and I have a very grand office of our own in this building with Noel Coward Inc. on the door in gold letters. It's very cheap so we're going to keep it permanently—we must have somewhere to put our papers and contracts (all three!) ... I haven't heard from [Philip] Tonge yet but I dread the telephone. Don't miss me *too* much.

November 3rd: ... we open cold at the Klaw Theatre on the 16th, my lucky date, they're all going to be frightfully good, Francine Larrimore particularly. She's small and red haired and very sexy and as far as I can gather has already made plans about every man in the cast so she ought to be well in her element. ... I'm still searching wildly for someone to play *Fallen Angels* with Ruth Gordon but it's very difficult. Still, perseverance is my middle name. (Basil is directing) *This Was a Man* beautifully and has great ideas about *Semi-Monde* if we can raise enough money. About twenty new buildings have shot up into the air since last year and five million more motor cars, consequently one can't move anywhere ... Gertie opens next Monday in the new Gershwin show ...

November 11th: Here goes for my weekly letter. The moment the play opens I am going away for a fortnight to Hot [he meant White Sulphur] Springs which is in the mountains and very quiet because I want to write a little. I shall only send you the address in case you fall down stairs or burn your finger or get pneumonia or have twins or something. Nigel Bruce is driving everybody mad by being completely and abjectly stupid and trying far too hard and not listening to what he's told and it's all frightful but we feel it will be all right on the Night! Please don't be in the least annoyed by [Hannen] Swaffer's remarks—he doesn't worry me at all. The more frightful things he says the more sympathy *I* get and it doesn't matter what the papers say anyhow good or bad. I'm far beyond being harmed in any way by the Press. Gertie opened in *Oh Kay* here on Monday and was really marvellous, she carried the whole show and made a huge success. I spend my time pursuing elusive actresses for *Fallen Angels* but they're all *very* tiresome. Linda Porter arrived yesterday and I am gracing a grand party given for her tonight. I spent this week end on Long Island in an enormous house party with all the Vanderbilts and Astors and Shufflebottoms—altogether Society's pet. The dining room sounds perfectly charming. I'm longing to see it all.

November 18th: ... I had a tremendous party given for me last night and it was rather fun, George Gershwin played and we all carried

on like one o'clock. Jack took me to the Yale v. Princeton Football
game on Saturday. It really was a marvellous sight and terribly
exciting—65,000 people all screaming their heads off. Jack lost all
control and beat me on the head whenever Yale scored anything.
I shall miss you dreadfully at my first night—It's going to be very
smart and there's a huge demand for seats. I shall want my grey-
haired Mother hung with Woolworth pearls to clutch! But never
mind I'll write and tell you all. I met Jack's complete family and
Mamma is writing to you to tell you how well I look—I haven't
had a day's illness since I left England except for my usual frightful
heart attacks and my lumbago, varicose veins and that dreadful
hacking couch that *never* stops but everyone is very kind and my
eyesight is slowly returning! All love darling.

November 25th: Shadowstone, Lawrenceville, New Jersey.
Darling, This is Thanksgiving Day and I'm spending it in the
Wilson home en route for White Sulphur. The play dear has *all* the
earmarks of being a failure! Gladys and I sat grandly in a box on
the First Night and watched it falling flatter and flatter and I must
admit we got bad giggles! They were all expecting something
very dirty indeed after the English Censor banning it and they were
bitterly disappointed [the Lord Chamberlain had refused it a
licence]. Francine Larrimore was very good and A. E. Matthews
too tho' he forgot most of his lines. Nigel Bruce who has never
understood what it was all about from the first was all right but
extremely dull and Auriol [Lee] was good but also dull—for some
unknown reason they played it so slowly that there was time to
go round the corner and have an ice cream soda between every
line. We suffered a little during the first Act but gave up suffering
after that and rather enjoyed it. There weren't any real calls for
Author so I remained coyly in oblivion. Of course it may pick up
and be a success but I doubt it. I find on close reflection that I
am as unmoved by failure as I am by success which is a *great*
comfort. Perhaps *Fallen Angels* will go better and if it doesn't I
don't really mind. I like *writing* the plays anyhow and if people
don't like them that's their loss. I hope you won't be depressed
about it because I'm really as bright as a button. I always get bored
anyhow if everything isn't a smashing success *immediately*! I've
just started a play for Marie Tempest but as there are several
illegitimate children in it I doubt if Lord Cromer [the Lord
Chamberlain] will care very deeply for it. We've had an offer for

the film rights of *The Young Idea* which was *very* surprising, it will mean about Three Thousand Pounds so that's quite cosy ... Oh dear I've made it up with Osbert Sitwell and it's all very funny—I wrote him a note saying that as we were both in a Foreign Country we ought to put an end to The Feud then he came round and suggested quite pleasantly that I should apologise publicly to Edith in all the papers! I gave him an old-fashioned look and explained gently that he was very very silly indeed which he seemed to understand perfectly and we parted very amicably. It really was becoming a bore because he wasn't being asked anywhere poor dear owing to my popularity being the greater so that's that. The Queen of Roumania with son and daughter came to the party after the First Night so we were all very grand. Reinhardt arrives in December and is very anxious to do *Semi-Monde* which would be one in the eye for everyone and place me on such an intellectual plane that I doubt if I should ever come down! I have just eaten the most enormous Thanksgiving Dinner Turkey and plum pudding and I'm blown out like a football but look very sweet. *The Constant Nymph* opens on the 9th and I don't *think* Glen Anders will be as good as your handsome son. I've written some nice new songs. All love my dearest darling, your unwanted unappreciated unabashed uncared for and untidy son. Snoopie. I do *hope* you won't think I'm smiling through my tears!

Jack accompanied Noel to White Sulphur Springs, and he wrote happily enough from there that they were in bed by ten, and were up early riding for two hours through pinewood forests and past wild gurgling torrents, Noel for once having found a horse that was mild and sweet, if a little flatulent. 'I lie flat on my back and write all the afternoon, a lovely comedy for Marie Tempest [*The Marquise*], at five o'clock we swim, laze about until dinner, after which they show a film in the ballroom. There is an awful married couple in the next room and they fight like cats—Jack and I spend hours with our ears glued to the wall. I'm drinking a lot of milk and getting *far* too fat!' He wrote on December 8th: 'I am sending this cheque early so as to get to you in time for Christmas, £5 for Poppa, £5 for Baby Erik, £5 for Vivacious Vida and £7 for yourself and don't spend it all on sweets. We are leaving here tonight for New York. I'm feeling wonderfully well the holiday has done me a tremendous amount of good!'

But all was far from well. Noel had all this time been dissembling to his mother about the true state of his health, and had been keeping his worries and troubles from her. At last he had to tell her the truth and wrote from the Gladstone in New York on December 14th:

Dearest Darling, I will now proceed to explain all! The moment I got back here I began to ache in every limb and have headaches. So three days ago I called in a specialist who examined me thoroughly, you will be relieved to hear that organically I am completely healthy—lungs, heart, everything perfect, but I am in a bad way as far as nerves are concerned—he said that I have been living on nervous energy for years and now it has given out and that I must go away at once! I was about to do a Revue ... but that must be sacrificed. He said a long sea voyage was the thing and a complete break with my present interests for at least two months. I know he's right so I am going to Sarawak—I leave for San Francisco on Saturday, Jack goes with me as far as Chicago, I sail from San Francisco on Christmas Day and go to Honolulu, Yokohama, Kobe, Shanghai and Hong Kong where I change boats and go on to Singapore where the Rajah [of Sarawak]'s yacht is sent for me ... I feel I must get away from all the people I know for a while, not only from the point of view of health but for my work as well. From now onwards I'm not going to work so hard, Jack will have charge of all contracts and things and I shan't think about anything. It will be heavenly to be stuck on a boat with *nothing* to do, I shall probably be bored stiff at first but there will be lovely places to see and I'm a keen traveller. Nerves are extraordinary things, I sleep for eleven hours and wake up *dead* tired with legs aching as tho' I'd walked ten miles! It's not serious yet as I haven't had a breakdown but the Doctor says I'm on the verge of one and warding it off is no good—I must get right away and clinch it finally. I expect your vivid imagination is now at work conjuring up pictures of your beloved son gibbering like a maniac and telling everyone he's the Empress Eugénie, but as a matter of fact I'm not the Empress Eugénie, I'm Napoleon! I'm dining tonight with Mary Garden and Reinhardt, I'm allowed to go out at night as long as I am *in bed* by twelve, so you see I'm not dying. I know I shall be dreadfully lonely and bored on that dreary boat but ... it will be nice staying with the Sarawaks and seeing the dawn come up like thunder out of China 'crost the bay, wouldn't it be awful if I became a second Rudyard Kipling. I shall be arriving back *just* at the right time for Aldington and the Marsh —oh Darling I do hope you won't cry much at the thought of two

more months without me, but you *do* see don't you? If I came
back to England now I'd be embroiled with Marie Tempest and
Basil and Films *however* much I tried to avoid them and I should
rush over to Paris and back and go to First Nights and do myself
in! I'll cable you the name of the boat and everything, cable me on
Christmas Day to San Francisco. I know I shall be terribly Mother-
sick Oh Dear Oh Dear. Your Wandering boy, Robinson Crusoe.

Jack wholeheartedly disapproved of Noel's violent decision to go off
alone for more than two months when he was in such a precarious state
of health, refused to say goodbye in Chicago and insisted on staying
with him until the last possible moment. Noel wrote from the Fairmont
Hotel, San Francisco, on Christmas Eve:

Darling, Here I am in California at last! Jack is here with me and
he goes back to New York tomorrow after I sail. He's been so
sweet trailing all out here—I don't know what I should have done
without him. We stopped in Chicago to see Syrie [Maugham]
and I just had lunch and dinner and went quietly to the theatre
and straight back to bed and felt perfectly *awful*. I get tired far too
quickly so the sooner I get well away from everybody the better.
I feel rather scarified going off all by myself but I know it's the
only really wise plan. I shall be home about the 8th of March ...
I save more than a week by getting off at Naples and coming
overland ... Have my little white bed ready at the cottage as I shall
probably wire you to meet me at Dover in Lulu [Mrs Coward's
car] and I'll go straight to Aldington. I'm looking forward to
coming home with wild excitement and my one comfort over this
trip is that it's all on the way once I start! What a Godsend that
cottage was—It's the *greatest* comfort to me to feel that you're
away from Ebury Street and have a nice peaceful place to wait for
your Wandering Boy!
Christmas Day: I'm finishing off this letter today I've just got
all the family cables which I loved. San Francisco is really divine,
we motored out to Burlinghame to lunch, everything green
and fresh and roses out! The streets are steep like Edinburgh,
and Chinatown right in the middle of everything. There's a Rock
just outside the town by the Golden Gate *covered* with seals!
They're so sweet. I sail at four o'clock this afternoon. It's now
9 A.M. which means about 5 P.M. in England if you've had
your Christmas dinner I expect you're all lying about stuffed.
Diana and Iris send their love, they're on the same floor as we

are, we had a grand party last night with Reinhardt. When you cable just put Well—Love because it will be expensive. I'll do the same from every port. Good bye now my darling—Give my dear love to Daddy, Vida and Erik and all. Be a good Snig and don't have too many nightmares about shipwrecks, this is *not* the Typhoon season! Hugs and kisses, Snoop.

Jack turned once and waved as Noel watched him walk down the gangway from the *President Pierce* just before she sailed that Christmas afternoon. Now Noel was quite alone as the doctor had ordered, cut off from all familiar faces of friends and family, and on his way to unknown destinations. He missed Jack, and at the same time knew that he had to get away from him. It must have been on this first of his numerous long and solitary journeys that he discovered his personal panacea for all disturbances and crises, mundane or emotional: geographical distance. This cure-all stood him in good stead when in the centre of many a turmoil in the future; 'I can't wait for the end of March,' he would say, 'geographical distance will do the trick,' and it always did, for him. But now, at the age of just twenty-seven, he had not yet found this comfort: the immediate future seemed grey, for the first time his mind was inactive and remained blank of plans; his imagination and even his urge to write non-existent. He despaired of himself during the seven-day passage to Honolulu, his unhappiness magnified by nightmare uncertainties; had too much happened to him too soon, had he burnt himself out, his talents already spent? Could he ever write again? Even sleep, always his especial solace, his great restorer, was denied him night after night until he began to have fears for his sanity.

Exactly two weeks before Christmas Day the specialist in New York had declared Noel to be organically sound, and there is no doubt that throughout his life more than a few of his illnesses were unconsciously self-induced. This was probably the first of them, certainly the first major example, but psychosomatic illnesses are nevertheless known to be positive and real and by the time the ship docked at Honolulu Noel was feverishly weak, with a temperature of a hundred and three. Louise Dillingham, at that time the uncrowned queen of the island with her husband Walter as king, had arranged a large welcoming luncheon for Noel; he could barely remain upright, everything swam before his eyes and he fled from the table before the end. As there was no question of continuing the cruise, he then had to face the ordeal of packing and getting himself and his luggage off the ship and, after enduring an endless half-hour in Customs, to the Moana Hotel at Waikiki, where he collapsed into bed.

He woke to find Paul Withington in the room. Paul Withington was the Dillinghams' doctor, and Noel never forgot him, his calm manner or his infinite patience and understanding. For a week Noel kept to his bed in the hotel, gazing out at the bright blue sea, the emerald shallows in the lagoon, the dazzling yellow sand and the beach-boys riding with effortless agility the long rollers from the far-off reef. As he watched he wondered whether he would ever recover enough strength to use his limbs again. Paul Withington could diagnose nothing until from an X-ray he settled for Noel's old TB scar which gave Noel something to fight against, and on the good doctor's advice he decided to stay for at least another month and do nothing but lie in the sun and fill his lungs with the beneficial air. The Dillinghams owned a ranch thirty miles away at Mokuleia, among their miles of bananas and sugar-cane. They placed this at his disposal and did him the supreme benevolence of never coming near him. Apart from Paul Withington's pleasant weekly visits, bringing books from the Dillinghams and flowers from their garden, he saw no one except briefly at meals which he ate with the French-speaking caretaker and his wife. His only companion was a vicious bull-terrier called Auguste, who growled and bared his teeth until Noel offered his hand and said, 'You want to bite my hand? All right, go on then, bite it. Go on, bite it.' Auguste looked at him shamefacedly, then with admiration and even affection and from that moment never left his side.

Noel couldn't prevent one tune, *A Room with a View*, from tumbling into his mind one day while dozing in the sun, but apart from this—which wasn't work—did no work whatsoever throughout his long stay. He read and reflected while burning himself black in the sun, and gave himself enough time, he said, to round up an imposing array of past mistakes:

> People, I decided, were the danger. People were greedy and predatory, and if you gave them the chance they would steal unscrupulously the heart and soul out of you without really wanting to or even meaning to. From now on there was going to be very little energy wasted, and very little vitality spilled unnecessarily.

At last a day came when he wearied of gaudy tropics and his mind's eye ached for the softer greens and gentle greys of Kent marshes. He decided there and then to pack his traps; the longing for England and home had become too insistent to be denied. When recounting this Hawaiian episode, he almost always ended, 'I pulled myself up by the bootstraps.' Somehow, from the depths of dark despair, he had surfaced to a more stable physical and mental tranquillity. He dropped his leis one by one into the sea as the ship pulled out, and his wishes were granted; he returned many times to Hawaii, always with gratitude.

The rejuvenated Noel returned to New York so invigorated that every prospect pleased him, and Gladys and Jack appeared to his fresh eye to look younger and nicer than ever. Lornie, too, he found in fine fettle when he got to London. He made haste on his first night there to the Criterion to see Marie Tempest in *The Marquise*, and enjoyed the curious and rare experience of watching his character come to life exactly as he had imagined the Marquise de Kestournel when he had written the part in White Sulphur Springs. From the moment she walked in through the french windows, Miss Tempest looked radiantly delicate, 'everything I had envisaged; the tricorne hat, the twinkle in her eye, the swift precision of movement,' and she brought to all his lines every crisp and witty inflection he could have hoped for. This experience was never to be so perfectly repeated: a peculiar pleasure.

Noel found out that the freehold and the land of Goldenhurst Farm were for sale at what was even then an absurdly low price, and quickly bought it. During the very first weekend he and Jack spent there after the return from America, they discovered that above the shoddy plaster ceilings were oak beams which were not only beautiful but, when surveyed, proved free from decay. Behind and below layers of unlovely wallpaper and makeshift linoleum, Goldenhurst was in fact a fine old seventeenth-century farmhouse. The 'heaps of plans' Noel had promised his mother in his letters were now, in the spring and summer of 1927, carried out to his and Jack's satisfaction, if not always to Mrs Coward's. The transformations already described were made, and although she and Auntie Vida continued their lifelong squabbling they were settled happily enough in their quarters. They resented the suggestion that they should be moved to the 'new' part, and Mrs Coward accused Noel and Jack of wanting to get his family 'out of the way and show off to their new-found crowds of grand friends'. Noel soon solved this by leaving them where they were and reserving the so-called new part for himself, Jack, and the house-guests, but no sooner had this more spacious half been expensively beautified by Syrie than Mrs Coward found the old part poky and gave large cock-tail parties in the Big Room to as many locals as she could round up as soon as Noel's back was turned. As Noel pointed out to her, it was now she who was doing the showing-off.

Up until this time Noel had been only too glad to leave the household arrangements to her; she had been mistress of their various habitations and loved doing all she could to make him comfortable and happy. Now for the first time she felt left out of things, of 'her' side of his life. Also Noel felt more drawn towards his Aunt Vida, who kept quietly in the background, unlike his mother. Scenes were made and acrimonious letters written and posted or left for Noel to find on arrival; as these letters are obviously written in the haste of hot temper they are not unnaturally incompletely dated but the following is a typical example. It seems strange that Noel should have kept them and not —with his equally quick temper—have torn them up or thrown them in the fire. Perhaps he felt that he simply had to take them to London to show to Lornie, for it is she who filed them, under M for Mum:

She [Vida] has been a mischief-maker all her life, and has done me any amount of harm. She has a wicked and unkind tongue, that is why she has no friends, or ever has had, and she has always been eaten up with jealousy. She can't be jealous of you, so you don't know much about her. My deafness has always been a source of joy to her. Vida should never have been here, and now you will not find it easy to get her out of this house, in spite of my unkindness, for she loves the luxury and grandeur—*I* love the place too but I would far rather have peace. So wouldn't it be possible to find a cottage for Arthur and me to live in? Arthur would live his life and I could live mine. It is much better for *me* to go as I am up against Jack too. I ought never to have mentioned the French room, fruit on the sideboard etc. etc. but having been mistress of a house for so many years, it was difficult though very stupid of me not to realise that Jack was boss. I promise never to make any remark about anything again. I have too independent a spirit, and feel my *entire* dependence keenly. I should have had a decent husband to keep me in my old age, then you would have had no right to speak to me as you did last Thursday. It is untrue to say that I am spoilt, and too grand, or that I am unkind to Vida. Your not coming this weekend made me a little more sad and unhappy, if that is possible, but that doesn't seem to matter much to anybody. Snig.

Don't worry about Vida being wretched, she is wildly excited and as her health is so wonderful, much better than mine or Arthur's, you may safely count I think on her outliving us both. You are quite at liberty to show this letter to Vida, or Jack.

Noel allowed the year 1927 to pass without himself making an appearance on the stage of any kind; the first time this had happened since his debut as a boy actor sixteen years before and most likely the result of the fright his breakdown had given him and of his resolution never again to overdraw on his reserves of energy. He did however finish a play that summer called *Home Chat*, and then, all unconscious of its doom, went off gaily to Venice for a holiday with Cole and Linda Porter, the three of them perpetuated with Elsa Maxwell in some famous snapshots, including one of Lady Diana Cooper standing on her head.

He returned to start rehearsals in optimistic high spirits and all went smoothly and suspiciously well; but Basil Dean had once more directed the play at a snail's pace which even Madge Titheradge's lively tempo could not quicken on the first night. The audience fidgeted, a smell of disaster little by little permeated the theatre and the evening ended with volleys of boos from pit and gallery. Noel with mistaken bravery took the then customary author's call and in the hush that followed his appearance a voice called clearly, 'We expected better.' Noel retorted quick as a wink, 'So did I,' and this brisk exchange just about summed up everybody's attitude towards the fiasco.

Worse was soon to come. The decision had already been made to put *Sirocco* into rehearsal and there was no going back on this for Noel or anybody else concerned, in spite of *Home Chat*'s failure. This was yet another youthful play that ought not to have been taken out of the drawer, but Basil Dean had for a long while been anxious to produce it and Noel did his best to tidge it up. The reader may remember that the play was inspired by the rather tawdry *festa* that Gladys and Noel had attended in Alassio in 1921 and, as they had arranged in the pact they made so long ago, Gladys designed the sets and clothes. Frances Doble and Ivor Novello were the two glamorous stars, though as it turned out neither of them at that time had enough weight or experience to carry their difficult parts in so shaky a play. The catastrophic first night of *Sirocco* marked the most spectacular failure of Noel's life in the theatre, to remain as deeply engraved on his memory as that of *The Vortex* was, for exactly the opposite reason. Not only the gallery but the entire house seemed to Noel to have been hostile from the start and by the end the theatre became a bedlam of noises—catcalls, boos, hisses and raspberries. Noel, by that time fighting mad, walked on to centre stage and added fuel to the conflagration by bowing very low as he kissed Frances Doble's hand, thus sticking his bottom out at the truculent audience, and then, without looking at them, marched contemptuously off again. When he did come back the fearful noise abated as he led Frances Doble forward, but unfortunately she could only, with tears streaming, utter the words she had prepared: 'Ladies and Gentlemen, this is the happiest moment of my life.' This was too much for Ivor, who typically got the giggles and caused Noel to laugh outright, which so enraged the gallery that some of them spat at him when he eventually left by the stage door.

Noel's first impulse on reading the explosion of abuse in the press the next morning was to leave the country, but he wisely took Lorn, Gladys and Jack to lunch at the Ivy instead, to face the music and be seen by 'everybody'. Noel observed that Ivor took failure with the same grace with which he had always taken success, and had decided on the same tactic himself: there Ivor was at a nearby table with his own coterie. Like Noel he had the gift of resilience, his gaiety seemed genuine enough and so the two tables joined up for coffee over which they sat laughing loud and long.

Sirocco is the only instance of Ivor and Noel working together professionally, but they had become and always remained boon companions since they first met in Manchester in 1917, each recognizing and respecting in the other the same qualities: strength of character, loyalty, generosity, determination to succeed in their different ways in the theatre, and what is known today as pressing on regardless. Not unnaturally, as they were both playwrights and composers, it was widely thought by public and press alike that they therefore must be rivals, when—to my knowledge in Noel's case and I feel sure I can say the same for Ivor's—there was not one scrap of jealousy between them. Noel admired the lovely melodies that flowed from Ivor with no apparent effort; his admiration was less unbounded when it came to Ivor's straight comedies and the books of his musicals. They were honest with each other about such matters, and on two occasions— Ivor's *Downhill* and *The Rat*—Noel was called in by anxious friends, Constance Collier and Sir Gerald du Maurier, to deal with the grave situation. There were very serious talks indeed over luncheon at the Ivy about Ivor's terrible new play: 'You must deal with it, you are the only one he will listen to. We must all go down to Brighton and you will see for yourself; it is too ghastly for words, we cannot *allow* him to bring it in. You must stop him.' Noel did as he was bid and told Ivor the uncompromising truth, to which he appeared to listen gratefully, then did exactly what he had planned to do all along; open in the West End where the plays ran for many months to audiences packed with Ivor's adoring fans.

Noel went on trying, even after these experiences; he would go to Ivor's latest play and writhe with embarrassment at some of the dialogue and acting and then steel himself to go round to Ivor's dressing-room and face him. Before he had time to speak, Ivor would smile delightedly, hug him and make a noise difficult to describe—a long drawn out A-a-a-a-ah, in which he combined deep pleasure and complete satisfaction: 'A-a-a-a-ah, ducky. I *knew* you'd like it!' Looking back on all this with affectionate recollection, Noel used to say, 'He always defeated me. All along the line.'

After the failure of *Home Chat*, the absolute débacle of *Sirocco* might well have deterred a lesser man to the point of ending his career. Noel admits to a certain vague scurry of apprehensions, and that inside he was scared. To offset these debits of self-doubt he had little on the credit side to comfort him, he had no new play or even an idea for one, and *Sirocco* was the last of the small pile of plays which had been for so long his standby in the drawer. To start all over again—which is what he would have to do—would require much more courage than he had needed ten years before when he had had more than most men's share of youthful assurance and no self-doubts whatever. Later he would state that these failures one after the other had been salutary, had pulled him up with a jerk; indeed, he would maintain he had been lucky in having to suffer them at exactly the right time and that few other young playwrights had been granted his good fortune. After a long run of success the pendulum of public favour must, it seems, swing the other way and he would watch and wait for his young successors to prove whether or not they had enough guts to survive this dip.

Noel in fact realised quite quickly that the *Sirocco* affair was only a nine days' wonder, if that; a ripple in the small theatrical pond soon to dissolve, forgotten by everybody except himself. Later still, and with more equanimity, he could admit that the failures of *Sirocco*, *The Rat Trap*, *This Was a Man* and *Home Chat* were deserved. They were nowhere near good enough, as has been proved by the fact that, though Heinemann in England and Doubleday in America gallantly published all four in Volume Three of their six volumes of Noel's *Play Parade*, they are, out of all his plays, the only ones not revived, nor are they done in repertory or by amateurs, and Volume Three never sold very well either.

But at the time, November 1928, in his dire situation, Noel needed all the stamina and pluck he could summon up. The faith of his intimates in his future remained of course unimpaired, and he was also greatly helped by Charles B. Cochran, who, when the first shock had subsided, began to go ahead confidently with the nebulous plans for a revue as though nothing had happened. What is more, this time, without being asked, he charged Noel with the whole show, music book and lyrics, eventually to be called *This Year of Grace*.

Some time before this, Lynn and Alfred had come to England bubbling over with the idea that Noel should play Alfred's part in Sam Behrman's comedy *The Second Man*, which they had played in, and enjoyed, in New York. He had agreed and was therefore committed to Messrs Macleod and Mayer who, to his pleased surprise in the still prevailing anti-Coward climate, would not hear of him relinquishing the part. But he was still haunted by small forebodings about appearing before another possibly cruel audience, especially as he had to play an author and be called upon at a certain point to tear up one of his own manuscripts with a bitter cry of 'Trash, trash, trash!' Would some wag cry out fervently, 'Hear, hear!' and the gallery hoot with derision? Not at all, the reception on his entrance was polite verging on warm and next day he received considerable praise for his performance, the critics for the first time taking him seriously as an actor, though some put their good opinion in the annoying form of stating that he was much better as an actor than a writer. 'The world will readily lose an unequal dramatist for a player of such quality,' said one. The dialogue of S. N. Behrman's play was witty and sophisticated and there were those who made up their minds that it was Noel, too frightened to face more criticism, who had really written it cowering behind a pen-name.

The three other characters in *The Second Man* were played by Zena Dare, Raymond Massey and Ursula Jeans, and they were a happy foursome, enjoying their smart success. Noel adored playing with Zena who looked smashingly chic, poised and cool, though inside a constant prey to terrible fears of dry-ups or the tiniest deviation from the script by the others, when she would whisper, 'Agony dear, what shall I do, where shall I go?'

She was so light-hearted when the long run came to an end that she and Ursula Jeans played a practical joke on Noel. He had to riffle through the pages of a book, which he found at the last performance they had filled with dirty pictures; he not only looked at these with a poker face but went across stage and pointed them out to Zena, which frightened her to death. She and Ursula Jeans had a long scene together, yet to come, during which he slowly poured water from a teapot into a tin can, so that from nearby they heard the tinkling sound of piddling into a chamberpot, which reduced the two of them to jellies and, Noel told them, served them jolly well right.

From eight o'clock onwards on the night of March 22nd, 1928, Noel watched part of the first performance of *This Year of Grace* at the London Pavilion, and then rushed down to the Playhouse for *The Second Man* at nine, which was played that night at such breakneck pace, and the intervals cut so short, that the bewildered audience found themselves out on the pavement long before their cars arrived. Then he rushed back to the Pavilion in time to watch the last part of the revue and see and hear its triumphant reception. The twenty-four numbers, astonishing in their variety, had all gone well. There was an ultra-chic scene on the Venice Lido ('one gets bitten by rats so, in a palazzo'), followed by a mackintosh-clad proletariat miserably enjoying the English equivalent. Mrs 'Arris gave her little Vi a smack round the chops for telling lies ('Cissie Parker's seen a whale!'), but the whale turned out to be everybody's favourite, Maisie Gay, who then made a spirited entrance as Daisy Kipshaw the Channel Swimmer and sang, 'Up Girls and at 'Em' to rousing cheers from the crowd. Jessie Matthews sang and danced entrancingly; Holland and Barry, long-legged and graceful, danced a whirlwind 'Blue Danube'; and Tilly Losch, prima ballerina from Vienna, stepped slowly down from a Gothic arch to dance to music by Bach. Noel wrote some very funny Potted Playlets, in one of them summing up the social snobbery and moral laxity of Frederick Lonsdale's characters in one line: 'Kiss me as passionately as you did last Wednesday in the Royal Enclosure at Ascot.' There was Miss Elsie, a splendid *dompteuse* with a whip, trying to control a horse called Pogo — the Griffith Brothers inside him — with very limp legs that kept on getting twisted, and there was Snowball, a little Negro whizz-kid of a banjo player, and much much more.

I have sometimes wondered whether it was my country bumpkin adolescence that still makes me think of *This Year of Grace* as the most abundant conglomeration of beauty, wit, elegance and gorgeous low comedy that I shall ever see; but it cannot have been, for the mature and distinguished St John Ervine in the *Observer*, trying, he said, to be careful with his superlatives, then proceeded to use them all up alphabetically: 'The most amusing, the most brilliant, the cleverest', until he got to 'the most uberous, the most versatile, the wittiest—blow, "x" has stopped me! After that marvellous exhibition of self-restraint, I will now let myself go and say that if any person comes to me and says that there has ever, anywhere in the world, been a better revue than this, I shall publicly tweak his nose.' Virginia Woolf, not so unlikely a fan as one might think, for she and Noel conducted a mutual-admiration flirtation for some years, wrote to him: 'Some of the numbers struck me on the head like a bullet. And what's more I remember them and see them enveloped in atmosphere— works of art in short.'

7

'THE CONGREVE OF OUR DAY'

LONGER than the Thirty Years War, the Coward Family strife continued until it petered out with Mr Coward's illness and death in the late 'thirties; hostilities reached a high point in the Battle of Goldenhurst, fought in 1928 and the four or five years that followed. Noel blithely hoped that his mother and father, Aunt Vida and Erik (with Aunt Ida Makeham living not far away on the outskirts of Folkestone) would get along together under such a very large roof.

111 Ebury Street was sold (though he maintained his own suite of rooms there as his London residence, paying rent to the new owners, until he moved to 17 Gerald Road two years later) and his father and Aunt Vida came to live at Goldenhurst. From this moment on, however, Mrs Coward avoided them as much as she could and, just to show them, spent much of her time in the company of her sister-in-law Aunt Ida.

The following letter is a specimen from the tempestuous time when the family for once banded together in resentment against Noel for wanting to move them to 'the cottage':

Darling, I did not mean to answer but your pose of being misunderstood is too ridiculous to allow it to pass. Also the terrible motives I ascribe to you and the working of your mighty brain! You can hardly call *facts* motives. After comfortably settling me in this house you want to send me to live in the cottage. Your motive, as you told me, was to have your house to yourself. Nothing very obscure about it. My one regret now is that I ever left Daddy and my work, even if I had died. How much better to have gone while you still loved me, and no crowds of grand friends and success had come between us! I must stay the week-end as I have to fetch Henry from the vet on Monday, but I have furnished two

rooms in the cottage and shall stick over there as much as possible.
I shall put Bobby Andrews in my room so you and he and Jack
can cuddle up together. Why not have Lorn and Gladys in the
guest room? Your really devilish and wicked beast of a Mother.

'Mum really was a wicked old devil, wasn't she,' Noel used to say
whenever he re-read these letters from long ago; re-read with great
enjoyment, I should add. He and his mother were two of a kind, both of
them when younger enjoying a jolly good row, though Noel—unlike
his mother—was seldom if ever spiteful. Except for Mrs Coward's
letters, when the spitfire words were irrevocably down on paper,
many of these family rows could be very funny, often ending in
laughter; if they did let the sun go down on it, their wrath might
easily be expunged from their minds by tomorrow morning. One
could say that they all had a talent for quarrelling; perhaps this is why
family quarrels are such a marked characteristic of every one of Noel's
comedies. In these he brilliantly builds up wildly funny, coruscating
altercations out of almost nothing at all, from the gossamer-like
beginnings of the squabbles in *Private Lives* to the Kilkenny Cat
slanging matches in *Red Peppers*.

Erik was by now twenty-three, a rather shadowy figure who comes
to life, and then only a little, in his letters to his mother. She has
already mentioned his particular and separate place in her heart; he
remained her baby son, her Benjamin, until his death at the age of
twenty-eight, and that is how she thought of him for ever afterwards.
When I asked Gladys about him during these years she described him
as 'a grey, very unmemorable figure, and not taken much notice of as I
remember. An allusion to him from Mum now and then but no real
tie with Noel somehow ... ' He was not unlike Noel in features, height
and physical appearance in the many snapshots of him, but the carbon
is blurred. His only close companion, also to die too young, was his
and Noel's first cousin, Leslie Makeham, Aunt Ida's son. During their
spare time, their cricketing Saturdays playing for Lensbury—'I had
the satisfaction of making my highest score, 76, so am feeling full of
beans'—their weekends, their holidays on the Norfolk Broads, they
seem to have been inseparable. To have been Noel's ungifted younger
brother cannot have made life easier for Erik, but through these years
he cherished a dream of travelling and making a life for himself in
Ceylon, which dream of course he shared with his mother and Leslie,
though not with Noel. Evidently he was without jealousy; Noel was
dazzling Noel, and that was that. Meanwhile he touchingly settled for

keeping out of the way—'Leslie and I will come down on the 1.15, Noel will have plenty of time to have departed,' or, 'Goodbye till Monday unless of course Noel changes his plans.' He and Leslie emulated Noel as much as they could, indulging in the craze for sun-bathing and constantly being photographed in pyjamas or dressing-gowns breakfasting in the sun at weekends and on the Norfolk Broads. (A year later Noel wrote one of his most famous lines, 'Very flat, Norfolk': did the partiality of his 'dull' brother and cousin for Norfolk give him the idea?)

Erik's and Leslie's jobs in the City involved irregular hours and are difficult to define: 'Leslie is staying with me all this week as we are working till 12 every night at Samuels on an issue of Debenham shares, we get a guinea a night so that's not so bad either'; 'Julian is going to start the wine business again so I don't suppose there will be any chance of my salary being raised'; 'got my cheque from Samuel's, £61.19.4., so that's *that*.' Judging by extracts from these always very loving notes to his mother during the first six months of 1928, his ambitious plans for a life in Ceylon were already under way: 'Nothing from Ceylon but there is a mail in on the 15th'; 'The Ceylon business which must be talked about [with her], writing would be inadequate.' And then: 'The Secretary of the Ceylon Association was very nice to me, though I mustn't tell Noel that. I am to go to Mr Jacques and he will arrange my passage. He is a dear old man of 65, quite encouraging ... says one is unlikely to make a fortune but can always make a com-fortable living and the life is perfect.' Exactly when he broke the news to Noel is not clear—they seem only to have met 'for a minute' by chance when one was leaving the house and the other coming in—but on July 11th Erik wrote:

My Darling, Daddy has just arrived with your letter and news of the general fracas and wiles which once more seem to have arisen through no fault of mine. I am writing at once just to say the obvious thing is for me to go out. You think so. And after all you are the one who counts most. Both Auntie Ida and Daddy think the same and I refuse to do anything else but go. Noel is apparently prepared to provide £350 provided he hears nothing further on the subject. Well and good. We'll grab it with both hands and feet and the business side, the guarantee I give him with regard to the money I receive under Grandmother's Will, can all be arranged through Jack. I understand Noel intends seeing somebody interested in tea. But he won't interest me as none of his friends

are ever any good in that way at all ... It's kind of Noel to be so
liberal and I really do think he is anxious for me to go, but his
hardness so gets the better of him that he trusts nobody and nothing that isn't a stone cold certainty. I know he has a pretty poor
opinion of me and that's what probably made him hesitate in the
first place. But he will receive a pleasant surprise one of these
days. Now darling please don't worry and be stupid and emotional
—not to mention *tenacious*. I'd come down this week-end, only I
should have to return on Monday as Noel is coming down and
you'd only upset yourself unnecessarily. I ought to cable Ross and
tell him I've decided to come out. Goodbye for the present my
love and don't think the end of the world has come just because
little Erik Brighteyes is going all the way to Ceylon. Leslie sends
you his love. Erik.

He sailed at the end of August in the S.S. *Gloucestershire* of the Bibby
Line, and dutifully wrote long, descriptive letters, posted from every
port they called at. These vary from the blasé at first, 'more than half
the passengers are *too* terrible, shopkeepers and barrow-pushers doing
the short trip to Marseilles, bouncing about all over the ship and either
can't or won't dress for dinner,' to the excited young man seeing his
first school of porpoises and later 'my first *shark*!' He made some useful
friends on board, returning planters, some married, some single, who
gave him helpful advice and with whom he stayed at the Galle Face
Hotel at Colombo before going, way up in the mountains above
Kandy, to face a somewhat lonely new life on a rubber and tea plantation at Karandagama. During the three years he was there, just like
Noel when separated from his mother, Erik wrote to her without fail
on Sunday mornings; she carefully kept every single letter, and after
his death tied the bundle up with bright red tape and stored it away in
'Mum's Suitcase'.

One fleeting haphazard occurrence, its repercussions echoing to this
day, happened to Noel this same summer of 1928. Mrs Peake, wife of
Ronald Peake with whom Gladys and Noel were staying in Surrey,
chose to put on a record of *Die Fledermaus* to while away the time before
their departure. Noel's mind was flooded by the sweeping music, the
Viennese waltzes most of all, and his hitherto vague ideas of one day
writing a romantic operetta immediately changed to definite determination. He and Gladys talked of nothing else during the drive to
London, Gladys visualizing glittering uniforms and dresses enchant-
ingly bustled, and at the end of a long talk after they had pulled up the

car, the story of *Bitter Sweet* first came to life under a tree on Wimbledon Common.

The new-born had to be nourished and encouraged to grow at the back of his mind for the time being; he had already promised Cochran he would appear in the New York production of *This Year of Grace* that autumn. He and Cochran sailed for New York in July to scout for talent, a lovely excuse to see all the new plays on Broadway and at the same time give themselves a larky holiday, while their first-class travel and hotel costs could be put down to Managerial Expenses. Above and beyond the call of duty, one of the shows they saw was Mae West in *Diamond Lil*, taking Constance Collier with them. Two years earlier Miss West and the entire company of *Sex* had been carted off in a prison-van after the first night for indecency (they were released next morning). As Miss West had herself written *Sex* and *Diamond Lil*, when they all went backstage to see her Noel, as one playwright to another, asked about her plans. 'Sure I'm writ'n a noo play,' she said; Noel, thinking she'd already gone about as far as she could go, inquired about the plot. 'Wal, y'see, it's about this guy. He's a cocksucker and ... ' One must remember this took place nearly fifty years ago: Constance's face turned pink then red and Cochran's purple and he gave way to such a spectacular fit of coughing and spluttering that it distracted everyone's attention and they had to leave. Noel's frustration knew no bounds; he said he had never heard a plot begin with so much promise.

Noel and Mr Cochran were forced against their will to share a cabin in the *Berengaria* on the voyage home, and to their surprise enjoyed the cosiness; neither of them snored, Noel reports the conversation after lights out as stimulating, and he managed to get a rough draft of the first act of *Bitter Sweet* down on paper, enthusiastically encouraged by 'Cockie'. In those days Almina Countess of Carnarvon's Nursing Home was 'the' place to go when ill, and it was to Lady Carnarvon's that Noel went after his return to London to undergo an operation for piles. While there, in marked contrast to this humiliation, he wrote the charmingly romantic second act; a constant visitor was the delicate pink-and-white porcelain Marie Tempest. Rather unexpectedly, though as he said he should have known better, piles were piles to Miss Tempest, not haemorrhoids, and she insisted on Noel explaining every detail of the operation.

Beatrice Lillie starred with Noel in the New York production of *This Year of Grace*, taking over the role Maisie Gay was still playing in London. Beattie behaved as usual like an absolute fiend from the first rehearsal until the curtain went up on opening night, and as usual like an absolute angel from the moment it came down and for the rest of the run; sweet, funny and a delight to play with. Gertie was starring nearby in *Treasure Girl*, and the three of them were asked and went 'every-where' together; no party could be considered an out-and-out success unless they graced it. The critics, as they had done in London, praised Noel to the skies for his triple feat of writing, composing and directing the show; Robert Benchley going so far as to say that, 'unless someone in America is able to do something that approximates to Mr Coward's feat we shall always feel it was a mistake to break away from England back there in 1776.'

1928 to 1934 were Noel's golden years. Year after year, under Charles B. Cochran's bright banner, he produced his most splendid successes, the titles that will always spring to mind in association with his name: *This Year of Grace, Bitter Sweet, Private Lives, Cavalcade, Words and Music*. Then in America *Design for Living* and in 1934, in London again with Cochran, *Conversation Piece*.

In a preface to a volume of three of Noel's plays which was published during these years of unparalleled success, Somerset Maugham wrote:

> For us English dramatists the young generation has assumed the brisk but determined form of Mr Noel Coward. He knocked at the door with impatient knuckles, and then he rattled the handle, and then he burst in. After a moment's stupor the older playwrights welcomed him affably enough and retired with what dignity they could muster to the shelf which with a spritely gesture he indicated to them as their proper place ... and. since there is no one now writing who has more obviously a gift for the theatre than Mr Noel Coward, nor more influence with young writers, it is probably his inclination and practice that will be responsible for the manner in which plays will be written during the next thirty years.

Maugham was out by four years — *Look Back in Anger* was produced twenty-six years after those words were written — but even so I do not think John Osborne would refute that he writes as he does (I am thinking of *Hotel in Amsterdam* in particular) as a result of Noel's changing everlastingly the manner of writing dialogue for the English theatre: the last traces of rhetoric and fustian were banished for ever.

Noel wondered how his hero, Saki, would have reacted to

that much-maligned period now glibly referred to as the Hectic Twenties, when upstart Michael Arlens and Noel Cowards flourished like green bay trees in the frenzied atmosphere of cocktail parties, Treasure Hunts, Hawes and Curtis dressing gowns, long cigarette holders and enthusiastically publicised decadence. He would undoubtedly have found many subjects for his sardonic wit but I have an instinctive feeling that it wouldn't really have been his cup of tea. His satire was based primarily on the assumption of a fixed social status quo which ... finally disappeared in the gunsmoke of 1914.

Writing to Beverley Nichols in 1957, Noel took a retrospective glance at the 'twenties to be incorporated in Beverley's book *The Sweet and Twenties*:

Gertrude Stein, one of the Oracles of the Twenties, once made the following pronouncement 'Everything is the same and everything is different!' This utterance, like most of Miss Stein's, is remarkable for a certain magnificent simplicity. However my purpose is not to discuss Miss Stein but to consider the profundity and truth or otherwise of her phrase as applied to the Twenties and Fifties.

I'm afraid she was right, they are awfully the same and they are dreadfully different, so different that I might go so far as to say that the Fifties are much much worse ... First the similarities. The Bright Young Things are just as determined to be bright as were their fathers and mothers; parapets are still walked at midnight it seems, and dinner-jacketed young men are still falling or being pushed into swimming pools or the river to round off successful parties. The desperate endeavours of the League of Nations are perpetuated by those of U.N.O. Cocktail parties, God help us, are still with us. Most musical comedies still have to come from Broadway. The latest dance from America — which shall be nameless because it will have become outmoded and been replaced in the short interval before these words get into print — is just as convulsive as the Black Bottom and the Charleston. Skin-tight jeans are just as exaggerated as were Oxford Bags ... The same hectic determination to have a good time is presumably due to the fact that younger people to-day are just as 'Post-War' as their mothers and fathers were and as resolved to catch up on their youth and any good times they may have missed during the years of austerity. And I don't blame them one bit.

... I will pass lightly over the many differences for the worse – H. (or even X.) Bombs, television, the general decline in standards and the crushing down of initiative, originality and ambition, the lack of incentive etc., because your book is about the Twenties and not the Fifties and in any case one must never, never say that things were better when one was young. Of course a great many changes have been for the better; people are healthier, better paid and there is little unemployment, hardly any of those pathetic ex-servicemen's bands in the streets and no ex-officers trying to sell writing paper at one's door. Whether people are happier or not is another matter, but then happiness is well known to be elusive.

Were we happy in the Twenties? On the whole I think most of us were but we tried to hide it by appearing to be as blasé, world-weary and 'jagged with sophistication' as we possibly could. Naturally we had a lot of fun in the process. I remember I had a lovely time writing a play called *Ritz Bar* which you, Beverley, most kindly tried to get the Norwegian Ambassador in Paris to back, – why I can't think. Anyway, *Ritz Bar* was as jagged with sophistication as all get out; the characters were either demi-mondaine or just plain mondaine, shared their apartments and their lives with members of the opposite, or the same, sex and no wife dreamed for one instant of doing anything so banal as living with her husband. The play was typical of the phase we all went through and, taken by and large, quite harmless: to call it good clean fun would perhaps be going too far, but at least it wasn't about the Death Wish and compared with Existentialism it becomes *Rebecca of Sunnybrook Farm*.

We all got over this period in our mental growth, or most of us did, and I can't feel we were any the worse for it. Should it be a matter for pride that we got over it without the help of psychiatry, considered so indispensable to-day, though not by me?

Taken all in all the Twenties was a diverting and highly exciting decade in which to live and I wouldn't have missed it, not – as they say – for a King's Ransom.

Ritz Bar – afterwards retitled *Semi-Monde* – judging by the frequency with which it is mentioned in their letters, seems never to have been forgotten by the friends to whom Noel read it privately. One and all appear to have had the same 'lovely time' listening to it as he had had in writing it. Most probably through the enthusiastic influence of Diana Cooper and Iris Tree, to whom he read it when they were appearing in *The Miracle* and he in *The Vortex* in Chicago, it was translated into German by their dear 'Kaetchen', Rudolf Kommer, and the great Reinhardt quite definitely wanted to produce it. But 'it escaped production by a hair's breadth and faded gently into oblivion' or, as he puts it elsewhere, 'mercifully never saw the light'.

Noel finished the book of *Bitter Sweet* with no trouble, but the score would not come so easily; try as he might the one big waltz number, always so necessary to him in his musicals, refused to materialise. After a matinée of *This Year of Grace*, driving across town in a taxi to get his precious, sacred rest between the shows, the tune of 'I'll See You Again' dropped into his head in its entirety during a long traffic jam, with drivers honking their klaxons all around him. This was one of the miracles which forever mystified Noel and which no one, least of all himself, could explain: 'How can a theme come to me complete like that? How can it be accounted for, and where does it come from?' Stuck in the taxi, however, he had no time to question the miraculous but went over and over the melody in his head for fear of losing it. When he did get to his apartment (he could not write music down and this was long before the days of tape recorders) he had to play it over, over and over again on the piano until 'I'll See You Again' was fixed in his memory. His rest between the shows was considered 'absolutely necessary'; he got none that afternoon, however, but from then on — as he knew it would once he had his *leitmotiv* — the remainder of the score came effortlessly.

Rehearsals of *Bitter Sweet* started in May 1929 in London, with Peggy Wood and Ivy St Helier already cast well before that in the roles which they later made so famous, Sari Linden and Manon la Crevette. Also before rehearsals started, Cochran and Noel decided to go on another of their talent-hunting expeditions, this time to Berlin and Vienna in search of someone to play the leading man, Carl Linden. Noel describes their search as 'arduous'; be that as it may, they at last found a handsome young tenor named Hans Unterfucker. Once again Cochran turned purple, this time with laughter inflamed by Noel insisting that however the name might be pronounced in German, still he would like to *see* it on every hoarding in London and on every bus. Cochran finally became so helpless, groaning with laughter, that they didn't even go round to see the poor young man but went back to London and engaged George Metaxa, who had been there all the time.

When Noel read and sang and Elsie April played the completed score to Cochran, the latter said, 'If we can put this on the stage as I visualise it, it cannot fail,' and from then on his enthusiasm was limitless. '*You* seem in exceptionally high spirits,' his general manager said that night. 'I've got an old-age pension: Coward's operetta is a gem, with a great title.' (It was Alfred Lunt who had thought of the perfect title.) Frank Collins, Cochran's production manager, was not so sure: 'It has no comedy, and the hero is killed at the end of the second act.' That it defied all the accepted conventions of a musical was the opinion of many: 'According to the rules of the theatre it should have failed,' Cochran said later, 'but I always contend that there are no rules.'

Bitter Sweet was beautiful to behold. Gladys's clothes and sets were, up to then, the loveliest she had ever done, and Professor Ernst Stern's set for the second act a delicious evocation of Vienna in 1880. Tilly Losch choreographed the dance of the Prater Girls and Orellana brilliantly orchestrated the score. Cochran handed the entire production over to Noel and kept well out of the way. When he did come to the final run-through, he stood up at the end, thanked the company, told them he was very proud of them and that he wouldn't part with his rights in the play for a million pounds. So everybody set out for Manchester with a high heart, and they were not disappointed. Their reception on the first night was rapturous, the whole audience standing at the end to cheer, some of them standing on the seats to do so. The audience at His Majesty's was less enchanted on the opening night; the audience was tremendously fashionable, led by Prince George and Lady Louis Mountbatten, and were for the first half at any rate 'as responsive as so many cornflour blancmanges', and in the intervals could be heard saying they couldn't see much in it. The men complained that the gals weren't up to standard (Mr Cochran's Young Ladies were usually very beautiful, comparable to Mr Ziegfeld's in New York, but these had been chosen for their voices and there was no chorus line as such), and worst of all, '*When* is Coward going to give us some funny lines?' There was however cheering at the end, greatly helped by Cochran clapping and shouting 'Author!' from the back of the circle and Gladys and Noel up in the dome clapping and shouting, 'Cochran!'

Noel complained that the next day's notices were remarkable for their tone of rather grudging patronage; what he did not mention is that on the following Sunday James Agate, London's leading critic, accorded him the most glorious paean of praise imaginable.

Noel dedicated the score to Elsie April, 'in gratitude for all the unfailing help and encouragement you have given me in music', and the published book to Charles B. Cochran, 'My help in ages past, My hope for years to come.' After a shaky few weeks during which Cochran 'nursed' the show – probably financially impossible today – *Bitter Sweet* ran for almost two years, counting the pre- and post-West End tours, was seen by very nearly one million people, and Robertson's launched a nationwide advertising campaign for their new Bitter-Sweet Marmalade, which Peggy Wood described as 'yummy'.

A New York production starring Evelyn Laye, then at the height of her beauty, was planned for that autumn by Cochran, in association with Archie Selwyn and Florenz Ziegfeld, to run at the Ziegfeld Theatre, but Cochran, up to his eyes with a new revue, could not get away from London. Noel therefore found himself in New York having to battle alone against the two eminent and experienced impresarios, both of whom had grave fears for the success of *Bitter Sweet* in its English form on Broadway. At first they tried to wheedle him with helpful suggestions for putting some zip into the show; the great Florenz Ziegfeld, unable to envisage a musical in the Ziegfeld Theatre of all places without his legendary long-stemmed American Beauty showgirls, insisted that Noel should somehow drag a bevy of them into the plot – his own public would *expect* to see the Ziegfeld Girls and besides, they would help to make the show more sexy.

After nearly a week of their interference Noel lost his temper, told them to mind their own business while he minded his as author and director, and forbade Mr Ziegfeld to show his face, even though it was in his own theatre, at any more rehearsals. The tryout was in Boston, and Noel wrote from the Ritz-Carlton to his mother, who was in Ceylon on a month-long visit to Erik:

Darling, the show opened here last night and caused a riot, they stood up and cheered and screamed and that was that. We had an awful time, Ziegfeld and Selwyn were so depressing and said everything was awful and I've had to fight every step of the way. They wanted me to alter everything and I wouldn't; now of course they're delighted and say they *knew* it was a success all along! We've had to change our leading man three times, Evelyn is marvellous and has set the town on fire, but Oh Dear it has been a business. We're living here in state at the expense of the management and keep ordering very expensive food at odd hours ... Your battered but loving Snoop. I think fighting agrees with me.

The 'word from mouth', as Garbo used to call it and perhaps still does, was so good from Boston that before the show got to New York tremendous excitement had been engendered. After the first night on November 5th (one critic said, accurately, that Evelyn Laye was 'the fairest prima donna this side of heaven'), Noel wrote:

> Well Darlingest, the show opened last night and was a complete riot, some seats were sold for as much as $150 (Thirty pounds!). All the celebrities were photographed coming in and all the traffic was specially controlled by the Police Department. Evelyn made the most triumphant success I've ever seen when she made her entrance in the *last* Act in the white dress they clapped and cheered for two solid minutes and when I came on at the end they went raving mad. How right you were about Evelyn she certainly does knock spots off Peggy. Tonight I took Cissie Sewell and Elsie April to see *Whoopee!*, they deserved a treat having worked like dogs, and Eddie Cantor stepped forward and said he wanted to introduce the greatest Theatrical Genius alive today and they popped a spotlight on me and I had to stand up and bow to my great American Public! All this mind you in the middle of some-body else's show! I've just had a wire from Ziegfeld saying that the theatre will never die as long as there is a genius like me in it which made me laugh quietly considering how *convinced* he was of failure before we opened in Boston! There's been a complete disaster on the New York Stock Market everybody is losing millions, poor old Syrie has lost practically all she had, but it really serves them right for gambling. Thank God Jack has only invested my money in gilt edged securities and never speculated so I'm perfectly safe, but it really is horrible, people hurling them-selves off buildings like confetti. I must stop now darling as I am exceedingly tired but very relieved and happy. Give my love to Erik and a good hug to yourself, if that's not possible get an Anaconda to do it in a *nice* way. All love, Snoopie. I've only got 283 telegrams to answer! Evelyn is weeing down her leg with excitement she's been such a darling. I'm delighted with her success.

Noel now left New York for a six-month voyage halfway round the world. On the second stage of his long journey, while the train was passing through New Mexico, he wrote to Mrs Coward, who was still in Ceylon:

Santa Fe Railroad. Hello Ma, Here I am trundling across the continent. I left Chicago where Jack saw me off yesterday morning early and arrive in Hollywood tomorrow night. I've been in bed ever since I got on this train and intend to stay there, it's so lovely just relaxing after all the fuss and furore. I had a hectic time in New York everyone gave farewell parties for me and handed me expensive presents and I departed in a blaze of glory. All the movie magnates are putting their cars at my disposal in the hopes that I'll work for them which God forbid, but I shall use the cars. I've caused more of a sensation in America this time than ever before, 'Bitter Sweet' is the only show playing to capacity during this appalling Stock Market crash. It's really very enjoyable.

Among the expensive presents he had been given was a rather large Cartier two-fold gold travelling clock from Gertie, which when opened displayed very clearly on the left leaf the time and on the right, under a photograph of Gertie, a loving message about the play he had promised to write for her. He grew to hate this clock, reminding him as it did of time's inexorable passage when he woke each morning with the comedy still unwritten, until he longed to fling it across the room or out of the porthole into the sea.

Noel had started to write a novel called *Julian Kane*, about a man who committed suicide because he was bored. He pressed on with it during the *Tenyo Maru*'s eight days from Honolulu to Yokohama, his enthusiasm daily decreasing until it petered out completely and he felt that any future reader would find ploughing through it as wearying as the tedium of writing it had become to him. He put the novel to one side for good and all; in its stead he racked his imagination, his mind wandering through Second-Empire salons and chromium cocktail bars in search of an idea for Gertie, but with no result. Nothing seemed to click. At last he gave up, remembering that he was supposed to be on holiday.

His first glimpse of the Glamorous East was however of a thick, icy blizzard raging as the ship docked at Yokohama, followed by the long drive to Tokyo through a downpour of sleet. A wheel flew off the taxi halfway, and Noel sat inside in a pool of water while a small crowd of Japanese—very excited, far from inscrutable—put it back on. The Imperial Hotel, where he had arranged to meet Jeffery Amherst, proved to be all he hoped it would be: large and comfortable. (He had by now formulated his ideal of an hotel, to which he stuck for always.

Apart from comfort and good service, the hotel had to be large, if possible so large that he could get 'lost' in it and thus ensure himself anonymity, or at any rate privacy from the curious.)

On arrival he found a cable from Jeffery to say he would be three days late for their rendezvous since he had missed the boat from Shanghai. Noel went early to bed the night before Jeff did arrive, because the boat was due at seven next morning; but he got no sleep. As unbidden as 'I'll See You Again' in the traffic jam, Gertie appeared as he switched out his bedside light in a white Molyneux dress on a terrace in the South of France, and by 4 a.m. he had mapped out *Private Lives*, title and all. For once he made no haste to write it. He had learnt, he said, the wisdom of not rushing an idea for a play too early, and he did not mention it in his next letter home.

While he was half the world away he thought often and nostalgically of Goldenhurst, of his Mum, Daddy, and his tiny Aunt Vida, 'probably at this moment battling through the weather with a trowel to attack the weeds in the orchard.' His nostalgic imaginings gave him a far from accurate picture of what was going on. Mrs Coward, fresh home from Erik and Ceylon, had once more dipped her pen in vitriol and written this letter to her husband:

Dear Arthur, This letter will probably come as a shock to you, I have made friends so often and it has taken a long time to kill my affection for you, but you have at last succeeded in doing so ... As long as I can remember, not once have you ever stood up for me or the boys when we have been in any little trouble, you have *always* taken the opposite side and been against us. I remember so many times when you have failed me: and this has been the last straw. How *dare* you behave as you have been doing lately. I have never been so miserable in my life as since I came from Ceylon, and who are you to dare to make my life so unhappy. What have you ever done for me or for either of your fine boys to help them on in life. You have never done anything to help anybody, and everything has been done for you. And yet you are so far from being ashamed of yourself that you plump yourself down on us, full of conceit, selfishness and self appreciation and spoil our lives for us. No one with any pretensions to being a gentleman could ever bully any woman as you bully my sister. It is *shameful* in front of those children too. [Presumably Noel and Erik.] She has as great a right to be here as you have. Noel chose to give her a home before he gave you one, and why are you not earning your living? You are strong and healthy and will no doubt live to be 100, a burden on Noel, not to speak of putting your wife on him too. Now I have come to a decision. I am going to add still more to poor Noel's burden and ask him to provide you with another home. If he agrees I will find you a cottage somewhere, with a little less grandeur than you have here which will do you good. Noel has always understood your character and what I have been through, and will do anything he can to make me happy again. For the present things must remain as they are and I must put up with you, but in a different way. I shall never stand up for you again as I have always done, and I tell you definitely, everything is over between you and me. The last scrap of my affection for you has gone and it is entirely your own fault. Violet.

Noel had no notion of the existence of this letter until years afterwards. Mrs Coward 'put up' with her husband by the expedient of making him move his room as far away from herself as possible to the other side of the house, though she had to endure the boredom of most of their meals in common. By the time Noel arrived home four months later, in May, an uneasy truce—for it cannot be called peace—must have been made and this state of affairs dragged on for the next two years until Mr and Mrs Coward were reunited, though never closely, by grief at Erik's untimely illness and death.

Noel had been mulling *Private Lives* over and over in his mind all this while until, after being smitten with influenza in the Cathay Hotel in Shanghai, he got it down on paper in roughly four days, sitting up in bed, writing with an Eversharp pencil on one of the foolscap-size, narrow-lined writing-blocks without which he never travelled. There used to be a metal plaque on the door of the room to mark the event; one wonders if today's communist masters would be interested enough to have left it there, or whether they disapproved so strongly of the lack of social significance in the play that they removed it.

Another event of importance happened to Noel in Shanghai; from there he made his first voyage as a guest in one of H.M.'s warships. He had always adored the sea and this voyage marked the beginning of his lifelong love-affair with, and his respect and admiration for, the Royal Navy. From then on some of the happiest times of his life were passed in many of its ward-rooms and mess-decks and swimming from its launches: 'The secret of naval good manners is hard to define; perhaps discipline has a lot to do with it and prolonged contact with the sea; perhaps a permanent background of such dignity makes for simplicity of mind.' The bandmaster hurriedly bought the parts of *Bitter Sweet* before the ship sailed, through which the ship's band struggled nightly during dinner, and Noel and Jeffery picked up enough naval jargon and etiquette not to disgrace themselves during the voyage.

8

PRIVATE LIVES
AND CAVALCADE

WHAT was probably the first meeting between Noel and T. E. Lawrence took place in August 1930, for on the 15th Lawrence wrote to Charlotte Shaw:

> On Wednesday I lunched with Philip Sassoon, with whom came Noel Coward. He is not deep but remarkable. A hasty kind of genius. I wonder what his origin is? His prose is quick, balanced, alive: like Congreve's probably, in his day. He dignifies slang when he admits it. I liked him, and suspected that you probably do not. Both of us were right.

Rehearsals for *Private Lives* had started in London in July; with Noel and Gertie were Laurence Olivier and Adrianne Allen, Noel also directing. Unlike most directors he loved to have a friend or two in front at rehearsals, and in this production, with himself on the stage most of the time, he found them a boon; they provided him with someone to 'play to' and their praise was sweet at the end of an otherwise boring day. Lord Lloyd was among these friends; George Lloyd, whom Noel thought a great man in many ways, with vitality, humour and a kind and generous heart. One day Noel astonished the company by telling them that not only was Lord Lloyd coming that morning but he was bringing Lawrence of Arabia with him. Everyone was thrilled, but of course did not show it, working away as though it were a run-of-the-mill rehearsal. They then went out to lunch together, not to the Ivy, but to an obscure restaurant in St Martin's Lane where Aircraftman Shaw's anonymity would not only be respected but where he would probably go unrecognized; this proved to be the case. Adrianne remembers that she liked him very much, that he was quiet and seemingly shy and that he seldom took his eyes off Noel, fascinated

by him. The whole day was a great success and Lawrence came to
several more rehearsals.

His and Noel's acquaintanceship was furthered both by their
mutual friendship with the aforementioned Sir Philip Sassoon and by
the latter's association with 601 Squadron, Royal Air Force, which was
stationed at Lympne, close to Sir Philip's house Lympne Castle and also
near to Goldenhurst. Lawrence had by this time exchanged what he
called 'the shallow grave of public duty' for comparative obscurity in
the ranks of the R.A.F. under the pseudonym of Aircraftman Shaw.
Their friendship lasted until Lawrence's life was, to use Noel's words,
'snuffed out in one blinding, noisy moment on that idiotic motor
cycle', though it tailed off towards the end, because by then Noel had
found his behaviour rather tiresome and had come to the conclusion
that he hadn't one grain of real humour in his body. His tiresomeness
was exemplified when he came for the weekend to Lympne, which he
knew would entail a visit to 601 Squadron. He was off duty and could
easily have worn a suit, but no, he had chosen to wear his aircraftman's
uniform, which he must have known would by rights only entitle him
to be entertained in the airmen's mess. He caused a lash-up; as he was
supposed to shrink from the limelight and loathed attention being
called to himself, Noel found it surprising he should choose the one
sure way of getting both:

> As a man I found him strange and elusive. He neither drank nor
> smoked and, as far as I could see, very seldom ate ... In most of his
> writing, particularly *Seven Pillars of Wisdom* and the Air Force diary,
> one can discern a certain bitterness directed against himself, a
> contempt for his smallness of stature. There was in him, I am sure,
> a terrible area of discontent ... I believe that there must always
> have been, deep down in that strange, mystic, dynamic mind the
> seeds of despair, and an impulse towards self-martyrdom.

But back in 1930 each was intensely interested and intrigued by the
other and the other's work; Lawrence fascinated by the dynamics
of the theatre, and Noel's hero-worship for the legendary figure
strengthened by his admiration for him as a writer. It was in fact their
writing that drew them together, Lawrence promising to come to
more rehearsals of *Private Lives*, eager to 'watch the wheels going
round' and also making a considerable leap forward in their friendship
by lending Noel his 'Air Force diary' to read and seeming anxious for
Noel's opinion on it. His R.A.F. notes, as he called them, were in 1930

a private matter, shown to none except close friends, Bernard Shaw among them, and publication (because of their then unprintable though accurate use of barrack room language) unthinkable. They remained unpublished until 1955 when they emerged as *The Mint*.

338171 A /C Shaw, R.A.F. Mountbatten, Plymouth, 15.vii.30. Dear N.C., Here are your R.A.F. notes. After looking at them you will agree with me that such tense and twisted prose cannot be admirable. It lacks health. Obscenity is vieux jeu too: but in 1922 I was not copying the fashion! Don't be too hard on them, though. They were meant not for reading, but to afford me raw material for an introductory chapter to my mag. op. on an airman's life. Unluckily I survived the Depot only to be sacked when on the point of being posted to a Squadron, the real flying unit. There followed a long spell of army life, wasting the novelty of barracks, till I broadened out into the present commonplace and lasting contentment. Obviously these notes libel our general R.A.F. life by being too violently true to an odd and insignificant part of it. So out of my head and with no formal notes I attempted a Part III to show the happiness that came after the bullying. Only happiness is such a beast to put on paper. Meeting you was a surprise and pleasure to me. I had often (and quite inadequately) wondered what you were like. Now I'll try to work the rehearsal you suggested into some later raid upon London. The going round of wheels fascinates me. So I found Wednesday wholly delightful. Yours, T. E. Shaw. Please do not keep them longer than you can help — or I shall forget where they are, and be troubled!

Adelphi Hotel, Liverpool, August 25th. [*Private Lives* had opened on tour.] Dear 338171 (May I call you 338?). I am tremendously grateful to you for letting me read your R.A.F. notes. I found them even better than I expected which is honestly saying a good deal. Now I'm faced with the problem of expressing to you my genuine and very deep admiration of your writing without treading on your over tender, hero worship Lawrence of Arabia corns! Really it has nothing to do with all that. I think you're a very thrilling writer indeed because you make pictures with such superb simplicity and no clichés at all, and I disagree flatly with you when you say you're photographic. Your descriptive powers far exceed flat photography. Cameras are unable to make people live in the mind as your prose succeeds in doing, China, and Taffy and Stiffy and Corporal Abner are grandly written with heart and blood and bones. I found so many things I want to talk about which in writing would sound over effusive and pompous, so please come to London one Saturday if you possibly can. My play was a great success in Edinburgh and we're opening here tonight in a theatre the size of Olympia which will be very disconcerting. I am terribly pleased you thought it good. I owe you a great deal for the things you said about my writing. Valuable praise is very rare indeed and beyond words stimulating. Please come to London and see some more wheels going round if it interests you. I am enormously pleased that we've met. Yours, Noel Coward.

Lawrence's reply on September 6th:

Dear N.C., It is very good to laugh: and I laughed so much, and made so many people laugh over your 'May I call you 338' that I became too busy and happy to acknowledge your letter ... Your praise of my R.A.F. notes pleases me, of course, more than it puzzles me. I'm damned if I can see any good in them. Some artifice—yes: some skill—yes; they even come off here and there: but the general impression on me is dry bones. Your work is like swordplay; as quick as light. Mine is a slow painful mosaic of hard words stiffly cemented together. However it is usually opposites that fall in love. At any rate I propose to go on looking forward, keenly, to seeing more of your works and work, and perhaps of yourself, if a kind fate lets me run into you when you are not better engaged. I'm hoping to get to London some time in October, for a week-end perhaps. Yours, T. E. Shaw.

Charles B. Cochran, Gertrude Lawrence, Noel Coward: *Private Lives* was deck'd in a glorious sheen of success before it started, and in addition was chosen to open Sidney [now Lord] Bernstein's Phoenix Theatre, a smart new ornament to London's theatreland and an event in itself. Laurence Olivier and Adrianne Allen played Victor and Sybil perfectly, as Victor and Sybil should always be played. Noel made a mistake in writing too early on that they are extra puppets, lightly wooden ninepins only to be repeatedly knocked down and stood up again: this led to productions everywhere in which they were usually portrayed as unattractive oafs. This can never be right, else why would Amanda and Elyot give them a second glance, let alone dream of marrying them? Sir John Gielgud was 'on' to this (as was Noel by then) when he directed the last major revival with Maggie Smith and Robert Stephens: 'We've got to have two people as attractive as Larry and Adrianne were in the first place, *if* we can find them.' This led to James Villiers and Polly Adams, both of them charming, funny and clever, and the proper balance of the play was restored. Johnny was also 'on' to the one other important risk in the play, which is the dangerous turning-point of the first love scene between Elyot and Amanda, when they are suddenly called upon to prevent the audience's laughter and she is desperately asking about his travels in an attempt to prevent him declaring how deeply they still love one another:

AMANDA: How was the Taj Mahal?

ELYOT: Unbelievable, a sort of dream.

AMANDA: That was the moonlight, I expect, you must have seen it in the moonlight.

ELYOT (*never taking his eyes off her face*): Yes, moonlight is cruelly deceptive.

AMANDA: And it didn't look like a biscuit box did it? I've always thought it might.

ELYOT: Darling, darling, I love you so.

AMANDA: And I hope you met a sacred elephant. They're lint-white I believe, and very, very sweet.

ELYOT: I've never loved anyone else for an instant.

AMANDA: No, no, you mustn't—Elyot—stop.

ELYOT: You love me too, don't you? There's no doubt about it anywhere, is there?

AMANDA: No, no doubt anywhere.

Gertie and Noel looked so beautiful together, standing in the moonlight, that no one who saw them can ever forget; and they played the scene so magically, lightly, tenderly, that one was for those fleeting moments brought near to tears by the underlying vulnerability, the evanescence, of their love.

The tour of *Private Lives* was, as Noel said, swathed in luxury, with first-class trains and hotels provided by Cochran. Adrianne Allen remembers their first train-journey to Edinburgh and the four of them having their first meal of the tour together, slightly shocked by Larry's behaviour at the end of it, throwing bits of bread at Noel and then anything stickier he could lay his hands on until the two of them turned the fight into a Mack Sennett custard-pie comedy. Noel adored

Larry, there is no other word for it, and Larry adored Noel. He, Larry, was then the worst giggler on stage that Noel had ever encountered, or ever did. The slightest thing would set him off; he had already been sacked from a production for giggling, and was very nearly expelled from Birmingham Rep for the same reason. Noel thought this a very serious matter and solemnly warned Larry of his intention to *try* to make him break up at every performance until he was cured. Noel could himself be as wicked as he liked on stage and keep a straight face; judging by the merriment with which he used to recount the tale, he evidently enjoyed administering the cure. He invented a dog called Roger, unseen but who was always on stage with them when he and Larry had a scene together. Roger belonged to Noel but was madly attracted by Larry, especially to his private parts both before and behind, to which he invisibly did unmentionable things in full sight of the audience. 'Down, Roger,' Noel would whisper, or, 'Not in front of the vicar!' until in the end, as though this time the dog really had gone much too far, a shocked 'ROGER!' was quite enough. The day did eventually come when Larry could not only stand up to this without a flicker, but beat Noel at his own game. He had a line which ran, 'A friend of mine has a house on the edge of Cap Ferrat'; Noel quickly ad-libbed, 'On the *edge*?' 'Yes,' Larry said firmly, 'on the *very* edge,' and looked Noel straight in the eye. His cure was complete. What is more he got a big laugh; and the line was slightly changed and incorporated into the play.

The opening night in London glittered with success on both sides of the footlights: a 'Noel Coward First Night' had by now become and would remain something special, usually graced by royalty, far more fashionable than anybody else's first nights and far more difficult to get into. Noel himself retained two memories of that first night. He seems to have been haunted by rude words at inopportune moments. (Or did he attract them? Certainly he enjoyed them.) Adrianne made her second entrance in the first act, very bright and pretty—this was going to be their honeymoon night—and said with clarity, 'Elli, can I have a cock?' (The line was afterwards changed for safety's sake to 'Cocktail, please'.) When I asked Adrianne what happened, had it been first-night nerves, she said, 'No, no, no; I hadn't a nerve in my body, I was young and knew we were a success. The "tail" part of the word just didn't come out, I shall never know why.' Noel's singing with Gertie and his playing of 'Someday I'll Find You' had been one of the highlights of the evening, and his second memory was Mrs Patrick Campbell's entrance into his crowded dressing-room. Every head turned. 'Don't you love it,' she cooingly inquired of the assembly, 'when he does his little hummings at the piano?'

Heinemann rushed out in book form the text of the play within a week. *The Times* found it 'unreadable'. T. E. Lawrence wrote:

Dear N.C., I was at the second night, and wondered to see how perfectly the finished product went. Just once it slipped, when she [the maid] drew the curtains and the daylight took 20 seconds to come! Yet I'm not sure that the bare works you showed me that afternoon were not better. For one thing, I could not always tell when you were acting and when talking to one another. So I would suggest my coming to another rehearsal, only there seems nothing to prevent these plays of yours running for ever, and so you will probably never write any more ... The play reads astonishingly well. It gets thicker in print, and has bones and muscles. On the stage you played with it and puffed your fancies up and about like swansdown. And one can't help laughing all the time; whereas over the book one does not do worse than chuckle or smile. For fun I took some pages and tried to strike redundant words out of your phrases. Only there were none. That's what I felt when I told you it was superb prose. You'll be sick of letters about it, so I'll shut up. Yet I had to tell you how much delight it gave me. Yours, T. E. Shaw.

In contrast to the critics' continual chorus of 'thin', 'tenuous' and 'brittle' Noel received much praise of this sort from the literary eminent of the time; so far as I can find out Arnold Bennett was the first to call him 'the Congreve of our day'.

Less than a year before this, Noel had come across an English touring company in Singapore called The Quaints with, to name a few, *The Girl Friend*, *When Knights Were Bold* and *Hamlet* in their repertory. Among The Quaints he discovered John Mills and Betty Hare who, once back in England, became his friends and worked with him a great deal from then on. He rashly agreed to appear with them as Stanhope in *Journey's End*, with John Mills as Raleigh giving the finest performance of that part Noel had ever seen. Apart from his overemotional performance and some hilarious mishaps — in his grief over the dead Raleigh, Noel's heavy tin hat fell off on to Johnny's genitals, bringing Raleigh back from the dead for a startled moment — Noel was strongly affected by the poignancy of the play itself. So much so that in the P. and O. ship between Ceylon and Marseilles he had written his own 'angry little vilification' of war, its futility, stupidity and sacrifice of so many young lives. He wrote this in play form, the best known to him, and the result was, he says, similar to his performance as Stanhope: confused and hysterical. He called the play *Post-Mortem* and never regretted writing it for a moment; it had purged his system of accumulated acids. During the run of *Private Lives* he wrote to Lawrence that he might inflict upon him the script of a play he had written, not to be produced—it was for publication only—and he would deeply value his opinion. Eight months went by, until on June 10th, 1931, Lawrence wrote:

> I have read your play (which? Why, your war one, of course) twice and want to admire you. It's a fine effort, a really fine effort. I fancied it hadn't the roots of a great success. You had something far more important to say than usual, and I fancy that in saying it you let the box-office and the stalls go hang. As argument it is first rate. As imagination magnificent: and it does you great honour as a human being. It's for that reason that I liked it so much. Mrs Humphrey Ward (before your time) once asked Matthew Arnold (also before your time) why he was not wholly serious. People won't like you better for being quite so serious as you are in this: but it does you honour, as I said, and gave me a thrill to read it ...

Noel was well towards production of *Cavalcade* by the time he wrote to thank Lawrence for his praise, and added a postscript to his letter: 'I'm doing a very fancy production at Drury Lane in September, so if you want to see *real* wheels going round let me know.'

Noel remained adamant in his intention of playing *Private Lives* for only three months, to the annoyance of nearly everybody, from Cochran to the general public, for they were sold out solid from the time they opened. As a needed change from his straight plays with a small cast and usually one set, he had for some time been fiddling with the idea of writing and directing something on a vast scale, a terrific spectacle in a huge theatre. Cochran encouraged him, as who would not with Noel on this successful peak of his career, but Noel became stuck with something along the lines of Reinhardt's *Miracle* or perhaps a thrilling chariot race with real horses galloping round the revolving stage at the Coliseum. He had by now moved into 17 Gerald Road, near Eaton Square; the upper part of a quite large house, from now on usually referred to as 'the studio'. It lay well back from the road, ensuring quiet, and was approached by what *Vogue* kindly described as a garden passage (true, there were two nondescript trees in tubs) but which in reality consisted for the most part of a tunnel, unlovely but a boon in wet weather. He took over the lease from Frankie Leveson, a dancer who was also an interior decorator of taste. The very large studio room itself had a raised dais all along one wall—a stage in fact, with a grand piano at each end and a prodigiously large window above it—and in this room Frankie Leveson's influence could still be seen. The handsome pale oak doors and other fixtures had been antiqued in a vaguely Spanish way, and Noel also bought from him some matching furniture. But Noel soon made his own personality felt, as he always did in a house, by choosing good modern fabrics, zebra-striped cushions and objects—a few of chromium and more of heavy Lalique and other glass —which today would be worth a small fortune as Art Deco.

It was from 17 Gerald Road that Noel set out one day to browse among the bookshops of Charing Cross Road, and in Foyle's by happy chance came across some bound volumes of the *Illustrated London News.* The first fell open at a picture of a troopship leaving for the Boer War: he bought the lot and on the way home his mind filled with the music-hall songs of the period and of his early childhood—'Goodbye My Bluebell', 'Goodbye Dolly Gray' and 'We're the Soldiers of the Queen, My Lads'. They rang a bell in his head, and he somehow knew he had found what he wanted for his spectacular; he was still singing and playing the songs in the big room by the time G. B. Stern arrived for tea. 'Peter', older than he, remembered the excitement of the Boer War vividly: the hero worship of 'Bobs' (Field-Marshal Lord Roberts, V.C.); scullery maids sent scurrying up area steps for newspapers with the latest news from South Africa, of Mafeking Night and of Queen Victoria's last illness and death. She became as enthusiastic as he, and Noel later dedicated the play to her in gratitude for the sparks she struck during those two productive hours. They even found the title; Noel knew he wanted something like Pageant or Procession until he finally, Peter said, shouted 'Cavalcade!' 'A procession on horseback': Noel's successful use of the word as a title has been adopted ever since, resulting in its debasement, and one can nowadays read of a cavalcade of cars following the hearse, or the announcement of a Cavalcade of Ice Skating.

Noel spent Christmas with Jack at Goldenhurst, a week in which he turned out four songs for *Cochran's 1931 Revue*, two of which—'Half-Caste Woman' and 'Any Little Fish Can Swim'—remain durable. He sailed in January of that year to appear with Gertie and Larry in the New York production of *Private Lives*; Jill Esmond, Larry's bride of a few months, replaced Adrianne, who had to make a film in England. Among his luggage were his copies of the *Illustrated London News* and a stack of books for research on *Cavalcade*, which was never out of his mind for long; he had promised Cochran to complete it that summer for production in the autumn. *Private Lives* repeated its London triumph on Broadway, the reviews were rapturous, Walter Winchell thought it 'something to go silly over', and Noel sold the film rights for what was then a great deal of money to M.G.M., as he did those of *Bitter Sweet*, outright and for ever. (Authors sold properties outright in those days and were glad to do so, but lived to regret it. Television was then only a dream in the minds of scientists, but contracts contained the words 'and any other rights of mechanical reproduction whatsoever', and many a future goldmine was lost to them.)

'I'm not very keen on Hollywood,' Noel wrote to his mother, 'I'd rather have a nice cup of cocoa really.' A political crisis was brewing in England and he wrote among other things in his Sunday letters that he was glad Father was fighting for England but 'if *you* start getting Political I should think there'd be hell to pay in the dear old country!' He wrote that he had sold the four Cochran revue songs, Beatrice Lillie was doing two of them in the new *Little Show* and the other two were going into the *Ziegfeld Follies*; everyone thought he was *crazy* to close after three months while playing to capacity; and Cochran had cabled he couldn't get the Coliseum for *Cavalcade* but had fixed the Theatre Royal, Drury Lane, which was more dignified but this was a secret and she wasn't to tell anyone except Sacha, the dachshund, and he would sail for home on the *Bremen* in May.

He and Gladys worked all summer long at Goldenhurst, every day from eight until five with a one-hour break for lunch, until *Cavalcade* was finished; she on the twenty-two sets and hundreds and hundreds of dresses, and he on the book. This was the story of two families under one roof, covering dramatically the history of England from 1899, the year Noel was born, up to that day, when he himself was thirty-one. The central figure was Jane Marryot, around whom the story revolved, played by Mary Clare. Otherwise there were no stars as such in the huge cast but Noel, ever loyal, found parts for many friends; Irene Browne, the young John Mills, Moya Nugent, Maidie Andrews, Arthur Macrae, Betty Shale, Betty Hare, Phyllis Harding and Anthony Pelissier among them, and there were also Binnie Barnes, Una O'Connor and Strella Wilson the Australian soprano.

Noel wrote Jane Marryot's story with no foreknowledge, how could he have had, that the first night on October 13th, 1931, would coincide with a national crisis of the first order, that just before then Great Britain would be shaken by having to come off the gold standard, that symbol of security, or that the Labour Government would be thrown out a few days afterwards.

Patriotism was at fever pitch, and from the moment the curtain went up, *Cavalcade* was an assault on the emotions and the senses such as one receives when a military band comes blaring down the street. But the band did not pass; the emotions were assaulted all evening long, Noel using those old recruiting songs that had sprung to his mind in Foyle's bookshop to devastating effect, culminating in his own 'Twentieth-Century Blues' sung in a scene of chaos:

> What is there to strive for,
> Love, or keep alive for?

Noel had given the public his spectacle all right, one big and extravagant scene followed another, with a cast of hundreds; but it was in the smaller inset scenes that his good, spare writing combined with inspired stagecraft became the most telling. Queen Victoria's funeral for instance; we saw the Marryots waiting in their drawing-room to watch the procession pass:

JOE (*the smaller, younger son*): Why did Queen Victoria die, Mum?
JANE: Because she was a very old lady, and very tired.
JOE: Could I have another piece of cake?

We only saw the backs of the family as they went to the balcony to watch, then we heard in the distance the dreadful brass sound of the Funeral March, combined with the rumble of the gun-carriage approaching with the tiny coffin, the clop of many horses' hooves and the heavy tread of the marching soldiers, until the noise crescendoed as the procession passed by and then slowly died away into silence. The family turned back into the room.

JANE: Five kings riding behind her.
JOE: Mum, she must have been a very little lady.
       (*The lights fade.*)

We had seen, felt we really had seen, the funeral of the great Queen Victoria.

Then there was a scene, set in the early evening of April 14th, 1912, with Edward, the elder Marryot son, leaning over a ship's rail, on honeymoon with Edith, his boyhood sweetheart. They were speculating on whether they would live happy ever after, as his father and mother had done.

EDWARD: How long do you give us?
EDITH: I don't know—and Edward (*she turns to him*) I don't care. This is our moment—complete and heavenly. I'm not afraid of anything. This is our own, for ever. (*Edward takes her in his arms and kisses her.*)

As they turned to walk away she took her evening cloak off the rail and the audience was horrified to see revealed on a ship's lifebelt the name S.S. *Titanic*, and to hear the orchestra swell into 'Nearer My God to Thee'.

The play ended after the Chaos scene, with the 250-strong company on stage to sing the National Anthem, with the Union Jack glowing in the darkness behind them. The audience to a man sprang to its feet and, except for those with voices too choked, sang it with them. The cheers and applause were tumultuous and no one would leave, until Noel had to come on. He made a speech which ended, 'In spite of the troublous times we are living in, it is still pretty exciting to be English.'

The praise was overwhelming, the play became a national sensation; King George V with Queen Mary and the immediate members of the Royal Family attended a performance two weeks later on the night of the sweeping National Government election victory—an evening of thrilling fervour—until Noel felt that his play about that simple, decent family had become distorted. Partly his own fault, the Union Jack and all that, and his 'pretty exciting to be English', and partly the fault of its coincidence with a time of national unrest which some papers blew up into 'Coward's Call to Arms' to the youth of the nation. Others called it a 'shrill blare on a trumpet' and the lefter weeklies saw it as a cheap descent into jingoism, a cashing-in on what was to them anathema: patriotism. The whole fuss and fume was, Noel thought, best summed up by Sara Allgood, who stopped by his table at the Ivy and gave her verdict in her rich brogue: 'There's some say it's clap-trap, but Oi loiked it.'

Letters poured in by the shoal, most from fans which Lornie could answer, but so many from the special and the famous that they had to make a *Cavalcade* section in the Celebrity File instead of separating them alphabetically. Dowager Peeresses abound in this section, some of their letters very touching: 'I saw the evening through a haze of tears'; 'my entire life passed before me'; 'I lost sons in both those wars, the Boer War and this last one.' Then there were those who amongst their praise brought up small points of military or social behaviour in those far-off days; 'the wounded were not carried off the train head first', and so on. Scene 8 of Part One (a splendid ball at which we know for the first time from the major-domo's announcement, 'Sir Edward and Lady Marryot', that Jane's husband has been honoured) caused a lot of fun. The Hon. Maurice Baring, the poet and novelist, wrote the funniest of the social settings-right. Mr Baring used a language of his own in which Noel Coward became 'Numble Cumble', and so on; here is his letter, typed as it was with his trembling fingers:

18 Cheyne Row, Chelsea, S.W.3. October 17 1931.
My Dear Noel, I wnr to Cumble Cumble last night and I was thrille from beginning to end and a mop of tears most of the time. I do congratulate you on the magnificent way you hav planned this work and the etraodin r y skill you have shown in carry ing out your idea. The cen of th eoldiers moving up the hill is wonderful and I mnot sure I didn't like the Queen Vic scene best of al There ought to be line about him he myust be called the German Emperor not the Kaiser in th se days. I hear Lord Lurgan is th authority for black wai coats at the ball. I cant help thi nking hes mixing it up with dinners. Myseldf I ever saw or wore a balck waistcoat at a ball. WEn to my first Stafford House in 1894. I have still ome 1900 hite waiscoats. But if you ant docimentary evidence look at the Vanity Faif caryoons which w re done from life and you will find as far back as uly 1870 a Gordon lennox described as a man of fashion and politics dressed for a pary putting on hi whiy gloves and wearing a whit waiscoat The you have in Jan 18 74 As Lumley a famous cotillon leader aslo putting on his gloves picture called 'Cotillon' and in awhite waiscoat then you have in 1887 Lord Henry Manners afterwards Duke of Rumble daxzzling in white waiscoat and shirt front and I expect her are many others. Anf if this is true of people so far back it is truer of 1903. But I do remeber coming back froma Russia in the nineteen hundreds and sudd nly being aware for the fisrt time that it was a floater to o out to dinner in a black waiscoat. Hiertho one ha alwasy bee n able to dine out ei a black wai coat bu not to go to a ball or big party. Im rather sorry there wasnt an air raid signal in one ofthe London scenes but one cant have evrything I like it all,

from beginning to end and I do congtarul te you with all my humble. Yrs Mumble.

Noel stayed on in London for a fortnight, up to a point revelling in all the adulation and hullabaloo, but the tempo of the last months had gone on intensifying alarmingly until in the end he was thankful to sail away with Jeffery from Boulogne on a grey November morning. The ship was making the gentle and increasingly warmer South Atlantic crossing to Rio de Janeiro; soon they were able to sunbathe on deck and watch the flying fish. Their plan was to stay away for nine months, after Rio to explore the tropical jungles and rivers, the vast mountains and vaster deserts of South America, so on the voyage Noel listened to Linguaphone records in order to brush up his Spanish until there was 'little I couldn't tell you about La Familia Fernandez straight off the bat'. He also trudged manfully through John Green's *History of the English People* and H. G. Wells's *Outline of History*.

Their first view of Rio de Janeiro did not let them down; it was as sensational as they had expected it to be, 'the Sugar Loaf mountain climbed up into the sky and the other mountains behind it emerged from the morning mist, shedding their clouds gracefully and looking a little self-conscious as though they had been caught washing their hair.' Their three weeks in Rio were dizzy with social activity; on the very first day the American Ambassador, Edwin Morgan, called and invited them to an enormous and glittering party at the Embassy that evening, so that they met all the top-notchers of Rio society in a trice. Out of the continuous gaiety two enduring friends emerged, the kind and beautiful Baby Guinle (now Mrs Kenneth Pendar) and Daan Hubrecht, son of the Dutch Ambassador. Noel also got in with a hearty English major with a black patch over one eye who, after he felt he knew Noel well enough, blushed like a maiden and confessed that he had been writing poetry secretly for years. Noel swore that the first poem the Major shyly handed him ended with the lines:

> Oh simple shepherd praise thy God
> That thou art nothing but a sod.

Daan was at this time twenty-one, 'tall, handsome and dashing, and only needed side-whiskers and a moustache to have been a credit to Ouida'. He was embroiled in a rather perilous love-affair with an Englishwoman married to a Brazilian, and when Noel and Jeffery asked his parents if he might come with them for at any rate part of their journey into the interior, they assented and made no attempt to conceal their relief.

Noel's Sunday letter from São Paulo begins, 'Well, we've got away from Rio at last. It was difficult to leave because we were having such fun. We made a striking exit—had to jump into the train while it was going. Crowds came down to see us off and it was all very funny.'

Noel had a passion for snakes, and on arrival at São Paulo made an immediate bee-line for the famous snake-farm. He left with the gift from Doctor Amliera of a coral snake as a pet. He christened it Eugénie, and Eugénie went everywhere with him, frightening people to death at cocktail parties when they saw her peeping out of his breast pocket. Eugénie eventually died of drink: an entire dry martini lapped up out of a saucer put down by Jeffery. Why did he allow Jeff to do it? He never satisfactorily answered this question, but it is no exaggeration to say that he mourned her always, often remembering 'how pretty she was, and how sweet'.

On Christmas Day 1931, Noel wrote from the Plaza Hotel, Buenos Aires:

I haven't written for two weeks because arriving here was very hectic. We had a marvellous expedition. We were the guests of a Matè (sort of Tea) Company, just Jeff and Daan and me. We had a special car from São Paulo, hitched on to the end of the train, we travelled for three days in it and then arrived at the Parana river where we got on a very peculiar boat and drifted down to a place called GUAYRA. It was really very interesting because only *very* few white people have ever made that trip, the jungle on each side of the river is absolutely virgin forest and quite terrifying. You can't walk more than a few yards and it's filled with snakes and orchids and parrots and it stretches on the right side for almost *two thousand* miles! We stayed in Guayra for two days, then we went on down river to the Iguassu Falls which are immense and twice as big as Niagara. Then on for days and days, changing boats all the time, until we arrived here. The last boat was very grand and the beast of a Captain refused to allow us to come on deck or have meals in the dining-room because we were not suitably dressed (riding things). He actually sent for the Police to put us off which they refused to do. So we were sent below where we remained for two days. All the first-class passengers were delighted with themselves. We remained quite happily below and gave a cocktail party to all the stewards. Then on the morning we arrived we stepped off the boat *exquisitely* dressed, were met by a very grand car and several commissionaires [*sic*: perhaps Commissioners? But it was in fact the British Consul, a Mr Gudgeon], we cut the Captain and shook hands with all the stewards. There has been the most awful row about it, all the Directors of the Line have apologised and the Papers have been full of it. I almost feel sorry for the Captain now! The fuss that was made over us in Rio is *nothing* to what's happening to us here. The Brit. Ambassador and Lady MacCleay are charming and take us everywhere, we're going to stay with them next week at Mar del Plata. [Noel notes elsewhere that 'Lady MacCleay cheated in the Casino at Mar del Plata. Very enjoyable scene.'] Then we're going to stay at a lovely Estancia on the borders of Chile where the Princes stayed. [The Prince of Wales and Prince George had very recently toured South America.] I have had to make a few official visits to Museums and Art Galleries, followed by a string of beetle-browed directors. It's very funny and my Spanish is improving rapidly.

The British Ambassador had asked Noel if he would mind being 'used'; the Princes had been an enormous success with the Argentines but had not paid quite enough attention to the English residents, causing some resentment. 'In fairness to the Princes I had to admit that I rather saw their point. I was naturally flattered to be told that by opening a flower show and making speeches at one or two clubs I could in any way enhance the prestige of my country, so I agreed. My official appearances were brief and quite painless and as a matter of fact I rather enjoyed them.'

Noel often wished to write a travel book; not, he said, of the *Through Tibet on a Bicycle* variety, nor could he hope to emulate the real travellers and explorers, such as Sir Richard Burton and his wife (though Noel could never forgive her for burning her husband's last manuscript, 'the silly old bitch'), and in our own time Peter Fleming, Rose Macaulay, Freya Stark and Lesley Blanch, all of whose books he devoured. Noel's would of necessity have been different. For one thing, although he admitted to the childish and egocentric pleasure of saying that he had been to Peru, or 'here I am, actually looking at the Great Wall of China', he was not by nature a see-er of sights. The reality as a rule came nowhere near his expectations, or up to the florid colours of travelogues seen from the comfort of a cinema seat (Angkor always the exception, surpassingly beautiful beyond imagining). And then quite often ill-luck would thwart him, as on these present travels, when after he and Jeffery endured much discomfort to see the Iguassu Falls, owing to some freak of Nature the entire area was densely clouded with large black mosquitoes. He preferred places and people to the recommended sights; Rome was to him the Via Veneto, as Bugis Street and Raffles Hotel constituted Singapore. He has left some accounts of his travels with Jeffery in 1932 which give a good idea of what his book would have been. His love of movement, of travel for its own sake, emanates from the pages; he puts up with adversity and hardship but only if he is forced to, preferring whenever possible to travel in comfort. Then too he belonged to a time when people — and his fame placed him in that class of person — went automatically on arrival at their destination to sign the book at Government House or the British Embassy, and he delights in the subsequent invitations, the luxury and the grandeur, after a spell of roughing it. One can be sure that his book would have abounded in vignettes such as this description of the night before his and Jeffery's attempt to see the Iguassu Falls:

There was nowhere to spend the night except on board an ancient, long-discarded pleasure steamer which had a sinister Outward Bound atmosphere and contained a few cockroach-infested cabins, a vast dark dining saloon and a mad steward dressed in a greyish-white bumfreezer, ominously stained blue trousers and multi-coloured carpet slippers. He had two complete rows of brilliantly gold teeth and, as it was his habit to go into gales of high-pitched laughter whenever we asked him for anything, we were almost blinded. Apart from him and us and the cockroaches, the only other living creature on board that macabre vessel was an incredibly old mongrel which had no teeth at all, gold or otherwise. Its name was Peppo. The food needless to say was disgusting ... After our nasty meal we sat out on the deck listening to the river muttering by and chain-smoking cigarettes to discourage the insects. Later on in the evening Peppo made a determined effort to get into bed with me but I succeeded in repelling his advances and he finally retired, wheezing down the dark corridor.

Before the end of their stay in the Argentine, Daan had had to leave them to return to Rio; they sadly missed his gay and charming company but pressed on for three nights and two days in a very hot train through a dust storm, from which they emerged covered in grit to stay for a week with Leonora Hughes. She had been the partner of 'Maurice', the same Maurice who had been at Davos that exciting Christmas of 1922, whom Noel then described as the best dancer in the world. Leonora Hughes and Maurice were almost as famous in England as Vernon and Irene Castle had been in America, and danced with the same whirlwind grace. She married Carlos Basualdo, eldest son of one of the wealthiest families in the Argentine, and they now provided the dusty travellers with one of the contrasts Noel so much enjoyed; the last word in luxury, perfect food and a marble bathroom to every gloriously comfortable bedroom, in a house set in the middle of hundreds of miles of wild, untamed country in Patagonia, verging on the Chilean Lakes.

The next stage of their journey, to the railhead for the train to get them to Valparaiso, involved constant changes in ramshackle little steamers to get them across a series of lakes, and, in between steamers, treks on disagreeable mules to transport them and their luggage. They arrived at the railhead in the early hours of the morning and spent the long hours waiting for their train sleepily playing Russian Bank on the top of a suitcase and watching their fellow travellers.

After Valparaiso their next stop was at Santiago, Chile, again at the Embassy. Noel does make slight apology for the profusion of Ambassadors littering his notes, but adds that the Chiltons were un-ambassadorial to a degree and did not know the meaning of the word pomposity. He spent one lazy afternoon with Jeff in the shade of an exotic tree with an unpronounceable name in the Embassy garden, enjoying all the theatrical gossip of London and New York in the packet of mail that had just caught up with them. That is until he came across a very severe jolt indeed in the form of a cable from the Lunts: OUR CONTRACT WITH THEATRE GUILD UP IN JUNE WHAT ABOUT IT?

He knew what they meant by IT, all right: his thoughts flew back eleven years to the pact the three of them had made. Looking back from the shady coolness of the Chiltons' garden, the idea seemed to Noel to have been little more – however earnest their belief in themselves – than a far fetched and over-ambitious pipedream. But a great deal had happened in those eleven years, they *had* all become established stars in their own right, and in addition Noel *had* become a successful playwright, as he had sworn that night he would. Now it was up to him to complete the plan; his promise that he and no one else would write a comedy for the three of them to play in, and of course at the age of twenty-one he had promised them that it would be 'brilliant'. The time had come, and what is more the play would have to be finished by June; the Lunts, once they were free of their Theatre Guild contract, would be scrambled after by every management in New York. To write a play for one star personality is no easy matter, but to provide three star parts in the same play, at the same time giving each equal status and equal opportunities to shine, would be a formidable assignment, easier said in 1921 than done in 1932. Noel did not panic, he would write quickly once he got a theme, but from then on his traveller's joy became less happy-go-lucky, overshadowed by a sense of urgency.

He journeyed on with Jeffery through jungles and over mountains, crossed Lake Titicaca to Cuzco, and saw the source of the Amazon gurgling out from under some small stones. They travelled hundreds of miles in something called an auto-carril, a small Ford car the wheels of which were presumably of the same gauge as the railway, for he says that it was wisely shunted into a siding when there was any danger of meeting an express train head-on.

Finally they got to Lima, but decided that Peru was 'too restless' after experiencing an earthquake and a revolution on one and the same day, and moved on to relax in the tropical heat of Panama. Their months of adventure ended at Colón, where they had to part company; Jeff for England, while Noel had the great good fortune to snap up the Owner's Suite in a Norwegian freighter, Los Angeles bound. The ship was small and there was no other passenger accommodation, not a soul to repel or bore him or on whom he would have to exert his by now well-known Noel Coward charm; he thought those ten days crawling slowly up the Pacific coast were among the most enjoyable he had ever known. All day he wore nothing at all, then put on a pair of shorts as a concession when dining at six sharp with the Captain, who to look at had stepped straight out of Joseph Conrad's pages, and with a sense of humour which failed him only at the mention of God, in whose existence he held a stern disbelief. The remainder of each evening Noel spent in long sing-songs and potent 'piss-ups' as he called them, with the crew in the fo'csle.

Noel spent his mornings writing *Design for Living*, the idea for which slipped easily into his mind on the first night out at sea, and he wrote steadily away every day—a painless birth with no moments of despair except for one when his typewriter ribbon ran out, but then he found that after all he had a spare one with him. The script was neatly completed and typed with two days still to go before docking at Los Angeles; the Captain shed his Nordic severity that evening and joined the crew in celebration so enthusiastically that Noel was surprised to find the ship still on an even keel the next morning.

Jack was waiting on the dockside in a state of highly nervous anxiety. Noel had to take him below and give him some gin in a toothglass while he explained that he had been rushing from one shipping office to another for over an hour. Noel attributed this to his never having had to meet a ship smaller than the *Queen Mary*, but to be fair, Noel's ship was so small that no official had heard of it, and Jack kept asking how a Norwegian freight boat could possibly be called the *Toronto* — a question no one, Noel included, could answer.

There then followed another hectic visit to Hollywood, this time highly charged with days in the studios watching films, rough-cuts and rushes, the evenings attending sybaritic dinner parties in palatial homes, after which a screen either rose up from the floor or descended from the ceiling, on which to show yet another brand new film starring (almost invariably) the hostess. Noel's first sight of the M.G.M. film of *Private Lives* was, however, mercifully shown in the afternoon, a pleasant occasion with few people present; he sat between the film's two stars, Norma Shearer and Robert Montgomery. Just before the film started Montgomery handed him a small red box. The box contained what was obviously a very expensive initialled gold watch: 'This', he disarmingly said, 'is to prevent you saying what you really think about my performance.' It didn't, however, because Noel thought both stars' performances were perfectly charming. The film had already proved a box-office success and in consequence his visit proved profitable; the film rights for *Bitter Sweet* and *The Queen Was in the Parlour* were easily sold, and so were those for *Hay Fever*, though no film of the latter was ever made.

The film rights to *Cavalcade* had not been sold. The play was still running at Drury Lane and a dear lady, to whom Noel was forever grateful, went to see it on the last night of her holiday in London. Mrs Tinker — for that was her lovely name — was so impressed by what she saw that she cancelled her next day's passage to America and went that night to see *Cavalcade* a second time. She cabled Mr Tinker, who happened to be a Fox Films executive, that it was imperative they buy the film rights in spite of every other major Hollywood studio having refused to do so. Mrs Tinker had her way and so did Mr Tinker, although he only had his wife's word to go on and also met with strong opposition from the rest of the board.

During this stay in Hollywood Noel was invited to attend the first technical conference before shooting began on the film, in fact his first film conference, his first sight of one of those forbiddingly long shiny tables, the pads and pencils and carafes and glasses of water. Everybody aired their views, the scriptwriter — later replaced by Reginald Berkeley, who wrote a very fine script — gave it as his opinion that the film should open with a wintry shot of a little bird perched on the bare branch of a tree, bird and branch both snow-flecked. As we watch the little bird the music should swell and before one's eyes the branch should burgeon with tender leaf and blossom, the bird would be joined by its mate and together they would build their love-nest, and suddenly it would be spring! Noel thought he had never heard so much tommy-rot talked in his life; exasperated beyond endurance he suddenly remembered a previous appointment and fled, leaving them to it. To finish the story, Fox displayed little interest in the film beyond engaging Frank Lloyd, a British director, and an excellent one, who had for some time been unemployed. He in turn engaged a first-rate cast, none of whom with the exception of Clive Brook could be described as top-flight film-stars; Diana Wynyard, Irene Browne, Frank Lawton and Ursula Jeans. Lloyd was left to make the picture straightforwardly and in peace, all the big-shots' dangerous suggestions for 'improvements' being directed elsewhere. Hardly anybody came near the set (though Noel liked to think that Mr and Mrs Tinker would have had access at all times and been provided with those mandatory canvas chairs, but with *their* names emblazoned in gold). The picture was almost finished before word began to seep out that Fox had a humdinger in *Cavalcade*, and a humdinger it turned out to be.

9

DESIGN
FOR LIVING

THE Hollywood visit ended with Noel falling into his bed on the Super Chief at Pasadena, so exhausted that he slept nearly all the way to Chicago. On arrival in New York he found that Lynn and Alfred were more excited and pleased with *Design for Living* than even he could have hoped for and, as he had foreseen, every important management in New York was after such a prize package and doing its utmost to entice the three of them. Noel was deluged with flowers, Napoleon brandy and cases of champagne, and in the end gave the play to Max Gordon, who hadn't sent him so much as a Hershey Bar. This was brought about by Max arriving at the apartment and announcing that unless Noel let him present *Design for Living* he would cut his throat—his own, not Noel's. Noel had been fond of Max ever since he had come round, a comparative stranger, after a performance of *Private Lives* and told Noel he thought the play brilliant, as were Noel himself and Gertie, so what the hell did the two of them think they were doing, overacting so disgracefully in the third act? This shocked Noel into calling a rehearsal the very next morning, and he had admired and been grateful for Max's honesty and courage. Noel did not know when Max made this present generous gesture that at that moment Max had not enough cash to pay the cast of his current play come Friday night, two or three days hence, or that Max rushed out and on the strength of Noel's promise immediately raised enough money not only to pay his cast but also to present *Design for Living* in a dignified and first-class manner. Max Gordon was back on the map in one bound, and has remained there ever since.

Lynn, Alfred, Noel and of course Max Gordon were in such a state of excitement that they longed to go into rehearsal at once, but common sense had to prevail; it would have been folly in those days to open in New York at the beginning of summer. Besides, Noel had promised Cochran a new revue for that very summer in England.

He was happy to get back to Goldenhurst and looking forward to rehearsals and production of the revue, which was by now entitled *Words and Music*. At an early audition he saw and met Master Graham Philip Payn for the first time. Graham's mother Sybil advised her fourteen-year-old son to sing one verse of 'Nearer My God to Thee' to show off the purity of his boyish treble to the best advantage, and then to go *quickly* before anyone could stop him into a tap dance, to show his versatility. Noel was not exactly impressed; he always said he had been so taken aback by this combination that he engaged Graham on the spot, and gave him the parts of a pageboy in a white satin suit in 'The Midnight Matinée' and an urchin street-singer in 'Mad About the Boy'.

Noel was by now in a position to dictate his wishes to Cochran instead of the other way round, and insisted he could do without three of what Cochran had up to then considered the most essential ingredients of his revues: one or more glamorous star names, sensationally good dancing and an assembly of brilliant designers. (Gladys had triumphantly designed the whole of *Cavalcade* and could do the same with *Words and Music*, which she did.) To add to Cochran's dismay, the revue contained some rather downbeat songs and too much satire for his—and he felt sure for the public's—liking. Cochran was right; though the critics were lavish with their praise, *Words and Music* ran for barely five months instead of the two years Noel had hoped for. Looking back on it all Noel remembered the warning of Emma, his old nurse, when he was a little boy: 'You're too sharp by half, you'll cut yourself one of these days.'

But from the beginning, and for the first few weeks of the run, the show had all the hallmarks of a Coward smash hit. This time no one could wait for London, but trooped up to Manchester for the final dress-rehearsal or first night there: Lord Lloyd, Lord Moynihan, Lord Derby, Lynn Fontanne, Alfred Lunt, Peggy Wood, Francis Lederer, and one yellowed clipping promises that the Marquess of Anglesey intends to bring a party of twelve, seats have been booked for a party of one hundred, including Mr Coward's friends coming from London, and—her name always news value—'I was told to-day that Lady Diana Duff Cooper is also making an effort to be present.'

Manchester over, Mrs Coward's scrap album gives an idea of what was going on socially in London. From *Vogue*: 'It was past three when Noel Coward sat down to the piano at York House to delight the Prince [of Wales]'s guests with numbers from his *Words and Music*. The next day very much the same company were seen at Noel Coward's cocktail party in his home at Gerald Road, in Frankie Leveson's old studio, with the addition of a number of lovely people from the world of the theatre such as the guest of honour, Joan Crawford and her husband [Douglas Fairbanks Jr].' A newspaper continues: 'Several people invited ... asked their host casually who was going to be there. "Oh, just ourselves." Just ourselves turned out to be a tremendous crowd which packed his studio ... some people still humming the tunes he had played at the Prince's party for Lady Louis Mountbatten.' *Vogue* goes on:

> Dorothy Dickson with her lovely daughter [Dorothy Hyson], Laurence Olivier with his wife Jill Esmond, Lady Louis was in a tiny hat and blue sailor suit, Lady Brecknock very compact in her usual mushroom hat, clean collar and clean-cut tailor-made, Lady Ravensdale very romanesque with a red neck band ... the studio, very Spanish with its interior gallery. There were Madonna lilies and concealed lighting and much sitting around (we rested when we could those last hectic days). It was a party in the enlightened tradition, all very white and witty.

Two of Noel's most famous songs, 'Mad About the Boy' and 'Mad Dogs and Englishmen', emerged from *Words and Music*, to stay. He personally was stuck with them for the rest of his life, always expected to sing one or the other at parties or cabaret appearances, unthinkable from his audience's point of view that he should not. These were later joined by a third, 'Don't Put Your Daughter on the Stage, Mrs Worthington', his very individual interpretation of which made it equally obligatory for his audiences. He was so weary of having to sing 'Mad Dogs' that by the time he got to Las Vegas in 1955, in order to do something, anything, with it for a change, he took it at such a terrific clip that Cole Porter said it was the only time in his life he'd heard an entire song sung all in one breath. He was delighted when he and 'Mad Dogs' achieved the immortality of *The Oxford Dictionary of Quotations* in its 1953 edition, but a little worried that the phrase might not be entirely his. Many fans had been sending slight traces of its origins from obscure books of travel, the earliest in *Rough Leaves From a Journal* by Lt.-Col. Lovell Badcock, published in 1835: 'It happened to be during the heat of the day, when dogs and English alone are seen to move.' The first mention

of mad dogs we ever came across was in an 1874 *Guide to Malta* by
the Reverend G. N. Goodwin, Chaplain to the Forces there: 'Only
newly arrived Englishmen and mad dogs expose themselves to it.'
Of course the *O.D.Q.* is right; the present neat shape of the saying is
Noel's.

On June 29th, Erik wrote to his mother:

> My Darling, By the time you get this I shall be on the high seas
> and *Home* before August. I am being sent home on 3 months
> sick leave as my tummy is all over the place and the doctors
> say that a sea voyage and good food are the only things that
> will put me right. This is an awful scribble but the mail is just
> going and the Doctors have only just finished examining me.
> Now *don't* worry. It's not serious & all expenses are being paid
> by the Company. So there! Snaps and snips, Erik.

This was followed by another note from Colombo, before he sailed:
'I got your cable this morning and like you I'm wildly excited. After
all I've had four years and a certain amount of illness so a change is
obviously what I want. My dear I *do* hope Cavalcade will last until
I get home. It would be maddening to just miss it. Give everyone
my love. I shall see you soon and snap you hard and often.'

The end of the Manchester tryout of *Words and Music* coincided
with Erik's return; Noel spent that weekend at Goldenhurst and
was so shocked by Erik's shrunken, gaunt appearance that he immediately feared the worst. He got him into Lady Carnarvon's Nursing
Home as quickly as he could, where Lord Moynihan's opinion confirmed Noel's fears—he was suffering from a lethal form of cancer
and could not be expected to live for more than six months. Erik
was in his room anxiously awaiting the verdict, and very frightened.
Lady Carnarvon was as usual a rock of strength and kindness; she
hurriedly searched a medical dictionary for a disease that was ultimately curable and settled on Hyperplasia of the abdominal glands
(Erik's cancer was abdominal). She and Noel went to Erik and
explained that it was a serious illness which would take a long time to
cure, that he would have to be patient and expect to get worse before
he could get better. He could go to Goldenhurst and slowly con-
valesce with a nurse, and then in a moment of inspiration Noel told
him he could busy himself by making an accurate and detailed index
of his hundreds of gramophone records.

Noel has left two confusing accounts—and no wonder—of the

order of events that followed, but it is evident that Erik was up and
about and got his wish to see *Cavalcade* just in time. He was sitting
in the stalls on the last night with his mother, both of them unconscious
of his fate, smiling and waving gaily to Noel in his box. The same
thing happened, agonising for Noel, who sought comfort in glasses
of brandy held below the level of the box, on the first night of *Words*
and Music at the Adelphi, when 'Erik and Mum were merry as grigs'.
His next miserable assignment was the breaking of the news to his
father and mother: 'This ghastly interview, organised with consummate tact and sympathy by Lady Carnarvon, took place in her
private sitting-room. I do not wish to enlarge upon it because even
after so many years I find the memory of it intolerable.'

After his gruesome afternoon he went alone to a movie at the
Tivoli and then walked across the Strand to the Adelphi to look in on
his pals in the cast of *Words and Music*, Joyce Barbour, Johnny Mills
and Romney Brent, who did their gallant best to cheer him up. Finally
Joyce and Romney induced him back to Joyce's flat, where they
and her husband Richard Bird deliberately made him blind drunk.
Then they must have driven him back to Gerald Road, undressed
him and put him to bed; he remembered nothing of it. Noel wrote:

> I think my relationship with Erik requires a little explanation
> principally because he played such a small part in my life that
> many people would have been surprised to know that I had a
> brother at all. He was five years my junior. Perhaps this five-year
> difference was either too long or too short. At all events I have
> to admit, a trifle guiltily perhaps, that I never found him very
> interesting. I tolerated him, was occasionally irritated by him
> and, engrossed as I was by my crowded and exciting career as a
> boy actor, paid very little attention to him. He was there ... but
> no real intimacy between us was ever established. I was reason-
> ably fond of him but I cannot honestly say that we were ever
> very close until perhaps the last sad months of his life.

The last sad months of Erik's life, with their only possible, inevitable
ending, hung like an evil cloud over Noel, a cloud which haunted him,
which would not lift. For him to have stayed on with his mother at
Goldenhurst would have served no purpose, but then this left her alone
in her grief, except for her husband. Apart from all the emotional
stress, Noel had been working hard for months on the revue, and badly
needed a break before the months of work ahead of him with *Design*

for Living. The Navy, to which he now instinctively turned, came to his rescue in the form of an invitation from Lord Mountbatten to join his ship H.M.S. *Queen Elizabeth* in Greece. On his way there he stayed with Lady Mendl at the Villa Trianon, Versailles:

> Darlingest, I'm trying to take your advice about not thinking of you but it's very difficult as I find I think about you all the time. Everything is so tragic and cruel for you and my heart aches dreadfully for you but that's no good either except that it proves even to me (who didn't need much proof) how very very much I love you. The next letter I write to you won't be like this at all, it will be crammed with gay description. This sort of letter only makes us both cry, and that's sillier than anything.

Noel arrived in Greece almost simultaneously with the severest earthquakes that country had suffered for years, the worst manifestation being at Ierossos. He went on with the Navy to Egypt, in the end sailing from Port Said to Genoa and thence back home to England. His farewells to Erik and to his mother before leaving for New York and *Design for Living* were heartrending, a dreadful experience. The play went well and smoothly from the first rehearsal, but he describes it as an unhappy and difficult period of his life: 'Alfred and Lynn I need hardly say were marvellous to me and continued to be consoling and sympathetic without overdoing it.' In addition to the task of writing letters to his mother on a hairline between sounding cheerful and not sounding callous, he had to write to his brother as though nothing were wrong at all: 'Well Master Erik, I haven't written as much and as often as I should have but that's me all over—careless!' He gave him the good news that the *Cavalcade* film had opened in New York and was a super success, he had never read so many superlatives, and so ended the letter: 'Your heroic National minded Patriot Bro. Don't forget to play the CHANTS D'AUVERGNE on the gramophone. All my love to you and hand some out to everybody and get well soon.' At the same time he wrote to his mother: 'I couldn't be so silly as to wish you a Happy Christmas but please buy yourself something completely unnecessary and think of me when you're doing it.' He tried hard to cheer up his mother whenever he could: he knew she would enjoy the following scrap of news because Philip Tonge had been the most handsome and sought-after boy actor in London, getting all the plum parts while Noel was struggling, and the two mothers had been bitterly jealous rivals on their sons' behalves. Mrs Tonge had always in those days emerged the winner, to Mrs Coward's fury, which she was forced to conceal beneath a very very thin veneer of friendship, calling her 'stuck-up' behind her back. 'I've given Philip Tonge a small part in the play and I've had a heartfelt letter of thanks from poor old [Mrs] Tonge so that's a good deed done! He has just one scene with me in the Second Act. It does seem funny when I look back and remember how much in awe of him I was, life certainly plays very strange tricks on people.'

Design for Living opened in Cleveland on January 2nd, 1933, then Pittsburgh and Washington. Two days before they were due to open at the Ethel Barrymore Theatre, New York, on January 22nd, Noel received a cable from his mother to say that Erik had died peacefully in his sleep at Goldenhurst. He cabled immediately that she and Aunt Vida were to come to New York as soon as ever they could, and made reservations for them at the Beekman Tower, just round the corner from his rented apartment at 1 Beekman Place.

Lynn, Alfred, Noel and the play became the talk of the town from the night they opened. Brooks Atkinson wrote that they were an incomparable trio of light comedians, and that they gave the play the sententious acting that transmutes artificial comedy into delight: 'The acting supplies the final brilliance. Miss Fontanne with her slow, languorous deliberation, Mr Lunt with his boyish enthusiasm, Mr Coward with his nervous, biting clarity ... Skill, art, even erudition of a sort, have gone into this gay bit of drollery.'

But privately, to begin with, Noel was far from gay; his mother's and Aunt Vida's arrival only accentuated for him the misery of the months she had had to endure and the strain of the whole dismal business of Erik's illness and death. Alfred arrived at Beekman Place one Saturday morning and said with gentle accusation, 'Noely, you've been crying again.' Noel replied that his voice had gone completely and he could not play that matinée and evening; if only he could rest, his voice would be all right by Monday. In spite of the fact that he and Lynn had recommended an expensive understudy and engaged him, Alfred said that they would refuse to play without Noely, they would close the theatre: 'And that's final!' If only Noel would make the effort he, Alfred, would speak as many as possible of his lines for him. So Noel dragged himself shaking to the theatre and Alfred dried up dead at Noel's first entrance. This so enraged him that he shouted the line at Alfred in a voice that Chaliapin would have envied and played both performances without a croak. All of which, Noel said, 'only goes to prove that the Theatre is a remarkable profession, that Mary Baker Eddy definitely had a point and that actors are very curious animals.'

The play was such a success that Noel for once readily agreed to play for five months instead of his rule of three. Mum and Auntie Vida returned to England, and gradually his sadness lifted until he was able to say that *Design for Living* was one of the happiest engagements he ever played in. Lynn and Alfred were a joy to work with; Alfred and Noel so flexible in their scenes together that once when one inadvertently spoke the other's line, they played the whole scene with lines reversed until Noel remembered that there was a burp coming which Alfred technically could not produce, and neatly switched back again. They both thought they had been frightfully clever, and came off delighted with themselves until Lynn the disciplinarian deflated them: 'I don't think anything either of you did was even remotely funny.' But neither of them ever forgot the fun they had had while doing it.

With the run extended, Noel decided to leave Beekman Place and rented a little cottage in the woods at Sneden's Landing on the banks of the Hudson. He had always loved Sneden's and was to grow to love it more in the years to come, staying there as often as he could with Katharine Cornell and Guthrie McClintic, the only other couple who, for cosy theatrical companionship, could be mentioned in the same breath as Alfred and Lynn. Although Sneden's Landing was only thirty-five minutes by car from the stage-door, it was utterly remote and peaceful; his cottage, though primitive, was well heated and the view through the trees to the Hudson River enchanting. Though he maintained he could write nothing while performing eight times a week unless forced to, the cottage was so ideally quiet for a writer that it was here, during the long mornings, he started work on his autobiography *Present Indicative* and made good progress. He was looked after by a genial, round, Negro gentleman called Henry, who had enjoyed a spell of glory when young, playing the head eunuch in *Aïda* at the Met. 'His voice was understandably very high indeed, and he fussed over me, cooked for me, cosetted me and only very occasionally, sang.'

Special police had to be called out during the last week of *Design for Living*, so great were the crowds in the street. For the latter half of the run Noel, for the first and last time in his life, had to employ a bodyguard, his own private detective. Kidnappings and abductions were rife, scares swept America, Noel received several threatening letters, and the cottage at Sneden's was isolated. So Tommy Webber never left him, drove with him back and forth and sat at the side of the stage at each performance, 'bulging with armaments'. Tommy shadowed Noel right up to the cocktail party he gave in the ship before sailing for Bermuda; he had been very cheerful and friendly, but Noel was relieved when Tommy gave him the last playful poke in the ribs with his loaded gun before he vanished down the gang-way. The ship that Noel caught to Bermuda was on a cruise, crammed with tourists who for three whole days and nights drank themselves silly, though Noel suspected that the majority of them were fairly silly to begin with. Middle-aged ladies, fried to the gills and wearing paper caps, frequently banged on his door in the middle of the night; the noise they made all day was equally hideous and he was forced to spend most of the time locked in his cabin. This was Noel's only experience of an honest-to-goodness jolly cruise and those dreadful three days must have been responsible, he considered, for the emergence of *Sail Away*, his musical satire of a cruise ship and its tourists, almost thirty years later.

Once arrived at Bermuda, he joined H.M.S. *Dragon*; and he thought that this cruise of the Caribbean was, out of all his cheerful gallivant-ings with the Navy, one of the happiest. His hosts were Admiral Wells, whose flagship it was, and 'Joe' Vian, he of the piercing blue eyes and aggressive eyebrows, later to become famous (which he hated) as Admiral Sir Philip Vian, hero of the *Altmark*, who first spoke the legendary phrase 'The Navy's here'. When a few days out to sea, Noel happened on a book, still delightful to read, called *The Regent and His Daughter* by Dormer Creston. Jane Austen apart—and she being timeless is not obviously representative of it—the period of the Regency had never attracted Noel. In fact he admitted that the whole stretch from the end of the French Revolution up to the Second Empire was for him undiscovered territory. Yet somehow *The Regent and His Daughter*, and Brighton during the Regency especially, re-mained in his mind, and during his voyage home to England from Trinidad in a ship called the *Flandre*—so slow she reminded him of a black-coated fat old concierge waddling through the water—he had completed the libretto for *Conversation Piece*.

He was astonished to find waiting at Gerald Road, at the early age of thirty-three, a copy of the first biography of himself: *The Amazing Mr Noel Coward* by Patrick Braybrooke, F.R.S.L. Astonished, because it was his first intimation that a biography could be written without the permission of the subject or word or contact of any kind from the author. The book contained more than a few inaccuracies; but was well-intentioned, the author writing about his subject with an admiration amounting to a schoolgirl crush, unhesitatingly calling Noel a genius on the very first page. Noel was, it seems, even active while still in his cradle, making rough mental notes for the future, and preparing himself for his life's work, 'and the river rolled on quietly through Teddington': the newsboys were so concerned shouting the bad news from the Boer War that they quite forgot to call out the good news from the English front, that 'December 16th, 1899, was a red-letter day for England, one of those days set apart for the birth of a man of genius.' Noel said he thought that the Thames really might have changed its course for him, or had a Tidal Wave or a Great Bore or *something*, and not just rolled on peacefully: 'Very unkind of it.'

Throughout the 1920s Noel had been to Paris whenever he could, and there, if she was playing, he would go before anything else to see Yvonne Printemps in her latest *opérette*: 'She was for me the epitome of that so often misapplied word "Star". She was the true, authentic article from the top of her head to the soles of her feet. In addition to this indefinable but unmistakable quality, she had one of the most individual and lovely singing voices I have ever heard. She also knew with instinctive artistry how to use it.' He now, back at Goldenhurst, began to compose the score for *Conversation Piece* with Yvonne in mind. He confided this ambitious project to Cochran as a dead secret, but Cochran at once released it to the press, and Yvonne cabled from Paris that she would be delighted. He went into retirement at Goldenhurst and slogged away for ten days, but, as with *Bitter Sweet*, no major waltz theme would materialise. At the end of the tenth day, late at night, he gave up, not so much in despair by then but in a rage with Cochran for forcing his hand. He made up his mind to cable Cochran and Yvonne the next morning that he had cancelled the whole enterprise, walked to the door of the Big Room and switched off the lights. But the one on the piano remained burning; he marched back in a worse temper than ever to turn it off and sat down and played 'I'll Follow My Secret Heart' straight through.

The rest followed fairly easily and was finished in November, and from then until Christmas there was for Noel much to-ing and fro-ing between London and Paris. Yvonne proved to be one of the nicest women in the world with an unexpected quality of jollity: '*Quelle splendeur!*' she cried when confronted with a large rice pudding at luncheon at Goldenhurst. She was a Star all right; enormous black velvet hats, three rows of pigeon's-egg-sized pearls and two of the tiniest dogs you have ever seen, always in imminent danger of being trodden to death but for the rows of bells forever tinkling on their collars. Though she was never, so far as I know, given to blazing rows, there was usually a star-sized drama of some kind going on, and after her first flush of enthusiasm she announced before Christmas that she wasn't going to play the part after all. True, she couldn't speak a word of English and was terrified at the prospect of having to learn it, but Pierre Fresnay, later to become her husband, whose English was good, guaranteed to teach her her part before rehearsals started in January. She never did learn English, but spoke her part parrot-fashion and held back her voice until very late in rehearsal. When she did at last sing full out the sound was heavenly, and nobody was unduly worried when one phrase emerged as 'a clood has pissed across the sun'. Meanwhile Noel had what he thought was going to be another drama on his hands; he felt that Romney Brent wasn't up to playing the leading man's role and he would have the painful job of asking Romney to relinquish it and of telling him that he would play it himself. But Romney said, 'Oh yes, gladly! *Providing* you let me still come to rehearsals and watch you find out what a bloody awful part it is.'

After the excitement and success of the opening night it became obvious that Yvonne would never settle for the boring routine of a run; nearly every evening she would produce one of her glamorous dramas. One of her little dogs was dying, and an unheard-of telephone call to Paris — as thrilling then as television from the moon nowadays — was put through from the stage door. Pierre held Kiki up to the telephone, Yvonne heard her one last tiny gasp and played the rest of the performance with a breaking heart.

Another night, after she had been singing with the nearest she could ever get to a croak and had whispered to Noel, '*Je ne peux plus. J'ai une migraine affreuse, je crois que je vais tomber en syncope,*' he pointed to Kreisler sitting on a chair in the wings (at Noel's invitation; there wasn't a seat in the house). 'Mon Dieu, c'est Kreeslair!' and out poured 'I'll Follow My Secret Heart' as loudly and gloriously as ever it had. 'Better get Tauber for tomorrow night,' said Danny O'Neil.

In April, Pierre Fresnay replaced Noel, which was very nice for him and Yvonne, in love as they were, and — Romney Brent had been right — a great relief to Noel.

In the London theatre, 1934 was one of the most exciting years there had ever been. First, in January, came Lynn Fontanne and

Alfred Lunt shining with all their might in *Reunion in Vienna*, with Yvonne Printemps and Noel in February. Noel went to Dover on April 1st to meet that beautiful, chic and funny lady Ina Claire, come to star with Laurence Olivier in *Biography*. 'April Fool's Day—hey?' was her greeting. Elizabeth Bergner was at the Apollo in *Escape Me Never*, playing with enormous power the frailest imaginable little waif. The exotic imports apart, all our own stars too were brightly shining that same year. Seymour Hicks at Daly's; John Gielgud in *The Maitlands*; Diana Wynyard in Joyce Carey's play *Sweet Aloes*; Edith Evans, infinitely touching as Gwenny in *The Late Christopher Bean*; John Gielgud again in *Hamlet*; Ivor Novello, Zena Dare and Fay Compton in *Proscenium*. Later in the year came one of the biggest treats of all; Marie Tempest, Madge Titheradge and Laurence Olivier in *Theatre Royal* (the English title of Kaufman and Ferber's *The Royal Family*), directed by Noel.

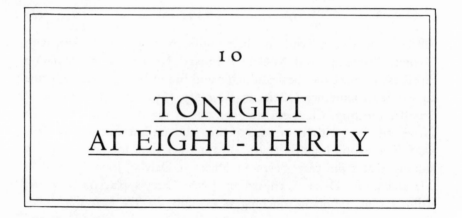

10

TONIGHT
AT EIGHT-THIRTY

NOEL had by now reached the heights of both his theatrical and social careers, and there is no doubt he revelled in combining the two: dashing off to stay with Lord and Lady Mountbatten in Malta, then rushing back to replace Pierre Fresnay in *Conversation Piece* because business was dropping, a dramatic collapse during a performance and an operation next day for acute appendicitis. Soon he was tearing off again with Louis Hayward to Cannes to board the yacht *Maara*, which he had chartered: 'A disastrous saga finishing up with a total wreck in Corsica. Terrible night in the storm with a fainting French Captain, me at the wheel, upheld by gin and my ex-appendicitis truss.' In October he was off again, this time to Ottawa in the *Empress of Britain* with Lady Louis to stay with the Governor-General and Lady Bessborough. One can imagine the good time they had, for Lady Louis and he could each spark the other off, and very often did, into fits of unconquerable giggles, hugely enjoyed by both. She was the embodiment of one of his aristocratic heroines; slim, exquisitely chic and with outrageously funny Noel Coward dialogue springing naturally from her lips. One gets glimpses of her in the Amanda of *Private Lives*, and Noel gladly admits that she was the inspiration for Piggie (Lady Maureen Gilpin) in *Hands Across the Sea*, as indeed was Lord Louis for Commander Peter Gilpin, Piggie's husband in the play.

Just after *Conversation Piece* Noel made the far-reaching decision to leave C. B. Cochran and his management. The letter announcing this bombshell remained anti-climactically unanswered for some long time. When tackled, Cochran said it must have been chewed up by the dog, who often did this to letters lying on the doormat. So the argument became a verbal one and ended by Noel as usual doing what he intended to do. A company was formed of himself, Lynn Fontanne, Alfred Lunt and John C. Wilson, and was given the name Transatlantic

Productions. Whether the break with Cochran was wise or not no one can say—none of the musicals Noel afterwards wrote really succeeded—but all ended well years later when the company worked with, and eventually merged with, H.M. Tennent, personified by Binkie Beaumont, with whom he had years of success and friendship.

Below the studio at 17 Gerald Road at this time lived a Mrs Mary McLeod and her son Rory, who was given to singing Elizabethan madrigals almost continually, sometimes accompanied by a friend on what may have been a recorder, I am not sure. This was not helpful to Noel when he was trying to compose in the studio directly above; in fact it drove him raving mad. He recorded having paid Rory, known to Noel and Lornie as Johnny-One-Note, five pounds a week 'silence money'. This cannot have been very effective, as he was still torturing Noel when I came on the scene two years later; by which time his name had been transmuted by Mrs Wray the charlady into One-Thumb-'Arry. The matter was eventually settled by Lornie finding and paying for a room in Kensington where Rory could madrigal all the livelong day and far into the night if he wanted to.

On March 14th the "great Doris Burton Hoax" was brought to light by a *Daily Mail* reporter. She had been going about for some time getting money out of people by saying she was Jack Buchanan's cousin. When at last faced by Jack she said that actually she was Noel Coward's cousin. Jack at once rang Noel and the fat was in the fire. She had been using both names to extract money. Whether she did this to found a theatrical company I do not know, but there is a note saying, 'Lorn met her and her amateur company in the Poland Rooms', and on the 19th, 'Lorn interviewed Mr Parker'. (One of her victims?) On the 26th she called to apologise, and the next day she was arrested— apologies obviously unaccepted. Noel gave evidence at Bow Street on April 7th and on the 10th she was committed for trial at the Old Bailey. Noel had a consultation with St John Hutchinson K.C.; perhaps in consequence of this he did not have to appear, and 'Doris Burton was sent briskly to prison'.

Every celebrity, I suppose, attracts a certain number of Maddies. By this I mean people who become more than fans and dream of passionate love with their idol with such intensity that the dreams eventually become reality to the dreamer. Noel had one such called Nelly, who lived opposite Harrods, almost within stone-throwing distance of 17 Gerald Road, so she could drop her love letters through the box at all hours. This went on for years and caused unease until it became frightening. Who knew whether—a Woman Scorned—her love might not turn to hate and she might not appear at the stage door or lurk in the shadows by the gate with a revolver or a dagger? Her letters became more matter-of-fact as time went on, writing as she did from the reality of her dream world: 'The children will be home on Wednesday, for the Easter Holidays. I shall expect you at seven, come before if you can', or, 'We really must do something about the lampshades in the drawing-room.' She plagued Noel and haunted him to such an extent that he left London to appear in a play on Broadway with relief. But when the curtain went up on the opening night, there she was, all by herself in a box near the stage.

To the end of his life Noel was never without a Maddie, usually more than one and most of them tediously persistent. But there was one, just after the war while we were still being rationed, a dark gentle girl who made no demands and kept her adoration to herself. Each week, just inside the wicket-gate to the courtyard, she laid her touching tribute; three rashers of bacon, two ounces of butter and her half pound of sugar.

In April came a letter asking Noel to become President of the Actors' Orphanage in place of Sir Gerald du Maurier, who had recently died, suggesting that he should be a figurehead only. 'Certainly not, I shall accept the Presidency with its full responsibilities,' he replied. This he did, though not without opposition from some members of the Committee, led by Cedric Hardwicke. 'Cedric,' Noel said, 'answer me just one question: where *is* the Actors' Orphanage?' Of course he didn't know, and that was that. Noel and Lornie, new brooms, went there often with Jill Esmond and did Queen Mary-like probings into kitchen stoves, cupboards and store-rooms, causing ructions at future committee meetings. Officials were replaced; one master, as well as displaying marked favouritism, also took far too keen an interest in the girls' evening baths, saying they looked like 'pretty little pink seals'. There was the Theatrical Garden Party to be organised each year; a tremendous task especially for Lornie who, as soon as one was over, began to worry about the next. Crises arose and were dealt with, and there was always a drama in the offing about at least one of the children—shop-lifting and bed-wetting were the most frequent, almost run-of-the-mill, offences. One boy set a cornfield alight and another time managed to remove the huge tyres from a tractor and sell them. This boy was always a source of rather exciting trouble, and I used to wait for Lornie to come back from committee meetings to hear what he had been up to this time. His pranks went on until Noel decided to go down to the Orphanage and give him a talking-to. They went for a walk in the grounds and sat on a bench. 'Now look here, nobody knows better than I what fun it is to be naughty. But surely always being the Worst Boy in the School must become boring. You are intelligent, why don't you try being the Best Boy for a change? Give it a trial. I have always believed in bribery; if you will try for a month to be the Best Boy in the School, I will give you ten shillings.' The bargain was struck, the boy became and remained the Best, and is now a well-known film-director.

Under Noel's twenty-year Presidency, the Orphanage became well-run, more financially secure and the children better fed and educated.

Rehearsals for *Biography* started in April, with Noel directing. S. N. Behrman was the author, Ina Claire and Laurence Olivier the stars; all great friends of his, so the production was on the whole a happy one. Ina, a perpetual source of fun and laughter and a dazzling pleasure to the eye—she still is—never stops talking from the moment she wakes until (if she can get someone to stay up with her) next daybreak. Noel once asked her towards the end of luncheon how she came to go on the stage. She told us, and we got up from the table at ten to five, our heads spinning. We have only once known Ina speechless; at the end of Princess Lee Radziwill's début on television in *Laura*. She seemed to be dumbfounded. We told Lynn about this phenomenon of Ina silent, hoping she would enjoy it. Lynn thought for a moment, then said, 'Perhaps they're great friends, darling, and Ina didn't like to say anything.'

Miss Anderson, the Scandinavian housekeeper at Gerald Road, left Noel's service in September. She had given him and Lornie great enjoyment from the beginning. Noel had returned from some far-flung holiday on Miss Anderson's very first day and he and Lornie had had a very serious talk about correct behaviour on their parts in front of the staff, from that moment on. When Miss Anderson brought in the tea a little later, the first thing she saw was Noel coming into the room quite naked, except for a funny hat. Almost never without a cigarette between her lips, Miss Anderson could perilously maintain the ash intact, nearly down to the butt. She was a spiritualist, and her gentleman friend, a Mr Booth, who lived in the suburbs, shared her beliefs. They sometimes wandered about the studio—once watched by Noel who was reading with a small light on—with their eyes closed, arms outstretched and sniffing deeply. For ectoplasms, he wondered? Miss Anderson was a great one for leaving things lying about, notably when Noel brought home some friends and found a beautifully set-out buffet supper and also, in the middle of that large floor, the most

revolting old slipper he had ever seen. Why only one? Had she gone
on hobbling about in the other and never missed its mate? Then one
night Noel got into bed to find for a bedfellow what he described as
a large white mutton-dish. When taxed, 'I must have left it there'
was her only explanation. Whether there is the After Life she so
fervently believed in or not, Miss Anderson has already achieved her
immortality as Miss Erikson in *Present Laughter*.

Also in September, rehearsals started for *Theatre Royal* with Noel
directing. Marie Tempest and Madge Titheradge headed the cast,
with Laurence Olivier consenting to play for only two weeks of the
pre-London tour as he wanted to do another play, *The Ringmaster* by
Keith Winter. At the end of the two weeks he was to be replaced by
Brian Aherne. But Larry gave such a terrific performance, blazing
with vitality, that Noel, Marie Tempest and the entire cast were absolutely mad about him. More important still, so was every audience,
to such an extent that the idea of him leaving became unimaginable.
Brian gives his version of what followed in his autobiography *A
Proper Job*, but I must give Noel's version as he always told it. Although
in both stories Brian emerges as an innocent lamb — which indeed he
was — Noel, in his, appears a wicked schemer. About the time Brian
went to Glasgow to join the company, Noel telephoned Guthrie
McClintic in New York and asked if he still wanted Brian to play
Mercutio. (Guthrie was about to direct his wife Katharine Cornell as
Juliet in what became his memorable production of *Romeo and Juliet*.)
'Yes, of course I do.' 'Well don't say anything, but I think you'll be
able to have him. Leave it to me.' He then took Larry for a walk and
started to put out feelers. 'Suppose Brian were to break his leg?'
'He won't break his leg.' 'But supposing he did, then you'd have to
play, wouldn't you? You couldn't let us down.' 'What about *The
Ringmaster*?' 'Fuck *The Ringmaster* and leave it to me.' (Larry, as
Brian says, probably knew what a rattling good part he had dropped
into and was not unwilling to change his plans.) There followed a
scene which both describe as 'painful' — Brian says Noel was 'friendly'
— and at the end of which Brian released the management from their
contract. So the innocent lamb was led, not to the slaughter, but to a
brilliant success as Mercutio in New York and Larry to a brilliant
one in *Theatre Royal* in the West End.

Dame Marie Tempest was an autocrat in the theatre. Her discipline
was so severe that everyone backstage from the highest in the cast
to the call-boy walked in fear and dread. Madge Titheradge, herself
a big star with experience ranging from high comedy through melo-

drama and *Peter Pan* to Shakespeare, was determined to avoid Dame
Marie's temper or ugly scenes of any kind with her. This she managed
to do and was all sweetness and light throughout the run, even when
Noel found her one night sobbing in her dressing-room. 'Midge [as
he called her], what on earth's the matter?' 'The little darling hit me
with her stick,' was all she said through her tears.

It must have been in November that Noel went to New York to
start rehearsals for *Point Valaine*. 'All very difficult. Rehearsals fairly
beastly. Gladys's sets too heavy and highly untropical. The Lunts
tetchy and not happy. Finally opened in Boston on Christmas night
with everything going wrong including rain effect and most of the
lighting. Nobody pleased.'

He had directed four productions in twelve months, written one
of them—*Point Valaine*—and appeared in another—*Conversation Piece*.
How could he cram so much into one year? All his life this remained
an annual wonder.

In *Point Valaine* Noel tried to break new ground by writing a play
as far removed as possible from anything he had done before. This he
succeeded in doing; he also succeeded in making the characters so
unsympathetic that they failed to extract one iota of compassion from
the audience. In any case the audiences wanted to see the Lunts as
their own beloved Lunts; what they got was Lynn as the disagreeable
owner of a gloomy hotel in the tropics and Alfred as a sinister Russian
waiter. So nobody was happy, either in front of the curtain or behind
it. Especially behind. One shocking night in Philadelphia a scene
change—end of Scene One, Act Three—was made too soon. Alfred
was revealed in full working light and no other scenery, standing
quite still on a rock, unable to jump to his death and be eaten by sharks
because the mattress to jump on to had also been whisked away. The
curtain came down to some laughter and a little puzzled applause.
This accident—as did others throughout his career—became to Alfred
a tragedy of Shakespearean proportions with himself as Lear. He fled
the theatre and wretchedly tramped the streets of Philadelphia for two
hours. Alexander Woollcott, Lynn and Noel went back to the hotel
and had their supper, having, I suspect, rather enjoyed the mishap,
and waited for Alfred's return. He finally turned up distraught and
vowing never, never to appear on the stage again as long as he
lived.

He and Lynn opened in the play in New York on January 16th; a
dreadful first night, and Louis Hayward got what few good notices
there were. Also in the cast was Osgood Perkins, a good actor and

the father of a baby son called Tony, now the film star. *Point Valaine* ran for only fifty-five performances.

Soon after the opening, Noel started work on *The Scoundrel*, his first film since his few days with D. W. Griffith and Lillian and Dorothy Gish in *Hearts of the World* in 1917, and therefore his first as a star. Ben Hecht and Charles MacArthur wrote and directed the picture, though Noel said they played backgammon all day long, let him change or invent whatever he liked and only tore themselves away from the board during an actual 'take'. With Noel in the film were Julie Haydon, Alexander Woollcott and Hope Williams. He had undertaken to do the film on the understanding that Charles MacArthur's wife, Helen Hayes, would play the female lead, and he was greatly looking forward to acting with her. He ended up with Julie Haydon instead and I think that this, as far as Noel was concerned, put Miss Haydon in the dog-house from the start. She couldn't, for him, do anything right and was preternaturally concerned at all times with her *coiffure*, which drove him mad. When it came to the big emotional scene he took the crew to one side and asked them to go on shooting whatever happened. They started, Noel dishevelled her careful hair-do and tugged at it and pulled it; she screamed and sobbed and – if Noel is to be believed – when the film was shown she won an Award for the Best Emotional Performance of the Year.

The Scoundrel, when released, was a success in the big cities – *succès d'estime* that is – and subsequently in art houses all over the world, but never in what is known as the sticks. Noel didn't get much money from Paramount for it; he was given a share of the profits, which went back into the next Hecht-MacArthur film *Down to their Last Yacht*. It flopped, and taught Noel to read the small print in a contract more carefully in future. *The Scoundrel* is still, after nearly forty years, being shown somewhere or other, so it must have become a minor classic. Or even a classic.

With the picture finished, it is apparent from his notes that Noel was again about to indulge in and give way to his two passionate urges – to travel and to write. 'I Travel Alone' was written about this time; haunting, a little sad, it is to me one of the most indicative, self-revealing songs he ever wrote:

> The world is wide, and when my day is done
> I shall at least have travelled free
> Led by this wanderlust
> That turns my eyes to far horizons

Though time and tide won't wait for anyone
There's one illusion left for me
And that's the happiness I've known — alone.

I travel alone
Sometimes I'm East
Sometimes I'm West
No chains can ever bind me
No remembered love can ever find me.
I travel alone
Fair though the faces and places I've known
When the dream is ended and passion has flown
I travel alone.
Free from love's illusion, my heart is my own;
I travel alone.

He told me he had learnt early that we are all essentially alone all our lives, and from the moment of that realisation he had determined to make the best of it.

He was always an efficient traveller, priding himself on never being late for train, ship or plane though admitting to some hair-raising near-misses. He never lost his luggage and seldom forgot anything in his packing; certainly never forgot his lined foolscap-size writing pads, portable typewriter and a bursting bookbag. This last held the latest good novels, two or three classics — Dickens, Trollope, Tolstoy, perhaps — and always Roget's *Thesaurus* and Clement Wood's *Rhyming Dictionary*, two books on which he depended, was faithful to and loved. Thus armed he was happy and could combine his passion to write and to travel at the same time.

So, in March 1935, he made one of those long train-journeys he loved so much, trans-continent from New York to the West Coast. In Hollywood he found himself 'the belle of the ball and fêted all ends up'. He was also, not unnaturally at that high point of success, offered the earth to stay there, either as a writer, film-star or both. The enormous offers were enormously tempting; he enjoyed them and the bribes and enticements that went with them — ceiling-high baskets of flowers, cases of champagne, the proffered swimming-pooled mansions and chauffeur-driven Rolls-Royces. He very nearly fell for it, but somehow managed to keep his head and blessed Edna Ferber ever after for sternly saying, 'What is there in it for you? You are a writer. Go away and write.' He had been induced by Irving Thalberg to make a screen test and never even stopped to see the result, but

sailed next day in the *Tatsuta Maru* for Honolulu. In the meantime he
had once more made new and lasting friends; Ruth Chatterton for one,
with whom for many years his great bond was to eat slices of raw
garlic on bread and butter, even at tea-time, and Joan Crawford,
lovingly known by Noel as Stinkpot at that time.

After a glamorous send-off, once on board the *Tatsuta Maru*, he
was delighted to find he had a 'lanai' suite – that is, a cabin with a
little outside verandah where he could sunbathe while writing. He
was still working on *Present Indicative*, which was, apart from his
youthful attempts at novel-writing, the first serious prose he had
undertaken. But it came easily and well and *Present Indicative* remains
not only enjoyably readable but one of the best, certainly the funniest,
theatrical autobiographies ever written.

After Honolulu he sailed for China and stayed at a hotel where
'Lickshaws are natulary plovided flee' then on to Yokohama, Tokyo
and Kobe, where he went to a Sukiaki dinner party and the 'whole
caboodle blew up, covering all of us with a shower of dainty but
dreadfully sticky bits of food'. Shanghai next, Singapore, and then
Bali, where he stayed for three weeks with Walter Spies in his beautiful
house which was on the edge of, almost in, the jungle, with monkeys
and cranes in the garden and indoors two Steinways and a python.
Walter Spies was a painter, a very individual one; his pictures Douanier
Rousseau-like of figures in the jungle but even more surrealist and
diffused with a vivid unearthly light. Noel was angry when he found
there wasn't one for sale, and absolutely furious when he found out
later that Barbara Hutton and Charlie Chaplin already had several.

To Batavia next, then back to Singapore where he was a guest of
Sidney and Mary Smith at the Air Force Base. He went up with the
Squadron and, when coming down, saw Arthur Rubinstein's name
on a large poster over the Victoria Theatre. He reports 'an enchanted
evening and an enchanting supper with Arthur afterwards'. While
at the Air Base, news came of his friend Lawrence of Arabia's tragic
death: 'The whole Air Base shocked and depressed and everywhere a
dreadful sense of loss.'

On the voyage home he wrote *Fumed Oak* and *Hands Across the Sea*,
and on arrival in London he fixed Gertrude Lawrence – who was 'very
busy being bankrupt' – to appear in them with him in *Tonight at
Eight-Thirty* that autumn. 1935 was the year of King George V's
Silver Jubilee, and in July Noel was summoned to a Garden Party at
Buckingham Palace. Sir Louis Grieg, an old friend, came up to him
and said the King had asked to talk to him; as they approached, Sir

Louis whispered instructions in his ear, whereupon Noel started to laugh and couldn't stop, even while making his royal bow. King George asked, 'What are you laughing at?' 'Louis told me not to stick my bottom out: the King hates it.' At which the King threw his head back, roared with laughter himself and everybody said, 'There's Noel Coward being witty again.'

He always had the gift of being able to plunge into a conversation or to start one when silence fell at a luncheon or dinner table. Most of us avoid the subject when introduced to, say, someone who has had a leg amputated; but not Noel, who would immediately say, 'Tell me, *how* did you come to lose your leg?' and he was right, the other person was invariably quite happy to tell him. At this same Garden Party he noticed that Queen Mary, when he was presented to her, hesitated slightly for something to say and as usual he plunged. Anything. 'How beautiful the gardens look, Ma'am. I've never seen anything so lovely,' and they were off—to the Queen's relief, he felt. From then on there was never any shyness between them. Years later, when Princess Elizabeth and Prince Philip gave their first dinner-party at Clarence House and he found himself next to Queen Mary at table, he broached, of all things, the subject of the Abdication and asked the question he had been longing to ask: 'Is it true, Ma'am, that you said, "Here's a pretty kettle of fish"? ' She said, 'Yes, I think I did,' and from then on, he said, they had a lovely time. They must have had, because Queen Mary also asked him to sit next to her during the film shown after dinner, and later Queen Elizabeth the Queen Mother told him she had telephoned the next day to say how much she had enjoyed Mr Coward's company, and what a bright and clever young man he was. This pleased him greatly, being fifty-two at the time.

Noel spent most of that summer of 1935 at Goldenhurst, Gladys never far from his side, writing and composing the songs for the remainder of the nine one-act plays that constitute *Tonight at Eight-Thirty*. One peaceful Sunday evening, the village postmistress, who also worked the tiny switchboard, telephoned; Noel could tell from her voice that she had been frightened to death by a call from California. It was Marlene Dietrich, whom he had never met, and he always marvelled at the trouble she must have taken to track him down to that little village six thousand miles away. She had just seen *The Scoundrel* and wanted to shower praise on him for the film and particularly for his performance, never having seen him act before. They talked for a long time; seeming, although strangers and so far apart, to leap at once into intimacy, each asking the other's plans for the next few months and swearing to meet as soon as ever they could. Thus started their lifelong *amitié amoureuse*, which survived through many ups and downs; the latter always overcome by love – only really understood by themselves, not always by their friends – and the fierce loyalty that bound them.

The three-month tour of *Tonight at Eight-Thirty* started in Manchester in October and was from beginning to end, as *Private Lives* had been in 1930, swathed in luxury and success; with the exception of Gertie who, on the rare occasions when she thought of it, really did try to dress and live economically as a gesture to her bankruptcy, and always failed.

The tour ended just before Christmas, for which Noel went off to Scandinavia with Jeff Amherst again his companion. First they went to Copenhagen, where he complained of feeling very tired and being made much too much of. He must have recovered by the time he got to Stockholm, where he went to a lot of jolly Christmas parties. Greta Garbo was there too, not always escaping being mobbed by the press and the public, and when Garbo *and* Noel Coward were seen together the international press understandably went mad with excitement. According to many papers there was certainly a romance between the two, and the world-shaking announcement of their engagement might be expected daily. They enjoyed one another's company enormously, but what was really happening was Noel's adamant refusal to meet her at some obscure address wearing dark glasses and with their faces hidden by turned-up coat collars. Instead, he was wheedling and coaxing her, then, when that failed, bullying her steadily and relentlessly until she would in the end consent to go to a theatre or a restaurant with him – or to the party given by the great actor Gosta Eckman when, as they were going up in the lift, Garbo refused to go in the door, saying, 'Believe me, Noel, I really and truly cannot go in, I cannot face it.' Noel said he shook her, rang the bell and said, 'Yes you bloody well *are* going in,' and when the door opened he pushed her. Once inside she soon became the charming, easy, gay person she really is and refused to leave till three in the morning. She can often be funny, loving to laugh at other people's jokes, and I suppose there is nothing more beautiful to be seen than Garbo laughing, especially in profile – that flawless profile, with the laughing head thrown so far back that the shining long pageboy-cut flows down the perfect neck.

The holiday ended with a New Year's Eve party at Prince William's 'Slottet', where a very good time was had by all until Noel shut his

finger in a door while playing hide-and-seek and nearly cut the tip off.
At two a.m. it was difficult to find a doctor, but at last one came and
put in steel clips to hold the flesh together. He had no anaesthetic with
him to relieve the pain and everyone was fainting in coils except Jeff
and himself, Noel said.

Whether there really was a romance between him and Garbo during
that holiday, or whether they thought it funny to continue in private
the one made so public by the press, one does not know. I do know
that they exchanged affectionate telegrams and telephone calls for
some time after, calling each other 'My little bridegroom' and 'My
little bride', and that she had said she 'wished the newspapers was
right'.

Noel and Gertie opened in *Tonight at Eight-Thirty* in January at
'their' theatre, the Phoenix, and on March 28th, 1936, I went to work
for the Master. As this book is about Noel I intend to spare the reader
a detailed account of my birth and upbringing. The usual boredom
of the author's ancestry can be dealt with speedily; my mother's
family's births, marriages and deaths have been recorded in the Parish
Register of the church of SS. Peter & Paul, Farningham, Kent, since
the register was started in 1603. So although I cannot say that my
ancestors came over with William the Conqueror, I think I can safely
say they were already there, probably serfs living in a hovel. I had a
most happy childhood, had always been lucky, and I learnt when about
eleven or twelve that dreams really do come true. With some other
boys I had, one summer evening, been leaning over one of the hurdles
fencing off the Tennis Club, watching the play. It was Wimbledon
time, at the time of the great players – Lenglen, Tilden, Helen Wills,
Lili D'Alvarez, Cochet and Borotra – and I was longing with all my
might to learn to play and, who knows, perhaps be a star at Wimbledon
one day. An impossible dream; no money for racquet and balls and
years to wait until I'd be old enough to join the club. But I wanted to
be able to play tennis then, at that moment, more than anything in
the world. Play stopped, my schoolmates drifted away, and Mr Grey,
President of the club, came up to me and asked me to walk home with
him – we both lived at the other end of the village. 'I've been thinking,' he said, 'we really ought to start a junior tennis club and teach
you youngsters how to play. Would you be interested?' Next day
he brought me back from the mysterious place where he worked
called the City a gleaming new Slazenger racket and a box of snow-
white tennis balls. Except in my story-books, never had a wish been
granted so quickly.

But by 1936 the time, with me, was rather out of joint. I had left home at twenty for the bright lights of London, the theatre lights to be exact, for I was stage-struck. Not to the extent of wanting to be an actor; quite enough heady excitement just to go to the theatre, wait at the stage door for Evelyn Laye, June or Alice Delysia to come out, and when at home to paste their pictures in my album. This I could do more often now that I lived in London, it had been the whole point of my leaving home. But what of my future? I had quite a good job in which I had been lucky and spoiled by my employers, but I knew it could lead nowhere. I had not been trained for anything specific and, young as I was, I had already faced the fact that I had no creative talent. You had to be happy in your work I knew, or life would not be worth living, but what direction should I take? This fateful question was never far from my worried mind. At last, one completely sleepless night in my bedsit in Chester Row (my bed a bunk, the room a ship's cabin at the whim of the owner's son) the answer came. If only I could get a job with someone I admired and respected – preferably someone famous of course – I could be content. I would do anything for him or her; scrub floors, anything, whatever they asked of me. But how to find the perfect person to whom to devote the rest of my life? Still sleepless at six in the morning, I remember thinking, Well, of course Noel Coward would be ideal, combining everything, especially the theatre I loved so much. But he was too remote to hope for, too high in the heavens; silly even to think of him.

Hundreds and hundreds of times I have been asked how I 'had the luck to get my job with Noel Coward'; luck indeed it was. Two months after my night without a wink, I had occasion to look for lodgings at West Wickham in Kent. I got out of the train and there, at the newsagent's near the station, was a board with notices on drawing-pinned postcards, 'Lost', 'Found' and 'Rooms to Let'. Among the latter was one whose wording and good, strong handwriting appealed to me more than any of the others, so I went to Mrs Curtis at 16 Queensway. She was small, black-clad and with the pale face and sombre eyes of those who can see the future. Through six inches of opened doorway she looked at me for what seemed like a minute, then opened it wide and asked me to come in.

During the weeks I stayed with Mrs Curtis, she took a deep and kind interest in me and my career and nightly tried, by consulting the stars and the cards, to discover what the gods had in store for me. On the evening of November 24th she read my hands and I immediately wrote down what she foretold: I still have the notes I made and every word has been proved accurate. Forty years ago, though, what was to come was still unsure and I longed for something less hazy, something more precise. Sure enough, the night before I left I got back to find her in a state of excitement and quite definite about my more immediate future. This time it was numerology and something wonderful, perfectly wonderful, was going to happen on my next birthday, 6.3. 1936. Two threes, two sixes and a nine coming together! Moreover, the whole, when added up, boiled down to ten (631936 = 28 = 10)! ('The ancients called the number three a perfect number because it was expressive of the beginning, the middle and the end. The number nine was a mystical number, being thrice three, hence the perfect plural and represented perfection or completion ... Then ... the mother of all, the all-comprising, the all-abounding, the first born, the never swerving, the never tiring holy ten, the keyholder of all.') I had three snail-paced months to wait.

Three—again three—friends, took me to dinner on 6.3.1936 at Pinoli's, 3/6 a head including wine, and then to see an enchanting *Pride and Prejudice* at the St James's Theatre. Afterwards, I was left with Jimmy Gregory, a chum from schooldays, and, as he lived near me, we walked home together. I remember feeling let down, anticlimax had set in. So that, after all, was my birthday, no golden sign in the sky, not one small auspicious portent had appeared. I twice refused to go in for a drink when we got to Jimmy's until he insisted, 'Well, coffee then, your birthday isn't over yet.' Soon after he had put the coffee on, the telephone rang in the next room—a long conversation, unheard by me. He reappeared and said, 'It's Harry Edwards, he'd like to say hello.' Harry, who worked at the Phoenix where *Tonight at Eight-Thirty* was playing, hoped I'd had a happy day, we inquired after each other's families and then talked about the weather and the crops until at the very end, about to hang up, he said despairingly, 'I don't know what I'm going to do. I've promised Mr Coward I'd try to find someone to go to work for him; Jimmy says he'll try to think of someone. You don't know anyone do you?' I looked at my watch; there were eighteen minutes still to go till midnight. I knew that this was it, and said, 'I'll go.'

I should never have had the courage to face the ghastly upheaval of leaving my job, or face the disapproval of family and friends, had it not been for the certainty with which Mrs Curtis had made her prediction. Was it destiny that made me pick out her card from among all the others? It must have been. And what if I had gone straight home and missed that haphazard telephone call? From that moment on, for the rest of my days, my life had taken a wonderful turn for the better.

Yes, Mrs Loraine would be pleased to see me at four thirty on Monday, Mr Coward would be back from his weekend at Goldenhurst by then. Lornie's office was at 1 Burton Mews in Belgravia, back-to-back with 17 Gerald Road (the two houses knocked into one), and was oak-panelled, with over the fireplace the *Daily Mail* placard (the only newspaper placard ever devoted to a review of a play) of *Cavalcade*; GREAT DRURY LANE PLAY in big red letters. Lornie, at her desk, was brusque and tried hard to be businesslike, but I thought I saw through this and that I should like her very much. Noel in *Future Indefinite* inaccurately says that I went to him as a cook-valet; nothing so grand, my duties were never clearly defined, and all I knew was that he needed 'someone to replace Charles', who was leaving him. In those days I knew almost nothing about cooking, but I think I did lie and said I could 'produce a little something for Mr Coward before and after the theatre' if needed. After some more questions, I mentioned the modest salary I had been getting and Lornie to my joy said, 'I think we can do better than *that*.' She left me, went up the few steps leading to the Studio and said to Noel—he told me long afterwards—'There's a young Clive Brook in the office and he seems much better than likely.' He came springing into the room, vital, friendly, and although just up from the country faultlessly dressed in the grey checked suit later familiar from the famous photograph by Horst, used as the frontispiece for *Present Indicative*. What he said I cannot much remember, because the interview was for me a mixture of knee-knocking terror and pleasure, the latter due to his charm and his going out of his way to make things easy for me. I do remember his parting shot—'I think you will do very well if you play your cards right.'

This I was only too eager to do when I started work in a week or so. I was such a paragon, my behaviour the pink of such perfection that, Lornie told me, behind my back I was known at that time as Jesus Christ.

I am sure I worked much harder than I need have, but no matter; it was bliss, paradise for me to be able to go any evening I liked to the Phoenix and watch the plays. Not a seat to be had, I stood at the back of the circle and would just as gladly have stood on a bed of nails. I had seen and adored Gertie and Noel in *Private Lives* but now there were three different evenings and nine different plays, no less, to delight in.

So much for the enchanted evenings, but the daily round was another matter and not such undiluted pleasure. Leonard, my first name, Noel said he loathed and hated. (I had been proud of it since I learnt as a boy that it meant 'strong and brave as a lion', though I was neither.) What was my second? When I said it was Cole, he pounced on it and so Cole, then later Coley, I became. (There was only one other Cole in that particular world at that time and that was Cole Porter, also known as Coley, which later led to confusion among the friends we shared and may have been one of the reasons Mr Porter and I never really got on.) I could not accustom myself to it for a long time, 'Cole' sounded cold and unfriendly to my ear; added to which Lornie and Noel treated me rather distantly. I could not know that this was because they had been let down badly by my predecessors; partly their own fault perhaps — they had been too free and easy with them. This time they were determined that the newcomer should be kept at a distance and not become spoiled. Weeks went by before the first joke was cracked and the ice broken. 'What would you say to a little fish?' I inquired about luncheon. 'I should say Good Morning, little fish.' Not tip-top Coward, but wonderful to be going on with, and from then on Noel knew he had in me a pushover as an appreciative audience.

I felt we became still closer when some now-forgotten disaster happened. One should tell the truth and shame the devil I knew, and this, heart in mouth, I did. Instead of the expected wrath he laughed, put a hand on my shoulder and said, 'Well, we must press on and rise above it, mustn't we?' Though I didn't know it then, this was his unvarying philosophy throughout his life and one would be hard put to it to find a better.

A few more weeks and then the time had evidently come for me to be given some praise. He was sitting up in bed in his minstrel's gallery of a room, from which, when the wooden shutters were opened, one could look down on the big studio below. He catalogued my virtues and I listened as though he were talking about somebody else; I couldn't believe it. (He always did this, I realised later, both in the theatre and out of it. His praise was generous and always freely given for work well done.) 'Above all,' he finished, 'you have good manners and they are very important, you know. If you behave well over small things, it means you will behave well when it comes to the big ones, and you can be relied upon in a crisis.' This had never occurred to me, and was the second lesson I learnt from him.

Even during the probation period there was much for me to enjoy. The theatrically, socially and politically famous came constantly to the studio and I found talking to them on the telephone stimulating to put it mildly, for they were frequently surprisingly forthcoming. Among the first callers was Jose Collins, who said she would be turned out into the street at the end of the week, grand piano and all, unless Noel lent her five pounds. My heart broke at the idea of the Maid of the Mountains penniless and hungry, but Lornie calmly said, 'Grand piano, my foot — she only wants the money for drink.'

Lady Cunard rang to ask if Mr Coward would come on Thursday after the theatre; she was having a quiet supper for the King. (King George V had died in January, the Prince of Wales was now King Edward VIII, and the Court was still in mourning.) A thrilling message to pass on, I thought, but Noel shouted, 'I am sick to DEATH of having quiet suppers with the King, AND Mrs Simpson. Tell her I can't.' All very exciting, and one never knew what would happen from one minute to another.

Noel went on holiday after *Tonight at Eight-Thirty* closed, to Venice, Dubrovnik and then to Rhodes, where he finished writing *Present Indicative*. It was during this visit to Venice that Admiral of the Fleet Sir Dudley Pound's flagship had put in and Noel and his friends were often invited on board. The friends, a merry band, included Lady Castlerosse, Valentina, Douglas Fairbanks, Sr, with Lady (Sylvia) Ashley, and Ivor Novello. When the Admiral and Lady Pound decided to give a large and official cocktail party on board, they told Noel and Lady Castlerosse that they might ask whoever they liked. When the hour drew near, Lady Castlerosse said, 'Noel, I have a dreadful feeling we've asked too many queer people.' Noel bade her not to worry: 'If we take care of the pansies, the Pounds will take care of themselves.'

From Rhodes he went on to Cairo, where he stayed with Lord and Lady Killearn while the former was in process of giving up being High Commissioner and becoming our Ambassador. There were unceasing social carryings-on, including a party given by the Prime Minister, Nahas Pasha, which became so big it had to be held in two ships instead of one. Noel enjoyed so much high-up Egyptian hospitality that by the time he got back to London Anthony Eden told him he must be the one to give the official reception for the delegation coming to sign the Anglo-Egyptian Treaty. Dismay at Gerald Road; how did one even begin to give such a grand political affair? Noel, never dismayed for long, said, 'Come on, let's make it a rout and enjoy ourselves,' and invited every single stage- and film-star in London, including the visiting Americans — Fred Astaire, Douglas Fairbanks, Jr, and Miriam Hopkins among them. The party was to be given on Tuesday August 25th, followed by another at Goldenhurst on Saturday 29th, which was also Jack's birthday. Jack was in New York, so Noel cabled him:

For Dab's return we've planned a celebration
A really lovely birthday treat
At which the whole Egyptian delegation
And everyone in London here will meet
T'will be a night o' nights with champagne flowing
But darling Dab don't think that is the worst
A few days later on with trumpets blowing
The Air Force comes en masse to Goldenhurst.

The Egyptian party was the first big test of my efficiency, and Lornie and I swung into action. Frightfully important-looking gilt-edged cards were printed; banks of flowers and masses of food and drink were ordered. The only available loo for the ladies was the size and shape of a small sedan chair and dreadfully shabby, but Lornie discovered some new-fangled stuff called quick-drying paint; a misnomer, for it remained tacky all through the party. How many famous bottoms were sanctified by white haloes we never knew but people remained in there an awfully long time—Hedda Hopper especially, who in any case was wearing such a large hat that I had to bend the brim down to her shoulders to get her in, and much later out, through the narrow door. We had been wakened early in the morning of the party by green-baize-aproned men who took away most of the furniture, leaving a hundred and fifty tiny gilt chairs scattered throughout the house, which Noel said depressed him. Panic set in at four in the afternoon: who would announce the guests? Who could pronounce the unpronounceable foreign names? A short call to the Egyptian Embassy produced a silver-haired major-domo, the spitting image of the late Lord Curzon, even to a blue riband across his white waistcoat, but the splendid effect was ruined early on by the heel coming off one of his shoes. His gait became a comic limp and then, owing to frequent nips from whatever bottle was handy, more and more erratic as the night went on. Still, he managed the Egyptian names beautifully, though when it came to the English and Americans he never recognised one of the world-famous faces, announcing Fred Astaire loud and clear as 'Mr Stair!' and bestowing a title each on Joyce Barbour and Bobby Andrews.

The delegation arrived and clung together till three in the morning in a nervous knot. Not only they but everybody else was shocked into silence when a likeable funny-faced young American called Ethel Merman got up on to the dais and sang 'You're the Top' and 'I Get a Kick out of You' marvellously, her voice brazen and stirring as a call to arms. Noel played and sang, Evelyn Laye, dazzling to the eye, sang 'Tell Me What Is Love' at a brilliantly fast tempo. Towards the end, at the slightest sign of flagging, Hedda Hopper would loudly call, 'One more for the black boys!', meaning the already dazed delegates, and the Treaty was signed next morning with what must have been trembling fingers.

Noel was teased for ever after by Lord and Lady Mountbatten, Mr Eden and his other political friends, who blamed his 'Egyptian Party' for the decline thereafter in Anglo-Egyptian relations and were still blaming him, years later, for the loss of the Suez Canal.

The party successfully behind us, we thought nothing of having nearly two hundred people for cocktails at Goldenhurst only four days later. Noel was Vice-President of Lympne Flying Club, Sir Philip Sassoon, our neighbour at Lympne Castle, the President, and an Air Rally was held each summer. Noel and Sir Philip filled their houses with guests, and competitors came from all over the Continent as well as the British Isles; Noel always gave his rout on the Saturday, when the day's flying was over. Dubonnet cocktails were then the order of the day and I made 'the best I have ever tasted, I *must* have another' by putting in only enough Dubonnet to give colour; the rest was gin. So again the affair became a riot; there are photographs of Lord Boothby and Godfrey Winn frolicking on the lawn; I remember Hermione Baddeley being frightfully funny, her pouting face and drawling plummy voice making everything funnier; and Sir Philip Sassoon saying almost continuously to his dog, 'Blazer, Blazer, Blazer—oh—*you're—so—* SWEET!'

This was my first time at Goldenhurst and from then on it became the accepted thing that I should go every weekend to help. Lornie warned me it was madness to work seven days a week, staying up till all hours, but I was young and for me Goldenhurst was not work. Eternal summer gilded it; I loved the drive down in the Rolls on the London–Dover road, passing through my native heath, Farningham, Kingsdown and Wrotham Hill, and I loved the drive up on Mondays, the back of the car stacked with branches of roses, huge peonies, delphiniums and lilies with which to bedeck the studio. Then the weekends themselves, the house filled with jolly guests. Joyce, Alan Webb, Jack Wilson and Princess Natalie Paley—beautiful, delicate, chic, a tremendous giggler and soon to become Jack's wife—were the regulars, and Gladys came daily from her house not far away, a mill-house with a little river running through the drawing-room. Rebecca West came that year, Owen Nares, Binkie Beaumont, Alexander Woollcott,

Alice Duer Miller, Zena Dare, Adrianne Allen, Bobby Andrews, G. B. Stern—the visitors' book goes on for pages.

Also that summer I got to know Noel's father and mother and his Auntie Vida. To use Noel's words, his father was 'very spruce' both sartorially and in his manner, usually in a pale grey flannel suit with a blue tie, and when available a cornflower buttonhole to bring out the colour in his twinkling eyes. Noel never cared greatly for his father but I think he owed much of his physical make-up to him; his height for one thing, and the eyes. Mentally too; who knows whether his musical genius—'sounds snatched from the air'—did or did not come from his father, who 'improvised at the piano'? Charm was innate with both him and Noel. I recall Mr Coward once exuding what I thought unnecessary charm on the grocer's boy, but neither he nor Noel could resist turning it on if they saw fit on anybody, or just as abruptly turning it off. Noel's sharper wit came from his mother, but his father too dearly loved to make a joke, of a kind at which Noel sometimes squirmed. As when they still lived at 111 Ebury Street and gave a tea party for the lodgers, to which they also invited Jane Cowl, at that time starring in Noel's *Easy Virtue*. Noel came in to find Miss Cowl, magnificent in leopard-skin, but bewildered and for her unusually silent, and to his horror heard his father say, 'Have a tongue sandwich, that'll make you talk.'

Mrs Coward I found to be small and pretty except for a very determined mouth, which Noel inherited; apart from that she looked as though she were made of pink-and-white china. Auntie Vida was an almost exact replica, mouth and all, but even tinier. (When Mrs Coward saw Auntie Vida in her coffin, she said, 'Doesn't she look pretty, like a little snowdrop. It's a pity she looked so disagreeable when she was alive.') From his mother Noel also inherited much besides her mouth, including her quick mind, quick temper and an indomitable fighting spirit, and I thought it easy to see how a combination of the genes of his parents might produce such a phenomenon as their son. Mrs Coward was very deaf most of her life, her deafness caused by a mastoid while at a convent school in Brussels where, she said, the nuns had done nothing more efficacious for her than pray. In spite of, or perhaps because of, her deafness, she was a demon at the wheel, even when well over seventy, usually wearing a small ostrich-feather hat; thus clad she once drove straight through a shop window in Ashford into a pyramid of glass jars, covering the bonnet of the car with Robertson's Golden Shred Marmalade. The local paper never mentioned the incident and she thought them fools for having missed such a scoop.

I now began to see and hear for myself the famous quarrelling I had heard so much about, Auntie Vida going so far as to pull up all the pansies Mr Coward had just put in. At Christmas when Auntie Vida said, 'It's peace on earth you know, Arthur, can't we make it up?' Mr Coward said, 'No, we can't,' and walked away. They were always feuding with friends as well, which on the whole Noel really rather enjoyed. When Mrs Coward found an unexpected Christmas gift of a calendar from an enemy she asked, 'Vida, did *you* send a card to Chrissie Alexander?' To which she got the defiant reply, 'Yes, I did.' 'Then you're a dirty dog,' she said to her flower-like little sister, and threw the calendar at her.

So when we arrived at Goldenhurst, often very late at night, to see the light still on in Mum's window, we knew there had been trouble and the ebb and flow of the week's battles were to be recounted and the recounting, exhausted as we were, had to be endured. By the same token, Maggie Cogger, the housekeeper and a dragon with the staff, would be waiting in the hall so as to get her version in first. 'Well, Cogger, how are things?' 'Ooo, Mr Noel,' in her Kentish burr, 'ut's bin turr'ble, summun turr'ble,' was the reply we expected and nearly always got. If it wasn't the family it was the staff and in either case it was dramatic. 'Annie didn't get in till half past ten on 'er day off and then she come in with bits er straw all over the back of 'er coat.' Noel, who had come for some peace after a crowded week in London, would lose his temper: 'Now look here, Cogger, I don't care if she has a bit of nooky all night long on every haystack from here to Folkestone, so shut up.' Then he would go upstairs to face his Mum.

All through this summer and autumn I became increasingly fond of Mrs Loraine. My first impression of her turned out to be accurate—behind the would-be businesslike exterior and the often caustic-sounding voice was to be found darling Lornie, always ready for fun and laughter, kindness, good advice and some gin on the stroke of six. She came of good Scots descent; an aunt, writing under the name of Miss Macnaughtan, had been quite a famous authoress with a best seller, *Christina MacNab*, to her credit, a book I had loved so much as a child that I was at first thrilled to get to know the niece of the author. Then I grew to love Lornie, for ever.

In September *Mademoiselle* opened at Wyndham's, brilliantly directed by Noel, with Isabel Jeans dazzling, Cecil Parker witty and both of them playing at great speed. Madge Titheradge was almost unbearably moving when required, and there was also a young, clever actress of obvious talent and promise called Greer Garson. Noel wired Audrey and Waveney Carten, who had adapted the play from the French:

> About this play of Jacques Deval's
> You've been extremely clever gals
> Although it swings from fun to gloom
> It may evade its rightful doom
> Although it jerks from gloom to fun
> I think the bloody thing will run.

On September 30th Noel sailed in the *Queen Mary* for the New York production, of course with Gertie and again a complete success (except for the critics who were patronising), of *Tonight at Eight-Thirty*. I woke him at 5 a.m. and helped him to finish packing and to catch the unusually early boat-train. In addition to a signed photograph he gave me a princely five pounds and a silver pencil from Asprey with my initials on it. When we got to Waterloo, I—thinking the subject had better be cleared up—asked him if he wanted me to go on working for him. 'Good God, yes,' he said with more than usual deliberation, 'until the grave closes over us,' and waved *au revoir* from the train window.

Noel returned from America on May 3rd, in time for the Coronation of King George VI and Queen Elizabeth on the 12th. He had had a happy holiday with Joyce and Alan Webb in Nassau after closing the successful run of *Tonight at Eight-Thirty* in New York owing to a nervous breakdown, presumably from exhaustion—eighteen months of work, off and on, had gone by since the start of the British tour of the plays. Meanwhile during the previous December King Edward VIII had abdicated, Noel's attitude being that a statue should be erected to Mrs Simpson in every town in England for the blessing she had bestowed upon the country. Feelings ran high about the abdication, the dearest of friends quarrelled violently; when Winston Churchill at luncheon asked why the King shouldn't be allowed to marry his cutie, Noel—summing it up for most people—said, 'Because England doesn't wish for a Queen Cutie.' The table roared at this but it could not have endeared him to Mr Churchill, who did not care for being worsted verbally or otherwise, and I think Noel's sometimes too quick wit was the main reason their friendship never became quite as close as it might otherwise have done.

Noel had been friends with the Duke and Duchess of York and the Duke of Kent since they were all young together and, when the latter married, with his wife, Princess Marina. But the Prince of Wales and he never really hit it off, Noel's opinion of him very early on being that 'he had the charm of the world, with nothing whatever to back it up'. The Prince put the lid on it when, having kept Noel up till all hours to supply piano accompaniment to the Prince's ukulele, he cut him dead next day in Hawes & Curtis, where all the smart young men of the time went for their famous backless evening waistcoats and haberdashery in general. When, on Noel's next visit there, he saw the Duke of York he pretended not to notice, but the Duke, in marked contrast, came over to him and was as friendly as could be—as, in fact, he always had been. Noel naturally never forgot this and from that afternoon as far as he was concerned his friendship with the future King George VI was cemented, and his admiration increased. So Noel was invited to the Coronation and to the many festivities including the Naval Review. By way of return—all London was *en fête*—he kept open house at the studio each evening from cocktail- until dinner-time.

It would be fair to add to the foregoing that by about 1950 the Duke and Duchess of Windsor and Noel became friends again, this time for good—the Duchess particularly, with her unfailing good manners, her quite remarkable gifts as a hostess and her sense of fun, often going out of her way to be kind to Noel, who never forgot her flowers and presents and her concern for him when once he was suddenly taken ill in Paris.

After the Coronation, again a golden summer, mostly divided as before between Goldenhurst and the studio at 17 Gerald Road. Rave reviews of *Present Indicative* appeared and the autobiography was a highly satisfactory success on both sides of the Atlantic.

Noel, instead of the then ubiquitous sports coat and grey flannels for the country, brought back from Paris and wore all this summer a wardrobe of navy-blue casual clothes relieved with white—shirt, shoes or scarf, perhaps—in which he looked very elegant indeed. He must always have unconsciously influenced men's fashion to a certain extent, starting with his polo-necked (then known as turtle-necked) pullovers at the time of *The Vortex* in 1924, which were much copied. Very comfortable they were, too. Then his beautifully tailored dressing-gowns, for use not only in the bedroom; over trousers, shirt and tie they were acceptable, and more colourful for informal wear in the drawing-room and, again, comfortable. His influence continued right up to his buying some Italian-tailored linen jackets with stand-up collars in Las Vegas in 1955, which, by the early 'sixties, became a craze and were known as 'Nehru' jackets. His brown dinner-jacket suits, made by Douglas Hayward and worn with matching bow tie and shoes, became famous, and he wore them right up to his last public appearance at the New York Gala of *Oh! Coward*. Examples of all these typically Noel Coward clothes are to be seen today in the Theatre Collection of the Museum of the City of New York, the Mander & Mitchenson Collection and, perhaps the most representative, in Mrs Doris Langley Moore's Museum of Costume at Bath.

Noel spent the end of June and most of July with the Royal Navy, joining Admiral Sir Philip Vian in H.M.S. *Arethusa* at Juan-les-Pins. The Mediterranean cruise ended up—because of the Spanish Civil War—at Valencia and Gibraltar. Out of the three Services it was to the Navy that Noel gave the most affection, and it was on his return to London from Gibraltar that the first discussion took place with Lord Mountbatten about the formation of the Royal Naval Film Corporation. The object of this enterprise was to obtain enough projectors to enable most ships to provide film entertainment as often as required, in whatever part of the world the Senior Service might find itself. Noel offered to liaise with the film industry to provide a flow of films, and spent much time with the Navy finding out from all ranks the kind of films they most wanted to see. George Formby, Jessie Matthews, Cicely Courtneidge, Jack Hulbert and Madeleine Carroll topped the poll. He and Lord Mountbatten worked hard for this project and it was due to their labour of love that most of H.M.'s ships eventually obtained the films and the equipment with which to show them.

While in London Noel agreed to Binkie Beaumont's and Jack Wilson's suggestion that he should direct *George and Margaret* that autumn for ultimate presentation on Broadway, and went to stay with Eleonora von Mendelssohn at Schloss Kammer am Attersee in Upper Austria. Eleonora was, or gave the effect of being, romantically beautiful and she was also, perhaps, a little too intense. She emanated the slight air of melancholy—which Noel could of course dispel—that sometimes accompanies beauty, so it seemed in keeping that her love-affairs should seldom be entirely happy and even that she should in the end commit suicide because of one. Her great love at this time was for Toscanini; he was at Kammer and so, to Noel's joy, was Fritzi Massary, whom he had seen and adored in operette in Berlin. It was from Fritzi that I heard of Toscanini playing the piano at Kammer one evening after dinner. He played exquisitely, and cast a spell so strong that he ended in a silence too complete to be broken. Eleonora, typically, rose to her feet during the hush, then walked across the room, theatrically took a painting off the wall, brought it back in homage to the Maestro and said, 'This is my Guardi. It is for you.' Then the hubbub and applause did break out, only to subside when Toscanini consented to play once more. But the expectant silence was shattered by Eleonora's mother's loud cry: 'All ze ozzer pictures on ze wall are mine.'

Fritzi and Noel became friends and it was during this holiday that he first conceived the idea of writing an operette for her. Her husband had died not long before, she had retired and, with Hitler rising to more maniacal heights than ever, it was becoming urgent that Fritzi, who was Jewish, should leave, come to England and eventually join her daughter in America. So Noel started then and there on the first version of *Operette*, plans were made for next year, he would ask Peggy Wood to co-star, and Fritzi promised to improve her erratic English. 'Who ees thees Piggy Wood?' she asked.

George and Margaret opened in Manchester in August. Noel mistakenly had a lot of it re-written and it never recaptured the hilarity and success of its long run in London. 'I bullied everyone,' he notes, 'Irene Browne very co-operative' (which means they enjoyed themselves buying barbaric beads and loose jumpers to transform the character of the ordinary middle-class housewife, which Irene couldn't play), 'the rest of the cast none too pleased.'

He sailed for New York on September 1st, getting there in time for the wedding of Jack to his Princess Natasha in what Noel described, quoting Dorothy Parker, as the twenty-first fine careless rapture. The ceremony took place at Jack's house in Fairfield, Connecticut, attended mainly by Jack's family. One of the exceptions was the elegant Baron Nicolas de Gunzburg; he and Noel made up the words of a ribald song, to be sung to the tune of *La Petite Tonkinoise*:

> On se sert de vaseline
> Pour faire gli- gli-, pour fair gli- gli-, glisser la pine
> C'est pratique, c'est bon
> Et après on
> Retire sa p'tite machine.

This they could and did sing as loudly as they liked at the reception in the garden, being understood by nobody except the unblushing bride. The wedding was supposed to have been a very quiet one, almost hush-hush, but Lornie cabled:

> In every paper of the English Press
> Are photographs of Dab and his Princess
> Although a deep dyed secret latterly
> All London sends its love to you and Natalie.

11

END
OF AN ERA

MEANWHILE at Goldenhurst the family and staff upsets continued dramatically. Cogger the housekeeper left in an outburst of fury, one of the staff having thrown a pat of butter in her eye. She was missed only by Noel and me; the house seemed strange without her, and we had become rather fond of her—which Mrs Coward explained away with, 'Oh of course she always sucks up to the *men*.' Sweet and gentle Kitty Macdonald took over from her, ran the house with calm and quiet confidence, never uttered a cross word and produced delicious meals for no matter how many and at however short a notice. (Kitty stayed with Mrs Coward through thick and thin, became her companion and looked after her with tender care—which cannot always have been easy—until her death, for which devotion Noel loved her and provided for her to this day.)

Mrs Coward reported all the family quarrels to Noel—by now in Canada with *George and Margaret*—in violent detail, his pacifying replies only aggravating her further, for she wrote, 'I shall keep your twaddly letter to show you one day. To think that *you* could write such tosh!' The squabbles had gone on endlessly until, before he left England, Noel firmly decided that Daddy should move to the pleasant rooms over the garage, at sufficient distance from the house to ensure an armistice. He made the move, but by this time his health had begun to deteriorate, requiring the services of a male nurse, and his mind began to wander. He had for some time been friendly with a local lady named Miss de Pomeroy, who seems to have been very kind to him; their friendship, at his advanced age, can only have been platonic. But Mrs Coward saw her as the Other Woman and said, 'She may be called de Pomeroy but she's no Vere de Vere.' (To say that a person was 'no Vere de Vere' implied that she was common, a dreadful stigma.) The fancy often took Mr Coward to go to see his friend; this could sometimes be averted by a record of Yvonne Arnaud playing on the piano a particular *morceau* which seemed to soothe him. When Yvonne Arnaud failed there was nothing for it but for the nurse to get the car out at whatever hour of the night and drive him to Miss de Pomeroy, who would give him a hot beverage from which he would return contented and go to sleep. He died peacefully that autumn and Lornie made the funeral arrangements. It was feared by Mrs Coward and Auntie Vida that Miss de Pomeroy might make a dramatic scene at the graveside, but she didn't even appear. The only mistake she made, and that a terrible one, was that the wreath she sent was bigger than Mrs Coward's.

Mr Coward failed to make a success of his life, but since he was of a happy disposition I think that on the whole he had enjoyed it; Noel had never been close to him, finding nothing in his father to admire or respect and he only notes, 'Father died at Goldenhurst. Left Toronto immediately and went to Genesee to stay with Lynn and Alfred. *George and Margaret* opened in New York to faint praise.'

By now people were beginning to ask me what Noel Coward was *really* like. Wasn't he 'difficult', demanding, selfish, temperamental? Didn't he make awful scenes? At that time the answer to all those questions was yes; he was all those things, and he did make awful scenes. He could fly into a rage over the slightest mishap. The most fearful dread of us all was to make sufficient noise to wake him up, especially from his sacred 'bubbers', his afternoon nap. ('If *God* rings up, tell him I'm not in.') We were fortunately protected by the double doors between the studio and the Burton Mews side of the house but a dog barking or nearby hammering, not our fault, would release his rage on us just the same. Hammering! Truly Noel was pursued by hammering wherever he went, all his life. He had only to go to a remote hotel in Fiji for hammering to start as though at a given signal, its irregular rhythm particularly driving him mad.

The scenes he made varied enormously, ranging from the histrionic bravura (captured by himself in the tirade near the end of the third act of *Present Laughter*) to suicidal despair. The former he consciously enjoyed as he went on, until the cause was forgotten, torrents of rapid and brilliantly chosen words pouring out to his and our admiration until we would all collapse in laughter. The despairing scenes could be equally funny once I had learned, which took me a long while, not to take them too seriously. A collar-stud popping out, flying like a bullet to some inaccessible cranny under the chest of drawers, could cause a nervous collapse accompanied by loud wails of 'Life deals me blow after blow', or 'I wish I were dead'. (He waged a constant war with inanimate objects, claiming that his glasses, pen or pencil had devilishly hid from him on purpose.) Once, having lingered too long in bed, he made himself late for some important occasion and dressed in a flash, only for me to discover that the car was not at the door. At this he fell flat on the bed, repeatedly crying, 'What *am* I to do?' with his face buried in his hands at the dreadfulness of this calamity with which he could not deal. I rang for a taxi, which thank God came quickly. He seemed astonished at, and grateful for, my resourcefulness in such an emergency; which taught me never again to allow his tantrums to upset me.

When he was really and truly angry, that was quite another matter. Then there would be an ominous quiet about him, his face pale with the concentration of his anger and the words shooting from his mouth with the deliberation of a slow-firing machine-gun. Then there was nothing to be done except to submit to it, until perhaps at the very end one might be able to coax him back to a more reasonable view. If not, one might have to wait days until his basic honesty with himself came to the surface and he would admit that he had been silly to allow, even for a moment, so supremely unimportant a matter to upset him.

So much for his being 'difficult' and temperamental. As for his selfishness, it was total; but if he only thought of himself and getting what he wanted when he wanted it, this was because he very genuinely believed that other people did, or should do, the same and were fools if they didn't. So his lack of consideration for others, such as keeping me up very late without ever thinking that I couldn't sleep as late in the morning as he could, was understandable. To his way of thinking I should have said, 'Well, I'm going to scapa now,' and gone. When he seriously told me that I simply must see the new cabaret at the Dorchester, the star—whoever she was—was marvellous, I was amazed at his unbelievable lack of comprehension that this would have been way beyond anything I could possibly afford: actually it sprang from his generous, though unthinking, assumption that everyone around him had enough money to do as they pleased. Again he was in his own way right, irresponsible as it seems; he didn't know then and he never knew, when he died, what my salary was. He didn't want to know—'how can what you do for me be measured in terms of money?'—though he would have been shocked had I not been given enough, which fortunately for us both was never the case. He gave his trust over financial matters, sometimes unwisely, to those around him. But between him and me it gradually became a subject of pride to both of us that my salary had never, in all those years, been mentioned. It only cropped up once, to our embarrassment, at a company meeting, when he got to his feet, said, 'I'll come back when you've made a decision,' and left the room.

Trying to describe him as he was in 1937, I must in all truth make it clear that I *expected* a star like Noel Coward to make scenes, and however many demands he made I was only too pleased to fulfil them. My reward came that autumn when we went to Goldenhurst and stayed there while he was writing *Operette*. This was the first Noel Coward score I had heard being composed; my happiness was complete each evening when I would draw the curtains of the Big Room and, over our drinks, he would play and sing his day's work several times and then play the score, as far as he had got, all through. Thrilling for me to be the first to hear the Master's brand-new songs and I freely and gladly gave him all the praise I later learnt that any creative artist has to have at this immediate point. I also learnt later that this is indeed the happiest time of all, while the work is fresh and seems to be perfect and before it has to be mauled about and cut for other people's often legitimate reasons and often for the good of the show when it comes to actual production. Even then the mauls and cuts can bring nothing but pain to the composer or writer.

The weekends were enlivened by Gladys, who was working on the sets and costumes for *Operette*, and by several visits from Fritzi Massary, vital and small, every inch a star. Lady Castlerosse came, bringing her own crêpe de chine sheets and pillow-cases, her maid, chauffeur and Rolls-Royce. The two latter had to be put up at the Walnut Tree, and the maid impressively ironed the sheets each day. The whole entourage made a glamorous exit on Monday morning in time to lunch with Mr Churchill at Chartwell. Binkie Beaumont was there that same weekend; young as he was, he looked much younger, and Lady Castlerosse named him the Baby-Faced Killer almost immediately.

Soon it was Christmas, for which Noel went to Paris and gave Edward Molyneux an exquisite Cartier-looking pencil which had actually come from a New York drugstore. In return Edward gave him a costly and beautiful Boudin water-colour, to his 'hideous mortification'.

After a dress-rehearsal with an invited audience, which Noel describes as 'a great mistake. I must have been barmy,' *Operette* opened at His Majesty's on March 16th, 1938. The distinguished cast included Peggy Wood, Fritzi Massary, Irene Vanbrugh, Griffith Jones and Phyllis Monkman; it was, according to Noel, 'the least successful musical play I have ever done'. Irene Vanbrugh celebrated her stage jubilee during the four-month run and Noel, at a special matinée to mark the occasion, spoke a poem to her written by Alfred Noyes. Twelve years later at an All-Star Matinée for the Irene Vanbrugh Memorial Fund he spoke another, this time written by himself and which at first included—for Lornie's and my entertainment—the to us immortal lines:

> Over fifty years
> Have passed since young Miss Vanbrugh's quality
> Was stamped indelibly on Margate's mighty heart.

She had indeed made her début at Margate, but of course this had to be changed. It became instead 'indelibly upon the hearts of Londoners', though when he got to the change at the Matinée he gulped, his mouth twitched and he very nearly 'went', Margate being by this time stamped indelibly upon his own heart.

The failure of *Operette* came as a blow to me; I had loved it from its inception and Manchester seemed to have loved it every night for four weeks. Noel accepted the blow with 'It simply isn't good enough', but I had to learn over the next thirty years, and so had he, what can cause a musical which has shown shining promise to fail. In this case it was fundamentally the book, and it almost invariably is; eventually Noel came to the conclusion that the book of a musical is almost certainly the most important ingredient. The loveliest and wittiest score cannot save a weak book, nor can the most sensationally beautiful and expensive sets and costumes. All the great successful musicals have strong books, the Cinderella story being the safest bet, *My Fair Lady* for example, or good triumphing over evil as in *Oklahoma!* To pull in the theatre parties and the coachloads the book, if not good, has at least to be the right kind of story for that particular public and have a kind of innocence about it. But oh dear, the expense of spirit and the long years it took to learn this.

Noel went on writing and directing his own musicals and I could not help wondering whether his leaving Cochran had not been a mistake and whether Cochran's experience, flair and guidance were not the hand that was missing to stir the perfect mixture. Even when the example of *Oklahoma!* burst upon us, Noel, enormously as he admired it, did not learn from it and the change it had brought about, that the songs should in some way further the storyline. To aggravate and confuse this mistake still further, he managed in every single show to write at least one song, nothing whatever to do with the plot, that was an absolute show-stopper. 'The Stately Homes of England' and 'Three Juvenile Delinquents', right up to the 'London' sequence sung by Tessie O'Shea in *The Girl Who Came to Supper*, belong to this category; they did eventually come in very handy indeed for his cabaret appearances and later still for the revues *Cowardy Custard* and *Oh! Coward*.

Most of April 1938 Noel spent on holiday: 'Went off again in *Arethusa* with Vian and Wells. Port Said, Jerusalem the Golden where we were shot at by Arabs, Cyprus and Albania.' While in Jerusalem he had surprisingly—for him—climbed the Mount of Olives. Summer was spent between London and Goldenhurst except for a visit to Rome when he 'went to a Fascist Rally, thought Mussolini looked like an over-ripe plum squeezed into a white uniform and laughed so dreadfully and had a seat so close I had to leave for fear of being flung into jug.' He also had an unlikely dream about Mussolini, stripped to the waist and wearing a Dolly Varden hat. But there he was soon after, thus unclad and wearing a big hat in pictures in the papers, helping to clear the Pontine Marshes.

Lilia Ralli came to Goldenhurst, and when asked if she had slept well replied that she hadn't slept at all, but had spent the night reading *Toads and Toad Life* by Jean Rostand. When pressed she said she thought there was something peculiar about the room, though not unpleasant; she had been quite happy with her book. She occupied the French Room, so called because the furniture and chintz were French and so were the engravings and books. This was the second intimation that the French Room might be haunted; I think Noel said the first had come from Gertie Millar. But how could it be haunted? It was the new guest-room Noel had had built off the long passage, less than ten years old, connecting the farmhouse and the barn. After this we never said a word to guests who were there for the first time, but it became usual for them to report a noise in the night or a lamp fallen over. This went on for all the years until we left, the most definite description coming from Mary Martin and her husband Richard Halliday who said the window had blown open and the looking-glass and the lamps on the dressing-table blown over; a gust of wind, they thought. We were rather shaken by this and questioned Old John the gardener, who said we were not to worry.

It was well known in the village that a ghost had walked the path over which the new room had been built; a local lad of long ago going nightly to keep a tryst with his lass until he discovered that she was unfaithful and had drowned himself. 'But 'e doan mean no 'arm.'

The sun seemed to shine all summer long while the shadow of war began to darken our lives. Hitler screamed and raved from our wireless sets and, while hating and despising him, it was also possible to laugh at him; he looked and sounded comical and Gladys Henson cheered us up with her theory that he was so hysterical and had such wide hips that actually he was a woman sporting a false moustache. But it wasn't possible to laugh at Neville Chamberlain; for him we felt nothing but utter contempt and hatred, much more than for Hitler. From schooldays on one had known that you have to stand up to a bully—appeasement was only another word for giving in, and to our ears sounded worse. We knew that had Winston Churchill been in power he would never have given way one inch and would have frightened the life out of Hitler, which made Chamberlain's cowardice all the more despicable. Noel was almost constantly in a rage with the latter, calling him 'that bloody conceited old sod' and maintaining you can never trust a man whose neck is too thin for his collar.

In the years to come he would often surprise Graham and me by saying, 'I've been sitting here wondering who I've hated most in my life.' Hannen Swaffer was soon dismissed as not being worthy of his hatred. Lord Beaverbrook, in spite of his twenty years of belittling and annoying Noel in all his papers—persecution is too strong a word—had made it up when they became neighbours in Jamaica, and Noel was the first to say that 'the old devil had tremendous charm'. It always ended up by him having to admit that he had gone through life without hating anybody except Neville Chamberlain. Our heroes were Duff Cooper and Anthony Eden, both of whom finally resigned from office in protest at the folly of Chamberlain's policy. They were also Noel's friends, as were Lord Vansittart, Lord Lloyd, Robert (now Lord) Boothby and others, all strongly anti-Chamberlain and all much frequented and consulted in London or at Goldenhurst. Lord Boothby lived not far away at the French House and describes those days as halcyon, when Noel used to take the stars of the theatrical world to see him and he used to bring 'some drab and wide-eyed politicians to Goldenhurst in return, and Philip Sassoon (and all he stood for) was a phenomenon which will never recur.' Laughter predominated at both their houses. He was a Member for East Aberdeenshire and was going through a period of trying to popularise the herring. These he gave weekly to Noel in wooden boxes and, rolled in oatmeal, gently grilled and served with mustard sauce, they were delicious; all friends were made—were in fact delighted—to eat them.

Alan Webb was a very close friend and came down every weekend; in those days he enjoyed throwing spanners in works, in fact became famous, infamous rather, for it. Clashes were so frequent, pro- and anti-Chamberlain, that all day long the noise of battle roll'd, and often into the night, many of the battles, even in front of the Edens, instigated by Alan. One evening he said so often to Lady Carlisle (now Dowager Viscountess Monckton of Brenchley), 'I give you India', that she felt personally responsible for India's sad plight by the time she got to bed. Noel identified himself so strongly with his political friends and their anti-appeasement policy that many of his theatre friends thought him a bore on the subject; he records that at Binkie Beaumont's party after the opening of *Dear Octopus* 'everyone flew at me for my hatred of Chamberlain'. When the latter came back from his meeting with Hitler waving his worthless piece of paper and saying—how dared he—Peace With Honour, Noel became even angrier, and angrier still with those of his friends who joined the crowds at Buckingham Palace to cheer him. He and Ivor went to a movie at the Tivoli; the newsreel showed Chamberlain smug and grinning as he got off the plane and when Ivor—reflecting the general feeling of relief—burst into tears, Noel hit him. He never felt so strongly about anything before or after.

Not all these days were spent in quarrelling, of course. There is much else to remember; lovely outings driving across the Marsh to double-feature movies in Folkestone, Hythe and Deal, even as far afield as the Dreamland Amusement Park in Margate, Noel loving funfairs and especially roller-coasters all his life. Lord Boothby remembers the *frisson* that swept through his office in the City when a telegram arrived one day addressed to him: MEET ME TONIGHT IN DREAMLAND IO PM NOEL COWARD. Lynn Fontanne and Alfred Lunt, Natasha and Jack Wilson came for the same weekend as Mr and Mrs Eden. Eden was at the height of his fame and good looks, and I suppose it was his importance that made us think we had better pull our socks up. We found to our horror that Mrs Coward had gone on buying the same white wine Mr Coward discovered some years before during an economy drive. It was labelled a Sauterne Type

and cost 2/9 a bottle; Mr Coward had said, with the air of a con-
noisseur, 'If you ask *me*, it's streets ahead of Graves.' We rectified this
but then went too far in the other direction and bought a bottle of
good port to be handed round, after the pudding *and* a savoury, with
dessert. This was a dead failure, refused by everybody; Noel got the
giggles at such unaccustomed grandeur and said, 'For Christ's sake
let's go and have some whisky and soda.'

I can remember Noel unexpectedly saying, 'Oh you pretty little
zinnias,' to a bed of them. I can remember Mr Eden sending for me and
us having a discussion about the best trains on Monday while he lay
in his bath. I certainly remember Somerset Maugham's visit and how
charming he was; I had expected him to lash everybody with his
tongue. Dorothy Dickson, star of so many musicals in London,
came the same weekend as Mr Maugham; golden, lovely, funny and
photographed for ever on my brain when on the Sunday evening she
came into the Big Room, more golden than ever in a lamé dress from
Vionnet. Dottie appears to float smiling vaguely through life, though
vague is the very last thing she is. When I heard her being cornered
by 'If you can't lunch on Tuesday, how about Wednesday, Thursday
or Friday? Or even Saturday?' she smiled up at her tormentor, her
blue eyes wide, and said, 'The answer is in the evasive.'

I could repeat the same kind of memories about those summer
months, the good times as well as the violent arguments, when I
come to those of 1939, but I shall not. As Noel wrote: 'For me the
pre-war past died on the day when Mr Neville Chamberlain returned
with such gay insouciance from Munich in 1938.'

The next personal excitement was that Noel was going to New
York to produce a revue, *Set to Music*, starring Beatrice Lillie, and
he asked me to go with him. I had never been to America and like
everybody else who has never been, I longed more than anything in
the world to go. The boat-train left Waterloo at just after five p.m.
on November 5th, Guy Fawkes' Day, so that there were bonfires
burning and fireworks exploding in, it seemed, every garden on
both sides of us all the way to Southampton. The *Normandie* I thought
was beautiful, and I suppose she was; with Art Deco now in vogue
she would be even more keenly appreciated today. She was fairly
new and vibrated too much; the joke was that however you ordered
your eggs they would in any case be scrambled by the time they got
to you. Larry Olivier was on board, he and Noel still great cronies
since *Private Lives*, so they were happy as bird-dogs. Leslie Howard
too was on board, so were Lady Ravensdale and a Rothschild, Victor

I think, who gave Noel a handsome donation for his Actors' Orphanage. Anna Neagle and Herbert Wilcox too, on their way for the première of Anna's *Sixty Glorious Years*, the first full-length British film to be shown at Radio City Music Hall. I had a great friend on board, Angus MacDougall, who was travelling steerage, so Noel quickly got us a *laisser-passer* from the Captain. I don't know whether we had more fun when he came to me or I to him but anyway we had the run of the ship and I do know that we drank much more in third class, feeling we should cheer up the Czechoslovakian refugee with whom Angus shared a cabin. After paying his fare he had nothing except thirty-six dozen pairs of ladies' kid gloves with which to start a new life, and I have hoped ever since that he got the gloves through all right, became rich and lived happily ever after in the Land of the Free. New York was then known for the champagne-like quality of its air, and it was quite true; when still twenty-four hours out from the city one began to feel exhilarated and remained exhilarated, needing less sleep, for the whole of one's stay.

Rehearsals started for *Set to Music*, Beattie again behaving as she had in 1928, a devil all through and right up to the opening, after which she became an angel of sweetness. (She explains in her book, *Every Other Inch a Lady*, what a terrifying, lonely nightmare it is for a comic trying to be funny in dingy rehearsal rooms and empty theatres with, after a day or two, no laughs coming from your by then *blasé* fellow-actors.) Once the curtain went up on opening night, however, the audience was as happy to see Beattie as she was to hear them laughing; she made a huge success and all was forgiven. The English members of the cast arrived and Noel gave a party for them in the apartment; Helen Hayes and Ruth Gordon were, I thought, much gayer and funnier than Dorothy Parker, who looked miserable verging on the disagreeable, emitting not one Parkerism for us to treasure. However she made up for this with one at about that time, which remained Noel's favourite. She produced a personable young man, of which she seemed to have a supply, to fill in a last-minute cancellation at a literary dinner-party. Faced with such distinguished guests, through nerves he knocked back too many martinis and was drunk by the time he got to table, from which he soon got up, loudly announced, 'I wanna piss,' and staggered from the room. 'He's very shy,' said Mrs Parker. 'Actually he only wants to telephone.'

The Edens arrived off the *Aquitania*, Mr Eden having to make many tactful post-Munich, and therefore difficult, public speeches which he managed to do brilliantly well. Mrs Eden adored staying up late in noisy night-clubs, to which Noel escorted her. Much as he loved her, this was his most unfavourite form of entertainment, but he did it, he said, for Britain.

Our train-journey to Boston, where the show was to open, was again illuminated on both sides, this time by Christmas trees lit up in snow-covered gardens, coloured lanterns and holly wreaths on the doors of the houses, none of which I had seen before. Also for the first time, the first of many, I stayed at that friendly, luxurious home from home, the Ritz-Carlton Hotel. And again for the first time which was also to prove the first of many, Noel and I had a serious quarrel. We seldom really quarrelled except over his musicals, about which somehow we never fully saw eye-to-eye; he resented my criticism because, I think, coming from me it was unexpected and he was hurt by it. We had many real rousers over the musicals in the future but this one started harmlessly enough. After the first run-through, in which there was only a brilliant solo by young Bronson Dudley, whose tap-dancing was accurately described by Brooks Atkinson as bizarre, I said I thought the revue would be perfect when the other dances were in. 'But there aren't going to *be* any other dances,' he stormed, 'that's the whole *point*, you bloody fool. Why do you think I called it *Words and Music* [as it had been called in London] in the first place? Because that's all it's going to *be*—words and music, so you can shut up.' I then knew—and I had been thinking of Cochran and *This Year of Grace*, which had been bursting with dances and star dancers—that this important ingredient would be missing and my remonstrations were in any case too late. I still think I was right. The show, though enthusiastically received, remained lop-sided and only ran for 129 performances in New York.

We ended 1938 with a New Year's Eve party, a very larky one, given by Noel and with Beattie and Gladys Henson as hostesses. There was much kissing and Auld Lang Syne-ing, and when I at last achieved my room I was still grinning happily and drunkenly into the glass as I untied my tie, until I saw a black cavern where my right front-tooth should have been. What had happened to my tooth I never found out and didn't dare to ask, as Beattie had started a very funny story going round the company about a tooth having to be extracted, not from the gum but from a lower part of someone's anatomy. So I spent next day in the merciful darkness of a Boston cinema watching Garbo and Charles Boyer four times over in *Marie Walewska* (*Conquest* in America) until it was glisteningly replaced at five thirty, as the dentist had promised.

Back in New York, Noel had a renewed attack of wanderlust and asked me to find out all I could about Pago-Pago, where he had never been and very much wanted to go. I knew it was pronounced Pango-Pango but didn't know, until an informative gentleman at American Express told me, that the printers of the very first map didn't have enough 'n's and sent the map home as Pago-Pago, which spelling has remained. To my 'Well, we live and learn, don't we?' he came back with 'And we die and forget it all', which depressed me and still does. Noel never did get to Pago-Pago. He got as far as Hollywood, whence he sent a telegram, BUTTERING NO PARSNIPS, changed his mind and went to Honolulu instead. He 'rented a beach shack at Mokolaeia, lived in it completely alone and was as happy as a clam. A Japanese lady used to appear each morning, clean the shack and give me breakfast and lunch. I drove into town once a week for supplies and managed to write nearly all of *To Step Aside*. A very very happy and peaceful interlude.'

To Step Aside is a volume of short stories, which was yet another new departure for him. He evidently enjoyed trying to master this new form, for he went on writing short stories, on and off, for the next thirty years: four volumes in all. In this, his first book of them, his inexperience hardly shows except in 'The Wooden Madonna', and Maugham's reprimand over 'Aunt Tittie' is in fact a compliment: 'You had material there for a great picaresque novel which probably no one but you could write and it is a shame to have squandered thus such a wealth of splendid stuff.' Dame Edith Sitwell, when Noel gave her his *Collected Short Stories* in 1962, wrote with typical generosity:

> There are no short stories written in our time that I admire more. I think 'Aunt Tittie', for instance, a real masterpiece. I am not a cry-baby but it brings tears to my eyes every time I read it—and I have read it over and over again. I can't think what you must have gone through, piercing into the hearts of those two forlorn human beings. The end of the story is almost unbearable, you have done more, so quietly, than most writers do by yelling at the tops of their voices. All the stories have that extra-ordinary quality of reality, so that although the endings are perfect endings, one feels that the people go on living after the stories, *qua* stories, are finished, and one wants to know what happened to them, beyond the stories.

After a brief return to England, he went at the end of April to Lausanne to finish the book. In spite of Mrs Parker—or was it Kathleen Norris?—describing Switzerland as beautiful but dumb, Noel loved it. He loved the Beau Rivage Hotel, with its view from his balcony of the changing colours on the lake and on the French Alps beyond; of the little boats, some with coloured sails, bobbing up and down near the shore; of the lake-steamers 'gliding like swans' to and from the Ouchy landing stage a little to the right. He worked all morning, then took a boat out to the clear waters in the middle of the lake, where he bathed, ate a delicious box-lunch provided by the hotel, and then sunbathed, unhampered even by bathing-trunks, lying in the boat. Taking one of the lake-steamers across to Évian late in the afternoon was a leisurely pleasure, with an overtone of adventure from having to take his passport for the landing in France and the prospect of an evening of chemin-de-fer at the Casino. He was a dashing gambler (though wise enough not to exceed the sum he had allowed himself to play with) and much more often than not a very lucky one. During this holiday he had such a sensationally long 'run' one evening that a crowd of other gamblers gathered round his table to watch. The excitement spread along the lakeside and then back again with news that the last, the midnight, steamer would wait for him, and so it did, for twenty minutes, and there were jubilant drinks all round, all the way back to Lausanne.

One of his stories, 'Mrs Ebony', is set, though the hotel is not identified, in the Beau Rivage, as are the three plays contained in *Suite in Three Keys*. He was happy and content 'on the bonny, bonny banks of Lac Leman' on which, as he said, there was no lack des cygnes. Exactly twenty years later he bought a house there, at nearby Les Avants, above Montreux.

The Theatrical Garden Party in aid of the Actors' Orphanage, with Noel as President, was held at Ranelagh on June 6th, opened by Lady Louis Mountbatten, who then gallantly accompanied him to every single side-show. The star attraction was Mary Pickford— from the mid-'thirties on it had become a film, not stage, star who drew the big crowds. Miss Pickford nearly caused a riot; in fact to be in the smallish tent to which Noel brought his friends for a short rest and refreshment at times became frightening, the poles of the tent swaying and creaking and the canvas billowing inwards from the surging of the crowds surrounding it until it became safer to go outside and face the excited mob. Miss Pickford was so tiny that hardly anybody saw her at all.

This interruption apart, Noel spent most of his time at Golden-hurst writing a play called *Sweet Sorrow*, which title was rightly changed to the gayer *Present Laughter*, it being a very funny comedy. This must have come swiftly, and so must its twin *This Happy Breed*, as there is a note that the latter was finished at exactly eleven thirty a.m. on June 29th. As he was himself planning to star in them he again wanted more than one vehicle, not only to exhibit his versatility but to avoid monotony, his bugbear. While working on these, he asked to be called at six thirty, which I thought to be an unnatural and unnecessarily early hour. But he sprang willingly from bed and bathed, shaved and dressed, while I lit a fire in the library in front of which he ate the breakfast Kitty had prepared; a cooked one, most often his favourite grilled pork sausages with bacon, extravagantly splashed with Worcester Sauce. Kitty and I 'did' his room while he ate, as it was also his workroom—a big scrubbed oak table in front of the window facing Romney Marsh serving as his desk. I grew to love these mornings with only the three of us up and about, and the military precision with which we all carried out our allotted parts, and soon saw Noel's point that this way he could be at work by half-past seven.

I became more involved with these straight plays than I had with *Operette*, when Noel had necessarily spent many hours alone at the piano. He worked all morning, no telephone calls allowed, his only break being when at the stroke of eleven I took him some coffee. I went in, put it down by him and went out quietly but firmly—he would have hated anyone to creep—without either of us saying a word. When he knew he could rely on this rule he then began quite often to break it with 'Sit down, I must read you this. I'm rather pleased with it', or 'Sit down, I'm in despair', and he would talk about his troubles, helped I think by simply talking about them. One bad morning came with *This Happy Breed* when he was stuck for a funny line for old Mrs Flint; I was happily able to tell him what my cousin Audrey and I had overheard in the Victoria at Dymchurch the night before: 'Eleven o'clock she was out doing her shopping and she was putting 'er joint in the oven at twelve—nice leg of lamb it was too—and at half-past one she was flat on 'er back on the operating table.' This he incorporated at once and my pleasure knew no bounds.

One evening, perfect for Glyndebourne, he went there and walked out stating that, in his considered opinion, Mozart was like piddling on flannel. He expressed this opinion for ever after, always getting a laugh except from those who like myself think Mozart can do no wrong. He got to know that this joke annoyed and embarrassed me, so of course he used it all the more, even when he had ceased really to mean it. But on August 28th, 1964—I made a note of the date—at a Yehudi Menuhin concert in Montreux, Yehudi's then son-in-law Fou Ts'ong played the Piano Concerto K271 so exquisitely that the audience stamped and yelled. Of course I couldn't smirk, 'What have I always told you?' so I looked straight ahead at the platform, but Noel leaned across and said, 'That was one of the loveliest things I've ever heard in my life,' and meant it, thus more than making up for all the years of pinpricks. But Mozart was never really for him, nor were, after many tries, the *longueurs* of Wagner—'I wish he'd get on with it,' he said. Verdi and especially Puccini with their sweeping melodies and crashing chords were 'my boys'; *Turandot* remained his favourite, with a soft spot, kept open always in his heart, for *Madam Butterfly*.

There were readings of the two plays at the studio late in June with Binkie, Gladys and Joyce present, also Leonora Corbett, who was to play the female leads opposite Noel. Anxious to make a good impression she had had her hair done for the occasion and on arrival asked me where there was a looking-glass. She scrutinised the result from every angle for a long time, never once touched it, only said, 'I try too hard, you know,' and then bravely walked in to face the music. Rehearsals went very well indeed, though Noel had all along had a presentiment that the plays would not be produced as planned that autumn.

'This dismal clairvoyance was ultimately justified,' he wrote, and war was declared—one cannot say broke out—on September 3rd. On the 5th Noel left for France to take up his already allotted job of setting up an office from which to liaise with the French *Commissariat d'Information*, which he most sincerely believed at that time, and so did I, to be his job for the duration and the one in which he could best serve his country.

Ten days later I left to join him; like him I was not allowed to reveal where I was bound and my grandmother, with memories of her sons in Flanders fields in the First World War, cried at the dangers of my unknown destination, which I am afraid was in fact the Ritz Hotel in Paris. The city was virtually deserted during those very early days of the war, though the Ritz, except for the rue Cambon side being temporarily closed, seemed to be more or less its usual self. Lady Mendl had expressed her determination that this should be a gay war, and I have a vivid memory of her bedroom, the bedcover made of pink ostrich feathers and everything on her bedside table made, it looked to me, of gold. On one landing there was a mountain of Vuitton suitcases and cabin trunks belonging to Barbara Hutton. (Was there not enough room in her suite for the mountain? Or had she taken the whole floor?) Noel and I never forgot the sight of Chanel's entrance into the Ritz air-raid shelter during an alert, followed at a respectful distance by her maid bearing her gas-mask on a cushion. These may have been two separate necessities put together for convenience but we preferred to remember their overwhelmingly royal effect.

Noel had difficulty at first in making contact with his French counterparts who seemed, except for Jean Giraudoux, never to have heard of him or of Sir Campbell Stuart and his London office, who had sent him. Nor did they take him seriously at first; perhaps the Ritz was too frivolous an address. It was in any case too expensive, so he soon took over the lease of an apartment on the other side of the Place Vendôme, in Van Cleef & Arpel's corner. We liked the apartment on sight; a string of six rooms painted white, all facing the sun, and, when there was no sun, still giving the impression of air and light. Curtains and carpets were bought with the lease, the curtains of white satin in some rooms, in others of a blue just brighter than navy. Noel tackled his first decorating job without Gladys's or anyone else's advice by going to Samaritaine de Luxe and ordering with quick decision natural wood furniture throughout, with upholstery of the same blue as the curtains, but in tweed. A few scarlet cushions here and there and *voilà*, how chic it looked. There was something wrong with the corner near the door though, something missing, so he ordered a very large three-fold screen, one fold painted red, the others white and blue. The thought of this screen gave us malicious comfort all through the war; once we learned that the flat was requisitioned for German officers we enjoyed thinking of them having to live with our big French flag.

Yvonne Garnier, fortyish, pretty and plump, came to us as maid and cook. As she was *Marseillaise*, her bouillabaisse was wonderful and so was the amount of garlic she put into everything else. Noel thought she would be good for my French and perhaps she was—I learned a lot of argot—but her accent certainly wasn't. When a barber told me he was astonished I was English I hoped he thought me *un vrai Parisien*, but no, from my accent he said he would have sworn I was an Egyptian.

Noel's office in the Place de la Madeleine was by now also in good working order, thanks mainly to the efforts of young Lord Strathallan and his staff. When they were joined by Lord Gerald Wellesley and Lord Reay it follows that the office quickly became known as the House of Lords. Apart from their propaganda duties they were expected to entertain visiting bigwigs, who soon, now that Paris was filling up again and the phoney war in full swing, found every excuse to come to Paris. After blacked-out, rationed England, Paris, which wasn't so blacked-out as all that, the apartment and Yvonne's cooking inevitably became an attraction with lunch or dinner at Maxim's an even more enticing alternative.

Spies were reputed to be everywhere; our building, more than most, was supposed to be a nest of them. Noel, not being allowed to explain what he was doing in Paris, was a prime suspect, which I think he rather enjoyed. Our neighbour in the next flat, the tall and strikingly beautiful Iya, Lady Abdy, certainly looked like one, so when she went away for a probably innocent three days it became gospel truth that she had been taken away for questioning. A Madame Walther was seized in the middle of the night, driven to Versailles and shot, which I am sure was as untrue as the rest of the stories but exciting in the telling nevertheless. Spying apart, our neighbour on the other side was a gentle lady named Madame Fahmy, said to be the famous Madame Fahmy who had shot her husband some years before in the Savoy Hotel in London during a terrific thunderstorm. When I asked Yvonne why she had done it, she said, '*Parce-qu'il a toujours fait l'amour par la derrière.*' This, with the brilliance of her defending counsel, Sir Edward Marshall Hall, and taking into account the thunderstorm and all, had resulted in her acquittal, which left her a rich widow and with an understandably high opinion of British justice. We of course never mentioned the *crime passionel* and only knew her as our nice pro-British neighbour with whom we played many a game of Chinese checkers on the back stairs during air-raid warnings, and whom we could hear every Sunday morning playing, for reasons best known to herself, 'Someday My Prince Will Come' on the piano.

There was an outbreak of poetry during the war, everybody writing or reading it, for which I believe there is a psychological reason. Whatever the reason, Field-Marshal Wavell's anthology *Other Men's Flowers* was never far from Noel's reach, nor was the *Oxford Book of English Verse*, and he wrote to all his friends in verse—or, let's face it, sometimes doggerel—as they replied to him. Even in the office the staff left their memos in rhyme, this from Squadron-Leader Bill Wilson:

The dear Air Attaché arrived back to find
His good lady Letty disturbed in her mind
Because of digestive disorders within her
She humbly regrets you'll excuse them from dinner.

There is a thick folder of these letter-poems which Noel re-read so
often with reminiscent pleasure that I must quote a few. (It should
be noted that he could sometimes get to London for weekends on
an official plane though never with any certainty that a seat would
become available until the very last moment.)

Dearest Mrs Lorn Loraine,
Please allow me to explain
That I'm feeling so much better
Since receiving your sweet letter.
Now sweet Lornie close your eyes
For a wonderful surprise,
Close your eyes and cross your feet
For a fast approaching treat,
MASTER IN A DAY OR TWO
WILL BE COMING BACK TO YOU!
Either Saturday or Sunday,
Failing this, at latest Monday,
In the quite near *avenir*
(French for future, Lornie dear)
You will hear your Master's step
Swift, decisive, full of pep.
You will hear your Master cry,
'Lornie, Lornie, it is I!'
You will feel the honied bliss
Of your Master's welcome kiss.
Just imagine, if you will
What excitement! What a thrill!
Tell my aged, widowed Mum
Deaf maybe but far from dumb
That her long-lost son once more
Is returning from the war.
None the less my heart is light
As a mocking bird in flight
Knowing it so soon will rest
Close to Lornie's largish breast.

Lornie was never allowed to forget for long that her hair was straight and far from thick. Here is her reply:

> Upon my bosom, broad and strong
> As fair Ben Lomond (famed in song)
> The Master, ere much time has passed
> Will lay his noble head at last.
>
> And I will laugh and I will sing
> And fill the house with carolling
> And toss my pretty curly hair
> Like golden king-cups in the air.
>
> Oh hurry Master, get here soon
> I cannot wait to start my tune
> I cannot *wait* to feel you press
> Your head upon my dusty dress.
>
> So hurry, hurry through the sky
> And wake the love-light in my eye.

Again from Noel, this time to Joycie:

> Beastly, horrid, idle, vile Joyce Carey
> Throwback from some ancient ghetto
> Why, by all the tidings brought to Mary,
> Do I get no wire, postcard nor letto?
>
> I who once was loved but now forgot
> Starting the New Year in pain and wonder
> Realize the bleakness of my lot
> Absence does NOT make the heart grow funder!

Joyce's wire, two days later:

> More numerous than all those loaves and fishes
> Sent down by Dod to feed the girls and boyce
> Are the devoted, half-semitic wishes
> That reach you hourly from your loving Joyce.

Although your stern reproaches I deserve
Think Christian thoughts and grant this tiny boon
Just blame my lack of news, not lack of lerve.
Herewith my heart: a letter follows soon.

I see from the foregoing that Baby Talk had started to creep in, Dod or Doddie being B.T. for God, but the dark days of 1940 are not a suitable time to expand on it and I shall postpone this disgraceful pleasure until after the war by which time it had become our daily prattle.

When Noel reached the age of forty on December 16th, 1939, one magazine asked him if he would agree that a creative artist does his best work after the age of forty. He replied:

Certainly. Look at Michaelangelo, Leonardo Da Vinci, Verdi, Bernard Shaw and me. Mind you, with regard to the last-named, opinion seems to vary as to whether it is my 'best' work, but I do not propose to let that worry me in the least. For who is to say with any certainty which of an artist's works are his best? Everyone knows that contemporary judgment is not to be relied upon and in fact it is a fairly safe rule to take the opposite view to the current one. Even Time will not tell, for an artist is sometimes remembered and loved for his more popular works rather than his best ... You will notice that the artists I mentioned have one thing in common—certainly the only thing I have in common with them—*a large output*. They worked hard before they came to forty year, and then went on working hard for the rest of their productive lives. I do not see why a writer should lay down his pen on the stroke of forty any more than a mechanic his spanner or a surgeon his scalpel.

'This is the way that boys begin. Wait till you come to forty year,' from Thackeray's poem 'The Age of Wisdom', had for a long time been a favourite quotation of his. We celebrated the occasion well and truly with a party in the Place Vendôme apartment, and when the last guest had gone we had one last drink and a long heart-to-heart talk in which he advised me to take Thackeray's and his advice when the time came. The day had been a milestone much to his liking; he could recommend being forty, it was quite true that it was then life really did begin. One was older and wiser, the questings and doubts of youth were, thank God, over and one had come to terms with life and with oneself while still young enough to make merry. We were, he said, both blest with the gift of making friends and had many of them, for which we must forever thank our lucky stars. We were—except for the probable Armageddon hanging over us all —without personal troubles, gay and carefree, and by the time we had had one more last drink we had sworn to take Herrick's advice as well as Thackeray's and gather the rosebuds while we could; tomorrow they might well be dying.

This oath we kept. Paris was full again and during the first months of 1940 the war had come to a standstill, the Maginot Line was impregnable and pleasures were hectic. The apartment filled almost every night from six till nearly nine—the martinis so dry they were known as *dynamites*—and by nine o'clock everyone was on the town, making their way to their formal or less formal engagements. Maurice Chevalier was at the Casino, marvellously holding his audience enraptured for the entire second half of the revue. At L'Amiral, a *boîte* not far from the Arc de Triomphe, everybody went night after night to see and hear a young singer called Edith Piaf, white-faced in her black dress, passionately singing her passionate songs—'*C'est lui qu' mon coeur a choisi*' and '*Je n'en connais pas la fin*', long before '*La vie en rose*'. The telephone never stopped ringing and Noel had at least two admirers too many. One was a very attractive lady who expressed her love through serendipity, this faculty enabling her to provide us with necessities and luxuries when nobody else could find them. The other was a youth, son of a famous father, so sick with love that he was unable to express it but would sit bolt upright, open-mouthed with adoration until Noel, having torn himself to shreds with one-sided conversation, would say, 'Well, you must bugger off now,' which he seemed content to do having had, let us hope, all he asked, a glimpse of his idol.

So much for the nights; for Noel his days at the office had become monotonous. There were many meetings, much talk and very little achieved, it seemed to him. By March his restlessness had become obvious and he was encouraged by Sir Campbell Stuart to take six weeks off in April and go to America. When the Germans invaded Norway and Denmark the pulse of the office suddenly quickened and the interminable Phoney War in fact was over, but to Noel's surprise Sir Campbell told him he thought it even more important that he should go to the States, keep his eyes and ears open, and any reports that he sent home on American reaction—whether there was less isolationism for instance—might prove extremely useful. He sailed from Genoa on April 18th, having hidden what he called The Papers under the drawing-room carpet. In May the Germans invaded Holland, then Belgium, finally got as near as the French Channel Ports and Lord Strathallan began telling me I must go home to England. But how could I? What would Noel think of me and what should I think of myself, running away from the Germans at the first sign of danger? Besides, all my French friends pooh-poohed the idea, how could I even imagine the German Army in Paris, it had got as near as the Marne in the last war but never got to Paris and I wasn't to be so silly. I listened to them, and, stubbornly, not to Lord Strathallan, to whom I must have been a nuisance and a responsibility. I stayed till June 9th when, after quite a cheerful dinner, I came out on to the Boulevard de l'Opéra to find an ominous change had taken place on that sunny Sunday evening; a sinister silence everywhere and no traffic to be seen until one car, crammed with people and luggage, went by at great speed. The sight of a rolled-up mattress tied to the roof gave me goose-pimples and I ran through the Marché St Honoré to the back entrance of the flat.

The telephone could not have been ringing with extra urgency but it seemed to me as if it were; it was Lord Strathallan, this time 'I'm ordering you, do you understand?' to leave tomorrow. He had got me a place with some of the British Embassy staff on the one o'clock train from the Gare du Nord, and told me I must only take what luggage I could carry myself. I got The Papers from under the carpet, devoted one suitcase to Noel's things, the things I knew he cared for, and one to my own. I hadn't dared tell Lord Strathallan that I had no exit permit so, after no sleep, I got to the Préfecture de Police by seven o'clock to queue for one. So had hundreds and hundreds of other people, Italy having declared war at midnight—their infamous Stab in the Back—and after a day spent slowly shuffling I got my permit late in the afternoon. When I called Lord Strathallan I could hear the controlled exasperation in his voice: '*Now* what are you going to do? That was the last train you missed. All the stations are closed to keep them free for troop movements. Well ... stay put in the apartment and I'll see what I can do.' A car came in about an hour, driven by Emanuel, the kind chauffeur from the office who had always driven Noel, the car loaded with documents to be taken to Tours, to which the French Government had already quickly moved. We joined the long, hot, crawling one-way procession of refugees who were in those dreadful days blocking all roads leading south from Paris; tormented from time to time by alerts and German planes overhead.

We felt lucky to have reached Tours by three o'clock next morning. There we had to part, Emanuel insisting on giving me what francs he had in his pocket because 'God knows what will happen to you.' The story of the remaining four days it took me to get to London is one of the usual refugee stories of that time, hunger and no sleep; I retell it rarely because it now seems incredible that it happened to me; it must be some other person I am talking about.

Noel wrote: 'On looking back now on those strange, frustrating months I find it difficult to believe that I ever lived them at all. They seem in my memory to be not exactly vague, but irrelevant, almost as though I had dreamed them.'

The dream wasn't quite over, but it had a happy ending. I got to the studio on the afternoon of Friday 14th, my key still fitted and in the letter-box was the *Evening Standard* with GERMANS ENTER PARIS in big black letters. I had never cried since childhood but I started to cry then, weak from reaction I suppose after my five days' tribulations and from sorrow at the German Occupation. Gladys soon appeared from nowhere and by way of comfort sensibly said, 'What you need is a prairie oyster,' and made me one. This did the trick, I began to cheer up and then, miraculously, the door opened and Noel walked in. He had been to most of the major cities in America, but with the ghastly news of the collapse of Europe coming in hourly had cut short his itinerary and caught the first Clipper he could to Lisbon. He spent several days there, urgently trying to get to Paris, with no way of knowing 'whether there was fighting in the streets and whether or not Cole and David [Strathallan] and the office had got away in time'. Sir Walford Selby, our Ambassador at Lisbon, had finally forbidden him even to try to get to Paris and had firmly put him on a plane for London that very morning. That we should be re-united within one hour after our long and entirely separate adventures is the kind of coincidence you only come across in a bad novel, or in life, but we were all together again—Joyce and Lornie soon joined us—and for the time being we asked for nothing more. Our very real grief over France's humiliating surrender was only somewhat assuaged by a fan of Noel's who, feeling as deeply as we did, had been moved to write a poem beginning: 'France, France, what *have* you done?'

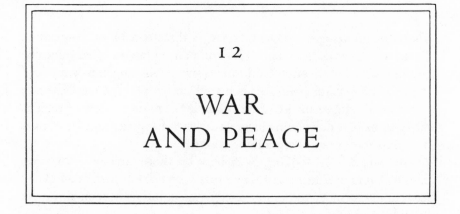

I 2

WAR
AND PEACE

THE next few weeks were indecisive for Noel. The tempo of the war had increased, his political and service friends were in office, and though he tried them all, nobody seemed to require his help or the use of his abilities. I wanted more than anything to join one of the services but said nothing about this to Noel or to anybody else. At last, one evening in June, Lord Lloyd came to the studio for a drink, bringing a definite suggestion from Duff Cooper that Noel should return to America, but with an indefinite idea of what his job was to be. His unofficial position was even less clearly defined; he was just to look around, keep his eyes and ears open and report back anything he thought might be of use. Lord Lloyd said, 'Of course you'll want Coley to go with you,' and I shall never forget Noel's immediate understanding when I refused because I wanted to join up. I had expected 'Don't be so bloody silly', or 'Let's talk about it later', followed by arguments trying to dissuade me. Instead he said, 'I do see. Of course you must. But on the strict understanding that you have a nice retaining fee for pocket money and come straight back to me the minute the war is over. And this is your home whenever you come on leave.'

So Noel went to America in July and I joined the Royal Air Force as soon as I could. My career was inglorious, but I spent four on the whole happy years with 231 Squadron, a mobile unit, which meant that we had to be constantly ready to be moved anywhere within twenty-four hours. We therefore had no permanent base, were looked down upon as a raggle-taggle lot despised and unwanted by the smart geranium-window-boxed R.A.F. stations on which we were foisted, which made our camaraderie and pride in our squadron the greater. Old-fashioned and quaint as it now sounds, I longed to serve my country and help to win the war and spent much time begging and filling in forms for an overseas posting. I had no ties, could speak

French and was used to knocking about the world; but no, it was always the chums with sweethearts and young wives to be torn away from who got the postings, while I remained in nissen huts in turnip fields, though admittedly in the lovely surroundings of Northern Ireland and the even lovelier Lake District.

Noel too tried desperately hard to serve his country but his efforts during the first part of the war were unsuccessful and came to naught. The just-mentioned visit to America caused open hostility in the British press, and his two friendly invitations from President and Mrs Roosevelt to the White House were interpreted as Noel helping to make high-level and far-reaching decisions as to the future conduct of the war. The fact is that the President and Mrs Roosevelt enjoyed Noel's company, he made them laugh; the only remark of any importance was the President's 'Well, I've got you your destroyers', to which Noel replied 'Thanks very much!' The *Sunday Express* of August 4th thought ' ... we should give the Americans our news, whether it be bad or good, and leave them alone to form their opinions on it. Nothing is more irritating than to be told about your duty by somebody else. For example, the despatch of Mr Noel Coward as special emissary to the States can do nothing but harm. In any event, Mr Coward is not the man for the job. His flippant England – cocktails, countesses, caviare – has gone.' Questions were asked in the House of Commons, to which Sir Harold Nicolson, speaking for the Ministry of Information, replied that Mr Coward 'possesses contacts with certain sections of opinion which are very difficult to reach through ordinary sources'. This caused the *Daily Mirror*'s caustic Cassandra to write next day: 'Mister Coward, with his stilted mannerisms, his clipped accents and his vast experience of the useless froth of society, may be making contacts with the American equivalents ... but as a representative for democracy he's like a plate of caviar in a carman's pull-up.'

All the facts and dates are there in his own *Future Indefinite* but the book somehow is not wholly satisfactory. It is not an apologia but one is left with a slightly uneasy feeling of an (unnecessary) attempt at self-justification; unconscious, I am sure, but why did he devote the book to the war years only? He didn't have to justify himself, he was well above service age anyway. The publication of *Middle East Diary* in 1944 was undeniably a mistake. He had worked very hard indeed giving troop concerts in North Africa, but it was difficult for the war-weary British to feel sympathy for his exhaustion, alleviated next day by lying in the sun by a swimming-pool with a drink. The book gives the impression that this part of his war work was done *en luxe* — Government Houses, special cars and planes, luncheons and dinners and always plenty to drink. Much of it conjures up a holiday in sunny North Africa; unpleasing reading for people back home, rationed, blacked-out and sometimes bombed-out, with no possibility of getting abroad for a nice change. In the average reader at that time it could only arouse envy and animosity.

I think the truth is that Noel started his war by getting off on the wrong foot. The political company he had been keeping for several years had given him the idea that he too should have a post in which he could use his brain. When he asked Churchill's advice a week or so before war broke out as to what he should do, Churchill thought — to Noel's annoyance — that he had meant Intelligence and advised him to stick to entertainment instead. 'Go out and sing "Mad Dogs and Englishmen" while the guns are firing,' he said, which annoyed Noel more than ever. After the petering-out of the job in Paris, he tried hard to find another and, after many months, he was at last offered an assignment by Sir William Stephenson, whose organisation in New York represented British Intelligence in the United States. 'Everything okay,' he wrote, 'very very excited. Feel at last I can be really utilised properly. I am to pick my own staff in London. All blissfully efficient. Very thrilled about everything.' This was on March 28th, 1941, and only two days later he was told that London had cabled making a postponement, about which he felt there was something sinister, but Sir William's staff reassured him; it was merely a priority hitch at Lisbon or something. Transatlantic planes in those days usually flew to London via Bermuda and Lisbon, and Noel got as far as Bermuda, where he stayed with Hamish Mitchell, also one of Sir William's 'boys', as they were known. Noel lunched at the Bermuda Yacht Club, spent a pleasant evening with Hamish, but was summoned by him next morning by telephone to get a boat and to come at once to his office in Hamilton. Noel's voices had been right; Sir William in New York had received a cable in cipher from London:

APRIL 2ND FOLLOWING FOR NOEL COWARD (A) REGRETTABLE PUBLICITY GIVEN TO YOUR VISIT LONDON BY ENTIRE BRITISH PRESS WHICH WOULD INCREASE ON YOUR ARRIVAL UNFORTUNATELY MAKES ENTIRE SCHEME IMPRACTICABLE (B) COMPLETE SECRECY IS FOUNDATION OUR WORK AND IT WOULD NOW BE IMPOSSIBLE FOR ANY OF OUR PEOPLE TO CONTACT YOU IN ENGLAND WITHOUT

INCURRING PUBLICITY (C) WE ARE ALL VERY DIS-
APPOINTED AS WE HAD LOOKED FORWARD TO WORKING
WITH YOU BUT THERE ARE NO FURTHER STEPS TO
BE TAKEN TEL ENDS I COPY ONLY.

Noel was 'utterly stunned. Unable to believe I have been let down so
thoroughly. Determined to get back to London. God, what enemies I
must have. Suspect whole thing has been done in by Beaverbrook plus
Churchill. Angrier than I've been for years, also utterly miserable.
Know I could have done the job well. Slept hardly at all.'

He did get back to London and found himself up against a stone
wall, unable to discover who had sent the cable; he never really did
discover, though he always suspected it was Churchill who had
caused it to be sent. Major William Dwight Whitney, an American
who at that time was in the Scots Guards and married to Adrianne
Allen, brought him comfort months later. Bill, who undertook various
missions for the U.S. Government in liaison with that of the U.K., had
seen the exchange of cables at the time and assured Noel that there had
been no wicked mastermind at work. The obstacle really and truly had
been his celebrity value.

Noel, though angry at the treatment he had received, found England
looking its loveliest in the spring; he had deeply comforting reunions
with Lornie, Gladys and Joyce, and found to his surprise that for the
first time since he had left it, he felt really happy to be back in London:
'How very odd, that deep-rooted content at being home, in spite of
war and black-outs and air raids, a profound and very real peace of
mind.' There was no money (he had paid most of his travel and all his
personal expenses during his 'war work' visits to America), there was
much income-tax to be paid—'obviously however hard I work I shall
never be able to save any money'—Gerald Road had been blasted out
by bombs dropped nearby and Lornie had got him much too grand a
suite at Claridge's; he was determined to economise and so he went to
Fortnum & Mason's and bought himself a bicycle and, for the first
time since his early youth, pedalled about on it all over the West End,
rather dangerously. For a time he lived in the spare room at Gerald
Road, all that had been repaired, until the Savoy always a second home,
gave him special terms and, as always, he was happy there. His disappointment over the war job receded: 'I don't care any more anyhow.
Bed, with the guns banging away like mad.'

The quotations used above and those which follow are taken from
the diaries which Noel began to keep this year and which, in one form

or another, he kept for the rest of his life. He started by giving only the facts of each day but before long he could not prevent Noel the writer beginning to appear in little glimpses: 'Saw my Godson who shrieked like an engine whistle', and 'André Gide was quite sweet but oozing with super-dignified French eminence'. The entries become longer, one of them ending, 'Good night, dear happy little journal. What a hell of a record you are going to turn out to be.' But the diaries do not truly evolve into journals until 1953, when he abandoned the daily details (of which there are too many, e.g. 'Got up at six and caught the early train') in favour of writing every Sunday morning about those events of the past week which had remained uppermost in his mind. In these weekly journals he could spread himself much more and enjoy himself; in the meantime the factual diaries are invaluable for reference and do contain from time to time patches of 'writing', either funny, touching or in some way effective, as we shall see.

With the tiresome and disappointing story of Noel's attempts to get an official job out of the way, the rest of his war makes much happier reporting. He was absolutely determined to make some lasting contribution to the war effort and at this point decided that this should be in his own field, that of entertainment, which was what Churchill had so strongly advised in the first place. Not in the sense that Churchill had meant though, as an entertainer; he had deliberately chosen the words 'lasting contribution' and his contribution would therefore have to be made as a writer. He made up his mind to write one really good play, one really good song and, because stories had begun to reach him of the sinking of H.M.S. *Kelly* and had given him an idea, one really patriotic film. One is astonished to read that he achieved all three of these formidable ambitions within four months, from the beginning of May to that of September 1941. *Blithe Spirit* was written between May 4th and 9th inclusive, made the nation laugh and has made many nations laugh ever since. Four songs, all 'patriotic' in intent, were written from June 2nd onwards, including 'Imagine the Duchess's Feelings', 'Won't You Please Oblige Us with a Bren Gun', and 'There Have Been Songs in England', but of the four it is 'London Pride' which has lasted and is still played and sung and loved.

With much help and advice from naval friends of all ranks, up to and especially including Lord Mountbatten, and through him encouragement from King George VI, by July 30th the idea for the film had jelled. He had never before written a film script, but seven days later, on August 6th, he had begun to tackle *White Ensign*, as *In Which We Serve* was called at first: 'Personally more thrilled with it than anything I can remember, but terrified of everything not being absolutely right and accurate [i.e. the hundreds of technical naval details]'; on September 2nd he finished the script 'flushed with triumph'. Although this script turned out to be the first of several and *In Which We Serve* could not be made until the following year, the actual writing—bulls-eyes on all three of his targets—was done, and he rightly felt pleased with himself and proud of his efforts.

While preparing accuracy of detail for the film, he spent two days at Plymouth:

Drove to Grand Hotel through terrible devastation. A heart-breaking sight. Had drinks at hotel with Dorothy the barmaid. She told me stories of the blitzes here, quite without conscious drama, therefore infinitely more touching. It certainly is a pretty exciting thing to be English. Spent next morning with [Nancy] Lady Astor walking round the devastated town. A strange experience. Lady Astor very breezy, noisy and au fond incredibly kind, banging people on the back and making jokes. The people themselves stoic, sometimes resentful of her but generally affectionately tolerant. The whole city a pitiful sight, houses that have held sailor families since the time of Drake spread across the road in rubble and twisted wood. [At lunch] Lady A. delivered tirade against Winston. Also said apropos of Bruce Lockhart that he could not be a really good appointment because he had written a book discussing his travels in Europe with his mistress. This point of view baffling and irritating. How sad that a woman of such kindness and courage should be a fanatic.

Watched the people of Plymouth dancing on the Hoe. A large dance floor, white coated band, several hundred girls gaily dressed, dancing very well with sailors, soldiers, marines etc., in the strong evening sunlight. A sight so touching, not that it was consciously brave but because it was so ordinary and unexhibitionist. The English do not always take their pleasures sadly, at least not when they are surrounded by death and destruction.

Meanwhile, in New York, Mrs Coward was once more proving tiresome. Less than a year before, Noel had, after endless string-pulling, managed to obtain passages for her and Aunt Ida to enjoy the safety of New York, away from the air raids in England. Aunt Vida refused to go, evidently preferring to endure bombing rather than what might be a very long stretch of close confinement with her sister, and so the

good-natured, even-tempered Aunt Ida went instead. Noel's apartment at 450 East 52nd Street, which he had taken over from Alec
Woollcott, was supremely comfortable for one person, but cramped for
two, though at first all went well. Mrs Coward was taken up and made
a fuss of by most of Noel's grander friends, such as Eleonora von
Mendelssohn and Mr Woollcott, who were delighted to take her to
theatres and smart restaurants, also by a younger set, headed by John
La Touche, who found her great fun and charming—both of which she
could be when she chose—and who took her to less expensive though
equally enjoyable delights, such as movies at Radio City Music Hall or
a day at Jones Beach. Aunt Ida seems to have been left Cinderella-like
in the apartment, and Mrs Coward absolutely queened it over her
arch-rival of days gone by, Mrs Tonge, mother of Philip, with whom
she now renewed their always shaky friendship. Aunt Ida stood the
humiliations and constant friction for months, and then in desperation
courageously bought a passage for the dangerous sea-voyage home to
England.

On August 30th of this same year, 1941, Noel heard from Jack that
his mother now wanted to come home. There followed a brisk and in
the end touching exchange of letters between Noel and his mother,
now aged seventy-eight. First, he told her firmly she must behave
herself because he had heard she had been saying some very silly things
about England. 'You must NEVER while you are in America speak
against this country, because if you do you are letting me down very
badly.' (Mrs Coward had by now become lonely, desperately homesick
and longing for a sight of her son.) 'But for the gallantry and ideals of
the fighting services there would be no England for you to come home
to and no ship to bring you.' The letter is long, much of it verging on
the pompous, but he does end with a joke:

> I wouldn't be surprised if you are not responsible for the whole
> war and it's only a matter of time before Hitler and his hordes join
> hands with Mrs Tonge, Auntie Ida and at moments Auntie Vida,
> Cogger and other oppressed peoples to encircle you with an
> extremely nasty pincer movement! Love and hugs, you wicked
> girl.

Mrs Coward, true to form, returned as good as she got:

> You neglected me for months because you had no time to write,
> and then found time to type pages of a pompous lecture at me.

How dared you! Hitler is not governing us yet and I have as much right to my opinions as you have, even if you have spent so much time in the Navy. Please don't bother about my coming home, it is impossible anyhow and I don't mind much ... I can't always be miserable and shall probably survive all this beastly war and come back with a few more wrinkles, and probably using a stick but as wicked as ever. 9 years ago today my Erik died. What a tragedy! I feel so very far away and so alone.

This angry letter crossed with 'a lovely one' from Noel, which she intended to take as a reply, although she knew it was written before he received her pages of anger, 'because I can't bear this horror any longer and have drawn down a shutter on the past. I can't be *all* bad and have had a very rotten time, but as in the nature of things I cannot have many years longer to live in this beastly world, I can't afford to throw away the only thing that is worth having, and that is you and your love.'

Poor Mrs Coward was forced to spend months of increasing loneliness and longing for England and her son. Aunt Ida had been lucky in getting away when she did; for all his considerable influence Noel could not get his mother home, though pleading for compassionate priority on the grounds that her only sister (Vida) was seriously ill in Devonshire and she was 'frantic with anxiety'. No less than four times she packed her bags and made her way to the dock or airport, only to be told that after all there was no place for her and back she would have to return, bitterly disappointed, to the apartment. Nearly a year passed, until in August 1942 she got a seat on a plane via Shannon to London, where Lornie had found her a little house in Boscobel Place, conveniently near to Gerald Road. Aunt Vida recovered; Kitty, who had been with her, happily came back and looked after Mrs Coward while Aunt Vida moved to a ladies 'club in Hamilton Place where, it seemed, she spent her days reading the *Daily Telegraph*.

1941 was not yet finished with Noel; on Thursday, October 16th, while working at Gerald Road with Gladys and Lorn on further scenes for *In Which We Serve*, they were 'cruelly interrupted by a shattering blow. Two Police Inspectors arrived with two summonses from the Finance Defence Department. I am to appear before a court and am liable to a fine of £22,000, for having broken certain rules about which I knew nothing and now know very little.' Neither his English nor his American accountants had warned him of the regulation whereby he should have declared his financial holdings in America. Legally he was guilty, although up to then he had been in ignorance of this war-time regulation. Four days later he was served with three more, separate, summonses. Under a foreign currency law passed in August 1939 he should also have declared the New York bank-balance into which his U.S. royalties were still being deposited by Jack, and not have spent a single penny of it in any circumstances whatsoever. Therefore his spending of it, principally on his goodwill tours under the aegis of the Ministry of Information, was a criminal offence. The outlook was unrelievedly black and the charges could not have been brought at a more unfortunate time. He was certain to be landed with a press scandal; he had already suffered criticism for daring to play—he, the lightweight comedian—the part of the Captain of a destroyer in a serious film about the Royal Navy. Also he and Lord Mountbatten had, after long struggles, only just succeeded in obtaining promise of co-operation from the Admiralty, so essential for the making of the film. 'Obviously I can expect no mercy. My years of success must be paid for.'

Two good things emerged from the gloom. First he engaged the services of the eminent lawyer Mr Bateson, later to become Sir Ding-wall Bateson, sometime President of the Law Society, and to remain, until 'Dingo's' too early death, Noel's trusted English lawyer. The second was another example of George Bernard Shaw's kindness to Noel; two days before the case was due to be heard he wrote reminding Noel that there can be no guilt without intention and he was therefore to let nothing induce him to plead guilty. And if his lawyers advised him to do so, he was to tell them that *he*, Bernard Shaw, advised him not to. Noel was deeply touched that G.B.S. had thought of him in his trouble, felt certain he was right, and against all legal advice, pleaded not guilty.

On Thursday October 30th, Noel appeared at Bow Street with Lornie and Dingo. Joyce and Gladys were also there.

Counsel for the Prosecution a snarling little rat, started by saying I was liable to a £61,000 fine. Magistrate rather grumpy. I went into Box about 12 o'c after Dubois [his accountant] and Cooper had suffered loss of memory and made asses of themselves. Gave my evidence quietly and, I think, well. All the truth of my war activities came out except the secret stuff. Sammy Hood was in Court, presumably to protect the interests of the Ministry of Information. Prosecuting counsel tried hard to prove that I was not sent to America officially by Duff. Fortunately M. of I. ticket was produced. Was cross-examined and kept my temper ... Magistrate asked Prosecuting Counsel what the British Government had expected me to live on, upon arriving in the U.S.A. with only £10. Brilliant speech by Geoffrey Roberts [his barrister], then careful summing-up by the Magistrate, Mr McKenna, who finished by fining me £200 on one summons and nothing on the other two, the minimum fine being £5,000. This was absolute triumph. Left Court in a daze of relief and gratitude for the most important fact of all, and that is that English justice is worth fighting for. I was treated fairly, courteously and without prejudice. Enormous headlines in the evening papers.

The next day he dictated a letter to Jack saying that never again must there be any muddling of his financial affairs. But all was not yet over; he still had to face the further charges in seven days, this time in front of the Lord Mayor at the Mansion House. (Why, Noel always wondered; they were virtually the same charges.) The Lord Mayor of the year made it evident from the start, Noel wrote, that he was bloody-minded, wanted to show off—*he* was not going to be as lenient as Mr McKenna had been. In addition, he had bad adenoids. He fined Noel £1,600, iniquitous compared to Bow Street, but Noel refused to appeal, considering the whole proceedings to have been beneath contempt. He is again grateful to report that the press had all been very good: not one dirty crack had been made.

Noel's mistrust of Jack's handling of his financial affairs arose from these two cases. At some point in the 'thirties Jack had caused a partnership agreement to be drawn up, which preposterously made over half of Noel's earnings to Jack in return for his business management and services, and which Noel signed, as always trusting others where his money was concerned. He now blamed himself for his foolishness, saying that he should have had his head examined. He was with reason angry with Jack; Dingo Bateson used the word 'iniquitous' to describe the agreement but Jack cabled that he too was angry and hurt when Noel demanded it should be cancelled. Here are Noel's words:

I feel sad that he is so upset but not as sad as I felt when I was being tried at Bow Street for a crime that I had no idea I had committed and which Jack, in his capacity of financial adviser, should have warned me about at the time. Obviously he didn't know, but as in the partnership he contributes his business and managerial

ability and I my talent, it seems to me that the balance of contribution is a trifle lopsided.

It is pleasant to record that, once Noel had, so to speak, taken
Churchill's advice to work in the field of entertainment, Churchill more
than made up for any annoyances he may have caused. Both before and
after *In Which We Serve* had opened to world-wide acclaim, he asked for
several showings to be arranged because he admired it so much and
was not ashamed to admit that it brought tears to his eyes. Then on
October 11th, 1941, 'a message from Beatrice Eden that Anthony wants
to take a party to *Blithe Spirit* [which had been running with great
success since June] on Tuesday—the Winston Churchills, Winants,
Beaverbrook and Averell Harriman. Prime Minister apparently mad
about the play and wants to see it again.' A few days later, 'Anthony
told me that Winston was raving about *Blithe Spirit* and had told
Beaverbrook that I had been disgracefully treated by the press; to
which Beaverbrook replied, "I cannot attack the Government. I must
attack someone." Anthony also said that Winston gave him my record
of *London Pride*. It's very sweet of him to be so determined in my
cause. Apparently Dickie [Mountbatten] has given a record of *London
Pride* to President Roosevelt.'

Mention should be made at this point of the Knighthood That
Never Was. King George VI had taken a personal interest in the film
from the time he read Noel's screenplay; with the Queen and the two
Princesses he had visited Denham Studios during shooting, and in
October 1942 the film was shown at Buckingham Palace after the
official dinner to welcome Mrs Eleanor Roosevelt to England. The
party included the Prime Minister, Field-Marshal Smuts and the
American Ambassador. All present were genuinely moved and
thrilled by the film; Churchill said he admired it even more having seen
it for the second time, and Lord Mountbatten that he liked it as much
the third time as the first. From existing correspondence and Noel's
diary for that year it is evident that a discussion had arisen regarding
the inclusion of Noel's name in the next—the New Year's—Honours
list, the King making it clear that he felt some kind of recognition was
overdue and that he would give the proposal his personal support. His
only worry seems to have been that Noel might refuse because of the
difficult times he had been through, ever since the beginning of the
war, with the press, but Noel at once sent a message to say that if it
was the King's wish, he would of course be honoured to accept.

It now seemed certain that nothing could prevent him from becoming Sir Noel Coward on January 1st, 1943. But two months passed with no official intimation forthcoming and on the last day of the old year he wrote, 'sabotage had been at work, so that's that and I shall not reconsider the matter.'

Who had been responsible for the 'sabotage'? Noel suspected Churchill and Beaverbrook, or more likely the latter's strong influence over the former, but when several years later he asked someone in a position to know he was told that it was Sir Kingsley Wood, dead by then but Postmaster-General at the time, who had led the objectors on the Honours Committee. Which was on the face of it an absurdly lame explanation, for supposing that Churchill and Beaverbrook *had* given their support to Lord Mountbatten and the King himself, how could the Postmaster-General have over-ridden so formidable a quartet? The feeble excuse only served to strengthen Noel's suspicion into conviction that Churchill and Beaverbrook had been the 'saboteurs'. The real obstruction was, in fact, Noel's technical breach of currency regulations two years before.

Gladys and Noel were inseparable for more than a year during the making of *In Which We Serve*; she planning the highly technical sets and designing the clothes, he acting and co-directing with David Lean. For this important task she obtained leave of absence from the Mechanized Transport Corps. Gladys leaned somewhat towards the barbaric in jewellery, and refused to follow everybody else's fashion in clothes: Noel summed this up in verse when she exchanged her rainbow wardrobe for the khaki of the M.T.C. (Blackheart, her nickname, was soon shortened to Blackie, and she has remained Blackie ever since):

> Where are the bright silk plaids of happier years
> And all those prawns that used to deck your ears?
> Where, in the mists of yesterday, oh where
> Is that small watch that formed a boutonnière?
> Where is the twist of Mechlin lace you had
> And called a hat before the world went mad?
> Where's the harpoon that fastened up your coat,
> Where those gay *mouchoirs d'Apache* for your throat?
> All, all are gone. The leopard skin, the sheath
> Of striped percale. But perhaps beneath
> Your blue and khaki, so austere and cold,
> My Blackheart is my Blackheart as of old,
> With shoulder-straps of shagreen and maybe
> A brassière of lapis lazuli.

Gladys fought side by side with Noel every inch of the way, from the
first battle to get the film made at all and through many more during
the actual making with various government departments and with
some of the crew at the studios, who at times were more than ob-
streperous. Gladys never failed him, not even when a War Office
telegram came saying that her only son Hugo was reported missing in
Burma. She told Noel while driving home after work on the film was
finished for that day, saying, 'There's still hope, we must wait and see —
I can't quite talk about it now.' Noel wrote, 'I feel low and wretched —
there is nothing to be done except to play up to Gladys's supreme
integrity.' Not until more than four weeks later, when the second
telegram arrived, saying that Captain H. D. Calthrop was now
reported killed, does one read:

> We talked about Hugo's death. Gladys has had a letter from his
> C.O., a very nice letter but somehow almost unbearable to read.
> Apparently when his party was surprised at night by a whole
> battalion of Japanese, from all reports Hugo dashed out alone
> with a tommy-gun and there is very little doubt that he was killed
> outright. Gladys's control over the whole thing is really superb.
> I know she is more deeply unhappy than ever before in her life.
> She is looking round and inside out and getting herself together.
> I am lost in admiration.

Clemence Dane, the famous novelist (*Broome Stages*, *The Flower Girls*,
Regiment of Women) and playwright (*A Bill of Divorcement*, *Will
Shakespeare*), should have put in an appearance on these pages long
ago. Her proper name was Winifred Ashton, and to her vast circle
of friends she was known as Winifred. She and Noel had known one
another for some years, but it was the war that suddenly brought them
together; from the beginning, even during the Paris days, whenever
he could get to London, he flew like an arrow on his very first evening
to Winifred's cosy, crowded little house at 20 Tavistock Street, Covent
Garden. To Noel and his close friends, allied with Winifred's own,
notably Richard Addinsell, Victor Stiebel and Joyce Grenfell, Tavistock
Street became a symbol of home and security. Winifred was endlessly
engaged in writing scripts for radio or films, all directly or indirectly
helping towards the war effort by calling up the spirit of England, so
that the shades of Shakespeare, Henry V, Drake, Nelson, Queen
Elizabeth, Alfred the Great and all our national heroes were never far
away when you were in Winifred's company. There was never any
question but that we should win the war.

The other inhabitants of Tavistock Street were Olwen Bowen, Winifred's friend and secretary, and Ben, a neurotic and snappy fox-terrier who was as much disliked as Olwen was loved. Some or most of the friends seemed always to be there of an evening, the party enlarged by any visiting firemen ranging from the Lunts, Katharine Cornell, Douglas and Mary Lee Fairbanks, David and Hjordis Niven and Mary Martin to any Admirals or Generals who happened to be about. Through this throng in the far from large sitting-room Winifred strode, more than Junoesque, with a nobly beautiful countenance, gowns—one cannot call them dresses—to the floor and with her rich and resonant voice put to good use. Her vitality and her enthusiasms were inexhaustible and sometimes exhausting. Her genius lay in the infinite amount of sheer creativity that sprang from her all day from the moment she opened her eyes in the morning. Just as much of her generous self went into the making of a steak-and-kidney pudding as into her latest play, novel or film script.

She had studied painting under Tonks at the Slade and she also sculpted; her oil portrait and her bronze head of Noel are now in the National Portrait Gallery and are the truest likenesses made of him. She painted boldly and with veracity—'Paint what you *see*' was her credo. Her paintings have never been on the market, the friends to whom she gave them rightly never dreaming of parting with them.

Painting and sculpting, though, were only two of her extra enthusiasms. Many a big tube of flake white was trodden into many a Wilton carpet and many lumps of clay flew in every direction before all was discarded in favour of 'throwing' pottery, a period much dreaded by her friends. Worse still was when she made large—everything about Winifred was large—fan-shaped flower arrangements in shallow dishes brimming with water, given to you on leaving. Even Noel was seen, trying to sway with the rhythm of a jolting train or taxi, swearing like a trooper and with his trousers soaked; but not for long, he soon rebelled. Noel's adoration for Winifred became tinged with annoyance, leading to fierce quarrels when he could not follow her into some esoteric realm of knowledge. If Winifred went too far, 'showing off about English Literature', and Noel was cornered, he would resort to pulling her leg and would in passing mention, let us say, Scatchwick. To her raised eyebrows he would say, 'Winifred! You've never read Scatchwick's Essays? Shame on you!' and then discourse on Scatchwick's merits until the penny dropped and Winifred would say, 'Oh No-el! What a wicked tease you are!'

He absolutely revelled, as we all did, in Winifred's Garden of

Bloomers. The first I can remember was when poor Gladys was made by Noel to explain to Winifred that she simply could not say in her latest novel, 'He stretched out and grasped the other's gnarled, stumpy tool.' The Bloomers poured innocently from her like an ever-rolling stream: 'Olwen's got crabs!' she cried as you arrived for dinner, or 'We're having roast cock tonight!' At the Old Vic, in the crowded foyer, she argued in ringing tones, 'But Joyce, it's well *known* that Shakespeare sucked Bacon dry.' It was Joyce too who anxiously inquired after some goldfish last seen in a pool in the blazing sun and was reassured, 'Oh, they're all right now! They've got a vast erection covered with everlasting pea!' 'Oh the pleasure of waking up to see a row of tits outside your window,' she said to Binkie during a weekend at Knott's Fosse. Schoolgirl slang sometimes came into it, for she was in fact the original from whom Noel created Madame Arcati: 'Do you remember the night we all had Dick on toast?' she inquired in front of the Governor of Jamaica and Lady Foot. Then there was her ghost story: 'Night after night for weeks she tried to make him come ... ' Why could she not have used the word 'materialise'? But then if she had we should never have had the fun.

Noel said he ' ... never published a book or produced a play since I have known her without first indulging myself in the warming radiance of her enthusiasm and the kindly but nonetheless perceptive shrewdness of her criticism. She has enriched my life with her warmth, her vitality, her knowledge and the unfailing generosity of her loving heart.'

Noel of course saw Lornie every day at Gerald Road, their mornings starting with Lornie's arrival in his bedroom carrying a tray full of newly arrived letters to be gone through and answered. (A pretty accurate picture of this usually hilarious ritual can be obtained from Garry Essendine's scene in the first act of *Present Laughter* with his secretary Monica, and Monica's line: 'The studio becomes rather active round about eleven. People call you know, and the telephone rings.')

Joyce also was never very far from Noel's side during these years of the war. She, like Gladys, also worked in *In Which We Serve*, and gave one of her finest film performances, particularly in her heart-rending death scene. One of Joyce's many bonds with Noel was her mastery of parlour games, with or without paper and pencil, and their mutual addiction to backgammon, six-pack bezique, and later canasta. Mention must be made of their most devilish game of all, because it reached its heyday during this time of Winifred's evenings at Tavistock Street and

Noel's own parties at Gerald Road. This was based on a complicated code given to Noel by Cary Grant, and they complicated this still further, calling for prodigious feats of memory from them both. The name of anybody among the millions born since Adam would be written on a piece of paper and handed to one of them, who would glance at it and then say, 'Last Tuesday week Cornelia Otis Skinner covered herself in treacle.' The other would then say 'St John The Baptist', which was indeed the name on the unseen slip of paper. As nobody could break the code some people, amused at first, became bored to death; others became more and more fascinated and determined, shutting Joyce up in a distant room, or even trying them when they were separated, telephoning Joyce in her flat in Chesham Place, but after Noel had spoken his jabberwocky, Joyce never failed to give the correct answer to the would-be solver of the mystery. Their fame spread until in the end the crack official code-breakers of MI5 and the Ministry of Information were called in. The reason the experts failed as shamefully as everybody else and the code remained forever unbroken was because Joyce and Noel had also evolved a great many seemingly telepathic short cuts: a few tra-la-la's of a Chopin mazurka evoked 'Charles Chaplin' because Chopin died in 1849, the year of the first Gold Rush. And because an actress named Everest had recently played her, 'Mount Everest' was enough for an immediate 'Queen Anne', and later, the name of any old mountain would do, even Popocatapetl.

And so Joyce was for Noel the ideal companion and fellow-actor for the six-month tour of Great Britain with *Play Parade* which Binkie began to plan in the summer of 1942. *Play Parade* was the omnibus title for three of Noel's plays: two of them were new to the public because their production had had to be postponed on the outbreak of war in September 1939 – *Present Laughter* and *This Happy Breed*. The third was *Blithe Spirit*, still running in London but new to the provinces. Noel wrote: 'I am very glad I am going out on tour to do the thing I really know about and to be no longer dependent on Civil Servants and Government decrees. How little did I dream at the beginning of the war that before so very long my fine schemes for working for the country officially would be frustrated and I would be back in the theatre. At least they can't take that away from me.'

Rehearsals began on August 24th, and Noel was delighted with the all-round excellence of the cast; Judy Campbell darkly beautiful and alluring as Joanna in *Present Laughter* and poignantly touching as the commonplace housewife in *This Happy Breed*. James Donald was the first Roland Maule and remains the funniest and best; he played the part with such deadly serious intensity. But before rehearsals started, Binkie had the excellent idea that Noel should try his wings by taking over the part of Charles in the long-running *Blithe Spirit*, which would at the same time allow Cecil Parker a well deserved holiday. Six years had passed since Noel had last appeared on the stage in *Tonight at Eight-Thirty*. He spent the day of his first appearance strangely unnervous though exceedingly apprehensive, but had only been on for a few minutes when the old, well-remembered magic began to happen, he began to time and listen and space his lines and in the end gave a good performance. He was happy. But, six days later,

A dreadful morning. The Duke of Kent was killed yesterday in an air crash. I can hardly believe it but of course that is nonsense because I can believe it only too well. It is never difficult to believe that someone young and gay and kind is dead. They are always dying. The Duke of Windsor, Hannen Swaffer, etc. remain alive but Prince George has to die by accident. There goes a friendship of 19 years. He may have had faults but he was kind always and I feel absolutely miserable. Years ago I stopped being impressed by him being Prince George, especially in the last years when I have seen him so much and have been so close to him. [He and Princess Marina lived at Coppins, not far from the studios, and Noel had been seeing them constantly all through the making of *In Which We Serve*.] I talked to him on Sunday and made plans about him coming to rehearsals. And now suddenly I must know I shall never see him again. I am taking this resentfully and personally. I am so deeply sorry for the poor Duchess. I wrote to her this morning of course, a rather inarticulate letter. In memoriam I say, 'Thank you for your friendship for me over all these years and I shall never forget you.'

He got himself to the St James's Theatre that evening in a sort of daze, but had to pull himself firmly together when Fay Compton gently reminded him of the dangers inherent in the performance that lay ahead. That one is usually playing in a comedy when a personal sadness occurs, Noel well knew; but *Blithe Spirit* would be worse than most, for a great many of those funny lines—and he would have to play them as usual and get the laughs—are concerned with the subject of death. He could never remember how he got through the performance. 'I got through it somehow,' was all he ever said.

The funeral was on Saturday, August 29th:

Drove to Windsor and got to the Chapel just before 11. Was given a seat in the Choir very close to everything—almost too close to be borne. The Service was impressive and supremely dignified. I tried hard not to cry but it was useless. When the Duchess came in with the Queen and Queen Mary I broke a bit and when the coffin passed with flowers from the garden at Coppins and Prince George's cap on it, I was finished. I then gave up all pretence and just stood with the tears splashing down my face. I was relieved and heartened to see that both Dickie and the King were doing the same thing. I suddenly find that I loved him more than I knew. The thought that I shall never see him again is terribly painful. After it was all over and the King had sprinkled the earth and the Royalties had gone away, we all went up one by one to the vault and bowed and secretly said goodbye to him. Then we went out into very strong sunlight. Margot Oxford came up to me and said, 'Very well done, wasn't it?' as though she had been at a successful first night. I thought this offensive and unforgiveable.

With the twenty-six-week tour of the plays, Noel experienced most of the day-to-day wartime hardships, plus the weekly journeys to the next town or city, often in bitterly cold trains to colder hotels (there were exceptions), the sound of bombs dropping nearby during performances, and food shortages. In the hotel at Cardiff the food was so meagre and unpalatable that he and Joyce only survived the week by the head-waiter's promise on Monday of roast goose on Saturday. All week they drooled at the thought of the piping hot plumpness and succulence awaiting them. What they got was a 'slice of grey flannel in some tepid gravy'. 'I think a grave has walked over my goose,' Noel said.

Noel's long concert-tours must not be forgotten; of Australia and New Zealand, raising a great deal of money for war charities, and his three months tour of South Africa in aid of the Red Cross and Mrs Smuts's Comforts Fund. Then there were his troop concerts in Burma and elsewhere, at Imphal notably, for the troops in the front line with the Japanese line at some points only four hundred yards away. In addition to the strain of these concerts, holding and keeping the audiences entertained single-handed, he visited service hospitals, sometimes three and four a day. He was outstandingly good at this, always having had a special talent for visiting the sick, combining jokes with common sense and with sympathy when necessary. For those patients too ill, wounded or otherwise unable to write, he offered to write to their families or sweethearts, and all these promises were scrupulously kept. As if this were not enough, there were on all these tours constant interviews with the press to be given and speeches and broadcasts to be made; an extra effort because, contrary to general expectation, he was never a natural impromptu speechmaker.

Noel always looked back with pride on his struggles and eventual achievements during the war, and on how he had overcome his many setbacks.

The evening of Victory Day, May 8th, 1945, Noel spent, as he had spent so many evenings of the drab days, with his closest friends at Winifred's welcoming house in Covent Garden: 'The room looked as comforting and relaxed in Victory as it had in Disaster.' After dinner they walked through the singing, dancing crowds in the streets to Buckingham Palace to cheer the King and Queen when they appeared on the floodlit balcony. Noel cheered the loudest but felt desolate beneath the gaiety, remembering all the people who had gone, and there was, he said, still the future to be fought.

Everybody got lit up when the lights went up in London after nearly six years of darkness. After months of anti-climax since the Normandy landings, everything seemed to happen at once. Only a week before Noel had written: 'Report on the deaths of Hitler and Goebbels. Mussolini shot yesterday, hung upside down in the street and spat at. The Italians are a lovable race ... Winston described Mr Attlee as a sheep in sheep's clothing.' Two nights later Lady Juliet Duff gave a dinner for Winston, Noel and Mrs Venetia Montagu, just the four of them. 'The Prime Minister was at his most benign and suddenly at the same moment we all became emotional about him. He was immensely touched and simple about it. It was a strange but I suppose a very natural moment. There he was, gossiping away with us, the man who had carried England through the black years and he looked so well and cheerful and unstrained and in addition was so ineffably charming that I forgave him all his trespasses and melted into hero worship.'

In January 1945 the R.A.F. discharged me after insisting that I have four monotonous operations in as many years for hernias which had given me no trouble at all, so incipient I didn't know I had them. I was awarded the King's Badge for Loyal Service, given a gratuity of ten pounds and a pension of seven and six a week for a year. Oh, the bliss of being back in my own little room in Burton Mews and having one last nightcap with the Master, and then another while we hatched plans for the future. Our greatest private pleasure was to dream of our

With Gertrude Lawrence at Goldenhurst, 1935

With Jack and Natasha Wilson and
Anthony Eden at Goldenhurst, 1938

Tennis at Goldenhurst, 1935.
This scene inspired 'That hedge
over there is called Cupressus
Macrocapa', from *Shadow Play*

Arriving in New York aboard
the *Normandie* with Leslie Howard, 1938

With the children of the Actor's Orphanage

Mrs Coward in New York, 1942

With Marlene Dietrich in New York
in the early 'forties

Mrs Coward with Laurence Olivier
and Vivien Leigh at the première
of *In Which We Serve,* 1942

King George VI, Queen Elizabeth and Princess Elizabeth
on the set of *In Which We Serve*, 1942

Graham Payn, 1947

Clemence Dane at Blue Harbour

With Alfred Lunt and Lynn Fontanne and Cecil Beaton, 1952

>

With Beatrice Lillie
and Queen Elizabeth at a
charity show, 1950

With Mrs Coward on opening night
of the French production of
Present Laughter, 1948

In cabaret at the Café de Paris

As King Magnus in *The Apple Cart*, with Margaret Leighton

Noel and Cole Lesley relaxing on the South Downs during
the Brighton run of *The Apple Cart*, 1953

>

Goldenhurst, 1956

With Graham Payn, Cole Lesley and Joyce Carey in the studio at Goldenhurst, 1956

Playing the piano at Goldenhurst, 1956

Rehearsing with Mary Martin
in Blue Harbour, 1956

Firefly Hill

With Marlene Dietrich and
Douglas Fairbanks, Jr, at the
London Palladium, June 1954

With Merle Oberon and Judy Garland
after the live televising of *Blithe Spirit*,
Hollywood, 1956

Las Vegas, 1955

return to the much-loved Paris apartment. We had learned by then that it was 'all right' though a friend wrote: 'The place has been occupied by what must have been a particularly unpleasant pair of Gestapo hounds, never properly housebroken ... there are some remarkable stains on the bed, notably on the brown satin headboard which, if my deductions are correct, are a remarkable commentary on the acrobatic agility of the occupants.'

We also learned that Yvonne the maid had, with the Germans almost at the gates of Paris, beguiled a man—at which she had many years' experience—to drive her in his lorry to Moulins, where she had a cottage. First she had put the grand piano into safe storage, then had hidden our personal possessions (fourteen suitcases and trunks in all) behind a false wall she had had built in the cottage. This had been papered and then sealed up in the presence of a Public Notary as being the property of Monsieur Novel Covarrr, as she always pronounced it. As luck would have it, when Gaul was divided into two parts by the German Occupation the line of demarcation ran clean through Moulins and for four years Yvonne helped, or perhaps did not help, people to cross the border. Her head was shaved at the Liberation, she was arrested for collaboration and sentenced to ten years *Indignité Nationale*. She was soon out and about in mink and wearing an Elizabeth Taylor-size diamond ring. All this was none of our business and as far as we were concerned Yvonne had been valiant, so when Noel went to Paris in March to appear at the Stage Door Canteen with Marlene Dietrich and Maurice Chevalier, he went down to Moulins, the *Chef de la Gendarmerie* formally broke the seals and Noel triumphantly returned to London with his and my clothes. We couldn't believe our eyes—all those shirts, pyjamas and dressing-gowns from Sulka—or our luck, in those days of a few clothing coupons a year.

Noel wrote, that night of his return, 'It is so sweet to be back in London again with the people who are my own closest ones.' There was a great deal to talk about, for 1945 was a year of bustle and plans. From its beginning there were the songs to be composed and written for a new revue, *Sigh No More*. *Private Lives*, with John Clements and the enchanting Kay Hammond, was enjoying its first major revival and playing to packed houses. Noel thought he would drop in to have a look at *Blithe Spirit*, still running after four years, and was delighted to find that he had to stand. But what we talked about endlessly, though, was where we were going to live.

Goldenhurst was still requisitioned by the Army and we had to find a smaller house in the country. Noel had a friend, the Hon. Kay

Norton, who had always given us pleasure, especially by her manner of speech which was aristocratic with a slight rasp, sprinkled with many a 'doncherknow': 'No, Joyce, I'm taking *you* to lunch. You're a paw person, doncherknow.' Kay had an elegant little house in a dramatic position at the very end of the beach at St Margaret's Bay in Kent which she said she thought she'd have to sell, doncherknow. Noel drove down to see it on a sunny wintry day, and thought it would be ideal for him—'I don't think I can fail to be happy here'—and so he bought it as quickly as he could. He adored the sea, and Kay's house was almost in it; depending on the weather the waves either lapped against or lashed the end wall of the house, and this was to become the wall of his bedroom, against which was the head of his bed. The drama of this situation of course appealed strongly to him, the drama intensified by the White Cliffs of Dover rising steeply on his right, only a yard or two from where he lay. To his left he could look at, or step out on to, a little low-walled lawn beyond which stretched the changing colours of the sky and the English Channel; the never-ending traffic on the latter further enhancing the visual pleasure.

But to move into 'White Cliffs' was not an easy matter. The house had been requisitioned, windows and doors blown out by bomb-blasts, and the floors were ankle deep in rubble. Building and re-decorating permissions were at that time difficult to come by, and when we did get the precious bit of paper it was only for one hundred pounds. Noel, ever since he had been a naughty schoolboy, had only to be told that he mustn't or couldn't do something for him to do it with increased determination. He wanted to move in to the house quickly and no minor obstacles such as rationing and housing restrictions were going to stand in his way. Luckily Gladys, who had been looking for and found a house nearby, produced with the help of Jeff Amherst a wonderful young man called Harry who could turn his hand to anything, and did. Noel and I painted walls and ceilings with white paint and breaking backs while Harry coped with plumbing, electricity and other mysteries. This he did with such skill, speed and good nature that Noel soon declared he was just wild about Harry and 'I *think* Harry's wild about me'.

Goldenhurst was not far away; Noel drove over to find it locked and empty; the Army had left it clean and in reasonably good condition but had never let him know they had left it at all. The garden was wildly overgrown and he found it all a bit heart-breaking. At last he discovered a door that would open so he 'went all over the house, pushing aside the ghosts. What is past is past.' The lovely Goldenhurst furniture had for six years been in store in Tankerton in a disused cinema which had twice been flooded by abnormally high seas. Going there to pick out what we wanted was a bit heart-breaking too; there it all was in a huge, sad, higgledy-piggledy pile, the beds, sofas and chairs—all old friends—on their backs with their legs in the air, looking pathetically helpless. We quickly chalk-marked what we needed and were glad to get back to sunny White Cliffs and press on with our tasks and occupations.

More and more people over the years came to Noel for his advice, with which he was always generous and usually helpful, about their love-affairs, broken marriages or their careers. He was sympathetic, but as in everything he did he favoured attack and would tell them firmly where they had gone wrong or what they ought to do instead of what they were doing, so that these talks soon became famous as Noel's Finger-Wags. He enjoyed giving them and we were all treated to a jolly good one from time to time, and he started to use the phrase himself: 'I can see I shall have to give him one of my Finger-Wags.'

On March 30th, 1945, he wrote: 'Good Friday. Graham Payn came to lunch and was lectured firmly.' Graham's Finger-Wag was about his future in the theatre; Noel had been the night before to the opening of Leslie Henson's *Gaieties*, in which Graham played one of the leads and which Noel said was the most deplorably incompetent production he had ever seen. Graham had a clause in his *Gaieties* contract which allowed him to leave and fulfil his promise to appear in Noel's revue, *Sigh No More*, so one can imagine the lecture he got about last night's lash-up and how he must set himself far higher standards in the future. He had been in *Words and Music* as a boy of fourteen and he and Noel had been meeting again more often towards the end of the war, but this luncheon was the first time I had met him, and I liked him very much on sight. Everyone who knew him liked him, and his innate good humour and sense of fun were infectious. His looks and personality were charming, he had enough height and his figure was good. On stage he used his light baritone voice well and appealingly and his dancing combined vigour with grace. He was quick and intelligent although his I.Q. as such was not spectacularly high; Noel more than once calling him an illiterate little sod to his face. Noel's circle of friends was bright, open and candid enough, but Graham brought even more fresh air into it. From the first he had cut through the famous legend and got to Noel himself, his irreverence such that it amounted to an attack until Lornie, 1 and Noel himself would warn him he was dicing with death. Once, when he was dicing dangerously, Lornie tried to caution him by singing *sotto voce* from one of the songs in the revue, 'Dear little lad unheeding'. We thought this funny and used it as a code signal so often that it stuck, and Little Lad became and remained his name. A few weeks after that Good Friday Noel wrote 'Matelot' for Graham which, with its haunting plaintive melody and nostalgically tender words, proved to be one of the high spots and best-remembered songs in *Sigh No More*. This particularly, coupled with all the other work on the revue, brought us close together. Almost exactly two years after the Good Friday luncheon, Graham moved in to stay, because his flat in St John's Wood had been let, and since then we have seldom separated. The temporary move turned out in fact to be for the rest of our days. Friends at the time were bemused by our threefold relationship: Jack asked me to lunch at the Carlton for what turned out to be cross-questioning. 'Now come on, you're always so god-damned sweet about everybody but you can tell me the truth. Don't tell me you didn't hate his guts from the moment he walked in the door.' We are still asked if it is really true that Graham and I have never quarrelled, and the rather dull but very happy answer has to be, 'No, we never have.' All the qualities glimpsed at first—his enthusiasm, honesty, generosity of spirit and pocket, his kindness and his love—have increased and remained steadfast for thirty years.

All through that beatific summer we drove whenever we could to White Cliffs, bathed, sunbathed and ate delicious box lunches from Madame Floris, the Soho confectioner famous for making Sir Winston Churchill's birthday cakes, each one photographed for the papers and more spectacular than last year's. Too impatient to wait, long before the house was ready, Noel and I moved in on October 18th; Graham was in *Sigh No More* and drove down late every Saturday night for the weekend. The discomfort was great; windows were missing and there was no heating or electric light, but no matter—we managed with Beatrice stoves, Calor gas and candles and bought a lot of bright coloured long-sleeved pullovers called Sloppy Joes. Gladys had already moved in to her house on the cliffs above us, called 'The Moorings', but because of its Suburban-Grand appearance re-christened 'The Stockbroker's Paradise', and to her we went most evenings for hot baths and piping-hot dinners. Since his success with the Paris flat Noel henceforth planned his own interior-decorating; furnishing materials were still scarce, but such a trifle could not for one moment deter him, he simply bought yards of vivid green plastic for curtains instead. He loved books *qua* books and lined one wall of the drawing-room from floor to ceiling with them; when Winifred remonstrated that no one could possibly reach the top shelves he said airily, 'I know. That's why they're filled with trash.' He spoke too quickly and could only pray she could not recognise some of her own novels at that height. From now on he would exercise his flair for decoration; he also developed a permanent passion not only for buying houses and doing them over but also for building them to his own design. When not actually building, he dreamed of building houses high up and remote, himself the first to admit that it was a madness like Ludwig of Bavaria's.

On the long beach of St Margaret's Bay there were only four houses, of which White Cliffs was the brave leader to the sea with three followers stringing close behind. They stood empty and Noel of course immediately wanted them, to ensure his privacy he said, but was not allowed to have them in those days of housing shortage. We got round this by Lornie taking the first house in her name and I the other, semi-detached half of it and, as when trying to find suitable titles for his plays, we had endless fun discussing possible names for the houses. Lornie's half became 'Lorn's Bluff' and mine (because Baby Talk had changed my name to Tole) became 'Tolegate'. Eric Ambler and his wife Louise made perfect neighbours in the second, easily named 'Summer's Lease' because theirs had all too short a date. Noel's Mum and Auntie Vida were by now of a great age and therefore called the Girls; we changed this slightly, and when they moved into the third house I don't think they ever knew why it was named 'The Gulls'. All this was an enjoyably naughty way of Noel getting what he wanted without breaking the law, but before long there arrived a Paul Pry from the Ministry of Works intent on making trouble, as they had received an anonymous letter about the building (fortunately in-accurate) of a house for Noel Coward the actor. As night follows day, next morning came the *Daily Mirror*; Noel 'got rid of him tactfully but I am getting a little sick of being persecuted'. Questions were asked in the House of Commons about Mr Coward's extensive repairs, but the Minister of Works replied that his licences and permits were in order. Noel thought this was all a lot of cock and that Parliament should put its time to better use.

After two months of the smell of paraffin, the benison of electricity was bestowed upon us, and as it was by then early December we only had proper heating in the very nick of time. All these past uncomfortable months had been so unlike the popular image of the sybaritic, silk-dressing-gowned Noel Coward that I think they should be remembered. He had worked and fought to achieve some comfort in the face of comparative hardship, and his resolution never to accept less than what he considered to be the best was an impressive and constant facet of his character.

Eggs were still hard to come by, so we bought ten hens and a cockerel which pecked behind wire-netting at the back of the house. The hens at once lost almost all their feathers — could it have been too much chalk in their White Cliffs of Dover diet? The back of the house was perforce the only entrance, and what with the bald hens, the limp wire-netting and three dustbins it was, as Noel said, no Blenheim. Beach strollers sometimes penetrated thus far and we heard one of them say, 'Whoever 'e is, 'e's got a scruffy-looking lot of chickens,' but we didn't care, all ten produced rather small eggs each morning with alarm-clock regularity.

The house itself was now complete, we were delighted with it and longed to show it off. Gladys popped down constantly from The Moorings and Joyce and Graham drove down on Saturdays bringing a stream of weekend guests. Gertrude Lawrence came with Daphne du Maurier, Gertie smart as paint in casual navy blue and white with gold sandals. She interrupted when Noel embarked on a rather long story with 'But you've told us that already!', which shook Noel dreadfully; it was the first time he had ever done such a thing and one knew he was making a strong mental note as he said, 'One martini too many. I must watch it,' angry with himself for having lost control.

By the following April Noel was in Paris and 'went to Schiaparelli's for cocktails. A gay mix-up including Mary Pickford. Dined with Edward [Molyneux] and promised to come over in May to do a Gala for the R.A.F. Sounds as if it is going to be another lash-up like the Stage Door Canteen.' (That was when some lesser luminaries had refused to appear with Maurice Chevalier because of his supposed collaboration with the Germans. He was making his first appearance since the Liberation and therefore it was of great importance to him; Marlene and Noel refused to appear unless he did, got their way and from then on Maurice was back in public favour.) After a month at White Cliffs he was again in Paris for the Gala:

A beastly morning spent in that nightmare hall with everything in chaos, Grace Moore [whom he loved] being rather tiresome and saying she would not appear because really she was a great singer etc. She left and came back again and finally sang 'Rose Marie' too slowly, 'The Merry Widow' much too slowly and 'The Lord's Prayer' a great deal too loudly ... [In the evening, the Gala was] chaos with no organisation. Diana and Duff [Cooper] as Patrons and Guests of Honour, arrived. 'The King' was played off key by our R.A.F. Band, after which 'The Marseillaise' rang out even more off key. Then I went on and introduced Josette Somebody, a tough little music-hall girl who though professional and quite good, went flat. Then Graham who was nervous; he did his numbers well but was not relaxed enough. Then came Marlene who went marvellously. Then I did my act and got them completely with 'Marvellous Party', after which all went terrifically; they kept quiet as mice and roared and screamed at the end. Then Grace came on, apologised for having a bad throat, sang one refrain of 'Rose Marie' and without warning anybody, walked off. I flew up from my dressing-room, rushed on to the stage and sang 'Mad Dogs' and 'Don't Let's Be Beastly', neither of which I had rehearsed. This really tore the place up which was jolly gratifying and I felt was deserved, as I had behaved well all day and not lost my temper.

Since the early 'thirties Noel had painted from time to time in water-colours, usually seascapes with ships, in sepia or low-toned keys; rather naive but, as in everything he attempted, with a style of his own. Sir Winston Churchill changed all this. Noel went to Chartwell one Sunday and I think they painted together; at any rate by the end of the day Sir Winston had commanded him to stop painting in water-colours and paint in oils, and Noel came back converted. There was an empty room in Tolegate and the side facing the sea was all window; what could be more ideal for a studio? So we went to Lechertier Barbe in Jermyn Street and bought everything a painter's heart could desire; all Noel now had to do was to paint. He got off to a flying start by using oils exactly as he had used his water-colours and produced a perfectly lovely seascape in misty pastel tones with a woman in red leading a small dog. I didn't need much persuasion when he insisted that I too must paint, and I very quickly caught the infection. Graham complained that he now had nobody with whom to play canasta, do the crossword or go for a walk, and says that Noel bullied him into putting some green paint at the bottom of a canvas and some blue at the top and that this first picture he ever painted was entitled 'Landscape'. All three of us became painting maniacs from two o'clock onwards every day; tea was brought at four and drinks at six and we had to drag ourselves unwillingly to dinner. Even then, more often than not we would sneak back before going to bed to make one more terribly important dab. I tried hard to paint like the Impressionists—it looked so easy—until Noel said, 'Monet, Monet, Monet; that's all you think about.' Gladys took Graham to a Matthew Smith exhibition from which he returned to paint in large splashes of colour so violent that he was known as Touch and Gauguin. No matter how hard we tried to be critical, we couldn't help admiring our own works and were impatient for their beauty to be enhanced at once by the best possible frames. Of course it was Noel who solved this problem in a trice by taking the station wagon to local junk shops and buying old paintings in ornate frames, ten and twenty at a time. We happily painted away over the canvases for which we had instant frames, but I hate to think of the value those Victorian paintings might have today, even if they weren't Old Masters.

Much laughter issued from the studio. When I painted a crowded vicarage garden-party all the figures were so extremely thin and very tall that Noel and Graham had only to look at them to split their sides. I found out later from a learned book on vision that I (though not, alas, by virtue of my Talent) was of a small band which includes Modigliani and El Greco; to this piece of information Noel said witheringly, 'Then I can only advise you to keep better company.'

At first we learned by trial and many errors, but soon were given the benefit of advice from three guests who happened to be very good painters indeed. Edward Molyneux was the first. As one of the world's top *couturiers* he knew most of what there was to know about design and colour, and as the then owner of one of the finest private collections of Impressionists he had absorbed from them knowledge of paint and how to use it. Derek Hill, although still young, was already a formidably good painter. Derek himself had been influenced and helped by Edward and later by Bernard Berenson, and he is now represented in the Tate and many other galleries of note. He kindly and patiently taught us much technically, including especially the colour with which to prime our canvases; up until then we had been painting straight on to the bright whiteness. Winifred (Clemence Dane), whose brave and colourful canvases have already been mentioned, was the third of our teachers and the one from whom we learned the most, because she visited us more often and stayed for longer periods, notably for one long holiday years later in Jamaica. She taught us many things, especially to use only a palette of colours any of which would tone with the others, from which safe point one could paint with the courage and attack which she so strongly advised. Noel, who never knew the meaning of the word fear, latched on to this. He was far and away the best painter of the three of us, Graham and I both sadly lacking in originality compared to the individuality he made manifest on his canvases. When you come to think of it, very few if any people have painted the tropics with success, except for Gauguin, who had the sense to do them in orange and mauves and magenta, thus avoiding lesser mortals' Reckitt's Blue travel-posters. Noel also avoided this danger when, in the years to come, he painted so many pictures of Jamaica. I don't know quite how he achieved this; the paintings of Jamaica—which are among his best—are not representational, but somehow he has caught the essential spirit and the many moods of that lovely island. It is true to say that all those countless hours he spent at his easel were among the most carefree and happy of his life.

While on the subject of happiness, Noel always maintained—as do some other great stars—that he had never experienced private happiness at the same time as his greatest public successes. He, and the several others who confided in us on the subject, felt that there was some rigid law of the gods against their having the two at the same time. Conversely, if they were allowed felicity at home then they must suffer professional disappointment. And so, for the next almost twenty years, it was with Noel.

To return to the post-war years, Noel was astounded when Beverley Baxter asked him at a luncheon if he thought he had survived the war; 'Yes—but have you?' was his reply. When he came home he told us, and added, 'Like Mother Goddam, I shall always survive.' There is no doubt that during those years of happiness beyond measure most critics—not all—had relegated Noel as a playwright to the Has-Been Department and would not even grant that his four or five best comedies were all they had been cracked up to be in the first place. When Tallulah Bankhead starred in *Private Lives* in New York, Noel wrote: 'The critics overwhelmed her with ecstatic praise. "How grateful," they said, "should the author be to this great and shining comedienne for endowing the dried bones of his old-fashioned trivia with such glorious life." ' At their very kindest, critics would only allow that his post-war efforts were 'not vintage Coward'. But when had they ever been? Of the original production of the same play Ivor Brown wrote: 'Within a few years the student of drama will be sitting in complete bewilderment before the text of *Private Lives*, wondering what on earth those fellows in 1930 saw in so flimsy a trifle.' Within a few years! How Noel always relished those four rash words, secure in his knowledge that ever since Ivor Brown wrote them, somewhere in the world the play is always either in production or rehearsal and unbewildered students are at this moment taking it in their stride in their drama courses.

Noel had all this time been working on the music, lyrics and book for *Pacific 1860*, the musical which was to reopen Drury Lane and in which Mary Martin was to star with Graham. Noel had for years played a lovely game of creating his own tropic island in his head; it was called Samolo and he was to use it as the setting for *Island Fling* with Claudette Colbert in America, later re-named *South Sea Bubble* for London, starring Vivien Leigh, and for a short story, *Solali*. It was now to be used for the musical, and we had great fun—perhaps too much— making the island as real as possible. With help from the atlas we pin-pointed it in the Pacific, and from the *Encyclopaedia Britannica* fixed its terrain, flora, fauna, annual rainfall etc. We wrote a Baedeker-like guide to the island. It was of course a British Possession and of course its climate was equable with abundant sunshine and, except in June, few tropical storms. Samolo was remarkable for its loveliness; beaches of the finest white coral sand abounded together with limpid lagoons, secluded coves and palm-fringed inlets. The natives were more than friendly, of Polynesian beauty, happy-go-lucky in their sex-lives and infinitely preferring to wear nothing but a hibiscus flower behind their ears rather than the Mother Hubbards imposed upon them by the missionaries. Noel did try to be fair to the latter in the *History of Samolo*, but for instance among the fauna is a poisonous snake called a Beo-Beo 'but nicknamed by the natives Miss Woodward, after a missionary nobody liked'. Noel drew a detailed map of the island which I painted in water-colour, almost of the Here-be-Dragons variety, the outline of which Gladys used as background for her crinolined lady on the posters and song covers for *Pacific 1860*. We compiled a dictionary of the language with enough verbs and vocabulary for us to talk it and for Noel to write one of the songs in it. Just to give you an idea, a flower was *lalua*, thunder *buumbalo*, nuts *kraaki-kraaki* and to copulate was *klabonga*. Noel dearly loved this island of his very own, and by the time he successfully used it for his novel *Pomp and Circumstance* he knew the names of every headland, river and mountain without having to refer to our map.

From the *History of Samolo* Noel traced the lineage of all the characters in the musical. This was the first time he had ever done so much research on his characters and I have dwelt on this Samolan occasion because it was not, alas, the last. From now on he developed a habit, which turned out to be a bad one, of fixing the characters in his plays from their birth until the moment they stepped on to the stage.

Useless to argue that neither he nor anybody else had known or cared a fig where Amanda and Elyot and Madame Arcati had come from; he now enjoyed the precise research and said he had to have it, so instead of the five fruitful days spent in writing *Blithe Spirit*, it now took him as many weeks before writing even the first lines of *Quadrille* and *Nude with Violin*. This may well be the reason why the later plays lack some of the spontaneity and timelessness of the earlier ones. It was certainly because of this precision that they sounded more dated to the ear; he would write 'I met her in 1941' instead of, as previously, 'I met her years ago', but don't rush to the *Collected Plays* to check on this. I always read the proofs after Master and Lornie, and before they were sent back to be printed I changed those definite dates to 'a few years ago' or 'a long time ago' or whatever, as often as I could. When very much later I confessed to this, all he said was, 'You clever little thing.'

We indulged ourselves in two crazes to which we gave full rein during these years immediately following the war: Fractured French and Baby Talk. We were not alone with the former — Fractured French was widely prevalent at the time; English-speaking schoolchildren have always perpetrated it, and it had become popular with grown-ups ever since Terence Rattigan wrote *French Without Tears* in 1936. Of our friends, Arthur Macrae provided the best samples. *Cuir de Russie* was his French for a Russian homosexual; Buckingham Palace he renamed *Mal Vu*; *pas encore* was Father's Second Song; artificial fur became *feu d'artifice*, and so on. Another friend tortured the language to such an extent that *La vie en rose* could become, if you tried, French for pink aeroplane. Noel fractured French with the next man, loved it, continued to use it for years and many good examples — or bad if you think the game unfunny — pepper his letters.

There is less excuse for our reprehensible use of Baby Talk except that it amused us, and I am afraid that a lot of it stuck. Joycie became Doycie, I Toley, and then Noel with his zest for nicknames Frenchified these childish familiarities to Lornette la Blanche and Doycette la Blanche etc. Mabel Lucie Attwell, the illustrator and writer, was the original malefactor who introduced Baby Talk into our and many other people's lives when we were young. Her picture-postcards sold in millions; drawings of small girls and boys whose chubbiness amounted almost to elephantiasis. Their age was indeterminate; far too sturdy for toddlers, they seemed to have become about four or five years old, yet with no command of English whatever. It would not be correct to say that they were 'behind' in learning to talk because they used the more complicated 'ickle me' instead of the simple pronoun 'I'. 'Does oo fink i'se pwetty?' is a fairly average sample of Miss Attwell's captions to her drawings. But she must not bear the blame entirely, for there were also many sentimental songs in our childhood and youth about ickle childwen whose parents had died and gone to heaven. From dismissing this jargon as nauseating when he was the young and cynical Noel Coward, with the passage of time he began to think it not unfunny and revived it, and always had a great success with his rendering of a sickening song about an ickle boy whose mother came to visit him in his dreams, after Nurse had tucked him up for the night:

> She holds me vewwy kind and tight
> And talks about a Land
> Where all the flowers are boys and girls
> Wiv muvvers close at hand
> And when I want to go wiv her
> She says, ' 'Twould never do,
> Cos Daddy would be lonely, Son,
> Wivout a man like oo.'

This language could only be used in public at great risk. Once, we settled ourselves in the restaurant car of a train with a Squire Toby at the next table who did what was known by us as a Don't Look Now to his wife (a whispered 'Don't look now, but that's Noel Coward'). The waiter brought our tea with a teaspoon missing and Noel said, 'Toley; Noley hasn't dot a poony.' I can still hear Squire Toby's snort of disgust. We were never completely cured of this disease. Only a few years ago, when I felt it was past our bedtime, I said, 'I'se tiredy-poos.' Noel said sternly, to Wendy Toye's astonishment, 'You must *never* talk like that! You must always say *Pease*, I'se tiredy-poos.'

In addition to Fractured French and Baby Talk there was yet another lingo frequently used by Noel, of Mayfair origin he thought, much in use during the days of the Bright Young Things. To the question, 'I say, isn't Sheila getting a bit thick round the middle?' one might receive the reply (Noel always used a languid voice for this), 'Preggers, darling.' This was quite useful for shortening *Blithe Spirit* to Blithers and White Cliffs to Whiters, and so on.

I think I have done all I can to help the reader decode some of the letters from Noel which follow in this book. (If his mixture of endearments with Baby Talk emerges as camp, this cannot be helped; he was the last person to use camp intentionally.) The reader will now know, I hope, that a letter with the heading 'Bombers, darling' does not necessarily express affection; it means he wrote it while staying in Bombay.

Pacific 1860 had to be postponed until the autumn because of endless frustrations over repairs to the bomb-damaged Drury Lane Theatre; delay in the required permits, the still-present shortage of materials and labour, and then in the end the application for a licence to repair was turned down flat. Noel never knuckled under, to officialdom especially, and was a great one for going straight to the horse's mouth; in this case it was round the corner from Gerald Road to the house of the Minister of Works, Aneurin Bevan, and his wife Jennie Lee. Noel never forgot their instant understanding and Nye's instant promise of a licence, declared he was mad about them both and would like to commission Dame Laura Knight to do a pencil portrait of Mr Bevan so he could say that Knight was drawing Nye.

This postponement meant that we could make our eager return to Paris in the spring of 1946, and what is more that Graham would be free to join us and see the much-loved Place Vendôme apartment for the first time. He and Noel made the journey in Noel's M.G.; I went ahead on the Golden Arrow to make a shining welcome for Graham. Whatever mess the Nazis had left had been cleaned up, and all I could find missing were the motor of the fridge and Lady Mendl's photograph. By the time Noel and Graham arrived the place had begun to smell like home again; the most delicious smell as soon as you opened the door of I don't quite know what—wood-smoke, freshly ground coffee and that very strong dark-brown bath-oil called Abano were the chief components. I remember filling the drawing-room with every branch of white lilac I could lay my hands on in the market, and on their arrival going like an arrow to the well-remembered drinks table to make three *dynamites*. The next weeks passed in a whirl of pleasure and Alka-Seltzer. So many reunions with old friends to celebrate, and celebrations with friends newly made; a determination on Noel's part to catch up on seldom-seen operas at the Opéra Comique, such as *Lakmé* and *The Pearl Fishers*, out of most of which we walked halfway through to return to a table outside the Café de la Paix and indulge in his favourite occupation of watching *le beau monde qui passe*. His name for it, though of course the *monde* wasn't always *beau* but never mind, the curiouser the people were the more he savoured them; 'But she's Toulouse-Lautrec's *uncle!*' he would exclaim, or, to a head-in-air of either sex, 'What-ho, my Proud Beauty!'

Sir Duff Cooper was our Ambassador at Paris, with Lady Diana Cooper a radiantly beautiful Ambassadress. Ever since I first saw Lady

Diana in the early 1920s, a white and pink and gold wraith, in a colour film called *The Glorious Adventure*, with a young pugilist called Victor McLaglen also starring, I had worshipped her from afar. Now it was inevitable that we should meet and I must prepare to meet my goddess. This I did with my feelings a mixture of thrilled anticipation and fright. Her beauty close to was blinding, some people said; others that unless you got off on the right foot her manner could be icy. She arrived at the apartment with Lady Juliet Duff, who greeted me with 'Coley, I'm so terribly pleased to see you. How are you? How lovely to see you again.' Sir Michael Duff came in moments later and used exactly the same words. Lady Diana, good comedian, put on an empty soup-plate expression and said, in a voice for all to hear, 'I've never met Coley before, but I'm *terribly* pleased to see him again.' The good comedian was pleased with the laugh she got, and my voices told me I was home and dry. And that is where I am today—still home and safe and dry and warm in her friendship.

Graham at first did not have my good fortune. Brush-off is too strong a word, but he had to put up with two or three vague passings-by which Diana's friends ascribed to myopia. The fourth time he said firmly, 'My name is Payn. P-a-y-n without an "e".' So that was all right, and long ago. For years now the two of us have been her boys: 'I want to see my boys,' she calls without preliminaries into the telephone.

Noel and Diana loved one another and on either side their loyalty was rock-like. 'Our loving friendship began', Diana wrote, 'in the Chicago of 1925 when my dearest friend, Iris Tree, and I were exhausting ourselves playing—sometimes three times a day—Max Reinhardt's perennial production of *The Miracle*. Noel was acting in his own play *The Vortex*. From those long lost days to these, the skies above Noel's head and mine have always been luminous and lovely. Rainbows here and there, yet without cloud or menace.'

From Paris Noel and Graham motored in the M.G. to Biarritz to stay in Edward Molyneux's apartment for a holiday. While there, they

> ... dined with Liv Ramoneda. Very chic. [Prince] Felix Yous-soupoff sang really quite sweetly with a guitar. He is made up to the teeth. I looked at him: a face that must, when young, have been very beautiful but now it is cracking with effort and age. I imagined him luring Rasputin to his doom with that guitar and dem rollin' eyes. It was all a little macabre. I sang but not very well. Graham [nobody, including Noel, knew that he had learnt

four songs in Russian when he was a boy soprano] was really wonderful. He was not only socially vital and attractive but he suddenly proceeded to sing in Russian so much better than Youssoupoff and his friend that the whole party was astonished.

Noel gives full rein to his passion for nicknames and Fractured French in a letter he later sent me from *La Résidence* at Val d'Esquières. His worry over money is because of the very small English travel allowance then in force.

Août le quatre 1946

Cher et aimable Charbon, Nous y sommes enfin après un voyage et des aventures assez amusant. L'adorable M.G. a couru comme un ange mais malheureusement elle a développé une fuite de l'huile qui est devenu un peu cher! Mais maintenant tout va ever so bien. Nous avons tâcher mille mille fois de vous téléphoner de Biarritz mais à cause de cette fartarsing grève il était impossible de vous attraper! Cet hôtel est excessivement luxe, excessivement bien placé et aussi plus qu'excessivement expensive on account of étant en pension which sounds tout droit jusqu'on découvre que tous les plats agréable sur la carte sont supplémentaire. Moi je m'en fiche parce-que je had my fortune told by a Russian lady in a château just au dehors de Marseille et elle m'a dit que I was surrounded by amour et argent et triomphes! Elle a dit aussi que I could dire merde au monde! So ici je suis, disant merde à tous! c'est très commode. Le Petit Garçon sans souci vous envoie son amour et ses embrasses les plus cordiales. Nous espérons tout nous deux que vous êtes heureux et gai comme un oiseau-mouche, où peut-être comme une libellule, et que votre vacance est as jolly decent comme what ours is si vous savez quoi je mean et je *pense* you do. Biarritz de toutes pointes de vue était a fucker véritable— le temps faisait froid et gris tout le temps sauf pour deux jours lorsqu'il était so bloody hot that nous ne pouvons pas bouger. Envoyez-nous un gentil télégramme quand you receive this parce-que j'ai des brefs moments de peur que ma mère et ma petite tante sont mortes comme mouton et que Falaises Blanches is incendie'd down et que vous avez cassé vos jambes tous les deux â cause d'excès d'amour.

Assurez-vous, sucré Charbon, de mes sentiments les plus distinguées. x x x x

MAÎTRE

Back in London, Noel bought a large blazing *fauve* Vlaminck on Edward Molyneux's advice for £1,000, and a smaller one of a dramatic navy-blue and white tempest for £450. These were the first 'important' paintings he had bought and were the start of his ultimately good collection. His premonition about his dear little Aunt Vida came true; she died aged ninety-two in her sleep on November 8th. Of his many aunts she was his favourite. He had always understood her and the trying times she had had with his mother and father, and she him, always being the one to give him the best birthday presents and unexpected treats. 'I must say she chose the perfect way to die. Just sleep and the light flickering out. Death is kind to the old.'

In December *Pacific 1860* at last opened in an ice-cold Drury Lane Theatre. Mary was enchanting from every point of view (not her fault that she was somewhat miscast), Graham sang and acted with attractive charm and danced with verve, and Gladys's costumes were more ravishing than ever. But it was no use. With the honourable exception of *The Times*, Noel's lovely music was barely mentioned, nor were his lyrics, although some of those to the ballads are lightly brushed with poetry; James Agate dismissed the book as mindless bosh.

Noel started 1947 by waking up

> in a still dark rage. Had a long think and decided that I am sick of being screamed at and abused. I have had to face a possible flop, vile notices, Matelot's death [his poodle] and a great deal of weariness and disappointment. Everybody roaring and stamping their feet and squealing about their integrity. I have been exceedingly forbearing with the lot of them but now I have decided to be forbearing no more. Anger is a healthier emotion for me than self-pity. Made a brisk but firm New Year's Resolution to stand no more nonsense.

A few nights later he had dinner with Gladys at the Ivy, in course of which he had a slight set-to with James Agate and firmly (and presumably briskly) called him a stupid old man to his face.

He never forgot the disappointment of *Pacific 1860*. The next show at Drury Lane was the terrific success *Oklahoma!*, to which in his enthusiasm he went several times. He would look around the lovely theatre feeling a little pang for 'poor old *Pacific 1860*' until the curtain went up and he would be carried away by 'Oh What a Beautiful Morning'. And always in the future when listening to the cast album of *Pacific 1860* he would suffer the same small pang. This sadness may have been prolonged at the time because, through force of circumstances, he could not for once immediately 'get the hell out' when a production had been launched. That winter was a hard one; Arctic conditions with icy blizzards, made worse by endless power cuts and fuel crises. When at very long last the thaw came, several thousand tons of chalk crumbled with a frightening roar from the top of the cliffs to the beach, not too far from the house. Expert advice was asked, but we could get no reassurance from anyone as to whether or not the cliffs looming above the house would fall and either push us into the sea or crush us to pieces. In the end Noel paid £2,000 to have our length of cliff 'pinned back', and it remained pinned back until a year or so ago when we heard that it had at last crumbled and crushed the very room that Noel used to occupy.

Noel was resilient always. 'In spite of all the press have said about me, I seem to be loved by the public. It is a lovely feeling and I am very grateful.' Before long he and Binkie were planning a revival of *Present Laughter* at the Haymarket with Noel starring, before which he couldn't wait to start writing a play called *Might Have Been*. Saki, as we know a literary hero of his, had written in *When William Came* about the German occupation of England and London in particular during the First World War, and Noel was fascinated by the same possibility during the Second. What would everyday life have been like in London with German soldiers in the streets, Nazis in Whitehall and Hitler in Buckingham Palace? Which of all the people we knew would have quickly become collaborators, and which heroes and heroines, splendidly resisting until the last Nazi was driven from our shores? A further spur for Noel was that he had seen and enormously admired a play called *Power Without Glory*, brilliantly acted by a cast of young unknowns including Dirk Bogarde, Kenneth More, Dandy Nichols and Maureen Pryor; he did all he could to help save the play, but it was failing and he wanted them for his own new one and he must therefore work quickly. He got down to it and Lornie thought of a better title— *Peace in Our Time*—which Noel was strongly advised not to use; there would be an outcry if he desecrated Neville Chamberlain's famous phrase for such a theme. Of course he used it, only too delighted to do anything which might anger the pro-Munich lot.

Sick of interminable snow and ice he decided to go at the end of January to stay with Grover Loehning at Palm Beach and finish the play. While he was there, Neysa McMein also came to stay. He thought Neysa a rare woman and a great one, prodigal in her friendships. He had known her since the Alexander Woollcott days, not I think that she spent much time at the Algonquin Round Table; everybody went instead to her and her studio, trooping in and out while Neysa unconcernedly painted her not first-class but highly-paid-for portraits. She had that exceptional gift, as David Niven has, of telling stories against herself that were funny from the beginning right through to the end, accompanied all the way by ripples of laughter at each disaster, yourself catching the infection. She once elected to go to a fancy dress party as a cave-woman, her hair deliberately dishevelled, clad only in animal skins and rabbit's-fur slippers and brandishing a meat-cleaver borrowed from her butcher. The butler looked surprised at her appearance on the doorstep but she said firmly, 'Miss McMein. I'm expected,' and he showed her into a drawing-room containing six people wearing formal evening-dress. Neysa paused in the doorway and said, 'I'm afraid there's been some terrible mistake.' No need to say that she remained not only for drinks and dinner but friends for life with the host and hostess.

She was a very special friend of Noel's, the one who always enjoyed a visit to Coney Island as much as he did, or to see their adored Rockettes at Radio City Music Hall. So they were happy to be together again at Palm Beach, playing backgammon as often as they could when he'd finished his day's work on *Peace in Our Time*, and 'having long heart-to-heart talks about everything'.

Noel arrived back in England bursting with plans and vitality, having bought dressing-gowns and pyjamas from Sulka while on his way through New York. Rehearsals started for a revival of *Present Laughter*, and simultaneously he began the casting of *Peace in Our Time,* finding Kenneth More to be a nice and intelligent young man, his having been in the Navy for six years making an immediate bond. Dirk Bogarde he thought a very bright boy who didn't miss a trick. He did his utmost to prevent Dirk from tying himself down to a seven-year film contract, his argument being that Dirk should first obtain more stage experience. Noel genuinely believed this, but at the same time he did badly want Dirk for *Peace in Our Time*; Dirk was adamant, chose films and quickly achieved stardom.

Though the plays Noel wrote during the 'fifties received little or no critical acclaim, his personal appearances always played to packed and enthusiastic audiences. And so it was with *Present Laughter*, which opened in April 1947; never an empty seat and for himself always an ovation at the end. He played for his usual three months, after which the play, with Hugh Sinclair and later Peter Gray, ran for eighteen months all told. During his three months of eight performances a week he had also done quite a lot of recording, and had planned a whole series of broadcasts of his songs and music, for which, while driving from London to White Cliffs after two shows on a Saturday, he dictated to me no less than nine introductory speeches. No wonder he wrote: 'I am going through one of my periodical worry phases about time and how little there is of it. There is so much I want to write and so many people get in the way. It is difficult to get into the right frame of mind and concentrate in London.'

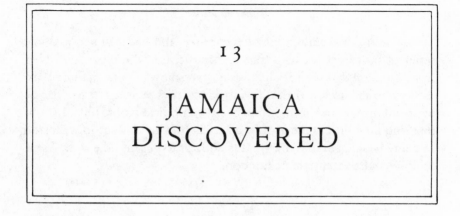

13

JAMAICA
DISCOVERED

The final rehearsals and the opening of *Peace in Our Time* were so arranged that Noel could 'get the hell out' as soon as possible after he left *Present Laughter*. The first-night audience were flat at the beginning but woke up towards the end and gave the play and Noel a terrific reception—he hadn't heard such a crack of noise in the theatre for many a year. Next morning the notices were on the whole grudging, but Noel felt quite sure the play was a smash hit (it proved not to be) and sailed with Graham for America happy in that assurance.

Once on board the *Queen Mary* Noel had 'an indescribable holiday feeling, nothing to do but read and relax'. A good time was had in New York, inevitably including an evening at Coney Island with Neysa, plus old friends Horst the photographer and Niki de Gunsburg. Noel's passion for roller-coasters was unbridled. He would refuse to get off, always saying, 'Just one more time,' until, as he admitted, he had shaken himself to bits, 'and then we all drove home singing and giggling.' Then came ten days at Martha's Vineyard (Graham's first visit) with Katharine Cornell, her husband Guthrie McClintic, Nancy Hamilton and Gert Macey:

Peace. Sleep. Swimming. Mint Juleps. Painting. Music and bézique. Mustn't grumble. Guthrie gave a vivid, exciting description of his forthcoming production of *Antony and Cleopatra*. When he is really excited he lights up like a carousel. One evening we had a clambake. Elaborate preparations; chickens, lobsters, corn, clams were buried under seaweed in the sand and cooked for hours and hours. Net result, nothing was cooked enough and everything was full of sand. Kit made a gallant effort to save the situation by building a fire and cooking the underdone dainties until they were burnt black and still full of sand. The white wine was delicious provided you waited until the sand had sunk to the bottom of the mug. Finally we all came indoors and had milk and angel cake, the lack of sand in which was somehow shocking.

If there was any business, or rather duty, to be done on this so far unclouded holiday, it was to go to Chicago to see what Miss Tallulah Bankhead was up to in *Private Lives*, before she brought it in to New York. This duty could be combined with what were for Noel two great pleasures; one was to travel there by train overnight on the crack Twentieth-Century Limited, and the other to join up with Lynn and Alfred to see the play and then go to stay with them at Genesee Depot, Wisconsin. Noel went to *Private Lives* with some misgivings, but to his relief and a certain amount of surprise Tallulah was extraordinarily good; he thought her a bit coarse in texture but her personality formidable, that she played some of it quite beautifully and all of it effectively. He thought Donald Cook, her leading man, was comedy-conscious and rather obvious but by no means bad. While he was upstairs talking to Donald Cook, Lynn, Alfred and Graham went to Tallulah's dressing-room, Lynn opening the proceedings with, 'Darling, I thought you were wonderful.' Her reward for this graciousness was, 'I don't give a fuck what you think. Where's my author?' Lynn froze, Tallulah trying to make amends but actually making matters worse by saying, 'It's awfully funny, Lynnie darling, Estelle Winwood and I were talking about you only the other day and wondering where you'd be without Alfred.' 'Playing *Private Lives*' should have been Lynn's answer, but alas she didn't think of it till next morning. Noel, all unconscious, then came in and found Tallulah touchingly thrilled that he liked her performance and ecstatic when he told her she could play it in New York: 'She is a curious character; wildly generous [she promised him and did eventually give him an Augustus John], a very big heart and can be both boring and amusing. Well, well.'

Noel and Graham went with Tallulah and her sister on the Sunday to dine at Chez Paree in order to see Carmen Miranda in the cabaret. She was extremely good and after the show came to sit at their table. A nervous young man came up and asked Tallulah for her autograph but did not, as expected, ask Noel or Carmen Miranda for theirs. To help him along Tallulah, with a wave of her arm, said, 'And this is my author,' but the young man got into a double muddle about the author and the play and said to Noel, 'Oh! Tell me, how is *The Iceman Cometh* going?'

From then on the evening became a nightmare. Tallulah was nicely thank you and proceeded to be noisy and vulgar. Carmen Miranda wisely disappeared. Tallulah screamed and roared and banged the table and I wished the floor would open. From Chez Paree we drove all round Chicago to a dive where there is a trombonist, a saxophonist, a drummer and a pianist who play the latest swing and bebop. The audience, mostly callow youths, became hypnotized and began to wriggle and sway and scream exactly like a revival meeting. To me, the whole thing was completely abominable. I loathed it. The heat, the violent noise, and Tallulah still shrieking. From there we went on to hear Dixieland music. We were driven back into Chicago to a beastly little club and given a table right under the trumpet, whereupon I walked out and came home. I am 47 and sane.

Next morning Tallulah was apologetic, and when Noel and Graham asked for their hotel bills at the Ambassador East there were none. Tallulah had already paid them.

From Chicago Noel and Graham went as arranged to stay at Genesee. They had such a peaceful, lazy holiday that Noel found he had nothing much to report beyond the loving kindness of Alfred and Lynn, which actually was beyond reporting. 'They have an imperishable magic for me. To be one of the family in this house is a very real thing. Lynn gave a mannequin parade of all her new Molyneux dresses before dinner. I must say Edward has done her proud.' Alfred is as great a cook as he is an actor; each meal an exquisite experience, not to mention the delicious breakfasts. Noel, with his small appetite, thought he was going to burst, and then, towards the end of the week reports: 'Dinner tonight was the *coup de grâce*; shrimps à la Créole, corn peas, pimentoes, custard pie tartlets and a series of explosions of wind that are still continuing as I write. Graham is blowing himself in and out of the room like a pop-gun.' Graham adds that Noel broke wind so loudly that Lynn called out 'Bravo!' from two or three rooms away.

Off and on during this American holiday there had been plans for a revival of *Tonight at Eight-Thirty* with Gertie playing her former parts and Graham playing Noel's. All Noel's instincts were against this but everybody—Gertie, Fanny Holtzmann and Jack as director—was enthusiastic and the producers produced backers instantly. Noel again received a fantastic proposition from Hollywood; if he would guarantee Paramount three commitments, either as actor, writer or director, they would pay him five hundred dollars a week for twenty-three years. Once more it was Edna Ferber who helped him to decide. She completely understood his cancellation of a greatly looked-forward-to weekend with her, his need for solitude, to 'get away from the whole boiling lot' and go to Lake Placid and write.

While there he met someone referred to only as John, with whom he had drinks, dinner and went to a movie called *The Kiss of Death*, which wasn't bad. 'Afterwards I found myself talking to him about England so very proudly, though I was talking about England in the War Years when her gallantry and commonsense were married by emergency. It is all very confusing. I think I had better get after *Future Indefinite* and get some of my confusion down on paper.' What he actually did was to turn 'What Mad Pursuit', one of his short stories, into a play called *Long Island Sound*. He worked hard and quickly and when he returned to New York he read the play to Jack, Natasha, Neysa and Martin Manulis. They didn't seem very impressed, Jack prophesying that the press would crucify him for it, and Noel went to bed feeling flat after having so much looked forward to the reading. None of them ever mentioned the play again. It was as though he had never written it.

Jack had by now become a successful director of plays as well as producer, his biggest successes being with *Kiss Me Kate* and *Gentlemen Prefer Blondes*. He also ran the theatre and directed productions at Westport, near his and Natasha's house at Fairfield, Connecticut. He loved to tell the story of Grace George, who behaved like the big star she was from the very beginning of the first rehearsal. She took a chair to stage centre and announced, 'Now. *I* shall sit here, and Mr Wilson will tell the rest of you where to go.' It was Texas Guinan who begged him at lunchtime to find her a seat—anywhere—for that night's première of a Broadway show he was presenting. He rushed one to her by special messenger who brought it back with a note, 'Miss Guinan wouldn't sit in Row M, not even for the Resurrection.'

Jack's status as Broadway producer inspired the following from Lornie. I must repeat that these verses, up until the Partnership Agreement trouble—there were none after—were jokingly written and received.

> Long years ago when first we knew
> Our dear John Chapman W.
> His latent talents were confined
> To efforts of a simple kind.
> A homely wit, a merry sense

Of fun at your and my expense
A criticism here and there
Of Peggy Wood and Mary Clare;
A trifling bagatelle may be
Of error in accountancy,
Pictures and books—a brooch or so
Those were his limits long ago.

But as the years that speed apace
Have added girth to Baybay's face
They've stretched the fields of enterprise
On which he casts his penny eyes.
Where wicked murmurs once were heard
All Broadway trembles at his word
The acid jokes that used to be
Reserved for Blackheart, you and me
Are now the bon mots of the day
In syndicated U.S.A.
And—Oh it only goes to show—
That oaks from little acorns grow ...

It used to be enough for Dab
To pinch, appropriate or grab
Such trifles as he wished to use
From Goldenhurst or Burton Mews.
But, as a child outgrows its nurse
So Baybay's pocket and his purse
Now finds investors just the thing
To suit light-fingered pilfering
And when he's had his fill from them ...
OH DO BE CAREFUL M.G.M.!

As we have seen, Jack married Natasha in 1937 and, being American
and living in that country, they and Noel seldom met during the five
years of the war. Noel felt that he and Jack were slowly growing
further and further apart during the long separation, the split made
wider by the financial disagreement. On the other hand he had grown
ever closer to Natasha from the war's beginning and even earlier
because of her European outlook and sympathies, about which he
wrote with gratitude. At war's end all three had many a happy reunion
but now, 1947, it was no use; Noel's friendship for Jack grew less and

less while his love for Natasha increased. Jack by then was drinking heavily, a fault which in anyone Noel found unforgiveable and with which he had no scrap of sympathy.

However, plans had gone ahead for the *Tonight at Eight-Thirty* revival, with Jack as director, and rehearsals started; it was during this four-week period that Jack's past and present perfidies, both personal and financial, were one by one revealed to Noel. The first was an accidentally overheard conversation in which Jack betrayed his loyalty to Noel:

That he should show his disloyalty to a complete stranger has done something dreadful to my inside. I made a joke of it at the time but when I got home I was sick. I feel this is the end of the friendship between Jack and me. So many things add up over the years, including the partnership, leading up to the reading of *Long Island Sound* the other night. It is a bitter revelation that I can no longer trust him.

More financial disclosures revealed Jack's breaches of trust. Worse—in a way—was the fact that Jack was a witty, incorrigible and indiscriminate gossip; inevitably his witticisms got back to Noel or went the rounds of the company, so that the atmosphere in the theatre became painful to work in. A showdown had to happen, and it did; Jack was relieved of the direction and Noel took it on, to everybody's relief. The company came to life immediately and began to enjoy themselves. Natasha's position all this time must have been unenviable but Noel only records her kindness and understanding, the long heart-to-hearts in which she allowed him to pour out everything, and her help in his difficult dealings with Jack. Gertie was his other support, perfectly charming through all the crises to everyone, but especially to Graham, to whom she gave all the unselfish help she could, while she herself remained from first to last undaunted.

Noel had his emotional relationship with Jack primarily in mind when writing in 1958 'The Best Advice I Ever Had' for *Reader's Digest*. After passing on the good advice he had received professionally, he went on to quote Madame Hubrecht, mother of his Dutch friend, Daan Hubrecht:

I remember so well on a certain occasion in Rome, she leaned a little forward, looked me gravely in the eye and spoke these words with quiet authority, 'Never demand from people more than they are capable of giving.' Madame Hubrecht knew something that I didn't myself realise at the time, which was that apart from the swans which really were swans, I had a dangerous capacity for seeing nearly all geese as those beautiful birds: dangerous for me, that is — the geese naturally enjoyed it enormously ... perhaps I have wasted too much time before realising that a number of them were not even geese but only lame ducks. It is in these moments of disillusioned discovery that I remember Madame Hubrecht's words and wish I had paid heed to them ... There is a whole universe of difference between discovering and encouraging hidden capabilities in other people and over-estimating non-existent ones ... Alas, it is a mistake we often make, especially when looking through eyes misty with love, that notorious impairer of hitherto perfect vision. Then, with our eyesight still off-true and rose-coloured, we heave the loved one on to a pedestal, an insecure lodging at best, and are unreasonably embittered and discouraged if the loved one should totter and fall. No, no — never demand from people more than they are capable of giving.

Noel went with the company to Princeton and Baltimore to see the tour launched very successfully. They went on to further triumphs in Boston and San Francisco while Noel returned to London for Christmas at Gerald Road, during which he suffered for the first and only time in his life a painful attack of gout. He persuaded Lornie to cast aside her hitherto ironclad insularity and undertake the sensational adventure of accompanying him on the *Queen Elizabeth* to New York and then across America by train to see *Tonight at Eight-Thirty* in San Francisco, but on January 1st he wrote:

The New Year starts with me in bed, feeling weak and jolly mouldy. Fortunately I have no more pain in the foot except when I move it or attempt to put it to the ground. It has been arranged for an invalid chair to get me to the boat on Saturday. Today [January 2nd] I arose from my bed and walked; and lo it was a miracle although it hurt like buggery; and lo there came unto my house Joyce the daughter of Dame Lilian and Edward [Molyneux] and Binkie and Ronnie Neame and Gladys and Arthur [Macrae] and Boxer [Arthur's dog]; and Boxer, the son of a bitch, sprang at my foot and worried it like a rat, but he was so beautiful and newly washed that he was forgiven. Mum came to say goodbye; she really is remarkable, not a tear nor a complaint.

The next day everybody, from Victoria Station till he reached his cabin in the ship, was so charmingly solicitous to Noel in his wheelchair that he swore that he would never travel any other way, even if it meant he had to invent a broken leg. After three whirlwind days of showing New York to Lornie and Lornie to New York, they were off to San Francisco, where he found that the standard of the show had been kept up very well and was enjoying continued success. Graham was off for two performances with 'flu and Noel admired Gertie's courage more than ever, playing with an unsatisfactory understudy: 'She was transcendental, I had tears in my eyes at the valour and charm of her performance up against such fearful odds.' Next day, to help her, he played the matinée himself: 'I flew down to the theatre, started rehearsing at 1.20 and was on at 2.30, proud of the fact that I didn't dry up once. Performance not bad; the company and audience were thrilled but it was all rather exhausting.' Three weeks in Hollywood followed, where a socially good time was had by all, but underneath he felt agitated, and wished that they were already opened in New York and anxieties were over. How he found time to type the following letter on the way back to New York is difficult to imagine, with Marlene Dietrich, Katharine Hepburn and Gertrude Lawrence all on the train and much time spent in their company. Someone had just published a list of the Film Stars who were Biggest Poison at the Box Office, with Marlene and Kate heading the list with Garbo. A notable argument arose, with Kate insisting that figures proved she was the biggest poison, but Marlene considered herself the winner and didn't need figures to prove it; Paramount had simply paid her good money *not* to make her next movie. Another type of discussion arose between Marlene and Gertie regarding the size and splendour of the gifts given them by their admirers. This time it was Marlene's turn to lose, although it was a near thing; she had never been given a yacht, and Gertie had.

Dearest Toley, Here we are exhausted but happy on our way back to New York. 'We' consist of Little Lad, Gertie, Marlene and Katie H. It's really quite fun and we're catching up with some sleep. Hollywood was gay but terribly wearing. I was the belle of the Thing and behaved ever so nicely and everyone outdid themselves to give parties and more parties and the whole thing was stinking with glamour. Our favourites were Irene Dunne, Clifton [Webb] and Gene Kelly but I must say everyone was really mighty sweet. Joan [Crawford] gave the largest, Mrs Calthrop on my left

so we had a good time and watched the big shots disporting themselves. It was well done, good food and drink and the entertainment
was really wonderful on account of Jack Benny, Tony Martin,
Celeste Holm and Dinah Shore who all sang divinely and as they
did it as a gesture to me I was very flattered and had to sing
'Marvellous Party' out of sheer self-preservation and it topped the
lot and that was jolly gratifying too. We had a nightmare visit to
Tia Juana over the Mexican border in order to get Little Lad's quota
number. He drove me and Fanny [Holtzmann, the most famous
woman lawyer in America, a friend of Noel's and an even closer
friend and adviser of Gertie's] and Fanny's nephew Howard;
Fanny never drew breath and went on buzzing and moaning in
our ears like a mad black-water beetle—four hours there and four
hours back—and it was unmitigated hell except that we got the
bloody number. All the agents in Hollywood have been trying to
cash in on me and Del Giudice went trumpeting about and giving
my script of Long Island Sound to all the studios and I finally got
very very angry indeed and decided that in no circumstances would
I have anything to do with any of it. I don't care for the movie
racket much in England but in Hollywood it is much much worse.
Leonard Spigelgass who got fried that week-end at White Cliffs
turned out to be a darling duck and gave a madly gay soirée with a
whole lot of different faces. It was great fun, particularly a rather
beautiful Czeck [*sic*] lady called Florence Marly who looked oddly
like Peter Glenville but she spoke lovely French and Spanish and
was rather sweet. Janet Gaynor and Adrian gave a dainty dinner
without really warning me that it was sixty miles away. It was nice
when I got there except for Joan Fontaine's titties which kept falling about and a large rock python which was handed to me as a surprise. I didn't mind but everyone else was jolly frightened and
Claudette [Colbert] had to spend the rest of the evening washing
her hands in a sort of Lady Macbeth frenzy. Peggy Cummins
appeared looking as though she had been carved out of opaque
glass. We saw some lovely bits from the new Fred Astaire–Judy
Garland *Easter Parade* which was exciting. You had better share
this letter with Mrs Marco Polo [Lornie, who was by now back in
London from her exotic journeyings]. J'ai reçu a très gentil lettre
de ta part which made me rigole beaucoup. Je ne crois pas vraiment
that there is any more nouvelles except that we are all in a slight
état about opening next Friday. Little Lad is giving a jolly fine
performance but has had to be slapped down for a slight but very

perceptible tendency to overact! Figure-toi! Le petit violet—
Quelle Bearnaise! Give my dear dear love to all and be a sweet
Tolette and ecrire again and again and again. La la la la. Le Maître.

They were right to have been in a slight 'état'; *Tonight at Eight-Thirty*
opened on February 20th, 1948, to notices that were abusive to the
point of insult for Noel, and all but two of them crucifying Graham.
After weeks of playing to packed houses and happy audiences on the
road and a terrific ovation the night before, such unanimous condem-
nation came as a sock on the jaw, especially for Graham, making his
first appearance on Broadway: 'His honesty and moral courage are
remarkable and I feel a great respect for him. I fear we are a flop and I
have always believed in putting geographical distance between myself
and a flop. Now, as far as I am concerned, the sooner we close the
better and then for Jamaica and some sun and some peace.'

Noel's first visit to Jamaica had been in 1944, when Sir William
Stephenson, known as Little Bill, who would have been his boss if his
wartime job had materialised, had insisted on sending him to Jamaica
to rest before embarking on a long and strenuous tour of charity
concerts in South Africa. The day was cloudless and the island's lush
green mountains set in the azure sea became visible from miles away,
attracting him at first sight. That two-week holiday had brought him
so much tranquil pleasure and peace of mind that he vowed to return
one day to what had become his dream island, with its pleasing tropical
scents and breezes and its cheerful friendly people. Now, four years
later in New York, he heard that Ian Fleming's new house, Goldeneye,
at Oracabessa, might be to let. Ian soon appeared; he also had been one
of Little Bill's 'boys' during the war, very hush-hush, and he and Noel
became instant leg-pulling and laughing friends. The first battle of
their war of chaff and banter, which was to last till Ian died, was fought
immediately. Ian *said* he had already let Goldeneye to very rich Americans but of course he would cancel the let if *Noel* wanted it. Noel
maintained that Ian had invented the Americans in order to fleece more
money out of him and nothing on God's earth would induce him to
pay the extortionate rent of fifty pounds a week. After two weeks of
argument and suspense, Noel lost, and had to pay it.

Tonight at Eight-Thirty lingered on for four depressing weeks. The
curtain came down for the last time to an enthusiastic audience, what
Noel always called 'sixteen curtain calls and close on Saturday', while
backstage the smaller part players tried to comfort him with, 'It's an
absolute *sin* to close.' He and Graham got on the sleeper for New

Orleans the next day, where Graham gave way to his one and only breakdown over the whole miserable affair, after which, and a good night's sleep, he was as merry as a lark; Noel read *The Loved One*, Evelyn Waugh's brilliant and bitter satire on Hollywood burial customs, which cheered him up. The weather was balmy during their four days in New Orleans; it was their first visit and Noel thought the Vieux Carré looked as vieux as Brooklyn Bridge, then did begin to admit the charm of the place and discovered that 'everything goes on behind the façade'. The mint juleps were many and delicious and a telegram from Ian agreed that Goldeneye was Noel's for the next six weeks.

They sailed for Kingston in a refined little ship which, three days later, arrived five hours late and rammed itself head-on into the landing pier. (Noel seldom had a holiday without incident.) An A.D.C. from King's House, sent by the Governor and Lady Huggins, was there to greet them and so was kind and efficient Charles D'Costa, who lent them his car in which to drive across the island on the spectacular Junction Road, and then on to Oracabessa. 'We arrived at Goldeneye just before dusk. It is quite perfect; a large sitting-room sparsely furnished, comfortable beds and showers, an agreeable staff, a small, private unbelievable coral beach with lint-white sand and warm clear water. We swam after a delicious dinner and lay on the sand unchilled under a full moon. So far, it all seems too good to be true.' It was; though only to the extent that this rhapsodic first impression had to be modified after a few days. The comfortable beds were then more accurately described as 'bed *and* board', the delicious dinners became a monotonous succession of either salt fish and ackee or curried goat followed by stewed guavas with coconut cream, all of them tasting of armpits and so dreaded by Noel that he used to cross himself before each morsel. As for the spacious sitting-room, the long window-sills had been so cunningly designed that they entirely cut off the view as you sank on to the sofa upholstered with iron shavings. This exaggeration became even more built up after Noel designed his own house and he and Ian outdid themselves in descriptions of the horrors of having to stay or eat a meal with the other. 'All you Flemings revel in discomfort; Peter lived for months on cowdung in Tibet and loved it,' Noel said to Ian, at which Ian threw back his head and gave rein to his very individual laugh, with a drawl and a chuckle in it.

Apart from the discomforts, much distorted, Noel and Graham were extremely happy; they had brought oil-painting materials and hours passed in a flash while they painted every afternoon, and Noel started to write his second volume of autobiography, *Future Indefinite*, at which he worked in the mornings. As for the evenings,

> the stars are enormous and very bright and infinity is going on all around and I really don't care a bit about the notices of *Tonight at Eight-Thirty*. We discussed over drinks the possibility of building a shack somewhere isolated on this island and how wonderful it would be to have such an idyllic bolt-hole to return to when life became too frustrating. The climate is so equable and lovely. There are no insects or pests. There is, above all, peace. I am thinking very seriously about this. Something tells me that the time has come to make a few plans for escape in the future.

They searched the island without success, Noel's low finances playing an important part in their considerations, and always returned to a magical spot two miles before you enter Port Maria from Oracabessa. You turn a corner and behold, spread before you is a ravishing view of the sea, with Port Maria Bay to the right, the small town almost hidden by coco-palm and banana plantations and in the middle of the bay a funny little green islet, called Cabarita, the exact shape of a round flat bun. Beyond and also to the right stretch a series of headlands to the far horizon, and behind and above all this beauty is the long range of the Blue Mountains, visible up in the sky in the clear evening, sometimes forget-me-not, sometimes almost purple, always blue. On an oblong piece of cardboard nailed to a tree were the words 'For Sale', but the property was well known to be landslide and therefore quite unsuitable, dangerous even, to build on.

Violet, the cook-housekeeper at Goldeneye, became famous in her own right later on, for an account of which see John Pearson's *The Life of Ian Fleming*, in which you will find more dispassionate views of her cooking; Peter Quennell for instance 'seems to have got used to it'. Noel and Graham became fond of Violet in spite of her cuisine; she gave them good advice about the island and its ways and indeed provided a momentous turning-point in our lives. Graham, anxious to experience every aspect of local life, drove her to the early Friday-morning market in Port Maria, packed with strange fruits and excited townsfolk dressed in every colour, and on the way back stopped to look at the lovely useless property. 'Naw, Naw, Mister Peen,' she said, 'him not all lanslide; this part him solid rock.' After a careful survey she was proved right and Noel bought the whole lot for a song; he decided to build and call the house 'Coward's Folly':

The die is cast. Now I must really admit how excited I am. Scovell
the architect came and we drove over and he was genuinely enthusiastic. If we dynamite the cove it will bring white sand in. When
he had gone we stayed behind on the point and watched the sunset
gilding the mountains and the sea. We also saw a double rainbow and
for a few moments the whole land was bathed in a pinky gold light.
We drove home and I thought of a name for the house, Blue
Harbour. It is a good name because it sounds nice and really
describes the view. The house is to be built against the hill on
different levels. It will be ready in December. I am very happy.

More luck and excitement were to follow only two weeks later. He
and Graham, in search of something and somewhere to paint, drove a
little way inland and then took a pretty road which unknown to them
ran parallel to the sea. When they came to an inviting-looking track
branching off to the right Noel said, 'I wonder what goes on up there?'
and they agreed to drive up and see for themselves. The track rose
steeply through shady foliage, a hairpin bend and more of the same
steep climbing; then they came out on to a four-acre plateau and caught
their breath. One thousand feet below them lay Blue Harbour, and
because of the height the view was even more spectacular, spreading
around them to all points of the compass. To the north in the distance
one could see Galina Point, nearest point to Cuba ninety miles away,
and to the south in the direction of Kingston, range upon range of
mountainous hills, gloriously beautiful but which Lynn Fontanne
later on refused to look at because they reminded her of rows and rows
of empty theatre-seats. More than all this, the place itself held a potent
charm, a romantic spell had been cast upon it, and there was even an
old and roofless ruin half-covered with tropical vines and creepers. At
last they settled down to paint and worked away till dusk, when fireflies
larger and more luminous than they had ever seen appeared until there
were a myriad twinkling in the trees and bushes. They sat there entranced, watching the stars come out and talking nineteen to the dozen about
their discovery until they had to drag themselves away for Violet's
dinner at Goldeneye, intoxicated by all they had seen and by the thermos
of ice-cold dry martinis they had had the foresight to bring with
them.

They started next morning to make inquiries and learned that the
name of the arcadian spot was Look-Out, so called because it had been
used for that very purpose by Sir Henry Morgan the buccaneer, three
hundred years before. Sir Henry owned a property named Llanrhum-

ney—he was Welsh—on the far side of Port Maria and had also built or bought another house at Look-Out, of which the pretty ruin must be part, for it has stone walls a foot thick, narrowly embrasured; here he had maintained men to guard and keep watch and send runners to Llanrhumney should any ship dare to deviate from the main sea route on the horizon and try to put in to 'his' bay of Port Maria. The land belonged to an old Jamaican family named Lindo, of which Blanche Blackwell is a member; Blanche has been a friend and good neighbour of Noel, Ian and all of us for many years, and it was her brother Roy Lindo who had greatly helped Noel over the purchase of Blue Harbour. Roy was a kind man, alas now dead, a fervent Noel Coward fan who insisted that the price should not be raised because of Noel's name and fame, in the teeth of opposition from his partners in the deal. Noel now noted on May 8th that he had driven up to Look-Out, 'where Roy has promised me some land at £10 an acre' but Noel, even though having to watch his budget, must have felt that Roy was carrying kindness much too far, and paid him £150 instead of forty for the four acres. Even so it was the best buy of his life. Noel, characteristically looking far far ahead, wrote: 'It is enchanting and I want to buy it ostensibly as a writing retreat, but really with a view to making it lovely for the future, living in it, and letting or selling Blue Harbour.' Characteristic, but nonetheless astonishing to find that he could write this less than two weeks after buying his 'ravishing' property at Blue Harbour where the house he already planned to sell or let consisted of no more than a few pegs in the ground to mark out its foundations.

Gladys flew from England to join Noel and Graham at Goldeneye and in the infectious excitement bought a house called Trade Winds to which she never returned. Apart from Noel's early-morning writing, the lazy days were spent indulging in orgies of painting, ending at Look-Out with the ritual of sunset, fireflies, stars and the flask of dry martinis on which all three got very nicely, thank you, rolling on the ground helpless with laughter as they blamed the high altitude for their intoxication. The idyllic holiday came to an end on June 1st.

Noel fortunately never sold Blue Harbour, but all the rest of his dreams for Look-Out came true. He soon bought the land from Roy and over the coming years would often talk of his determined hopes for the property, 'One day, when I have enough money ... ', loving to discuss and plan his very own castle in the air. Sufficient money suddenly materialised from the improbable source of a cabaret appearance at Las Vegas, and eight years after the foregoing entry in his diary the house was built, designed and geared to suit the needs of one person:

himself. He rechristened the property Firefly Hill and kept the promise made to himself to make it even lovelier by planting many flowering trees. His instincts had been right. For him the place breathed solace, a comforting quietude. Now he lies, buried in the plot he loved so dearly, at Firefly Hill.

14

JOYEUX CHAGRINS

NOEL'S diary for the summer of 1948 makes dizzy reading. We shuttled between London and White Cliffs with twice-weekly frequency and seemed almost as often to be catching the Golden Arrow for a few days in Paris, until the stewards on both boat and train became old friends. Kiki and Cameron McClure, friends from South Africa, were in London that summer, as were Alfred and Lynn, and also Joseph Cotten and his wife Lenore, lovingly known as the Noisy Cottens. In turn they motored down with us on Friday nights after a theatre in London, the journey enhanced by the inevitable flask of martinis, to spend Saturday and Sunday at White Cliffs lazily sunbathing or playing canasta or Scrabble. Lynn actually preferred the Scrabble board upside down, facing away from her, and making phenomenally high scores from that position with words such as 'exheel' with the 'x' of course on a red square. Alfred would remonstrate, 'Why Lynnie! I've never seen such a word in all my born days!' Inexorably Lynn would say, 'It's a man who used to be a heel, darling,' and coolly go on with the game.

Noel seems to have been in demand professionally and socially every waking moment of the days he managed to spend in London. There were many discussions with Maggie Teyte, who longed for him to make *The Marquise* into an operetta for her and for whom he would have loved to write the music. He attended, at Herbert Morrison's invitation, the preliminary meetings of the Council for the 1951 Festival of Britain, at which he thought much time was wasted, a great deal of balls was talked and he feared the whole thing would be a monumental lash-up. Meetings of the Actors' Orphanage Committee with last-minute ideas for the Theatrical Garden Party; the Garden Party itself at Roehampton, from which he returned to Gerald Road exhausted but delighted to have made four thousand pounds in spite of the rain. Long discussions with Charles Russell and Lance Hamilton, who had ambitious plans to form their own company with which to produce Noel's plays, which resulted in their taking out a tour of *Fallen Angels* that autumn. An appearance with Lord and Lady Mountbatten at the Burma Rally at the Albert Hall; he introduced the artists successfully but 'speeches too long and the B.B.C. man going out of his mind'. When *Present Laughter* finished its long run at the Haymarket, he took on the rehearsals for the Australian tour with Peter Gray in the lead. He worked with a Señor Rodriguez on a broadcast he had promised to do in Spanish and finally did the broadcast, rather proud of himself because the script had been so badly typed and difficult to read. More long discussions, this time with Sydney Box, planning to make a film from some of the *Tonight at Eight-Thirty* plays. He wrote a foreword for *Peace in Our Time* and then, because it was so dull, 'had to redo the whole damn thing'. All this he seems to have taken in his stride, together with many social occasions late into the night, theatres and suppers with Princess Marina, 'a huge rout at Olive [Lady] Baillie's, very chic, to which all London came; Prince Philip, Edwina [Lady Mountbatten], Mollie [Duchess of] Buccleuch, Poppy Thursby, Princess Marina etc etc', and the next night 'a small select party at the Mountbattens including Prince Philip and Sophie Tucker'.

In the thick of all this activity, Noel took on yet another task; one of greater magnitude than he had bargained for. When André Roussin sent the first act of his adaptation of *Present Laughter*, Noel while reading it not unnaturally began to see and hear himself as Garry Essendine — the showy star part he had written for himself and had by now made famous — but this time playing it in French in Paris. Why not? It would be fun, an exciting adventure. He was well aware that his actor's ear helped his accent and made his use of the language sound easier and more flexible than in fact it was, but his French was fluent enough, with hard work could be improved, and he loved to use it. He adored Paris, and there was the apartment simply asking to be lived in while he played a three-month season; then he went too far too soon and started to worry about who would follow him in his great success: Pierre Fresnay? Maurice Teynac? Fernand Gravet? His French theatrical agent at that time was Marguerite Scialtiel, brilliantly renamed Grey Daisy by Joycie, for although amiable and kind, she did indeed emanate a nebulous grey aura; difficult, well-nigh impossible, to associate this quaker-coloured lady with the photographs of her playing a saucy young soubrette in *A Little Bit of Fluff* in 1913. Grey Daisy for once became quite animated at the prospect of Noel Coward coming to act in Paris more or less under her aegis, negotiated for the Théâtre Edouard VII and obtained it, and, on the night we went with her to see *The Little Hut*, got carried away with excitement. In fact, we all did; we were so enchanted by Roussin's comedy, and by the acting of himself, Pierre Gay and the adorable Suzanne Flon that Noel, over supper with all of them at the Club Mermoz, undertook to make the English adaptation of *The Little Hut* if only Roussin would hurry up with the other two acts of *Present Laughter*. Both authors were thrilled that they had found perfect adaptors, and Grey Daisy, with all these feathers in her cap, sat there actually beaming.

Our trips on the Golden Arrow became more frequent, our sojourns in the Place Vendôme of longer duration—there was so much to be done—and our efforts during these visits to speak nothing but French left us exhausted. Noel always tried to get home by midnight when, with him flat on his bed, I would draw up a chair and over a nightcap we indulged in our great treat of forgetting the French language alto-gether and struggling with *The Times* crossword for relief. But André Roussin appeared one morning triumphant with the completed script of *Joyeux Chagrins* (*Present Laughter*), which was of such fearful bulk that Noel said he had peur like anything. He now realized fully that the part of Garry Essendine was actually longer than that of Hamlet, and he had set himself the vast labour of memorizing it in French and then, worse still, having to get his tongue round it and having to produce hitherto little-used vocal processes for hours at a time. André Roussin, now assured of immortality in the valhalla of the Académie Française, was then a young man, looking younger, short, vital and funny, and with his great crony Louis Ducreux (who wrote the words of the theme song for the film of *La Ronde*) was an immense help; one or the other, or both, came every morning to the flat and worked with Noel on his part until lunch-time. Another worry also made evident to Noel at this time was the near-impossibility of capturing in the French language the very English flavour of the wit in his comedies. Especially his genius for the funny use of the most ordinary place-names; 'Uckfield', in this very play, always gets a laugh when Roland Maule says that is where he comes from; and 'It's very near Lewes', 'Then there's nothing to worry about, is there?' gets an even bigger. Why, nobody can explain; though perhaps the gentleman who said that humour is the unexpected juxtaposition of incongruities got nearest to the mark. Although we searched the map for the names of every small town and village in France, no satisfactory equivalents were ever found, not even when Ginette Spanier—as at home in France as she is in England—joined our brain-racked circle. I remember St Cloud was given a try and was received in stony silence, except from Noel who slayed himself by unexpectedly coming out with St Clew on the first night.

Ginette Spanier and her husband, Paul-Émile Seidmann, now came into our lives to stay. She was already directrice of Balmain. Paul-Émile was an eminent doctor, tall and handsome, and his manner was as gentle and charming wherever you met him as it was at your bedside. He at once became our doctor, and he and Ginette our saviours during these sometimes tempestuous, always incident-packed, four months; their big and rambling apartment at 70 Avenue Marceau our haven. In his foreword to her book *It Isn't All Mink*, Noel wrote: 'Ginette is in no way a hostess in the brittle, accepted sense of the word. She could no more plan a "smart" dinner-party than submit an original design for a space-ship. To say that she "entertains" is a misnomer. She does not entertain, she is entertained.' This is true. In its heyday, Noel, Marlene, Vivien and Larry, Lena Horne, Lilli Palmer, Claudette Colbert, Maria Montez, Jean-Pierre Aumont and Danny Kaye formed the nucleus of the 'regulars' at the Avenue Marceau, with a constantly changing fringe of every film- and stage-star in Paris or from London and New York. And it still goes on; only recently Colin Higgins, author of *Harold and Maude*, asked if he might bring a girl-friend, to whom Ginette took such an instant liking that they embraced at parting, and Ginette asked her name, she hadn't quite 'caught' it. As Noel said, in the flat itself 'names' don't get in the way; the name the girl wrote on the telephone pad was Bette Midler.

Apart from all the invitations springing naturally from these relaxed and happy gatherings, and before rehearsals started for *Present Laughter*, Noel was receiving and accepting invitations from Coco Chanel, Schiaparelli, Elsa Maxwell, the Duke and Duchess of Windsor, or entertaining them in his own apartment. Then there were Lady Mendl's Sunday luncheons at Versailles. Noel remembered for ever—who would not—one particular luncheon at the Villa Trianon when, over coffee in the garden, Lady Mendl announced her plans for landscaping: 'And on this side, all the way from here to the end of the garden, I'm going to have hundreds of arseholes, covered in roses.' Noel and Howard Sturgis realised too late—they had already collapsed—that she had given a French word—*arceau*—the English plural.

Casting began on September 14th: 'A morning of great va-et-vient and confusion. Actors and actresses arriving to read scenes and then buggering off again. The young man for Roland Maule rehearsing by himself in the dining-room at the top of his lungs.' Next day he found a

perfect Joanna, Michèle Lahaye, and the day after that the poor girl was
dead out of luck because Ginette produced Nadia Gray. In walked
Nadia, beautiful and intelligent, and she read so well that Noel decided
on her then and there. The day after *that*, drama set in; Michèle
Lahaye had broken her contract to appear as Joanna, but Noel remained firm as a rock about Nadia and said, 'Everybody else must deal
with everything.' The morning of the first rehearsal Noel had an
appalling fit of nerves, which he dismissed as 'really quite idiotic'. All
went fairly well—though Noel found the concentration required a
terrific strain—until, five days later, Black Monday set in with a
vengeance. French Equity discovered, or had been informed, that out
of the cast of ten no less than seven people carried foreign passports.
Only one foreigner was allowed by Equity ruling; Noel and the other
six were in despair, made worse by having solemnly to sign stern
documents renouncing their contracts, and to stop rehearsing at once.
After two depressing days Equity met and graciously allowed the seven
aliens to work 'in the very special circumstances', in return for which
the poor management had to engage six French actors at full salary as
understudies. Gladys arrived from London to do the set, tremulous and
quite obviously on the edge of a nervous breakdown, and this, apart
from causing Noel great additional worry, upset him emotionally; he
hated having to watch her struggling to get through each day, yet on
the other hand to have sent her home with the job unfinished might
have made her breakdown complete.

These were dreadful days; Noel felt flat, stale and irritable, driven
mad by the elderly crone of a prompter, in mourning for her life, whose
rasping voice was too frequently heard when at this late stage it should
not have been heard at all. Eleven days before the try-out in Brussels
Noel woke bunged up with cold and catarrh; he struggled to rehearsal,
where he staggered about and forgot his words until he had to come
home to bed, shivering and shaking and very near collapse. Paul-
Émile kept him in bed for nearly a week, popped in and out, popped
piqûres in and out of him, and was an abiding comfort. Noel, terrified at
the loss of time with the opening so near, went over and over his
words with me for hours on end and well into the night. After fourteen solid hours of sleep on the fifth night he woke up cured as suddenly as he had collapsed, breezed through the next week of rehearsals,
read *Vanity Fair* for the first time but by no means the last ('the most
wonderful novel I have ever read'), and bought a very smart dressing-
gown from Sulka for the second act. Leslie and Rex Benson gave him a
beautiful silk one for the first act, predominantly pink. The fact must

be faced that through all these weeks in Paris, off and on all through the summer, Noel had been eating far too many rich French meals, the entrées blanketed with sauces and the puddings smothered with cream. For the first time in his life he lost the lean and elegant figure for which he had been so famous and was furious when he ultimately saw the photographs of himself in Leslie Benson's dressing-gown; how *could* Graham and I let him appear looking like a vast pink sausage? He took good care never to let such a thing happen again; until his more sedentary old age he kept his figure, eating smaller meals of simpler food—apart from very sweet puddings, which he loved—which were anyway much more to his liking.

We all travelled together to Brussels, four hours freezing in a train unheated because of a strike. Elizabeth Taylor—not the film star or the novelist, 'our' Elizabeth Taylor—had come from London to help Gladys through her ill-health, a never-to-be-forgotten blessing. Grey Daisy, Ginette and Paul-Émile were all there in time for the first night at the charming Théâtre des Galeries. Noel had been through so much that he was not nervous, he was past caring; he made up, got dressed for his entrance and then settled down with Miss Mitford's *Our Village*, by which he was immediately entranced. He whizzed through the first act, people crowded backstage in the first interval to tell him how simply marvellous he was, but he quickly shooed them away and went back to *Our Village*. He reluctantly tore himself away to play the second act, at the end of which he got a tremendous ovation, and by the end of the play there was no doubt that we were a sellout success for the week in Brussels. For some weeks there had been talk of giving an extra performance in a place called Anvers which, though unheard of by us, had a theatre large enough to make a lot of money for all concerned. The sound of the name 'Onvair' haunted us, and then at last the great night arrived and had to be faced. We were driven through Simenon-like country for miles, foggy and dark with secrets—it was November —until at last we reached the outskirts of the mysterious city and Noel cried, 'Onvair! My God, it's good old Antwerp!'

Good old Antwerp turned out in force for Noel, and the evening proved to be one of the most curious he ever experienced; that very funny comedy was received in total silence. The more Noel tore himself to shreds, the straighter became the faces. At the end the huge audience rose to its feet and cheered its head off. It transpired that they had been told they were going to see a great English actor and had watched his antics with the hushed reverence they would have accorded John Gielgud in *Hamlet* or Laurence Olivier in *Lear*: 'I was assured by the management that the evening had been one of the greatest theatrical occasions Antwerp had ever known.' There was a crowd at the stage door, he waved and smiled at them from the car and they could see but not hear him mouthing the words, 'I'll sing Carmen for you another night.' Then he sank back in his seat: '*I* thought it was fucking awful and I'd like to garrotte every man jack of them.'

We got back to Brussels at two o'clock in the morning and were woken at six thirty to catch the train for Paris. To quote Nancy Mitford, 'Up before seven, *dead* before eleven', and such was the case, worsened by having to wait hours after missing the train because of the management's ghastly muddle over our tickets and luggage. By the time we got to Paris that evening, after hours in the cold and the strain of Antwerp the night before, Noel had lost his voice completely. We were due to open in three days' time, and nightmare ensued. Noel stayed in bed all next day trying to save his voice by not speaking a word and being cossetted. Joyce arrived from London, and my own diary entry for the day after that is headed: 'Disaster! Went *three* times to the Gare du Nord to meet Mrs Coward, Kitty, Graham and Sybil [his mother] and they finally arrived *six hours late*!' Graham somehow got them settled in their hotel while I rushed back to Noel and somehow got him, tottering, to the final dress-rehearsal. He laboured manfully through the first act, but it was no use; after that he had to capitulate and postpone the opening for a week. My next day's entry is headed 'Torture!', which is hardly an exaggeration. The trouble of getting Noel settled into a room in the American Hospital at Neuilly without forgetting a single one of his many necessities and comforts Graham of course shared with me, as he did the responsibility of looking after the aged Mrs Coward, Kitty, and all our other guests. My own particular hell was the re-allocation of Noel's large block of first-night seats which, with *Tout Paris* (the *gratin*, at that) to be there, headed by the Windsors, had been complicated enough in the first place. The telephone never stopped for the next week and I had to be more tactful, and in some cases more firm, than ever, until I felt like shooting myself.

Noel meanwhile stayed peacefully enough in hospital reading yet more Victorian novels, among them *Barchester Towers*. Was this, one now wonders, an escape from the ordeal in the French language still hanging over him, into the pleasure and security of good straightforward English? He was a brave man, but were these illnesses unconsciously self-induced from fear of his ordeal? I surmise that they were.

Noel says in his diary that he has nothing to report about the first night, nine days later, except that he was almost bored, not nervous, and played to the most chic, smart, glamorous and truly awful audience he had ever known. He thought he had made a success but that they did not like or understand the play, and he was right up to a point. We later found out the trouble; his accent had been too good—if only, in a comedy, he had played with more English accent they might have laughed and found it as adorable as England and America found Maurice Chevalier's French one. That the play was not a sell-out soon became evident and Noel began to call it the most ghastly flop of his life. I used to help him with a quick change early in the play; he would come down a little ladder into a tiny sort of cellar under the stage and say, 'There's *no one* in front tonight! There is ... quite ... literally nobody there ... at ... *all*!' An exaggeration of course; I think we never played one week at a loss and Grey Daisy even bought a fur coat from her proceeds with a hat to match, so her name was changed to the Leopard Woman: 'If the Leopard Woman comes in tonight and tells me once more that business is healthy, I warn you I shall throttle her!'

The name Théâtre Édouard VII had a dignified ring, whereas in fact it was one of the most rumbustious theatres ever known; there was an exhibition in the lobby of mud-coloured pictures painted by the manageress, and matinées of a perfectly horrid children's play called *Bidibi et Bonbon* which played to audiences much larger than Noel's of 'perfectly horrid French children'. Half way through the run the management asked Noel to the opening of their new night-club in the big room above the stage, to which he untruthfully replied he would be delighted; to his fury loud dance music and a thunder of dancing feet started above his head during his quiet love-scene in the second act. I flew upstairs to stop it and was told that it was not possible. 'Ce soir est gala!' They soon stopped it, however, when Noel tore up there in the interval and let loose a more eloquent flood of French abuse than he knew he was capable of. But his worst humiliation came on the days when, between *Bidibi et Bonbon* and *Joyeux Chagrins*, there were concerts of *le Jazz Hot*, when we had to fight our way through hordes of screaming teenage fans just leaving, so that Noel could get in to face his smattering of an audience.

Henri Bernstein tried to help matters by writing a kind and generous article about Noel and the play, but the cheaper, weekly, papers were vile: 'All left-wing and attacking me personally. I certainly seem to be going through a bad patch these years but I don't intend to let it get me down. All the same, it is disappointing. I expected a warm and loving welcome from Paris and got a sock in the kisser. Heigh-ho ... I suppose this succession of failures is good for my soul but I doubt it.'

The succession of failures was to be prolonged for several more years, and the bravery with which Noel faced these bitter disappointments must not be under-estimated or forgotten. I stress this because he gives little indication in the writings he has left of the indignities and unhappiness he endured professionally during this decade. All he allows himself is always more or less as above: 'Heigh-ho ...'

Interesting among the diary entries is evidence of a curious trait Noel had of making himself sound one year older than he was. He was forty-nine this December 16th, yet he ends his entry for the 15th— presumably made after midnight—'I am now in my fiftieth year'. This went on after each birthday all his life. 'No, you're not,' I would firmly reiterate.

The flop apart, there was gaiety to hand in Paris every day and far into the night until the run ended on December 26th. There were always celebrities in front, or friends, or both; Noel's dressing-room was usually full to bursting, and afterwards most of us would repair to what was known by every actor in Paris simply as the Club, just off the Rond Point, for onion soup or *oeufs au beurre noir* and not a few drinks. Lornie, who you will remember had at last taken to foreign travel, came over and was eager not to miss any of the sights, from the Winged Victory in the Louvre to the gentlemen dancing together at La Vie en Rose. Then Gladys returned, recovered from her breakdown and in effervescent form, to our delight. Joe and Lenore Cotten had us with Orson Welles to supper in their suite at the Lancaster on Christmas Eve, and their presents were lavish. Mine included a toy white rabbit, with long silky fur, which could hop across the room on its back legs while beating two little drums together with its front ones. Orson became insanely jealous of my rabbit and begged me to give it to him— by now it was around four o'clock in the morning and the vodka had been flowing—but I couldn't bear to part with it and refused. He swore he would never forgive me, and at the big party after the last night of *Joyeux Chagrins* was still pointing me out to everybody as 'that old meanie [and much worse] who won't give me his white rabbit'. The party, unlike the play, was a great success, given by Noel in the apartment—Larry was there, I remember, with Vivien a vision in white; it lasted until after five in the morning and we sank into our berths on the boat-train next evening still feeling terrible, slept until the train passed Orpington, and just got dressed in time to step out at Victoria Station.

All through these hectic months Noel had been comforted by the thought of his return to Jamaica, now imminent. The house at Blue Harbour was finished in time as promised, and he excitedly gave me glowing descriptions of the beauty of it all—the colour, the bougain-villea, hibiscus, oleanders, the swift and magical twilights, the night sky star-spangled, and by day the joys of swimming and sunbathing wearing nothing at all. He had not unnaturally assumed that I should go with him, and it came as a blow when I told him I could not; the telling was for me one of the most painful things I have ever had to do in my life. We had neither of us yet learned the wisdom of separation for a while, after a long stretch of proximity almost every waking moment of our days. I had foolishly undertaken to try to do every-thing myself during the four long months in Paris; I ran the apartment and, apart from Clothilde the cook, did every other household chore that had to be done. Moreover, there had been no Lornie as there was in London, and for the first time I coped with the always large personal mail by myself. In addition to all these activities it had seemed the most natural thing in the world for me to continue, after all the rehearsals and the play had opened, to go as usual with him to the theatre and act as his dresser, which in any case was my only excuse for being there and not missing one minute of the fun. Sensible Lornie always warned me that I overworked with not nearly enough sleep or rest, and I paid no heed. Jamaica would be no rest, I felt sure; a move into a new house would simply mean another huge job to be undertaken. And, subtly, something else had occurred which strengthened my purpose in this difficult decision. Nervous breakdowns were something that happened to other people, they could never happen to me; but I had so recently watched Noel through two illnesses amounting to breakdowns, and then one day alone with Gladys in the flat I saw her give way com-pletely (with every reason on that particular day, I must add) and as I watched I became aware that I too was fallible, that it *could* happen to me. I was on the edge of a breakdown now, knew that I must rest and not go to Jamaica. The distress to Noel must have been considerable but he only notes that he 'spent an almost sleepless night with my brain clicking, torn between irritation and affection'. Some of the close friends were shocked, they could not imagine anyone refusing Noel anything and looked upon my defection as a betrayal; I heard little or nothing of them until Noel returned. But Noel's own understanding, once he had recovered from his anger, was remarkable; he went ahead

with the plans for Graham and himself to sail as though that had been
the arrangement all along, and left me fairly happy with the job of
making the word-for-word translation of *The Little Hut*. They travelled
via New York, whence he sent me a copy of *The Kinsey Report* inscribed,
'Don't let this go to your head', and after they were settled in Jamaica,
wrote to me as sweetly as ever. I might have known he could be
depended upon.

I think that in the long run this minor revolution on my part was
good for both of us; each respected the other more than ever, and we
never again had a major upset. All the while he was away I longed for
his letters and longed for his return.

Noel's and Graham's arrival at Blue Harbour was an occasion of
great disappointment, relieved by some hilarity. They approached it
from Port Maria, and once past the last headland, the new house
became visible. The sight that met their eyes was such a shock that they
gazed at it in disbelief. The house had not been built back layer by
layer to follow the lie of the hillside as Noel had wished; instead it
stuck up straight, white and naked, its height made to look more stark
because many wild almond trees and every bit of the thick tropical
brush around the house had been chopped to the ground by the workmen. The silence in the car can only be described as stunned, until Noel
said, 'My God, it's the Flatiron Building!' and they started to laugh and
drove on. When they reached Noel's seashore House Beautiful, the
shock when they entered the living-room was even more severe.
Reggie Aquart, the agent, had furnished it with everything Noel most
disliked; all the woodwork was of gloomy dark cedar, the curtain
material was a design of stripes of sickly green and sicklier beige, and
dark parchment lampshades with galleons on them abounded. Noel
took in the horror and then said, 'It reminds me of the station waiting-
room at Hull.' They inspected the rest of the house, met the staff
Aquart had engaged and then flew quickly over to Goldeneye for stiff
drinks with Ian Fleming, Ann Rothermere and Edward (Lord) Stanley
who, Noel wrote, 'were welcoming and sweet. Back home, we had one
more martini and sat on the verandah on rockers, looking out over
the fabulous view and almost burst into tears of sheer pleasure.' The
disillusionments are not mentioned.

A few days later he did write, 'Worried about the Surbiton look of
the sitting-room. It is quite definitely "Kozy Kot". Something must be
done.' All the dark cedar was quickly painted white; days of intensive
shopping in Kingston replaced most of the hideosities; Jack and
Natasha sent from New York dining-chairs, table and sideboard of

bamboo, and Ellen Doubleday, wife of his American publisher Nelson Doubleday, sent some good-looking pieces of early American furniture, all of which are still in use. Kozy Kot or not, from the first the house seethed with guests: Ian and Ann and their guests, Lord and Lady Birkenhead: Sir John Huggins, the Governor, with Lady Huggins and their three daughters; Clive Brook; Lucinda Ballard; Gladys Cooper; Sir Harold and Lady Mitchell; Kitty Lehman, later Kitty Reiner, later still Kitty Spence but always the same sweet Kitty ('Kitty suddenly arrived with fourteen friends but they all behaved very nicely and went early'); Babe and Bill Paley; Vincent Astor and his wife; Ivor Novello, Bobby Andrews, Zena Dare and Olive Gilbert, all four of whom stayed two nights, Zena later reporting in London that 'Noel's house is a target for all the winds that blow'. To continue the list would be tedious, but mention must be made of the *rapprochement* with Lord Beaverbrook after twenty years of warfare open and declared in all the Beaverbrook newspapers. The *rapprochement* had been engineered by mutual friends in the ship on the way over, Cuckoo Leith in particular, but Loelia Duchess of Westminster, Lord Porchester, Evelyn Waugh and Coco Chanel were also on board, and everybody including Lord Beaverbrook cocktailed and dined with everybody else. On the first night, 'Max very amiable and asked me to stay with him in Montego'; the next, 'Drinks after dinner with Max. Long talk about the past, a polite duel which on the whole I won': the night after that, 'further conversation with Max who was more charming than ever. He is a witty old bastard and though he has done me much harm I can't help finding him excellent company.'

In Jamaica, although Noel did not go to stay, Ian Fleming helped still more by arranging several meetings between the two; 'Drove to Montego with Ian, lunched with Max Beaverbrook, who I must say couldn't have been nicer.' And in a letter to me, Noel wrote: 'The Baron Beaverbrook came to lunch the other day oozing amiability and went really dotty about the maison and the garden and the view. There was a distinct glint of green envy in the baronial eye. He turned on masses of charm and fell heavily for Natasha who looked and was divine as usual.' That is about as far as it went; their renewed auld acquaintance was I think soon forgot by Lord Beaverbrook, and by Noel seldom brought to mind.

In the same letter Noel wrote:

There have been great carryings on about Lady R. [Ann] and Commander F. [Ian]. She arrived in a blaze of Jamaican publicity and announced that she was staying with me. So when a *Life* photographer arrived here we had to send Little Lad [to Goldeneye] chaud pied to fetch her. There then began a very natty high comedy scene in which she kept forgetting she was a house guest and asking us what we had been doing all the morning etc. We then all traipsed over to Montego Bay for a night and Elle et Lui discreetly (i.e. indiscreetly) had breakfast together on the balcony of his room! After this I descended upon them both and gave them a very stern lecture indeed. I must say they are very sweet but ... I have grave fears for the avenir.

The cooking at Blue Harbour may have been one up on Violet's at Goldeneye but nevertheless wasn't really up to snuff for such distinguished visitors, and Noel wrote asking for some easy-to-make but tasty dishes:

Dearest Toley, Thanks for yours like anything et mille mercis pour les jolis recipes which have caused a minor race riot dans la cuisine. We had some soft, damp fried bread for breakfast this morning cuddled round some old bacon rind. It was but delicious! Evan Williams, our homme à tout faire, is full of enthusiasm and tries like a mad thing. He is very sweet and coffee-coloured and I have to keep on buying him trousers. He will never *quite* supplant you in my affections on account of his inadequate knowledge of French (*and* English) and not being very good at crosswords. Little Lad alternates between savage irritation and hilarious joy at his film being postponed. Personally of course I am delighted because he can go on bashing about in the jardin and rolling in manure and putting things in upside down and generally enhancing the House Beautiful. The H.B. as a matter of fact is coming along a treat and is a seething mass of dark gentlemen of the sonnets hammering and fixing and smelling jolly poignant. Mrs Calthrop's abandoned dwelling sits on the top of the hill with half a verandah and looks at us reproachfully every time we pass. I seem to hear it sighing, 'Please send out someone to make me uncomfortable.' Dennis Price came to stay and liked everything including the plumbing which proves that kind hearts are far superior to coronets any day of the week. We have a tayny white titty-poo called Evelyn and an equally tayny puppinger called Jellyby on account of he keeps on getting his head caught between things and screaming like all fuck. I've put in the word fuck so that if ever this witty letter is published in your memoirs they will be able to put in four dots—perhaps starting with F and ending with K. I hope you are happy as a bee and working away at La Petite H[utte]. Kindly write again in two minutes from now and dites-moi tout and be dood as dold.

The tayny white titty-poo was so beautiful that at first sight Natasha exclaimed, 'Doomed!'; it was named Evelyn, either contingency thus being covered until it was ascertained whether it should be named after Evelyn Laye or Evelyn Waugh. She soon cleared up this mystery by becoming a child bride and giving birth to six equally beautiful kittens; while they were still at the breast she could be seen up the nearest tree having, according to Noel, 'the living daylight fucked out of her'. She steadily pursued her amorous course for years until at one point there were no less than seventeen cats and kittens, mostly products of incest, clawing the furniture in the living-room. She came as the gift of Charles and Mildred D'Costa in Kingston, and was famous during her life and a legend after her death for her beauty and fecundity; today her numberless blue-eyed white descendants can be seen all over the very large Parish of St Mary.

All his grown-up life Noel had a deep interest in medicine and an insatiable curiosity about surgery; the latter, to me, amounting to the gruesome. He made friends with every doctor he met, pumped them with questions and, whenever he could, induced them to let him attend operations. He once watched a well-known American actress undergoing surgery and it wasn't until many years later in Bermuda she choked over her cocktail when Noel told her he had seen her ovaries being removed. There is no better description of this lively curiosity than Noel's own, written during this same visit to Jamaica:

Tuesday April 12th: Interesting morning. Went to Port Maria Hospital and watched Dr S. doing a big abdominal operation (short circuit) with only a local anaesthetic. It was strange and macabre to talk to the patient, who although frightened, was completely conscious and out of pain, while his whole stomach was outside his body and being treated like an unwieldy Christmas parcel. He couldn't see what was going on and, apart from slight pain during the preliminary injection, felt nothing at all. His whole organism, however, was affected by shock because I watched his eyes and also the sudden acute trembling of his body. The human body is a most extraordinary mechanism; I watched those pulsating, throbbing organs and tissues being cruelly set upon with steel and catgut and was once more amazed at the body's capacity for healing itself. When the stitched and operated-upon areas were done with they seemed to slip back inside with an audible sigh of relief, so that they could get on with the business of healing in their own way.

On Friday May 13th, day of ill omen, Noel received four cables to say that his dearly loved Neysa McMein had died. One of the jokes between them had been that upon receipt of the date of his arrival in New York, Neysa would cancel any and every engagement. Even were she to be asked to dinner with the President, she swore she would say, 'No Mr President, I can't. Beauty is coming to town.'
Noel wrote:

Neysa is dead. I spent a lonely wretched day [Graham had returned to England] unable to concentrate on anything but the thought that I would never see Neysa again. I so wanted her to come here and see the house and play games and laugh as we have done for so many years. New York will be dreadful without her. I had just written ordering her to cancel all engagements for the week I was there. Fortunately she got the letter and it made her laugh. She has always cancelled every engagement for me; this one she could not cancel. I shall miss her always. She was good and kind and true and above all, gay. I feel a dreadful sense of loss but I must be prepared and armed for the future. I shall be 50 in December and as one gets older people begin to die and when each one goes a little light goes out ... So many of my friends have gone; Alec [Woollcott], Alice [Duer Miller], Bob Benchley, Bea Kaufman, all the ones who made New York particularly gay for me. Now Neysa whom I loved more than any of them. I shall never forget her.

Noel did miss her always. Over the years he would from time to time say, 'I could have done without Neysa dying, you know.'
All through this five-month welter of social gaddings-about and emotions both grave and gay, Noel worked religiously most mornings. His work too was a welter, his mind teeming with so many ideas that he was hard-put to control them. He wrote the preface for *Play Parade Volume Two* and a short story, 'A Richer Dust': 'I must admit I adore writing fiction. I must certainly do a novel soon.' But songs would

keep popping into his head for a vaguely formulated musical, *Over The Garden Wall*, eventually called *Ace of Clubs*: 'Had a long think about what I really want to do, a play for Gertie or for me or both, short stories, a book or a musical. Wrote three lyric refrains for *Josephine*, worked at the piano. Suddenly a new and lovely tune appeared. Felt the authentic thrill. All right, the musical it shall be.' Only four days later, 'Suddenly while re-reading *Vile Bodies* an idea for a comedy for Gertie fell into my mind. It rang a loud bell so I constructed it then and there and everything seened to fall into place. The title is *Home and Colonial'* (later changed to *Island Fling* and finally *South Sea Bubble*). He meant to work on it next day but the piano tuner came, so he continued to write lyrics; but the day after that he wrote eleven pages of the play and also painted a picture, 'a poor man's Cézanne, nice and thick and chunky'. After four weeks of hard work, interrupted by having to write several more songs because he couldn't suppress them, he finished the play for Gertie.

Four months had gone by; for most of this time, since Graham's departure, Noel had been by himself. On May 23rd, his last night at Blue Harbour, he dined alone and was touched to find that the staff, who had been tearful all day, had decorated the table with pink begonias and Russian violets, spelling in big letters BOSS SAFE VOYAGE. 'These people are so gentle and kind and I am so fond of them. I know how nostalgic I shall be for this divine place when I am far away, but I am always restless. I am longing now for White Cliffs and all my loved ones.'

He travelled via New York and saw masses of friends, all of whom mourned with him the loss of Neysa. Whatever misunderstandings there had been between himself and Mary Martin and Richard Halliday over *Pacific 1860* were now cleared up for ever. He went twice to see Mary in *South Pacific* and thought she was enchanting: 'We had a real reunion. Mary was genuinely in tears and truly happy and relieved that we were making up, it was really touching. I feel as though a weight had been lifted from my shoulders. I hate quarrels and feuds and she really had a bloody time in England and I have felt uncomfortable and unhappy about it. Now all that is over and I could not be more pleased.'

He caught up on all the new plays, among them *Death of a Salesman*: Irene Selznick had already told him it wasn't a play, it was an experience, and Leonora Corbett—when told it was a play with a message— had said, 'Then I shan't dress.' He went with Mainbocher, and wrote:

Well, we're the boys who're out of step. I found it boring and embarrassing. Lee Cobb overacted and roared and ranted. Mildred Dunnock was good, so was the rest of the cast and the production was occasionally effective. All that symbolic wandering about is considered an innovation. Basil Dean did it in *Hannele* in 1912 and the Germans did nothing else for years. The play is a glorification of mediocrity. The hero [Willie Loman] is a cracking bore and a liar and a fool and a failure; the sons are idiotic. At moments the writing was literate and good and when it was, it was out of key with the characters.

When *Death of a Salesman* came to London, Rebecca West found herself at the first-night party next to a man who asked her what she thought of it. She didn't know he was Arthur Miller, the author, but even if she had I suspect her answer would have been the same: 'Twaddle! What was he going on about? Judging by the backdrop he owned one of the most valuable bits of real estate in Manhattan.' Inevitably, in London Noel was again told it wasn't a play, it was an experience. With all the regret in the world in his voice Noel replied, 'I wish it had been a play.'

'Oh dear, I really think I love White Cliffs more than anywhere else in the world!' was Noel's reaction when he returned there and settled in for the summer. There was peace and quiet and above all there was time; plenty of time to work and paint and read and sleep. All this was true up to a point; we listened to stacks of records of classical music, attacked *The Times* crossword every day ('*very* good exercise for the brain') and we did as a rule go early to bed. But then we got badly bitten by the canasta bug. Fierce battles raged over the long weekends, increased in ferocity when Ian Fleming and Ann moved in to Summer's Lease, the house next door to us. We became canasta-crazy to such a point that Noel travelled with his folding, felt-covered knee-table, so that we could start playing before the train left Charing Cross on Friday afternoons, and reverse the process on the way up to London on Mondays. Happily, Winifred captured on canvas one Sunday-evening canasta game, with excellent likenesses of Ann, Joyce, Ian and Noel at the card-table in the drawing-room, in a mist of cigarette smoke. Only once that summer do I remember a train journey when instead of canasta we all answered a long questionnaire in a magazine about our likes and dislikes which, when added up, promised to give a true picture of our characters. It worked quite well, except that Loelia surprisingly emerged as 'Dear Old Dad'. The name stuck, and this should be recorded, or readers of letters and diaries in the future will never know that 'Dear Old Dad' was at that time Loelia, Duchess of Westminster.

In the weeks that summer of 1949 when we did not go up to London, our days at White Cliffs—far from being as tranquil as Noel had prophesied—passed in a frenzy of activity. Noel worked all morning on the book of *Ace of Clubs*, while Graham and I were also engaged on the score and book for a musical. Graham had for some time been composing songs for which I wrote the lyrics: our musical was called *Ghost of a Chance*, and we slaved away until it was completed. For reasons beyond our control, let us say, it never saw the light, but in the meantime we had captive and appreciative audiences in our friends. Poor Master, how much suffering we caused him we shall never know; after the first few songs he wrote politely that Graham's music was really fairly good, if melodically simple, and his harmony needed strengthening, he praised my lyrics, and said our libretto was very good. Ian Fleming was far and away our best audience for the funny songs, rolling about with laughter; and he assured me that I must go on writing, promising to help in any way he could, even to 'placing' anything I wrote. I never availed myself of his kindness, but writing this book has made me very conscious of Ian's encouragement all those years ago.

The afternoons were spent frenetically painting; for the first and last time that summer we tried to emulate the Impressionists to the point of painting out of doors and trying to capture the light; the station-wagon was piled high with stools, easels and three complete sets of painting paraphernalia, and we drove for miles to find subjects that appealed equally to us all. We ended up by admiring the Impressionists more than ever for sheer tenacity alone; for us the elements were seldom friendly, gusts of wind blowing our easels over at the end of an afternoon's work, and we would have to come home with grass and dirt sticking to our masterpieces. Noel did manage to bring one splendid large canvas safely home, only to have Joe, the black poodle, jump into the car to welcome us, slide across it and remove hours of work on to his behind and tail. The damage he did, 'though funny, was awful and irreparable'; and from then on we never again painted out of doors in England.

Interruptions to our peaceful existence were many and varied. After rain, hordes of beach flies crawled under the french windows in a thick, wide, dark-brown procession, and headed straight for the fire in which they committed suttee in hundreds, leaving a disgusting smell of rotting fish. Large companies of Royal Marine Commandos often appeared from their nearby school and swarmed all over, or hurled themselves up and down, the almost perpendicular cliffs; and then there were the Channel swimmers, covered in lard, who were from time to time washed up on the beach like stranded whales and who then had to be rolled up in blankets and carted off to Dover.

Other diversions were movie-going and reading; there were innumerable outings to enjoyable double-features at the Odeons in Ashford and Folkestone, and Noel read greedily. He got through no less than twelve of Trollope's longer novels during this time, and he also read Monica Baldwin's *I Leap Over the Wall*, of which he said, 'Very interesting. It has strengthened me in my decision not to become a nun.'

Work started early in June on the film *The Astonished Heart*, adapted from Noel's one-act play of the same name, and very early on he went to Pinewood to see some rushes. He thought that Celia Johnson and Margaret Leighton were brilliant but that Michael Redgrave was not quite right. Next day he reports a luncheon which became 'mostly a duologue between Mike and me. Eventually he suggested that I should play the part myself. He behaved really and truly superbly and I will always respect him for it.' Noel took the part and there now began a very pleasant month or more of work at Pinewood Studios. His scenes for the first ten days were exclusively with Celia, who, with Trevor Howard, had proved herself in *Brief Encounter* to be a perfect interpreter of Noel's carefully controlled emotional writing. This film, more than any other of his works, brought home to millions of people, especially in America, that he could when he wished discard his flippant wit and write with tender and true understanding of the workings of the hearts of (for want of a better word) 'average' men and women. Celia was an ideal companion during the inevitable, interminable 'waits'. We got as much of *The Times* crossword done as we could in the car before we got to the studios at eight o'clock in the morning, but Celia had always done more. Some days we were defeated by one or two impossibly difficult clues, and we never forgot the day we saw Celia play a scene so poignantly that our eyes were brimming with tears; the director called 'Cut!', Celia walked straight off the set and said, 'Fourteen across is Rabbit.'

After Celia came days of scenes with Margaret Leighton, another perfect interpreter of Coward dialogue, but Maggie arrived with an inferiority complex about succeeding Celia as a companion. 'I'm not nearly as brainy as she is, and I'm an absolute duffer with the crossword. And I warn you I'm a bore. I don't mean I'm a *crashing* bore: I'm one of those perfectly ordinary bores you know, the ones who just go droning on and on.' Of course she was nothing of the kind; we laughed our heads off then, and always did whenever we were in her company, until her tragically early death in 1976.

Work ceased on *The Astonished Heart* during the first half of August: a State of Emergency was declared because of dock strikers defying the Government; after Sir Stafford Cripps had said it would never, never happen the pound was devalued; a financial crisis followed and the allowance for foreign travel was very small. Noel reports on August 29th: 'Back to the factory. Everyone rather lax but cheerful after their holiday. All the staff have been abroad to Étretat, Dinard, Brittany and the South of France. I presume that Clacton and Southend have been bequeathed to the upper classes.'

The film, though it contains some fine and moving scenes quite beautifully acted, was not a success. Particularly with Mrs Coward, who told her son she thought it perfectly awful, and that he had looked hideous throughout.

On November 22nd, Noel dined at the American Embassy with the much-admired Ambassador and Mrs Lewis Douglas:

Sat next to the Queen [now Queen Elizabeth, the Queen Mother] at dinner, who was perfectly enchanting as always. Afterwards played canasta with Princess Margaret as partner. We won. Then I sang all the new songs [from *Ace of Clubs*] for the Queen and she most obviously loved them. Princess Margaret obliged with songs at the piano. Surprisingly good, she has an impeccable ear, her piano playing is simple but has perfect rhythm and her method of singing is really very funny. The Queen was sweet on account of being so genuinely proud of her chick. Altogether a most charming and gay evening.

Long gone were the days when everything Noel wrote for the theatre had been so eagerly snapped up by André Charlot and Charles B. Cochran. Eighteen months of vicissitudes and humiliations had to be endured by him since he had, alone at Blue Harbour, so enthusiastically written his comedy for Gertie and started to compose the score for the musical. (They both suffered so many changes of title that they will be referred to from now on as *South Sea Bubble* and *Ace of Clubs*.) *Ace of Clubs* did not reach production until July 1950, by which time the comedy had mortifyingly not been produced at all, and in fact seven years were to pass before *South Sea Bubble* saw the light, with Vivien

Leigh starring, in 1956 in London. Gertie dickered and dithered about 'her' comedy for months until Noel, angry with her 'frigging about in New York', offered it to Kay Hammond and John Clements. They were at first delighted, and Noel happy in the assurance that Kay would be enchanting, but then at last they decided that none of the men's roles were important enough for John. A grave disappointment; Noel sent the script to Diana Wynyard, but nothing came of that either, and then, after more than a year of dashed hopes, Binkie telephoned. He said

> that Vivien and Larry violently disliked poor *South Sea Bubble* and had flown at him for encouraging me. They said they loved me far too much to lie to me, and I was not to do the play as it was old-fashioned Noel Coward and would do me great harm. This is a surprising and salutary jolt and I have a strange feeling that they are right. At all events I love them for their honesty and moral courage. They may be wrong, but I must admit the play didn't come easily in the first place ... I shall think carefully and probably shelve it for at least a year.

With Jack of necessity separated from Noel all through the war and heavily engaged ever since with direction and production on Broadway, all Noel's plays had been presented in England since 1939 by H. M. Tennent Ltd. Tennent's was exemplified in the attractive, persuasive, amusingly talkative person of Binkie Beaumont. Binkie, despite his powerful position, remained to the public a mystery man to the end of his days, loving anonymity and coolly practising it. He was more than slightly wicked when it came to business, even with close friends, but business apart, he was the staunchest friend imaginable. Like Vivien, he never seemed to want to go to bed, yet he was the first on the telephone in the mornings, his voice buoyant with the latest private and professional news of the most famous names in the theatre in England and America. Although the news he imparted was often hair-raising, given long before it reached the newspapers, and sometimes so hair-raising and private that it never reached the papers at all, he seemed always to trust one's integrity implicitly, flatteringly taking it for granted that the scandal would go no further. Violent and occasional business flare-ups excepted, Noel and Binkie were more than friends: they were the deepest, closest cronies, and it was therefore to Binkie that Noel turned with *Ace of Clubs*.

But in those days Binkie knew little about big musicals, Tennent's did not then present them, and Binkie handed it over to his associate, Prince Littler. There now followed many months which were to Noel affronting and shaming; as the pattern was repeated three times with successive managements, one explanation will suffice. With the American musical-play invasion of England, new methods had become obligatory and no management would risk the increasing costs of a musical, not even by Noel Coward, until they, and all henchmen involved, approved every aspect of it. Noel now had to 'sell' his work like everybody else, like an inexperienced beginner having to audition. He accepted the inevitable, but to soften these blows to his pride he mistakenly turned these occasions into friendly parties at Gerald Road, at which he could play the host. There was good food and drink, and Noel of course read the book so well and sang and played the score so brilliantly that these evenings ended with much clapping on the back, expressions of esteem and admiration and a firm assurance that they would be honoured to present *Ace of Clubs*. Then, very gradually over a period of weeks, a rot set in, enthusiasm waned, conferences were held at which everyone and everyone's assistant was allowed their say, until hopes would fade and at last be extinguished. The blow at the end of the second episode of this dismal serial came in the form of a cable from Binkie which said that Val Parnell did not consider the book strong enough and would not do the show. The cable ended by Binkie's apologising for the gloomy news and sending his fondest love: 'That at any stage of my career Mr Val Parnell's opinion should be of the remotest importance is indeed gloomy news. I cabled back "Fondest love my foot".'

Third time was luckier, with Tom Arnold and his manager Clem Butson, but the same humbling experience had to be gone through yet once more: 'Telephoned Clem to find out how things were going. His voice sounded strained, with every reason, as he stumblingly explained that he and Tom were not satisfied with *Ace of Clubs* and that unless it were drastically reconstructed and re-written they would not do it. I must admit I felt battered and inclined to self-pity on account of having had my fair share of slaps in the kisser just lately.'

Through most of 1949 and half of 1950 these humiliations had run concurrently with his disappointments over *South Sea Bubble*, and as though all these slaps in the kisser were not enough, he received at the same time still more from *The Astonished Heart*. The film had opened to scathing reviews in New York, and in London he had wakened one morning to read 'filthy notices, really very vitriolic'. He cared still more when, over a quiet dinner, Ian Fleming attacked him and told him how awful it was. 'Oh dear. I really seem quite unable to please.'

There is little doubt that this period was the lowest ebb in Noel's professional career, and certainly the most prolonged. For once it would be untrue to say that he remained undaunted; in addition to the critics the general climate of opinion that he was 'finished' was so strong that it could not but affect him. Always honest when alone, as we all should be, he subjected himself to sessions of soul-searching before going to sleep at night—*was* he old hat? Had he written himself out? He had the relief of getting these doubts off his chest next day, to whichever of his near and dear ones happened to be about, but he did not ask for soothing reassurance on these occasions, he wanted to face facts fair and square. By the end of one of these long heart-to-hearts, it was not difficult to comfort him. Of course he was not finished, he had made that evident during the course of the talk. 'I shall always pop up out of another hole in the ground. I shall twitch my mantle blue, tomorrow to fresh woods and pastures new. Oh I do wish people wouldn't always misquote that line. And now let's have a drink.'

The newer pasture to which he referred was the field of fiction. All through this troubled period he had found one deeply satisfying distraction, and one that would last—unlike a play that might be taken off after a few nights. He had written four short stories. He sent them to his publisher Alexander Frere and his wife Pat, who displayed such warm enthusiasm that if he would write two more, Frere said, Heinemann would publish them in January. This was not only the life-line he so badly needed; a whole new prospect, peaceful and at the same time fertile, opened out before him. Imagine the blissful simplicity of writing something to one's own satisfaction and then seeing it in print exactly as one had envisaged it! Not, as in the theatre, mangled and twisted to other people's demands after months of wrangling, until one's perfectly formed brainchild was born crippled and distorted. That is what he would do, what he could always do in the future if he wanted: write fiction. Who knew, he might even one day write a full-length novel, he would see.

Meanwhile he had to press on with writing *Future Indefinite* and more urgently—one has to salute his determination—again completely rewrite *Ace of Clubs*. Once the first set-to with Tom Arnold and Clem Butson was over and Noel had reconstructed the book to their wishes, they proved a pleasant management to work with. Pat Kirkwood, with Graham and Sylvia Cecil, headed the cast, and the predominantly youthful company were great fun and everybody had a good time both onstage and off. There were troubles while on the road, over Gladys's too-heavy sets and Pat's dresses, but 'Pat behaving well, as she always does' and 'what a good character, she is such a dear'. Troubles were overcome and the tour was successful. On the first night in London,

> the theatre was tingling with tension. I got the usual ovation and the show went magnificently. Sylvia stopped the show with 'Nothing Can Last for Ever', Graham had a rip-snorting triumph with 'America' and Pat got them roaring with 'Josephine' and 'Chase Me Charlie'. The whole thing went marvellously and when I walked on to the stage at the end there was a lot of booing. I stood still and waited while a free fight broke out in the gallery. Finally I silenced them and made my speech and that was that.

Next day the notices were mixed, some silly, some insulting, some adulatory, but nearly all good for the box-office. *Ace of Clubs* had at last got off to a good start.

Noel had been taking a beating for too long; why he had been booed on the first night we never really knew, perhaps it had been anti- and pro-Coward partisans who had fought in the gallery. He could not wait to get away from it all—'I must take up the tangled threads of my life'—and once in his seat in the Constellation on the way to Jamaica, he started to read the first volume of *À la recherche du temps perdu* as an antidote to absolutely everything. Back in the 'twenties Noel had known Proust's translator, C. K. Scott-Moncrieff, quite well, during the years nearing the completion of his stupendous labour, and he had for a long time intended to read right through his edition of twelve volumes. He arrived at Blue Harbour expecting tranquil weather in July, but not at all; there was a strong Norther blowing, the sea was choppy and grey, and in consequence his beach was a sorry muck-up of blown-in debris. A perfect excuse to sit in a corner of his verandah out of the wind and persevere with Proust: 'A really idle day immersed in Mr Proust whom I find enthralling. It is wonderful writing and leaves vivid pictures in the mind, but he does I think carry intricacy of style and design a bit too far. Still, his characters are clear as crystal and the atmosphere so well done that you can almost smell it.' Arthur Macrae in London wrote that he too was carrying out the same self-imposed task, in one letter warning Noel that one of the characters had just taken twenty minutes, by Arthur's watch, to get from the top step of the stairs to the bottom. Noel got through all twelve volumes, very glad indeed that he had done so, but

vowing that nothing on earth would induce him to do it again. That
his enthusiasm wore thin by the end can be gathered from this letter,
which also gives an eloquent report of the weather in Jamaica:

Dearest Tolette, I have now had two lettines from you and so it is
haut temps that you got one back. The biggest hurricane since
Tallulah Bankhead has just avoided the island and is on its way to
Miami. We had a dear little earthquake on Saturday morning but I
was on the loo at the time and put the strange rumbling down to
natural causes. Apparently in Kingston quite a lot of ladies rushed
into the street holding sponges over their pussies and crying
Hilfe! Hilfe! Apart from these minor caprices of Mother Nature's,
life is very peaceful and the weather now divine. Tell Little Lad
that I went to the Moneague Hotel and that we were very foolish
not to go before as it is perfectly enchanting. It is run by a stout
gentleman called Tom Macauley who, although far from being as
normal as blueberry pie, is a really wonderful cook; his cordon
couldn't be bluer and he has promised to take some poor wretch
into his kitchen and train him or her as a cook for me next winter.
Jolly good luck! His hotel is perched on the top of a highish
mountain and is crammed with gout — you know, Bristol, Sheraton
and old Spode. It is all very strange. I am going up to New York
for about ten days to buy some braid and a thing for making ice
cubes which is made of rubber and plugs into practically anything.
I shall then return and plug it in and hope for the best. I have now
finished with Mr Proust. He is worth reading but Oh la la how
jolly tiresome. I am furious about Ace of Clubs not being a real
smash and I have come to the conclusion that if they don't care for
first rate music, lyrics, dialogue and performance, they can stuff it
up their collective arses and go and see King's Rhapsody until les
vaches se rentrent ... I am happy as a bee writing my stories and I
have a strong suspicion that there is a novel in the offing. I need
hardly tell you that this holiday has done me more good than I
could have believed possible. I feel smooth as silk and look quite
wonderful. Give my dearest love to all and a great deal to yourself.

His wonderful looks had come about because he had been dieting, and
was slim again, and 'not one drop of the demon alcohol has sullied
these chiselled lips' since he left England. 'I feel very proud of myself
and my self-discipline. I have wasted too much time during these last
five years. I have drunk too much, eaten too much, and played too

much. The only trouble about not drinking is that other people who are drinking are liable to look a little silly.'

With all the writing he had had to do and his head teeming with ideas for the future, he had handed over what small amount he had done on *The Little Hut* to Nancy Mitford, and as we all know, Nancy's adaptation ran successfully for ages and is still being played somewhere or other. Another big financial chance cropped up and was turned down during the just-referred-to ten days in New York, when Richard Rodgers nearly persuaded him not only to direct *The King and I*, but also to play the King. The money involved was tempting, the idea exciting, and flattering to his bruised ego. Everybody urged him to accept until, yet again, Edna Ferber said over dinner, 'Nonsense! Why should you do a thing like that when there is no "food" in it for you.' 'I could have kissed her. I went home and found a cable saying Ace of Clubs was up £500 last week.'

He got back to London on October 1st, his suitcases bulging as usual with splendid presents for everyone. Before returning home he would make a careful list in which nobody, from his mother to all members of his staff, was ever forgotten. He regarded this as a serious duty, and always allowed several days for what he called 'intensive shopping for prezzies'. He excelled in making quick decisions in the shops and unusual choices, invariably perfect for the recipients. That he thoroughly enjoyed the shopping itself, the extravagant spending and the actual giving of the presents, does not detract from the fact that this was a lovable and generous aspect of his nature.

'October is such a mournful month!' as Judith Bliss exclaims in *Hay Fever*, and from the 23rd to the 26th we were faced with the melancholy occupation of packing up and saying goodbye for ever to the Paris flat. It had come up for sale and Noel was offered it for what was, even in those days, a snip; but currency regulations were still stringent and he dared not risk another breach of regulations by finagling. We were efficient and ruthless about disposal of the contents, and were absolutely miserable while doing so. We loved the flat so much, the place had spelt happiness and gaiety for us, and now that charming chapter in our lives was closed. He decided on a valedictory dinner at Korniloff's, just the two of us, to mark the sad event. He was 'back on the drink again': we dined solely on the caviar for which Korniloff's was famous, accompanied by innumerable thimbles, constantly refilled, of neat vodka. When I said I thought it was time we went to the theatre which we had planned, we found we were two and a half hours too late, we had talked so much. The only thing to do was to move to a table out on

the boulevard and drink more vodka. The night was still, and fragrant
with the smells of Paris; I felt I could hardly bear the thought of never
seeing the flat again. We reminisced about all the adventures we had
had, in which Place Vendôme had played so large a part for ten years;
the mischief we had got up to; the summer evening when Yvonne
Printemps had sung so divinely that all the other open windows in the
courtyard had filled with faces listening to the lyrical sounds; the night
Grace Moore stuck her tongue out at Marlene behind Marlene's back,
and much much more. Though not actually crying into our vodka, we
had drunk far too much and become bleary when Noel said, 'Now we
must stop all this. Who do we think we are, Madame Ranevsky?
Regrets are useless: no more looking back, on to the next thing. We've
had good times and they're over that's all, and we shall have others.
Let's just be thankful we've been so lucky.'

From Paris, Noel went to Florence for the first and only time in his
life, to stay with Derek Hill, in Derek's cottage at the end of Bernard
Berenson's garden. But the weather turned chilly, there was no central
heating, and Noel caught cold. In London I received a cable: HAVE
MOVED HOTEL EXCELSIOR COUGHING MYSELF INTO A FIRENZE.
His cold got better and he dutifully 'did' the Pitti and the Uffizi. But
Florence had no real message for him, and before he left, Derek
received a finger-wag: 'For a young painter like you to try to paint
here surrounded by all these simpering Madonnas is like someone
sitting in Rumpelmeyer's trying to make fudge.'

Noel could not wait to get back to Jamaica and the sun. There had
for some time been a sad scare that Edward Molyneux might be losing
the sight of his 'good' eye, which caused him constant pain. Afraid of
over-tiring it, he sold the business of his famous *maison de couture* in the
rue Royale, though his name and the premises were retained. He had by
now become an extremely good painter and painting was his greatest
joy, but even that had to be abandoned, and he seemed at an absolute
loss to know what to do with himself. Doctor Jamaica had become
Noel's cure-all for every ill, so he took matters firmly in hand and
Edward sailed with him in the *Liberté* on December 8th. But no good
deed goes unpunished; Edward had brought a party of friends with
him who yapped and squabbled to an extent that, after only two days at
sea, Noel felt he would rather he were going to Hull to stay with the
Littlers. They would ruin his lovely smiling Jamaica for him. An eye-
specialist in New York pronounced that there was little wrong with
Edward's eye beyond over-strain, and that he might even paint again in
moderation. Immense relief all round; but Jamaica let Noel down

badly. The arrival in sheets of pouring rain at Blue Harbour was disastrous, the long path from the garage to the house had become a muddy swamp through which they had to trudge, and after Edward had been settled in the guest house he later reappeared soaked to the skin and announced that to look over his verandah railing gave him vertigo, that if there were any sun he couldn't sit in it, the one thing he could not stand was the sound of the sea, and to crown all he hated bananas. Everything was wrong, and nothing was right for Noel either—even his expensive new sea wall to the bathing beach didn't work; it had brought in a great deal of sand, as the builders had promised, but it had also kept out the water. On the whole he kept his temper for the next few weeks, the strain alleviated by the two young members of the party, who soothingly watered down angry messages and notes between Noel and his friend of such long standing. Christmas Day passed with just enough good will to ensure that nobody flew at anybody. Happily, before they left, Edward had fallen in love with Jamaica and ultimately built himself a splendorous house at Montego Bay, in the grounds of which, except for the grass, all was white and pale yellow from the beds of flowers to the dustbins. Also before leaving, he prodigally gave Noel the present of a tropicalised grand piano, on which Noel worked and played happily in the years to come.

The run of *Ace of Clubs* ended on January 6th, 1951, and three days later Graham flew out to join Noel at Blue Harbour. A few weeks after that I, in London, received a letter:

Dearest Tolette, I have decided in my fluffy little mind that it would be well worth the spondulicks expended if you were to come out and be a comfort to your aged Master on account of I feel a certain lack of spiritual nourishment without you. Also the new lilos that Doycie sent me are much easier to fall off than the other ones and I long to open my lattice and watch you being constantly dashed against the reef. Niki [de Gunzburg] will be coming and also perhaps Marlene, so just you go snaking up to the hard-faced Mrs Loraine and keep on hissing in her ear, 'Master wants Toley and money's vulgar anyhow', until by sheer persistence you wear her down.

This was my initial taste of the tropics. Graham and Noel met me at the airport, and I can clearly remember my first drive across the island, over two ranges of mountains to Port Maria, Noel driving. Sensational hairpin bends; the myriad greens of the sometimes jungly vegetation;

the vivid young green of waving bamboo; the viridian of banana leaves made iridescent (I learnt later) with pale blue anti-pest spray; all this occasionally splashed with the orangey scarlet flowers of the tulip trees, or the white foam of waterfalls. Noel pointed out all the beauties and the landmarks with an almost proprietory pride: 'This river is called the Wag Water,' he told me as we crossed a long ungainly metal bridge. 'But there's no water,' I said, 'it's dried up completely!' 'Like Ellen Terry,' he said.

I took to the life at Blue Harbour from the first. All day long, until one dressed up to go out in the evening, we and any guests lived in a state of undress next to naked. A small towel round the waist sufficed, to be shed immediately one reached the bottom of the garden, the more to enjoy the delights of sunbathing, and above all swimming, wearing nothing at all. Thus unclad, on my very first morning I slid off one of Joyce's lilos to which I clung upside down while the waves went on washing it and me against some jagged volcanic rock. Although I was drowning, no one came to help, but at last I made sense out of all the shouting and stood up to find that the water came to just below my knee. I had quickly fulfilled the wish Noel had expressed in his letter, and of course he flew to his lattice when he heard the shouting to watch and enjoy the drama, just as he had hoped.

The evenings were in sharp contrast; after a rest and a cool shower we peacocked in shirts patterned in bright tropical colours, the cotton woven and printed in Manchester, bought in Port Maria and made up locally for a shilling or two. Every evening, usually with Noel demonic at the wheel—we drove with our guests—Rosamond Lehmann, or Larry and Vivien, or Lynn and Alfred, or Natasha and Jack—back and forth along the North Coast to cocktail and dinner-parties with friends who owned pleasant and comfortable houses on neighbouring plantations. Running through this year of 1951, and for many years to come, was the happy fact that Ian and Ann, soon to be joined by James Bond, were just along the coast at Goldeneye.

Jamaica was booming, it had become 'the' place to holiday in the winter—Noel, Ian and Ann and their friends heading the post-war pioneers—and hotels began to spring up all along the North Coast. Oliver Messel was staying at Jamaica Inn, happy as the day was long at his easel, painting portraits of the Jamaicans against tropical foliage, so enchanting that Noel bought one and Oliver gave him another for good measure. Agnes de Mille was among Noel's troop of fascinating visitors, and we saw a great deal of Roald Dahl, accompanied the following year by the ravishing Patricia Neal, soon to become his wife.

Pat taught us to cut off the top quarter of green coconuts, fill the rest of the nut and its soft white flesh with lamb, prawn or chicken curry, seal the top on again with a paste of flour and water and stick the whole thing in the oven for as long as you like. Marvellous for picnics; when the top is removed, even after several hours, the delicious inside has retained its piping heat. We became so mad about this dramatic looking dish that Noel named it Cocomania.

Errol Flynn, his lovely young wife Patrice Wymore, and his yacht — he called her a schooner — the *Zaca*, were along the coast in the other direction at Port Antonio. Joycie and Niki de Gunzburg were staying at Blue Harbour; Niki and Errol were playmates of old and we were all asked over. First of all, drinks under striped awnings on the deck of the *Zaca*, beautiful in the evening light. Then we went ashore to feast on one of the coral beaches of Errol's own island; the table covered with jade-green banana leaves, decorated with scarlet hibiscus, gleaming with candles and silver and crystal, and a baby sucking-pig slowly roasting over a pit in the sand a few yards away. When an enormous moon came up out of the sea, everything seemed too much: it was piling Pelléas on Mélisande, Noel said. Joycie and I had not met Errol before and I don't know what we had expected, but all four of us agreed on the way home that, in spite of all we had read, he was one of the most charming, kind and courteous hosts we had ever known. If only he had lived longer; the kind, civilized man is revealed in parts of the autobiography he left behind him, but he was no longer with us to receive the praise.

All this gaiety notwithstanding, Noel worked away every morning like a beaver. He wrote the verses which make the links between the songs on the album of *Conversation Piece* and flew up to New York for a few days to record them. Lily Pons sang Melanie's songs and arias, and the part of the young leading man was spoken by Richard Burton. Even as long ago as 1951 two hundred dollars was a pittance to Richard and he told his agent to refuse it. His telephone rang — Noel was always one for the direct approach — and he heard the firm tone in the well-known voice: 'You will do it for two hundred dollars and like it,' and Richard did it. Whether he liked it I don't know, but Noel was very fond of Richard, had admired him as an actor from the beginning, and his voice on the record remained for Noel a source of pleasure. After Noel's routine morning stint, he came down to the beach at noon and we would go through the mail while we soaked up the sun. (Once four long pages of dictation blew irrecoverably out to sea and he was very angry indeed: the letters all had to be dictated a second time and were much shorter and sharper in tone.) On March 23rd, which he described as *very* Good Friday, he came down to the beach bubbling over with an idea for a play which refused to be suppressed; Joycie was still there and greatly helped with working out the construction of *Relative Values*. Noel's firm determination to write fiction and not get involved with the turmoil of the theatre went into sudden reverse; a few days later he exclaimed, 'Oh, the bliss of writing dialogue after trying to struggle with prose!' He also wrote the lyrics and music for a song, 'Don't Make Fun of the Fair'; by the end of April he had finished the first draft of the play and it was time for us unwillingly to leave Blue Harbour, Noel on a round of visits in the Bahamas, and Joycie and I London-bound.

Spring in London that year was a lively one: it was the year of the Festival of Britain, Kay Thompson was back at the Café de Paris, plans were well afoot for *The Lyric Revue*, and the last two events were for us inextricably entwined. Kay Thompson had come into our lives the year before with the velocity of a rocket when she opened at the Café, backed by four talented young singers and dancers, the Williams Brothers, one of whom was before long to become the world-famous Andy. Kay's angular elegance and grace have already been mentioned, her legs so long they seem to have been put on above her waist; then there was her yellow hair scraped back flat and ending in a pony tail held by an elastic band, and the extreme thinness of her gothic face somehow transmuted into beauty. Everything about her quick as a flash—singing, dancing, piano playing and the extraordinary language in which she spoke; it was as if (if I may borrow the key word from Kenneth Tynan) she communicated in morse.

She had a flat round the corner at Chesham Place, came at weekends to White Cliffs and as good as lived with us at Gerald Road, where she flew to the piano to improvise and compose and ate nothing except very thin slices of bread burnt black, piled thick with Tiptree jam. We went to see Kay and her cabaret act every night we could, so that by the time Noel appeared there the Café de Paris and its matchbox dressing-room had already become a second home.

Graham was in any case in the cast of *The Lyric Revue* and had also written the music for one of the songs, 'This Seems to be the Moment', for which I wrote the lyrics; Noel's 'Don't Make Fun of the Fair' proved to be one of the funniest numbers, and Kay composed 'Lucky Day', with brilliantly fast choreography especially for Graham, one of the hits of the show. So we were all involved in the revue and its fate. The cast were young and highly talented—Dora Bryan, Joan Heal,

Irlin Hall, Ian Carmichael, Myles Eason, Jeremy Hawke and the rest, and everything was roses until the show went on the road and flopped miserably. What few people came didn't laugh at the sophisticated jokes, resulting in torture for both actors and audience. At one lowest-ebb matinée in Cardiff, John Perry, who had produced the show, heard one woman utter the dire words, 'You can see they've gone to a lot of trouble. But I don't know ... ' From the moment the curtain went up on the opening night in London however, a heady smell of success was in the air, and the revue ran for so long that, although the royalty from my one lyric was tiny, well before the end I could afford to buy my first (and my last) gold cigarette-case.

The Theatrical Garden Party took place in June and for the first time Noel forsook his role of the tail-coated, silk top-hatted President signing autographs and auctioneering. Instead he gave a series of twelve half-hour concerts, almost non-stop, in a tent with a placard saying, NOEL COWARD AT HOME. Norman Hackforth, his friend and trusty accompanist through the three months of wartime charity concerts in South Africa, and ever to be relied upon through the discomforts of many a troop concert in Ceylon, Assam and Burma, was at the piano. It was like old times for them both and Noel enjoyed himself: 'My shows were happily triumphant and all of them rapturously received.' Lornie was again worrying over the low state of finances, and by the end of July Noel and Norman, encouraged by their triumphant Garden Party concerts, had agreed to open at the Café (at that time we all called it the Kafe) in October.

Noel had first appeared at the Café thirty-five years before with a girl called Eileen Denis, singing and dancing during dinner and supper, for which they each got two pounds ten a week. They performed a slow waltz, a tango and he said, 'a rather untidy one-step. Later, owing to popular demand (from Eileen Dennis's mother) we introduced a pierrot fantasia.' He had decided to strengthen their act still further with a solo number by himself; he came on with great zest and all the brashness of his sixteen years and then, after only one chorus, forgot his words completely, tapered off into a string of ever fainter la-la-la's and made a very tame exit. He emerged from the kitchens (where he had to dress, Miss Dennis occupying the matchbox) to hear a bewildered colonel-type diner say, 'What an extr*ordnry* young man that was. Nothing but la-la-la: I can't get over it!'

The Café de Paris was one of the most perfect rooms in the world for cabaret — the size, the luxurious décor and furnishings, its oval shape, all were exactly right. The performer was happily placed and so was the

audience; its tables close enough, though not too close, to embrace him
or her on three sides. Best of all, from street level, two gracefully curv-
ing staircases ran down to right and left of the small stage, and these
were a gift to the performers who knew how to use them to advantage
—Marlene and Noel were the best exponents, with, to my mind,
Hermione Gingold third. Hermione waited at the top until her
applause at last died down and then, with a warning finger to her lips,
said in a voice promising all kinds of wickedness, 'Hush! Hush!
whisper who dares! Old Mother Gingold is coming downstairs.'

Noel dramatically lost his voice on the afternoon before his opening
night on October 29th. John Musgrove, the best throat-specialist in
London, was called in and he, after 'pulling out my vocal chords and
twiddling about with them', equally dramatically forbade Noel to
utter one word until he was safely down on the stage on the stroke of
midnight. Who knew what would happen then? Only John seemed
confident. The crowded audience of course was unaware of the
impending drama, there was quite enough excited anticipation as it
was; more than a few people, we were well aware, were there expressly
to watch Noel come a cropper. The crush was terrific; the Café
glittered with celebrities, with Princess Margaret and Princess Marina
impressively heading the list.

Anyone who ever saw Mistinguette make one of her celebrated
entrances down those long flights of stairs at the Folies Bergère—and
Noel saw her many times—knows that she looked straight out front as
though the stairs didn't exist. Noel descended the stairs that night,
smiling as though he hadn't a care in the world and, like Mistinguette,
never once looked down. Once he was *bien descendu*, he opened wide his
arms as though welcoming the audience to a marvellous party, bowed
low and then, with a graciously modest gesture, silenced the applause.
John Musgrove's treatment, or some other magic, had done the trick.
From the moment he opened his trap, as he liked to put it, the sounds
that issued when he went into the medley of his most famous sentimental songs were surprisingly mellifluous. That afternoon's scare
apart, he was at this time singing better than he had ever done before,
cooing like a baritone dove, as Kenneth Tynan accurately described it.
Less percipient reviewers didn't know what to make of it; one paper
called it 'a shocking voice', but then went on to say that it held the
audience spellbound. Another critic made an ass of himself for ever by
saying that Noel massacred his own songs, when in fact (songs and
arias from operettas excepted) nobody has ever sung his songs as well
as he did himself. He excelled as was to be expected in the 'witty Noel

Coward' ones, their often outrageous couplets always allied to a pretty, charming or rollicking tune, but the excellence cannot be quite fully gleaned from the recordings alone; he had to be seen to be believed. Sometimes exuberant, slapping his thigh with glee as he prophesied that there were 'Bad Times Just Around the Corner', he more often used complete repose, so that only the slightest gesture, a sideways glance or a raised eyebrow, was needed to produce a devastatingly funny effect. He had immense variety: the unbelievable speed of 'Mad Dogs', the wistful melancholy of 'World Weary', and the terrible vehemence with which, in the last refrain, he forbade Mrs Worthington to put her daughter on the stage. He had learned years ago never to go on too long; thirty-five minutes and, with seeming reluctance, he left us, giving us a benign wave as he walked up the stairs. Of course he had to come back, sometimes down the other staircase just to make a change, to acknowledge the continuing applause and yells of bravo. And then, once more having to induce silence, he sang gently and really rather movingly:

> The party's over now
> The dawn is drawing very nigh
> The candles gutter
> The starlight leaves the sky ...

And that was that, forty-five minutes in all. For the next six weeks, every night became a Noel Coward first night; sables, ermine, jewels and celebrities abounded and there was never an empty table. In fact there were never enough tables. We didn't, as he asked us in the last song, hurry home to bed'; when we left, we left unwillingly, it had indeed been a marvellous party. Noel was back, right up there where he belonged, his first appearance in cabaret an overwhelming success. He had, as he had said he would when so many people thought him finished, 'popped up through another hole in the ground'.

Rehearsals started for *Relative Values* before Noel opened at the Café, and it became evident from the first that Gladys Cooper was going to make her biggest success in London since *The Shining Hour* nearly twenty years before. From their first skirmish during the famous Christmas party in Davos in 1922, and in between other, later skirmishes, a firm and enduring friendship had built itself up between Gladys and Noel, and this was now to be put to its severest test; Gladys could not learn her words and her part was enormously long. Especially in his comedy dialogue, not one of his carefully chosen words must be misplaced, or another word substituted, and to listen to Gladys stumbling became torture for Noel; counting rehearsals and the pre-London tour he suffered two and a half months of this torture. Gladys, with her many years of stardom and experience, seldom actually dried up, but filled in the many gaps with er, er, er, which was even more painful to his ear. We went up to the opening night in Newcastle, in agony because of her insecurity, though she herself flew brilliantly through the play with every outward sign of star-sized assurance, and so beautiful that Noel called her the Hag, or simply Hag. Theatres were packed all through the tour, but even as late as the week in Brighton, the list of Gladys's mistakes amounted during one performance to no less than twenty-eight, including when, instead of saying she was going into the study, she announced that she was going into the understudy. Good trouper that she was she rose word-perfect to the occasion of the first night in London, and she and the play got an ovation at the end. Next morning: 'Well, well, what a surprise! Rave notices. All, with the exception of the dear little Daily Mirror, enthusiastic and wonderful box office. This should mean a smash hit — very nice too.' Though never entirely forgotten, all was forgiven; Gladys remained his Darling Hag to the end, and there were no more skirmishes.

15

BACK TO GOLDENHURST

THROUGHOUT that year, 1951, with Lornie in London as always and Graham working happily away in *The Lyric Revue*, Noel stayed as many days of the week as he could at White Cliffs that spring and summer, and I suppose that period was the longest he and I ever spent alone together in England. Mornings were devoted religiously as always to work, very busy. After he had rewritten and polished *Relative Values*, he worked on the characters and construction of a romantic Victorian comedy for Alfred and Lynn (*Quadrille*), and then one evening at the end of an enjoyably heated discussion on modern art the idea came to him for *Nude with Violin*, an idea so good, we felt, that he had to drop everything else and get it down on paper while still fresh in his mind. As for me, Jean-Pierre Aumont had asked me to make the English adaptation of his comedy *L'Île heureuse*, which was a task not only congenial but thrilling, for it was intended as a vehicle in which his wife Maria Montez, then at the height of her fame as a film-star, was to make her début on the stage in London. Maria, in the leading role, was of course going to play a glamorous and temperamental film-star wearing gloriously beautiful clothes; everything about the enterprise promised excitement, and we even found a perfect title — *Stardust*. Noel read what I had written each day, generously helped with advice and some criticism, on the whole enjoyed what he read, and approved. The finished script was rushed to Jean-Pierre, who quickly telephoned that he and Maria were delighted with it and asked if he could pop over from Paris that very Saturday to discuss immediate plans. Then the unbelievable happened. There we were on the Friday evening expecting Jean-Pierre the next day when the papers arrived with 'the appalling news that poor Maria Montez died this morning. Apparently she fainted in her bath and was drowned. Poor Jean-Pierre will be demented.' My adaptation quite apart, the shock was great; he and Maria had been our friends ever since our first initiation into Ginette's circle in the Avenue Marceau.

Aside from this tragic calamity, those summer days at White Cliffs seem in retrospect to have been long and tranquil. Our pleasures were so gentle, reading and painting, that we quoted Jane Austen's 'You know how interesting the purchase of a sponge-cake is to me', and an outing to the movies became an event. From the screened advertisements at the Odeon we learned that Cadbury's Bournvita ensured sound and restful sleep and we faithfully drank it or Horlick's or Ovaltine, last thing every night, Noel sitting up in bed and wondering what his fans all over the world, who pictured him constantly sipping champagne, would think of the reality. Then we switched to slightly more sophisticated sleep-inducers, such as jasmine or mint tea, or tisanes of *tilleul* or *fleurs d'oranger*, when Noel would say, 'Let's have a Tisane for Twosane at half-past ten.' Noel had a great capacity for sleep always, a need for it, often sleeping ten or eleven hours a night, as well as the cat-naps he took in the afternoons when he could sink into deep sleep at will for half an hour or more. He loved supper in bed at the end of these White Cliffs days, the noise of the sea so close to his bed; 'a little eggy something on a tray', followed by no small quantity of chocolates from Charbonnel & Walker in Bond Street, 'Mr Coward's special mixture', all soft centred, half coffee and half vanilla with a sprinkling of rose and violet creams for variety.

We talked endlessly in the evenings, mostly about our current reading, arguing and exchanging views and opinions. It can be said that by now his taste in literature was formed for life, although it had always been catholic. There were always piles of the latest books published in England and America waiting to be read, novels and more especially biographies. His favourites of E. Nesbit were re-read annually and there were certain other books to which he constantly returned, of which Stefan Zweig's *Marie Antoinette* was one, and he also bought any and every other book about her. His reactions to the Zweig never varied: when about half way through he would say, 'I suppose Marie Antoinette was one of the silliest women who ever lived', and then expatiate on her silliness until he came to the flight to Varennes. From then on he became more and more moved by her increasing courage and sweetness of character in adversity, and finally by her unassailable dignity at her trial and execution. Noel coupled her with Mary Queen of Scots for silliness, but in the latter's case could find few if any redeeming features, yet tormented himself by reading every new book about her. Mary Baker Eddy also held an eternal fascination; he returned time after time to *Mrs Eddy* by E. F. Dakin and it never failed to rouse him from grudging admiration of her achievements to anger. 'Oh that wicked old woman, I suppose she has been responsible for more deaths than anyone except Hitler.' The story of her life is a dramatic one, which is undoubtedly why this book so attracted Noel, plus the powerful sway she exerted over so many people from her day to this, and finally the star quality she must have possessed, a quality which he endlessly tried to analyse. She also provided him with a lot of fun. Once when I was ill in bed he sent me some medicine with the following note: 'God is *Love*. There is *No Such Thing* as pain. It is all error and *Malicious Animal Magnetism* strongly laced with *Dialectic Materialism*. Under separate cover please find two Tuinals, two Amytals and one flacon of God is love there is no painkiller. I remain Yours in Science, Mrs Molesworth.' He also composed the following song, sung with gusto to a racy tune:

> Steady, steady, Mary Baker Eddy,
> You've got to play the final scene.
> Admit that it's distasteful
> To say that pain ain't painful
> What about some more morphine?
> In your great fight with sin, come
> Admit you made an income
> Far greater than your friend the Nazarene.
> Steady, steady, Mary Baker Eddy,
> *What* a saucy girl you've been!

His greatest heroine of all was Queen Elizabeth I, the person out of all the world's history he would most have liked to meet. 'I think we should have got on, don't you? I don't think I should have been frightened of her, I should have stood up to her and I think I could have made her laugh.' He admired everything about her; her splendour, courage, statesmanship, her love for England, and even her faults he transformed into cleverly cunning virtues. Her scholarship astounded him, and he loved the noble English of her letters. He could never read Neale's *Life* often enough, and later Elizabeth Jenkins's *Elizabeth the Great*; in fact he saturated himself with reading not only about the Queen, but all who surrounded her, the Cecils, Essex, Leicester and especially those courtiers who so miraculously combined their dashing navigation or soldiery with the art of lyrical poetry. Of these Sir Philip Sidney and Sir Walter Raleigh were his favourites; sometimes he over-

did his reading until he couldn't resist a nonsense parody of the lovely
stuff he had just read:

After a Surfeit of Sir Philip Sidney

Oh womb from which hath 'merged
My true love chaste
By love hath not begat
My old time's waste.

Queen Elizabeth and Shakespeare, he idolised them both, the latter
becoming in fun 'my colleague Will'. He adored the Sonnets and knew
many by heart; he dutifully ploughed through all the plays, most of
them never to be ploughed through again, but constantly marvelling,
as who does not, at the miracles. 'She was a lass unparalleled,' for
example. 'What in God's name inspired him to choose the word
"lass" for the Queen of Egypt, and then to put it together with
"unparalleled"?' Noel thought people wasted an inordinate amount of
time trying to prove that Bacon wrote Shakespeare. He finally got this
verse off his chest as his own small protest at this silliness:

Christopher Marlowe or Francis Bacon
The author of *Lear* remains unshaken
Willie Herbert or Mary Fitton
What does it matter? The Sonnets were written.

The business was clinched once and for all by an American gentleman
with whom Noel was in absolute agreement. 'It is my belief,' he
declared, 'that the works of Shakespeare were written by William
Shakespeare himself and by nobody else. *Not even another man of the
same name.*'

Winifred somehow convinced Noel he must read Dickens; if he
could get through Proust, then it was certainly his duty to get through
all of Dickens. He took her advice, at first rather like a good little boy
doing his lessons, and then very soon finding that Dickens brought him
immense satisfaction and at some points made him laugh aloud. Some
of the novels became favourites, to be read over and over again, but he
did as he was bid and read them all, even *Little Dorrit.* 'What a horrid
girl, but what a wonderful novel!' he wrote in his diary the night he
finished it.

Winifred's most surprising command was that Noel should read the

King James Bible from cover to cover and, even more surprisingly, Noel obeyed her. This task took several weeks and I never knew what to expect over our cup of Bournvita. He hadn't got very far when he beseechingly asked if he really had to plod through all those 'begats' and I assured him that even Winifred wouldn't expect *that*. Then there were the nights when he had come across one of the stories in the Old Testament which appealed to his sense of humour, and he would say in a special Mayfair accent of his, 'My dear, I really *must* tell you about Susannah and the Elders. There was this *sweet* girl, up to her arse in dirty old men ... ' More often, though, he was struck by the magnificence of the language and would say, 'Listen to this!' and read aloud the passage which had captured him by its beauty. Again he enjoyed the incongruity of the popular conception of Noel Coward and the reality; reading the Bible and drinking Bournvita.

Another very favourite author was Anthony Trollope; here I could not follow him, agreeing with V. S. Pritchett (I think) who said that reading Trollope was like walking down endless corridors of carpet, but Noel devoured the novels time and again, with great pleasure. Oscar Wilde irritated him beyond endurance, yet, as with Mary Queen of Scots, he bought and read every biography and memoir as they appeared and tormented himself all over again. As for the trial itself, the stupidity of everyone's behaviour—from Oscar Wilde, Lord Alfred Douglas and Lord Queensberry to the judge, jury, the press and the public—nearly drove him mad. The brilliant wit of the plays of course appealed strongly to Noel, it was very much his own kind of wit; but the physical appearance and the character of Oscar Wilde repelled him. He was someone whom Noel would *not* have liked to meet, he said. The very idea of someone 'holding' the luncheon table with their wit until half past four was the antithesis of Noel's quick, short, spontaneous and unexpected comments, and he felt sure that Oscar Wilde's being consciously witty for hours on end would have bored him to death. Nevertheless he pressed on:

> I read the unexpurgated *De Profundis*. Poor Oscar Wilde, what a silly, conceited, inadequate creature he was, and what a self-deceiver. It is odd that such brilliant wit should be allied to no humour at all. I didn't expect him to enjoy prison life and be speechless with laughter from morning to night, but he might have had a little warm human joke occasionally, if only with the Warder. The trouble with him was that he was a Beauty Lover, a podgy pseudo-philosopher.

Then there were the everlasting piles of new books of all kinds waiting to be read, one or two towers of them always leaning Pisa-like on his bedside table, promising who knew what delights. He hated who-dunits, but loved good thrillers—Eric Ambler, Helen MacInnes, John le Carré—a love dating from E. Phillips Oppenheim and Sax Rohmer in his early youth. He tried to keep abreast of new trends and up to a point succeeded, but 'pornography bores me, squalor disgusts me', he wrote, and the pleasures of modern poetry—if such there are—evaded him. T. S. Eliot at one point said he doubted that Mr Coward had ever spent one hour in the study of ethics; 'What has that got to do with the price of eggs?' Noel wanted to know. He tried to read Eliot and other moderns and derived no benefit from them; though he enjoyed *The Cocktail Party*, he marvelled that anyone lacking the magic of the Elizabethan playwrights should go to the extraordinary bother of putting a play into so-called blank verse, only to put the actors to the still further bother of having to make it sound like colloquial speech. One explanation was proffered by a friend of ours, Michael Barber, who was appearing in a play by an imitator of Eliot's: 'I don't think he meant it to be blank verse,' he said, 'it isn't. I think he happens to have a narrow typewriter.' Of course Noel seized on this and liked to think that a narrow typewriter accounted for a lot of the rot he saw, without rhyme, reason or scansion, in otherwise intelligent magazines. For real poetry of the kind that brings the shiver of wonder and delight, Noel returned with relief to trusty Wordsworth, Keats, Meredith and Matthew Arnold.

He lamented that no new writers of the stature of Henry James, Edith Wharton and Scott Fitzgerald (he tired of Hemingway early) had emerged since them in America, nor any poets to equal Edna St Vincent Millay and Emily Dickinson. On the other hand, he immensely enjoyed the big fat modern America novels with narrative quality, such as *The Caine Mutiny*, all Irwin Shaw's best-sellers, and up to *The Godfather*, the last he read; the kind you 'couldn't put down'. Of course he couldn't resist making fun of some examples and he had James Gould Cozzens's vastly over-rated *By Love Possessed* in mind when he wrote the following: 'A modern novel can be forgiven anything providing it is long enough and this, on the American market at least, has been triumphantly proved. Acres of words, regardless of their content, closely printed on seven to eight hundred pages and bound handsomely in heavy cloth, can hardly fail to remain on the Best Seller lists for several months.' A special target for his fun was certain American lady novelists with triple-barrelled names, which he regarded as fatal even before he started to read their books. They could be relied upon to butcher the English language he said; he cringed at every split infinitive, and said of one that she should have her 'overly's' removed.

Noel had his own difficulties as author and composer. Here are a few notes taken from his diaries, which dispel the legend of the 'facility' for which he had become famous:

> I am writing daily ... letting myself wander about at will. It can all be revised and shaped later. It is astounding, this passion for writing, and I wonder how it came about that I was born with it. It is a strange, austere, satisfying happiness and hell hard work at the same time ... Made a little progress musically today but my mind and hands feel heavy. I know nothing so dreary as the feeling that you can't make the sounds or write the words that your whole creative being is yearning for ... A frustrating day. I only did two pages and sat and stared at the typewriter.

We had six very happy years at White Cliffs, but on July 2nd, 1951, Noel wrote:

> I sat in the sunshine with the beach crowded with people and dogs barking and children yelling. I tried to paint—gave it up and went to bed. I decided that I am going to give this up and go back to Goldenhurst. It is my own land and so much quieter. I shall miss the sea and the ships but I shall have the Marsh and the trees, the orchard and the croquet lawn. White Cliffs has given me immense pleasure but ... there is something curiously distracting about it; someone crunches by on the beach or a big ship passes and one's concentration snaps.

Noel swung into action immediately, and so did everybody else. The next four months were beset with the same frustrations we had endured when moving in to White Cliffs; permits were still necessary for repairs and alterations, and the Army's depredations since the requisitioning in 1940 had reduced the lovely house to a sorry state. Patience Erskine, kind friend of many years, had occupied Noel's suite of rooms with her two dogs since the Army had finally evacuated, and that was all. Patience had taken care of the very large house, the garden and the grounds—she is a gardener by nature and from deep-rooted love of it—but the thought of getting at least thirty rooms shipshape from their stark and war-scarred condition was daunting.

No matter, I was as excited and eager as Noel at the thought of 'coming home'. Goldenhurst really was home, which White Cliffs never quite had been, and we would end our days there ... we thought. Patience moved into a caravan parked near the pond until the pleasant rooms over the garage were converted into a flat for her, and we all worked with a will. The only people who didn't bestir themselves were the bestowers of permits, until Noel became incensed at their dreary delays. After all, for his house to have sheltered the Army for so long came under the heading of helping the War Effort; surely his country would not now prevent him restoring it? It was his house and he was bloody well going to do what he wanted and move in before Christmas. There was one particular grumpy old devil in the local council offices who seemed to be the stumbling block, so Noel decided to go and beard him behind his desk, using 'the well-known Coward charm'. To our astonishment this ogre turned out to be a young man in his twenties. Noel tactfully invited him over for a drink, to see for himself the amount of work that must be done. After his second glass of sherry, 'I set about him. He is rather nice really and curiously honest— he admitted to being jealous of people having things he could not have, and to an inferiority complex and a chip on the shoulder. He is a good English type really, trapped into small-town pettiness by circumstances. His war record was valiant and he has a flair for words. I think maybe I did him a bit of good.'

The permits were granted (though far from liberal) and Patience moved into her flat—known as The Lodge from now on—where one could rely on good talk, an abundant supply of Scotch whisky and a loving welcome. She now ruled her kingdom as head gardener, Old John and his brother Ted her lieutenants, soon joined by a Kentish lad, John Brooks. Young John adored Patience, and indeed helped and served her faithfully until he died too young, twenty years later. For the next weeks we all mucked in, including Noel at weekends, wielding paintbrushes, staggering under the weight of innumerable books, and hanging pictures. Noel succeeded in getting his way against all the odds —at midnight on December 15th, the last night of his season, he descended the stairs at the Café de Paris, the band played 'Happy Birthday to You', the crowded audience stood up and sang 'For He's a Jolly Good Fellow', cheered him three times three, and the next day he moved back in to Goldenhurst. 'Probably the nicest birthday I have ever had—the house and land seemed to envelope me in a warm and loving welcome.' On December 31st, he wrote: 'It has been on the whole a good year. There have been the successes of the Lyric Revue, the Café de Paris, Relative Values and the return to Goldenhurst. Let us hope that 1952 will be as amiably disposed.'

Noel had been a sympathetic conspirator from almost the beginning of the romance between Ian Fleming and Ann Rothermere. He loved them both, dearly. In the early days, when secrecy had been essential, everyone closely concerned had pretended that Ann was staying at Blue Harbour when she was not, and since then — caution as good as blown to the winds — they had been, both literally and in terms of friendship, our closest possible neighbours at White Cliffs. With our move back to Goldenhurst, Ian took over the lease of White Cliffs itself, though not without the abusive banter between him and Noel to which we had long become accustomed; Ian as usual ramming home the squalor of Noel's residences, in this case the dustbins at the front entrance, and souvenirs such as the limp wire-netting, now rusty, which had once housed our featherless hens.

Dear Ian, As our two solicitors seem to have completely divergent views regarding the matter about which you wrote ... and as we offered to leave the bookshelves and you particularly asked us to remove them I am using the good old British plan of compromise and enclose a cheque for Fifty Pounds. If you do not want it I can give you a few suggestions as to what to do with it when you come to lunch on Sunday. With regards and also with smacking great kisses. Cordially, Noel Coward.

On March 24th, 1952, Ian and Ann were married at the Town Hall, Port Maria. Noel and I were their witnesses, and the two of us alone constituted the congregation. We took our duties very seriously; wore ties (unheard-of for Noel in Jamaica) with formal white suits, our pockets full of rice, and got to the Town Hall early. We attracted a crowd of six and a smiling though toothless black crone who entertained us with some extremely improper calypsos, including one called 'Belly Lick'. Then the happy couple arrived, Ian wearing one of his blue linen, belted, moujik-like shirts, and Ann in eau-de-nil by Dior, or rather a copy by the local dressmaker. No photographer, alas, recorded the occasion. The Town Hall is large and lofty, and was then dominated by a big oleographic reproduction of Winston Churchill, surly, glowering and obviously disapproving of the whole proceedings, and from the beginning we were all attacked by giggles. The Registrar had such terrible breath that Ann and Ian kept their heads averted as they made their vows, and as they passed us on our way to sign the register Ian muttered, 'Try to keep upwind of him.' The ceremony concluded, and after an animated argument, Noel and I decided that we should have to precede the bride and groom in order to throw our rice over them as they emerged, but by this time we had lost all control and it wasn't until we reached Blue Harbour for what Ian called *le vin d'honneur* that we found out Noel had tied the old shoe to the bumper of his own car. *Le vin d'honneur* took the form of dry martinis without anyone having to ask, except that Ian insisted, as 007 was later to insist (had already insisted if only we'd known) that they be made 'without bruising the gin'. We later repaired to Goldeneye, plus Niki de Gunzburg, for the wedding breakfast—dinner by that time—the menu carefully chosen by Ian in collusion with Violet, but he wasn't allowed to get away with a thing. Noel compared the turtle, which Ian was so proud of having caught, with chewing an old Dunlop tyre, and the delicious black crab served in its shell as exactly like eating cigarette ash out of an ashtray. He had more reason to criticise the wedding-cake, made of unidentifiable ingredients and covered with viscous pale green icing, but Violet peeked through the door to observe our enjoyment of her creation and heard him comparing the icing to bird-lime and saw Niki, with the skill of a bricklayer, plastering his slice back into position in the cake. By this time we were beyond caring and, as Noel reported, 'we sat there speechless with laughter and the tears running down our faces.' He had composed a calypso especially for the occasion, one chorus of which ends

> Hey for the blowfish, blowfish,
> Ho for the wedding ring
> Hey for the Dry Martinis, old goat fricassee, Old Man's Thing.

The festivities ended that night with Ian preparing Old Man's Thing, a ritual reserved for high occasions such as this. There was much of the schoolboy still in Ian, and in Noel, and at the very mention of Old Man's Thing they always started to laugh. A crockery punchbowl was fetched from the kitchen, into which Ian peeled an orange and a lime (or a lemon will do), never failing to peel the rind in one long spiral; a point of honour with him. Then over these two whorls he poured a bottle of crude white rum of appalling potency and, in the dark, set the whole thing alight to cheers from the company. When the flames died down we drank the strong concoction with many toasts to their happiness, finally reeled to our car, and Noel miraculously drove us home through the dark night without accident. Ian and Ann left next morning for New York, Ian with the script of a novel called *Casino Royale* safe among his luggage.

Goldenhurst and White Cliffs were not too far apart and, once back in England, all through that summer and autumn there was much to-ing and fro-ing, Noel delighted to find he could happily revisit White Cliffs unclouded by nostalgia. Ann and Ian often brought their guests to Goldenhurst for rather rowdy meals on Sunday evenings; guests such as Somerset Maugham, Evelyn Waugh, Cyril Connolly, Cecil Beaton or Peter Quennell. Mr Maugham no longer held any terrors for me, but I was nervous of meeting Evelyn Waugh for the first time. 'What would you like to drink?' I asked. 'Something I'm sure Noel hasn't got,' and then, surprisingly, 'some sweet Martini.' Only a few days before, Noel had berated the butler for ordering a bottle, and told him he never wished to see the stuff in his house again. 'Of *course* he has,' I was pleased to be able to say. Towards the year's end Noel drove over alone to see Ann and Ian and records his pleasure at finding them so happily married, and at being asked to stand as godfather to their son, Caspar Leander Fleming.

Noel finished *Quadrille*, his Victorian comedy for the Lunts, earlier in the year, and it proved to be a great success on the road. Lynn and Alfred loved the play, were very happy in it and both gave brilliant performances. Cecil Beaton designed beautiful sets and exquisite clothes; he still thinks one of the sets in particular among the best he has ever done. The play was due to open in London at the Phoenix Theatre on September 12th.

Saturday, September 6th was a day that started gaily and ended in misery. The gay part was going to Folkestone Races where we had great fun, backed several winners, and drank rather a lot of cherry brandy. We also, naturally, had to back a horse called Bitter-Sweet, running in the first race at a course somewhere in the north of England. After the last race I ran to get an evening paper to find out if Bitter-Sweet had won, turned to the back page, and in the Stop Press was stupefied to read in large black letters: GERTRUDE LAWRENCE DEAD. Noel's grief was dreadful to see, his face ashen during the drive home, and once at home he broke down completely. The telephone was ringing and never stopped ringing for the rest of the day, the press of the world agog to know what he had to say. But what could he say; he couldn't have got the words out even had he been able to find them. Fanny Holtzmann rang from New York incoherent, only managing to get out that Gertie had known she was dying and had asked for Noel.

He told Fanny he could not fly to New York for the funeral, it would be too much for him, unbearable. Then he did promise *The Times* that he would write an obituary, a task to which he sat down immediately at his folding table by the fire in the library, at moments unable to see the paper for the tears which he had to brush away. When Noel had last seen her in New York there had been pressure brought to bear for her to leave *The King and I,* and he had tried to induce her to come to London and appear in *South Sea Bubble,* which as we know he had written specially for her, but she had refused out of loyalty to the rest of the cast. (She never knew that there had been complaints from audiences about her singing so poorly, which we now painfully realised had arisen because she was so near to death.) Gertie's last letter to Noel of a few days before was fresh in our minds – of course she wouldn't be able to come to the preview of *Quadrille* in aid of the Orphanage, but sent a cheque instead, wished that she could be with us all and see the new play. Her letter ends: 'So, it seems that there is not too much to worry about – I just struck a bad patch and you came and sat in it!' Then the last words ever from Gertie to Noel: 'Oh dear – and it's always you I want to please more than ANYONE.'

The emotions of the following days are so mixed and so many that they were and still are impossible to separate; Noel had to swallow them as they were, in a dreadful sort of lump. We soon learned that it was from cancer of the liver Gertie had died, and at this same time Noel's cousin, Doris Dalton, lay in Guy's Hospital, overthrown by the same disease. The only cousin Noel had remained close to and fond of, Doris was attractive and kind, of exactly the same age as Gertie, and we were now aware that their fatal courses would run parallel. Doris lasted little more than two weeks longer: 'Went to see Doris in the hospital, she is more or less unconscious. Her face looked very peaceful with all the lines ironed out. No fear or conflict and the Sister assured me that there was no question of the slightest pain. Approaching death is a curious spectacle – in this instance touching rather than agonising.'

Then there was the first night at the Phoenix hanging imminently over Noel and Lynn and Alfred, from all points of view made painful by Gertie's death when it should have been the joyful occasion for which they had planned, worked and looked forward to for more than a year. Lynn and Alfred sent Noel no message of sympathy; instead they seemed to find his grief excessive, and it is not difficult to see why. For years they had heard from Noel what a bore Gertie could sometimes be, how silly she could be, and above all how often she had committed the, to them, unforgivable sin of badly over-acting to the point of driving Noel mad. They knew how often he had passed through New York without even calling Gertie. They did not seem to realise, perhaps they had never known, that underneath all this she had remained his darling old Gertie who never did a mean or unkind thing, that he had loved her since he was twelve and he always would. Lynnie, with her own ordeal of opening in a play by Noel facing her, was bewildered and hurt to read in *The Times* what he had written of Gertie: 'No one I have ever known, however brilliant and however gifted, has contributed quite what she contributed to my work.' Lynn and Alfred, needless to say, did try their best to understand. After the last preview Alfred, after apologising for muddling a minor laugh of Lynn's, asked Noel why he was still so unhappy. Noel explained that he had heard that Gertie had suffered much pain before she died and that he had been torn apart by the whole thing. Alfred then put his arm round Noel to comfort him and told him that they were specially making him his favourite chocolate cake as a first-night present on the morrow. Noel understood completely all Alfred meant by this, and from then on misunderstandings began to melt away.

Twenty-two years before, Noel and Gertie had triumphantly opened the Phoenix Theatre with *Private Lives*, and packed it six years later with *Tonight at Eight-Thirty*. Now Noel had to sit through the first night of *Quadrille* in the same theatre, haunted by memories and ghosts. He was glad when the curtain fell. It fell to tremendous applause and cheers, the play he felt was unquestionably a success, and Binkie's party at Lord North Street afterwards was very gay and enjoyably optimistic. The press next morning were unanimous in their praise of the Lunts and in their abuse of the play itself, which they viciously tore to pieces. This Noel found 'very interesting. We are virtually sold out until Christmas.' He popped into the Phoenix two nights later, where he found everyone in fine form, the business fabulous, and was told that audiences loved it and gave it a wonderful reception at the end.

Quadrille has faults; the plot is somewhat static, a variation on *Private Lives* with less of that play's wit and sparkle, and precariously thin in places. It is also over-written; Noel had become more than a little drunk on words, perhaps influenced, one cannot help wondering, by all the 'good writing' he had lately been absorbing, as already described. Ian Fleming warned him of this, tried to tell him how dangerous it was. Noel's style was unique, and for him to read 'better' writers would either result in an inferiority complex or, worse still, in an attempt to write 'better' himself, and perhaps this last was what Noel had unconsciously done. (Ian said that he went so far as never to read a single book while engaged upon one himself.) This said, it is now difficult to see why that gentle play, at times touching, at others witty, should have aroused such malevolence as it did in certain quarters, especially in the *New Statesman*: written as a vehicle for the Lunts, it succeeded.

Noel did a second and equally successful season at the Café de Paris. Lena Horne was packing them in at the Palladium at about the same time. Noel went often to see her and she to see him; she and her husband Lennie Hayton were already old friends from Ginette's salon at Avenue Marceau. Lena seemed to be more beautiful and to be singing more wonderfully than ever, if two such impossibilities can be imagined. She and Lennie came back to Gerald Road one night, and after supper the telephone rang; we heard Noel say, 'Then get in a taxi and come round at once.' Gene Kelly came in ten minutes later, Carol Haney with him. Lennie, a fine musician, was already at the piano; Lena, cross-legged on the floor by the fireplace, soon began to sing, quietly though with her inborn potency and rhythm, and then, very gently at first, Gene began to dance. All three gradually and excitingly increased the use of their powerful talents until Gene was dancing up and down the steps of the dais, on the dais, over the chairs and all along the back of the big sofa. Magic filled the room, something that could never have been deliberately conjured up, something we all knew in our hearts could never happen again, something we never, never forgot.

All the Maughams now played a large part in our lives. Viscount Maugham, one-time Lord Chief Justice, by repute every bit as much a dragon as his brother, turned out to be a smiling, witty, dear old gentleman, at least when in Noel's company. Noel sat to daughter Honor for a portrait in pastels to be sold for charity, son Robin became our friend for life and, like everybody else who knew her, we adored their sister Kate Mary. On October 25th Noel wrote:

Four hours with Kate Mary and Honor, conversation very enjoy-able—the Maughams are a highly interesting family. When they had gone I began to imagine a play about a devoted, well-bred, professional-class family. It is time someone sang a small song in praise of the indestructible decency of 'nice people', neither aristocratic nor proletarian—just intelligent and well-educated, not only by schools but by their own ingrained tradition.

Noel had all his upper teeth extracted this November: he had, especially in the last few weeks, though in fact for the last few years, been suffer-ing much trouble and pain—something I could never understand, considering he went to one of the best and most expensive dentists in London. When this last long bout was to end in an operation under general anaesthetic at East Grinstead, he resolved to get rid of the lot. His mother had had all her teeth removed at the age of twenty-six and was still employing the same dentures supplied in 1889. Imagine: sixty-three years free from toothache, abscesses, dentist's chairs and dentist's bills! This fact greatly predisposed Noel to follow her example, an action he never regretted. He made no secret of his false teeth, told anybody who was interested all about them and was liable to take out his plate to show you how splendid it was. Years after, over lunch at the Colony in New York with Rex Harrison and Kay Kendall he did this and extolled to Rex the pleasures of a plate and its many advantages (without success, I think). But Mrs Roosevelt, while cleverly maintaining the conversation at her table alongside, visibly inclined to her right, cocked an ear and listened to Noel's praise of his clackers with absolute fascination. Noel came out of the anaesthetic at East Grinstead with his new teeth miraculously already in place, but at first had difficulty in speaking. Four days later there was great excite-ment in the press because a Communist on trial for his life in Prague confessed that Noel, while with Intelligence, had given him instructions to become a British agent. Noel longed to say to the press, 'Owing to a little dental trouble, my lips are sealed.'

Binkie tried to persuade Noel that it was his duty to do *something* to celebrate the coronation of Queen Elizabeth II in 1953. Noel protested that he had already promised to contribute to the festivities by again appearing at the Café de Paris, for two weeks before and two weeks after Coronation Day itself on June 2nd, and that would be quite enough, thank you. But Binkie was extremely skilled and experienced at planting seeds in people's minds. A little later he said he *thought* the Theatre Royal, Haymarket, would become available, well knowing that to Noel the Haymarket was the most perfect theatre in the world, not only from the audience's point of view, but a joy to act in. Besides, the 'Theatre Royal' appealed to Noel as sounding exactly right for this sovereign occasion. Then, over supper for two at 14 Lord North Street—Binkie's venue for clinching his plans, aided by many a well-filled glass—he produced a copy of Bernard Shaw's *The Apple Cart*, not with the air of a trump card but merely asking Noel to take it home and read it before he said No. Binkie was quite right, as he was about most things professional; Noel immediately saw himself as King Magnus.

The first thing to be done was to learn it, and our winter holiday in Jamaica was devoted in great part to this long task, for King Magnus is on stage for nearly the whole of the play. His very long speech in Act One Noel called 'a bit of a pill'—a phrase used by Joan Sutherland when we asked her what it was like having to sing the whole of *Norma*. After working on *Future Indefinite* until noon each morning (which he did too hurriedly; he had to write it all over again later in the year) he came down to the beach where I cued him and heard him declaim his lines until, as he said, there was not one seagull on the North Coast which couldn't have prompted him.

Two events of that Jamaican winter remain in the memory; the first is Mr and Mrs Winston Churchill's stay, not too far away at Prospect, Sir Harold and Lady Mitchell's flower-covered estate. Mrs Churchill came to Blue Harbour on the second evening, with her daughters Sarah and Mary and the latter's husband, Christopher Soames, and at her request we initiated her into the pleasures of Jamaican rum punch. This she found so delicious—ice-cold on a tropical evening—that she quickly asked for more and as quickly finished it, Noel and I a little worried, though we need not have been; the only result was a merry party. Noel wrote:

Mrs Churchill was very charming indeed. We had a long heart to heart which was fairly illuminating. She was honest about Randolph and, considering that she is his Mum, extremely trenchant. She loathes and has always loathed Max Beaverbrook who she says is malicious and loves giving pain. She very sweetly gave me a £30 order for 'Designs For Living' [Noel's own local charity]—the publicity of this will help the shop enormously. She also appeared genuinely impressed by my banana paintings, and carried a large one away with her, frame and all, to show to the Prime Minister.

The second happy memory is of Katharine Hepburn and Irene Selznick twice coming to stay for several days, sensationally arriving in an open sports-car, unheard-of then in Jamaica and still rare today. Up until then Noel had been firmly warned of the danger of sunstroke and made by his Jamaican friends to use a closed car. He soon followed Kate's lead and from then on always used open cars in Jamaica, for which, among other things, we have blessed her ever since. While Kate and Irene were with us Serena (our much-loved dog, of indeterminate

breed) gave birth to four puppies, Charlotte, Emily, Anne and Bran-
well. Emily took to Kate at once; Kate holding the fat little beige
sausage-roll in one hand while Emily gazed up adoringly at the famous,
beautiful face. Emily we kept always. Apart from her angelic character
she was, unlike her namesake, a born comic. Also she 'knew' everything, even spontaneously bringing an old, large mutton bone to be
placed among the presents on Joycie's birthday morning. Secretly as
we did our packing and hid the suitcases, she knew exactly when we
were leaving, as do some other dogs, but Emily, with supreme tact,
always disappeared into hiding the day before our departure, sparing us
and herself the sorrow of having to say goodbye.

Twenty-five years had passed since Noel had appeared in a play
(*The Second Man*) by an author other than himself. Of the first night of
the try-out of *The Apple Cart* in Brighton he wrote: 'Curiously enough
I was not nervous and this made all the difference. I intend never to
indulge myself in first-night nerves again. It is waste of time and
unnecessary. This is big talk but I am determined to strain every unnervous nerve to carry it through.' In this intent he succeeded, both at
the opening of the play on May 7th, and on the 26th, when he went on
from the Haymarket for his other first night at the Café de Paris. He
enjoyed the challenge of Shaw, in which he was greatly helped by
Michael MacOwan's direction; he was forever grateful for Michael's
indication that there is an underlying vein of sadness in King Magnus's
character. This gave Noel a key which he seized on, knowing full well
that he could handle the comedy side with ease. We are unlikely to see
a better production of *The Apple Cart* in our lifetime. The play surprised by its topicality, which with Shaw's defence of monarchy made
an aptly perfect choice for Coronation Year. Loudon Sainthill designed
three extravagantly beautiful sets, notably the opulent boudoir for
Margaret Leighton as Orinthia. Pierre Balmain created a stunning
confection for Margaret; it remains the design for the stage of which
he is most proud. The top was velvet of the clearest yellow; not being
able to find what he wanted for the voluminous skirt, he cut up his own
black-and-white zebra-striped bath-towels, new from New York; the
skirt he then overlaid towards the back with yards of turquoise
chiffon, all of which Margaret 'used' spectacularly well.

Margaret and Noel, happy to be together again, gave a firework
display of high-comedy acting which ended in a rough-and-tumble fight
on and off the enormous sofa. Loudon's set for the Terrace of the
Palace in the last act had more than a hint of twilight melancholy, of
which Noel took advantage, making the lonely weight of the crown

touchingly apparent. He looked attractive in his splendid dark-blue uniform, scored a personal triumph, and in many people's opinion gave the finest performance of his life. He liked to think that Shaw would have been pleased with him, and with the entire production. Noel as usual had something wrong with him, as he always had during the later half of his life when performing; this time acute lumbago caused, he thought, by pulling Margaret too violently over his shoulder during the try-out in Brighton:

> I have been living on codeine and Veganin and have had a physio-therapist to massage me and at last, at long long last, it is better. It really is maddening, with only two and a half weeks more to play ... I love acting and I love the Theatre but oh Christ, how people can play heavy parts for long runs I shall never know. I feel now, with the holiday stretching before me, as though a sky-light had been opened in my head.

Noel's holidays! As already hinted, they—especially the motoring ones—were packed with incident, usually of a disastrous nature, and this year provides a representative example. Here is Noel's version, telescoped for brevity. His Jaguar, of which he was proud, had been taken to a famous car firm off Piccadilly, which in turn, if memory serves, had sent it to the Jaguar people themselves for a thorough, complete and expensive overhaul, after which Noel could set out for a carefree holiday. After a diversion to the Jaguar factory at St Germain to get the hood fixed, Noel wrote from the Hotel de la Poste, Avallon:

> Well, the holiday started with a bang. The bang was at six yesterday evening when the back axle broke in half in front of a War Memorial. Today we hope a Jaguar expert will arrive with a new one, in the meantime we are stranded. Napoleon, on his way *from* Italy in 1815, stayed one night in this hotel; we, on our way *to* Italy, look like staying a bloody sight longer. There is no way of leaving except by an autobus to Dijon and we have far too much luggage to get on to an autobus anyhow. Yesterday was further complicated by Little Lad having an appalling attack of wind after eating Lobster Gâteau at Barbizon, made with a lot of cream and washed down with vin rosé, in such pain that he could not move. We hope that when he wakes [this morning] the wind will have subsided, if not he will have to hobble to the local hospital and have a nice enema ... [Next day] the new back axle duly arrived,

was affixed and we drove off, merry as grigs, at six p.m. The car went like a bird for an hour or so and then ejected clouds of steam and stopped. We limped along to a tiny wayside garage where it was discovered that the ventilator fan had not been greased and the rubber tube which supplied the engine with water had rotted! ... the garagist tinkered away for an hour, and off we went again to Geneva ... Hotel Palace, Montreux: A Victorian-Edwardian hotel, filled with heavy furniture and tortured woodwork. One can imagine Mrs Keppel lying about on chaises-longues while her faithful maid did her nails. The Jaguar returned to us looking shiny and a trifle self-conscious ... Castello di Urio, Como: Yesterday was definitely strained ... we drove without mishap to Brigue and over the Simplon, lunched in a scruffy hotel in Domo-dossola, after which we drove for fifty yards down the main street filled with Sunday traffic when there was a sharp grinding noise in the gearbox and the car refused to move forwards, backwards, or even sideways. In an inferno of hooting and imprecations we waited forty minutes until a garage man arrived with a truck, managed to jack up the Jaguar and tow it to the side of the road. After another forty minutes it was towed to a garage where we waited gloomily for two hours, then told the gearbox was hope-lessly jammed and could not be mended under twenty-four hours! We were fairly frantic, so we hired a Lancia and its driver, loaded all the luggage on to it and drove off at breakneck speed to Como, through, I believe, lovely scenery of which I saw little as I kept my eyes tight shut. The Jaguar we hope will be returned to us tomorrow or the day after. I am seriously thinking of suing the Jaguar people for negligence, irresponsibility, arson, slander, libel and sexual perversion.

Castello di Urio, Como, 16th August: The Jaguar returned to us with only a slight knock in the engine. In the house, in addition to our host [Paolo Langheim] there is a desiccated voluble gentleman who is the Chilean Chargé d'Affaires, married and has three children but travels with a boy friend who is pretty, young and fairly idiotic. He speaks French and Italian more quickly and violently than anyone I have ever met. We have, during the week, visited one Principessa and one Duchessa. The former was born Ella Walker in America and is fabulously rich. She was a friend of Mussolini and had to flee to Switzerland where she lived for two years in an elaborate clinique, without enough eggs. She is eighty-four, very chic, has forty-eight gardeners, twelve manservants, three cooks, one Tiepolo, one Guardi and two dim grand-nieces in white broderie Anglaise who seldom utter and are so comme il faut that it is difficult not to call them Ma'am.

The Duchesa Sermoneta lives on the top of a mountain in a small square house which she fondly imagines is in 'le style Anglais'. She is only about seventy, has had asthma for two years and is exceedingly grand. These rich, grand, drained old ladies belong to a past that is dead-O and sigh for the times that are past-O. La Sermoneta had as guests an elderly English queen (grey moustache, Corps Diplomatique, beauty-lover), his brother who is a Catholic priest (rather nice), and a startled young man fresh from Oxford with over-eager teeth. I don't know *what* he could have been doing there but I have my ideas. Mussolini, who of course they all bum-crawled to like mad, was caught and shot just near here on the border. He wasn't, however, hung upside down until they took him to Milan.

There is to be a Ball in Biarritz on Sept 1st, given by the Marquis de Cuevas. This is of tremendous social importance and is now in jeopardy owing to the general strike in France. Nobody can get in touch with anybody else to find out what costume Zuki, Norman, Nada and Nell will or will not wear. It is clearly understood that Titi Something-or-other is going as a red parrot, perched on the shoulder of someone else as Man Friday. Apart from this concrete information we have little definite to go on. The excitement is reaching fever-pitch and Chili Pom Pom [the Chilean *Chargé*] is beginning to show signs of strain. So, as a matter of fact, are we, and are leaving tomorrow for Lago di Garda.

By the time Noel got back to Goldenhurst the saga of the Jaguar's catastrophes had become a hilarious set-piece, with Graham's terrible wind after the Lobster Gâteau and the car's blowing up at the same time in the middle of the street as the highlight. Ian, wiping the tears from his eyes, begged Noel to tell it all over again, and not miss out a single detail, and brought his guests over on the following Sunday specially to hear it. Noel noted without comment, 'Cole looks sunburnt and well after a perfect holiday in the West Country during which the Hillman never went wrong once.' Soon after his return, Noel wrote:

This weekend there is no one here but Coley and me and it has been very restful. Last night we played my early records and I retired to bed inadequately lulled by the echo of my thin feathery voice and the realization that I am getting old. It is a curious sensation to listen to one's younger voice and to become suddenly aware of how swiftly the years march by. The songs I sang were sung twenty years ago, some nearly thirty. I tried to remember, listening to them, what was going on in my life at the time they were recorded, but I failed ... although there is a certain charm in my voice here and there and the phrasing, even then, is excellent, they are not really very satisfactory.

One boost to Noel's morale was provided by Erica Marx, our near neighbour, who had for some time been publishing the best of the young post-war poets, well printed on her Hand And Flower Press at Aldington. Her admiration for the literary aspect of Noel's work stood out from her all-round love of it, and she decided she must do something to help counteract the fairly low critical estimation then current. She commissioned young Robert Greacen, a critic and himself a poet, to write *The Art of Noel Coward*, and Erica's beautifully turned-out volume appeared this autumn of 1953. The assignment cannot have been an easy one for Mr Greacen at that particular moment, but he succeeded in writing a graceful tribute to Noel as an author of wide range. This naturally gave Noel pleasure; his one criticism being that perhaps Mr Greacen had not been critical enough, considering the prevalent climate of opinion.

16

AN ENGLISHMAN'S RIGHT

THE New Year of 1954 we saw in with the Douglas Vaughans at Brimmer Hall, Port Maria. During our absence a swimming pool had been built on the seashore at Blue Harbour, its length facing out to, and almost in, the ocean. Designed and built with local labour by Pat Marr-Johnson at the now unimaginably low cost of £450, it still stands solid, having withstood several earthquakes. Douglas announced at the New Year party that he proposed to show some home movies, to which Noel responded, 'Oh no you don't, home movies bore me to death. I'd rather lie down in the road and let a truck run over my head.' 'I think you'll be interested in this one,' Douglas said, and ran the movie in colour

> of a dolphin being devoured by sharks right in the enclosed part of my beach. This was startling because I have until now subscribed to the blind, comforting faith that *no* big fish could get through the reef. Actually there were about a dozen sharks and the dolphin itself ... and on the flat sandy bit where we always bathe a twelve-foot shark was lassoed and dragged in shore, thrashing its angry blue-black tail and champing its dreadful jaws. I must try to veil this information from my guests. It is comforting to reflect that I have built a pool.

He was at this time occupied with writing the score for his musical adaptation of Oscar Wilde's *Lady Windermere's Fan*, called *After the Ball*, 'the music flowing from my fingers'. Norman Hackforth came out to 'take down' the music and eventually take it back to London to be orchestrated, for production in March. Norman's arrival happily coincided with the official opening of Round Hill on January 7th. For a long time young John Pringle had had the ambitious, and at that time novel, plan of building beyond Montego Bay a luxurious hotel, not large, with a colony of cottages which were only to be bought or rented by the Beautiful People, and rich at that, of the day; the whole would in fact become a very exclusive club. This seemed an impossible dream, but John was determined and convincing. He offered one of the cottages (when built) to Noel for the peppercorn rent of a shilling a year; Noel's name would attract the social register of America as well as the English smart set, and so it turned out. When it was nearing completion, Noel felt he recognised a good thing when he saw one, and bought his cottage like everybody else. He now felt involved, and responsible for giving the project a successful launching. 'Mr Noel Coward requested the pleasure' of every bigwig on the island; he and Norman would oblige at midnight with Noel's repertoire from the Café de Paris. The news spread to New York, the American glossies we were told would send a small army of reporters, and the affair blew up to such proportions that Noel began to call it the Great Beach Barbecue Bonfire Bugger-My-Wig Party. Knowing all the hazards from his troop concerts, Noel had a horror of performing in the open air, but all went wonderfully well. The night was still, little white wavelets lapped the sandy beach above which we sat and Noel sang; John lit rows of flaming bamboo torches as far as one could see, huge bonfires blazed spectacularly away on zinc rafts twenty yards from the shore and 'thanks to God and a perfect mike', Noel sang well. What the press never knew was that Round Hill was far from ready that evening: Mrs Everard Gates rushed round putting lights in all the cottage windows to make them look inhabited, and after *Vogue* had told Noel how *clever* he was to build his patio around it, Liz Pringle and Graham had to take it in turns to hold upright a rootless tree. Natasha emerged with a piercing scream from the ladies' room, and with her skirts round her waist, explaining that when she pressed the flush gallons of hot water had boiled up at her. Noel enjoyed the rent from 'Noel Coward's Cottage' for several years without having to go near it, except for two nights, and eventually sold it at a profit—the first time he had ever made money from an investment.

Although *After the Ball* had opened on the road in England and we had heard disquieting reports, Noel resolutely determined to stay for the three months he had allotted himself in Jamaica, happily engaged in writing *Nude with Violin*. Even at three months' end he would not hurry, but stopped off for several days in Miami 'to buy shoes'. This had become a joke, inexplicable to his grander friends who had their shoes made by Lobb in St James's, but in fact he enjoyed Miami, spending lavishly on presents and on the bargains he found for himself. He loved driving 'along the flat interminable streets, looking at the Bar-B-Q signs, the Hamburger Heavens, and the posters advertising the imminent arrival of Jesus'. But this time Miami let him down; and I had watched him board his plane, the other passengers all young mothers with babes in arms and a lot of tiny staggerers:

Cher La Blanche, I have enjoyed my stay on the whole but the Miamians have a theory that this is tropics and this is, like the Immaculate Conception, an *inaccurate* theory. I have been frozen stiff ever since my arrival on account of icy weather and *no* Central H. I have done some dainty shopping and bought a great many shoes. The babies shrieked incessantly in the plane ... the K.L.M. pilots have a nasty habit of speaking every few minutes through a deafening loudspeaker and explaining what you are passing over. This noise precludes true relaxation, however I had André Maurois and my thoughts. I bought a dakron, wool, nylon, plastic, cardboard, aluminium-blue suit in which I think I may look very ha-ha indeed. It was only 40 bucks. I also slipped into a linen number in grey which has a tiny suggestion of Alcatraz uniform. I also bought a very very very pink sports coat for Sunday evenings at Goldenaggers. Don't forget my *pink* belt to clash with my *pink* coat. P.S. I am in the pink.

After Miami, New York, in order to catch up on the new shows. He saw no less than seventeen in twelve days:

The most impressive was *The Caine Mutiny* acted to perfection by Hank Fonda, Ina Claire in *The Confidential Clerk* was exquisite and beyond praise. *Tea and Sympathy* was well acted by Deborah [Kerr] but the play itself a mixture of naiveté and dishonesty. Homosexuality is à la mode this season and in this particular instance it is treated untruly and lasciviously. *The Immoralist*, a gloomy little number whipped up from André Gide's turgid preoccupation with the same theme, bored me to death when it wasn't giving me the giggles. Apart from these theatrical forays, I saw a film of Helen Keller's life, shown privately for me by Kit [Cornell] and Nancy Hamilton who wrote it. Aside from two or three moments when its nobility spilled over and became unintentionally funny, it was immensely moving. Helen Keller herself, whom I met and loved instantly, emerges as a great character, which obviously she is. I have enjoyed New York this time, perhaps because I devoted myself to theatre-going and stayed on Broadway [at the Astor Hotel]. I felt at home again in New York, a feeling that I thought the idiocies of the war had killed for ever. In theatres strangers were suddenly sweet to me and convinced me that I must play on Broadway again before I am too old. The Park Avenue lot I saw little of. Marlene I saw most of; she is sweet company and a permanent pleasure to the eye. She drove me out to the airport and saw me off, as she always does.

After the Ball opened at the Globe Theatre on June 10th, 1954. Nine months earlier Noel wrote: 'I had completed the first rough draft of *Lady Windermere's Fan* and done it very well—that is, I had cut out the more glaringly melodramatic of Oscar Wilde's lines and divided the remainder into sections ending with a suitable "cue for a song".' Noel was probably more happy while writing the score for *After the Ball* than while writing any other. He felt completely at home in the period and the music poured out effortlessly: 'I can scarcely go to the piano without a melody seeping from my fingers, usually in keys that I am not used to and can't play in: it is most extraordinary and never ceases to surprise me.'

After the day's work one evening at Goldenhurst we watched Mary Ellis in an effective play on television; Noel called immediately to congratulate her. She had first appeared at the Metropolitan Opera House at the age of eighteen, had also sung *Louise*, and had created the role of *Rose Marie*. To Noel's question, Mary replied that she was singing as well as ever, and though I am sure that Mary herself believed this, in the event it proved to be quite untrue. After another call a few nights later, Noel strode back into the room, gleefully rubbing his hands and announced, 'Well, I've got Mary Ellis for Mrs Erlynne, so it's fuck Lady Windermere isn't it.' There followed a blazing row between us, only worth reporting because our quarrels were of such blue-moon infrequency. My point, to which I stuck until we parted angrily at bedtime, was that it could never be 'fuck Lady Windermere': Mrs Erlynne is a part of cast-iron strength, while Lady Windermere's character is that of a colourless goose, and it was her, not Mrs Erlynne, to whom Noel must give every help he could to try to bring her to life, above all in this production, a musical. This argument, never again referred to by Noel, had nothing whatever to do with the inadequacy of Mary's voice, of which we remained blissfully unaware for months. The only, sad, point of the story is that the 'help' he insisted on giving Mrs Erlynne consisted of his writing for Mary some lovely entrance music, two arias, and a duet with Lady Windermere, all of well-nigh operatic quality, among the best music he ever wrote, and of which he was rightly proud. His diary for the six weeks of the tour, after he saw — and heard — the show for the first time at Bristol, makes painful reading. One by one Mrs Erlynne's numbers had to go, though Noel held on to them until in the end he could no longer bear to listen and then, late in the tour he cut the last — her vocal entrance: 'Seven minutes of my best music and most charming lyrics sacrificed.' Other disappointments had to be surmounted, the conductor replaced and new orchestrations made, which Phil Green fortunately did brilliantly.

Through all the bad times, director Robert Helpmann's wild sense of humour helped Noel to laugh at many a dashed hope and difficult situation, and he remained professional and calm. Noel thought it a great tribute to them both that they surmounted so many danger points without conflict. Doris Zinkeisen's sets and clothes were a visual pleasure; Vanessa Lee as Lady Windermere, in glorious voice, gave no trouble and worked like a Trojan to carry the show musically; Mary Ellis played Mrs Erlynne with impressive star-quality; Irene Browne was splendidly *grande dame* and funny too as the Duchess of Berwick, and Graham and pretty Patricia Cree made an engaging pair of young lovers. Robert Helpmann created for them the most ecstatically happy polka-like dance ever seen, to celebrate their engagement; Noel watched him choreograph this in three-quarters of an hour and marvelled — he thought it had the shine of genius upon it. What praise there was from the critics was tepid except for Harold Hobson in the *Sunday Times*, who waxed lyrical, and *After the Ball* managed to run for six months.

Fifteen months before this Noel had first had fears that his mother was like to die: 'I want to be near her when she does, just to hold her hand — she has held mine for fifty-three years,' he wrote. The last decade of her life had for the most part been happy. Lornie had found for her a charming ground-floor flat in Eaton Square, with walls of apple-pink, at the large drawing-room window of which she could sit and watch the passing show, and the seasonal changes of flowers and trees in the square. With her almost total deafness, her pleasures perforce were visual; she went to the cinema once a week with Kitty, and then we hit upon the perfect outing for her — a matinée at the ballet, at which she gazed entranced, no longer maddened by being unable to hear the dialogue of a straight play. From then on, late in life, she became a confirmed balletomane. These were her autumn and winter diversions. Then, so very like her son, she became restless and looked forward with Noel's eagerness to the next change of scene: 'Won't it be lovely to get to Goldenhurst; I don't want to miss the spring flowers and the blossom.' Towards summer's end she would begin to fret for Eaton Square: 'It's so much more *lively*. I do miss seeing all the people, stuck down here.' Her all-year-round great pleasure had been reading, but this was gradually denied her until at last she could no longer see the print, not even with her big magnifying-glass. She celebrated her ninety-first birthday on April 20th, a birthday date she had for years been forced to share with Adolf Hitler – at that time a cause of much leg-pulling from her son.

This spring of 1954, she did not go to Goldenhurst. On May 30th Noel wrote:

> The poor old darling can hardly see any more, and it is agony to visit her because she makes such gallant efforts to hear and understand and I know that the moment I leave she relapses into exhausted melancholy. Old age is a protracted, cruel business. It is heartbreaking to see her waiting for me so eagerly at the window and then barely recognising me when I walk into the room. I don't think she can last much longer. I dread her dying but I also long for it.

She had for some time told Noel that she was 'sick of all this hanging about', and two years before had prepared an envelope addressed in a quavering hand, 'On the event of my death.' The letter reads: 'My darling Noel. This is just to tell you that I have left everything I possess to you. Don't fret for me my darling. Except [for] leaving you, I shall be glad to go. I have outlived all my friends. God bless you my precious darling, always Snig.'

On Wednesday June 30th, a much-heralded eclipse of the sun took place – not total, but Mrs Coward died when the eclipse seemed to be at its darkest, at about one thirty in the afternoon. Noel had had a premonition that morning that this would be likely to happen; it seemed to him fitting that that redoubtable lady's light should be extinguished at the same time as the sun's. He, Lornie and I hurried round to Eaton Square at eleven o'clock.

> She recognized me for a fleeting moment and said, 'Dear old darling.' Then she went into a coma ... I sat by the bed and held her hand until she gave a pathetic little final gasp and died. I have

no complaints and no regrets. It was as I always hoped it would be. I was with her close close close until her last breath ... Fifty-four years of love and tenderness and crossness and devotion and unswerving loyalty. Without her I could only have achieved a quarter of what I have achieved, not only in terms of success and career, but in terms of personal happiness. We have quarrelled, often violently, over the years, but she has never stood between me and my life, never tried to hold me too tightly, always let me go free. For a woman of her strength of character this was truly remarkable. She was gay, even to the last I believe, gallant certainly. There was no fear in her except for me. She was a great woman to whom I owe the whole of my life. I shall never be without her in my deep mind but I shall never see her again. Goodbye my darling.

Ten days later:

One thing has impressed me deeply and that is the kindness of people, apart from intimates. Never let it be said that letters of condolence are useless or a bore: they are curiously warming. I had so very many, some of them from most unexpected and unlikely people. Lots of them were silly and filled with godliness and flowery vicarious grief but all of them were kindly meant. On the evening of the day she died I had arranged to dine with Rebecca West. I didn't put her off because I felt that her clear astringent mind would be a comfort. I was right. We dined quietly at Ziggy's and talked of all sorts of things. She knew of course that I was miserable and made no effort to cheer me, she merely talked away and we laughed a lot and she cheered me a great deal.

Aside from the inevitable pang when Mrs Coward's small coffin was first brought into the church, Noel was able to bear her funeral three days later at St Alban's, Teddington, almost with detachment. Aunt Ida, with so many Coward relations buried nearby, among them her dearly loved only son Leslie (Erik's friend), gave way in the churchyard to an abandon of grief and slid on the sloping artificial grass surrounding the grave. Helping hands prevented her at the very brink from joining her sister-in-law six feet below, which drama greatly helped to relieve the tension for Noel. He caught the four-thirty plane for Paris that afternoon, thinking a change of scene would help. Ginette and Paul-Émile were a comfort, and he had to have discussions with

Grey Daisy and Paul Geraldy about the French adaptation of *Quadrille*. Paul Geraldy was apt to become emotional over his inability, he said, to capture the 'poetry' of Noel's play in the French language. On the whole, though, Noel thought his week had been fairly idiotic: 'I have drunk a lot, not excessively, seen heaps of people, gone through each day and night not tragically, but dully ... Mum, with her usual tact, has been content to sit quietly in my subconscious and not bother me.'

He was, in fact, trying to be too brave too soon. He wandered about the South of France and all over Italy through July and August, at the end of which two months he felt he would have been better advised to have stayed quietly and soaked himself in the peace of Goldenhurst. The physical pleasures of sunshine, heat, suntan and beautiful sights had all been spoiled by an inside dreariness, a feeling of nullity. Sleep became elusive and his mother haunted his dreams; not uncheerfully, but still, there she was every night, to make his waking every morning the sadder. He unburdened himself of these troubles once he was home, which immediately helped; but in the meantime he kept them to himself while showering us all with funny letters and postcards. Much of his holiday he had of course enjoyed. Curiously enough he had found peace while staying with Mr Maugham at his exquisitely comfortable Villa Mauresque: 'Willie merry as a grig and mellow and sweet. I would like to be certain that I shall be as entertaining and cheerful when I am rising eighty-one.' Then five days in Venice with Valentina; Kate Hepburn was there, and Constance Collier, and Natasha, but he made a solemn vow never to go to Venice in August again. Then two weeks in Capri, where he joined up with Beattie Lillie and her large and cheerful entourage and where they all had several jollifications with Gracie Fields. Sam Spiegel arrived in his yacht and they spent some very funny days together. Paolo Langheim, who seems to have had palazzos everywhere, then whisked Noel off to his island villa at Posillipo, which, though unfinished, Noel thought a paradise, and then Paolo 'bitched the whole enterprise by inviting hordes of chattering Contessas and Principessas'.

Noel was able to get along in Italian quite well, but during these two months he set himself the task of really mastering the verbs, in which he never entirely succeeded. In the meantime he enjoyed playing with the language, just as he had fractured the French; this letter must have been written before all the Contessas arrived. ('It doesn't matter about me: I only wrote *Cavalcade*,' was one of his stock phrases.)

Just after I dispatched my omnibus letter ieri a large bunch of letters arrived questa mattina. I don't intend to come back until the centre of September, so ne worry pas about Io perche Io ne count pas, escrito solamente Cavalcado. A cui the weather she has changed and the sea she is making immense vagues. The shutters also are making bangalato and I am very very contento on account of there are no social engagements and I can myself put down for un poco. The Napolitani on the whole are sweet but molto molto dirty and make caca everywhere probablamente perche they eat troppo di olio but it makes not good for strolling barefoot, however I have never been a grande uno for walking barefoot at the migliore of tempi so non importa. You will gather from this that I have veree little Inglese and even less Italiano. I will escrivo quanti paroli a Piccolo Raggazzo. In the meantempo have a really buon viaggio and give my all embracing amore to tutto. xxxx

(Baci)   Maestro.

Night of a Hundred Stars took place in June of this year, and made a clear profit of no less than ten thousand pounds. We couldn't believe it—one night at the Palladium had made more money for the Actors' Orphanage than years of Theatrical Garden Parties put together. *Night of a Hundred Stars* was the brain-child of Charles Russell and Lance Hamilton, who had had the bright idea of collecting every star available in London and putting them together in unlikely juxtaposition: Dame Edith Evans with Hermione Gingold; Vivien, Larry, Danny Kaye and John Mills in a musical number; Ty Power singing and dancing with a bevy of chorus girls, each one of them a star in her own right, for the huge enjoyment of the audience. Ham (as Lance was known) and Charles rehearsed what might have been an unwieldy show, got it into good running order and produced what Noel called a miracle of smooth organization, to which was added the beyond-praise efficiency of the lighting, sound and stage-management of the Palladium staff. Noel felt immense gratitude to Charles and Ham, and great relief—there was no reason why the show should not be repeated every year and the Actors' Orphanage could, after all, survive financially.

Charles and Ham had been intimates of Noel, Lornie and me all through the years since they had stage-managed Noel's six-month tour of three separate productions with such apparent ease, though this was actually achieved only through Herculean labour against the fearful odds of wartime conditions in Great Britain. They both have strong personalities, which perhaps is why they ultimately clashed with Noel, but until that sad happening they remained very much part of the family. The annual parties they gave for Noel in their flat in Greek Street were without doubt among the best theatrical parties of that era; a constellation of famous names jumbled up with charming people less well known who happened to turn up in London. The parties always got off to a flying start because Charles and Ham were themselves non-drinkers and didn't know how much they were pouring out; or perhaps they did, one couldn't be sure. After supper, chairs were pushed back and we got down to the serious business of the evening, which was The Game. Those were the great days of The Game, before it became mechanical and debased by too many code signs made with the fingers; then you really had to act your heart out, in dumb show, to convey the impossible word or terrible message on your slip of paper. By general consensus, because they were the best, Noel was always captain of one side at these parties and Kenneth More of the other. It was clearly understood (and dreaded) by all that the phrases on the slips of paper doled out by Kenny would be either of an erudite or of a deeply shocking nature. No one present ever forgot the exquisitely pretty Margaret Lockwood, a Fragonard-like figure, emoting away, viciously kicking from time to time, and Joycie inquiring of her, ever so gently, 'Darling, could it by any chance be "Take a flying fuck at a galloping mule"?'

This took place at what turned out to be the last of the big Greek Street parties: Charles and Ham that autumn took out a tour of *Blithe Spirit* with the enchanting Kay Kendall as Elvira, which involved Noel and me spending two extremely happy weeks in Dublin. On this, our first visit, we fell in love with Dublin, its eagerly enthusiastic theatre audiences and with the Shelbourne Hotel in particular. We also fell head-over-heels in love with Kay, and grew to love her more and more in the few years left of the short span of her life. Within eighteen months or so, Charles and Ham would become Noel's advisers in New York, an end-result of what follows.

One evening in October, during Noel's fourth (and what also turned out to be his last) season at the Café de Paris, a stranger detached himself from among the forest of tables and asked if he might see Mr Coward. The very sort of person, one thought, who had to be carefully screened before being allowed into that holy of holies, the Matchbox. But he was charmingly well-mannered, very American, and insisted that his business was extremely important. Once inside the tiny room, after some perfunctory compliments on Noel's performance (by which he seemed to us to have been bewildered) he got straight to the point. His name was Joe Glaser, a New York theatrical agent, and he had come to offer Noel thirty-five thousand dollars a week to appear in Las Vegas. Noel might just as well have been asked to appear on another planet. True, one had heard of Las Vegas, but only just, and in those days it seemed no more than a name, a far distant mirage in the Nevada Desert, a mythical El Dorado, and even if it really existed wasn't it peopled by gamblers and run by gangsters, who could not possibly ever have heard of Noel Coward, much less pay him any attention when he stood up to sing his sophisticated, very English songs. We didn't really believe any of what we had heard, but Noel managed to say politely—in rather a faint voice for him—that perhaps they could meet tomorrow.

Joe Glaser had happened by chance to arrive at a moment when Noel was in desperately low water financially. Only a week or so before, the accountant had blithely told Noel that his company, Noel Coward Ltd, was £19,000 overdrawn but that Noel was not to worry, some royalty cheques were due in the autumn. Noel was very worried indeed; he realised that apart from what little there was in his personal current account and the 'cushion' Lornie always put aside to pay the taxman, he not only had no money whatever but was £19,000 in debt, as he more realistically put it. He was made angrier still by the accountant telling him that he had used Noel's only nest-egg, his life insurance, to guarantee the overdraft. When Joe Glaser arrived at Gerald Road next afternoon he was faced with Noel, his lawyer Sir Dingwall Bateson, his accountant, Lornie and Charles. By the end of the meeting, after Joe had made it evident that his offer was *bona fide*, Noel said yes, he would gladly appear at Las Vegas next June, even if they threw beer-bottles at him.

This decision was the first in a chain of events which in the end made Noel realise that much-needed money was to be made outside of England, which made Charles and Ham his business advisers in America, and which ultimately led him to make his financial base elsewhere than in Great Britain.

Noel made his only appearance, during this season at the Café de Paris, in a Royal Command Performance at the Palladium:

A glittering occasion, crammed with stars, all shaking like aspens. The moment I arrived in the dressing room and found Bob Hope tight-lipped, Jack Buchanan quivering and Norman Wisdom sweating I realised that the audience was vile, as it usually is on such regal nights. In the entr'acte, Cole and Charles came round from the front and said it was the worst they had ever encountered and that I was to be prepared for a fate worse than death. This was exactly what I needed and so I bounded on to the stage like a bullet from a gun, sang 'Uncle Harry', 'MadDogs', and 'Bad Times' very very fast indeed and got the whole house cheering. I was on and off the stage in nine and a half minutes. The next day the papers announced, with unexpected generosity, that I was the hit of the show. This was actually true but it wouldn't have been if I had stayed on two minutes longer. Bob Hope had them where he wanted them and then went on and on and lost them entirely. I have quite definitely decided *not* to do a season at the Palladium, much as I love the theatre and the efficiency and niceness of all concerned, it's not really my ambience. Oh no. Me for the more intimate lark to my own type of audience. After the show we lined up and were presented to the Queen, Prince Philip and Princess Margaret. The Queen looked luminously lovely and was wearing the largest sapphires I have ever seen.

Then it was back to Blue Harbour, via Hollywood and Chicago, where Noel dined with Yul Brynner, '... in full make-up as the King of Siam ... our meal was made convulsive by autograph-hunters.'

We have a new maid [at Blue Harbour] called Maud who pongs dreadfully so we have sent for some Charm soap and Odorono. Alton [the chauffeur-butler], with foolish reticence, has withheld from us the valuable information that he had a bad case of scabies. On discovering this we sent him hot foot, and hot arms and legs, to the Doctor. Scabies are fearfully contagious and Coley and I examine each other hourly for incipient spots. I found some on my arm but think they are only insect bites. Today is Christmas Eve, that time of good will, and even here with the blue skyo, which is as grey as John Knox's arse at the moment, there is still that pall of kindliness and present-giving and card-arriving and general hell upon earth. Paul-Émile, Ginette and Johnny [Gielgud] who should have arrived on Tuesday, actually arrived at 5 a.m. yesterday, having been about forty-six hours in a crowded plane which was two days late in starting from London anyway. We met the plane in the pitch darkness that precedes the dawn and at long last packed them and all their luggage into the car and drove home through the sunrise which was spectacularly beautiful and comforted them no end. We stopped for a slap-up breakfast at Jamaica Inn and got to Blue Harbour about eight o'clock. Great enthusiasm on arrival, all the suitable adjectives [were used] and then sleep for all. Meanwhile [while waiting two days for them at Montego] Coley and I disported ourselves at Round Hill which has developed incredibly within a year and is now really beautiful. Charles Laughton and Paul Gregory were there and we had tremendous conversations about Dickens, Saki, E. Nesbit and Plato. Claudette [Colbert] and her husband are due to arrive for lunch and will stay for two days until Christmas is over and done with and the old tired year packed away. Now for the hellish despair of present wrapping and all sorts of Yuletide fun. Oh how nice it would be, just for today and tomorrow, to be a little boy of five, instead of an aging playwright of fifty-five, and look forward to all the high jinks with passionate excitement and be given a clockwork train with a full set of rails and a tunnel. As things are, drink will take the place of parlour games and we shall all pull crackers and probably enjoy ourselves enough to warrant at least some of the god-damned fuss.

We did enjoy ourselves. John Gielgud turned out to be a highly entertaining house-guest, the words tumbling out of his mouth in an avalanche, frequently having to wipe away his own tears of laughter at the funniness of the disasters he recounted, disasters always against himself. Claudette was at her gayest, sweetest and best; no matter how nippy we were, none of us ever succeeded in snapping the 'wrong' side of her face, some sixth sense warning her of a silent approach from the rear. We only tried to capture it for its rarity value—both sides looked lovely to a layman. Ginette and Paul-Émile stayed for a golden month, during which Noel read to them what he had written of his current short story. They vociferously insisted that it was too packed with incident to be wasted thus; he had more than enough for a novel.

Noel had not looked at his mass of material on Samolo since the failure of *Pacific 1860*, and was astonished at what he found. 'I had no idea I had been so thorough. Everything is there that I need. I feel so strongly about Samolo and its archipelago that I almost believe it exists.' Samolo took over and he scrapped the short story, which he had started 'laboriously at first, worrying about sentence construction, and the usual splurge of too many qualifying adjectives and adverbs, then suddenly it started to flow and before I knew it I had done several thousand words. I don't know who it was who said, "The only time I believe in God is when I write," but whoever it was said a mouthful.' He worked on the novel for four years, so intermittently that 'I really must get to Jamaica and finish my novel' became a joke. *Pomp and Circumstance* at last saw the light in 1960, but was conceived that January evening in 1955.

David Niven—always known as 'Dearest Chum'—arrived in March with his wife Hjordis, of the exquisitely beautiful face and figure. Their stay was packed with incident, much of it hilarious, though not for David. He arrived with a sun-rash on the back of his neck and shoulders, caught while staying at Roaring River, along the coast, and by next morning was threshing about in bed with a temperature fluctuating between 100 and 104, violently itching and with his far-famed face covered with angry spots. Our trusty village doctor was just leaving for three days in Kingston to participate in the sacred rite of watching a Test Match, instead of which Noel dragged him unwillingly to Blue Harbour. He hurriedly diagnosed chicken-pox, prescribed I forget what, advised a thick paste of soda-bicarb and water for the spots, and sentenced David and Hjordis to fourteen days in quarantine. David's good looks became fearful to behold in the next few days, what with the flaming spots and an ever-lengthening stubble of dark beard bristling through the white paste. Hjordis has many wonderful qualities, but those of Florence Nightingale-cum-*hausfrau* I think she will admit are not among them, though she did her best. Pathetic-looking trays of food and changes of bed-linen were left halfway on the long flight of steps leading to the guest-house, while Hjordis had to wash up the crockery and glass—too infectious to be sent to the kitchen—in their hand-basin. All fears of quarantine were however flung to the winds when she appeared, stricken, and announced that David was now suffering from yet another malady and would we please come and have a look. The trouble, quickly diagnosed by Noel, turned out to be grass ticks, also caught at Roaring River; they had by this time reached their Mecca, David's crotch, where they had been happily breeding away for nearly a week. The grass ticks on top of everything else really was too much and we all, including David, laughed ourselves silly. When we had pulled ourselves together we held a council of war and decided that Hjordis should go beetling back to Hollywood by the next plane available in case she herself caught the complaint and gave it to us and the staff in a sort of daisy-chain, and we should all be in quarantine for ever. All this was of course lovely grist for Noel's novel; Bunny Colville, the hero of *Pomp and Circumstance*, is laid low by chicken-pox when the plot is at its thickest.

The shadow of Noel's forthcoming début in Las Vegas in June

hung over those first six months of 1955; not heavily, because it would by its very nature be an exciting adventure, and Noel thrived on a new excitement. Then, one by one, events contributed towards dispelling any misgivings he may have had. First, Charles and Ham came to Blue Harbour with the astounding news of a concrete offer from C.B.S. of four hundred and fifty thousand dollars for three television shows, and that Mary Martin would be delighted to appear with him in the first of these, later in the year. All this money, plus Las Vegas, would mean that at last he could have some capital in the bank; Charles and Ham were as determined as he that at the end of the series as much money as possible should be set aside for his old age which, as he put it, was due to begin next Tuesday.

Even more important to Noel at that moment was that he could also afford to realise his long-cherished dream of building the perfect bolt-hole for himself on his beloved Firefly Hill. What with Round Hill now so fashionably successful, filled with friends anxious to come over to see him, and his own house-guests and the neighbours who came daily to Blue Harbour that season, all of whom he genuinely did want to see, he had nearly been driven to distraction. He even fled for refuge to the more remote Caribbean islands, Tobago, Grenada, Dominica and the rest, but returned disillusioned; he was set upon by people wherever he went. He could not escape the consequences of his own fame. Only by observing the strictest purdah at Blue Harbour until noon did he succeed in getting any work done at all. A house planned to accommodate only one person in the peace of Firefly Hill would be the perfect solution to this problem; his god-damned loved ones could mill about to their hearts' content down at Blue Harbour. He excitedly gave orders for building to begin as soon as possible.

Another comfort was that Marlene had by now assured him he would be successful in Las Vegas, though he was still unsure himself, and told him firmly that he must appear at the Desert Inn — it was for him the perfect, the only, place. He began to look forward to absolutely everything in this *annus mirabilis* and decided to fly to New York and from thence to Las Vegas to have a look-see, to case the joint. From New York he wrote:

In that breathless hush when everything has been packed upside down and Marlene is on her way to pick me up, I seize my ball plume to write to you. All has gone well. All is set for Hollywood (one week there before going to Las Vegas) and Mr Frank Sennes who runs Desert Inn *and* the Moulin Rouge is determined to give a

gargantuan party for us in Hollywood on May 29th. This should
be a *great* experience. Marlene is as bright as a bee but informed me
casually that *everyone*'s voice conked out in Vegas on account of the
dryness and altitude! I caught a hideous cold on the plane and
took some tablets called Super Anahist (which sounds like Ziegfeld's mistress) and it cured it at once with no side effects at all. A
miracle! I have bought eight thousand bottles. Columbia is going
to record several of my Vegas performances so that we can take
our pick. Kit was charming in 'The Light is Dark Enough', but
not up to our Ede. [Edith Evans had played *The Dark is Light
Enough* in London the year before. Noel always deliberately put the
title the wrong way round because, he said, it meant the same thing
— if it meant anything at all.]

Noel had contracted to give two shows nightly for four weeks at the
Desert Inn, instead of his accustomed one show at the Café; not only
that, there would be no nights off, not even on Sundays. He nervously
wondered whether his voice would stand up to the tremendous strain,
and on the other hand particularly longed to be in his best vocal condition. Mary Martin and Katharine Hepburn came to the rescue. They
both strongly advised him to go, as they had gone, to Alfred Dixon, a
New York vocal coach with unique methods, one of which was to
make a mooing noise with lips closed, starting very low in the scale,
gradually rising higher and higher and then slowly all the way down
again, until at last you had to stop for lack of breath. The result
resembled a loud, long air-raid warning emitted by a cow, repeated
over and over again. No matter how funny this sounded to other
people (the noise could be heard three dressing-rooms away), it was
the best loosener-upper in the world, and it extended the vocal range
with ease. Dixon's other dictum, revolutionary to Noel and of great
psychological help, was never to breathe deeply; even the longest
musical phrase could be sung—would be better sung—on very little
breath. Just inhale the merest sip only when you had to and it would
carry you through to the end. And sure enough, it did. There was his
voice, clear as a bell and with no fluff on it.

The last big difficulty to be overcome was that no American work-
permit could be obtained for Norman Hackforth. Where on earth
would Noel find another accompanist as sympathetic? He interviewed
eight people, none of whom were good enough, and then one evening
the telephone rang. This time his saviour was Marlene, who had been
loyally working away on his behalf. She was calling from the airport

and her plane for London was already boarding; had he got a pencil ready, quick, Pete Matz, this is his number, ring him at once and grab him. Pete came round next day. He seemed absurdly young, only twenty-six, dark and intelligent, with a great sense of dehydrated humour, and Noel knew in his bones that he was exactly what was needed. When Noel showed him the old arrangements he had been using at the Café, Pete said, not contemptuously but matter-of-factly, 'You're not going to use these, are you?' Noel lied quickly, 'Of course not, but who can make me new ones in the time?' Quite calmly Pete said, 'I will.' Noel had no way as yet of knowing how brilliant a musician Pete was. Later we discovered from experience that for instance there was no need for laboured conversation at the breakfast table; instead of Agatha Christie, Pete read silently from a Mozart score propped against the toast-rack.

Pete flew out to Hollywood a few days later and I flew from Jamaica to join Noel in Clifton Webb's house in North Rexford Drive. Clifton was away and so was his jolly but formidable mother Mabelle, dreaded by all Hollywood, who would willingly dance the can-can for you—her version—at the age of nearly ninety. Clifton's house was comfortable and lovely, but the windows were so creeper-overgrown that we lived in sub-aqueous light, as though in a Cousteau film. The life we led was curious. Noel made his Dixon noises off and on from the time he woke, as though a bull-moose had been let loose in the house. For his figure's sake we lunched off lettuce with cottage cheese and grapefruit quarters, or cottage cheese and pineapple, served on trays; lunch made convulsive by a remote-control switch at our fingertips which gave us a choice of eleven television channels, out of which we could never decide on one for more than two minutes.

Then came the great day of Frank Sennes's stupendous rout for Noel, to which three hundred people had been invited at the freak hour of four in the afternoon. We arrived on the dot and made desultory conversation in the corner of the garden with the host and his charming wife Lou, for an hour's eternity. The only other person there was a beautiful girl sitting alone at a distance, on whom I took pity and went over and jabbered away until at last, very long last, Charlton Heston and his wife made a welcome appearance. At this the girl said, 'Well, I'd better get to work,' stood up, and revealed the most generous length of fish-netted leg I have ever seen at a formal party; her demure black dress was slit right up to her waist. I was green to Hollywood's ways; a few moments later she hung a tray round her neck and offered everyone a choice of cigarettes or cigars.

From then on things went from fast to furious; people poured in and so did hordes of photographers, who were dazzled by Zsa Zsa in white, Greer Garson in mauve, Jean Simmons in blue ... Four cadaverous fiddlers played without zest until Jack Benny seized one of the violins and led them in and out of the throng to merrier tunes and made even the fiddlers laugh. Hundreds of camellias and thousands of rose petals swirled slowly round on the surface of the swimming-pool. 'You mark my words,' Noel said to me, 'Louella Parsons will come up naked out of it, looking *un*like Aphrodite.' 'Oh, no she won't. I'm right here by your side, Noel darling,' said the sawney voice. (Noel's theory was that that illiterate lady had taken the whole thing as a compliment.)

Noel has left his impression of Las Vegas as it was when he performed there, twenty-odd years ago:

This is a fabulous madhouse. All around is desert sand with pink and purple mountains on the horizon. All the big hotels are luxe to the last degree. There are myriads of people tearing away at the fruit machines and gambling gambling gambling for twenty four hours a day. The lighting at night is fantastic: downtown where the Golden Nugget is and the lesser dives, it is ablaze with variegated neon signs. In the classier casinos, beams of light shoot down from baroque ceilings on the masses of earnest morons flinging their money down the drain. The sound is fascinating, a steady hum of conversation against a background of rhumba music and the noise of the fruit machines, the clink of silver dollars, quarters and nickels, and the subdued shouts of the croupiers. There are lots of pretty women about but I think, on the whole, sex takes a comparatively back seat. Every instinct and desire is concentrated on money. I expected that this would exasperate me but oddly enough it didn't. The whole fantasia is on such a colossal scale that it is almost stimulating. I went from hotel to hotel and looked at the supper rooms. They are all much of a muchness: expert lighting and sound, and cheerful appreciative audiences who are obviously there to have a good time. I noticed little drunkenness and much better manners than in the New York nightclubs. The gangsters who run the places are all urbane and charming. I had a feeling that if I opened a rival casino I would be battered to death with the utmost efficiency, but if I remained on my own ground as a most highly paid entertainer, I could trust them all the way. Their morals are bizarre in the extreme.

They are generous, mother-worshippers, sentimental and capable of much kindness. They are also ruthless, cruel, violent and devoid of scruples.

Joe Glaser, whom I have taken a great shine to, never drinks, never smokes and adores his mother. My heart, and reason, go out to him because he at least took the trouble to fly over to London and see me at the Café and give me a concrete offer. If it all ends in smoke I don't think it will be his fault. I believe him to be honest according to his neon lights.

Joe was honest all right, and kind, always remembered Noel's birthday, and remained our friend until he died. He was also my cicerone to the niceties of life in Vegas. No matter if the taxi ride from the Desert Inn to the Sands only cost thirty cents, I must always tip one dollar, 'Never tip less than a dollar when you're with Noel. If you're going to play the machines, play the ones near the entrance. They pay off the most often, to lure people inside.' I tried this on our very first night, when we went across the road to see Sammy Davis at the New Frontier, and hit the jackpot. The most terrifying clatter as the coins continued to tumble out, and I stood there helpless until a girl came and shovelled them up into two big plastic cartons and finally got me folding money in exchange. Noel as usual had gone striding ahead and was annoyed by the delay; 'What in the name of God do you think you're doing? We shall be late for Sammy's show.' I never hit the jackpot again; still, I thought it was a good omen on our first night, and it was.

Pete had made brilliant new orchestrations for Noel; often musically witty, and always highly imaginative in their own right, yet they never obtruded on Noel's singing. They sound as fresh today on the record *Noel Coward at Las Vegas* as they did then, and so does Noel. He had never been in better vocal form, thanks to Alfred Dixon and his own strength of purpose, and the record is the best, the most truly representative, he ever made.

On the day of Noel's opening, to his consternation, Carlton Hayes the orchestra leader went down with the Las Vegas virus, exactly as Marlene had predicted 'everybody' would. Pete remained cucumber-cool, told Noel that he would take charge of the orchestra, and he was not to worry. But Noel was very anxious indeed. Pete at the piano would be upstage right with the orchestra way behind Noel, and Noel downstage centre, alone. He had never before performed without being able to catch somebody's eye—his accompanist's or the conductor's. They got through the afternoon rehearsal with no trouble;

neither Noel nor Pete once faltered and I could comfort Noel by telling him truthfully that the arrangement looked ten times more effective visually.

The two shows at night were known as the 'dinner' show at eight thirty and the 'supper' show which started at midnight. Noel was preceded by forty-five minutes of first-class entertainment, including a chorus line of lovely girls (one of whom, Janet Morrison, Pete fell for and later married), and which ended with a backdrop looking as unlike the façade of the Café de Paris as it possibly could, although a sign stated firmly that that was what it was, with NOEL COWARD flashing on and off in electric lights. The stage was then pumped knee-high with Nujol mist to represent a pea-soup London fog, sending diners at the front tables into paroxysms of coughing, and the entire company rendered a song which, Noel swore, consisted of the most heavenly lyrics he had ever heard, starting, 'So this is London, Land of Romance.' Then Noel came down the steps to the strains of 'I'll See You Again', and started to sing.

The audiences at the dinner shows, we had been told, were notoriously dull, something that had to be endured, but this just was not so in Noel's case. Never again could he think of those gamblers and their wives as morons. They warmly welcomed the start of each famous song with applause, sat quiet as mice and utterly attentive during the more serious numbers and were surprisingly 'on' to all his jokes in the funny ones. They loved him and he loved them. The place was packed; Joe Glaser and I had to stand at the back with Wilbur Clark, owner of the Desert Inn. Mr Clark watched the middle-aged Englishman on the stage, nonplussed. 'Who is this guy?' he asked. 'You must tell me more about him.'

The supper show, after this, was a riotous walk-over for Noel. Frank Sinatra had specially chartered a private plane from Hollywood for the great occasion and I suppose no plane ever carried a more precious cargo; Frankie himself, Judy Garland, Joseph Cotten with Lenore, David Niven with Hjordis, and Humphrey Bogart with Betty Bacall. Also with him at the front tables were Zsa Zsa Gabor, Jane Powell, Laurence Harvey, Michael Wilding, Rosemary Clooney and Joan Fontaine. Everybody trooped up to Noel's suite afterwards to celebrate, and the last guest left at four. We were far too excited to think of going to sleep, and relived each triumphant moment over one last drink. At nearly five a.m. an immense mauve teddy-bear was brought to the door, nearly the size of Noel himself; where had Zsa Zsa been able to find it at this impossible hour? The label round its neck read, 'Monsieur Noel Coward. En Ville', and in truth that was now the only address Noel needed in Las Vegas. He was touched most of all next day by Frank Sinatra, whose singing he greatly admired, going on the air and telling the listeners that if they wanted to hear how songs should *really* be sung, to hurry to the Desert Inn. Which, as Noel said, made a nice change from Mr Harold Conway's verdict in London that he massacred his own songs. He was equally touched by Sammy Davis, with his own rich talents, who twice nightly for the rest of his run commanded his audiences to go across the road if they wanted to see and hear a really great performer. Noel wrote: 'Well, it is all over bar the shouting which is still going on. I have made one of the most sensational successes of my career and to pretend that I am not absolutely delighted would be idiotic. I have had rave notices and the news has flashed round the world.' Noel is not exaggerating. Cables of congratulations started to pour in immediately.

The next four weeks continued to be just as intoxicating. There was never a night when celebrities had not flown in specially from New York, San Francisco and Hollywood. *Life* magazine sent photographers who took the famous pictures of Noel alone in the Nevada desert in a dinner-jacket, drinking a cup of tea. The pictures were taken in a temperature of 129 degrees. After half an hour in such scorching sun we burnt our fingers on the metal of the car door-handles; inside, the car mercifully had the, to us, new-fangled air conditioning.

Rita Hayworth's husband, Dick Haymes, opened at one of the other hotels and we saw a lot of them. Rita was looking her most beautiful, but Noel said, 'You look remarkably pasty.' She explained that pale lipstick was now *à la mode*, but he would have none of this and called her Pasty from then on. With Noel and Dick occupied, Rita and I were on the loose at night and discovered that once we had seen all the shows at the other hotels there was in those days nothing whatever to do but gamble. After we danced for a while at the Golden Nugget, the band melted away and, as elsewhere, the exit sign led you unavoidably into the casino itself. We could not find a cinema and so back we went to the Desert Inn in time to catch Noel singing 'Nina', which, because Rita had made her dancing début in Tijuana, he used to sing very pointedly at her.

One after the other, sure enough, we all went down with 'the virus', including Noel himself, who was distressed at having to be off for one night, though nobody else was, except the audience. It was to be expected, and there was great camaraderie among all the performers, so Gordon and Sheila MacRae pinch-hitted for him at the first show and Peter Lind Hayes and Mary Healy at the second.

The triumph continued,

> ... and is even greater than at first. I receive a screaming ovation at every performance. Cole Porter came and Tallulah and the Van Johnsons and it really was sensational. I was so glad because I wanted Cole to see me at my best and he certainly did. Last night Ina [Claire] and Bill, Edie and Bill Goetz, George Burns and Gracie Allen and Jack and Mary Benny. Also darling Kay Thompson. Tonight Joe Cotten again and Jeanette MacDonald. The business is fantastic and hundreds are turned away at every performance ... I am enjoying myself like crazy.

It was during this visit that Miss MacDonald reported she had been packing arenas and auditoriums all over with *Bitter Sweet*, had had the good idea of appropriating Manon's 'If Love Were All' for herself, and had also interpolated 'Mad About the Boy' into the late Victorian operetta, and could she take it to Broadway? With the breath taken right out of his body, Noel just managed to say, '*No*,' very firmly.

Then, at the beginning of July, it was all over:

> The bags are packed, the farewell presents given and the paper streamers drooping in the hot desert wind. Last night was exciting and strangely moving. The Management presented me with a beautiful silver cigarette-box, I made a speech and everyone became very sentimental. Ethel [Merman] was in the front row and in floods. Then I gave a party in the Sky Room to all the boys and girls plus Merman, Tallulah, the Lind Hayes and MacRaes, etc. At long last when all goodbyes were said, I lost fifteen dollars very quickly at Blackjack and went to bed.

> At this moment [July 11th] we are flying over the flat brown plains of Kansas, both Coley and I exhausted from far too much entertaining. There have been red carpets everywhere. [We had spent a week in Hollywood, Noel crowned with laurels and naturally loving every moment.] Merle gave a glamorous dinner for me, everyone *and* the dinner looked most nice. The Kirk Douglases, the James Stewarts, the Joe Cottens, the Van Johnsons, and Marlon Brando who was gentler and nicer than I expected. Frankie

Sinatra gave a tremendous rout for me at Romanoffs in the private room upstairs. He is a charmer and I love him. He was a wonderful host and a lovely time was had by all. He sang like a dream, I sang less alluringly, circumstances were not propitious, no mike and bad acoustics, however everyone expressed great enthusiasm, Charlie Vidor tore off his amethyst and gold buttons and links and gave them to me; I protested mildly and pocketed them.

We were on our way to Chicago for Noel to enter the Passavant Hospital for a general check-up, at Lynn and Alfred's suggestion. The bright particular star of the Passavant was Doctor Edward Bigg, the Lunts' own remarkable doctor, who would look after him. Noel's fame in the States at this point was such that he assumed, on his entrance papers, the name of Nicholas Cole. So did Alfred for his next check-up, which led to confusion when it came to my turn. Before signing myself in I discovered at the last minute that I had a wildly tangled medical history, had been born at Teddington in 1899 and had lost a kidney. (It was Alfred who had lost the kidney.)

We already know that Noel, though brave as a lion when seriously ill, kicked up the most terrible fuss when only having a routine check-up, and this occasion was no exception. The Passavant is a famous and excellent hospital, but Noel maligns the food and the nursing nearly to the point of libel in his journal. It is true that this stay was exacerbated for him by the fact that Chicago was enduring a furnace of a heatwave at the time, as well as an invasion of many thousands of Shriners holding their annual convention, and marching about to excruciating brass bands which assembled near the Passavant at nine thirty every morning. Noel thought it too cruel that this should be allowed in a hospital zone and even more cruel that a battery of pneumatic drills should start their day-long ear-splitting even earlier in the parking-lot below his window. He had a particularly sensitive dread of the barium enemas which were essential for his tests; on purely physical grounds the idea of the act of sodomy either passive or active gave him the shudders, and he faced these ordeals with the air of total resignation with which the Early Christian Martyrs must have gone to their deaths. Especially when friends told him that once inside you the barium turned to cement unless you were quick, and Margaret Leighton had even used the word concrete. When Lynn, Alfred and I anxiously rang up from Genesee the first evening to ask how he had survived this calvary, he said that it had been absolute torture, hell upon earth, but that as the barium had been administered the massed bands of the Shriners had struck up 'The Darktown Strutters' Ball', and he thought that the syncopated rhythm had helped a little, spasmodically.

In between the rigours of this dreadful week Noel read *War and Peace* with complete absorption and enjoyment and this, he maintained, together with Doctor Bigg, saved his reason. From now on Ed (as he soon became) was 'our' doctor and Noel returned many times to him and the Passavant, with all the latter's shortcomings, and telephoned him for advice from no matter what part of the world he happened to be in. Noel left the Passavant with the assurance that he was organically sound, and with Ed's counsel to remember that he was fifty-five and not twenty-five, and should not squander his vitality. He ended his catalogue of Ed's virtues, written on this his first acquaintance, 'I have found a new friend, for life.'

On arrival in London he hurried to the Café de Paris to catch Marlene and to 'introduce' her at her last performance as he had her first, a year earlier:

She was very good indeed, better than last year, but afterwards when we repaired to her suite at the Dorchester she was fairly tiresome. She was grumbling about some bad press notices and being lonely. Poor darling glamorous stars everywhere, their lives are so lonely and wretched and frustrated. Nothing but applause, flowers, Rolls-Royces, expensive hotel suites, constant adulation. It's too pathetic and wrings the heart ... we made a getaway and drove down here [to Goldenhurst] through the dawn. The road was clear all the way and it was lovely arriving in full light, with the birds chirping their heads off ... In two weeks' time Blue Harbour and the peace of Firefly Hill. What a fabulously enjoyable life I lead!

Noel wrote when the three of us got to Jamaica:

I am happy every minute of the day, and the long mornings are heavenly. On Monday we drove into Kingston for shopping in course of which, apart from meat and groceries, I bought a new Austin in which I drove home, and a beautiful Bechstein grand which was put on a truck and was waiting for me when I got back. I also bought a radiogram so that I can have music while I paint or play patience. A richly extravagant day and thank God for Las Vegas and, later on, American television. Lovely sunshine every morning and a nice Biblical thunderstorm every afternoon at 2.45.

The house looks spotless and the garden is a-growing and a-blowing. [The walls of the house at Firefly were halfway up, and most of the earth paths at Blue Harbour were now cemented.] Little Lad, Coley and Mr MacCrae have been busy with cement and now the outside of the kitchen looks like an Athenian pleasaunce and there is a fountain which, as yet, doesn't work. Coley and I have two new names for the property, his is 'Concrete Proposition' and mine is 'You Were Cement For Me'. Joke over. The dogs are well and rampageous and the cats are well and pregnant. How Evelyn can carry on with her flaming sex life at her great age is truly remarkable. In cat language she must be rising eighty. It must be the lack of religious scruples that has kept her so rorty.

The time had now come for Noel to start thinking seriously about the first of his three television spectaculars for C.B.S. in America. This was to be his début—his first major appearance on television—with Mary Martin, the two of them alone on the screen for an hour and a half with no scenery as such, no props, nothing whatever to hold the eyes and ears of the viewers for all that time except their talents and Mary's two beautiful dresses by Mainbocher. Considering the complexity and quantity of the lyrics and movements they had to memorize, and the fact that the show would be televised 'live' (not filmed as it would be today), the audacity and courage of Mary and Noel's achievement is breathtaking and, in retrospect, terrifying. They did in fact realize the immensity of their self-imposed task, and no show has ever been more meticulously rehearsed. They had the great comfort of Pete Matz to work with, and daily for the next two months, first in Jamaica and then in New York, the three of them worked like slaves.

By the time Mary, her husband Richard, and Pete got to Blue Harbour, Noel had already written their two opening numbers 'Ninety Minutes is a Long, Long Time', and 'Together with Music', which of course he played to them on their first evening: 'To my horror Mary took against "Together with Music" very firmly indeed. I admired her honesty but it was dreadfully irritating and disappointing. Actually I am afraid she's right, so I am now in the throes of rewriting and making it more romantic.' When the second version was completed, 'it is better than the first really, but it was bloody hell to do. However, now it is done and Mary's delighted and everybody's delighted.' Several squabbles arose during these two months, caused by Richard (as they had been throughout *Pacific 1860*), which only need to be mentioned as proof of the bond that existed between Noel and Mary, which had already been put to the test and survived, and was to do the same again. Mary must have been severely torn between divided loyalties, but stayed steadfast in her professional application to the immediate job in hand, which, after all the storm and stress, ended in strengthening and deepening their friendship.

The actual performance went without a hitch, and Noel and Mary sang and danced as though they hadn't a care in the world. The reception was rapturous:

> It had been a terrific week, a heroic, White-Headed-Boy-week, a thoroughly wallowing week. Wherever I have walked or driven or lunched or dined ecstatic strangers have loaded me with praise and gratitude: one lady who meant well said, 'I never liked you until Saturday night but now I love you!' Another, with wild blue hair, rushed up to me on Madison Avenue and cried shrilly, 'You're out of this world and I'm from East Orange, New Jersey!'

Noel had little time for resting on laurels when he got back to Blue Harbour. For one thing his novel was rushing along like a river, and there were many decisions to be made, the most difficult of these being to sack Grey Daisy. Word reached us that the Paris production of *Relative Values* had been appallingly bad and the notice in *Le Figaro* came right out and said it was the shoddiest production ever seen. Their use of the word 'shoddy' clinched it for Noel: 'She really is a blundering old fool and I've now had enough of her. I intend to write firmly and withdraw finally from her inefficient clutches. If it breaks her heart, very well it breaks her heart. I cannot afford to have play after play go down the drain just because I am sentimentally chary of hurting the feelings of a silly old ass.' To pay Grey Daisy her due, she wrote a dignified letter by return, accepting her *congé* gracefully. Doctor Jan Van Loewen in London stepped into her place, and Noel's theatrical business affairs, not only in France but all over the continent of Europe and in South America, took an immediate and sharp upward turn in his hands, at which high level they have remained ever since.

Most urgent of all, the second of Noel's American television shows had to be prepared and cast. *Blithe Spirit* had been chosen, and this meant that the three-hour-long play would have to be cut to less than one and a half hours' playing time, which Noel dreaded having to do. Certainly a lot of the best lines and the best laughs would have to go; painful surgery for an author to perform. But Noel had long ago learnt that when one had to cut, then cut ruthlessly, and he soon found himself really rather enjoying the process of pulling the play to bits and putting it together again. In the end he became quite proud of his successful operation, secure in the knowledge that *Blithe Spirit* now rattled along so rapidly that the viewers would have no time to be bored. He would play Charles, and Claudette Colbert Ruth; Mildred Natwick would repeat her successful Broadway performance as Madame Arcati and, since he had been so impressed by Lauren Bacall on television in *The Petrified Forest* with Humphrey Bogart, he would have no one but her for Elvira. As the telecast was to be made in Hollywood in early January, it was decided that he should fly there in time for his birthday on December 16th and, like it or not, he would have to put up with 'the hell of Christmas' in the film capital. As Graham, Charles and Ham were already there, I could be much more usefully employed by remaining in Jamaica; the house up at Firefly was nearing completion and I was to have it furnished ready for Noel to walk into on his return, down to the last ashtray.

Noel did not fly from Miami to Hollywood, but chose instead to make stop-overs at Havana and Mexico City, the last a particularly unfortunate decision as it was freezing cold and he was trapped into attending an open-air performance of Anouilh's *The Lark*, which play—as he was one hundred per cent allergic to Joan of Arc—he had been carefully avoiding in Paris, London and New York for years. Noel had rented a furnished house at 1573 Sunset Plaza Drive, Beverly Hills, where this letter, headed 'Boulevard Nowhere', was written:

Tolette, this is going to be a curious letter as I am doing it on the new Tippa Tappa [typewriter] et je ne suis pas certain of it. The house is sweet and *when* the fog lifts the view will be gorgeous. Oh dear there is so much to tell you that I don't know where to begin. Little Lad is in fine form, he is leaving Clifton's today for an apartment in the same place as Charles and Ham. He has handled the Clifton situation with consummate skill and every prospect pleases except that it was getting near the point of no return. Poor Clifton is always on the verge of Umbrage about something or other and this is not helped by Harry Pissalatums which happens very very often indeed indeedy. The cocktail party yesterday was a riot of fun and fancy and the girls came [our Goldenhurst neighbours, Erica Marx and 'our' Elizabeth Taylor] and Erica was mistaken for Millie Natwick by Betty Bacall who congratulated her on her performance in something. Erica finally said, 'Who *do* you think I am?' whereupon Betty said, 'Mildred Natwick Jesus Christ have I put my fucking foot in it!' and it all passed off in gales of laughter. Rock and Phyllis [Hudson] appeared and were very sweet. Marlene gave me a wonderful set of black silk pyjamas and dressing-gown to match. The Nivs are also very sweet and send you particular love and so do Betty and Bogey [Noels' spelling]. Havana was un-noted by me on account of the Ambassador giving an enormous buffet dinner-party for all the nobs the majority of whom were called Gonzalez-y-Lopez except for a few who were called Lopez-y-Gonzalez. They were all Sugar Barons. Mexico City was almost complete disaster on account of P. and V. being intolerably silly. They kept on taking wrong turnings and not knowing the way to anywhere and V. was playing the Dauphin in *The Lark* in the Round and I had to go and sit through it wrapped in a rug with a flask of brandy and it was a bugger to end all buggers. So bad indeed that I was bereft of speech. My only comfort was when Joan said something about not fearing the flames, a small, miser-able boy in front of me let such a loud fart that it nearly blew the brandy flask right out of my hand. She, Joan, was a bright amateur with her arse resting on her heels and a boyish manner. I expected her to say, 'Mumsie can't I play just *one* more set with Roger?' She had recently appeared as Serena in *Quadrille*! V. camped about and was quite inaudible and the whole thing was very very dread-ful. My maid is called Fredda. She has Sugar Diabetes and comes from St Ann's Bay. She is very sweet, not only because of the diabetes. I have not yet got a secretary but one I believe is coming which all points to the fact that I miss Tolette La Blanche but on the whole I am happy as a bird-dog, perched in my little housie, and mercifully alone, and with a great great deal to look forward to. Love Love Love and get after that turfing [at Firefly], Master.

My Spanish lessons stood me in good stead, I found myself gabbing away like crazy and making witty little jokes.
The Joe Cottens came to the party and made a very great noise.
I have a most wonderful car which goes fast fast fast up hill and down dale.
I am on a diet and not drinking.
My Irving [Irving Paul Lazar] sent me a Christmas Tree.
I hate Christmas.
The weather is very foggy.
I do not like foggy weather.

The boiler burst the day I arrived but happily it was mended before I froze to death.

I am now very hot.

Did I mention that Mexico City is a cunt?

The nicest Mexican I met was Roy Boulting.

Mabelle [Webb] is very well and much brighter than her son.

Bogey, justly celebrated for his Dix-Huitième manners, said to Clifton at the party apropos their own projected Christmas Eve Rout, 'Bring your fucking mother and she can wipe up her own sick!' Clifton was not pleased.

Alec Guinness was *very* pleased and we bowed low to each other like characters in a Restoration comedy.

It was all meant in a spirit of nice clean fun.

Betty Bacall passed out on Mabelle's bed for three hours.

All of this surprised the Rock Hudsons who are perhaps unused to high society.

Betty Bacall called Hedda Hopper a lousy bitch and kicked her up the bottie under my very eyes. Then there was an upper and a downer and now they are great great friends.

Comme la vie est etonnante, n'est-ce pas?

Voila c'est tout.

Two reflections from Noel's journal before we leave this year:

I remember distinctly lying on the bed, racked with pain and nausea, thinking of death and almost wishing for it. I thought, 'All right, if I never saw Goldenhurst again or my loved ones or the sun rising over the sea or Piccadilly Circus, so what?' I know when I was watching darling Mum die that she was neither scared nor unhappy. Death seems to me as natural a process as birth: inevitable, absolute and final. If, when it happens to me, I find myself in a sort of Odeon ante-room queuing up for an interview with Our Lord I shall be very surprised indeed.

I think on the whole I am a better writer than I am given credit for being. It is fairly natural that my writing should be appreciated casually, because my personality, performances, music and legend get in the way. Someday I suspect, when Jesus has definitely got me for a sunbeam, my works may be adequately assessed.

Claudette Colbert got off on the wrong foot as Ruth in *Blithe Spirit* from the first. Ruth is a part that many actresses do not like playing, thinking that Elvira and Arcati have all the plums, but they are wrong. Ruth, if played firmly and dead straight, driven to extreme exasperation by her husband and Elvira, can be very funny indeed. Fay Compton, Joyce, Adrianne, Louise Troy (in *High Spirits*) and Rachel Roberts, who were on to this, all made successes as Ruth. Claudette was determined to play her sweetly and sympathetically and was so sweet to Charles and Elvira that Noel said she made their relationship incestuous. It also gave Noel nothing to 'kick against', which drove him mad, and she had not learnt her words; it was not her method, she said. Noel had known Claudette since she first appeared in London in *The Barker* in 1928, and of late years she had become an enchanting friend, but anything but enchanting to work with, like Beatrice Lillie. The story of their quarrels is beginning to appear in theatrical memoirs, passing into folklore. (It is true that Claudette did say, 'It's funny, but I knew this scene backwards last night,' and he said, 'That's the way you're playing it this morning,' and that he said he would wring her neck if he could find it.)

The actual performance went well, as Noel's Journal shows:

We went on the air at 6.30, having worked up to 5.45. During this fascinating period I had about seventeen cups of black coffee, one hot dog and a Dexamyl. When the play started I bounced on and, thank God, the curious miracle happened again. I played without nerves and *on* nerves and felt oddly detached as though I were watching myself from outside. The result was that the performance went like a bomb [i.e. a smash hit]. Claudette played her hysterical scene well, her first scene too slowly and too sweetly. She wore tangerine lace in the first act, black and pearls in the second and a grey ghost dress that would have startled Gypsy Rose Lee. Her appearance throughout was charming and entirely inappropriate to the part and the play. God preserve me in future from egocentric female stars. I don't suppose he will, but I might conceivably do something about this myself. I really am too old to go through all these tired old hoops.

Noel was also too old at fifty-six to be living solely on the income from his royalties, with no capital whatever save the fees from Las Vegas and the TV shows. Something had to be done, and it was in 1956 that Noel had to make his 'Great Decision'. At the time of writing, the skilled and the famous are leaving England in swarms to avoid the Chancellor of the Exchequer's avowed intention of soaking the rich and no one pays much attention, but when Noel had to make the same sensible choice, in his case also a painful one, he was made a target for the slings and arrows of the press. Not only the press, but many of his closest friends wrote letters of expostulation; he of all people, who had written *Cavalcade* and *In Which We Serve*, and whose very name connoted patriotism, could not, simply must not, leave England. And so, to add to his trials, he had to write many laborious letters of explanation to the very people he had expected would understand. He was merely leaving England to make his remaining years comfortable, and on his lawyer's wise advice. As Sir Dingwall pointed out: 'You are unlike a businessman whose concerns will go on bringing in money when he is old and ill: you are your own factory, you carry your factory with you in your head. What do you propose to live on if you become incapacitated, if you have a stroke for instance?'

Noel was liable to have to pay in income tax anything between £25,000 and £50,000 every year; in those days a very large amount of money, but in truth the British Government could not wholly be blamed for the fact that this left him with little to spare. Goldenhurst and Gerald Road and their staffs' salaries ate up money; as he admitted, to maintain two large and expensive residences and then not live in them was an extravagance amounting to idiocy. The pattern of his life since his first successes had been to travel whenever he could and to exchange the English winters for the sun of the tropics for as long as he could; therefore the regulation that he could spend no more than three months each year in the United Kingdom would make no difference to him whatever. He seldom had spent more than that amount of time in England for many years, and three months would more than suffice for the future. Nevertheless ...

A cable from Lornie saying that Gerald Road had definitely been sold for eleven thousand pounds. This, although obviously good news, depressed Little Lad, Coley and me very much. It is worse for them than for me really because they will have to go back and pack it up and wander about those memory-sodden rooms, touching the walls and furniture like Madame Ranevsky and saying their adieux whereas I am at least making a clean cut. It is none the less horrid to feel that I shall never live there again, never have relish in the magic power of walking briskly up the alleyway, bounding up the stairs, leaving a 'To be called' note on the round table and retiring to my cosy little bedroom where, let's face it, a *great deal* has happened during the last twenty-six years. The myriad 'somethings on a tray', the mornings after opening nights, the interminable telephone conversations, the morning séances with Lorn, the ideas conceived and the plans made and above all the jokes, the rich, wonderful jokes with Lorn and Cole and Little Lad roaring with laughter and me hopping out of bed in the middle of all the hilarity and rushing down to the loo. As Sylvia Cecil sang with such lyric gusto in *Ace of Clubs*, 'Nothing Can Last for Ever', and as many a prima donna has sung with equal gusto and superior orchestration, 'Adieu Notre Petite Table'. I hope that whoever occupies that lovely place will have as happy and gay a time in it as I have had. None of this nostalgie du temps perdu is deflecting me for a moment from the conviction that I am doing a most practical and sensible thing. It must have been a wrench for Lornie to give up the office in Gerald Road after all these years but she was superb about it as indeed she is and has been superb about all the major decisions I have ever had to make. It is lovely to think that for thirty-six years she has been my friend and for thirty-three of them more closely associated with my life than anyone else. Her common sense and her humour have never failed me, nor has her intense loyalty. Goldenhurst of course I mind dreadfully about, but only sentimentally dreadfully, because after all I did without it quite comfortably for ten years and have only been back in it for five and I am certainly in a far less painful position than people who have had, owing to the tax situation, to give up the ancestral homes they were born and brought up in ... It is quite startling to receive so much more admiration, respect and enthusiasm in America at ten times the money and as I propose to appear less and less as time goes on I really do think I might as well do it for more than double the appreciation and ten times the lolly. Another important point is that I am in no way saying goodbye to England, I would never become an alien citizen and am only going on being as British as I can be in two British colonies. After the next eighteen months I shall be tearing back and forth as I have always done ... apart from a very few small pangs, everything in the jardin is couleur de rose.

Apart from selling the two houses, Noel had to show that his 'intention' to live abroad was genuine, and on Sir Dingo's advice he resigned from the Athenaeum, gave up his Presidency of the Actors' Orphanage after twenty years, and put his small collection of good paintings up for auction at Sotheby's. Most of the pictures made a profit but he afterwards felt that the advice had been over-cautious; his *fauve* Vlaminck would be worth a fortune today, and he always mourned the loss of his charming Bonnard, given to him by Mike Todd.

The full furore in the press did not break until September when attention was called to the try-out of *Nude with Violin*, taking place in Dublin because Noel was temporarily technically unable to set foot on British soil. He had sailed from New York to Cherbourg in the *Queen Mary*, and the press came aboard at a very early hour while she was lying off Southampton. He told the reporters that were he to go ashore it would cost him at least £25,000, meaning in income tax for the current year, which was interpreted (probably not deliberately) as what he owed to the Treasury, whereas in fact he owed not a penny (and his London company was to go on paying large amounts in tax for the next nine years). He was further harassed by the press during his short stay in Paris and spent most of his time eluding them; they would probably have loved to know that he was staying with Marlene *chez* Ginette and Paul-Émile, and that Marlene was in one of her tremendously *hausfrau* moods and washed everything in sight including his hairbrush which, he protested, was already perfectly clean.

Loel and Gloria Guinness lent him their plane and fortunately, as he said, their pilot, in which to fly from Paris to Dublin where

I was subjected to a press carry-on which would have made Marilyn Monroe envious. The whole business was far and away out of proportion to the event, but of course had nothing to do with my play, only my financial affairs. They asked me sly, bold, ignorant, insulting and entirely contemptible questions for over half an hour, in course of which I remained calm and kept my temper. It was a disgusting business altogether. *The Times* on the other hand came up trumps. Their reporter, one of those who interviewed me on arrival, had some common sense. He not only reported me accurately but flew back to England and interviewed an official of the Inland Revenue who explained the whole 'non-resident' situation clearly, concisely and without frills. This *The Times* published and it was the one note of sanity in a naughty world. I wrote a very good letter thanking them and that was published too so at last a small blow was struck for human dignity.

The British Inland Revenue behaved well all through the brouhaha and continued to do so, arranging matters when he exceeded his time because of the success of *Suite in Three Keys* in 1966, and compassionate when he had to do the same thing another year, owing to Lornie's last, long illness. He obtained more immediate comfort from a rather unexpected quarter, Winston Churchill, who summed up the matter once and for all: 'An Englishman has an inalienable right to live wherever he chooses.'

HOMESICK
FOR EUROPE

So it was that, on a January day in 1956, Noel arrived at the Bermudiana Hotel in Hamilton to look for a house (no income tax being payable in Bermuda). The weather was wild; together with a cold and gusty wind the rain crashed down and the flat shapes of the island were only just discernible through the mist. The outlook was disconsolate, the letters of attempted dissuasion began to arrive from friends in England and he felt depressed and tired after surmounting the difficulties of *Blithe Spirit* in Hollywood. But the die was cast and there must be no repining. Sir Dingo arrived within a few days and set up business meetings with bankers and lawyers, the latter to establish his residence in Bermuda and to form a Noel Coward company there. All of which, although everybody was charming and exceedingly helpful, bored him to death. He and Graham traipsed back and forth for days over the island roads with a pleasant house-agent in a tiny Morris, and none of the houses they saw, except one, were the faintest good. The exception, however, was an attractively sprawling, fairly large house on the other side of the Sound from Hamilton, in the parish of Warwick. Part of the house was three hundred years old, with giant beams and open fireplaces, and it was right on the sea. Its name was Spithead Lodge and Noel decided without hesitation to buy it, and they flew on to Jamaica with relief.

As I had promised, the last ashtray was in position in the new house at Firefly ready for Noel's return, and Alton and I had stayed up more than half the previous night until we placed the final sod of turf in position in the courtyard, which the builders had left a desert of dust. He arrived at midnight, more pleased I believe than anything at the sight of his bed—a lovely old Jamaican pineapple four-poster—turned down ready for his first night in the house he had for so long planned and yearned for: 'The house is enchanting and Coley has been working like a slave to get it looking shining and bright, and it does. I looked out at the stars twinkling in the sky and the lights twinkling in Port Maria and felt very exalté.' Pat Marr-Johnson, friend and architect, had done a good job; he had avoided the obvious and boxlike by designing the rooms on different levels, so that they were all approached by steps up or steps down. This gave a pretty effect which Noel became less keen on as he grew older. Pat called next morning, to be told by Noel how delighted he was, and he left showered with thanks and praise. That night Mother Nature arranged a spectacular storm in glorious grey technicolour and the roof leaked like a sieve. Patches of damp appeared on all the white walls, some with rivulets running down and forming pools on the floor. 'All right, I have got the house of my dreams,' Noel said in a voice of razor sharpness, 'would it be *too* much to expect it to be watertight as well?' In spite of an army of workmen everywhere, bashing and hammering for the next two weeks, he wrote that he loved the place so much that he still couldn't bring himself to go down to Blue Harbour.

We stayed happily in Jamaica for the next three months, during which we and all our friends had to put our shoulders to the wheel and help with Noel's local charity, Designs For Living. This was a shop in Port Maria which sold furniture and other objects made by the Quakers in Highgate, profits from which were ploughed back into the enterprise, and where local boys and girls of school-leaving age were trained in arts and crafts. (After years of hard work the worthy cause finally died a lingering death because the ungrateful boys and girls, when fully trained, left and set up shops for themselves.)

We had a long committee meeting during which directives were issued and agreed upon. It was hilariously funny at moments but on the whole rewarding. We should be able to pay for ourselves within a year or two without demanding further aid from the American Welfare Foundation. I am proud of this because I like to think that I have been able to contribute a little to the island that has given me so much happiness and peace and time to work. The opening of the new premises was a great success. The local Canon, with a bang, opened proceedings and blessed the enterprise, imploring the Almighty, without whose personal supervision the designs of men are but as nought, to look kindly on our endeavours. I do hope if he is really going to take an interest he will find some means of dissuading Mrs Phillips from sewing sequin flowers on to raffia baskets, but I fear that this is too much to ask. After the Canon had mildly thundered, Hurley Whitehorne said a few fairly well-chosen words, then I sprang on to a table and declared the whole thing open. It was all very sweet really, and lots of local friends rallied round.' [The Almighty in his infinite wisdom did not intervene; the tourists made straight for Mrs Phillips, and her baskets sold like hot cakes.]

At the beginning of April the three of us flew to New York, and thence to Bermuda for twenty-four hours, during which day we took down the measurements of every single room and window of Spithead Lodge in an exercise book, to find out what carpets, curtains and furniture would be of use if sent out from Goldenhurst and Gerald Road. While Graham and I flew back to England, Noel returned to New York, where he was to recite Ogden Nash's verses to Saint-Saëns's *Carnival of the Animals* with Kostelanetz and the New York Symphony Orchestra, in addition to casting *This Happy Breed*, which was to be the third of his TV spectaculars.

I made my debut on the historic stage of the Carnegie Hall and I cannot, much as I would like to, describe it as a triumph. I spoke the verses clearly and well but the lighting was awful, the atmosphere fusty and the presentation very bad. Kostelanetz insisted on doing Carnival second on the programme, so I came on before the audience was warmed up. I asked him to let me come on at the end but he said that it was impossible. I couldn't for the life of me imagine why until I realised that had I done so, it would have interfered with his encores! Last night [on TV] was much better. Ed Sullivan was really marvellous to me and I did a cut version of Carnival and finished with Mad Dogs, all of which brought the place down.

He was greatly in demand for television at this point and in a letter to us in England he described his *Person to Person* with Ed Murrow, which

was a fair carry-on and no error. I did it in Charles and Ham's apartment because my cocoa-coloured cavern really did look too beastly. The waiting about for hours was calculated to be nerve-racking but I refused to let it get me down and went into the kitchen and made myself a delicious omelette and cut my finger on a tin of Dundee Cake and finally appeared before the cameras calmer than any concombre you have ever seen. I made a few good jokes one of which was when Ed asked me if I did anything to relax me after a long day's work and I said, 'Certainly, but I have no intention of discussing it before several million people!' There he was in a studio in Grand Central Station and I had to snatch his questions out of the air. In any event it was apparently a great success and I crept in a personalised way into thirty-one million gracious American homes. In course of the whole lark I discussed poetry and read a bit of 'Dover Beach'. I will bring over the Kinescope together with 'Happy Breed' and we will have a Coward Film Festival in Paris France.

Case-hardened as Graham and I were by now to moving into and out of various habitations, the picking-out and packing-up of the contents of the two large houses really was a gigantic task. From nearly thirty years of accumulations we had to decide what would be needed to furnish Spithead Lodge completely, and also the flat he and I had taken on Chelsea Embankment, what would be of use at Blue Harbour and Firefly or in New York, and make sure that the thousands of objects would at any rate start off correctly to their widely different destinations. We were far too industriously occupied to have time for sentimental mopings, as Noel had feared. The only piece of furniture we were affectionately sad to part with was the stupendously long sofa Syrie Maugham had made back in the 'twenties. For us it emanated nostalgia: every famous bottom imaginable had perched upon it, and it had been the setting for so many memories, blossoming romances, pitched battles of violent argument, lovemaking, feuds begun, old vendettas condoned, tears and laughter. But it was no use, it was too big, and nobody wanted it. The incoming tenants offered a measly £32 for it, which we refused because the covers alone had cost well over a hundred not long before, and we felt guilty and unfaithful when we labelled it 'To be sold by auction'.

South Sea Bubble opened in London on April 26th. Because of Noel's enforced absence this was the only major production of one of his plays that he was never to see, which worried him only up to a point. Of course he would have liked to see Vivien in the part he had written so long before for Gertie, but on the other hand he was not sorry to be out of all the fuss and fume and hullabaloo of rehearsals, the first night and possibly scathing notices next morning, and wrote, 'O, *not* to be in England, now that April's there'. *The Times* thought the play 'not unpleasing' and the others trotted out the tired old adjectives. Harold

Hobson in the *Sunday Times* said, 'Naturally Miss Vivien Leigh is the splendour of the production. Her performance shines like the stars, and is as troubling as the inconstant moon,' and he was right—Vivien, radiating star-quality, packed the Lyric Theatre in the months to come.

At some point during the twelve months before we left Gerald Road for ever, Noel had received a letter from Raymond Mander and Joe Mitchenson. Those 'truffle hounds of our theatre' had already published two handsome volumes, *Theatrical Companion to Shaw and Theatrical Companion to Maugham*, remarkable for the vast amount of research involved and outstanding for the loving care for accuracy of detail evident in both books. They astonished us at this point, when Noel's playwriting career appeared to be critically at its lowest ebb, by suggesting a third volume, *The Theatrical Companion to Coward*. To put Noel up there with Shaw and Maugham, instead of putting him to bed once and for all—a write-off—as the majority of critics had done ever since the war! Noel was delighted; his faith in himself had stayed as steady as ever no matter what other people said about him, and besides, 'I love praise and can never have enough.' But we both felt we should ask them if they fully realised what they were doing, possibly exposing themselves to ridicule and almost certain to be pounced upon by the intellectuals of the time for according to Noel the status of a classic. I was delegated this job, but only got as far as a lame 'Are you sure ... ' to be overwhelmed by an absolute torrent of conviction, the words pouring out of them (simultaneously of course, they always talk at the same time) and I can only describe their handling of me as solicitous, anxious to put a sheep who has strayed back on the right path as gently as possible. 'The Master's only going through a dip, all great playwrights go through it. Shaw went through it at about Master's age and lived to become a classic in his lifetime. The same thing will happen to the Master, you'll see ... ' So they were given the go-ahead and access to the files in Lornie's office, becoming in the process tremendous cronies of hers, and of Joan Hirst, her assistant, over cups of tea or gins-and-tonic. Terence Rattigan wrote a preface to their book of such generous praise coupled with wit that Noel in the future would say from time to time, 'I've just been reading Terry's preface again. It always bucks me up.' The book was published in 1957 and is now in the process of republication, having been brought completely up-to-date.

Noel was, in April 1956, deeply engaged in New York with *This Happy Breed*, which would be going on the air less than two weeks later. Opposite him he had Edna Best, his friend ever since the far-off days of *Polly with a Past* and *The Constant Nymph*. After she had played with the Lunts in the Broadway production of *Quadrille* she had had a nervous breakdown, from which she was now recovering, and she came to rehearsals from her clinic, which Noel felt would be for her the best possible therapy. He judged correctly, and she remained unruffled to the point of giving him a reassuring wink with her off-screen eye as he made his first entrance.

Before the credits were over on the screen, C.B.S. had over a thousand telephone calls. Apparently I gave a really fine performance, a great deal of which I owe to Edna. She was calm and sure and infinitely touching ... it is so lovely for her after all those months of mental misery to come back like this, and she has been so dear all through that I am forever in her debt. The rapport between us was so strong that it gave the play a little personal magic that it has never had before. *I* know it was good and I feel proud of having done it. Edna rightly shares all honours and the entire cast got good notices and immediate offers of jobs from all over the place ... what touched and pleased me most last night was a red carnation and a telegram from the technical staff wishing me well and thanking me for my confidence in them.

We moved into Spithead Lodge in June. Noel wrote:

Bermuda itself is much much nicer than I thought it would be. In the past [on brief visits] I never cared for it much, but now, in the lovely heat of summer, I am becoming enchanted. I love the pastel-coloured houses and the little creeks and harbours and islands, the masses and masses of Oleanders and vast Flamboyants. The sea, in strong sunlight, is a bright almost hysterical turquoise, and from where we are, looking out across the harbour towards Hamilton in the far right distance, the water traffic is very gay—little boats, big boats, yachts, naval craft, ferry-boats and Chris-crafts go scurrying by.

The atmosphere of Spithead Lodge was immediately sympathetic. Owing to its age and its beamed low ceilings, the rooms were con-solingly reminiscent of Goldenhurst and all the furnishings fell naturally into place. The house was approached from the coast road by a long drive, actually a cul-de-sac road in itself because it ran beyond us to the spit of land sticking out at right angles from us, on which stood a lovely house, rose-gardened at the back, called Spithead. This house had been for many years the home of Eugene O'Neill, and one year when Spithead had been full to overflowing, he had rented our house, in which Mrs O'Neill had given birth to a daughter, Oona, who in 1943 married Charles Chaplin.

What had attracted Noel most about the whole layout was the separate cottage called Watergate, fifty yards away at the very entrance of the drive, overhanging the water, with deep clear rock-bathing, one big room with a picture window, loo and shower and a kitchenette. This he bagged for himself because, as always, he wanted to be on his own, away from telephone and house-guests, and away from Graham and me if he chose. He could enjoy complete independence in Watergate now that he had learnt enough to cook his own breakfasts, of which he was very proud. He performed some terrible experiments in his kitchenette, sprinkling his breakfast coffee with grated chocolate and then adding a large pinch of cinnamon, the idea of which, first thing in the morning, made us feel faintly sick, but which he strongly recommended.

The very first crate to come down the long drive was of such immensity that it might have housed a baby zeppelin. Awestruck, Noel cried, 'What in the name of God can be inside it?' It was the one and only mistake made by the removal people—our dear old Syrie Maugham sofa, which had quite evidently refused to be parted from us. It fitted perfectly into the drawing-room; we were overjoyed to see it and swore never to part from it again. It eventually made another Atlantic crossing, and unbelievably was again the first crate to come lumbering up the mountain to the house at Les Avants, where it still has pride of place. Graham chose to perfect his water ski-ing, to Noel's fury, while there were still fifty-two tea-chests of books to be unpacked, and he and I staggered about under the weight, covered with dust and dripping with sweat. Graham quickly changed this rite to six in the evening, when the day's toil was o'er, after which we always went across to Mary and Joe Huber, our Philadelphian neighbours at Spithead, who were friendly and hospitable to excess, and poured strong drinks down our throats. Either they gave us dinner or we weaved our way, stoned to the gills, back to Spithead Lodge, cooked ourselves eggs and bacon and then fell into our beds, exhausted.

Our labours continued for weeks, but we were happy as sandboys, wearing smaller and smaller briefs as the heat and humidity increased. A great excitement was the arrival of the S.S. *Queen of Bermuda* every Monday morning:

She is very large and grey and hoots reassuringly, so unlike our own dear Queen. On Wednesday afternoon she steams away again, her rails lined with tourists with peeling skins, cameras and curious straw hats. Every morning at about noon a crowded ferry-boat passes and the gentleman in charge announces places of interest through a loud speaker. His voice echoes across the still water and when the boat passes Spithead Lodge I hear him explaining that whereas the house was originally the home of Eugene O'Neill it is now the home of none other than Noel Coward. The first time I heard this I was swimming along doing a stately Margate breast-stroke with my head high out of the water. I looked up in dismay, saw about twenty nuns peering at me through binoculars and sank like a stone. I don't really mind this daily publicity but it does encourage the boat's passengers to spring into taxis the moment they land and come belting out to stare over the wall and take photographs. The other morning I was caught, practically naked and carrying a frying-pan in one hand and a slop-pail in the other. I paused graciously while they took their bloody snapshots, and then pressed on with my tasks and occupations. Noel Coward is *so* sophisticated.

Nancy Mitford had written to Noel, enclosing the illustrated brochure of a Club or Home for aged and penurious writers in which, she suggested, they might happily spend together the twilight of their lives. The end of Noel's reply was as always, Non-U:

July the Whatever it is 1956. Darling Pen-Buddy, Your Author's Club letter made me laugh like a drain, as Lady Blessington used to say. Oh Dear what a comfort it is going to be to us all except that I warn you here and now that I shall grumble continuously about the climate. I am sending this to rue Monsieur on account of you might have left Torcello and come winging your way back to Paris France with your manuscript under your arm and a dreadful smug gleam in your eye. I would like to be able to tell you proudly that I have written thousands of witty words since I saw you and that my novel is finished and a new play started. Unfortunately however it would NOT BE TRUE. What is true is that I haven't written a bloody word except a short note in the third person say-ing that Mr Noel Coward would be delighted to attend the Admiralty Fete and draw tickets for the Raffle. What I have been doing is what is laughingly known as 'Settling In'. Oh Ma Fois and Misericorde Quelle Brouhaha! I do not know if Brouhaha is really feminine or I would have brought it up before, but I shall give it the benefit of the doubt. The house is enchanting and my own little private cottage a veritable reve because it goes straight down into the limpidest sea. You really will have to force your frail body (in the best sense) on to a plane and come and stay and we can sit in the lounge, which is very tastefully furnished, and have a spiffing old natter about books because as you may or may not know, I am just mad about books and you being so brainy and all, that you might give me a few ideas which, I may say, would be bitterly resented ... I must now stop and go back to my tasks one of which is to frost a rather rubbery angel cake which I made yesterday. So ta ta for the present and drop us a p.c. when you have a sec. Love and kisses. Noel (signed).

Ever since their marriage, Larry and Vivien's relationship with Noel, and his with them, had become closer. Larry he had always adored, and his already strong ties with Vivien were made fast forever at the time of her withdrawal from the film *Elephant Walk* owing to a critical nervous breakdown. She was taken to a hospital for nervous disorders in Surrey, given shock treatment and placed under such massive sedation that all her nearest and dearest naturally felt it safe to leave her. In any case no visitors were allowed, and flowers and presents were useless for she would be kept almost continuously unconscious for at least two weeks. But Noel was adamant in his insistence that there should be something from him at her side in case she awoke. Vivien's resilient constitution proved stronger than the strongest drugs and she became conscious earlier than expected, to find nobody there. Most of the people close to her were out of England and all she had as a loving symbol to cling to was Noel's bottle of Miss Dior. Vivien never forgot; from time to time in the years ahead she would unexpectedly produce the small white card with Noel's message of love which she carried always in her handbag—'All I had to hang on to at that dreadful time.'

It was therefore a considerable shock for Noel in Bermuda to receive a letter from Vivien to say that she was expecting a baby and would be leaving the cast of *South Sea Bubble* in three weeks' time. Of course he sent a cable of congratulations and of course he sincerely hoped that the arrival of a baby would help to weld their already troubled marriage, but why had his friends waited so long to let him know? They themselves must have known for months, but now there was little time to find even an adequate replacement and, as he noted, 'capacity hits are hard to come by'. The other person deeply involved was Binkie, as management, and when Noel later discovered that Binkie had known but had not told him nearly four months before, he was even more hurt and bewildered. Had three of the people whom he felt kept no secrets from him been in some sort of league? Or had they not had the courage to tell him, but waited until he was safely out of the way in Bermuda? He felt he had been unforgivably let down. The whole affair makes a sorry story: Elizabeth Sellars replaced Vivien at Binkie's suggestion and business took a nosedive (though it later recovered) and the day after Vivien left the cast she tragically miscarried.

Noel much later made such a self-indulgent scene with Vivien and Binkie when he got to Dublin for *Nude with Violin* (Vivien had flown over specially to see him) that he wrote and apologised abjectly to Larry for it: 'Whatever I may have ranted and roared in my unbecoming outburst was neither valid nor accurate. Curiously enough I believe Puss [Vivien] knew this at the time. She was very sweet and understanding and, I *know*, forgiving.' His letter ends: 'Give my dearest love to Puss and tell her that she's a wicked, dull, common, repulsive pig and I never want to see her again except constantly.' And so it was: he did love Vivien and Larry and Binkie always, and the incident need not have been mentioned in this book except that Noel dwells on it at length in his journals, a mass of correspondence exists on the subject, and it cast the only shadow on our sunny first summer in Bermuda.

The greatest excitement was Noel's purchase of a speedboat:

It is a very smart little craft and I am learning by trial and a good deal of error, to handle it. To live here and *not* have a boat would be silly because it makes the whole difference. We go off to faraway beaches, drop anchor clumsily and have picnics. It is the first boat I have ever owned and I am mad about it. We have learned to moor it, unmoor it, bring it alongside—convulsively as yet—wash it, fill it with petrol, start the engine, stop the engine, spring out of it clutching tangles of rope, tie up, untie and spring back again. I have rammed it into the dock very hard, I have scraped it over rocks, but so far no serious damage has been done. It is a fearful joy and fraught with peril and we are christening it *Dingo* [as a tribute to Sir Dingwall and his successful advice; but for him we shouldn't have been in Bermuda at all].

Our exploits with the *Dingo* were perilous and many. The most ignominious took place in front of the smart people with their pre-lunch aperitifs on the lawn of the Bermuda Yacht Club, all of them quite obviously saying, 'Oh do look, there's Noel Coward with his speed-boat.' I knew my duties as crew and, after getting her filled up, gave the cord a sharp pull to start the engine, but after many tries, and for the first time, she failed to start. I stepped ashore for help, both of us feeling ashamed in front of the Yacht Club watchers, and even more humiliated when a small boy hopped on board, started her with the first jerk, and jumped ashore again. I had one foot on the *Dingo* and one on the dock when Noel shot off at tremendous speed while I, fully clothed, executed the splits spectacularly and fell into the sea. I stood on the dock sopping wet until Noel at last realized that I wasn't on board with him and had to come back to collect me, cross as two sticks and calling me a clumsy cunt. He did however laugh and wave when we made our final getaway, to applause from the crowd.

(The reader will have gathered by now that Noel was fond of using four-letter words on occasion—not overmuch—as was Lornie. After long and careful consideration they both reached the conclusion that out of them all, because it sounded the funniest, 'cunt' was their favourite.)

Apart from a statuesque lady called Doris who came in the mornings and languidly vacuumed, we had no domestic help whatever at Spit-head Lodge. A cook was not to be had for love or the large amount of money we offered, and so we did the cooking ourselves. I was by now an efficient all-round cook except that I scrupulously avoided anything to do with flour; the making of pastry, pies, cakes and soufflés to this day remains to me a deep mystery, and all these were the things Noel particularly liked to eat. He, knowing as little as I about the subject, regarded this as a splendid challenge which he of course would overcome, and he did:

> Our kitchen scenes are good sound slapstick comedy and the cursing and swearing and getting in each other's way adds up to some nice clean belly-laughs. It seems to me that I do nothing but buy things. I go to the Super Mart for one tin of tomato purée and come out wheeling a barrow piled to the skies with comestibles for which there is No Room at the Inn. But still, while the cooking craze lasts, I had better give it its head. We have electric frying-pans, waffle-irons, egg-beaters, percolators, pressure-saucepans, double-boilers, cake-tins, moulds and a sea of bowls. We also have shelves crowded with canned herbs, canned fruit, canned meat,

canned everything. I have so far made, unaided, pancakes, chocolate cake, coffee mousse, crab mousse and a sensational Yorkshire
pudding.

He also boasted that he had made a consommé devoutly to be wished.
A most unexpected sideline to Noel's culinary activities was that he
genuinely loved to do the washing-up. He didn't want to help to dry,
he wanted to plunge his arms up to the elbows in the greasy suds, and
scour the pots and pans until they were all shining bright and clinically
clean.

The weather in August became grillingly hot with high humidity
and so, although the kitchen was large and pleasant, one wore as little
as possible while the oven and the gas-rings were on. Noel, alone one
morning, was in fact wearing nothing at all except Doris's little plastic
apron patterned with rosebuds, when a dignified-looking gentleman
appeared at the kitchen door and explained that he had obtained no
answer at the front of the house and that he was the Bishop of Bermuda.
Noel said, 'How do you do,' and would the Bishop give him *one*
moment to see how his vol-au-vent cases were getting on. Bending over
to see how they were getting on involved exposing his bare bottom
(bare except for the rosebudded bow tied above it) and by the time he
straightened himself and turned from the oven, the Bishop had fled and
never called again.

Noel summed up this culinary summer in his foreword to Adrianne's
cookbook *Delightful Food*, which she compiled with Marjorie Salter,
and for which Oliver Messel drew the enchanting illustrations:

Among the trends of the present day—the trend towards Rock 'n
Roll, the trend towards self-immolation (known as the Death-
Wish among friends), the tendency to drop the H-bomb on the
neighbours, etc., far and away the nicest is the trend towards the
kitchen ... Of course this trend isn't new, nothing is under the sun,
and over three hundred years ago Robert Burton said 'Cookery is
become an art, a noble science; cooks are gentlemen', but I am
sorry to say that it wasn't until lately that I heard the call to come
into the kitchen. The year 1956, which is shuddering to its close as I
write, has been an eventful one for me and not the least eventful
part has been devoted to my culinary adventures. There was the
wonderful day when my soufflé rose to such heights that it hit the
top of the oven (the oven fortunately had a glass door so that I was
able to watch this phenomenon open-mouthed), the thirty-six

hours I spent first trying to make puff pastry, during which I had to cancel all engagements and lost a night's sleep into the bargain, the night the Oven Blew Up, the afternoon the lid flew off the Waring Mixer and sprayed unreachable parts of the ceiling with chocolate mousse, and the day I said, 'Leave the canapés to me,' and later found that several of the guests had taken one nibble and then dropped them, not I must admit without reason, behind the sofa. I am learning the hard way but I am proud to say that at the end of my first year I have more than once turned out a creditable three-course dinner for six. Up until this year I had always appreciated good cooking but never learned to cook and the only pronouncement I had hitherto made on the subject was, 'If it's rissoles I shan't dress,' a rule I made in 1929 and to which I still strictly adhere.

The idea of a comedy about modern art had persisted in Noel's mind for some four or five years, but he did not settle down to the actual writing of *Nude with Violin* until 1954, when he noted:

I have been carefully reading Wilenski's *Lives of the Impressionists* and really no burlesque however extravagant could equal the phrases he uses to describe the Abstract Boys. Quite a lot of it is completely unintelligible. He talks a lot about 'emotive force' and 'constant functional forms', etc., and after he has described a picture in approximately these terms you turn to a colour plate and look at a square lady with three breasts and a guitar up her crotch. The first part of the book where he deals with Manet, Renoir, Cézanne, etc., is very good and written lucidly and sanely. When the Dadas and Gagas rear their ugly heads he loses his and writes unmitigated bollocks. I can only presume the subject-matter defeated him. At any rate I am grateful to him for giving me a lot of hilarious material.

Sir John Gielgud, as well as playing the lead, also directed *Nude with Violin* and, after rehearsals in London, the play opened in Dublin in September 1956. Noel got there for the second night and saw at once that it needed stringent cutting and some rewriting, and that though Johnny had directed with loving care, much of the business was too fussy. ('I wonder why it is that my plays are such traps for directors, as my lyrics are for singers. Nobody seems capable of leaving well enough alone and allowing the words to take care of themselves. Neither my lyrics nor my dialogue require decoration; all they do require are clarity, diction and intention and the minimum of gesture and business.') He also felt that Johnny's own performance needed help; he had probably been too occupied with other people's, or had been unable to 'see' himself. At the end of two weeks' intensive hard work from everybody concerned, Noel was able to write: 'The outstanding behaver has been Johnny. He has never for one instant shown the slightest resentment or even irritation although I have changed his production. He has been enthusiastic and helpful and has concentrated on nothing but getting the play and his own performance right ... I think now that the play will be a success.'

Nude with Violin played to capacity when it opened in London with Johnny, to more than capacity because of standees when Michael Wilding took over (Michael was headline news because of his recent divorce from Elizabeth Taylor) and then with Robert Helpmann it altogether achieved a successful run of one year and four months. Almost all the notices had been bad for the play, some of them, Noel says, 'choking and spitting with venom. One critic, whose name eludes me, says that this play places me on the bottom rung of the ladder, which is where I fully deserve to be! It is certainly a curious sensation to be the recipient of so much concentrated hatred and abuse.'

Noel had been trying to keep abreast by sitting through more than a few turgid so-called plays, utterly without form, all of which had received critical acclaim and awards. 'I expect I am just a dear foggy-minded old has-been. Oh no, I don't expect any such thing! What I *do* know is that as long as I continue to write plays to be acted in theatres, I shall strain every fibre to see that they are clear, well constructed and strong enough in content ... to keep an average paying audience interested from 8.30 until 11.15. Here endeth the first and last and, for me, only lesson.'

We got to Jamaica well before Christmas, Noel happier than ever high in his domain on Firefly Hill, and in nostalgic mood:

Another lovely week has scurried by ... I am reading again through all the dear E. Nesbits and they seem to me to be more charming and evocative than ever. It is strange that after half a century I still get such lovely pleasure from them. Her writing is so light and unforced, her humour so sure and her narrative quality so strong that the stories, which I know backwards, rivet me as much now as they did then when I was a little boy. Even more so in one way because I can now enjoy her actual talent and her extraordinary

power of describing hot summer days in England in the beginning
years of the century. All the pleasant memories of my own childhood jump up at me from the pages. I remember Bay Tree Cottage
at Meon, and walking across the cornfields to Tichfield to buy the
Magnet and the *Gem*; I remember exploring for the first time the
'jungle' round Aunt Laura's lake in Cornwall and the old blue
punt and the creek and the wooden swing in the clearing. I can
also recapture clearly the early morning before-breakfast bathes at
Bognor and the smell of the seaweed and of the bacon frying when
we came back to the lodgings. E. Nesbit knew all the things that
stay in the mind, all the happy treasures. I suppose she, of all the
writers I have ever read, has given me over the years the most
complete satisfaction and, incidentally, a great deal of inspiration.
I am glad I knew her in the last years of her life. She certainly left
me a lot in her will.

Noel had, as we know, been writing verse (as opposed to his lyrics)
since boyhood, for the amusement of his friends and himself. He now
began to compose verses in a more serious vein, but refused to allow
anyone to call them poems; 'those dear old fairies at my christening at
St Alban's Church, Teddington, endowed me with many rich gifts but
a true poetic sense was not one of them.' He first embarked on a long
narrative in varying rhythms called *P. & O. 1930* which forms the
main body of his book of verse called *Not Yet the Dodo*, published a
decade later by Heinemann and Doubleday in 1967, and dedicated to
Lady Diana Cooper:

> I find it quite fascinating to write at random, sometimes in rhyme,
> sometimes not. I am trying to discipline myself away from too
> much discipline, by which I mean that my experience and training
> in lyric writing has made me inclined to stick too closely to a rigid
> form. It is strange that technical accuracy should occasionally
> banish magic, but it does. The carefully rhymed verses, which I
> find it difficult *not* to write, are on the whole less effective and
> certainly less moving than the free ones.

His zest for the lengthy *P. & O.* might have flagged in the middle had
it not been for the arrival of Winifred (Dane) and Gladys at Blue
Harbour for a three-week holiday over the Christmas season. They
both seemed genuinely impressed, and Winifred, who after all had
written *Will Shakespeare* in good blank verse and who knew a great deal

about poetry in general, continued loudly voluble in her encouragement until he finished his 'epic' of the ship and its passengers' voyage
from Shanghai home to England.

Winifred was in fact vociferous in her praise of everything from the
moment they arrived. Noel, owing her so much for so long, had given
her at the age of sixty-eight this, her first and only holiday in the tropics,
and felt himself richly rewarded:

> It was a lovely drive [late at night from the airport at Montego]
> with Winnie shrieking with enthusiasm at everything she saw.
> When we arrived Blackie looked like paper and was obviously
> worn out but not our Winnie. Oh dear no. She downed a couple of
> dry martinis—midnight!—and was all for swimming in the pool.
> This was discouraged but the next morning she was bouncing
> about in the pool at dawn and from then onwards. She has already
> painted a large picture of several oranges, very good, told us the
> plots of several classic novels, recited reams of poetry and dug a
> fork in her own neck while illustrating the way Shakespeare
> stabbed Marlowe. [Noel was the only person who dared call her
> Winnie, and she suffered this ungladly.] Winnie is the supreme
> Dominator. Her vitality is indestructible, her energy fabulous and
> her untidiness remarkable; she manages to wreak more havoc in a
> small space of time than an army of delinquent refugees. She talks
> wisely and informatively up to the point where she gets carried
> away and begins to show off. Then steps have to be taken. Our
> evenings are loud with argument. She is a wonderful unique
> mixture of artist, writer, games mistress, poet and egomaniac. She
> is infinitely kind, stubborn, and ruthless in her dislikes. She loves
> me dearly and so everything I do has a glow for her and if it
> hasn't ... her own affection for me proceeds automatically to manu-
> facture one. She only really knows little bits of me. These little
> bits on the whole she treasures, but there are other bigger bits
> which are completely beyond the range of her understanding. It is
> all fascinating and the visit, so far, is being a triumphant success.

As always, with Winifred in the house, there was never a dull moment.
With bombshell suddenness she insisted that we drop our painting
and must learn the joys of modelling, she would teach us. So we had to
drive into Kingston where we bought such huge quantities of clay that
much of it remains at Firefly to this day, and an extraordinary assort-
ment of sculpting tools; kitchen spatulas, egg-slices, meat-skewers and

knitting needles (for scratching the effect of hair and for poking in the pupils of the eyes): 'Now a new excitement has happened, I have started to model in clay. I did a negro head to start with and then two full-length statuettes. Really not bad for a very beginner. Coley did an exquisite little woman's head at first go off and now we spend hours walking round our masterpieces and admiring them from every angle.'

Binkie, Johnny Perry and Terence Rattigan were also there, and the three of them with Noel made the worst possible—or the best— audience for Winifred's never-ending stream of Bloomers. Meal-times were a terrible hazard because there was the ever-present danger of choking. Fortunately it was at the end of luncheon that she electrified us all by declaring that every man had five John Thomases. '*Five?*' asked Noel, wide-eyed but wickedly encouraging. 'But it's well known, dear! There's the actual John Thomas he keeps to himself, and there's also the splendid John Thomas of his imagination. Then there's the John Thomas he only allows his closest friends to see'—she warmed to her theme—'and the John Thomas of his *other* friends' imagination. And finally'—rising to a climax—'there's the John Thomas he presents to the world in general!'

Naturally everybody looked in on Winifred's modelling classes, anxious not to miss a word. 'No-el, dear boy, you must wipe your tool! You cannot work with a dirty tool!' Then, when we had covered the armature with clay, in a clarion voice, 'Now then, stick it right up, ram it, ram it and work away, either from the back or the front, which-ever comes easiest! Some people use a lubricant, I've used honey in my time! And remember, when you've finished you must withdraw it wig-gle wag-gle, wig-gle wag-gle, ve-ry ve-ry gently.' It was un-believable. Noel wrote that she said these hair-raising things with 'unmistakable Freudian compulsion'. Or was it genuine innocence?

Winifred left Blue Harbour with uncharacteristic tears in her eyes after, she assured us, a holiday of pure delight. Much of this she fortunately captured on canvas; views from Firefly to the sea, seen through a maze of bougainvillea or fruit-laden orange-tree branches in the foreground. What with all the large canvases, the armful of bleached driftwood she had gathered on the beach and a lot of big conch shells, B.O.A.C.—and Gladys—must have been very tolerant on the flight back to London.

Lornie came in March and the days passed pleasantly, driving up and down to Firefly for lunch and dinner, until at last she asked me hesi-tantly whether there would be any chance of her seeing Master alone before she left. I felt ashamed of my thoughtlessness and told her that I had been asked by Ian Fleming to go on one of the 'adventures' he liked to plan each year, up to Cinchona in the Blue Mountains. (A violent earthquake, changing to a sickening swaying movement of the ground beneath one's feet, shook the island while we were 4,500 feet up, but that is another story; meanwhile at Firefly Lornie and Noel lay flat on the floor with their heads buried in cushions all through the violence, though the needle on the gramophone never jumped but pressed gallantly on, playing Margaret Leighton and Noel in the love scene from *Present Laughter.*)

On my return Lornie told me her trouble had been that Noel's will had become hopelessly out of date since his mother's death, and she had had to discuss this with him and get him to draw up a new one. Everything was now all right. When, weeks later, the new draft arrived from London, Lornie had sealed it heavily, marked it PRIVATE in red, asked me to give it to him as it was, and ask him to sign it. A will is of course a very personal matter, so I left Noel alone with it and went away as far as possible. Edna Ferber had said not long before this that cellophane stood between her and everything she needed, and Noel fought the same running battle with scotch tape. Very soon there were loud cries and yells for help, and when I got to him panting, he said, 'It's no use, I can't undo the fucking thing. You'll have to do it for me.' This I did and again I left him. More shouts for help; this time it was, 'I don't understand one bloody word, it's nothing but whereas and thereof and heretofore. For God's sake sit down and let's try to sort it out.' It wasn't all that complicated. After his very numerous and generous bequests, with Gladys and Joyce comfortably enough off, there were, he said, only Lornie, Graham and me he really had to worry about, and this had been taken care of.

Four months later Noel wrote: 'One of the gayest incidents in my London stay was a discussion of my will with Lornie and Coley who had re-written it between them. As the late Queen Alexandra would say, "How we roared!"' After Lornie's death and before his own, Noel's will had to be remade two or three times and on each occasion the pattern of our behaviour was repeated. We always started very seriously indeed about the essentials, then he began to enjoy enumerating his bequests, imagining the recipient's pleasure (much as he enjoyed giving splendid presents at Christmas) and we always ended in gales of laughter. '*What* did I leave to So-and-so?' 'Your emerald links and studs.' 'The Coward emeralds! I must have been out of my mind! He can have the tourmalines and lump it … Who gets the money if we're all killed in the same plane crash?' 'The Public Receiver, I think.' 'Well he's bloody well not going to—I'd rather leave it to a cat's home,' and so on. He was, however, always relieved when the job was done; to know that everything was shipshape in the remote event of his death. It was only a precautionary measure, done for the sake of tidiness. He firmly believed that he would outlive us all, and so did we.

After Lornie's departure Noel took a vow, which he did not keep, that never again would he spend what is known as the Season in Jamaica. Although he had Firefly as a bolt-hole, there were for him altogether 'too many people and too much happening'. There were so many other Caribbean islands, said to be very beautiful, and perhaps on one of these he could find the complete hideaway in which to spend each January to March. It must be remembered that as well as his wanderlust he also had his Ludwig of Bavaria compulsion to build yet another castle in the air, and he set off for St Croix, St Thomas, Tortola, Martinique, Dominica and the rest with eager anticipation. He eventually returned from this odyssey with as usual a great many hilarious traveller's tales to tell but without having found his Shangri-La. Within a few days of his return he found that like the blue bird of happiness it had been at home under his nose all the time, 'a fabulous piece of land with a spectacular view over the whole of Kingston on one side, and on the other a deep valley filled with bamboo and the Blue Mountains rising up into the sky. The situation is miraculous. So that is that and I shall start building when I have time.' Noel bought the land immediately, but in the event never built on it. There were already no less than nine roofs in Jamaica and Bermuda constantly demanding to be kept in a state of repair, and we all breathed a sigh of infinite relief when he sold the land a few years later at a profit.

Noel had learned by now the sense of taking paperbacks with him which could be jettisoned along the way, and on this voyage he took with him a great many volumes of Balzac, Thomas Hardy, Henry James, all of Jane Austen, and *Wuthering Heights*, which he considered, blushing with shame, to be one of the silliest books he had ever read:

I admit it was remarkable that poor Emily, thrashing about in that rectory, could have had the endurance to write such a long novel at all, but apart from some fine moments of poetic description, I see little to admire. The whole thing struck me as being the gibberings of a sadistic, manic-depressive lunatic. I don't believe Heathcliff for a second, and as for that horrid old woman who

relates so untidily the most unlikely story ... I know this is
Literary Heresy but it can't be helped. However I am comforting
myself with *Sense and Sensibility* and the gentle, acid good manners
of Miss Austen.

After *Wuthering Heights*, Noel continued his orgy of debased self-
revelation

by confessing a terrible disappointment in *The Mayor of Casterbridge*. This is doubly sad for me because, just having read a
eulogy on Hardy and his works by Virginia Woolf, I was all set
and prepared to enjoy his novels one after the other. V.W. places
Casterbridge as being one of his greatest masterpieces, in which
case I can only say that his other opi will have to moulder away
unnoted and unsung as far as I am concerned. I have also waded
through a long biographical analysis of Henry James and his
oeuvres and oh dear my heart is in my espadrilles. I shall press on,
for from time to time he has interested me, but I have a feeling that
I shall be maddened. [He wasn't all that maddened, and for many
years enjoyed much of Henry James.] I am beginning to suspect,
now, two years and eight months off sixty, that I have an incurably
superficial mind. If this is true I regret it only very little because
taken by and large it has kept me considerably amused for most of
my years. [After writing this, he read a great deal of Balzac whose
narrative quality he found strong and compelling, and felt that the
crushing sense of his inadequacy in literary appreciation had been
slightly mitigated.]

Noel at this point tried to have another honest-to-God look at himself
as objectively as possible, this time physically, about his everlasting
weight problem. With his appearance on Broadway in *Nude with
Violin* approaching, he had subjected himself to too severe a diet:

I became too thin and with the thinness irritation set in—irritation
and tetchiness and a feeling of unease and dissatisfaction with
everything. Even Coley and Little Lad, who could not have
sweeter dispositions, began to get on my nerves. After a little
private séance with myself I managed to spell out the writing on
the wall which said, in so many words, 'This is foolish vanity.
Youth is no longer essential or even becoming. Rapidly approaching fifty-seven, health and happiness are more important than

lissomeness. To be fat is bad and slovenly unless it is beyond your control, but however slim you get you will still be the age you are and no one will be fooled, so banish this nonsense once and for all. Conserve your vitality by eating enough and enjoying it.' After this person-to-person reprimand I gained about six pounds and have felt better for it. My face is not my fortune but it must be watched, if only for professional reasons ... it is no longer a young face and if it were it would be macabre. It is strange to examine it carefully and compare it with early photographs. There it is, the same eyes and nose and mouth, but oh, the changes! I think for the better; mutton is so much more acceptable when not masquerading as lamb. I have no complaints. If I am happy and at peace and my nerves are cosily enclosed in enough fatty tissue to keep them from twitching, the people near me are also more likely to be happy and at peace. I would really rather be fat than disagreeable, but with a little horse sense there is no need to be either.

Nude with Violin at the Belasco in New York was not the smash hit it had been on the road; it was in fact rather a damp squib. Business was quite good, but for the first time on Broadway Noel had to watch those thin arrow-like gaps at the side of the stalls nightly lengthening and widening towards the back. The theatre parties, which were in fact what kept the play going, were absolute hell to play to; all those otherwise charitably inclined ladies arrived at the theatre already disgruntled and didn't laugh much because Brooks Atkinson and Walter Kerr in the *Times* and *Tribune* had as good as told them not to. Mona Washbourne bravely went on being very funny and Joycie, repeating the success she had made in the London production, was a great comfort to all, both on and off the stage.

Noel each night scrutinised the gently diminishing box-office returns and became dispirited. He was however determined to play his scheduled three months and equally resolute that the damp squib should not fizzle out altogether. He therefore decided to revive *Present Laughter* to play alternately with *Nude* and *not* invite the critics (the audience cheered the roof off after the first performance) and then take both plays to the West Coast for six weeks, where they would not only make more money but play to more warmly welcoming audiences. So we left New York behind us where, Noel reported more than once, Charles and Ham had been wonderful throughout the blizzards and the disappointments, and opened in San Francisco: 'The sun is shining with all its might. The city is beautiful. We are a smash success with both plays and got rave notices. I have been praised to the skies and am now ensconced in the Presidential Suite of the Mark Hopkins reading, for a change, glowing accounts of myself in the newspapers.'

There were good parts for the company in both plays, except that a glamour-puss had to be found for Joanna in *Present Laughter*. From the moment Miss Eva Gabor appeared everybody's spirits rose, Noel's especially. He describes Eva with exactitude as an adorable darling, and he loved playing with her—there was such warm rapport between them. Her theatre manners from the start had been impeccable; she had appeared in the prettiest, most graceful dress of orange chiffon, only to have Noel say, 'You're not going to wear it you know,' and was the first to laugh when he explained, 'If you wear that, nobody's going to look at *me*.' With no fuss, she settled for the same dress but the colour of champagne. It became the recognised thing for Noel to hang his felt hat on one of Eva's beautiful breasts during their quick change at the side of the stage until Eva's dresser removed it—'There's no time for messing about.'

Graham and I saw Eva not long ago in Chicago, where she and Zsa Zsa were appearing in *Arsenic and Old Lace*, looking like innocent schoolgirls as the two murderesses. We stayed up till two in the morning with Eva, laughing about the times gone by. 'He took all my lovers from me,' she said, which was true to the point where he exerted the Coward charm, they fell for it, and gave a series of expensively enjoyable parties for him, and for us all. (There may have been other, smaller parties at which I was not present, and have no idea of how they ended.) 'And you remember how I went out whoring for him?' Again true to the point where she persuaded her admirers that if they were really fond of Noel they would give him a token of their esteem, and she once came back from dear old Lou Lurie, who 'owned the theatre as well as half of San Francisco', and poured out a handful of cufflinks and a gold watch for Noel. 'Oh, I worshipped and adored the Master,' Eva said as we parted. 'It was the happiest time of my life.'

The tour ended triumphantly in Los Angeles 'with *no gaps* at the side', Noel gratefully reported. There was however a great sadness for Noel at the very end. His lucky star, watchdog since his birth, was still on guard; he might so easily have been in the same plane in which Mike Todd came to his untimely end. All week long, Mike had begged him to fly with him to New York for the dinner to be given in Mike's honour on the Sunday. Mike thought it a lame excuse that there was to be a company party on the Saturday night, and as for Noel's flying next day to Jamaica, that could much more easily be done from New

York than from Los Angeles, but in the end Noel remained adamant, and Mike flew on the Friday night. The dreadful headlines next morning were a shock and a grief for Noel. He had the nightmare of having to play the last performance of *Nude with Violin* at the matinée, the first act of which was full of comedy lines about death. He heard his voice break when he had to say, 'Until death wiped out the twinkle from his eyes he contrived to enjoy life to the full,' but managed to recover himself. 'He was a human dynamo, insanely generous, a great showman, and a wonderful friend,' Noel wrote.

With Mike Todd's fatal plane-crash still so fresh in our minds, our flight to Jamaica turned out to be the most frightening air journey we ever experienced. After Havana, our almost empty plane ran into an electric storm of such alarming violence that it battered the hell out of us and the plane itself. We expected the plane to disintegrate and, after being flung about for an endless amount of time, that is exactly what seemed to happen; we came out on the other side of the storm and dropped straight down through the air, causing the contents of the galley to hit the ceiling and then crash to the floor. Broken glass and crockery floated in the gangway, which was awash with Coca Cola, other beverages and effluvia from the lavatories. Joycie, Noel and I remained green-faced and dumb but Lornie, with not much flying experience, cried loudly, 'Oh, how I wish they wouldn't *do* that!', and after the plane had levelled out, we emerged hysterical and shaken at Montego and headed for the bar.

After swimming several lengths in the pool at Blue Harbour one morning, Noel stood up at the shallow end and said to me, 'I have made a great decision, so hold on to your hat. I am going back to live in Europe. It's awfully silly, having two houses in the tropics; I want to breathe some fresh air, cool air. I am sick of all our loved ones being on the other side of the Atlantic. I can't go back to England to live, and I don't want to for any length of time because of the climate. It's curious, but I always get homesick for France when I'm away too long, and this time it's a bit stronger than usual. I feel I want to put some roots down, somewhere in Europe. Don't you think a house in the South of France would be a nice idea?' Then he began to enthuse and enlarge upon the delights of living in the South of France—so many friends already living there; he had always loved the Côte d'Azur; he loved the dining outside, the French cuisine and being able to gamble at night if he wanted to. France was in any case so much more civilised than anywhere else. 'And besides, we can get from Nice airport to London, Paris or Rome in a jiffy.' So I had to agree and enthuse because I loved

the South of France as much as he did, though inwardly my heart sank
at the prospect of another tremendous upheaval such as we had
undergone less than two years before.

Edward Molyneux had built himself a beautiful house at Biot, inland
from Antibes, but built of such mellowed, warm, peach-coloured stone
that it looked as though it had stood among its fields of lavender,
roses and carnations for ages. The house had a smaller *dépendance*, the
charming Old Farm itself, which Noel rented from Edward's sister
Kathleen and in which we spent most of the summer. Lornie came out,
so did Graham, and never did we have a happier holiday. Noel and I
worked on *Look after Lulu*, our translation of Feydeau's *Occupe-toi
d'Amélie*, in the mornings and even that was fun (laughing uncon-
trollably at our own jokes, we probably inserted too many Coward
jokes for Feydeau's good). The sun shone steadily on the surrounding
fields of flowers and on the pebbly beach at Antibes where we bathed
and picnic-lunched among hoi polloi and its on the whole beguiling
babies and children, which was indeed 'so much more fun than being
imprisoned on holiday with the very rich'. In the evenings, after
blowing ourselves out at Félix au Port on bouillabaisse we went,
stinking of garlic as we must have done, to gamble; as a rule in the
intimate little Casino at Juan-les-Pins. Noel had the longest and most
astonishing run of luck at *chemin de fer*, night after night. He won so
much that he paid Kathleen the costly two months' rent out of it, and
for all the lavish meals, and bought all of us, including himself, several
top-to-toe new outfits of very smart clothes. Even then, there was quite
a lot left over. The only thing he failed to do, although we raked the
countryside, was to find the house he so badly wanted on the Côte
d'Azur.

He almost settled for one, perched on the top of Haut-de-Cagnes
and consequently with a glorious view, but providentially did not,
because:

A sadness occurred between me and Edward just before I left Biot.
My new French lawyer suggested that the best way to settle the
house business was to borrow half the price from a friend rather
than do it on mortgage. I said at once that nothing could be easier
because Edward would lend it to me. [Edward was very rich.]
However when I asked Edward he refused, explaining that it
would mean selling stocks when the market was low (untrue) and
that he had to think of Kathleen! He also added in rather a
fiustered voice that it would be horribly embarrassing if I were

unable to pay him back. Oh dear. Oh dear. 'A thing called Pennies'
—Edward's favourite expression! What dreadful havoc 'Pennies'
can wreak in the human heart. Poor poor Edward. I felt mortified
at having asked him and so terribly ashamed of him. We have been
friends for 38 years. I must remember more clearly in future *never*
to demand of people more than they are capable of giving. None
of it really matters ...

The whole of the year 1958 curiously followed the same pattern; it
passed cheerfully with Noel in fine fettle, bursting with incorrigibly
optimistic ideas and plans, but few of them came to fruition during the
year, and some of them never. *Lulu* was completed, but though Vivien
regarded it as 'her' play, she contracted to do *Duel of Angels* instead.
Noel was halfway through a play, *Waiting in the Wings*, but somehow
the essential eluded him, and *Pomp and Circumstance* still languished
unfinished. But music was fairly rushing out of him and he composed
the score and scenario for the ballet *London Morning* in less than two
months, with a lot of melodies and musical themes left over. What to
do with them? He first of all had an idea of shifting the Shires hunting
milieu of *The Young Idea* to Long Island and turning it into a musical
for the young Daniel and Anna Massey, who would play the twins. A
few weeks later he discarded this in favour of a musical based on that
jolly widow, Mrs Wentworth-Brewster, who you may remember discovered in a bar on the Piccola Marina, and in the nick of time, that
life was for living. It was to be called *Later than Spring*, and Ethel
Merman would play Mrs Wentworth-Brewster, of course. Then for
some reason Ethel couldn't or wouldn't and Noel switched all his
enthusiasm to Rosalind Russell: 'I took her to lunch at the Colony and
sold her the idea. She is not ideal, being a shade too elegant, but she is a
brilliant comedienne and an enormous draw.' Noel felt there was a
strong chance that she would play it.

There were two months in Bermuda, where music flowed out of Noel
in a gratifying spate, song after song; unlike the old days of having to
memorise his melodies, Noel could now capture them immediately on
a tape-recorder, 'a great relief and a lovely new toy'. He was by now
eager for Rosalind Russell, thought she would be marvellous and went
on writing with her in mind, but had to wait until December, when she
would have finished her TV of *Wonderful Town*, before she could even
listen to what he had done. At last the great day came: 'I read *Later
than Spring* to Roz and Freddie Brisson [in New York] who received it
in stony, non-committal silence. I pressed on gallantly in the face of

almost but not quite overwhelming odds. She still hasn't said whether or not she'll do it, tiresome bitch.'

A great excitement has now occurred about doing *Look after Lulu* almost immediately. The first idea for Lulu was Shirley McLaine but she was too tied up. Then I approached Carol Channing by telephone in Reno Nevada, sent her the script, certain that she would jump at it, but she turned it down on account of Lulu being a prostitute and therefore unpalatable, and because it would be too like Lorelei in *Gentlemen Prefer Blondes*. I said, fairly acidly, that if so, whatever she played including Lady Macbeth, would be exactly like Lorelei. Anyhow the silly great ox was adamant. [I hasten to point out that this was written in the heat and disappointment of the moment; Noel loved Carol dearly.] In the meantime Sam Zolotow announced in his column that she was going to play it, whereupon Vivien went up in smoke in London and I had to telephone and soothe her ... what a perpetual carry-on!

A few days later we flew to England, having sentimentally decided we should like to spend Christmas in London, which we hadn't done for several years. All the loved ones would be there and there would be lots of parties, especially Binkie's traditional rout on Christmas night, always packed with fun and incident. But ... Noel wrote from his suite at the Dorchester:

The Almighty, with an unerring aim, has struck me down and here I am lying in bed with pneumonia! I cannot honestly say that I mind very much, the 104 temperature and violent sweating are over and I am weak but peaceful. I had a curious feeling, after my arrival, that the pace was getting too hot. The telephone never stopped and invitations and demands came flooding in and I was beginning to get frantic and panic-stricken. There can be no two opinions about it, I know far too many people and have far too many friends. I love to see them, I am delighted by their attentions until there suddenly comes a moment when I wish them all at the bottom of the sea. This is not ingratitude, it is merely my physical vitality rebelling. The Almighty, whom I occasionally suspect of being on my side, realises this and when he observes me going too far, giving out too much and generally making a cunt of myself, he firmly knocks me out. I am most grateful to him.

Though rather frail and wobbly, Noel was determined to carry out his plan of taking us all—'the family'—to the Boxing-Day matinée of *Peter Pan*, every word of which he could still remember and quote at the drop of a hat. He was delighted to find the theatre packed and that present-day young mothers and fathers were still taking their excited children, just as they had always done ever since 1904. Some of the magic had flown, he thought, but Sarah Churchill made a satis-factorily good Peter. Next day, undaunted, we took Kay Kendall to the Caprice, where we ate two enormous helpings of steak-and-kidney pudding, and then, distended, to see *Where the Rainbow Ends*, which reeked with nostalgia for us all:

This really has gone down the drain, but still has its moments. Micheál MacLiammóir was wonderful as the Dragon King, Pat [Anton] Dolin sincere as St George ... and Markova waved her arms about very prettily as the Spirit of the Lake. These two Christmas productions were for me indeed a *recherche du temps perdu*. I played the Rainbow 48 years ago and Peter Pan 46. I find it difficult to believe that I have been at it for so long.

18

'HOME SWEET HOME AT LAST'

THE new year of 1959 found Noel and me at the Hotel des Bergues in Geneva, which city was known by Noel as Calvin's Hideaway. He had given up all idea of a house in France, to everybody's relief, but especially his lawyer's, who had advised him to 'emigrate' from Bermuda if he wanted to, but had begged him all along to settle instead in Switzerland:

> From the first of January I shall be a resident of Geneva as well as Bermuda. There are many advantages and few disadvantages. I shall be able to spend my own money in whatever quantities I like without asking permission from man or beast. The fact that all this is possible surely proves that there is something very basically silly about international finance and economics, but silly or not I am thankful for it.

Noel immediately plunged into the pleasures of Switzerland in winter. He bought fur-lined overcoats and boots and ski and après-ski outfits for us both, and then off we went for a week to the intense cold, sunshine, glittering snow and blue skies of St Moritz, where we stayed at the Palace Hotel. The entire Badrutt family, the owners, gave Noel an open-armed welcome, especially old Madame Badrutt—*Die Königin Mutter*—who gave us the entrée to the 'six o'clocks' in her private apartments, Swiss Baroque and dense with hothouse flowers. 'Everyone' was there: Princess Soraya, the von Thyssens, Stavros Niarchos, young Winston, Lady Caroline Somerset, Lord Astor and, above all as far as we were concerned, Loel and Gloria Guinness. Loel, kindest of men, advised Noel at length how to go about settling in Switzerland, such sound advice that we bless him for it to this day. Beautiful Gloria was undoubtedly the queen and the leader of the revels. Everything, according to Gloria, was 'fahntahstic', from the ice-cold caviar in piping hot jacket-potatoes to which she introduced us, to our daily run down after lunch at the Corviglia Club on *luges* back into the town. Sometimes we sledded so fast that we couldn't stop at the prescribed limit, and one day Gloria and I, who had gone skeltering ahead, watched Noel come round the corner and disappear completely under the front of a lorry, which was fortunately coming uphill very very slowly. Stavros Niarchos gave the large and cheerfully noisy farewell party for Noel in the Bowling Alley of the Palace Hotel, and we caught the night train for Basle and Paris. Noel, with his abiding passion for trains, thought it a very romantic journey, hurtling through the forests and mountains and prettily icicled, snow-covered little stations in the middle of the night.

We installed ourselves expensively in a suite at the Ritz in Paris, and though Noel said, 'We won't even *think* about the bill until the end of the week,' took the precaution of sending for the remainder of his winnings from Juan-les-Pins. We sauntered out at noon from the Ritz into the winter sunshine, laying our plans: 'We'll have an *orgy* of theatre-going.' (And we did: magical Marie Bell and young Jeanne Moreau in *La Bonne Soupe*, Jean-Louis Barrault and Madeleine Reynaud in *La Vie Parisienne*, and a joyful reunion supper with Yvonne and Pierre after we had seen them in *Père*.) Then he added, hugely as we had enjoyed all the junketing in St Moritz, 'And we have no social engagements whatever. Isn't *that* nice. And we won't make any either. I'll tell you what we'll do: we'll go and give ourselves a jolly good lunch at Maxim's.'

Maxim's was absolutely packed except for a table for two next to ours, and, after a flurry of waiters and then a hush, in came the Duchess of Windsor with the Marquesa Portago and sat next to Noel. 'Won't you please come to dinner tomorrow night,' she very soon said. 'We've got an awful lot of people we've got to get "done" before we leave for America. The Duke and I call it the Bore Hunt and you must *please* come and help us.'

The Duchess lived up to her reputation as a hostess the next night. The Duke was in a party mood and sang to us in German and then in Spanish, accompanied by a young, pretty woman who turned out to be able to play anything required of her. Then the Duke made some of us cluster near the piano and sing 'Alouette', and 'Frère Jacques' as it should be sung, as a round. When the music changed, the Duke unexpectedly went into a solo Charleston and called out, 'Come on, Noel!' Noel faced him and the two of them danced the Charleston of

their youth in the 'twenties, each egging the other on as they remembered all the variations. The Duke's face became boyish again
with his enthusiasm, his still slim figure youthful, the whole picture
clearly recalling at moments the days when he had been the idol of the
Empire. Next, of all things, he suggested a sailor's hornpipe, which
they danced merrily enough, again remembering the different movements of the dance one after the other. I watched enthralled, happy to
see them so happy together.

Now, after all these years, I find that Noel had looked on the
incident with other, sadder eyes:

The evening finished with everyone getting a trifle 'high'. Princess
Sixte de Bourbon was definitely shocked when the Duke and I
danced a sailor's hornpipe and the charleston but there was no
harm in it, perhaps a little sadness and nostalgia for him and for me
a curious feeling of detached amusement, remembering how
beastly he had been to me and about me in our earlier years when
he was Prince of Wales and I was beginning. Had he danced the
charleston and hornpipe with me then it would have been an
accolade to cherish. As it was it looked only faintly ridiculous to
see us skipping about with a will. The Princess needn't have been
shocked, it was merely pleasantly ridiculous.

Noel is wrong; he couldn't see himself and the Duke. They had not
looked ridiculous.

Before we finally settled in Switzerland Noel made one last attempt
to live in France. A house near, but not in, Paris he thought would
be the thing. Lady Mendl's Villa Trianon, so crammed for Noel with
nearly three decades of happy memories, was made available to him.
He wrote:

Coley and I drove via St Cloud through the enchanted winter
forests ... to the Villa Trianon which is empty. They took me over
it because Paul-Louis Weiller said I could have it if I wanted it. It
was a painful excursion. It had not been entirely dismantled and a
great many of Elsie's lovely things have been left to moulder away
in the dank cold ... We walked shivering through the rooms, so
full of ghosts for me. We looked at yellowing visitors' books and
photograph albums and there I found myself, over and over
again, the sophisticated young Noel Coward of the 'twenties and
'thirties without a line on his thin thin face and quite a lot of hair.

I blew a gentle and loving kiss to Elsie over the years. She was so very kind to me. How she would have loathed to see her *objets* left to die so slowly and so coldly. Even if I had wanted the house it is far far too grand and big and elaborate but I *didn't*—I wanted to get the hell out of it as quickly as possible. We walked back across the sad muddy garden and life returned to my bloodstream and the ghosts departed.

One morning soon after this a splendid glossy brochure came through the post with illustrations in colour of a new block of apartments outside Geneva. They looked magnificently light and airy, flooded with sunshine and standing in spacious tree-studded grounds. Why hadn't we thought of this before? An apartment would of course be ideal, Noel now thought; all mod. cons built in and laid on, and imagine being able to go away and light-heartedly turn the key in the lock without a worry in the world! We caught the first plane we could to Geneva, and then got into a taxi and went straight to the address, hoping and praying that these desirable residences wouldn't all have been snapped up; that just one would be left for us or, if God were on our side, we might even have a choice between two. The taxi dropped us at a site which conjured up Passchendaele after the battle in the First World War, and we trudged through the mire to where some disagreeable workmen were sheltering in a hut from the pouring rain. They seemed incredibly stupid, quite unable to direct us to our magnificent apartment building, and one of the workmen called us *crétins*. Finally another, kinder than the rest, explained slowly as though to idiot children that they were only just beginning to clear the site and that with luck the apartments *might* be ready in two years' time. So again we were still 'homeless in Europe', but after two Rob Roys before dinner at the Richemond Noel cheered up and declared that in his opinion we had been saved by the bell and that nothing on earth would ever induce him to live permanently in an apartment.

Look After Lulu, with Tammy Grimes, Roddy McDowall and an all-round excellent cast, extremely well directed by Cyril Ritchard, and with pretty, witty sets and costumes by Cecil Beaton, opened in New York in March 1959 and closed six weeks later. As with *Nude with Violin*, only to a more frightening degree, the same phenomenon occurred. All through the tryout and the previews and including the opening, we had watched the audiences night after night—I do not exaggerate—rock and roar and roll about with laughter. Except for one rave in a lesser newspaper, all the notices were damning. Although licking their own wounds, both Cyril and Noel hurried to the Henry Miller on the second night to jolly up the company, and we watched them give the same shining performances. All those sure-fire laughs met with a tomb-like silence and the atmosphere became creepy. Creepier still when one thought of the implications; how could a few hundred printed words in the *Times* and the *Tribune* exert such a powerful psychological influence upon an audience?

The same thing could not happen in London, Noel thought, and it did not. *Lulu* opened at the Royal Court in July with Vivien Leigh to generally disparaging notices, but Vivien and the play packed the theatre until they transferred to the New, where it played to marvellous business until it dropped below the get-out in the pre-Christmas slump, when the management took it off—foolishly, Noel thought, considering the good post-Christmas advance. Critically speaking, Harold Hobson in the *Sunday Times* probably came nearest the mark: 'If *Look After Lulu* is only half a success, the reasons are more than complimentary to everybody concerned. The trouble is that Mr Noel Coward is too witty and Miss Vivien Leigh too beautiful. For the kind of play that *Look After Lulu* is, beauty and wit are as unnecessary as a peach melba at the North Pole.' Noel felt that the other, more abusive notices only mildly exasperated him—he was by now so accustomed to them—and this time the company needed no comforting so Noel caught a plane for Athens the next morning to join Douglas and Mary Lee Fairbanks on the smaller Niarchos yacht, the *Eros*. From there he wrote:

The Fairbanks have been sweet and nobody has been irritable with anyone which is a remarkable achievement. The Yacht is tiny but fortunately a good sea boat which is a great comfort as I only have to set foot on board any craft to attract the most violent winds and tumultuous seas. We had two days of halcyon calm, gliding along past isles of enchantment and fetching up with Stavros and Mrs Stavros (who is a darling) and caviar and vodka and the Jaipurs, and the Niarchos children and an English Nanny with splendid clackers. Then we left the Mother Ship (the *Creole*) and Poseidon said in Ancient Greek, 'Fuck you for a start', and up came the wind and up came the sea and up came everybody's caviar except Doug's and mine. The Mistros (Mistral to you) has raged now for four days and we are back at Athens, our whole trip having been re-arranged in order for us to dine with the King and Queen [of Greece] at Corfu on the 13th. This means nipping through the

Corinth Canal and sailing due whatever it is. Yesterday poor Daphne was thrown across her cabin and concussed; the ship continued heartlessly to do the Cha-Cha and radios were despatched. Last night, at last in harbour, the Queen's doctor appeared and said that there was nothing wrong with her at all! So now we are off again. Mary Lee is a great one for sight seeing, *not* touching stray cats because of germs and allergies. I have bashed away at gouache (as a change from oil paints), fallen in love with Greek architecture and stuffed myself nightly with Enusital on account of sleeping in a curtained-off piece of the saloon. I have my own loo and shower. The colours are glorious, the discomforts indescribable and the fun considerable. The *Creole* is fantastic. Nothing but Monets, Renoirs, Cezannes, etc. Daphne is better this morning. All my love to all my loves. xxxxx Maitre. I'm doing fairly well in Greek but it is 'ow you say, *not* easy. We dined with the Niarchos's at Myconos, very 'paysan' with fishermen playing on their local organs and singing off-key. Then, in a howling gale, the *Creole* speedboat conked out and we were towed home (soaked) by a caique! One of those caiques that you can have but *not* eat.

Two weeks later he transferred from the *Eros* to the *Creole* itself,

... and am now ensconced in a super luxe air-conditioned cabin with white-coated waiters fluttering round me like moths. The Niarchoses are kind and hospitable but curiously remote, particularly Stavros. He is the stuff of which Dictators are made. Everyone is terrified of him, and the staff cringes and trembles with fear at his frown. To me he is charming but his Napoleonic quality forbids intimacy and he flies into tantrums easily. Eugénie [Mrs Niarchos] is attractive and has a fascinating voice. The two little boys are potentially sweet but of course spoiled. Oddly enough, amid all this luxe and all these Renoirs and Monets the food, except for the caviar, is mediocre. I was told that we were just going to be ourselves but I might have known better than to believe it. Last night just after we arrived here we had sixteen people to dinner! I still hold to my conviction that the very rich lead most unenviable lives. With all the luxury on board this yacht I was happier mucking in with the Fairbanks family on the little *Eros*. They are a devoted family and their affection for each other spreads over whoever is with them. The Niarchoses are also devoted but there are unscaleable barriers of money and power between them and other people. I am enjoying myself fitfully but I shall be glad to fly away home.

On Monday at Corfu the King and Queen came to dine on board accompanied by an immense clutch of minor Princes and Princesses, all of whom had to be bobbed and bowed to. The Queen [Frederika] has a deceptive laugh based on a strong Teutonic lack of humour. The King has a loud affable laugh based on nothing at all. The Queen, who is very *Bas Bleu*, embarked on a long and confused conversation with me about Physics, Nuclear Fission and advanced planes of thought and experience. She then proceeded to bugger up her scientific theses by talking about the After Life, etc. I behaved splendidly and agreed with exquisite subservience to everything she said. They didn't leave until 2.30 a.m. so they must have enjoyed themselves.

I remain here in exquisite durance vile until Wednesday when, hell or high water, I intend to get myself to Geneva. The life of the very rich is not for me and although it is enjoyable to observe at close quarters for a brief spell it is strangely deadening to the heart.

Noel's one and only ballet, *London Morning*, was produced at the Festival Hall in July. The music he wrote for it is all delightful, with particularly lovely themes for the young lovers' two romantic *pas de deux*. John Gilpin danced with brilliance. The choreography by Jack Carter was commonplace, but then Noel's scenario was not inspired either; merely a passing and re-passing of schoolgirls, businessmen, ladies of the town, etcetera, and a young American girl falls in love with an English sailor, against a background of sentries and the Changing of the Guard. The Festival Ballet's faithful audiences seemed to love it. Clive Barnes, then with the *Spectator*, proclaimed it 'as predictable an entertainment as all-in wrestling ... it takes place in front of Buckingham Palace and has everything except Christopher Robin who must have been saying his prayers when it was cast.'

We had known for more than a year that we were one day going to have to bear a heavy sorrow, and this came to pass on September 6th:

Darling Katie Kendall died last Sunday. She died gently without pain and without any idea that she was dying. I felt absolutely miserable. She was a gay and wonderful companion. Rex really has behaved very very admirably. I went to the funeral with

Vivien; quite small and quiet and nicely done. There were no
mobs or shaming demonstrations, only a few newspaper photographers clambering about on the cemetery railings and snapping
the coffin being lowered into the ground.

Katie was ravishingly slim and young and beautiful. She had infallible
chic, a generous heart and oh, how funny she was. There could never
be another Gertie, but she was Gertie's only possible successor. Now
it was brought home with a pang to everyone who loved her, that we
should never see Katie again.

Without doubt the most important event of the year for us was the
discovery of what was to be our happy home at Les Avants. We had
house-hunted sporadically for five months but had, if we had known it,
got off on the wrong foot at the wrong end of the Lake. Because of
U.N.O.What, as Noel called it, prices had rocketed all around Geneva
and towards the end of May in near-despair we settled for a house in
the village of Céligny, in gently sloping fields just above the lake. True,
we should have Richard and Sybil Burton as near neighbours, which
was a pleasing prospect, but the house wasn't really 'Noel' and was in
such spanking fine condition—somebody's else's good taste—that it
would have been no fun at all to move into. And it was going to cost
fifty thousand pounds, of which Noel would have to borrow at least
ten. The Coward luck still held. On the morning when Noel had
promised to give either a Yes or a No, a cutting from the *Daily Telegraph* arrived unbidden through the post from Leslie Smith, Sir
Dingo's second in London, of a chalet for sale above Montreux at the
extreme other end of the lake, with ten bedrooms, four and a half
acres, and going for twelve thousand pounds.

We caught the tiny toy railway-train that twirls up and up from
Montreux to Les Avants the next afternoon. The little village drowsed
in the hot spring sunshine in a blanket of Alpine flowers spread over
the lower slopes of the mountains which half encircle it, and above the
village stood the massive chalet. Scenically it was sensationally well
placed; Lac Léman lay two thousand feet below and on the far side of
the lake the French Alps towered. The terrain of the chalet consisted of
four large terraced gardens, filled with wild strawberries, lilacs, goose-
berry and blackcurrant bushes and a burgeoning English herbaceous
border. Of the chalet itself I was a little dubious. Although not exactly
ugly, it was after all 1899 Swiss, but the more percipient Noel quickly
whispered to me, 'The rooms are very well proportioned and the
ceilings lovely.' The staircases were built with the gentlest, shallowest

tread. 'The house seems solid to me and we shall never find anything better for the money. Let's say yes.'

On our next visit we found the chalet wrapped round with a thickly swirling, grey and dripping, mountain mist; calling to mind Wuthering Heights in winter. 'You couldn't see your thing in front of your face, even if you wanted to,' Noel said, and we fled and sat in the car, wringing our hands and moaning, 'Oh my God, what have we done?' However, the rest of the summer was bright and sunny; the owners, Colonel and Mrs Petrie, were kindness personified, letting us come as often as we liked to make our plans and giving us huge nursery teas of home-made cakes and scones and rhubarb jam into the bargain. '*Now* we can afford to spend some money!' Noel said, having saved so much on the buy; fatal words, but he strode through the house planning tremendous transformations. 'All these windows must go and we'll have big picture windows; everybody must have their own bathroom and we'll have wall-to-wall carpeting everywhere, *especially* in the bathrooms.' Pale apricot-coloured stone fireplaces were specially carved in Vevey and we happily chose bidets, lavatories and douches, expensive wallpapers and French chintzes until in the end, Noel declared, the whole thing had cost him exactly two million pounds, seventeen and twopence.

To use less of Noel's wild exaggeration, the chalet itself, with its gleaming new contents and comforts, and the cost of transporting the vast amount of Goldenhurst and Gerald Road furniture back again across the Atlantic, were all more than paid for by the two films Noel made during 1959. After the big personal success he made in Graham Greene's *Our Man in Havana*, with Alec Guinness and Ralph Richardson, he found himself in demand and once more started a career as a film actor. The second film was *Surprise Package*, with Yul Brynner and Mitzi Gaynor, directed by Stanley Donen, for which he was paid £35,000 and all expenses:

> This comes in the nick of time because we were running low in the dear Credit Suisse and beginning to get worried. I read the script in an hour and said 'Yes'. I would have said 'Yes' if it had been written in Sanscrit. Actually it's very funny ... I have already learnt quite a lot of the part and I'm really looking forward to it. I'm also looking forward to being able to pay for the house!

So as to be near the rebuilding, for that is what it almost amounted to, we moved for the summer into the Hotel Victoria, across the valley at

Noel as ex-King Pavel of Anatolia in Stanley Donen's *Surprise Package*, 1959

On location for
Our Man in Havana, 1959

With Vivien Leigh, Kay Kendall and Lauren Bacall at the Ivy, 1959

With Sean Connery on location
in Jamaica for *Doctor No,* 1963

With Sophia Loren in Montreux
during the filming of *Lady L,* 1964

Sunday morning in Trafalgar Square, 1964

With Kay Thompson at Les Avants

With Peter O'Toole

The Wink

<

Coward by Beaton

On the set of Richard Rodgers'
musical adaptation of *Androcles
and the Lion* for television,
with the composer, 1967

With Dame Edith Evans
at a rehearsal of *Hay Fever,* 1964

Firing the noonday gun, Hong Kong, 1968

With Queen Elizabeth the Queen Mother
(Elizabeth Taylor is in the background), July 1968

With Charles and Oona Chaplin

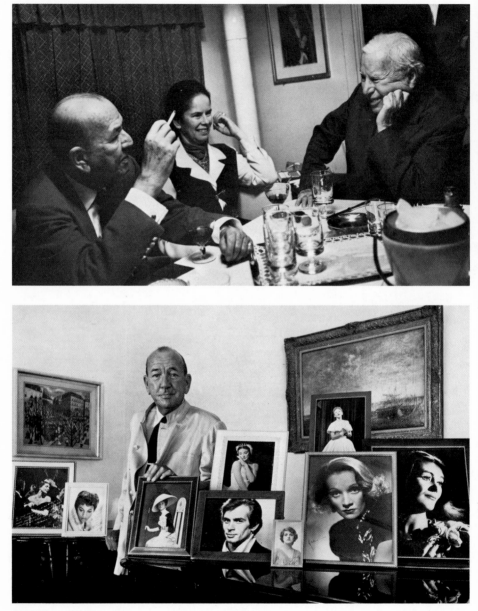

Noel Coward and friends

In the drawing room at Les Avants in the early 'sixties

Lornie at Les Avants,
January 1960

With Gladys Calthrop and
Joyce Carey on the occasion
of Noel's investiture as
Knight Bachelor,
February 1970

With Lady Diana Cooper,
January 1972

In repose, 1969

Noel's last photograph,
36 hours before his death

His grave at Firefly

<

Noel's last public appearance: with Marlene Dietrich
at a gala performance of *Oh! Coward,* New York, January 1973

Derek Hill's portrait of Noel

Glion. The atmosphere of the Victoria in those days reminded Noel of a Katherine Mansfield *pension*, which exactly suited him, but along with the retired couples and the well-to-do spinsters it surprisingly numbered among its clientele Edwige Feuillère, Suzy Delair and Margalo Gillmore, who were—unsurprisingly—attracted by Ernest the *concierge*, who provided every creature comfort, and by the excellent cuisine. One day, months later, in the car we passed a pretty girl who appeared to be sixteen, in a white cotton dress with her hair down her back, sitting under a tree and writing what I felt sure was a love-letter. 'I could have sworn that was Lillian Gish! But what would she be doing here?' Joycie asked. 'She'd be at the Victoria,' I said with certainty, and it was indeed Lillian. The love letter she was writing was the beginning of her book, *The Movies, Mr Griffith, and Me*.

Old friends appeared all through that summer. Adrianne and Bill Whitney were also at the Victoria, looking for a chalet, and found a lovely one just above the hotel; it was in fact Adrianne who had 'discovered' Glion if anyone had, and had brought her children, Daniel and Anna, there for summer and ski-ing holidays throughout their childhood. Many a riotous evening we spent with Van Johnson and his wife Evie, who lived nearby at Vevey, and then there was Edna Ferber on a long holiday at the splendidly Edwardian Palace Hotel at Montreux. Edna was a lady of iron will, famous for feuding and fighting in defence of her strongly-held opinions, and could lash with her tongue. But Noel, at the first storm signal, could usually manage to make her laugh, and he, Adrianne, Graham and I were proud of the fact that we managed to bask uninterruptedly in her friendship to the end of her life. Conversationally she was a spellbinder and had us riveted one evening with her revelations concerning that perpetual enigma, Jed Harris. Another evening after scrutinizing me carefully she said, 'The upper half of your head is rather beautiful,' which has left me dreadfully worried ever since about the more important lower half.

Queen Victoria Eugenia of Spain, who had for years been fond of Noel, now cropped up again in his life. The Queen's mansion near Lausanne bordered on that of Nicky and Mary, Comte and Comtesse de Chevreau d'Antraigues, and we were to see a lot of them all (Mary had been at school with Joycie) during the coming years. The Queen, majestic in looks and presence and, as she said, not Queen Victoria's granddaughter for nothing, could be quite startlingly forthright and took a lively interest in the progress of the chalet from the beginning. We had of course gone up there most days to watch this for ourselves, ever since work started in June. Then, one day in October, after luncheon the Queen said, 'Take my advice, my dear, and move in next Monday and *rough it*. Of course they will tell you you can't but do as I say. That's what I did in this house, I slept on a camp bed for weeks and I *goosed* the workmen every day. You must do the same.'

Never was better advice given. The workmen warned me that no one could exist in such conditions; it would soon be November, we were three thousand feet above sea level and there was no heat or light, let alone hot water. The ground floor was wide open to the winds of autumn, with no doors or windows. But when, true to my word, I moved into a little room under the eaves on the Monday, I found that the Swiss Family Heath Robinson (Noel's joke) had, with some precariously looped and vulnerable-looking wiring, provided me with everything, even to electric contraptions on which I could make toast and coffee for breakfast in the morning. 'You see,' the Queen said triumphantly when Noel telephoned that evening to report, 'What did I tell you. And now the work will go like *one* o'clock!'

The Queen also advised us on all kinds of other household matters. Did we know Mr Smith in Lausanne? 'Oh but you must, I shall arrange it. He is a friend of mine and extremely useful if you want to get rid of anything. He was a great comfort to me when my mother left me her collection of seventeen *chaises percées*.'

I very soon rigged up another room fairly comfortably and Gladys flew out to help me while Noel was in London finishing *Surprise Package*. Gladys and I were very happy roughing it, cocooned in sweaters and scarves. Hungry as hunters, we walked twice daily to consume hot meals at the Buffet de la Gare, and after the day's hard labour in the strong mountain air fell thankfully into the arms of Morpheus as our heads hit the pillow. On December 14th Noel arrived, in time for his sixtieth birthday on the 16th.

It is eight o'clock in the morning and I am sitting up comfortably in bed in my own house at last. Outside it is still blue dark but the sun is preparing to come up from behind the Rochers de Naye. The mountains are beginning to turn pink and the visible world is white with snow. I arrived cheerfully on Monday and was met by Coley and Blackie. The house is really beautiful, much more so than I would have believed possible ... we have all three worked like mad and filled up bookshelves and hung pictures. It has been great fun but exhausting. The main salon and library are done and look lovely. The French room done, the pink room done, and my

suite virtually complete and quite perfect. My workroom is a
dream and feels really shut away from the rest of the house, and my
multiple shower is sensational! I know I am going to be happy
here. It is a light, gay house, and the sun shines on most days, so
much so that it is dazzling and we are having sun blinds made for
all the windows.

The basic pattern for Noel's remaining years was now established for
good, as were the settings for those years, in Switzerland and Jamaica.
Quite apart from the advantage of Switzerland providing him with a
financial base in the Canton of Vaud, in which one gladly paid a
reasonable amount of income-tax, Les Avants became his home. All the
possessions about which Noel cared were at last under one roof; his
library, his collection of paintings, and all the furniture, by now much
loved through many years of familiar use. And for the first time there
was space enough to store all his published works, gramophone
recordings and sheet-music in quantity, and a lifetime of memorabilia.
Noel wrote for *Plays and Players* that month:

> Much faith is needed to believe in the Immaculate Conception,
> and I find that even more is required for me to believe in my
> sixtieth birthday. Both events seem to me to be removed from the
> realm of probability: of the two, the latter strikes me as being much
> the more incredible though, unlike the former, there is certainly no
> disputing it. Except when pulled up sharply by a very slight and
> very occasional twinge of lumbago I still think of myself as
> irrepressibly precocious, and capable of anything ... As with
> Queen Victoria, one Jubilee follows hard on the heels of the last,
> and it will soon be fifty years since I first bounced, with all the
> faith, hope and trusting innocence of a boy of eleven, on to the
> stage of the Little Theatre. It is unlikely that I shall drive through
> the streets in an open carriage to celebrate this event. But, like Her
> Majesty, I shall certainly hold a service of thanksgiving—on a
> smaller scale of course—for all the excitement and happiness the
> theatre has brought me, and for all the love and support the
> theatre-going public has so generously given to me for so many
> years.

In his own journal: 'There is an implacable ring to the word "sixty".
Ten years more and I shall be seventy if I am still a-growing and
a-blowing and then there will be old age. The fact that my story is

comparatively nearly over is something that must be faced. I hope indeed that my faculties will remain unimpaired for as long as possible but if they don't there really isn't anything I can do about it.'

On his way to Les Avants from London, Noel had had a long talk with Larry in Paris. Larry was in a bad state and confided that he was in love with Joan Plowright and had had to tell Vivien: 'He obviously hates hurting her but is equally obviously determined not to go back to her.' Vivien, after her arrival at Les Avants for Christmas, was 'desolate and missing Larry every minute but is behaving beautifully and her outward manner is gay and charming. Whether or not he will ever come back to her there is no knowing, but if only she would face up to the fact that he probably won't, and get on with her life until the old Great Healer does his job, it would be much better.' I think it is true to say that in her heart Vivien never completely gave up hope that Larry would one day come back to her, but the Great Healer helped as he always does, and she did bravely 'get on with her life'.

The press were not unnaturally burning with curiosity as to why Vivien Leigh was spending Christmas with Noel Coward and without Laurence Olivier, and a small posse of them gathered in the village. What were we to do? After an agitated huddle, it was decided to ask them for a drink before lunch. Vivien and Noel received them wreathed in smiles, were so excessively good-mannered and polite and charming, and Noel went on at such length about his new play, *Waiting in the Wings*, that no one asked a single embarrassing question. But it had been Close Shave Department, we all agreed: the news didn't break officially for another six months.

January 1st, 1960:

The new year has begun. The four of us, Coley, Blackie, Vivien and me, welcomed it in last night cosily and without fuss. We opened the window and heard festive sounds in the village. We kissed and drank each other's healths and settled down again in front of the fire and played 'Twenty Questions'. Vivien, with deep sadness in her heart and for one fleeting moment tears in her eyes, behaved gaily and charmingly and never for one instant allowed her unhappiness to spill over. This quite remarkable exhibition of good manners touched me very much. I have always been fond of her in spite of her former exigence and frequent tiresomeness but last night my fondness was fortified by profound admiration and respect for her strength of character. There is always hope for people with that amount of courage and consideration for others.

The year begins for me in a blaze of slightly tawdry triumph. I have had rave notices for my performance in *Our Man in Havana*. One paper carried a screaming headline and stated that I had 'stolen the picture' from Alec Guinness. It then went on to insult the rest of the cast and abuse Carol Reed. Delighted as I am to have made such a spectacular success in what is after all a minor part, my pleasure is tempered with irritation at being used as a flail against my fellow artists. This is not noble modesty on my part. I *am* very good, the picture *is* slow in parts and Alec *is* dull at moments. But I would rather have made a nice honest, deserved success which was not at the expense of other people.

I am worried about not getting on with the novel ... If I can't get it finished by the end of January, it will just have to miss summer publication and wait for next autumn to burst on to an ecstatic world.

I am being deluged with congratulatory telegrams and cables about *Havana*. Very gratifying because it means that my cinema stock will be high and I shall probably get some nice offers. Over this I intend to be choosy and wily. The new year is rich with promises. Let us hope it fulfils them.

After Vivien's departure, Lornie came to stay and to Noel's pleasure she seemed genuinely impressed by the house, *Waiting in the Wings*, and the nearly finished novel. Anton Dolin and John Gilpin joined us and one day took us to Gstaad to lunch with Princesse Antoinette of Monaco; a very happy day but a long one, involving much walking, at the end of which Noel started to complain of a pain in his right leg. The leg presented a frightening sight when we got home, so swollen that the skin was stretched very tight and in consequence shiny and in colour bright pink. John knew enough first-aid (from his years with the ballet) to ease Noel's pain through the night, but when the doctor came the next morning he diagnosed phlebitis at once; a much more scaring disease than we had realised, with a clot floating about in the bloodstream, and Noel was forbidden to put the leg to the ground in any circumstances. Luckily Piero, the young Italian butler, was strong as an ox and could carry Noel about like a parcel to the bathroom or to a chair while his bed was made. This went on for weeks until at last the clot dispersed, but because no one had warned us that Noel should have been doing deep-breathing exercises and certainly not chain-smoking while lying so long in bed, he ended up with severe congestion in his left lung. Each shallow breath he took was painful. Again luckily, our neighbour Mary Littleton was a first-class nurse from her war service and sweetly and efficiently came and nursed Noel through each night.

Jamaica was of course out of the question that winter. The long weeks of his illness had been far from uneventful and Noel had in fact been seeing a great many people. There had been the shocking and sorrowful news of his old friend Edwina Mountbatten's sudden death, albeit peacefully in her sleep, in Borneo. The happier news of Princess Margaret's engagement to Tony Armstrong-Jones. And the cheaper Continental magazines, ever to be relied upon for invention, began to state that Noel and Princess Marina intended to marry, that he was in consequence *persona non grata* at Court, and the Queen had forbidden his name ever to be mentioned again in Buckingham Palace. Glynis Johns came to stay and so did Ginette, Nancy Spain, Joycie and Graham. To the neighbours already mentioned, who all visited him, were now added George and Benita Sanders (Benita, Ronald Colman's widow, had been Noel's friend since the 'twenties) and William Holden.

The house was now in apple-pie order, the very last workman had vanished and so, during Noel's convalescence, the Queen of Spain could at last be asked to luncheon and to see the house. She approved of everything and especially liked my office, which, because of the 1899 art nouveau woodwork and the flock wallpaper, had already become cluttered with gifts of Victoriana. 'There's my grandmother!' she exclaimed and went straight to the Diamond Jubilee plate over the fireplace, 'and dear Osborne, and Balmoral.' After luncheon, the Queen said how greatly she enjoyed a cigarette with her coffee. For lack of matter, I asked if she had always smoked. 'Since I was seven,' she said, obviously delighting in my astonishment. 'My brothers taught me. They were nine and eleven and were already *heavy* smokers.' 'But Ma'am, you said you were brought up at Osborne with Queen Victoria! How did you manage?' The Queen's voice became confidential. 'There was a *very* convenient bush to the left of the main entrance. We used to crawl underneath, and once we were inside we used to *puff* away.'

As I have already said, one could not forget for a moment that one was in the presence of a very great and regal lady, but in spite of this the conversation would become racy, led by the Queen. 'We've only ever had one real drunkard in the family,' she stated, 'old Princess So-and-So,' to which even Noel could only manage a lame 'Oh Ma'am!' (He had met the Princess often.) 'Yes really. Sherry you know. She used to roll about on the floor!'

To complete his convalescence and get some sunshine, Noel went to Morocco in April. Two weeks later, from Marrakech (a rose-red city, half as Golders Green, was Nancy Spain's joke), Noel wrote:

I really am having a most peculiar holiday. Tangier was fairly ghastly except for David [Herbert] who was really sweet but it was *too cold.* I set off in a car arranged by 'Travel with Ferer, travel in terror' at 8 a.m. in a very old Consul with inadequate springs and a squat, idiotic, but careful driver. I bumped along in acute discomfort for nine hours to Mayigan which has changed its name to El Judida like Dorothy Cox changed hers to Diana Wynyard, where there was a bitter wind, freezing swimming-pool, a moderne-moderne French hotel with seven people in it. After two days of that I came here and it is HOT! I can hardly believe it. Marrakech is really beautiful and very much half as Golders Green. I have today been to a grand lunch party at the Breteuils when everyone started every sentence with est-ce que vous avez vu—or lu—as the case may be. We had Arab food, cous-cous etc: in fact damp mutton but vurry atmospheric deerr. The food in this hotel is lethal. I was served last night with a black rubber turd which was laughingly listed on the menu as steak au poivre. I sent it back with a flea in its ear.

I had a cable from Lornie saying that she has to have her left breast taken off as soon as possible. This is a dreadful shock and I feel miserable. I *know* that nowadays it's ninety-nine to a hundred certain to be successful, but I also know that the poor darling will have to endure hideous discomfort and a certain amount of pain. I love her so and I can't bear to think of it. I am well aware that we are all nearing the end of our lives but I don't want Lornie to go away yet. However, she is brave and sane and practical and will probably come through it all right. Thank God money is no object and she can have a lovely long convalescence at Les Avants. All the same, I *hate it.*

He wrote to me: 'Be firm with Lornie. She must not be guided by second-rate doctors, she must have the best of everything,' and promised to come hurrying home. This involved a stopover in Paris, where he stayed the night with Ginette and where

Coley called up and said Lornie's operation was entirely satisfactory and far less deep than anticipated. This was a wonderful

relief and I went out and dined with a light heart ... I arrived in
London on Wednesday and went straight to Westminster Hospital
to see Lornie who was as bright as a button and overwhelmed with
relief. Her room was crammed with flowers from everyone. I
warned her, wisely, that she would have a let-down later. She was,
if anything, too cheerful and I know that a serious operation is
likely to take its toll when the immediate fears and discomforts
have worn off.

Lornie, in spite of Noel's fears, made a good and quite quick recovery
and was happily spared to us for seven more years.

With Princess Margaret's wedding in the offing, he decided to stay
on and have what he invariably described as an orgy of theatre-going.
But this time it really was a veritable orgy; he had not been in London
for more than six months, and, anxious to miss nothing, he went to
matinées as well as every evening to the theatre and to two shows on
Fridays and Saturdays. He thought Larry was as usual superb in
Rhinoceros and the beginning of the play brilliant, but then it began to
drag and 'was directed into the ground by Orson. I am sick of these
amateur pseudo-intellectual scribblings—Ionesco in my opinion is *not* a
playwright and not a particularly original thinker. He merely tries to
be, which is fatal.'

He was therefore in no mood to go next night to see *The Caretaker* by
Harold Pinter at the Arts, but neither of us ever forgot the excitement
of the evening. The writing was an eye-opener:

> I went with fear and dread [but it was] *quite* another cup of tea. I
> loathed *Dumb Waiter* and *The Room* but after seeing this I'd like to
> see them again. I think I'm now on to Pinter's wavelength. He is
> at least a genuine original. I don't think he could write in any other
> way if he tried. *The Caretaker*, on the face of it, is everything I hate
> most in the theatre; squalor, repetition, lack of action, but some-
> how it seized hold of you ... Nothing happens except that some-
> how it does. The writing is at moments brilliant and quite unlike
> anyone else's.

From that evening on, Noel became an ardent Pinter admirer, saw all
the plays, and even, along with Elizabeth and Richard Burton, in-
vested in the film of *The Caretaker* which, as I write, is about to pay off
its original investment. How very pleased he would have been.

Noel always ended his account of the Ball for Princess Margaret's wedding with him and Margaret Leighton being 'swept out with the garbage'. In fact what happened was that they enjoyed themselves so much and stayed so late that when they emerged they were astonished to see the pre-dawn light and two dustcarts arriving at the Buckingham Palace Road entrance.

And now for the high Festivities. On Wednesday night the Court Ball at Buckingham Palace. Everybody looking their tip-top best and the entire Royal Family charming. From the pictorial point of view the whole affair was dazzling. The lovely rooms and pictures, the preponderance of red brocade and glittering chandeliers: the fabulous jewels and the excellent lighting and the whole atmosphere of supreme grandeur without pomposity. I had enjoyable conversations with Prince Philip, the Queen Mother, the Queen—brief but amiable—the dear Duchess of Kent [Princess Marina] of course and family, and the radiant engaged couple. He, the bridegroom, is a charmer and I took a great shine to him, easy and unflurried and a sweet smile ... Maggie arrived late and we wandered about and bobbed and bowed and had a lovely time. Her dress split and an Adonis footman produced a pin and we screened her while she fixed it up more or less satisfactorily. Finally, after she had borrowed half a crown for the loo from the bridegroom's father, we were swept out into the small hours with the garbage. A really lovely rout and something to be remembered.

Then, on Friday, the Wedding. God in his heaven really smiling like mad and everything in the garden being genuinely lovely. I escorted (not took, escorted) Maggie and we drove down Constitution Hill, along the Mall, through the Horse Guards Parade and along Whitehall to the Abbey. The morning was brilliant and the crowds lining the streets looked like endless, vivid herbaceous borders. The Police were smiling and gay, the Guards beaming, and the air tingling with excitement and the magic of Spring. One old girl in electric blue pranced in front of our car and sang 'Mad Dogs and Englishmen' waving a flag! The wedding itself was moving and irreproachably organised. We had good seats but couldn't see much, but it was thrilling all the same. The Queen alone looked disagreeable ... why, nobody seems to know. Princess Margaret looked like the ideal of what any fairy-tale Princess should look like. Tony Armstrong-Jones pale, a bit tremulous and completely charming. Prince Philip jocular and reassuring as he led the Bride to the Altar. The music divine and the Fanfare immensely moving. Nowhere in the world but England could such Pomp and Circumstance and Pageantry be handled with such dignity ... it was gay, lusty, charming, romantic, splendid and conducted without a false note. It is still a pretty exciting thing to be English.

After the ceremony a wild but beautifully organised lunch party for fifty people at Annie's [Ann Fleming's]. A glorious mix-up. The Duchess of Devonshire, Nancy Spain, James Pope-Hennessy, Jock and Betsy Whitney, Lucien Freud, Bob Boothby, Hugh Gaitskell, Judy Montagu, etc., etc. Great fun. I forgot to mention that during the week I met, at long last, John Betjeman and of course loved him immediately.

The Dublin opening of *Waiting in the Wings* was triumphant. Sybil Thorndike gave a beautiful performance, most moving in the scene with her son, played with strength ending in tenderness by William Hutt. Marie Lohr played simply and well and she too in her scene with Sybil moved one to tears. Graham was relaxed and charming and sang a touching little ballad written by Noel called 'Come the Wild, Wild Weather'. All the 'old guard'; Edith Day, Norah Blaney, Maidie Andrews, Nora Nicholson, Lewis Casson, Una Venning, Mary Clare, were provided by Noel with very funny or effectively contrasted parts, and the ensemble playing under Peggy Webster's direction could not have been bettered. Capacity audiences adored tham all, and the play, in Dublin, Liverpool and Manchester. Noel, as already reported, had fallen in love with Dublin and was having a lovely time:

I am enjoying Ireland. The pubs are peculiar and very very full of stage characters. In fact the Irish behave exactly as they have been portrayed as behaving for years. Charming, soft-voiced, quarrelsome, Priest-ridden, feckless and happily devoid of the slightest integrity in our stodgy English sense of the word. I had supper with Micky MacLiammóir and Hilton Edwards in their dingy but gentle house. We reminisced about *The Goldfish* and *Peter Pan*. Micky, who is two months and ten days older than I, has a jet-black toupée and a full Max Factor make-up and is full of charm and dubious sentiment. There is an atmosphere of amiable retrogressiveness over everything and everyone which, for a little while, is curiously attractive. The countryside is bathed in rain and magic light and feels like England—particularly Cornwall—felt fifty years ago when I was a little boy. One can drive for miles along excellent roads without meeting a car. There are occasionally little governess-carts and herds of cattle and the sight of a penny-farthing bicycle would not surprise me in the least. There is little television as yet [he means few aerials to be seen], hardly any hoardings along the roads and the minimum of Coca Cola. The Church has set its face against progress and I for one am grateful for it ... Elizabeth Bowen came to the play and was appropriately moved by it ... Brendan Behan appeared, strictly sober, very grubby and really very beguiling. We all adjourned to a pub and then to his house where we sat and roared at each other. I think he was surprised that I could say cunt and fuck as easily and naturally as he could. At any rate we got on like a house on fire and he appeared here [the Shelbourne Hotel] the next morning bearing signed copies of *Quare Fellow* and *The Hostage*. I was touched by this.

What touched Noel more than anything was the fact that he had put on a tie for the occasion.

Waiting in the Wings was presented by Michael Redgrave in association with Fred Sadoff. For the first time since the beginning of their long association, Binkie refused to have any part in the presentation of a play by Noel, and Noel was deeply hurt by this. Certainly Binkie was entitled to his opinion as to the play's merits or otherwise, but Noel felt badly let down; Binkie might have presented the play out of loyalty and for old friendship's sake and worked with him on it as he had so often done before, until it was licked into shape and more to Binkie's liking. He was of course grateful for Michael and Fred's belief in the play, and in the end, in a way, made himself respect the honesty of the finality of Binkie's decision. But then, one by one, examples of Binkie's perfidy came to light, of which only the major need be quoted:

At Larry's first night Gladys Cooper asked me why I had written a play about retired actresses and not offered her a part in it! I explained that I had written it *for* her, but Binkie told me that she had turned it down without comment. I originally planned it with her as Lotta and Sybil as May. This is rather shocking I am afraid ... the point is that Binkie just told a black lie. I am making no issue of this, but am wondering if Edith Evans, whom Binkie told me *loathed* the play, ever had it sent to her? It's not very nice, is it.

Noel also found out that Binkie had been discouraging backers from investing in Michael and Fred's production. He never—to my knowledge, at least—reproached Binkie for these duplicities or even mentioned them; he was accustomed to Binkie's devious ways in business. But it took a long while for Binkie to regain his place in Noel's heart as a friend.

Waiting in the Wings opened in September at the Duke of York's in London. I hesitate to weary the reader—but mercifully this will be the last occasion—with yet another account of the majority of the critics (perfectly justified in criticising the play if they felt so inclined) not even attempting to mention what they had seen happen in the theatre the night before, and therefore foisting an untrue and incomplete picture on their readers:

> The opening performance was an unqualified triumph from the moment the curtain rose until its final fall. The audience, unlike average first-night audiences, was marvellous, swift in all the laughs and quiet as mice when required. At the end there was a really tremendous ovation, and when I finally emerged from the theatre there were cheering crowds on both sides of St Martin's Lane ... next morning the notices. With the exception of *The Times* (guarded), *Telegraph* (kindly), *Chronicle* (good) and *Herald* (fair) I have never read such abuse in my life. The *Mail*, *Express* and *Standard* were vile, and the *Evening News* violently vituperative. I was accused of tastelessness, vulgarity, sentimentality, etc. To read them was like being repeatedly slashed in the face ... Even *Nude with Violin* at least won some praise for the actors. In this play poor Sybil's *great* performance, to say nothing of Marie's and the others, was barely mentioned. I am terribly sad for the company's sake. This ghastly cold douche after heartwarming triumph cannot but have laid them low inside. I know it made me frankly miserable. To be the target of so much virulence is painful however much one pretends it doesn't matter. It breeds hatred in the heart and that is unedifying and uncomfortable.
>
> The Sunday notices were mild and let us off with a caution. I cannot yet feel full repentance for having written a well-constructed play from my heart and seen to it that it was brilliantly directed and acted, but perhaps later I shall see the error of my old-

fashioned ways. I flew to Geneva feeling like chewed string ...
meanwhile *Waiting in the Wings* is playing to virtual capacity ... The
New Movement in the Theatre has been taking a beating lately
[he mentions some of the critically praised Turkeys] ... and that
staunch upholder of the revolution Ken Tynan has slithered backwards off the barricades and is now inquiring rather dismally
where all the 'destructiveness' is leading us and what is to be put
in place of what has been destroyed! What indeed? Nothing has
been destroyed except the enjoyment of the public and the
reputations of the critics ...

His novel *Pomp and Circumstance* came out at last and sold well, and it
remained among the top ten on the best-seller list in America for
twenty-six weeks. The English notices were snooty and Noel felt it
was no use, his legend was too strong and too exasperating, and he did
not now expect the critics to let him get away with anything.

At about this time, towards the end of 1960, he had occasion in his
journal to use the words 'What silly cunts they can make of themselves.'
Not with reference to the literary critics I must quickly add; he is
writing about certain ladies of our acquaintance. 'It's *quite* all right to
say cunt now because the *Lady Chatterley's Lover* case has been won and
already fuck, balls, arse and shit have been printed in the pages of the
Observer and the *Spectator*. Hurrah for free speech and the death of
literature.'

He felt strongly about this: in his opinion *Madame Bovary* was the
sexiest book ever written, and she the sexiest character, which proved
that you could achieve any effect you wished without the use of four-
letter words. His own lyrics are justification for this conviction of his;
he conveys the most outrageous possibilities—'took to pig-sticking in
quite the wrong way', for example—without giving offence. (His
enjoyment of four-letter words in private was quite another matter, and
his own affair.) He of course felt that the fight over *Lady Chatterley* had
been worth fighting and pleased that victory had been achieved, but
incidentally thought it curious that the case had had to be fought, as it
had with *The Well of Loneliness*, over a bad novel. *Lady Chatterley* he
thought meretricious and the characters cardboard, and felt thankful
that he had not been called upon to give evidence and have to defend
so important an issue arising from a novel with little, if any, literary
merit. 'What *should* I have done?' he often wondered.

Graham had to suffer many long weeks of strain that autumn. Sybil,
his pretty, comparatively young and sunny-natured mother, had for

some years been resisting the ravages of cancer, but at last he had to face the fact that there was no hope and that she was slowly, slowly dying. Noel had to be in New York, which enabled me to be with Graham to the last. Twice daily we went to see Sybil in Westminster Hospital. Her strong will to survive protracted the painful process; on some evenings Graham would have to leave her and go to give a cheerful, 'as usual' performance in *Waiting in the Wings*, knowing in his heart she could not last the night, only to find her next morning brightly planning her Christmas cards, or some other project. She spent a happy birthday on December 1st, but the next night we knew for certain that we had seen her for the last time; Graham went to give his performance and told the stage-door man to give him no messages — wisely, for she died while he was at the theatre. Noel happened to ring from New York just after we got home:

> His behaviour over the whole tragic business has been sane and brave and touched me deeply and made me love him more than ever. Thank God Coley was there, Sybil Thorndike has been angelic throughout and Lornie a rock of strength. This is his first major sorrow and I have no fears for him ever. He has courage, balance, humour and is much loved.

Death had also at last claimed Mabelle Webb, Clifton's apparently indestructible mother:

> Poor Clifton on the other hand is still, after two months, wailing and sobbing over Mabelle's death. As she was well over ninety, gaga, and had driven him mad for years, this seems excessive and over-indulgent. He arrives here on Monday and I'm dreaming of a wet Christmas. I am of course deeply sorry for him but he must snap out of it.

Those of Clifton's friends who were not in Hollywood telephoned regularly to try to cheer him up, Betty Bacall in particular, from New York. So did Noel, but Clifton wept so uninterruptedly that Noel finally lost his temper and said sharply, 'Unless you stop crying I shall reverse the charges!' which had an immediate effect. 'It must be tough to be orphaned at seventy-one,' was another remark of Noel's which went the rounds among the long-suffering friends.

Noel had prophesied aright. Although the sun shone, Christmas at Blue Harbour was indeed a wet one in the lachrymose sense. Apart from Clifton, the party consisted of Charles Russell, Jean Howard and Marti Stevens (known by Noel as the Blonde Beast), all three of them givers and by nature predisposed to enjoyment. What Noel and I would have done without them I really do not know. Clifton adored Jean, as we all did, and she was especially helpful at clamping down on Clifton's lamentations, but even she could do little after nightfall. He tried to be cheerful and succeeded during the greater part of the day. It was not until after the second martini before dinner that he began to tell sad stories of the death of friends in gruesome detail. Friends long since departed; Rudolph Valentino, Dorothy di Frasso, Jeanne Eagels, Lilyan Tashman and more. Mabelle and he had been great ones at overseeing their layings-out, and seemed to have had the entrée, refused to lesser mortals, to Mr Campbell's Funeral Parlour in New York for this purpose (and also no doubt to Utter McKinley's in Hollywood). Thank *God* they had gone to put the finishing touches to Rudy the evening before his thousands of grieving fans were admitted on the morrow. They had done Rudy's hair all wrong! Rudy never did his hair like that! It was *Mabelle* who had combed Rudy's hair correctly into position before his fans saw him. And Lil Tashman, renowned for her chic! Tears had by now begun to well. Whatever had been wrong with Lil's toilette—or hair—it was Mabelle who had righted it. Inevitably, as dinner progressed every evening, Mabelle's own laying-out drew ever nearer. She had been buried in her favourite evening dress (by Norman Hartnell) with all the correct accessories. Helen, Clifton's secretary, had been perfectly wonderful all through, but my God, at the very last moment they realised that they had forgotten the ear-rings to match! Clifton would never forget how Helen had driven all the way to North Rexford Drive through the night and all the way back to the funeral parlour so that Mabelle should have her ear-rings. At this point he would break down and sob and, as Noel said, there was nothing we could do except gaze at him in wild surmise and give him another drink.

The night was not yet over. Leaving Noel at Firefly, the rest of us had to drive down to Blue Harbour and get Clifton to bed. Charles and I, after the first night, decided it was silly for both of us to miss Jean and Marti's hilarious company, and so we took on the long job in turns. Getting Clifton undressed and into his pyjamas was only half the battle. After this, he sat on the edge of the bed and repeated word for word each night the same sad monologue: 'Ah, Coley [or Charles], you don't know. Nobody knows. Nobody understands. Nobody understands what it's like. Only Gloria [Swanson] understands. Marlene never called, did I tell you? *Not one word* from Marlene. You know what Gloria said when she called? She said, "Clifton, you've lost more than a mother. You've lost a sister, a friend and a lover as well." Only Gloria understands. Can you imagine, *not one word* from Marlene.' Poor Clifton. One felt dreadfully inadequate; with only Gloria understanding, one was left with nothing at all to add by way of consolation. Fortunately he had found a prayer which brought him comfort, and he would read this over and over again until he went to sleep.

The atmosphere was not conducive to a very Happy New Year; the air heavy with the knowledge that in all his seventy-one years this was the first New Year Clifton would have to see in without his mother. However when the time came he sensibly said he would not spoil our fun, he would in any case be unable to simulate gaiety, and would go early to bed. After he had finished his monologue, I left him with his prayer and went down to the pool, and we all became children out of school. The night was balmy and bathing slips were dispensed with. On the far edge of the pool, clearly outlined in a row against the sky, were champagne, champagne glasses and the big cheap clock from the kitchen, timed to go off at midnight. I can still see Marti at one minute to twelve, naked in the light of the full moon, fists clenched and in a fighting stance worthy of Muhammad Ali, shouting in an assumed tough accent, 'Come on, 1961! Get back there [with a violent kick] 1960, y'bastard,' then even more aggressively, 'Come *on*, 1961, I can take it! I can take anything! 1961, I'm ready for ya!' Then the alarm went off and we all raced through the water towards the champagne.

19

'GET ON
WITH LIFE...'

As Marti seemed to have anticipated, 1961 needed quite a bit of 'taking'; it was the year of *Sail Away*, the first big musical Noel ever 'created' in America. And in 1962, '63 and '64 Noel assisted in the creation of two more, *High Spirits* and *The Girl Who Came to Supper*. As always, Noel embarked on these three ventures with the highest hopes — 'It's going to be one of the best things I've ever done.' But as everyone who has been on the road in America with a new musical knows, many a battle must be fought between New Haven and Broadway, and at the end of these four years we were scarred for life. Like an old soldier looking back on his campaigns, sitting by the fire at Les Avants, Noel would sometimes exclaim, 'Oh aren't you glad we're going to have supper on a tray and go to bed, and we're *not* on the road with a musical in America?' Then we'd reminisce about past vicissitudes, among which the appalling hardships of the Taft Hotel in New Haven ranked high. Also high on his list were the wasteful hours of trouble caused by leading ladies' stubbornness over their dresses and hair, the violent quarrels, the screaming, the tears, the not speaking for days. Yes, when he eventually wrote his definitive book on the theatre he would write a *whole chapter* on leading ladies' hair and dresses. And, he always added, leading ladies' husbands would also come in for some acrid comment.

Before undertaking the first of these hazardous enterprises, Noel wrote three articles for the *Sunday Times* on the present state of the theatre from his point of view. He had tried with all his might to understand and appreciate the new wave of Kitchen Sink and Dustbin drama, as I know to my cost, having had to sit next to him through endless intolerable evenings watching hobos being unable to communicate. (Lack of communication between human beings was considered unbearably moving in those days, which it is, but of course in the theatre this did not make for spirited dialogue, on top of which the actors mumbled dreadfully.) 'Why doesn't someone go to a pub on a Saturday night for a change and write about that?' Noel inquired with reason. 'They're all as merry as grigs and communicating like anything!'

'Consider the public,' he advised the young writers of the day in the first of his articles, ' ... coax it, charm it, interest it, stimulate it, shock it now and then if you must, make it laugh, make it cry and make it think, but above all, dear pioneers ... never, never, never bore the living hell out of it.'

'My articles in the *Sunday Times* have appeared and caused an uproar,' Noel wrote. 'There have been so many letters for and against that they have been forced to publish only brief extracts. They have been on the whole idiotic ... One lady called Pamela Platt wrote that I should realise that my career was over and that it was unkind of the S.T. to allow "the silly old man to make such a spectacle of himself". This I consider to be on the rude side.' A week later: 'The press in London are still squealing like stuck pigs over my articles. Mr Levin in the *Express* outdid himself in insulting abuse. I really must write some more when I have time.'

For nearly eighteen months Noel struggled with *Later than Spring,* the musical he had started in Bermuda. Rosalind Russell had been right to turn it down; Mrs Wentworth-Brewster refused to come to life. She should have been an old duck of a character, and probably Miss Russell's chic image got in the way. So she had to go, and Noel substituted Mimi Paragon, hostess on a ship making a cruise from New York to the Mediterranean and back. He retitled it *Sail Away,* but made the mistake of retaining most of the other characters.

Last night I decided to perform a major operation and cut Max and Polly out entirely. They are neither of them real and never were ... they are hangovers from that abortive enterprise and have been worrying me ever since ... I have been working like a maniac since 6.30 this morning. It is extraordinary the way certain characters refuse to come to life. All the dialogue facility in the world is useless against fundamental falseness. It is always a mistake to try to rehash yesterday's cold mutton. Polly and Max are now, happily, dead as Dodos.

Five months later, in July in New York, Noel reported that everything was going so well that it was almost frightening. 'There is no doubt at all that Joe [Layton] is a brilliant choreographer. I don't remember since *Bitter Sweet* being so happy with a company. The whole thing is obviously headed for enormous success.' (Against which entry in his journal he later scribbled 'Oh dear!') Joe Layton and his wife Evelyn Russell became immediate and lasting friends; Joe co-directed with Noel and advised and assisted so closely that in the end the show was as much Joe's as Noel's. The show was a smash hit from the moment it opened in Boston at the beautiful Colonial Theatre, and was a complete sell-out for the month we were there. Excitement was in the air from the start; amongst those who came up for the opening were Judy Garland, Kay Thompson, Loelia Westminster, Lynn and Alfred, Cathleen Nesbitt, Sybil Burton, Richard and Dorothy Rodgers and Dorothy Hammerstein, and all attended the party afterwards at the Statler Hilton, which became a full-blooded jamboree. The heat was appalling, the sidewalks crowded, and the press went mad—flashbulbs and tension and hysteria. Elaine Stritch made an enormous success as Mimi Paragon. From then on there were celebrities every night and once two First Ladies within three evenings. Mrs Roosevelt came with Henry Morgenthau and was smiling and kind and congratulatory to all the company.

Some days before this I had received a mysterious telephone call from Adele Astaire; 'If I told you that a *very* important lady would like four seats on Thursday, you'd know who I mean wouldn't you? Right. Bunny and Paul Mellon are coming with her.' We never told a soul, but when the great night came a bellboy at the Ritz Carlton flew to the front desk and told the management that he had just seen Mrs Kennedy going up in the elevator. He nearly got a clip around the ears for telling lies, they told us later, but of course it was true, and while she was dining the news got out. Crowds gathered round the hotel and round the Colonial and the theatre became an inferno of reporters and photographers. Noel felt dreadfully embarrassed but Mrs Kennedy didn't seem to mind. She made it quite evident that she had enjoyed the show and was sweet to Noel and to everybody else, including the photographers.

Coley and I had a lovely day on Sunday. Paul and Bunny Mellon sent their private jet for us and we were whisked to Osterville on Cape Cod, an exquisite house, where we had a gay lunch with the President and Mrs Kennedy, both of whom were charming. I was impressed with him. Although the burden of the Western World is on his shoulders he resolutely insists on relaxing completely every weekend. They arrived on the *Merlin*, the Presidential motor cruiser. Secret Service gentlemen were festooned from every tree. She is pretty, cheerful and full of star quality. In fact they both are. She is also, to her everlasting credit, an ardent Coward fan. Adele was there, full of vitality and gaiety as always.

Dellie had met us with Mr Mellon at the airport, and in the car Noel told Dellie that he hoped she would behave herself in front of the President and *not* tell the story with which she had had such a success in Jamaica that spring, about the couple on their honeymoon night and the bride's gums being in a terrible condition. She did not tell the story, but the subject of dentistry cropped up with agonising frequency during luncheon.

I may have made Boston sound like the dream of delight which it was, but underneath the triumphant success we were suffering the first of our battle-scars; we were stricken with that age-old malady of musicals on the road, 'book trouble'. The notices in Philadelphia, though good, made it ruthlessly clear that the show sagged whenever the two singing leads came on to play their love story. They both sang Noel's songs beautifully but—not their fault—the characters of Verity and Johnny were essentially bores. Noel had done all he could to give them the breath of life and could do no more: he was despairingly drinking his breakfast coffee when Joe breezed smiling into the room. 'Why don't we cut Verity out altogether, give the best of her songs to Stritch, and have Johnny fall in love with Mimi Paragon instead?' It was as simple as that, and of course he was right, but oh, what this entailed; what dramas, what tears. No one had ever before entirely cut out an important star part, Equity had to be appealed to for a ruling, and we had to attend an arbitration meeting. The management, Haila Stoddard and Don Seawell, remained firmly in support of Noel during the hell that ensued. For two days Noel worked at high pressure on the scissors-and-paste job while the company, all of whom would be affected by the change, were in a state of suspended frenzy.

What was virtually a new show was rewritten, learnt, rehearsed and opened six nights later:

Stritch's performance was nothing short of miraculous and she sang 'Something Very Strange' so movingly that I almost cried. There is no doubt about it, I made the right decision. There are now no dull patches and James Hurst [Johnny] has come up a fair treat.

The [New York] *Times* notice was a rave. Walter Kerr in the *Tribune* was disagreeable but praised Stritch extravagantly ... there has been a line at the box-office since we opened. The first-night performance was magnificent, the audience chic to the point of nausea but, for them, enthusiastic. The party afterwards at Sardi's East given by the management was beautifully organised hell. Everyone in New York was there invited or uninvited from Adlai Stevenson to Jean Fenn. [It was Jean who had played Verity until the part was cut.] My little lot consisted of Marlene, who behaved fairly well, Dorothy Dickson who behaved divinely, Myrna Loy ditto, and Stritchie, and later Maggie Leighton. Everyone had gone out of their way to make it a tribute to me. My music was played incessantly ... and one room was entirely devoted to caricatures of me. I had millions of telegrams, masses of flowers and several expensive presents. When I pause to reflect on the numbers of people who seem genuinely to wish me well from all corners of the world, I am really very proud and pleased.

We flew after this to Jamaica as soon as we possibly could. Geoffrey Johnson, who because of *Sail Away* had come into our lives for good and still looks after Noel's affairs in America, came with us to help answer the 'millions' of telegrams and letters. Mornings were devoted to this tremendous task for several weeks; apart from this, the sensation of having nothing particular to do was extraordinary. Noel wrote to Gladys:

Darling Cockalino, Here I am after all the sturm and drang having a nice sitty down and contemplating my navel which looks lovelier than ever in a drained sort of way. I really must have it lifted. It has all been yolly interesting and novel and a bit epuisant and although I enjoyed most of it I really wouldn't wish to embark on such a gargantuan lark again for quaite a whaile. When I left Nueva York we were playing to our full complement of standees ... We recorded the cast album last Sunday and it was out on Wednesday! How's that for efficiency? Not very like our own dear His Master's Voice ... the company is really marvellous and I love each and every one of them. Stritch is divine and very funny indeed both on the stage and off it ... It's so absolutely lovely having nothing whatever to do and so it's out with the easels and on with the Naples Yellow. Hurray! I am very well indeed—I can't think why—and have remained so all through the whole alouette. Arrivederci for the momento and love to the dear [Alan] Mooreheads. Baci Baci Baci, Cockalino.

As will have been gathered, he had become very fond indeed of the mercurial Elaine Stritch. One never knew what aspect of herself she would next reveal; her devout Catholicism perhaps fascinated Noel the most. She and the larger proportion of the company were Catholics, and we loved the way they all flew to the callboard on arrival in a new town to see if there was what they called a Late Show, Midnight Mass on the Saturday, which would enable them to sleep late on Sunday morning. Noel thought this a very sensible idea. He wrote from Jamaica:

> Darling Stritchie, I hope that you are well; that your cold is better; that you are singing divinely; that you are putting on weight; that you are not belting too much; that your skin is clear and free from spots and blemishes; that you are delivering my brilliant material to the public in the manner in which it *should* be delivered; that you are not making too many God-damned suggestions; that your breath is relatively free from the sinful taint of alcohol; that you are singing the verse of 'Come to Me' more quickly; that you are going regularly to confession and to everywhere else that it is necessary to go regularly. I also hope that you are not encouraging those dear little doggies to behave in such a fashion on the stage that they bring disrepute to the fair name of Equity and add fuel to the already prevalent suspicion that our gallant little company is not, by and large, entirely normal; that you are being gracious and attentive to Pat Harty's manager; and that you are not constantly taking all those silly people to the Pavillon for lunch *every* day. They only exhaust you and drain your energy and however much you want to keep in with them, you must remember that your first duty is to Haila Stoddard, M.C.A. and the Catholic Church ... I remain yours sincerely with mad hot kisses. Annamary Dickey. [Miss Dickey was a character actress in the show.]

After twenty years of devotion, Charles and Ham's association with Noel, as part of his 'family' and as business associates, was terminated this autumn, with Charles's contract to expire formally the following April. Charles was ambitious and rightly so, for he seemed to possess every qualification for success. One can only assume that it was his relationship with Noel that was at the heart of the matter. A love-hate relationship on his side seemed to have developed; Noel's journal for this year records a long series of raging scenes followed by affectionate reconciliations, the latter always accompanied by great relief on Noel's part. None of us could ever explain exactly what had happened, and I certainly cannot explain it now. Nor do I wish to, it was too painful; they had for so long played such a large and happy part in our lives.

It was at this point that Geoffrey Johnson took over Noel's New York office with quiet efficiency. Slim, tall and good-looking, he at that time closely resembled Franchot Tone when young. He had already served nearly a year's apprenticeship, helping me through the turmoil of the tour of *Sail Away*, and in any case had the advantage of always having worked in the theatre and of being such a Noel Coward admirer that he possessed a knowledge of everything Noel had ever written, composed, filmed or recorded. Nothing had to be explained; Geoffrey knew it already. His advent at this point was lucky for us and perhaps even more fortunate for him—it meant that he got to know and be loved by Lornie before she died, he enjoyed the inestimable privilege of Katharine Cornell's friendship and of Noel's love to the end.

On Sunday evening, October 29th, 1961, the telephone rang at Blue Harbour; with difficulty, for the line was very faint, I took down a cable from New York to say that Jack had died that morning. Although not unexpected—Jack had been slowly disintegrating for years—this was a blow, another large part of our lives which had gone for ever. The telephone rang again, and fainter than before I could just make out the same words, 'Deeply regret to inform you', at which I shouted at the operator (she couldn't hear me either) that we had already received the cable. But she pressed on and I heard the name Guthrie; dear Guthrie McClintic had also died that morning. In his journal Noel wrote:

I shall always miss him. Jack of course is quite another matter. I cannot feel sad that he is dead. He has been less than half alive for the last ten years, a trouble and a bore to himself and everyone else. Naturally, now that he is dead my mind is inclined to fly back to when he was handsome, witty, charming, good company ... of course I am sad. Of course I feel horrid inside. But not nearly so much as I might have. To me he died years ago. [Here he pays unlimited tribute to Natasha and her superb behaviour through those trying years; he had become more devoted to her than ever.]

Ah me! This losing of friends and breaking of links with the past. One by one they go—a bit chipped off here, a bit chipped off there. It is an inevitability that one must prepare the heart and mind for. I shall probably live to see many other, more poignant deaths. Unlike Edna St Vincent Millay I *am* resigned. [One of her poems begins, 'I am not resigned to the shutting away of loving hearts in the cold ground … '] There is no sense in rebellion … I'd rather face up to finality and get on with life, lonely or not, for as long as it lasts. Those I have really loved are with me in moments of memory—intact and unchanged. I cannot envisage them in another sphere. I do not even wish to. If I were to see darling Mum again which phase of her should I choose? The last sad months when she was deaf and nearly blind? The earlier years when she was vital and energetic and frequently maddening? Or the earlier still years when I was tiny and she was my whole world? It's all too complicated. I'll settle without apprehension for oblivion. I cannot really feel that oblivion will be disappointing.

So many of Noel's friends and acquaintances had died during the last eighteen months—Jack, Guthrie, Sybil, Mabelle, Lady Mountbatten, Prince Aly Khan, Oscar Hammerstein, Clark Gable, Marion Davies, Ruth Chatterton … In moments of reasoning he would decide that through having such a multitude of friends it was only logical to have to suffer more losses than most people: 'The Great Reaper has been at it again.' (A friend of mine wrote that he had behaved more like a combine harvester.) Next he carried off Noel's darling Madge Titheradge.

'Coley and I had a long and cosy talk about Death the other evening, sitting up here watching the dark come and waiting for the fireflies to appear,' Noel wrote. We discussed what would happen if I died or if he died and came to the sensible conclusion that there was nothing to be done. We should have to get on with life until our turn came. I said, 'After all, the day had to go on and breakfast had to be eaten,' and he replied that if I died he might find it difficult to eat breakfast but would probably begin to feel peckish by lunch-time. But when the time did come my little joke—which Noel enjoyed and often quoted—went badly wrong on me. Neither Graham nor I felt peckish by lunch-time.

Not long after this Noel began to say that as his friends were dying like flies all around him the most he asked of people now was that they should survive through luncheon. 'Why lunch, sweetheart?' Marlene asked, and this joke too was to have repercussions years later.

Noel's lust for travel never lay dormant for long. He loved to shatter the tranquillity of Les Avants with a startling announcement: 'I long for the Far East again. I should like to leave tomorrow and spend *months* in a freighter getting there,' or, 'Why don't the three of us go round the world?' or, 'I must see Peking again. And Bali.' Some of these dreams did not come true, but he would spend the rest of the evening with his Oxford Atlas, happily planning these journeys exactly, until by the time we went to bed the whole thing had become reality and in his mind's eye he could already see the three of us in Singapore for example, at Raffles Hotel, or sitting watching the delights that Bugis Street had to offer.

He left in February 1962 for two months by himself in the Pacific, a holiday unique in that it was disaster-free, and which ended with him discovering by chance Bora-Bora, off Tahiti, which became and remained for him the perfect South Sea Isle. (He mentions his leg in the letters which follow because his doctors had warned him that the main artery on the right hand side, affecting his right leg, was beginning to harden, and Ed Bigg in Chicago had forbidden him to smoke because of this. Otherwise he had been given a clean bill of health.)

[Fairmount Hotel, San Francisco:] Coley saw me off in Kingston [and] I sped off through the bright skies at approximately the same moment that John Glenn Jr sped off in his capsule into outer space. He had been round the world three times before I landed at Miami airport. I did a little shopping and had my hair cut and while this was going on I heard over the radio that Glenn had landed safely. It was a tremendously exciting moment ruined for me by a blonde manicurist with a voice like a corncrake who made it almost impossible to hear what had happened.

[Hotel Tahiti, March 4th:] Me voici sitting bollock naked in a thatched bungalow because my luggage had to stay at the aeroport to be decontaminated on account of Rhinoceros Beetle. This takes two hours. I left Nadi [Fiji] at 5 a.m. and it is now 5 p.m. ... yesterday was Sunday the 4th and today is Sunday the 4th [he had crossed the date-line] which may or may not make me Happy Fanny Fields. Tahiti so far is divine—it is jolly gentil to hear Français spoken in toutes directions. I didn't much care for Suva, the social carry-on was tedious although I avoided as much as I could by shooting off in the ketch for three days with my Stan. My Stan is a story in himself, tough, ex-Merchant Navy and R.N.V.R. and twice married. The jet flying is really remarkable in these parts. I've flown over two thousand miles today and feel bright as a bee. My leg is a bit better ... I expect the no smoking has helped. Curiously enough I haven't minded so very dreadfully except for odd moments. I had rather a pang giving my carton of Salems to the barman at the Grand Pacific. What they say about the natives being amenable and friendly is sensationally true. I've really scarcely had a moment to myself. My bags have now arrived so I shall unpack and go for a drink on the town. Happy happy birthday. I'll cable you about Bora-Bora. Amour Amour. Maitre.

[Hotel Tahiti, March 7th:] Yesterday I set forth in a tiny chug-chug boat with a Teensy Frog who's the Kon Tiki type and sailed across the Pacific in a po or something. We went to Moorea which takes about two hours and made a tour of the island inside the lagoon. It was breathtakingly beautiful—violent mountains standing straight up out of the sea—glorious coral and coloured fish and white sand beaches ... the real South Sea stuff. I took a lot of jolly snaps with my Starmite. The trouble with Tahiti is that it is devoted almost exclusively to 'Con'. It really is thrown at you all the time and this is 'ow you say tres gentil if you happen to like it ... there is a café here on the port called Vaimar's where one can sit watching all the cons watching all the cons watching all the cons go by. It is picturesque but fairly dull. I am now burnt black and peeling like an old snake. Perhaps when I get to Bora-Bora I will put pen to paper but I rather doubt it, this is a lackadaisical atmosphere ... The petites Tahitiennes spend most of their time when not being rogered in emitting little squeaks. This is rather boring, however I have my ear plugs.

[Hotel Bora-Bora, March 15th:] This is being a really wonderful holiday. I have tried to work but have not persevered because there is so much to see and do and having come all this way I don't want to waste any of it. I am absorbing away like an old sponge. This is the loveliest place I have ever been to in my life. The hotel, which is excellent, is run by an American married to a Tahitian singer. There is a bar and a main restaurant, the rest separate bungalows all thickly thatched with a low overhang to keep them cool. The proprietor, Alex Bougerie, has a speedboat and I have crept like a hookworm into his heart. There are very few other guests and so we spend most of every day in the boat cruising about the lagoon and fishing from the reef. I have never taken so much exercise in my life. Yesterday we paddled the pirogue-

outrigger canoe out to the reef and back before lunch, a mile and a half each way! On the way we saw two large sting-rays having a go 'Arry Boy with a third looking on. This could only happen in a *French* colonial possession. We also encountered a very nasty sea-snake which I decapitated neatly with my paddle. The reefs are glorious beyond description, if you can multiply what we see at Goldeneye about twenty times this will give you a rough ahdee. [Noel's 'Deep South' for idea.] The varieties of fish are incredible and also the different sorts of coral. We went far out to the outer reef and I was snorkling away doing nobody any harm when I saw, as in a dream, a six-foot shark coming towards me. I kept my head and slapped the water hard with my fist. It gave me a look of infinite disdain and swam under me and away. In fact the whole thing is all that one has ever dreamed about the South Sea islands ... I am almost black and feeling marvellous except for my leg which, although better is *not* right. My bungalow is a goodish way from the main building and I have to force myself to go-slow-Johnny. I smoked not at all for a month and then decided that it was *too* mizzy and so now I have my first cigarette with my first drink at sundown. My average is five to seven a day! I must myself say I didn't find it difficult and *do* feel the benefit, no more dry mouth in the night for instance. I am sure the leg is circulatory trouble and can be dealt with. I have a great great deal to tell, I have taken five million photographs and am liable to be a great South Sea Bora-Bora. Show this communal effusion to any loved ones who would like it. Love love love to all. Master.

Noel was back in time for the casting and rehearsals of *Sail Away* in London in the spring. Joe and Evie Layton, Elaine Stritch and Grover Dale were there from the American production, joined by David Holliday, a fine singer and good actor, as Johnny. Loudon Sainthill designed beautiful and imaginative sets. We were all very happy together, and *Sail Away* repeated the pattern set in America; a packed and successful provincial tour, a triumphant London opening—Elaine tore the place up and received a tumultuous reception—and grudging notices. The show had an aura of great success around it for about six months and then, owing to a sudden and 'almost sensational lack of enthusiasm on the part of the public', it was withdrawn, as it had been in New York. Noel confessed that by now he had become rather tired of poor *Sail Away*; he had never really liked the book but he loved and would always love his lyrics and music. And rightly—the music is still played and the songs sung, especially 'Where Shall I Find Him' and 'Something Very Strange is Happening to Me'.

Earlier in the year Arnold Wesker had telephoned Les Avants from London and asked if he could see Noel; Noel, devoured by curiosity, invited him to come immediately. What Arnold wanted was for Noel to give financial support, or a preview of *Sail Away*, for his idealistic and ultimately unsuccessful project to take the arts to Trades Union audiences. This Noel resolutely refused to do on the grounds that, as he later wrote to Arnold, 'your first allegiance should be to your own rich talent and you should go on using it and enlarging it instead of wasting valuable time trying to bring art and culture to a great number of people who neither need it nor want it. After seeing *Chips with Everything* I feel more strongly about this than ever.' Arnold had won several important awards and had been hailed by the critics as a great writer. Now,

> he complained that he and his other avant-garde colleagues have been victimised by the press and is suddenly dismayed to discover that his plays (except for *Chips*) aren't box-office. He explained all this to me honestly. I reminded him that that was exactly what I had prophesied in my articles in the *Sunday Times*. He left next day rather desolate and, seized by pangs of guilt, I read his trilogy right through. He has undoubtedly got great talent.

There followed a short and somehow touching correspondence between those two so dissimilar playwrights who liked one another, proving to my mind yet again that Noel was not the reactionary he was at that time dubbed; on the contrary, he was ever open to try to understand the aims of the younger playwrights, providing their work was good enough, which Arnold's was. Here, in part, is a letter from Noel:

> I have got to talk to you more … you *have* been victimised by those foolish men, but your talent is too rich to be lastingly affected either by over-praise or over-blame. Please, dear Arnold, don't grumble so much in your heart about political and governmental injustices and stupidities. You can't change human nature. All you can do with your gifts is observe and comment with compassion and humour *and* as theatrically effectively as possible, so long as you continue to write plays. And *please* remember that 'Failure', unless written [about] with pure genius, is rarely entertaining. I

have deep sympathy for Beatie [in *Roots*] whom I feel will
eventually succeed with her own life. I have none for Dave, who
is conceited, stubborn, woolly-minded and incompetent. I *love*
Sarah who succeeds triumphantly as a human being. It seems to
me that the women in the Trilogy are conceived with more depth
and understanding than the men. *The Kitchen* from this point of
view is a great step forward. And now you are going to waste an
enormous amount of your energy and creative talent in coping
with mediocre little bureaucrats and organizing a Cultural
Revolution! *Do* me a favour! Leave those cheerful old girls to
enjoy their Bingo. Let the great majority enjoy itself in its own
way ... When you had left the house I had pangs of guilt for
having been so unresponsive to your project, but they have since
died away. I am unregenerate; still hopeful and eager to contribute
to the world's entertainment and transient enjoyment, but *only
after* I have contributed to my own integrity ... In the meantime I
wish you success and happiness in whatever you do, even if it is
only organising Maypole dances in South Shields. *Never* wear
your wife's sweater again, it is *not* becoming. Yours in Science,
Noel.

Noel's right leg had become so painful that he went into hospital in
Lausanne for examination under anaesthetic and was next day shown
the resulting X-rays. There was no doubt about it, he would have to
undergo major surgery; three operations in one for the choked-up
sections in the artery, one in the abdomen and two in the leg. The
success of the substitution of a plastic artery had at that time yet to be
proven, but Noel had already firmly made up his mind that this had to
be done and he had better get on with it. But now, perhaps unfortunately in view of later events, he was assured that there was no
urgency. He seized on this, and happily postponed the operation until
the following April, by which time we should have returned from
Jamaica.

Rebecca West came to stay, and while she was at Les Avants I had
occasion to ring Professor Paul Niehans at his world-famous clinic
nearby. He and his wife Coralie were our neighbours and friends. A
great many world-famous names came for the Professor's treatment
(and still do even since his death) and benefited; a minority came and
did not. The Professor was a saintly man; Noel wrote, 'I have a profound respect for him. He has I believe a stroke of genius.' He always
made it clear to us that he did not, contrary to popular legend, promise

rejuvenation or the restoration of a declining sex-life; what he did promise, and he numbered children among his patients, it should be remembered, was to find out by means of tests the deficiencies, if any, from which the body was suffering and to supply, to replace, them by means of injections of placenta obtained from a pregnant ewe. This made sense—we have many of us at some time been given extract of liver from a bottle and the principle is the same.

The news of Noel's pending operation spread among our local friends, including of course Professor Niehans and Coralie, and in the course of my chance telephone-call he begged me to point out to Noel —he was *not* interfering—that surgery was not inevitably the answer, and should only be used as a last resort, only when and if other means of effecting a cure have failed. In short, Noel went to see him and received his treatment, which included strict and total abstinence from nicotine and alcohol for at least three months; for how could the new cells form and grow if given those two poisons? The abstention from nicotine in any case probably helped Noel greatly, as his other doctors had already promised it would, (it also made him fearfully bad-tempered) and the pain did grow less, and in the end the artery was never operated upon.

With Rebecca in the house for more than two weeks—'Oh, that glorious intelligence,' Noel wrote—and with Lynn and Alfred's arrival during that time, the time passed eventfully. There was much leg-pulling on the subject of the treatment: Noel himself said, 'But supposing I am given a Non-U ewe! What will Nancy say?' and there were many suggestions as to what his theme song should be: 'Ewe Were Meant for Me', or perhaps 'I've Got Ewe under My Skin' was more apt?

On the very first night, I showed Rebecca to her room, and my parting words to her were, 'You know where my room is don't you, if you want anything in the night.' 'Coley,' she said, 'I've received many invitations in my life: *never* so direct a one as that. But must you put all the initiative so squarely on me?' Which I thought maidenly of her, and told her so. Peals of laughter accompanied our good nights, but sure enough, Rebecca did come to my room at quarter to five in the morning, like Lady Macbeth with hair and nightdress streaming, in appalling pain from a gall-bladder attack. Doctor Spuhler, in response to my call, came hurrying up the mountain from Montreux and injected her with morphine. She wrote: 'He [Noel] told me with such delicate falsity that I was causing no trouble at all, indeed suggesting that his household had for years been sitting about waiting for someone to come and stay who would oblige them by having a gall-bladder attack.'

By the time she had recovered, Lynn was giving Rebecca's hair some very searching looks and she finally suggested that she should wash and set it for her on the morrow. Lynn is a gifted *coiffeuse* but this Rebecca didn't know, and the piercingly critical looks continued all next morning (wondering how best to cut and set it, I assume) until Rebecca was reduced to sheer fright. 'What is she going to *do* to me?' she wailed, and I took a picture of her, her head bound up in white, a victim facing pitiless cruelty. But the day ended well; even Rebecca admitted that her hair looked splendid, and after our dinner guest had gone—there had been some political argument—Noel asked 'I wasn't *too* hard on him was I?' 'No, no,' Rebecca reassured him, 'I admired your forbearance. You took your hobnailed boots off before you trampled on him.'

During this visit Rebecca had a conversation with Noel during which he said, 'Coley paints better than I do, and is as funny as I am and often funnier, and he works hard to prevent me noticing it. How I wish I could thank him, but it would spoil it all.' Noel was too kind— I paint with no spark of originality, as he did, and who could possibly be funnier than he? This conversation was not published until after Noel's death, and so the only part that matters to me, his infinitely touching thanks at the end (owing to Rebecca having preserved his words) reached me after all. I have no way of expressing my gratitude to Rebecca for this.

Noel's friendship with Sir Osbert Sitwell had long since been resumed, back in 1955, in fact; and now at last the feud (if feud it could still be called after forty years) with Dame Edith reached its happy conclusion. As the reader knows, Noel bought any and every new book of consequence about Queen Elizabeth I, and had just finished Dame Edith's *The Queens and the Hive*, about which he wrote (with at first the dark hint 'in spite of what some other lady writers may say') that he had found it wonderfully readable and at moments brilliant. On our way back to Noel's suite at the Savoy late one afternoon, we found the door of the suite next to Noel's wide open and could hear an American voice on the telephone. Noel stopped in his tracks and said, 'But I know that voice,' looked round the door, and found George Cukor. George soon hung up and we had a boisterous reunion, celebrated with drinks all round. Late in the conversation Noel said to George, rather rudely he afterwards thought, that he had been quite startled to find that *The Queens and the Hive* was dedicated to

George. Elizabeth Salter in *The Last Years of a Rebel* wrote that in his eagerness to read the book, George skipped the introductory pages and had no idea that the book was dedicated to him until Noel pointed it out, but this did not happen, as Miss Salter says, over the telephone. George then said that he would be off in half an hour to Hampstead to see Dame Edith, whereupon Noel begged him to tell her what enormous pleasure the book had given him. 'I'll give her the message certainly, but,' he added firmly, 'write and tell her so yourself. You're always so good about that sort of thing, praising people's books and performances. Go on, write to Edith yourself,' and so Noel did, that same evening.

By way of answer he first of all received a telegram: DELIGHTED STOP FRIENDSHIP NEVER TOO LATE INVITE YOU BIRTHDAY CONCERT AND SUPPER FESTIVAL HALL OCTOBER 9TH 8 P.M. EDITH SITWELL.

Noel regretfully could not accept because the 9th coincided with his entry into hospital in Lausanne, already described. Noel seems not to have kept copies of his letters to Dame Edith, but the resumption and progress of their friendship can be gathered from Dame Edith's letters to him:

Dear Mr Coward, Thank you so much for your letter in answer to my telegram, and above all let me thank you for your charming previous letter [the 'fan' letter which started it all] which pleased and touched me very much. I had to answer by telegram, as I had acute writer's cramp (indeed I have only just emerged from bandages and a sling). How I wish that *un*professional writers would suffer, sometimes, from this disease! ... The 9th should be a day for all present to remember. Never before, I think, has anyone attended their own Memorial Service. (The press is madly excited at me being 75, and is looking forward avidly to my funeral.) I do hope you *will* find time to come and have a sherry or a cocktail with me when you are in London. Do please ring me up. I am giving Osbert your message. He is at Renishaw, so I send you love on his behalf. All good wishes. Yours ever. Edith Sitwell.

After the seventy-fifth birthday celebrations:

Dear Mr Coward ... Osbert and I were so very sorry you couldn't come ... The concert and supper party were fun, in a way. But it was all rather like something macabre out of Proust. The papers

excelled themselves—the Sketch particularly. I had never met the
nice well-meaning reporter who 'covered' the event, but according
to him he sat beside me as my weary head sank into my pillow,
and just as I was dropping asleep, I uttered these

Famous Last Words

'Be kind to me! Not many people are!' Very moving I think,
don't you? ... please don't forget that if you can spare the time,
you are coming to see me when you are in London. Yours very
sincerely. Edith Sitwell. Osbert sends his love.

Miss Salter describes their meeting delightfully. Dame Edith wore her
latest hat, 'her inevitable fur coat and slippers', and she and Miss
Salter awaited Noel's arrival with some trepidation, but for different
reasons, Dame Edith because she was going to receive the man she had
regarded as her enemy for forty years, and Miss Salter because she had
admired Noel since she first discovered his work at the age of seventeen. Neither Dame Edith nor Noel knew what to expect of each other,
though perhaps Noel had more idea, because so many friends, Natasha
especially, had told him for so long that 'Edith is such fun'. Their
reaction, Miss Salter says, was one of astonishment as well as delight.
Noel always maintained that regrets are useless, but by the end of their
meeting they both admitted regret for the wasted years, the fun they
might have had, as they had had that afternoon. As Noel left, Miss
Salter told him she felt she had been present at an historic occasion.
'You have been,' he agreed. Later Dame Edith wrote:

Dear Mr Coward, I cannot tell you what real pleasure it gave
me to see you the other day. I enjoyed our talk so much. [There
now follows Dame Edith's generous praise, quoted long ago in
this book, for his *Collected Short Stories*, which he had sent her; she
in turn sent him her *Notebook on William Shakespeare* 'with my
admiration and affectionate best wishes'.] ... I am having a rather
harassing time with lunatics, because I was televised the other
day. One wrote to say that I ought to be ashamed of myself, and
that I have senile decay and softening of the brain, which—oddly
enough—makes him respect me. Another has written me a very
long letter about Einstein, telling me I will never get into Space or
Time. I am sending you my notebook on Shakespeare. The cover
is so unspeakably appalling [she is not exaggerating] that I nearly
faint when I contemplate it. I do not know if it is meant as a

portrait of me if I turn blue, or if it is supposed to represent a map. I am not supposed to show any of my Autobiography to anyone at all, but I *can't* resist sending you my portrait of Wyndham Lewis, hoping it will make you laugh. [It did.] ... Please come and see me again very soon ... The American monsters who published my Notebook, not content with inflicting that scarifying cover on me, won't allow me to be an Hon.D. Litt. of Oxford. One shouldn't mind, but I do take it hard!

The last letter was on March 3rd, 1963:

Dear Mr Coward, I was so delighted to get your postcard ... Will you really give me a 'Coward Original'? I look forward to having it. You won't forget you have promised it to me, will you? [Noel had received *English Eccentrics* 'with affectionate best wishes for Christmas, from Edith S.' and he now kept his promise and gave Dame Edith one of his paintings.] ... A Club here have seized a poem of mine, 'Still Falls the Rain', without my permission, and have recited it with their heads out of a window! Evidently they don't know it is a poem about the bombing, but think it is an advertisement for mackintoshes! Some people might be rather cross. Osbert has just been here and sends his love. I look forward so much to seeing you when we both get back to England. Your *ancient* friend (ancient God knows) Edith.

Dame Edith's fan-mail had become a torture to her; apart from its size, she seems to have taken each letter more seriously than she need have done, haunted by letters from madmen and heartbroken by letters from cripples. Miss Salter helped overcome this by composing and having printed a form letter, polite and firm at the same time. Noel's postbag had also become unmanageably swollen; Lornie and Joan Hirst, her assistant, in London, Geoffrey in New York and myself in Switzerland were hard put to keep abreast of it and could never win the race because another shoal came in next morning. Noel's personal correspondence, always large, was more than doubled by the business letters regarding the stage, film, television, radio and recording productions of the plays, books and the endless amount of songs and music he had written and composed. All requests for autographs and signed photographs were scrupulously granted as they always had been; I would let them pile up for a while until we had to have an Autograph Morning, Noel sitting up in bed after breakfast signing away, grumbling at first and then philosophising, 'Well this is what I wanted when I was young; now I've got it.' The post also brought numberless other requests and problems as well until in despair I turned to Miss Salter for her formula—she had become Elizabeth by then—and she helped me compose the following printed message:

Mr Noël Coward regrets that, owing to pressure of work, he has had to make it a rule not to read unsolicited mss. or music and lyrics, answer questionnaires, contribute to anthologies or symposiums, or reply to questions on students' theses, etc. He receives so many of these and similar requests that he is sorry to say that it has become impossible to deal with them all and at the same time fulfil his own writing commitments.

All of which was perfectly true; no human being could have read, given a considered opinion on, and then answered all the material that was sent to him. Why hadn't we thought of the printed cards years before? We did of course quickly look at all the amateur scripts, anxious not to miss another such gem as the one we found in a mediaeval play when a Sister Anne gazed out of a castle embrasure and said, 'Some men are coming up the gulch. I do avow 'tis Uncle Pulesden.'

While on the subject of Noel's correspondence I had better tell the truth while I am alive, or dealers in autographed letters may go haywire in the future. Noel himself said that his handwriting looked as though Chinese ants had crawled all over the paper and it did; it is very small and not easy to decipher. Lornie, unable to type, had to solve her problem in her own way and this she did, as early on as *The Vortex* and before, by developing an extraordinary gift of being able to imitate Noel's handwriting, which she used for years. This was of course a boon to herself and to Noel and was done innocently enough because neither of them then dreamed that Noel Coward mss might one day become sought after and valuable. Handwriting experts will I am sure quickly detect the difference; Lornie's counterfeits are slightly more clearly written, and therefore more easily read. I must confess that I too could manage to forge a passable 'Noel' or 'Noel Coward' or 'Master', but no more than that, and these I only used when driven to it—for instance when Noel dictated a big batch of letters to 'polish them off' before going away and was in a plane halfway across the world before they could be typed and signed. Many of the most genuine Noel Coward letters, those to close friends including myself and which are used in this book, are not handwritten but typed by himself, even to the signature and the XXX's. Those manuscripts of his plays and books which are written by hand, and most of them are, were of course written by Noel himself, and no one else.

All through 1962 Noel worked hard on the score and lyrics for *The Girl Who Came to Supper*; Terence Rattigan's *The Sleeping Prince* transformed into a musical. Herman Levin, who presented *My Fair Lady*, was to present it, Harry Kurnitz wrote the book and from the first the show was planned and created at a high social level. Harry would come to Les Avants to write what he called 'some jokes' and then have to leave for yet another weekend with the Windsors—he was a great golfing buddy of the Duke's. Like Noel he was also a close friend of Loel and Gloria Guinness, and so we all went off for a Mediterranean cruise on Loel's yacht, Loel specially providing a piano in the yacht for Noel to work on. We spent several days in Portofino, everyone trying to induce Rex Harrison to play the Prince; in the end he would not and production had to be postponed until the following year. But early in 1963,

> A great surprise happened. Hugh Martin and Timothy Gray came to play the score of [their musical version of] *Blithe Spirit*. I was all set to turn it down because it really has been going on for far too long and I was sick of all the frigging about. Coley and I sat with our mouths open. The music is melodic and delightful, the lyrics witty and they have done a book outline keeping to my original play and yet making it effective as a musical. I am not only relieved but delighted. I have told them to go ahead.

Noel promised them he would direct when the time came. He was now in the curious, for him, position of being concerned with two big musicals and yet not entirely concerned with either. In fact he had nothing whatever to do with *The Girl Who Came to Supper* officially, except that he had written the songs; everybody else did everything else and he had to watch some things go wrong (in his opinion) and could do nothing to prevent them. Not only was the next twelve months to become a complex entanglement of these two shows; he had in addition promised to go in May to Australia to supervise the final rehearsals of *Sail Away* in Melbourne and see it launched. He slipped away with relief—he had longed to return to Australia—taking me with him and promising me a lovely holiday on the way there.

This we had, stopping off for several days each at Beirut, Bangkok and Hong Kong—known of course as Honkers—old friends of Noel's springing up wherever we went and entertaining us, notably the legendary Linda Sursock in her Arabian Nights Palace in Beirut which Noel described as an early Oscar Asche production with lots of stained glass, tinkling fountains and attar of roses.

Noel already had a big public for his work in general in Australia, for his music in particular, and was well-loved and remembered there for his concert tour of the continent during the war; he was big news, and from our arrival onwards he was photographed all ends up and never stopped giving interviews to press, radio and television, all of which he enjoyed thoroughly. *Sail Away* was a howling success in Melbourne, but did not do as well when it later moved to Sydney.

We parted company in Sidney, Noel for a tour of the Far East, me for Fiji and a week in Honolulu and thence to Ed Bigg and the Passavant Hospital in Chicago for an operation. I had had the four operations in the Air Force for quite inoffensive hernias and Ed promised to tidy up the jumble once and for all with a piece of nylon mesh. Noel wrote from the Peninsula Hotel, Hong Kong:

Fancy having a bit of mesh way down deep inside. I wonder if it will let the sand in. I knew the operation was going to be more tricky than you thought, Ed having warned me, so you can imagine how relieved I am that it is tout droit. Ed really is a darlin man and I have the most complete faith in him. You really must be good in future and not go on and awn and arn lifting pianos and double basses. You know what you are. I am pigging it here in an even larger suite than the one before. The sitting-room is the size of the Palais de Dance and sparsely furnished with hideously uncomfortable ORANGE chairs. The air-conditioning thing came away in my hand this morning and there is very very leetle wasser [there was a drought] but owing to being so luxe I have a tiny trickle which I help out with a lot of Moment Suprême and Givenchy's Monsieur. The voyage in the *Chitral* was a great success and fairly enhanced by the presence of R.S. who in the old days was a gynaecologist and used to fiddle about with the twots of Maud Gilroy, Ivy St Helier and even our own dear Mrs Loraine. He is the ship's surgeon and quite sweet and civilised if silly.

The Girl Who Came to Supper had the most glittering opening imaginable at the vast Broadway Theatre in December and ran for three months.

Noel's 'little lot' this time consisted of Lena Horne, Adele Astaire, Beatrice Lillie, Ruth Gordon, Garson Kanin, Joan Sutherland, Richard Bonynge, Katharine Cornell, Joan Fontaine, Lynn, Alfred, Stritch, Sharman Douglas and too many more to mention. The show itself had much to offer: Irene Sharaff's glorious costumes, Joe's brilliant choreography in the ballroom scene, with all the splendid Edwardian ladies and gentlemen dancing to what is now recognised as a 'Scott Joplin' rhythm, Irene Browne's regal appearance and manner as the Grand Duchess, and above all Tessie O'Shea's show-stopping sequence with Noel's four brilliant parodies (they might well have been the real thing) of music-hall songs of the period under the general heading 'London is a Little Bit of All Right'. The trouble, as Noel had privately foreseen, was that everybody concerned seemed afraid to use genuine sentiment, the late and forever lamented Harry Kurnitz being the chief offender with his 'book'. Larry had first played the Prince in Terry Rattigan's play in London with Vivien enchanting as the Chorus Girl, and then with Marilyn Monroe in the film; playing him as an extremely funny Teutonic bore. This was fine, but Noel strongly felt that in a musical the Prince must be played by a much younger man of great charm, or the 'romance' boiled down to a middle-aged man calculatingly wanting a one-night stand with a young and pretty girl. An enormous laugh was obtained by the Girl saying, 'Shall I ever be glad to get out of this dress!' as the Prince carried her into his bedroom, which drove this point home still further and which Noel thought was fatal. He may have been right; at any rate the theatre parties did not come.

Someone should write a book about the Taft Hotel, New Haven, now derelict. Someone indeed may well be writing one at this moment, for every ex-alumnus of nearby Yale University who is old enough now looks back on the Taft with fond nostalgia, all horrors forgotten. The Taft was a hideous building and the food was terrible, but never mind, for them it is crammed with memories of fleeting youth now fled for ever, for it was to the Taft that their sweethearts and girl friends came in droves for the noisy exciting weekends of the Yale-Harvard football games, or to dance in their arms, cheek to cheek, at the romantic Proms. The forbidding front desk of the Taft was considered sufficient chaperonage by parents in the far-off straight-laced days. New Haven used to be almost invariably chosen for the first week of the try-out of a show before going on to Boston and theatre people stayed at the Taft for the only but very good reason that it was next door to the Shubert Theatre, and for them the Taft also plays a very large part in their memories, not always as happy as those of the Yale alumni. The losing battles with room service, the confusion of opinions on the merits of the show left behind by friends and enemies who came up from New York, the recriminations and quarrels that took place there, and the slashing cuts made in the show or new scenes written and learnt at fever pitch: all these things are among the less happy recollections.

By the time we got to New Haven in January 1964 with Beatrice Lillie and *High Spirits*, Noel and I felt we had got the measure of the Taft Hotel and waged war accordingly. We changed all the gloomy little light-bulbs in the suite for brilliant 100-watt ones, also bought an electric kettle and made our own coffee and tea, laid in enough food for a small Arctic expedition, and bottles of milk and yoghourt stood in rows on the windowsills, refrigerated in six inches of snow. We lived the life of Riley in the nest we had made—we had of course also brought enough to stock a small bar—and felt very pleased with ourselves at having won the war.

Tammy Grimes, Louise Troy and Edward Woodward all sang with verve and gave tip-top performances in *High Spirits*, but Noel predicted as early as this, in New Haven, that the show would become *An Evening with Beatrice Lillie*, with Beattie as Madame Arcati, and this is exactly what happened. We endured two months of terrible tribulations on the road, among which Beattie's utter inability to memorise her lines loomed large at every performance. Noel wished this to be placed on record: 'I am patient, kind, forbearing, sensible and decisive. If I were not all these things I should now be nestling cosily in a straight-jacket in a Loony Bin. Day after day I have sat quietly with my nails dug into the palms of my hands while Miss Lillie stumbles, flounders, forgets, remembers, drives the company mad and is as much like Madame Arcati as I am like Queen Victoria.' After these eight weeks of suffering, *High Spirits* opened triumphantly at the Alvin in New York, to wonderful notices with raves for Beattie, and deservedly: 'Beattie came on with a star mixture of assurance and humility, took the audience by the scruff of its neck and shook it into a state of adoring frenzy.' It is quite a relief to be able to say that the third time was lucky in Noel's trio of Broadway musicals, and that *High Spirits* ran well over a year and made a lot of money.

The same unhappily cannot be said of the London production. Cicely Courtneidge could do little with Beattie's highly individual material, and if Cis could do little, nobody else could have done more. One realised too late that the attempt should never have been made in the first place.

The first small sign of Noel becoming Nationalised, as Terry Rattigan called it, was made a year before it actually happened, when Noel, far away in Bangkok, wrote with wonder in his journal: 'There has been a revival of *Private Lives* in a tiny theatre in Hampstead and it has had rave notices! Some critics even praised the play!' And then, two months later when the production moved to the Duke of York's— Noel by this time in Honolulu—'It has suddenly been discovered after thirty-three years that it is a good play!'

Our lives now fell into a pattern that was to remain permanent. Holidays and crowded, enjoyable trips to London, Paris or Rome apart, eight months of the year were spent at Les Avants up to and including Christmas and New Year, and from January until the end of April in Jamaica. After having lived in Switzerland for five years on a *Permis de séjour*, one was in those more carefree days given Swiss Residence without even having to ask for it and so, in that summer of 1964, Noel and I automatically became *bona fide* residents. Nine years had gone by since Noel relinquished English residence and yet he was still not enjoying all the benefits his advisers had promised him, and for which he had suffered so much abuse from the press. For instance the greater part of the basic income from his royalties still went through his London company and in consequence he was still paying up to fifty per cent in company tax to the British Government. Why, he wanted to know, after all he had been through? We ourselves had a sneaking suspicion that the advisers, plus Lornie, didn't really trust us and thought the money safer in their hands, regarding us as potential spendthrifts who would squander Noel's substance on we didn't quite know what—riotous living, perhaps?

Thomas Roe had for some years been Noel's lawyer in Switzerland and he was, at the end of this same year, to become involved in the Great Sausage Scandal along with George Sanders and a gentleman by the name of Denis Loraine. I was about to write, as I did about the Taft Hotel, that a book should be written about the Great Sausage Scandal, but in fact Her Majesty's Stationery Office published a quite thick White Paper on the subject at the time which sold out in a flash, so enthralling and, to anyone who knew Tom and George, hair-raising was the story. At any rate, before Tom was sent to prison (he has been out for some years now, as cheerful and Micawberish as ever) he performed more than a few good services for Noel, for which we have to thank him to this day. Tom it was who fell back in astonishment when we told him that Noel's royalties were still not flowing directly to him, and who flew immediately to London and goosed everybody concerned. The accountant said to Tom—best joke of all we thought—that Noel had only been gone nine years and that Rome wasn't built in a day. *'Only* nine years!' Noel said, 'the first part of that statement is silly and the second irrelevant.'

Not long after this Noel had the pleasure—a pleasure unknown to him for forty years, ever since he made over his financial affairs to Jack in the 'twenties—of handling his own money. We were fascinated when the cheques began to arrive, actually made out to Noel Coward, and even more by the accompanying statements. These told us exactly how much good old *Fallen Angels* had made in summer stock, how much his books had earned, how much his music had brought in via Chappell's, along with such pregnant facts as *Blithe Spirit* having been done by the all-girl theatre in Tokyo. Noel would have flown to Tokyo if he'd known, he said, just to see Doctor Bradman played by a geisha. All this brought an added excitement to the post for both of us, a naïve pleasure perhaps but a real one. Tom then saw the authorities, and Noel's Swiss income-tax was fixed at just over seven per cent; a reasonable figure to pay, we thought, and certainly an improvement on the fifty he had been paying in England. Need I say that like everything else the figure increased before very long but remained, and remains, reasonable.

The presentation of a play by Britain's National Theatre does not necessarily bestow upon it the status of a classic, but the National's production of *Hay Fever* in October 1964 seems to have brought with it that honour by general assent, from critics and public alike. Kenneth Tynan, so John Dexter told us, was the first to suggest the production, for which Noel was at the same time surprised and grateful, and Mr Tynan's suggestion was from the first strongly reinforced by Larry's unflagging and loving enthusiasm for the project. Larry's and Noel's telegrams on the subject are couched in terms of such love for one another that Joan (Lady Olivier) at the height of the exchange expressed the fear that one of them might be intercepted and they would both be arrested.

When I tapped out this little comedy so exuberantly on to my typewriter in 1924 I would indeed have been astonished if anyone had told me that it was destined to re-emerge, fresh and blooming, forty years later ... One of the reasons it was hailed so warmly by the critics in 1925 was that there happened to be an ardent campaign being conducted against 'Sex' plays, and *Hay Fever*, as I remarked in my first-night speech, was as clean as a whistle. True there has been no campaign against 'Sex' plays lately; on the contrary rape, incontinence, perversion, sadism, psychopathology and flatulence, both verbal and physical, have for some time been sure bets in the race for critical acclaim. I was therefore agreeably surprised to wake up on the morning after the first night at the National Theatre and read a number of adulatory and enthusiastic notices. Such (almost) unanimous praise has not been lavished upon me for many a long year and to pretend that I am not delighted by it would be the height of affectation.

It was noted ... that the play had no plot and that there were few if any witty lines, by which I presume is meant that the dialogue is non-epigrammatic. This I think and hope is quite true... To me, the essence of good comedy writing is that perfectly ordinary phrases such as 'Just fancy!' should, by virtue of their context, achieve greater laughs than the most literate epigrams. Some of the biggest laughs in *Hay Fever* occur on such lines as 'Go on', 'No there isn't, is there?' and 'This haddock's disgusting'. There are many other glittering examples of my sophistication in the same vein ... I would add that the sort of lines above mentioned have to be impeccably delivered and that in the current performance they certainly are. [The cast included Dame Edith Evans, Maggie Smith, Lynn Redgrave, Robert Stephens and Robert Lang.] In fact I can truthfully say that never in my long years of writing and directing have I encountered a more talented, co-operative and technically efficient group of actors and my gratitude to them and my affection for them is unbounded.

The brilliance of the performances on the first night (though Edith was a bit rocky), and the sight of the entire audience at the Old Vic helpless with laughter, remain in the memory. A third recollection is of Diana in a flimsy dress floating up the aisle in the interval, plaintively saying, 'Mother wants her gin,' and heading the procession of Noel's other guests: Margot Fonteyn, Rudolf Nureyev, Judy Garland, Liza Minelli, Lena Horne, Vivien Leigh, John Merivale, and Lady Alexandra Metcalfe with Benita Sanders and Sylvia Ashley not far behind. 'A squalid little group,' Noel said, 'if ever I saw one.'

Noel was now, after *Hay Fever* at the National, accorded a kind of affectionate reverence, which could not be better expressed than it was by Ronald Bryden in the *New Statesman*:

Who would have thought the landmarks of the 'sixties would

include ... the emergence of Noel Coward as the grand old man of British drama? There he was one morning flipping verbal tiddly-winks with reporters about 'Dad's Renaissance' ... the next, he was there again, a national treasure: slightly older than the century on which he sits, his eyelids wearier than ever, hanging beside Forster, Eliot and the O.M.s, demonstrably the greatest living English playwright.

The National Treasure now decided to take a winter holiday on the isle of Capri. His summer holiday had included Turkey, then Rome (whence I received a cable: AM BACK FROM ISTANBUL WHERE I WAS KNOWN AS ENGLISH DELIGHT) and then in Jacques Sarlie's yacht with Jean Howard and others to Capri. 'Capri swirled around us and we swirled around Capri. Nobody ever sat down to dinner before 11.30. Everybody bought shirts and trousers and pullovers. We visited the Blue Grotto in a rubber boat. The island is still wickedly enchanting and enchanted ... I really would like to know what it is like out of season.'

We were soon to find out. A very attractive and vivacious lady named Joan Baruch-Bové, patently aged twenty-eight but who said she was really sixty-eight, told Noel that he could use her exquisite house whenever he liked—she only used it for two months in the summer, but all the same she had had the forethought to instal central heating. Noel, Graham and I caught the aliscafe from Naples on a cold December day and arrived at Mrs Baruch's villa in the evening to find that the boiler had never been lit since it had been put in years ago. The daily lady had called in all her family and friends—twenty at least, counting the babies—to cope with the emergency, all of them terrified that the infernal machine would blow up in their faces. Dark smoke from a wood fire stung our eyes until tears poured down our faces, and the daily lady repeated '*la vita è una fregatura*' so often that we could only agree, and flee from the house to get something to eat. Graham and I saw Noel to bed, by now all alone in his luxury villa—the radiators were just tepid and the lavatory refused to work—and left him for our hotel, too tired to notice the geography, and fell into our beds exhausted. We woke to blazing sunshine, so hot that we breakfasted on our balcony, first removing our dressing-gowns, then our pyjama tops and finally having to withdraw indoors because of the heat. The telephone rang and it was Noel, complaining that he was slowly perishing to death in an icy room, with a pile of rugs and carpets on his bed. 'Then why don't you go out and sit in the sun?' He nearly exploded into the telephone: 'Because there *isn't* any sun, you bloody fool,' followed by much worse abuse for our stupidity. We were bewildered and hurried over to find that all he had said was only too true. Mrs Baruch's house was on the opposite side of the island, and though deliciously cool in the summer and with a view of Vesuvius, it obtained not one single glimpse of sun during the winter. We hurriedly packed his things and moved him over to join us in the hotel, but it was no use; it was destined to be one of Noel's Disaster Holidays. The weather changed with violent rapidity before we got there (he never completely believed that we had sweated in the sun) and from then on remained steadily *cattivo*, as he mildly put it.

Capri out of season is not only quiet but moribund. There is nowhere to go, no one to see, nowhere to eat except for two crummy restaurants ... in fact the whole thing is a bugger and I have decided that my head should be very thoroughly examined. I have in Switzerland a divine house, wonderful servants, exquisite food, everything my heart can desire and here I am sitting on a deserted rock in the pouring rain getting more decrepit and cross with every breath I take. This is not repeat *not* going to continue. I have decided to leave for Switzerland, home and beauty ... Capri in inverno non me piace e sono troppo stanco di non being comfortable.

In spite of his annual complaints — 'Christmas is at our throats again' and 'that terrible pall of goodwill hanging over us' — Noel enjoyed Christmas more than anybody. He filled the house with guests, with Gladys, Joycie and Geoffrey as the permanent nucleus, unless Joycie was working in the theatre. And he insisted on crackers from Fortnum and Mason with really good presents inside them and really good-bad riddles and paper caps; there was always a tree to the ceiling with a mountain of presents beneath it, much holly and mistletoe, and the rooms festooned with loops of the hundreds of Christmas cards he received. On Christmas Eve we would all troop next door to Joan Sutherland and Richard Bonynge for the tree in their enormous and beautiful music-room. Joan and Richard's house guests out-numbered ours by far and a platoon of them would come over to us on Christmas morning, by which time Adrianne and Bill had joined our own contingent. Pitchers of champagne cocktails were produced and served on the stroke of noon, for we found from experience that enough time must be allowed to undo the presents before the turkey at half past two. Coma relieved by alka-seltzer at last set in, and then early to bed, for we had to be up and about early on Boxing Day.

' "Boxers" with the Nivs' was the second part of the unalterable tradition; we caught the little train from Les Avants which wiggle-waggled its way through the snowy mountains to Château D'Oex, where the Nivens live, bearing three pillow-cases full of gifts. David and Noel gave presents of such increasing splendour that after a few years of this even David tried to call a halt; he rang up and begged for a sensible limit—no gift was to cost more than ten pounds. 'I'll tell you what we'll do,' Noel said as he hung up, 'we'll buy lots of very big presents and arrive with three *sacks* full and frighten the hell out of him.'

Our arrival at Château D'Oex always caused a sensation; there seemed to be hundreds of skiers about, half waiting to board our train and the other half to board a train coming from the opposite direction and due in a few minutes. The Nivs were always on the tracks to meet us, which called forth an excited chorus of 'Look, there's David Niven!', swollen a few minutes later with 'Look, there's Noel Coward!' The sensation became greater than ever this particular year, for the group of Nivs were holding large opened umbrellas made of vivid Union Jacks, David himself bearing a tray of bloody marys to be consumed there and then. But we had to scuttle for the platform to escape death from the oncoming train, to the enjoyment of the on-lookers, and our bulging sacks went unnoticed.

The Nivs would be joined by neighbours, Julie Andrews and Blake Edwards, Alastair Forbes, or Elizabeth and Richard Burton. Elizabeth must have received one of the first, if not the first, of the famous diamond rings from Richard for one of these Christmases. She was engagingly thrilled with it, a girl anxious for us all to share her enjoy-ment, to try it on for ourselves and make the facets catch the light. The room became full and the two of us sat on the floor. 'Let's sit opposite the window, then when the sun comes out we can blind everybody with it,' and the sun obliged. Too soon it was time for Noel and his 'little lot' to catch the train. One last nip of brandy in the Buffet de la Gare, more excitement from the crowd, and another happy Christmas was over until the next one.

2 0

A SONG
AT TWILIGHT

' ... AND they were sent to prison for having had unnatural relations.'
'Like my Auntie Ida, you mean?' Remarks like this shot from Noel's
lips unbidden, it would seem, lightning quick, almost before one had
time to finish the word 'relations'. How could he have had time to
think of it, let alone go off at such an unexpected tangent? But he did,
not all of the time, but most of the time; his everyday wit as opposed
to that contained in his plays. This spontaneity came to him effortlessly,
and up to a point those who lived with him were inclined to take it
for granted, one became so used to it, though at the moment it happened
it was always appreciated keenly.

The extreme brevity of his wit will be noted. Everybody nowadays
seems to have their favourite Noel Coward story, more often than not
spoiled by embellishment; every extraneous word should be pared
away if the teller's version is to carry the ring of truth. Another mistaken attempt to make a story sound like Noel is to insert 'dear boy'
as often as possible; he rarely used this endearment, though I expect it
is now too late for me to be believed. But William Fairchild's remembrance is true and bears this out. When Bill had to write the dialogue
for the Noel Coward character in the film *Star*, he handed the finished
effort to Noel, not without trepidation, and was of course relieved and
pleased when Noel told him he thought he had done a wonderful job.
'Haven't you *any* criticisms?' Bill asked. 'Too many Dear Boys, dear
boy.'

When not using a flat delivery, Noel's use of emphasis could be
equally effective. After a young Indian student at the next table had
been boring him for an hour, he found out that he came from Lucknow.
'Oh the re*lief* of Lucknow,' he muttered to me. It was never matins
or evensong with Noel, it was always Di*vine* Service, or 'She had to be
given Ex*treme* Unction'.

Noel, as with Oscar Wilde and 'Her hair turned quite gold from grief', enjoyed the substitution of another word—often the opposite of the original—in a platitude, such as 'There is less in this than meets the eye', 'Let me be the eighth to congratulate you', 'His thinking is a triumph of never mind over doesn't matter' and 'She suffered for years in a lack of concentration camp.' He gives full rein to this trick in his comedies, giving his characters banalities to say and then playing merry hell with them—'It will bring out the colour in your eyes.' 'Much better leave it where it is.' And, 'I'll never be able to hold my head up again, and that's a fact.' 'In that case we shall have to settle for it hanging down, shan't we?' All the comedies are sprinkled with examples of this.

The idea of self-conscious wit, for example a dinner-party given expressly for well-known wits who were then expected to perform, held little attraction for him. One seldom heard him use the word witty about himself or anyone else, but he loved to be thought of as frightfully funny, and by way of compliment much preferred Nancy Mitford wiping her eyes and saying helplessly, 'Oh Noel, you do make such jolly good jokes,' and her 'Au nom de Dieu, do come back to Paris soon, I could do with another shriek.'

After his renaissance this year, and with *Hay Fever* still at the National, by which time his major comedies had been acknowledged as classics and had been placed by many as in direct descent from Congreve, Sheridan and Oscar Wilde, he would put down paper or magazine and ask, 'Do *you* think I'm the wittiest man alive? This paper says I am.' What could you say except, 'I suppose you must be. Who else is there? Try to name a wittier.' He would consider, 'There might be someone at this very moment being witty as all get-out in Urdu.'

A major misconception is that his last play of importance, *A Song at Twilight*, is autobiographical. Since its successful and beautifully acted revival with Hume Cronyn, Jessica Tandy and Anne Baxter, reviewers have begun to state this as a fact. The idea for the play came to Noel when he read in Lord David Cecil's *Max* of Constance Collier's whirlwind visit to Sir Max Beerbohm, fracturing the tranquillity of his existence at Rapallo. Constance had been a flame of Beerbohm's when they were young, but they hadn't met for many years and her enthusiasms and vitality had left him exhausted, and relieved to see the back of her. Noel thought this very funny and started to write a comedy, but did not get very far. After all, he had already used the idea of people arriving, upsetting a household and then going away in *Hay Fever*. The character of Sir Hugo Latymer then began to take on overtones of Somerset Maugham. Noel himself had never written compromising love letters to a male secretary (or to anyone else of either sex so far as is known), much less been blackmailed for them. Neither had Mr Maugham to Noel's knowledge, but with him in mind Noel did think of the untypically outspoken and very moving letter Mr Maugham wrote to him when Gerald Haxton died. That was as far as it went, but dramatically he had to go on from there and thought of what might happen to *any* public figure in such a situation, should he be blackmailed. Sir Hugo in the play happens to be a distinguished author and some of his lines no doubt express the philosophy which Noel himself expressed late in life. But his character, crusty and somewhat disagreeable, in no way resembles Noel's, the circumstances of his private life still less, and he can in no way, apart from being a writer, be described as a self-portrait.

Here are some more popular illusions about Noel, taken from newspaper clippings of the last few weeks at the time of writing; printed as gospel and widely believed as such, but in fact wide of the truth.

'There was a brittle feminine streak in Coward that lashed out at those around him ... quite frequently he wounded or stung his prey into submission.' (Not true; I was around him for thirty-seven years.) And a current memoir gives these extremely unlikely words as having issued from Noel's lips: 'That [something Noel is supposed to have said] will appear in print one day and merely perpetuate my reputation for being a prime bitch.' He had no such reputation and in no circumstances can I imagine him using the words 'prime bitch'.

This misconception seems mainly to have arisen in America, where Clifton Webb first played Garry Essendine in *Present Laughter* as waspish and bitchy. Garry is a larger-than-life portrait of Noel, written by himself, which does give a good if exaggerated idea of what he was like to live with, and of his relations with 'those around him'. Douglas Fairbanks, Jr, is rebuked by this same reviewer and others for not playing Garry as Clifton did, and blamed for removing the venom. Douglas is playing the role as Noel wrote it and intended it to be played and as he played it himself—for its comedy value alone, and with likeable charm. Garry is quite funny enough as he is, without adding venom that is not there, and Noel disliked Clifton's portrayal very much indeed.

Two clippings from this same batch, using almost identical words, state categorically that Noel summed up his gift years ago as 'merely a talent to amuse'. It is Manon in *Bitter Sweet*, not Noel, who sings, 'I believe that since my life began, the most I've had is just a talent to amuse.' Sheridan Morley thought *A Talent to Amuse* a good title for his biography of Noel, which it was, and Noel gave Sheridan his permission to use it. But he himself never thus underrated his many gifts or 'summed them up' (and neither can anybody else) in those four words.

There will one supposes be no way of stemming the tide of these and other fallacies (including the one that he used a long cigarette-holder all his life). Noel, as so often, has the last word to say:

> The only thing that saddens me over my demise is that I shall not be here to read the nonsense that will be written about me and my works and my motives. There will be detailed and inaccurate analyses of my motives for writing this or that and of my character. There will be lists of apocryphal jokes I never made and gleeful misquotations of words I never said. *What* a pity I shan't be here to enjoy them!

Queen Elizabeth the Queen Mother paid an official visit to Jamaica in February 1965. Before Noel left London it had been arranged between Queen Elizabeth and himself that after her five days at King's House in Kingston—days crowded with official duties—she would come to luncheon at Firefly Hill as the first part of her two-day holiday, the rest of which she would spend at Tryall beyond Montego Bay. The luncheon was intended to be private and informal, which in the end it was, but a few days beforehand Noel wrote in his journal:

> The hubbub about the Queen Mother coming to lunch with me, far from being a secret, is the talk of the island. The whole place [Firefly] has been hopping with Security Police for weeks. [They returned again and again to spend an ominously long time with tape-measures in Noel's bathroom and always left sadly shaking their heads, which worried us considerably.] I sense bewilderment among the officials that she should wish to come to my tiny un-grand house when there are so many more apparently suitable ones. They just don't know the Queen Mother. Today Maureen Dufferin, Primrose Cadogan, Hugh Cruddas and Robert Heber-Percy are coming to lunch. We shall give them a dress rehearsal of what we are giving the Queen Mother, i.e. Lobster mousse, curry in coconuts [our old favourite specialité, cocomania] and rum cream pie.

Lynn and Alfred were staying and Noel also invited Blanchie to the luncheon. The weather remained slightly inclement for days; a worry, for the dining patio, a cool oasis on a hot day, became gloomy on a wet one. However Wednesday February 24th dawned crystal clear and developed into a peerlessly beautiful day. The morning was incident-packed. There were a thousand things to attend to, but in the middle of them all Noel pronounced that my hair looked simply terrible and that something must be done, so Lynnie gave me a quick back-and-sides in the garden. Blanchie arrived with a canteen of gold cutlery which up until that moment we never knew she possessed.

We could follow the Queen Mother's progress on the radio as far as her last engagement in Spanish Town, from which we learnt that 'Her Majesty was looking radiant in pale blue and yellow'—our own colour scheme for the tables, which was a great bit of luck. Drama set in over the lobster mousse which, in a metal mould the shape of a lobster, was of an unlovely grey and frozen hard as iron. To my suggestion that it should be placed on a chair in the sun to defreeze, Mae the cook shrieked, 'You can't do that, the cats will get at it!', but I had my way and Desmond the gardener was put on sentry-go. We paid anxious visits to the mousse from time to time; Noel at one late point reporting that it had now reached the consistency of an ordinary Slazenger tennis-ball. By the time I made one last despairing visit at twenty minutes to one, the mousse had begun to melt and my thumb went clean through it. Noel now assumed an air of authority: 'Everybody must remain perfectly calm. I can see that I shall have to take charge.' He made some delicious iced green-pea soup in the blender, spiked with fresh mint from the garden.

The Queen Mother arrived at 1.20, gayer and more enchanting than ever. Lunch was a great success, I had to make iced soup twenty minutes before she arrived. We sat on the verandah and introduced the Queen Mother to Bullshots, she had two and was delighted. The view was dazzlingly beautiful and absolutely at its best. She was supposed to leave at three for her long drive to Tryall, but she insisted on seeing Blue Harbour as well (which had *not* been frisked, to the Security men's horror, though not to the Queen Mother's) so I drove down with her through the cheering citizens of Grant's Town and she didn't actually leave till ten to four. Coley, Blanche, Lynn and Alfred inevitably fell in love with her. As for me, I am at her feet. She has infinite grace of mind, charm, humour, and deep down kindness. She puts everyone at

ease immediately without apparent effort. She did me great honour
by driving nearly eighty miles off her course to come and see me.
Ruth Fermoy, Martin Gilliat and David McMicking were funny,
relaxed and helpful. Everyone waited on everyone else at lunch:
Percival, by his special request, wore white gloves with his white
coat. It was all tremendous fun and the Queen Mother left behind
her five gibbering worshippers. She turned and waved to us all
the way until her car was out of sight, at Reef Point corner.

Our next house-guests were Joan Sutherland and Richard Bonynge,
then James Pope-Hennessy, to whom they took an immediate liking,
as James did to them. Noel first met James as long ago as 1943; the
friendship continued, though not very closely until now, with Noel
all the time much admiring James's writing. Noel's book of *Collected
Lyrics* was about to appear; with scrupulous care that his meticulous
rhyming should look its best on the printed page—particularly when
possible the 'inner rhyming'—the very long book had been retyped
three times and as often scrutinised by us until we felt we might lose
our reason when faced with the task of correcting the galleys. James
took this important burden off our shoulders and worked indefatigably
at it during his holiday; not without enjoyment, for he was reading
many of the lesser lyrics for the first time, and admitted to laughing
aloud when by himself, which was something, he said, he rarely did.
Out of gratitude, Noel dedicated the *Collected Lyrics* to James.

   A separate book could be written about Noel's attitude to religion,
it fluctuated so much and often depended on the last book he had read
on the subject. The only constant was the elementary instruction he
had received at St Alban's Church and from his mother in his childhood.
While he did not believe in the Holy Trinity, God the Father remained
for Noel rather real—a fairly fierce old gentleman with a white beard,
wearing a nightgown and inclined to lose his temper at the drop of a
hat. Moses and St Paul, in a way embodiments of God the Father, he
actively hated, for they had really existed and made beasts of themselves,
bossing everybody about, laying down the law and preventing people
enjoying themselves, which he found unforgivable. With God the
Father himself on the other hand he maintained a rather bantering
relationship, replying on television when David Frost asked whether
he believed in God, 'We've never been intimate but maybe we have a
few things in common,' and constantly referring to the Almighty and
the One Above in his writings: 'This will have to be left to the Almighty
and I sincerely hope that he will do something about it, and not just

sit there.' Then there was gentle Jesus, whose teachings Noel admired (and obeyed without consciously doing so) while forever deploring the sins his followers had committed for nearly two thousand years in his name. Noel's attitude to Christ is summed up, as it is for many people, by Lord Byron: 'The *moral* of Christianity is perfectly beautiful.' The Holy Ghost remained a puzzlement.

By and large Noel got along with this arrangement very well, doing unto others as he often *wished* they would do unto him, and never dreaming of interfering with, or trying to alter or prevent, other people's belief in God. But on to this tolerance a bombshell would drop from time to time in the form of a book. Two books in particular caused much trouble to Noel and even more to those around him. The first was G. Rattray Taylor's *Sex in History*, sent to him in all innocence by Arthur Macrae, which caused him to write:

The witch-hunting, the massacres, the intolerance, the wild futility of human behaviour over the centuries is hardly credible. And the laws as they stand today are almost inconceivably stupid. With all this brilliant scientific knowledge of atom splitting and nuclear physics, we are *still* worshipping at different shrines, imprisoning homosexuals, imposing unnecessary and irrelevant restrictions on each other. Hearts can be withdrawn from human breasts, dead hearts, and after a little neat manipulation popped back in again as good as new. The skies can be conquered. Sputniks can whizz round and round the globe and be controlled and guided. People are still genuflecting before crucifixes and [effigies of] Virgin Marys, still persecuting other people for being coloured or Jewish or in some way different from what they apparently should be. There are wars being waged at this very moment in Indonesia, the Middle East, Algeria, Cyprus ... The Ku Klux Klan is still, if permitted, ready to dash out and do some light lynching. God, for millions of people, is still secure in his heaven.

His friends would beg him to consider the good the Church had done during its two thousand years' existence, which equalled if not outweighed the evil; the many benefits of its teachings, its encouragement of learning and the arts through the Dark Ages and above all the inspiration and solace it had brought to millions of people. One did not beg in vain; he would listen and agree.

Then the second book arrived, written by Robert Ardrey and

illustrated by his wife Berdine—both of them friends. It was *African Genesis*, in which Bob puts forth a theory that we are descended from killer apes and not from those beguiling chimpanzees who hold such happy tea-parties in the Zoo. Noel seized upon this theory; it explained man's inhumanity to man and neatly fitted in with Mr Rattray Taylor's long list of cruelties we have inflicted upon our fellows since recorded time. Noel, it should be remembered, in spite of his natural gaiety and resilience, also possessed a curiously strong streak of pessimism regarding the human race which he had expressed ever since he started writing, though in those days in a minor degree—'World Weary', 'Poor Little Rich Girl' and 'What is there to strive for, Live or keep alive for'. In these songs and others he saw little hope.

Noel's temporary enthusiasm for these two books was such that he sent copies to a great many friends; their lack of equal enthusiasm, often expressed by total silence, passed unnoticed by him. In the meantime we, the people living or staying with him, had to endure his expounding of their merits, many evenings ending in angry disagreement or boredom from his repetition. At long last the hubbub died down and he returned, as he always did in the end, to his true bedside bible, *The Human Situation* by W. Macneile Dixon, a gentle, more philosophically comforting assessment of mankind's condition.

One evening, at the height of the *African Genesis* discussions, Joan, Richard, James and myself were sitting at the dining table at Blue Harbour with Noel at the head; James a devout Catholic, and Joan, Richard and me with our Anglican upbringing. Noel started again on the killer apes; 'Three quarters of a million years ago ... ', to which I said, 'But that's so long ago it sounds like the beginning of the Bible— in the beginning was the Word.' Noel banged his fist on the glass table, making a terrible clatter, and jumped to his feet. 'If that is all you have to say, *I* shall say good night.' He stormed to the doorway, said, 'Good *night*,' banged the door, went to his jeep and drove up to Firefly. I was appalled at what I had done, embarrassed and distressed and faced with the ruins of the evening. Joan and Richard eventually went to bed, but not long after there was the sound of someone at the verandah door. I went to it and there in the half-light stood God the Father, avenging arms outstretched, booming, 'I am on my way up to Noel and I'm going to frighten the hell out of him.' It was Joan, draped in a sheet and with a long cotton-wool beard. The blessed relief of laughter after my unhappiness is beyond description and then, after this, James and I sat on the verandah and talked late into the night. James's comfort can never be forgotten either: 'You mustn't worry

about Noel, there's nothing to worry about. He possesses all the
Christian virtues, and what is more he practises them.'

Winifred died in April:

She'd been in pain for months. Later I had a letter from Patrick
[Dr Woodcock, for many years our doctor in London] saying
that on the evening before, she rallied suddenly, tied a purple
nylon scarf round her head, slapped on some lipstick and sent for
Dick [Addinsell] and Victor [Stiebel] and had a little farewell
party with them for an hour. She was a gallant old girl. When I
think of all the war years and the fun we had in her little Tavistock
Street house and all the arguments and jokes and violent enthusiasms. I realise how much I am in her debt. What is particularly
horrid for me is that I wrote to her the day she died—a gay and
loving letter. If only I had done so a few days before. I would so
have liked her to hear from me and know that I was thinking of
her. Well, that's one more old friend gone—the cupboard is
getting barer.

There now began a long search, to last on and off for five years, to
'find an understudy for Coley'. If for no other reason than that it plays
a large part in the journals and letters of the period, it should be mentioned. With the financial and tax affairs now centred in Switzerland
and all major theatrical business decisions inevitably coming to
Noel and me, instead of my life becoming easier with advancing
years, I was working more assiduously than ever, although, I must
quickly add, having a wonderful time into the bargain. Nobody could
help me over this. Lornie and Joan in London and Geoffrey in New
York did all they could but naturally would not have known where to
begin to pick up all the threads of Noel's life in Switzerland and
Jamaica. Noel began to worry dreadfully over this:

We must have extra help ... it must be realised that if anything
should happen to Coley I should have *no one* who knew the ropes
and was au courant with all the complications of my complicated
life. I don't want one day to be faced suddenly with an emergency.
Much better to have someone waiting in the wings. Coley now
does all the letters, runs the houses, deals with guests, books all
reservations, organises all journeys. There are also lots of other
things such as the sorting of my private letters and journals which
he hasn't time to attempt. We have therefore been searching ...

It should have been easy enough. Numberless times I had been told by people that they would give anything to have a glamorous and exciting job like mine. That any replacement should be younger than me was a prerequisite. This was true of the three who gave it a try, but they all found in time that life in a little village in the Alps was not after all very exciting, while I was of an age to appreciate the peace of it after three decades of hurly-burly. They were all of them without exception eager to learn, started the job with enthusiasm, and when they left we parted amicably and they remained our good friends.

That lasting success did not come of their efforts was not their fault. Too late we realised that no one could suddenly be called upon to do what I was doing, which was the result of experience slowly gained over thirty years and was in fact not 'a job' at all. It had become my life—it was as simple as that—Noel's friends had become my friends and his interests my only interests. When the last of the 'apprentices' left, Noel and I knew that nothing more could be done; we knew that we should have to press on as we always had. I was born on a Saturday, and when I was little I thought the old rhyme cruelly unjust; why should one of my cousins be good-looking because he was born on a Monday while I must 'work hard for my living'? Only now I acknowledged that the old rhyme had helped me after all. I had accepted it since boyhood and never fought against it and, what is more, it tallied with Noel's eternal dictum that the only lasting satisfaction in life came from work well done. The remainder, the pleasures, were a bonus; a reward earned honestly. What were we going on about, Noel asked at five years' end. If and when I was under the sod I should anyway be completely unconscious of the pickle I had left him in, and I was not to fret about him should I die first. 'I shall manage somehow, I always have.' Our search had failed and we never tried again. Graham was there, ready and waiting to help when the time came.

All told, Noel had sixteen godchildren, among them Daniel Massey, Tarquin Olivier, David Niven, Jr, Lornie's daughter Meggie, Michael Attenborough, Juliet Mills, Alan Williams (Emlyn's son), Caspar Fleming, Simon Havelock-Allan and Stewart Forster's daughter Sarah. The last was Hugo Morley, Sheridan's son. All sixteen received a present of some kind at Christmas while they were children. The godson he saw the most of was young David Niven, because of encounters in Hollywood and later in Rome while David was working there and the proximity of the Niven chalet to ours in Switzerland. Noel dictated the following letter to David in September 1965, before flying to join Sam Spiegel and Burt Lancaster on Sam's yacht at Monaco:

Dear Sir, Mr Noel Coward, who is at present cruising in the Mediterranean, asked me before he left to tell you that he is outraged and disgusted by your insolence in asking for *two* of his paintings. Mr Coward's paintings, apart from their enormous artistic merit, also have great rarity value and nobody, not even Royalty or a Deserving Charity or a Great Hollywood Film Star, has ever had the brass to ask him for more than one.

He feels that your position at the William Morris Organization—such as it is, for nobody seems to know what you really do there though people who should know say that you are nothing more than a glorified office boy—has gone to your tiny head. Or that perhaps Something Has Come Over You since he, as your godfather, stopped giving you his invaluable religious instruction when you reached years of discretion (ha ha excuse me laughing).

Mr Coward has a very good mind to release the whole shocking story to Radie Harris to break in her column so the entire world will know how greedy and grasping you really are.

All right, Mr Coward will send you two of his beautiful pictures but, not to put too fine a point on it, he thinks you have a fucking nerve and are, *among other things*, a Saucy Sod. Yours etc.

There was at this time, and still is, some speculation as to whether or not Noel ever had his face lifted. He did not. But he did begin to develop a double chin, which displeased him. Lornie's opinion was that as you get older you must either suffer a scraggy neck like a turkey or a jowl, and a jowl is better. All right, he had a jowl, but Ina Claire said, 'Why not get rid of it? Get rid of all that garbage,' and Noel took Ina's advice: 'Thursday morning I was operated on by Matthew Banks [at Harley House in London]. Three hours on the table and had claustrophobic panic afterwards when I had half come round: apart from that lots of heroin and everything fine.' He was told weeks afterwards that the claustrophobic panic was caused by his heart having completely stopped beating for some long and frightening moments, hence the abnormal length of time 'on the table' and the 'lots of heroin'. Unaware at the time of this drama he blithely concludes the entry: 'Underchin jowls now completely gone! Must remain bandaged until Monday when I return to London to have stitches out.'

Noel set out in October 1965 for what was to be the last of his long holidays alone. He had conceived a yearning to visit the Seychelles, which many people assured him were an absolute paradise on earth, though he did keep in the back of his mind the fact that Ian Fleming had not taken to them, and his warning that everything in the Indian Ocean was twice as dangerous as anywhere else. In 1965 one could not get to the Seychelles by air; nowadays one can, and Noel's description of the conditions, written ten years ago, no longer holds good. He flew to Bombay, where he stayed for more than a week and where he caught the amoebic dysentery for which the Seychelles, because it was there that the illness manifested itself, were wrongly blamed for a while. From Bombay he sailed in a ship called the *Karanja* and (because he later wanted to continue the voyage to Mombasa and then visit the game reserves in Africa) was voluntarily marooned on the Seychelles for a month. This he looked forward to enormously; there would be peace, plenty of time to write and to visit all the other islands with their pretty names—Praslin, Félicité, Silhouette and Curieuse. We always looked forward to our separations, Noel to his holiday and I to mine and yet, the moment we were apart, we felt an immediate urge to write to one another, and our correspondence over the next two months became more frequent than ever before; Noel as usual writing hilariously funny letters and, if I had only known it, very brave ones. But at last he could be funny and brave no longer. He wrote:

Oh Coley I will withhold from you no longer the gruesome fact that ... I have been horribly ill again for the last week ... I sail on Thursday for Mombasa unless I can get on to the American seaplane on Wednesday which will bear this letter. If I am still feeling ghastly I shall forego the African part of my trip and fly straight back to Geneva ... These last few days have been lovely but too late to be of any good to me. I haven't even got enough energy to walk into the sea. Everybody has been very kind and one or other of the Oxfords [Lord and Lady Oxford and Asquith, he being the Governor of the Seychelles] come and visit me every day. The food remains indescribable so I stick to poached eggs and cornflakes and tea. I hate the Seychelles and everything to do with them. Everything is dirty and tatty and run to seed. I share my ghastly bungalow with a rat the size of a small collie and several centipedes. I haven't quite recovered my sense of humour and there have been some black moments. I haven't any more news except that I am counting the days ...

The gaunt, ashen, emaciated figure I found slumped on a seat at Geneva Airport was, for a moment, unrecognisable as Noel, so weak he could not stand or walk without help. How he had made the flight from Nairobi and the two-hour wait and change of planes at Rome I couldn't imagine; he said that everybody had been 'very kind' but that he had felt 'more dead than alive'. Three days later he could write: 'Home at last, I can hardly believe it. I have my own comfortable bed and delicious food. I am feeling fifty times better already, no more nausea and no more "trots". Dr Spuhler is looking after me. I'm still on a careful diet of course and still not drinking a drop but Oh the bliss of being home again!' Little by little Noel gained strength until at last he was up and about, and well enough to enjoy his birthday and Christmas as much as ever. But, Doctor Spuhler told us, tests showed that there was still albumen, later described as too many white corpuscles, and traces of blood in the urine which remained a mystery, and of these we had by no means heard the last, though Noel wrote, 'I feel fine so there can't be anything terribly amiss.'

For many years Noel had cherished a dream, rather vague at first, of appearing once more on the stage in the West End. It had to be in London, nowhere else, 'where I first started more than fifty years ago, to sort of round off the dinner.' The dream sometimes seemed unlikely to materialise; effective star parts for men in their mid-sixties do not grow on trees, and moreover both the part and the play would have to be certain, as far as one can ever be certain, of success. The idea of Noel appearing, possibly for the last time, in a failure was unthinkable. The idea was never far from his mind for long, and more and more it grew to be the one definite ambition left for him to achieve: 'I must search for or write a play to do in London as a sort of Swan Song. I would like to act once more before I fold my bedraggled wings.' In the end he decided that he would have to do what he had usually done and write the vehicle for himself and, as already related, he had the idea of the comedy about Max Beerbohm and Constance Collier. To confirm what I have already dwelt upon—that *A Song at Twilight* is not auto-biographical—Noel himself noted, when halfway through the writing, 'My play is now more sinister, and there is Maugham in it as well as Max.'

The play at last was finished, a good strong play with equally power-ful parts for Margaret Leighton and Irene Worth, Binkie was enthusi-astic and agreed to put it on for Noel's customary three months, and Noel was satisfied. He had successfully achieved the first part of his scheme. But then the thought hit him—Graham and I laughed in his face when he told us, he looked so horror-struck—the *monotony* of having to play the same part eight times a week for three months!—he would have to write one or two more. And so he wrote *Come Into the Garden, Maud* and then *Shadows of the Evening*, a gently melancholy title for the last play Noel ever wrote.

Margaret dithered about leaving Hollywood and coming to London to play the parts Noel had written for her. Lilli Palmer came to Les Avants for the weekend and Noel read her *A Song at Twilight*; at the end of another call to Hollywood with still no decision from Margaret, Lilli said, 'If I had that chance I'd start rehearsing tomorrow morning.' Lilli was very soon given that chance and early in January 1966, Lilli, Irene and Vivian Matalon, who was to direct, came to Les Avants for preliminary discussions and readings. Even from these it became evident that Lilli and Irene would give brilliant performances, and from the beginning Noel found Vivian a sympathetic director and increasingly relied on his opinion and advice. The set-up was perfect and Noel was happy—but then disaster struck. The amoebic dysentery recurred, this time more severely than ever, and the little party had to disband.

The six weeks Noel then spent in the clinic in Lausanne were for him one prolonged misery. The frustration of having to postpone the plays, indeed the possibility that he might never be able to do them at all, added to the already dark depression caused by his illness. We learned for the first time that the amoeba requires no mate but can reproduce itself, and that therefore Noel must for weeks take increasingly stronger antibiotics until the doctors were certain that the very last amoeba had been vanquished. Noel always inspired devotion, affection even, in his doctors and Doctor Claud Wild was no exception. He was unfailingly kind, tactful with Noel's foibles and sympathetic, and he worked closely by telephone with Ed in Chicago and Patrick Woodcock in London. He warned me that for the last two weeks Noel would be on the (then) strongest antibiotic of all, a drug called Emetine, and would feel suicidal. This, true to character, brought out Noel's fighting spirit. He felt suicidal all right and his lowness of spirit was dreadful to see, but he firmly made up his mind that all he was now suffering from was the hideous depression caused by the Emetine, that he was bloody well going to leave the Clinic *next Tuesday* and go to London and get on with the plays. Psychologically he was right, he could postpone no longer and he did go to London and rehearse and do the plays. He also made a resolution: 'I must never be ill in a foreign language again. The strain is too great.' Doctor Wild, however, tears in his eyes, begged me to the last to stop Noel leaving the Clinic; the rather sinister mystery of the sedimentation—the blood and the albumen—was still unsolved.

The success of *Suite in Three Keys*, as the three plays were collectively called, at the Queen's Theatre was as great as Noel had dreamed of and hoped for. He and Lilli and Irene provided a feast of good acting in nine diversified roles and their reward was spellbound admiration from capacity audiences for the entire run:

> Well, the most incredible thing has happened. Not only has *A Song at Twilight* opened triumphantly but the press notices have on the whole been extremely good. Most particularly the [Beaverbrook Press] *Express* and *Evening Standard*! Fortunately the *Sun* struck a sour note and said, 'Coward's Return Very Tedious', which convinced me that I hadn't entirely slipped ... the play is such a sell-out that we have had to engage extra people to cope with the ticket demand. [Ten days later:] We opened *Shadows of the Evening* and *Come Into the Garden, Maud* to a fantastic audience ... *Maud* was an absolute riot and the ovation at the final curtain was quite wonderful. I haven't experienced anything like it for many a long day and it made everything worth while. People came pouring on to the stage afterwards and it was altogether heartwarming.

Noel's dressing-room each night became a three-ring circus as it had always done, packed with friends and celebrities, and, as there had always been, there was a crowd of fans waiting at the stage-door for his autograph after each performance.

'I wish I felt physically better,' Noel wrote nearly halfway through the run, 'but nothing would induce me to disappoint these wonderful audiences. I feel a warmth and a genuine love emanating from the front of the house at every performance.' Although feeling exhausted and drained and in pain, he never did disappoint them. To add to the foregoing troubles, one of the most humiliating things that could happen to Noel happened now; he began to 'dry up'. He, of all people, who had always been word-perfect, had never fluffed and had rattled off all those intricate lyrics at such a rate, began to forget his lines. Irene and Lilli were perfectly wonderful at covering up for him; Lilli especially, who had to play with him what is in fact one prolonged duet in the middle of *A Song at Twilight*, was always one jump ahead, ready to help in a flash. She never failed to get him through the long dinner scene, for which he was forever grateful to her. His dryings-up were seldom mentioned in or out of the theatre, they were glossed over, but his distress was great and most of this he got off his chest to me and to Patrick Woodcock in the mornings. Patrick gave him strong vitamin injections and, even more effective, he had the invaluable gift of being able to cheer Noel up, to make him laugh and assure him that yes, he would get through all right. The real cause of the sedimentation in the urine would not be correctly diagnosed, and then accidentally, until months later. When it was, it became apparent that Noel had been seriously ill and must have been in pain all through what eventually was a four-month run; looking back, one could only admire such long-drawn-out determination and courage.

Before leaving London Noel had more medical tests. One specialist 'shoved an Eiffel Tower up my arse with a light on the end of it ... rather painful. However, what he saw apparently entranced him. I have *nothing* sinister wrong with me. Only this dear old spastic colon which, with enough rest, will cure itself.' The next months passed quite happily, most of them in the peace and sun of Jamaica, with Noel on a bland diet. He did not, however, improve in health; pain was never far away. We decided to give the complete rest and bland diet one more month, and if Noel did not feel better by then we would fly to Chicago, Ed and the Passavant Hospital. He grew steadily worse and the beginning of November found him in the Passavant and me in a hotel nearby: 'The merry Calvary has started. I dread further experiments and tests, my poor body would so much rather be left alone. But I am determined that from now on I am going to be well—if it kills me.' Ed took me to one side and explained that the sedimentation in the urine could be the symptom of about seven different diseases, three of which could prove fatal. Noel as usual behaved very badly throughout the week of intensive tests, taking each one as a personal affront, yelling blue murder at the barium enemas, and insisting on anaesthetics for others, for which anaesthetics are not usually given. A day came when Ed took me to see the latest batch of X-rays. Attention was still concentrated on the colon, which had become inflamed and infected and in one place perforated; all this was in the lower half of the X-ray, but a passing colleague of Ed's asked, 'What's that?' and pointed to a smudge in the upper half. Noel to his annoyance was again wheeled away for yet more X-rays and I waited with him for the result.

At last Ed and the surgeon, Doctor Greyhack, came into the room with smiling faces. 'We've got good news for you; what you've got is a stone in the kidney.' 'I have heard better news in my time,' Noel said. Ed's smile was of course one of relief that what was wrong with Noel was after all nothing sinister, nothing fatal—it was operable, and the mystery had at last been cleared up. The stone was so large, pointed at both ends, that one was not in the least surprised that Noel had been in such pain for so long. He correctly described it as being the size of a Victoria plum stone, and less accurately as being in 'an attractive setting of pink mucus'; he thought he might have it made into a brooch for Gladys for Christmas. He was rather proud of it and kept it in a glass by his bed for days until someone whisked it away for analysis, to his regret. The day of the operation lasted from his awakening at five thirty in the morning until a mad-looking night nurse literally wrenched the intravenous feeding tube from his arm at two o'clock the next morning; the exhaustingly long day had involved many other grim incidents and the wound necessitated thirty-seven stitches. The curious thing about Noel's behaviour was that there were no more tantrums as there had been during the tests. When it came to unavoidable pain or discomfort he bore it with fortitude and never complained.

Noel's working career reached its apogee with *Suite in Three Keys*—the remaining years were a postscription. Struggles were over, and honours and glory were to come. His life during those seven years was agreeable and happy enough; he even seemed to enjoy grumbling about the approach of old age. He began to act the part of an old man before he became one, moaning, 'I am old, Father William,' or simulating a wheeze or a querulous croak, 'I am old, and scant of breath.' Another joke was to have to be helped out of bed because he was so frail and aged, hobbling bent double on his way to the bathroom and then executing a snappy buck-and-wing before he went inside and closed the door.

The cause of the intermittent loss of memory during *Suite in Three Keys* must have been due to his gradually increasing arterio-sclerosis. He never completely regained his former remarkably easy ability to learn and memorise lines. This was again a source of mortification to him during the last television performance he gave (as opposed to the extempore talk shows with David Frost and Dick Cavett, in which he remained as quick-witted as ever). The show was Richard Rodgers's musical of *Androcles and the Lion* in New York with Norman Wisdom, and the failing was equally evident during the making of his last two films, *Boom* with Elizabeth Taylor and Richard Burton, and *The Italian Job* with Michael Caine. He himself was miserably aware of this, but again, tactfully, nothing was said by the others; the three sympathetic directors were respectively Joe Layton, Joe Losey and Peter Collinson. He never forgot the pleasure he derived from acting with Elizabeth (he had no scenes with Richard), her professionalism, the way she never 'lost his eye', her help, and above all the way her high spirits kept him and indeed the whole unit cheerful through the long and chilly hours of night shooting.

Physically he remained quite active after the stone had been removed; it was not until the very last years that the hardening of the arteries, diagnosed so long ago and aggravated by his stubborn refusal to take exercise or give up smoking, became acute, particularly in his right leg:

Walking! I've just got to walk so much a day from now onwards, even if it's only as far as the village. Those sweet little peripheral veins have *got* to be encouraged. Ah me! All I've got to console me now is bad weather, when it is raining or snowing too heavily for me to go out. I greet each radiant new day with a sinking heart. It is snowing violently today so I am happy as can be, but tomorrow will come and I shall have to go stumping down the bloody hill. I must *learn* to like it. [He never did, and what is more he never really tried.] My health is all right ... which I put down to excessive smoking. A reckoning will probably come, it usually does. I read [in these journals] a triumphant account of giving up smoking for ever, while in Fiji, Tahiti and Bora Bora ... after a few weeks I could bear it no longer, so back I went to the darling weed and have felt splendid ever since. It may of course shorten my life by a year or two but I haven't got all that much longer and I couldn't care less. It's been a nice and profitable buggy ride and I've enjoyed most of it very much. The loss of a few years of gnarled old age does not oppress me ... It is possible that with my constitution I might stagger on into the nineties which would mean nearly another quarter of a century! I cannot say I find this prospect very alluring. I would prefer Fate to allow me to go to sleep when it's my proper bedtime. I never have been one for staying up too late.

Oh how fortunate I was to have been born poor. [He had been reading Lytton Strachey and 'the Bloomsbury lot'.] If Mother had been able to afford to send me to a private school, Eton and Oxford or Cambridge it would probably have set me back years. I have always distrusted too much education and intellectualism ... There was something to me both arid and damp about dwelling too much among the literary shades of the past. My good fortune

was to have a bright, acquisitive but *not* an intellectual mind and
to have been impelled by circumstances to get out and earn my
living and help pay the instalments on the house. I believe that
had my formative years been passed in more assured circumstances
I might easily have slipped into preciousness; as it was I merely
had to slip *out* of precociousness and bring home the bacon.

'GOODNIGHT, MY DARLINGS'

MUCH of 1967 was spent in London, during which Noel stayed at the Savoy Hotel: 'The Savoy enfolds me in its expensive arms.' Mr Beverly Griffin, General Manager, gave an interview to the *International Herald Tribune*:

> The most precise guest in the hotel's history is named almost without hesitation. They say the prize has to go to Noel Coward. Like many people who deal or have dealt with the Savoy, he left clothes there so he'd never need a suitcase. Yet Coward was hardly that simple. 'Besides the clothes,' says Mr Griffin, 'he wanted five pillows and a large bed. Then he insisted that the tables, the chairs, his pills and even his water glass all be placed in exactly the same way every time he stayed here. It took some doing but we finally worked out a system. When we got everything the way he liked it, we had the room photographed and filed the picture in the index. From then on we simply followed the index to the minutest detail.'

The Savoy Grill had played a large part in Noel's life ever since the 'twenties. He now grew to love the hotel itself and, wrote Mr Griffin after his death, 'Sir Noel was a client deeply loved by us all.'

In July 1967 Noel wrote:

> I can't even remember the date of the morning that Coley came into my suite at the Savoy, suffused with tears, and told me that Vivien had died. The shock was too violent. She was a lovely, generous and darling friend. A day or two later Jack [John Merivale] rang me up and asked me to read the Address at her

Memorial Service. I lovingly but firmly refused. I truly do not believe I could have done it without breaking down and making a shambles of it. I know this was cowardly ... if it could have helped Vivien in any way I would have done anything, but it couldn't because she's gone for ever. I mind too deeply about this to go on about it.

Perhaps he felt the same sense of inadequacy when Lornie died in November of this same year, for no mention is made in his journal of her death. Or perhaps, because her last illness had been of such long duration and her death so long expected, there was nothing left to say. Months before she died he wrote:

Lornie has been one of the principal mainstays of my life for forty-six years. Loving, passionately devoted and one of the most truly important characters of my life. There will be no more of it now. Even if she lives on she will become increasingly ill and probably suffer more pain. For her sake it would be kinder if she could die. This is an intolerable sentence to have to write but I know, miserably, that it is the truth ... Of course I shall ultimately get over it and go on living my life as cheerfully as possible but I shall have lost something absolutely irreplaceable. The immediate future is dark with unhappiness. It is said that old age has its compensations. I wonder what they are.

Noel dreaded the memorial service for Lornie. I went to the Savoy to pick him up and we both felt wretchedly miserable, but the day brought forth, among others, two outstanding acts of kindness. Larry breezed in unasked while we were waiting, said briskly, 'Well, we've got a nice day for it,' and announced that he was coming with us; his support was invaluable. The second kindness was Diana's. The service was very well and simply done, but Noel found it almost intolerably sad:

I staggered blindly away from it and went to a gay luncheon at Diana's which was an excellent thing to do. She of course knew I was in misery, and why, and was utterly sweet ... Her beauty and her intelligence both seem to be indestructible. There is no subject on earth that I wouldn't freely discuss with her, except perhaps commonness of mind which would be a waste of time because she wouldn't know what I was talking about. A rare friend.

Life at Les Avants consisted from now on of longer stretches of very pleasant placidity. As always, Noel read endlessly; all the new books from both sides of the Atlantic interspersed with re-readings of all the old favourites. Long afternoons passed too quickly, painting in the well-equipped studio. He became allergic to turpentine and now painted in a medium akin to tempera, called casein; it was quick-drying, which pleased him, impatient as he had always been for rapid results. On the other hand he painted with much more care during this later period, covering large canvases with many small figures. I counted two hundred and forty-two people on one painting: 'Then I must have painted four hundred and eighty-four feet!' he exclaimed in a kind of wonder. These paintings are among his best; at all events his most striking, and in their way, because of their individual style and vivid colours, impressive. He was so proud of them that he gave three pride of place in the drawing-room; Boudin, Sickert and Innes were banished to the hallway and staircase.

The habit of a lifetime could of course not be relinquished entirely and so there was, if only nominally, always some 'work in hand'. For several years he worked on the third volume of his autobiography under the not very apt title of *Past Conditional*, but desultorily, and it remained unfinished:

> The urge to get something done in as short a time as possible, which I used to have, has diminished a bit [but] I find it pleasant to have something on the hob simmering away and requiring from me only an occasional progressive stir. I spend relaxed hours painting in the studio. Perhaps relaxed is not the word. Concentrated, oblivious hours is a better description.

Sunday mornings were no longer passed religiously writing to his loved ones. There was no need: we were together for good except for those in London, and a telephone call to Gladys and Joycie was more immediately satisfactory than a letter. And his other weekly task of writing up his journal was now less eagerly and less frequently under-taken: 'A journal by rights should be full of observations, psycho-logical reflections and witty comments on the passing days, not merely a flat report of engagements fulfilled. I stare at my engagement book blankly and it provides me with scant inspiration.' He did, however, continue with his reports, not always flat but rather the reverse, with some sharp comments on books read and films, plays and operas seen locally or in London and New York.

Noel's social life remained active. Visits to or from Joan and Richard next door, Adrianne and Bill, Charlie and Oona, Nesta Obermer, Monica Stirling, Topazia Markewitch, Brian and Eleanor Aherne, Norman and Erle Krasna, and Oskar Kokoschka and his wife Olde, all of whom are our neighbours. (Oskar Kokoschka, Noel wrote, 'remains and looks like an endearing and affectionate schoolboy of eighty.') We and all or most of the foregoing turned out in force every October for the visit of the Knie Circus. This circus is the National Circus of Switzerland, has been owned and run by the Knie family for more than a hundred years, and is now in the sixth generation, going more strongly than ever. It is one of the great circuses of the world, not too large, with sensationally good turns (proximity renders the feats of the trapeze artists more terrifying) and is presented with great taste and elegance—all the costumes are made in Paris. Charlie Chaplin, the most famous clown who ever lived, is always the guest of honour, gets a rapturous reception from the audience and out and out adoration from the clowns in the company.

The chalet had by now become known by the villagers and the post-man as the Chalet Coward, pronounced Covarr, and Chalet Coward it has remained. For many years it had been nameless, Noel finally resist-ing his urge to be funny and call it 'Swiss Cottage', or, a friend's suggestion, 'Shilly-Chalet'. Chalet Coward was seldom without one house guest or more; among the regulars were Peter and Molly Daubeny, Cathleen Nesbitt, Merle Oberon, Marlene, Robin Maugham, Biddy Monckton (Viscountess Monckton of Brenchley) and Diana Daly. Hester Chapman, the distinguished historian and novelist, was another, her visits particularly relished for the unexpected historical information she shot into the air: 'You know, Noel, it is now almost incontro*ver*tibly proved that Queen Boadicea is buried beneath platform eleven at St Pancras,' for instance.

Probably the most eagerly anticipated visits were Diana Cooper's, during the first week in September. Apart from her virtues and all the other qualities for which she is famous, what makes her perfection as a guest is an outstanding capacity to be game for anything, to take any-thing on and to enjoy it; dangerous drives through mountain roads on a dark night after Yehudi Menuhin's recitals at Gstaad, shopping with unerring taste for blouses and hats and shoes in the local department store, and our daily visits to the public swimming-pool in Montreux. Once inside the entrance of the pool on the first day, she stopped and gazed around at the glare of colour—the electric blue water, the orange marigolds, the blood-red roses and the shocking-pink begonias.

'Oh, I do love it so!' she said, 'it's so pretty and so gay, and not overburdened with taste. That's what I like!'

Derek Hill came with her and painted the portrait of Noel in his chair by the window in the library; perhaps the most 'alive' of all the portraits, though Noel complained that Derek had placed his eyes too close together. Another year Diana brought Cecil Beaton and her grand-daughter Artemis of whom, young as she was, Noel said, 'She is a permanent pleasure to the eye and to the intellect.' Cecil wrote to Noel, 'I think it is rare to find someone facing the later years with such added zest and interest and wisdom. Without losing any of your pepper you have become so *kind*.'

Cecil was right; it was during these later years that his kindness was made more manifest, although it had been there all the time. This became evident from the many hundreds of letters received after his death. Out of all the adjectives that might have been applied to Noel, this quality is surprisingly the first mentioned in the letters, nearly without exception.

Noel all his life attracted devotion from the people who worked for him, in and out of the theatre. In his households the staff had to be his friends; 'I cannot have people around me continually if I am not fond of them.' The danger of this was that he spoiled his employees. He trusted them without question, left money and valuables about, left them for long periods in his houses with freedom to use his cars and his accounts with the shops and pampered them with gifts. When disaster struck and someone had to go he reproached himself, but after long experience one could contradict him. No, it was not his fault, it had been up to them not to take advantage, and it was of course the ones with enough strength of character to remain unspoiled who stayed with him. Always blessed, Noel's last years were made smooth and comfortable by the dedication of those around him. In Jamaica, Mae Simpson, cook-housekeeper for twenty years, and Vernon Jaghai, head man for ten, between them did 'everything for the Master'.

In Switzerland his luck was even more remarkable. Binkie suggested that because of Noel's refusal to take exercise, he should be given massage to help his circulation; an excellent idea, but where to find a masseur? One day the telephone rang and the voice said that Monsieur Anton Dolin had told him we needed a masseur. 'When can you come?' I asked. 'Now,' was the answer. Fifteen minutes later I opened the door to Jean-René Huber, a blond, blue-eyed giant of twenty-seven, soon christened Fafner by Diana and the Six-Foot Cherub by Lynn. He had worked as a chef in the leading hotels in Switzerland;

massage was merely a sideline learned because of a burning desire to learn everything. He could also drive, garden, market economically, and very soon moved in, married and fathered a son and now, seven years later, still seems too good to be true. The rapport between Jean-René and Noel was immediate and exemplified the good relationship that can exist, but rarely does, between master and man. Fiercely independent, he was firm when Noel was crotchety and laughed when Noel called him a stupid cunt if he knocked over a salt-cellar. Because of his size and height he soon became known as *le plus grand con du monde*, or *mon cher petit con*, and enjoyed both titles. It was Jean-René more than anybody among Noel's staff who looked after and cared for his needs for the rest of Noel's life.

In contrast to the even tenor of life at Les Avants was balanced Noel's eternal restlessness, he still had to have 'the next thing' to look forward to, still longed to return to the sights and the smells of the Far East and the tropics. And so, in 1968, the three of us set out on what developed into a three-month trip round the world. We flew to Tahiti, making stops in London, New York and San Francisco for reunions with friends. Noel looked forward more than anything to showing off the delights of his beloved Bora Bora to Graham and me and in this he succeeded—our hopes were excelled.

We learned to lie flat and paddle about on the wide surfboards with perspex windows let into them, through which we could see the fantastic coral-heads in the lagoons and watch the myriads of coloured fish. Erwin Christian, king of such matters, took us out way beyond the reef every day in his powerful speedboat, to chase sharks whenever he spotted one, and to visit and feed two incredibly beautiful Imperial Peacock Angel Fish with whom he kept rendezvous on the stroke of eleven. Or Erwin would cut diagonally up and across huge incoming waves as they were about to break on the reef, until Noel stopped him; although thrilling, it really was too dangerous. Another great joy, about which Noel had never told us, was to visit one of the little islets far out on the horizon, only just visible because of their coconut palms. With a large ice-box and food from the hotel, Erwin would leave us marooned for the day, castaways on an uninhabited South Sea Island. Late in the afternoon, when we liked to pretend that we might have been forgotten and would have to rub two sticks together to light a fire and spend the night, we would see a speck and hear a chug-chug coming nearer and Erwin would arrive to 'rescue' us. I believe these Robinson Crusoe days to have been among the happiest of our lives.

After our long stay in Bora Bora, two weeks in Fiji, then via Sydney to Singapore and the Raffles Hotel with its huge punkahs slowly revolving and curries so hot we burnt our mouths. Nevertheless we asked for more every day and burnt our mouths all over again; Noel craftily getting the same table in order to eavesdrop shamelessly on two American ladies who never failed him. Among the pearls he treasured were, 'Ah but then you would never wear that particular shade of blue. Your taste is so elite,' and, 'I found out what that white stuff was we had in Japan. It was rice.'

On to Hong Kong, where Noel was invited to fire the famous noonday gun which he had immortalized nearly forty years before in 'Mad Dogs and Englishmen':

> In Hong Kong
> They strike a gong
> And fire off a noonday gun
> To reprimand each inmate
> Who's in late

There wasn't a mad dog or a solar topee to be seen among the crowd of onlookers, all of whom were nearly deafened by the report at such close quarters. The four officials whose daily duty it is to fire the gun looked nervous, I thought. 'I fired off the noonday gun which made the hell of a noise and scared the liver and lights out of me. However it all went off very well, with a bang in fact.'

In Bangkok we stayed more than happily at the Oriental Hotel. Noel's chief delight was to watch the traffic on the immensely wide river. His favourite was a tiny old lady in black who ferried passengers across the expanse in a (for her) very large punt and who danced three never-varying little dance steps between each plunge of the pole. Graham and I left Noel alone for four days to go and be ravished by the beauty of Angkor Wat, Angkor Thom and the rest of the magic city; he confessed in his journal to having got up to some highish jinks while our backs were turned, and then went on: 'This hotel is so much nicer than that beastly other one. There is a terrace overlooking the swift river where we have drinks every evening watching the liver-coloured water swirling by and tiny steam tugs hauling rows of barges up river against the tide. It's a lovely place and I am fonder of it than ever.' He was so fond of it that he left his mark, and perhaps it is no wonder that Patrick Campbell felt impelled to write as he did in the *Sunday Times*:

We had to leave ... and fly off to the Noel Coward suite in the Oriental Hotel, Bangkok. Two photographs of the Master in the sitting-room and below us the garden and the swiftly flowing vegetable soup of the Chao Phya, the River of Kings. Two Chinese fourposters in the green and gold boudoir, but no plaque to indicate in which of them the Master had laid his sweet head. Next morning on the lawn six impossibly beautiful Thai girls in national costume performed a stately dance to the sound of flutes and drums. After quite a long time a strange thing happened. From the shade of the surrounding trees there burst a horde of foreigners, looking lumpish and hot in their western clothes, each and every one of them armed with a camera. They fought and scrambled and fell over one another, taking happy snaps of the girls. Beside me, I felt the Master humming in that light tenor voice:

> In Bangkok
> At twelve o'clock
> They foam at the mouth and run.

Standing there at the window of the Oriental, despite the thundering engines of the river boats, the charter tours and the plethora of Japanese cameras, I felt I was right back again to the 'thirties, to *Cavalcade*, to all those Cochran revues, to 'Mad Dogs and Englishmen' and all the rest of the Master's brittle and brilliant music. Strange, the potency of luxury hotels.

Twelve months before it came to pass, Hal Burton saw Noel at the Savoy and started to plan Noel's Seventieth Birthday Week—seven nights of Noel Coward entertainment on B.B.C. Television was Hal's germ of the idea which eventually blossomed into a national event, reported in newspapers and on radio the world over. Hal had sent an emissary to Les Avants six months before this even, when the idea of his seventieth birthday seemed unreal to Noel, who said that he couldn't help still thinking of himself as a precocious young man of nineteen. He wrote that the idea did not appeal to him greatly: 'However it is inevitable and I must rise above it unless the Angelo de la Morta whisks me off in the nick of time.' He by no means turned down the idea though, and by the time Hal came to the Savoy he had become more enthusiastic and co-operative.

To Hal's scheme was now added Richard Attenborough's enthusiasm and months of planning: much of the fantastic success of Birthday Week was due to Dickie's untiring efforts and those of his wife Sheila and his brother David. David was head of the Outside Events department of the B.B.C. which covered many of the functions of the week, fees and profits from which went to the Actors' Charitable Trust (which had long ago absorbed Noel's Orphanage). T.A.C.T. now concentrated on the charming retreat for retired actors and actresses called Denville Hall, in which Noel took a personal interest, and which is the cause dearest to Dickie and Sheila's hearts.

Excitement began to spread among Noel's friends and the events of the week became so numerous that Diana Daly said, 'Noel, you're making me dizzy. I must go and fetch my engagement book.' 'Don't,' said Noel, 'just keep the whole week wide open.' 'All right. I'll just write Holy Week right across the page,' and that was how that little joke started and eventually spread.

By the time we got to the Savoy in early December Noel found himself engulfed in affection—letters, gifts, cards, cables and flowers endlessly flowed in from the four corners of the earth. The letters from those who had hitherto been total strangers were the most touching; 'We became engaged the evening we saw *Private Lives* when we were young,' or ' "Someday I'll Find You" has always been "our" song, and we named our daughter Amanda because of you and Miss Lawrence.' The effect Noel and his works had exerted on so many people's lives now became eloquently apparent, as did the inspiration his example had afforded to so many people from their youth onwards. It just so happened at this point that *Private Lives* with Tammy Grimes and Brian Bedford opened on Broadway to the most dazzling reviews the play had ever received, which helped to pile yet more praise and adulation on Noel's head. Betty Comden and Adolph Green, supreme examples of Noel's influence on the lives of the young, had already written their Transatlantic tribute in Roddy McDowall's book *Double Exposure*:

Noel was a light to us. He opened doors. To us he represented class ... and we don't mean that in the superficial sense. We mean the highest of wit, of style, of discipline and craftsmanship ... His candour, his irreverence, his impatience with falseness, his sharpness are well known. Happily, we have also seen his warmth, his kindness, and shared some small portion of his friendship. It is comforting to know that after all these years his Mother Country is finally beginning to recognise the enduring value and brilliance of his theatre works. We knew it all the time.

All Noel's friends who could be there were in London that week to surround him. Merle Oberon, with whom we had spent an idyllic holiday in Acapulco earlier in the year, flew from Mexico, moved into the suite next to Noel at the Savoy and, more beautiful than ever, inseparably arrived at every jollification on Noel's arm. The week so bristled with royalty and titles that every announcer got Radie Harris's name wrong, and she enjoyed Open Sesame to everything; her calls were put through immediately as Lady Harris. First of all Noel opened the Noel Coward Bar at his and Gertie's theatre the Phoenix, for which, as his birthday present, Edward Seago generously painted and gave to the Phoenix a reproduction of his portrait of Noel already hanging in the Garrick Club. The three-day-and-night climax to the week began on Sunday, December 14th, with a gala showing at the National Film Theatre of *In Which We Serve* at which the Prince of Wales, Princess Anne and Lord Mountbatten were present. The thirty-year-old film stood up as well and as movingly as ever until, as the papers said, there wasn't a dry eye in the house.

The idea for Noel's Midnight Matinée was Martin Tickner's, aided by Mr and Mrs Flint-Shipman, owners of the Phoenix, and Martin clung obstinately to his conception in spite of the pundits' warnings that such things cannot be done nowadays, they had gone out long ago with Marie Tempest and Irene Vanbrugh. True, Martin had the luck to find Wendy Toye with a month between engagements—something unheard of before or since. Wendy, with stars queuing up to take part, or hurt if they had not been asked, rehearsed them until the show moved swiftly and had on it a smooth polish usually only attained after a six week try-out. On the 15th, the eve of his birthday, Noel entered his box at the Phoenix on the stroke of midnight, Princess Margaret and Lord Snowdon the first to their feet, quickly followed by the crowded audience; the strains of 'Happy Birthday' were never heard at all, drowned by roof-raising cheers and applause. The cast, composed mainly of stars who had played with Noel or in his productions, and numbering a hundred and fifty, gathered on the stage at the end, when Noel came on to take his bow. The evening had been one long happy mixture of fun and nostalgia and love, and Noel confessed in his speech that that moment, surrounded on both sides of the footlights by hundreds of friends, was an emotional one and the most moving of his life. He was near to tears but had remembered in time the lesson his

Guv'nor, Charles Hawtrey, taught him when young: 'If you lose yourself, you lose your audience. When you have an emotional scene to play, play it down.' So instead he made the evening end with laughter, as he had so often done before. Champagne on the stage with the cast followed, and when he finally came out of the stage-door at five o'clock into the cold December morning, unbelievably there was still a crowd of his fans in the road waiting for him, as they too had so often done before. 'I wish darling old Gertie could have been there,' he said. 'My God, she would have been seventy-two!' he realised with a start. 'Still, I bet she'd have been a wonderful seventy-two.'

Late as he had been in getting to bed, Noel was naturally up in good time for his birthday luncheon at Clarence House with Queen Elizabeth the Queen Mother. Queen Elizabeth alas was laid low with a cold, but left him a charming message to say that she hoped he would manage with her daughters, and Noel 'managed' very happily with the Queen and Princess Margaret. It was at this luncheon that the Queen asked Noel if he had 'heard from the Prime Minister'. Yes, he had. And she hoped that he was going to accept? Yes, he had already accepted. Sixteen days later, on January 1st, 1970, Noel's name appeared in the New Year honours list as a Knight Bachelor, for services to the arts.

Hugely enjoyable and gratifying as Holy Week and the weeks preceding it had been, they had undoubtedly also been a strain on Noel, mentally and physically. In health he had begun a decline which would from now on slowly increase; he walked with a pronounced stoop, never entirely without pain. He tired easily. So many emotions had been aroused which had had to be surmounted and kept under control, and in addition he—the witty Noel Coward—was not unnaturally still expected to be 'on' during most of his waking moments. He had, however, got through his week wonderfully well, and it was with a sense of relief that he looked forward to the last celebration, the climax, as did those around him. This was his Birthday Party in the Lancaster Room of the Savoy, on the evening of the same long day. There was nothing for most of us to do except to sit back and enjoy the lovely party of nearly three hundred friends and 'have a good dinner', as the Prince of Wales expressed it in his telegram to Noel.

The speeches by Lord Nugent, Lord Mountbatten, Larry and Noel were televised nationwide by the B.B.C. Lord Mountbatten had made a list, which seemed as though it would never come to an end, of all Noel's talents, including admittedly some of the minor ones: 'There may be better [I am quoting from memory] singers, pianists, dancers, painters, etc., etc., etc., but there would have to be fourteen different people. There is only *one* Noel Coward and he combines the attributes of all fourteen.' His and Larry's friendships with Noel were lifelong, stretching back more than forty years, and Noel was inevitably touched by their remembrances of those years and moved by the abundant tributes they paid him in their speeches. 'All my life,' Noel said, 'my two great passions have been the theatre and the sea. Now tonight I have been honoured by a great sailor and a great actor. I am very proud.' The marvellous party was over. Never again would so many of Noel's friends be gathered together in one place as they had been in London for his Seventieth Birthday Week.

His knighthood gave great pleasure not only to Noel but again to thousands of people all over the world, and again the telegrams and letters of congratulations came thick and fast for weeks. Perhaps none were more delighted than his fellow knights in the theatrical profession. Alec Guinness put it this way: 'We have been like a row of teeth with a front tooth missing. Now we can smile again.'

The remaining years rushed by in a procession of successes, tributes, awards, honours and glory. Four months after his knighthood, Noel was awarded the highest the American theatre can bestow; a special Tony Award for Distinguished Achievement in the Theatre. In this he was reunited with Lynn and Alfred, who received the same awards on the same occasion—a happy completion to their fifty years of association. Noel was in high spirits and better physical shape after three months' rest in Jamaica and did not tire throughout the long Sunday of rehearsal and the show in the evening at the Mark Hellinger Theatre. The show, presented by Alexander Cohen, was by general consent considered one of the most exciting in the twenty-four-year history of the Awards. With Noel, Lynn and Alfred in the show were also Lauren Bacall, Tammy Grimes, Shirley Maclaine, Patricia Neal, Barbra Streisand, Mia Farrow, James Stewart, Michael Caine and Julie Andrews. Maggie Smith and Robert Stephens flew from London between Saturday and Monday performances to present the Awards to Lynn and Alfred; to Maggie and Lynn's dismay they discovered they had both elected to wear pale beige. 'Oh dear,' Maggie said, 'we shall look like a couple of sponge fingers.' The other awards remain secret until the sealed envelopes are opened on the stage, and to add to our personal excitement Betty Bacall won a Tony for her performance in *Applause*, and then so did Tammy for hers in *Private Lives*.

Noel kept everyone on day-long tenterhooks (especially Cary Grant, who was to present him the award) by refusing to disclose what he intended to say in his speech. He descended the immensely long Cecil Beaton staircase from the *Coco* (Chanel) set with all the aplomb of twenty years before at the Café de Paris, advanced to the footlights and said in a voice of appeal when the applause subsided, 'This is my first award, so please be kind,' and got a shout of laughter. (This statement was not strictly accurate, for he had already received the Award of the Year from the Plumbers' Association of America, for saying on television that good plumbing was one of the most important things in life.)

All of Noel's more predominant straight plays enjoyed successful revivals during these years, but not one of his musicals, nor have they since. Wisely, perhaps, for with the single exception of *Bitter Sweet* the librettos, always their weakest point, most probably would not stand the test of time. On the other hand, all the revues, operettas and musical comedies are goldmines of music and lyrics, asking to be made anew into revue form. Roderick Cook had already used this formula and had been playing Coward revues with great success in America and Canada for two years. In England, Sir Bernard Miles, with his affection and admiration for Noel dating from the time they appeared together in *In Which We Serve*, for a long time had nurtured a hope of doing exactly this, and Noel gladly gave his consent. After her triumph with the Midnight Matinée, Wendy Toye was the only possible choice as director. But what to call the revue? Nobody could think of a title, not even Noel. Bernard cabled while we were in Jamaica suggesting among others *Cream of Coward*, but Noel said, 'That would be *asking* for trouble': the train of thought is obvious and he added immediately, 'I know. Cowardy Custard,' but nobody except Noel cared for that either. But *Cowardy Custard* it was, and Noel's material emerged as extraordinarily apt and fresh as when it had first been written. The show had a triumphant first night at the Mermaid in 1972 and ran for a year.

The morning after the opening Noel was up with the lark to drive to the University of Sussex, where in an impressive ceremony the honorary degree of Doctor of Letters was conferred on Noel; his young godson Michael Attenborough received his own degree that same afternoon. In September there was another rapturous reception from the public for John Gielgud's production of *Private Lives* at the Queen's with Maggie Smith and Robert Stephens, which Maggie was to play one way and another for the next two years, miraculously ending up fresher than ever (she was by then the best Amanda since Gertie) on Broadway. In October *Oh! Coward* opened to ecstatic notices in New York and so, together with *Cowardy Custard*, Noel had three smash hits running simultaneously until well into 1973.

Before leaving 1972 mention must be made of the memorable party given for Noel in September at Claridges by Swifty and Mary Lazar. Elegant and gay as the party was, there is in retrospect a sadness. Out of the forty or so of Noel's closest friends who attended, the party was for many of them, though unaware of the fact at the time, his farewell. Patrick Garland wrote for *Vogue*:

> I was there and am unlikely ever to forget so perfect and vale-dictory an occasion ... When the cabaret was finished, the most touching highlight of which was Fritz Loewe singing 'We've grown accustomed to your face' directly to a visibly moved Noel Coward, the Master himself walked slowly over to the piano ... the celebrated diction, the characteristic *hauteur* were quite gone and he sang [Manon's song] with a sense of both regret and pain:
>
> > Night after night
> > Have to look bright
> > Whether you're well or ill,
> > People must laugh their fill ...
> >
> > Hey ho,
> > If love were all.
>
> The forlorn break on 'hey ho' was unmistakable, and I knew then where I had heard it before. It was *Twelfth Night* of course, where Feste is left by himself at the end of the play. The same Feste who, when Duke Orsino says, 'Take that for thy pains,' replies, 'No pains sir, I take pleasure in singing sir.' Here was Feste in black tie, surrounded by his friends and great contemporaries in the theatre, all those he loved and most profoundly trusted. When he left the piano the party dissolved straight away and several were in tears.

Noel arrived in New York in January 1973 to find two separate hullabaloos going on at once. One had been caused by Marlene giving a large press conference in which, with her producer Alex Cohen present, she announced to the world how terribly bad her hour-long television special—the only one she ever made and therefore eagerly awaited—was going to be on the following Saturday. This caused a sensation, and Mr Cohen was later reported as about to sue, but it may well have been deliberate publicity on Marlene's part; the entire nation watched, looking forward to the worst, but of course it wasn't terrible at all. But the sensational press conference had been by no means all. She had followed it by bewailing to another interviewer that she had no friends left—Hemingway, Cocteau, Remarque, Chevalier and the rest, all, all were gone. Marlene had already done this several times before, adding that she had no *real* friends left, the ones she could ring up at four in the morning, a category to which Noel said he was delighted not to belong. On this occasion she went further; to the suggestion that there was Noel, why didn't she go and spend Christmas with him in Switzerland, she replied, 'He could be dead before I get there.' We felt sure that it was Noel's old joke that he now only expected his friends to survive through lunch which had gone wrong; Marlene had never really grasped it. Her remark however did look callously shocking in print, all Noel's friends were immediately up in arms and Marlene was in the doghouse all round.

The second furore was the gala, black-tie, invitation-only performance of *Oh! Coward* on the following day. The New Theatre was so small that the allocation of invitations had presented a problem for weeks, reaching fever pitch during the days following Noel's arrival in New York. Speculation was rampant as to whom Noel would escort, Mrs Onassis being the most popular guess, and Noel himself had no idea who to bring when Katharine Cornell rang to say that she was not well enough to come after all. His eleventh-hour decision to ask Marlene was made for three reasons; first and most important because of their long-time *amitié amoureuse*; to rescue her in the most glamorous way possible from her doghouse; and because he had all his life been every whit as clever at managing his own publicity as Marlene had been at hers. In this he was right—Marlene was the last person in the world that particular audience expected to see make her entrance on Noel's arm. He warned Marlene that the interviewer in question would most probably be present at the gala. 'If I see him,' she said, 'I shall kick him in the balls. If he has any balls.'

None of us could know that Noel was making his last public appearance that evening. Both the gala itself and the large party afterwards were extremely happy occasions for him; his personal invitations had been based on his American Christmas-card list and so, as had happened in London, every single friend whom Noel cared for, many of them by great good fortune dear friends from the past whom he had not seen for years, were there to see him for the last time.

Noel was as ever impatient to hurry to the warmth of Jamaica and the quiet of Firefly Hill, but before leaving New York he gave the original manuscript of a poem to Nedda Harrigan Logan to be auctioned in aid of the Actors' Fund of America, the verses which have now become widely known as Noel's Last Poem. The poem has a curious history; the line about the peace of the changing sea strongly suggests that it was occasioned by his looking out at the view from the verandah at Firefly on which he always wrote. The manuscript fortunately came to light in the personal papers which were with him in New York, which enabled him to give it to Nedda, and must therefore have been written on the previous visit to Jamaica in 1972. It also very strongly suggests a sense of loneliness when he wrote it. So he may perhaps have written it when Graham and I left him to spend a holiday on Grand Cayman. Or on another occasion that year when we left him to go to Haiti; he seemed more than usually pleased—for him almost emotionally—when we returned safely. This possibility apart, the poem appears to have been particularly personal to him, for neither Graham nor I can remember him reading it or showing it to us as he usually did with his work. Now, in 1975, another longer version has come to light. Noel must have worked further since he wrote the manuscript and then carefully typed the finished version; it is typed in the lettering of his own typewriter. Perhaps he forgot he had done this; in any case so far as is known he had kept it to himself.

> When I have fears, as Keats had fears,
> Of the moment I'll cease to be
> I console myself with vanished years
> Remembered laughter, remembered tears,
> And the peace of the changing sea.
>
> When I feel sad, as Keats felt sad,
> That my life is so nearly done
> It gives me comfort to dwell upon
> Remembered friends who are dead and gone
> And the jokes we had and the fun.
>
> How happy they are I cannot know
> But happy am I who loved them so.

Noel's two-month holiday in Jamaica was as peaceful as he could have wished, and as sunny. He remained all through it if anything in better health than he had enjoyed for the last two years; so well that we had no occasion to call for a doctor. This peace was shattered for ever when the telephone rang at Blue Harbour on the morning of March 22nd. It was Joan, ringing from London to tell us that Binkie had suddenly died in his sleep the night before. At this point it should be stressed that apart from their business rifts and aside from his 'family', Binkie was for the last twenty-five years the friend with whom Noel had been in closest touch by telephone or letter and to whom he always hurried on arrival in London for another of their suppers at Lord North Street; evenings of incessant talk, drinks and jokes late into the night. Graham and I now had the dread task of driving up the hill to break the news to Noel.

Every detail of the hours we spent with Noel during the last four days of his life is etched on the memory. Because of the news of Binkie's death one's sensitivities to everything were heightened; an extra awareness of the beauties of the visual world, for Firefly Hill was looking its loveliest. From where we sat with Noel on his verandah, vividly perceptible against the sea and blue sky, the tulip trees we planted so long ago were in abundant scarlet blossom. Emotions too were more susceptible; there was an extra edge to our laughter and our sadness. Noel never completely recovered from the blow of Binkie's death; it seemed hauntingly unbelievable to him that Binkie's vitality had been snuffed out for ever, that never again should we see the attractive smiling face, listen to the wickedly funny gossip, or hear him laugh.

Up until receipt of the news we had been a merry enough crew of five. Gentle Geoffrey, whom Noel loved, was with us; the perfect friend, soothingly quiet and exceedingly funny by turns, of iron strength when required—and his strength was soon to be called upon. James Justice, another friend from New York, was also staying, and Jim's gaiety and unobtrusive sympathy were inestimable assets during those bewildering days.

Noel came to the end of the stack of new books he had ordered from our friends at Heywood Hill in London and Doubleday's in New York. The last book left was Anne Morrow Lindbergh's *Hour of Gold, Hour of Lead*, the second volume of her Diaries and Letters, in which we knew she would inevitably have to deal with her marriage to Charles Lindbergh and the birth, kidnapping and murder of their son. Noel's reading of this book is inextricably entwined in our memories of those last days. 'I don't know whether I can bear it,' he said at first, 'those two young people ... what they must have gone through. It's too dreadful to think about.' Our twice-daily visits to Firefly followed an invariable pattern. 'I cannot get Binkie out of my mind,' Noel would say upon our arrivals at noon and in the early evening. 'I still cannot believe it. Joycie will be so very sad and upset—I did cable her, didn't I?' Each time we would reassure him on this and other points. He worried especially about Elvira and Anna, Binkie's faithful maids, who adored him and who were old friends of Noel's. 'What will they do? Binkie *will* have looked after them, won't he?' Again we would have to reassure him. Gradually, gradually, we would lead him away from the subject of Binkie's death. Graham especially was supremely tactful and successful at this, changing the subject so imperceptibly that one hardly realised he had done so, and that Noel was miraculously laughing again. From then on all would be well. 'How are you getting on with Mrs Lindbergh?' 'Oh she is such a beautiful writer, her English is a comfort.' 'Have you got to the awful part yet?' At last he was able to say that yes, he had, and that it was perfectly all right. 'She handles it so well. She spares the reader. I might have known that she was to be trusted. I can't wait to finish it so that you can read it.'

Jim had to leave us on the Sunday morning, to our regret, but fortunately he persuaded me to photograph Noel the day before. This photograph was to become a comfort to the many people who wanted to know what Noel had been like, what he had looked like, at the end. There he is exactly; looking bronzed and well and happy, with the eternal cigarette, his favourite brandy and ginger-ale and Mrs Lindbergh's book on the table in front of him. We were able to show his friends how he looked, even to wearing the same floral-patterned red-and-white dressing gown, as we last saw him, less than twelve hours before his death.

When we arrived on that last evening, Graham again gently steered him away from Binkie's death, and Noel gave me Mrs Lindbergh's book. 'There you are, I've finished it at last. You're in for a lovely treat. I must write to her and I will.' We could not know that this was the last evening we should ever spend together, but even had we known and had planned it it could not have been more peaceful or more quietly happy, or more perfectly evocative of the countless evenings we had spent witnessing the Firefly pageant. ('What mysterious rite do the villagers think we come up here to observe?' Maggie Smith once wondered.)

First of all, while still light, came the Aquacade, one of Noel's keenest enjoyments, as though it were laid on specially for him. A swirling flock of Jamaican starlings would appear from nowhere, dart swiftly before us from right to left, and one after the other take their evening dip in the swimming-pool, below and in front of us. After the dip they flew a little out to sea and then turned, the first starling catching up with the last until they were all flying round in an endless circle. The sight was beautiful, thrilling even, while it lasted, and funny too, for there were always the comics—the over-daring ones who took too deep a dip and fluttered and wobbled precariously before they recovered balance and took swift flight again. The pool for five or ten minutes became their territory and we always kept silent and out of their way. As suddenly as they had appeared, as though at a signal, they would with one accord disappear up into the blue in a swarm, and the spectacle was over.

Next came the first loud croak nearby from Ezio the tree-frog, christened by Noel after Ezio Pinza in *South Pacific*, because his croak was equally *basso profundo*. After so many years, twenty-five all told, we decided he must be at least Son of Ezio, and if he was, happily he had inherited his father's voice.

The next treat, to be watched for in the very last glimmer of twilight, was Noel's white owl, flapping slowly on milk-white wings against the darkening trees. 'There's my lucky white owl! I do love him so. He always brings me luck.' This too was a pretty sight:

> Lovely are the curves of the white owl sweeping
> Wavy in the dusk lit by one large star.

By now it was about time for Miguel to freshen our drinks, ready for the sunset, the climax to the enchanted hour. Had Coleridge himself seen a tropical sunset he could not have described it more truly in *The Ancient Mariner*:

> The Sun's rim dips; the stars rush out:
> At one stride comes the dark.

Then the fireflies would emerge from the thickets, and the lights of Port Maria, to the left in the distance, come on gradually until they looked as though someone had carelessly scattered a necklace and left it lying, sparkling in the dark. We all agreed that we had had a lovely evening and the magic of Firefly Hill had been as potent as ever.

Noel over the years had had great fun, from time to time, speculating on what his last words would be. Would they be Famous Last Words? Of course, he said, he would like to utter something frightfully witty like '*Les flammes déjà?*' with his last breath, but couldn't bank on it. He thought he'd better settle for something simpler and for a long time promised he would try to remember to say—emulating Charles II, his eternal hero—'Let not poor Coley starve,' which would at least be touching. But then doubt crept in ... supposing he were to say something perfectly awful? Supposing—horror of horrors—he were to be tended at the last by one of those relentlessly cheerful nurses and lost his temper, and his final words were 'For God's sake bugger off, you're driving me mad'?

In the event, the last words Noel spoke to Graham and me were as simple and for us as touching as he could have wished. He called—we were half way down the steps of his verandah—'Good night, my darlings, I'll see you tomorrow.'

POSTSCRIPT

I was wakened early the next day by Jaghai knocking on my door. His face was sad and stricken for, even more than the rest of the staff, he truly loved his master. 'Master very sick,' was all he said. Graham and I scrambled into some clothes. Our village doctor, Val Harry, who had seen us safely through many an illness, had lately retired, and we knew of no doctor to whom to turn. Jaghai had already appealed to one who refused to come: Noel must come to him at Port Maria Hospital, like everybody else. And so, Jaghai said, we would try Doctor Akpabio, the new doctor. Doctor Akpabio, who was Nigerian by birth and had learned his medicine at London University, came to his door at our knock and said he would come at once, to our relief. But when we got to Firefly, Miguel was standing motionless on the verandah outside Noel's room, his cheeks wet with tears. 'Master died,' was all he seemed able to say.

This was unbelievable, something not possible after Noel's well-being of the night before. But we went in to Noel's room and it was true. Noel lay with his head on the pillows looking for all the world as though he had gone comfortably to sleep, and this in fact was what he had done. What had happened? Both Miguel and Imogene his wife are young; through their tears they tried to explain. Imogene had wakened unusually early and, unable to sleep, had taken a walk that sunny morning. Mercifully she did, for this involved passing the back of the house and she heard Noel calling. Miguel found him on the floor of his bathroom, evidently having had a heart attack, but by then his suffering was not great and he was able, helped and supported by Miguel, to walk and get back to his bed. Miguel made him comfortable and held his hand. Then what had happened? Miguel told him that he would send for Graham and me but Noel had said, 'No, it's too early, they will still be asleep.' His kind and touching thought of us apart, Noel's last words were of great comfort; they clearly meant he had felt no fear, but had calmly thought that the attack would pass, or even that it had passed already. 'Then he gave me a little smile and settled down and went to sleep. I went on holding his hand and then he gave a little sigh and he died.'

All his life Noel's wishes had been granted and now, even his wish as to the manner of his dying had been gratified. A peaceful death, no long, lingering and painful illness, and he was spared the infirmities and indignities of extreme old age, which he had dreaded. But, Graham and I suddenly wondered, what had happened to him after we had left him the night before? We questioned Winston the night watchman. 'Master read till quarter to twelve, then he turned his light off and looked out'—had looked his last on all things lovely—'then he called out, "Good night, Winston", like he always did and went in and shut his door.' What had he been reading? We hurried to see and there, on his table, were two E. Nesbits; he had read half way through *The Enchanted Castle* and left it lying open. His lifelong favourite; if he had ordained his end he could not have arranged it better. To the last detail, Noel's life had been rounded off to perfection.

To me and to my generation [Anne Morrow Lindbergh wrote], he was the epitome of youth and of the beauty and glamour of youth. And yet—perhaps this is why we adored him and his songs have lasted—he was always aware of how near the Hour of Lead was to the Hour of Gold. Just as—if I can judge from what I have read and heard about him from Nesta and others—he was able to perceive the gold, the joy, even through the diminishments of the latter part of life. I am grateful to him for such an example at both ends of life ...

The events of that day, Monday, March 26th, remain perfectly clear in my mind, yet I find difficulty in giving a lucid account of it; of how Geoffrey, Graham and I got through it. Noel and I had so often tried to anticipate his or my behaviour on such a day, both of us strong in the hope that we should behave sensibly and well, but we had been wide of the mark; no rules can be laid down for grief. The day was too much of a jumble for us, with no time for sorrow—grief must wait until night and dark hours when sleep would not come. The shattering event that happened in that remote little hamlet in Jamaica was, so far we thought, something that had happened only to us and yet, by the time we came down from Firefly to Blue Harbour, floods of cables had poured in. Among the first we opened were one from Pamela Lindo in Australia and one from Derek Adkins in Hong Kong, and we had to adjust to the knowledge that the news of Noel's death had already flashed round the world. How it did so with such startling rapidity we do not know to this day—an overheard telephone-call perhaps. Only now did we realise the importance of the news to thousands of people the world over. Linda Lee-Potter in the *Daily Mail* wrote in passing, more than a year later, 'I cried when Noel Coward died,' touchingly verifying what so many people cabled to us that day: 'The world is poorer, a sense of loss is everywhere.'

Whenever the subject cropped up, Noel asked us to bury, not cremate him, adding, perhaps irrationally—who can judge—that he would like to go back to the earth and do a little good. And we were to make no fuss, we were to bury him wherever he died. Adrianne telephoned that evening and said, quite simply, 'Why don't you leave him where he was happiest—at Firefly Hill?' which confirmed our own decision. Two years afterwards I found that Noel had ended his account of one of the earliest of his evenings at Firefly, twenty-four years before, with the words 'laughter learnt of friends, and gentleness, in hearts at peace, under a Jamaican heaven'. We chose as the site for his grave that spot about which he wrote so long ago, where he had sat with so many friends with their first drinks of the evening, looking straight out to sea, watching the sunset reflected on the long vista of coastline as far as the eye can see—the view he loved.

All went well. Jaghai, quietly firm, would allow no strangers to dig his master's grave; he, Miguel, Desmond, Egbert, and David Harrow, all friends and past and present employees, worked for two days and into the night with flares. To our misgivings that he was making the grave too big, he assured us that it would be all right, we should see. Far back in this book I wrote that to the end Noel remained faithful to walls of white, and it was now that Jaghai, by his own decision, caused this to become literally true. For Noel's tomb, he and the others built a spacious room, edged the four sides with long fern fronds inclining inwards and, as Noel would have wished, the walls were painted white.

Noel's burial, three days after his death, took place at four in the afternoon; perhaps the loveliest time of all, when the heat of the day is over and the sun is westering. We asked only Noel's and our own neighbours, whose friendships dated back to our first days in Jamaica—Mary Mitchell, Kitty Spence, Mildred and Charles D'Costa, Jeremy Vaughan—and there were of course his faithful staff, Violet from Goldeneye, Geoffrey, Graham and myself, that is all. The men wore white and the women light-coloured dresses. The private ceremony we planned, gradually and quite rightly in the intervening days expanded to exactly the proper degree of importance. First the British

High Commissioner asked if he might attend because, besides representing the government of Noel's country, he had a special reason for
coming that day—to bring flowers from members of the Royal Family.
With the British High Commissioner officially attending, we then felt
that Jamaica itself should be represented, and the Governor-General,
Sir Roy Campbell, and the Prime Minister, the Rt. Hon. Michael
Manley, sent their representatives.

Meanwhile members of the British press had arrived and were
staying nearby at the Casa Maria Hotel. Ian Ball of the *Daily Telegraph*
seemed to be their spokesman and asked if they might attend, gently
reminding us that we as well as they had a duty to perform—readers of
newspapers the world over would be expecting coverage of the service
on the morrow. They would stay to one side, he said, under the trees.
They were all young men, with, one felt sure, no idea of the hurts and
taunts their predecessors had inflicted on Noel decades before; all the
more touching to find, after they had gone, a sheaf of flowers with a
card: 'In affectionate memory from the British press.'

The villagers from Grant's Town walked up the hill in their brightest
clothes to say farewell, not to the famous Noel Coward, who was a
man they did not know, but to the man who had been kind to them
and to whom they called out, 'Hello Master', when he drove through
their village. The Bishop of Kingston, the Right Reverend J. T. Clark,
himself offered to come and assist our sympathetic vicar of Port Maria,
the Reverend Father Worrel, with the service. Both possessed beautifully clear, resonant voices, and they read the familiar words of the
Service for the Burial of the Dead simply and well.

When all the dignitaries had gone, there was nothing more natural in
the world than for us and our friends to take our drinks at six o'clock
and sit on the grass at that peaceful spot, where we had so often sat
before, and drink to Noel, and thank him for all he had given us.

And now ... Graham has given Firefly Hill to the nation of Jamaica
unconditionally. Jamaica in return has given assurance that Noel's
resting-place will be safeguarded and cared for in perpetuity.

On May 24th, 1973, a Service of Thanksgiving for the life of Noel
Coward was held at St Martin-in-the-Fields, with its ages of traditional association with the Royal Navy and the Theatre. To quote Sir
John Betjeman, 'this beautiful, great eighteenth-century theatre of a
church in the heart of London. Cheerful, wide, welcoming English
baroque; it is precise, elegant and well-ordered. Like Noel.'

The Vicar, the Reverend Austen Williams, spoke of Noel in words
well chosen and true. Lord Olivier read Noel's early verse and his

Last Poem. He told of Noel and himself going together when young to see *La Femme du Boulanger* and reminded us of the end of the film, by which I think he meant that Noel was the Baker's good bread and that we the congregation had all turned out, as the village did in the film, to rejoice in it.

Yehudi Menuhin, a lone figure in the chancel, played for his friend from Bach's Solo Sonata in E Major. Sir John Gielgud—the incomparable voice—read Shakespeare's Sonnet XXX:

> But if the while I think on thee dear friend,
> All losses are restor'd, and sorrows end.

Sir John Betjeman, Poet Laureate, composed and spoke the address:

> We are all here today to thank the Lord for the life
>   of Noel Coward.
> Noel with two dots over the 'e'
> And the firm decided downward stroke of the 'l'.
> We can all see him in our mind's eye
> And in our mind's ear
> We can hear the clipped decided voice ...

The two hymns were 'For All the Saints, Who from Their Labours Rest' and, as a token of Noel's fifty-year ties with the United States, 'The Battle Hymn of the Republic', with its many 'Glory Alleluias'.

When Graham and I got back to our hotel the telephone was ringing. It was Dame Rebecca West, her voice eager and happy with enthusiasm. 'Wasn't it *lovely*,' she said. 'Do you know what I liked best of all? That packed congregation of friends, all singing Alleluia for Noel at the tops of their voices.'

And now, recently, a letter from John Merivale:

> The Master never seems more than a breath away. I know of no one who conquered death with such ease. He's on the air constantly, singing away like a dicky-bird. And he's quoted and referred to with love and admiration not only on the air but wherever one goes—from drawing-room to four-ale bar. And always there's laughter and love.

BIBLIOGRAPHY

The major works of Noel Coward

A Withered Nosegay (satire), Christophers, London, 1922. (Published, with additions, in the United States as *Terribly Intimate Portraits*, Boni and Liveright, New York, 1922.)

Three Plays (containing *The Rat Trap, The Vortex, Fallen Angels*), with the Author's reply to his critics, Ernest Benn, London, 1925.

Chelsea Buns (satire), Hutchinson, London, 1925.

Three Plays with a Preface (containing *Home Chat, Sirocco, This Was a Man*), Martin Secker, London, 1928. (Published in the United States, with a Preface by Arnold Bennett, as *The Plays of Noel Coward*, Doubleday, Doran, New York, 1928.)

Bitter Sweet and Other Plays (containing *Easy Virtue* and *Hay Fever*), with a Preface by W. Somerset Maugham, Doubleday, Doran, New York, 1929.

Collected Sketches and Lyrics, Hutchinson, London, 1931; Doubleday, Doran, New York, 1932.

Spangled Unicorn (satire), Hutchinson, London, 1932.

Play Parade, Vol. I (containing *Cavalcade, Bitter Sweet, Hay Fever, Design for Living, Private Lives, Post Mortem*), Doubleday, Doran, New York, 1933; Heinemann, London, 1934.

Present Indicative (autobiography), Heinemann, London; Doubleday, Doran, New York; 1937.

To Step Aside (short stories), Heinemann, London; Doubleday, Doran, New York; 1939.

Play Parade, Vol. II (containing *This Year of Grace, Words and Music, Operette, Conversation Piece, Easy Virtue, Fallen Angels*), Heinemann, London, 1939.

Curtain Calls (containing *Tonight at Eight-Thirty, Conversation Piece, Easy Virtue, Point Valaine, This Was a Man*), Doubleday, Doran, New York, 1940.

Australia Visited (broadcasts), Heinemann, London, 1941.

Middle East Diary, Heinemann, London; Doubleday, Doran, New York; 1944.

Play Parade, Vol. III (containing *The Queen Was in the Parlour, I'll Leave It to You, The Young Idea, Sirocco, The Rat Trap, This Was a Man, Home Chat, The Marquise*), Heinemann, London, 1950.

Star Quality (short stories), Doubleday, New York; Heinemann, London; 1951.

The Noel Coward Song Book, Michael Joseph, London, 1953.

Future Indefinite (autobiography), Heinemann, London; Doubleday, New York; 1954.

Play Parade, Vol. IV (containing *Tonight at Eight-Thirty*), Heinemann, London, 1954.

Play Parade, Vol. V (containing *Blithe Spirit, Pacific 1860, Peace in Our Time, Relative Values, Quadrille*), Heinemann, London, 1958.

Pomp and Circumstance (novel), Heinemann, London; Doubleday, New York; 1960.

The Collected Short Stories, Heinemann, London; Doubleday, New York; 1962.

Play Parade, Vol. VI (containing *Point Valaine, South Sea Bubble, Ace of Clubs, Nude with Violin, Waiting in the Wings*), Heinemann, London, 1962.

Pretty Polly Barlow (short stories), Heinemann, London, 1964; Doubleday, New York, 1965.

The Lyrics of Noel Coward, Heinemann, London, 1965; Doubleday, New York, 1967.

Suite in Three Keys (containing *A Song at Twilight, Shadows of the Evening, Come into the Garden, Maud*), Heinemann, London, 1966; Doubleday, New York, 1967.

Bon Voyage (short stories), Heinemann, London, 1967; Doubleday, New York, 1968.

Not Yet the Dodo (verse), Heinemann, London, 1967; Doubleday, New York, 1968.

Works consulted

ALBANESI, E. MARIA: *Meggie Albanesi*, Hodder and Stoughton, London, 1928.

AMORY, CLEVELAND, and BRADLEE, FREDERIC (eds): *Vanity Fair: A Cavalcade of the 1920s and 1930s*, Viking, New York, 1960.

ARLEN, MICHAEL J.: *Exiles*, Farrar, Straus and Giroux, New York; André Deutsch, London; 1971.

BRAYBROOKE, PATRICK: *The Amazing Mr Noel Coward*, Archer, London, 1933.

COURTNEY, MARGUERITE: *Laurette Taylor*, Rinehart, New York, 1955.

DAMASE, JACQUES: *Les Folies du Music-Hall*, with a Foreword by Noel Coward, Anthony Blond, London, 1962.

GALLATI, MARIO: *Mario of the Caprice*, Hutchinson, London, 1960.

GREACEN, ROBERT: *The Art of Noel Coward*, Hand and Flower Press, England, 1953.

MCDOWALL, RODDY (ed.): *Double Exposure*, Delacorte Press, New York, 1966.

MANDER, RAYMOND, and MITCHENSON, JOE: *Theatrical Companion to Coward*, Rockliff, London; Macmillan, New York; 1957.

MOORE, DORIS LANGLEY: *E. Nesbitt, a Biography*, new edition, Chilton Books, Philadelphia, 1966; Ernest Benn, London, 1967.

MORLEY, SHERIDAN: *A Talent to Amuse*, Heinemann, London; Doubleday, New York; 1969.

PEARSON, JOHN: *The Life of Ian Fleming*, Jonathan Cape, London; McGraw-Hill, New York; 1966.

SALTER, ELIZABETH: *The Last Years of a Rebel*, Bodley Head, London; Houghton Mifflin, Boston; 1967.

SALTER, MARJORIE, and ALLEN, ADRIANNE: *Delightful Food*, with a Foreword by Noel Coward, Sidgwick and Jackson, London, 1957.

SPANIER, GINETTE: *It Isn't All Mink*, Collins, London, 1959; Random House, New York, 1960.

ZOLOTOW, MAURICE: *Stagestruck*, Harcourt Brace, New York, 1964; Heinemann, London, 1965.

INDEX

Coward's works are indexed under the entry for Coward himself

A NOTE ON THE TYPE

The text of this book was set on the Monotype in a type face called Garamond. Jean Jannon has been identified as designer for this face, which is based on Garamond's original models but is much lighter and more open. The italic is taken from a fount of Granjon, which appeared in the repertory of the Imprimerie Royale and was probably cut in the middle of the sixteenth century.

Printed and bound by American Book-Stratford Press,
Saddle Brook, New Jersey

Design by Earl Tidwell